EXCELLENT PUBLIC RELATIONS
AND EFFECTIVE ORGANIZATIONS

A Study of Communication Management
in Three Countries

LEA's COMMUNICATION SERIES
Jennings Bryant/Dolf Zillmann, General Editors

For a complete list of titles in LEA's Communication Series, please contact Lawrence Erlbaum Associates, Publishers at www.erlbaum.com.

EXCELLENT PUBLIC RELATIONS AND EFFECTIVE ORGANIZATIONS

A Study of Communication Management in Three Countries

LARISSA A. GRUNIG
Department of Communication
University of Maryland

JAMES E. GRUNIG
Department of Communication
University of Maryland

DAVID M. DOZIER
School of Communication
San Diego State University

The Excellence Study was funded through a grant from the International Association of Business Communicators (IABC) Research Foundation

I6 02 0I

 LAWRENCE ERLBAUM ASSOCIATES, PUBLISHERS
2002   Mahwah, New Jersey   London

Lawrence Erlbaum Associates, Inc., Publishers
10 Industrial Avenue
Mahwah, New Jersey 07430

Cover design by Kathryn Houghtaling-Lacey

Library of Congress Cataloging-in-Publication Data

Grunig, Larissa A.
  Excellent public relations and effective organizations : a study of communication
management in three countries : Larissa A. Grunig, James A. Grunig, David M. Dozier.
    p. cm. — (LEA's communication series)
  Includes bibliographical references and index.
  ISBN 0-8058-1817-0 (casebound : alk. paper) — ISBN 0-8058-1818-9 (pbk. : alk. paper)
    1. Corporations—Public relations—United States.   2. Corporations—Public
relations—Canada.   3. Corporations—Public relations—Great Britain.   I. Grunig, James E.
II. Dozier, David M.   III. Title.   IV. Series.

  HD59.6.U6 G78   2002
  659.2'85—dc21
                                                                    2002016471
                                                                    CIP

Books published by Lawrence Erlbaum Associates are printed on acid-free paper,
and their bindings are chosen for strength and durability.

Printed in the United States of America
10 9 8 7 6 5 4 3 2 1

DEDICATION

We dedicate this book to our friend and colleague Fred C. Repper, who died May 5, 2001, before he had the chance to read this final product of our collaborative work. Fred was a valuable member of the Excellence team. He provided insight into the world of working professionals to which we—as academics—do not have such ready access as he did. We remember fondly his insights, his support and encouragement, and the good times we had with Fred and his wife, Dorothy Repper.

Contents

Preface

During the summer of 1984, the IABC Foundation (now the IABC Research Foundation) issued a request for proposals for a research project that gave us a chance to conduct what is probably the largest study ever of the public relations profession. The IABC Foundation wanted to know "how, why, and to what extent communication affects the achievement of organizational objectives." Project director James Grunig assembled a research team of both scholars and practitioners from the United Kingdom as well as the United States. The team consisted of the three of us, James Grunig and Larissa Grunig of the University of Maryland and David Dozier of San Diego State University, along with William Ehling, then of Syracuse University and now retired, Jon White, then of the Cranfield School of Management in the United Kingdom and now with City University of London, and Fred Repper, the retired vice president of public relations for Gulf States Utilities in Beaumont, Texas.

This team demonstrated what true collaboration means. Together, we put together a proposal that promised to review the literature on organizational effectiveness to develop an answer to the question of how and why public relations has value to an organization. Because we believed that not all public relations units have value to their organizations, however, we also promised to do an extensive review of the literature on public relations to isolate the characteristics that make it more likely that a communication unit will add value to an organization. We could do that because each member of the team had been heavily involved in research on different, but complementary, aspects of communication management—such as strategic management, practitioner roles, gender and diversity, models of public relations, operations research, employee communication, organizational culture, and activism.

In the summer of 1985, the IABC Foundation awarded us a grant for $400,000 to conduct the project we had outlined. The literature review started out as a paper but expanded into the 666-page book, *Excellence in Public Relations and Communication Management,* edited by James Grunig and published by Lawrence Erlbaum Associates in 1992. As the book was in press, we developed three survey questionnaires, which you can see in Appendixes A to C, that we administered to heads of public relations, CEOs, and employees in more than 300 organizations in the United States, Canada, and the United Kingdom. In September 1991, The IABC Research Foundation published the first results of this study—the development of the index of Excellence described in chapter 3—as a report titled *Excellence in Public Relations and Communication Management: Initial Data Report and Practical Guide.* After finishing this initial report, we provided a report to each of the organizations participating in the study. The report explained the theory behind the study and provided percentile scores showing each organization where it stood relative to the other organizations on overall Excellence and each of the component variables of the Excellence scale.

We believed that our research would reveal much more about excellence in communication if we went beyond the survey results to do detailed case studies of some of the organizations in our sample. We chose 25 organizations to study in more depth. Most of these had scored at the top of the Excellence scale. A few had scored at the bottom. We, student assistants at the University of Maryland and San Diego State University, and John Blamphin and Jon White in London interviewed three people in each of these organizations and wrote a detailed case study of each organization. Larissa Grunig analyzed the case studies for patterns that would answer our research questions. The IABC Research Foundation published this qualitative analysis as a second report, *IABC Excellence in Public Relations and Communication Management, Phase 2: Qualitative Study, Initial Analysis: Cases of Excellence,* in 1994.

David Dozier, with the assistance of Larissa Grunig and James Grunig, wrote a short book—primarily for communication professionals—that summarized the results of the quantitative and qualitative studies. He was assisted by a team of IABC members who reviewed the book to help make the language and interpretation accessible to communication managers. In 1995, Lawrence Erlbaum Associates published this book, *Manager's Guide to Excellence in Public Relations and Communication Management.*

Over the span of the project, we have lectured or presented seminars to more than 150 professional groups in over 35 countries. Needless to say, the Excellence study has generated tremendous interest and debate worldwide.

Now you are about to read the final product of this 15-year program of research. This book puts it all together. It summarizes and updates the literature published in *Excellence in Public Relations and Communication Management.* It incorporates the results presented in the reports published by the IABC Research Foundation and in the *Manager's Guide.* This book goes well beyond any of the previously published reports on the Excellence study. It contains many new statistical analyses of the survey data and more details from the case studies. The book is intended for scholars, applied researchers, students, and informed professionals who understand the value of research in developing a profession such as public relations. Knowledge of quantitative and qualitative research methods will make it easier to understand the book. However, we believe we have interpreted the results in a way that makes the analyses understandable even to those with little or no knowledge of statistics and research methods.

The book discusses theory and data related to several ongoing discussions in the communication profession. How can we show the value of public relations? What is the value of relationships? How do relationships affect reputation? What does it mean to practice communication strategically? How can we measure and evaluate the effects of public relations programs? Should communication programs be integrated? How does the new female majority in the profession affect communication Excellence?

In a nutshell, we show that the value of public relations comes from the relationships that communicators develop and maintain with publics. We show that reputation is a product of relationships and that the quality of relationships and reputation result more from the behavior of the organization than from the messages that communicators disseminate. We show that public relations can affect management decisions and behavior if it is headed by a manager who is empowered to play an essential role in the strategic management of the organization. In that role, communicators have their greatest value when they bring information *into* the organization, more than when they disseminate information *out* of the organization. We show how communication programs for publics such as employees, consumers, or investors can be planned and managed strategically and evaluated to demonstrate their effectiveness.

We show that communicators can develop relationships more effectively when they communicate symmetrically with publics rather than asymmetrically. Symmetrical communication is especially important inside the organization where it helps to build a participative culture that, in turn, increases employee satisfaction with the organization. We show, though, that symmetrical communication inside the organization and participative culture largely result from the structure that top management chooses for the organization. Communicators cannot be successful, therefore, unless they are part of the top-management team that develops an organizational structure. We show that diversity is important in a public relations department and throughout the organization. Women and men are equally effective in top communication roles, but we also show that women have a more difficult time than men developing the experiences needed for a top communication role.

We show that excellent communication functions are integrated. However, they are not integrated through another management function, such as marketing or human resources. They are integrated through a senior communication executive—who usually has a background in public relations—or through a single public relations department. We found that integrated marketing communication (IMC) is integrated into the integrated public relations function. IMC should not be the concept that integrates communication.

Finally, we show that activism is good for an organization rather than bad. Activism provides the impetus for excellent public publics. Excellent public relations departments develop programs to communicate actively, and symmetrically, with activists. Organizations that collaborate with activists develop a competitive advantage over organizations that do not because they behave in way that is acceptable to publics and, therefore, make fewer decisions that result in negative publicity and regulation, litigation, and opposition.

This book, as well as the research that it reports, is the product of symmetrical communication and collaboration. William Ehling, Fred Repper, and Jon White collaborated closely with us in writing the first book and in developing the study. The three of us took responsibility for conducting the research, analyzing the results, and writing the reports and books that followed. James Grunig and David Dozier did most of the quantitative analysis. Larissa Grunig did most of the qualitative analysis. However, each of us had a role in all phases of the analysis. The order of authors for this book does not indicate the importance of each of our contributions. Rather, it reflects our desire to have a different first author for each of the three *Excellence* books to show that our work truly was collaborative.

As we finish 17 years of work together on this project, from the writing of the proposal to the writing of this preface, we wish to express a mutual respect for each other. We have learned from each other. We have argued with each other. We have challenged each other. Our research is better because it is the product of collaboration and not of one person. At the same time, we have had fun together.

At this point, we are ready to move on to new research challenges. The Excellence study has provided a comprehensive picture of how we think the communication profession should be practiced. It shows that public relations is an important profession for society. It can make organizations more responsible. It can give publics a voice in management decisions that affect them. It can enhance relationships and manage conflict. In chapter 12, however, we outline what we think the new challenges are for public relations research: globalization, strategic management and relationship building, ethics and social responsibility, and change. We hope you will join us in meeting these new challenges.

ACKNOWLEDGMENTS

We already have acknowledged the contributions of our three colleagues on the Excellence research team: Jon White, William Ehling, and Fred Repper. We also have acknowledged each other. Jim and Lauri Grunig acknowledge the tolerance and support of each other. David Dozier acknowledges the support of his wife, Lorri Anne Greene.

Many of our students have worked with us over the life of the Excellence project. At the University of Maryland, they have included Linda Childers Hon, K. Sriramesh, Jody Buffington, Judith K. Meyer, Kenneth D. Plowman, and John M. Blamphin. At San Diego State University, student assistants have included Jane Ballinger, Jo Nell Miettinen, Troy Anderson, Valerie Barker, Brian Ferrario, Danielle Hauck, Nancy Lowden, Susie Maguire, James Ritchey, Natalie Walsh, and Kimberly J. White.

Finally, we acknowledge the tremendous contribution that the men and women of the IABC Research Foundation and of IABC in general have made to this project and to scholarship in public relations. They have donated generously of their time and money in developing and carrying out the project. We are especially grateful to the many individuals and chapters who contributed financially to the project and to the other contributors. There are too many IABC members to name them all, but we especially acknowledge the chairs and board members of the Foundation who were instrumental in the development and support of the project: Linda Stewart, Louis Williams, Jean Cormier, Fred Halperin, Wilma Mathews, and Robert Berzok. We thank Robert Berzok for reviewing early chapters of the manuscript and Dejan Verčič who reviewed the entire final manuscript. We also thank Dejan Verčič for replicating most of the study in Slovenia.

Finally, we express our thanks to Lawrence Erlbaum Associates—especially to communication editor Linda Bathgate, her predecessor Hollis Heimbouch, and marketing vice-president Joseph Petrowski. They have embraced and supported our work and public relations scholarship in general.

Excellence in Public Relations and Communication Management: A Review of the Theory and Results

Organizations are effective when they have the expertise needed to respond to threats and opportunities in their environment. Although the necessary knowledge varies from situation to situation, organizations typically maintain expertise in several crucial management functions. For example, a perusal of the courses offered in a typical MBA program suggests that corporations need competence in accounting, finance, marketing, human resources, logistics, strategic management, manufacturing, transportation, information systems, and operations research. Most MBA programs also require courses in business and public policy, and a few require courses in communication. Few, if any, however, require courses in public relations—even though communication and public policy are essential components of the public relations function.

Some management theorists such as Hammer and Champy (1993) believe that functional categories of expertise, such as in marketing or public relations, will be less relevant in reengineered or reinvented organizations in which people work in teams to solve problems and to produce products and services. Nevertheless, cross-functional teams still will require different types of expertise even though the people holding that expertise no longer are segregated into departments.

At different times and circumstances, certain types of expertise have been more important than others for the survival and success of organizations—for example, manufacturing during the Industrial Revolution, finance when a takeover is threatened, marketing for new companies, or human resources during downsizing. Mintzberg (1983) pointed out that individuals gain power in and over an organization because of "some dependency that [the organization] has—some gap in its own power as a system . . . the organization needs something, and it can get it only from the few people who have it" (p. 24). Today, more and more organizations seem to depend on public relations.

1

Organizations are bombarded by demands from stakeholders both inside the organization and in their environments—employees, governments, communities, consumers, stockholders, and organized activists. As a result, organizations increasingly depend on someone who has the expertise to communicate with and build relationships with these stakeholder groups. The public relations profession has or should have the expertise to fulfill that organizational dependency. The purpose of public relations is to help organizations build relationships with the publics found within several categories of stakeholders.[1] Public relations professionals help to build relationships by facilitating communication between subsystems of the organization and publics in and around the organization. Public relations is communication management, the "management of communication between an organization and its publics" (J. Grunig, 1992a, p. 4). As a result of good public relations, both management and publics should behave in ways that minimize conflict or manage conflict effectively. To facilitate a good behavioral relationship, public relations must affect organizational policy, strategy, and decisions as well as the behavior of publics.

The fact that MBA programs are beginning to offer courses in communication and that most require a course in policy provides evidence of the gradual recognition of the need for public relations expertise in management, because public relations is about communication and about policy. Too often, though, both management educators and professional managers equate communication with techniques such as the writing of reports or letters, interpersonal communication, or publicity and media relations. Likewise, they divorce public relations from policy and create new titles for the function, such as public affairs, issues management, corporate communication, or external relations. In *Excellence in Public Relations and Communication Management* (J. Grunig, 1992a), we described the relationship between the management of communication and formulation of policy in this way:

> Public relations/communication management is broader than communication technique and broader than specialized public relations programs such as media relations or publicity. Public relations and communication management describe the overall planning, execution, and evaluation of an organization's communication with both external and internal publics—groups that affect the ability of an organization to meet its goals. . . .
>
> [P]ublic relations managers should be involved in decision making by the group of senior managers who control an organization, which we call the *dominant coalition* throughout this book. Although public relations managers often vote in policy decisions made by the dominant coalition, we argue that their specialized role in the process of making those decisions is as communicators.

---

[1]The concepts of stakeholders and publics often are used interchangeably. In the first *Excellence* book, however, J. Grunig and Repper (1992) defined stakeholders as general categories of publics linked to an organization, such as employees, customers, and investors. Several publics, varying in the extent to which they are active or passive, may exist within each of these categories.

Public relations managers who are part of the dominant coalition communicate the views of publics to other senior managers, and they must communicate with publics to be able to do so. They also communicate to other senior managers the likely consequences of policy decisions after communicating with publics affected by the potential policy. (pp. 4–5)

Although expertise in public relations may seem essential for organizations, organizations and their managers vary greatly in the extent to which they recognize and empower the function. Two reasons seem to explain why: (a) Senior managers with the most power in an organization—the dominant coalition—often fail to recognize and appreciate their dependency on the public relations function, and (b) public relations practitioners often lack the expertise needed to meet that dependency even if the dominant coalition recognizes it. A preliminary understanding of these two reasons for the uneven status of public relations, especially the lack of management understanding, motivated the members of the IABC Research Foundation in 1984 to issue the call for research proposals that eventually led to the study whose results are reported in this book. In addition, these two reasons together emerged in the study as sets of variables that distinguished excellent public relations programs from those that are less excellent.

This book is the last of three produced by the research team awarded a $400,000 grant by the IABC Foundation in 1985. The first book, *Excellence in Public Relations and Communication Management* (J. Grunig, 1992b), presented the results of an extensive literature review that led to the conceptual framework for the 10-year study reported in this book. The IABC Research Foundation has published preliminary reports of the results of that research.

The first research report presented some of the results from the quantitative study of 327 organizations in the United States, Canada, and the United Kingdom (J. Grunig et al., 1991). In the quantitative segment of the Excellence study, 407 senior communication officers (some organizations had more than one public relations department), 292 CEOs or other executive managers, and 4,631 employees (an average of 14 per organization) completed separate questionnaires that measured different critical success factors for public relations. The organizations included corporations, government agencies, nonprofit organizations, and trade and professional associations.

The second report presented in-depth descriptions from qualitative research on 25 of these organizations with the highest and lowest scores on a scale of excellence produced by the quantitative research (L. Grunig, Dozier, & J. Grunig, 1994). In addition, the second book, *Manager's Guide to Excellence in Public Relations and Communication Management* (Dozier with L. Grunig & J. Grunig, 1995), presented a user-friendly review and explanation of the theory and results of both parts of the study, written mostly for public relations practitioners.

This book presents the complete results of both the quantitative and qualitative segments of the study. Sufficient detail is provided on the methods, results, data and observations, and statistics and qualitative analysis so that scholars of public relations and related fields can evaluate and interpret the study and use it to generate new research. At the same time, we have attempted to explain the study and our methods as clearly as possible so that public relations professionals and students can use its results to understand excellence in public relations and explain it to those who use and work with public relations. As a result of this extensive program of research, we believe we have constructed, modified, and confirmed an explanation of why organizations depend on public relations for their success, along with other critical success factors, and why public relations is among the most important management functions for a 21st-century organization.

This first chapter reviews the theoretical foundation for the Excellence study developed in *Excellence in Public Relations and Communication Management*. It should provide enough background so that readers who have not read that first book can understand the results presented here. Readers who want a complete understanding of the theory and the literature that supports it should read the first volume as well. This chapter ends with an overview of the results reported throughout the book and suggestions for how to read the book if one wants details only from parts of the study.

RESEARCH QUESTIONS

In its request for proposals in August 1984, the IABC Foundation asked researchers to address the question:

How, why, and to what extent does communication affect the achievement of organizational objectives?

Most public relations professionals probably are interested only in the third part of this research question: *To what extent* does communication affect the achievement of organizational objectives? That is, professionals most want to learn or prove how much value public relations has to an organization. By including three questions in the sentence, however, the IABC Foundation called for research that made it possible not only to show that public relations does have value to an organization but also to explain *why* it has value and *how* to organize the communication function so that it can provide this value.

Two major research questions, therefore, guided the Excellence study. We have called these questions the "Effectiveness Question" and the "Excellence Question." The Effectiveness Question incorporates the questions of *why* and *to what extent* public relations increases organizational effectiveness:

How does public relations make an organization more effective, and how much is that contribution worth economically?

The Excellence Question asks *how* public relations must be organized and managed to be able to make the contribution to organizational effectiveness identified in the answer to the Effectiveness Question:

What are the characteristics of a public relations function that are most likely to make an organization effective?

A number of *excellence* studies have been conducted for management practices in general, the most famous of which was Peters and Waterman's (1982) study, *In Search of Excellence*. We reviewed this study and similar ones and integrated the results in the chapter, "What Is Excellence in Management?" of *Excellence in Public Relations and Communication Management* (J. Grunig, 1992c). Most previous studies of excellence, however, addressed only the *how* question of the three questions posed in the IABC Foundation's research question. Previous excellence researchers typically chose what they thought were excellent organizations using arbitrary criteria, such as six financial measures used by Peters and Waterman, and then searched for management practices that these excellent organizations shared. Generally, though, these researchers could not explain *why* the shared practices produced the financial results. That problem became especially acute when many of the excellent companies suffered financial declines or went out of business even though the management practices had not changed ("Who's Excellent Now," 1984).

In developing our study of excellence in public relations and communication management, by contrast, we began by reviewing the literature on the nature of organizational effectiveness, the nature of public relations, and the relationship between the two (L. Grunig, J. Grunig, & Ehling, 1992). That literature allowed us to answer the *why* question: *For what reason* does public relations contribute to organizational effectiveness?

With the answer to that question in mind, we then searched literature in public relations, communication, management, organizational sociology and psychology, social and cognitive psychology, feminist studies, political science, operations research, and culture to identify characteristics of public relations programs and departments and of the organizations in which they are found that answer the *how* question: By what means do excellent public relations departments make organizations more effective?

Finally, we searched the literature for concepts that would explain the value of individual public relations programs and the value of the overall public relations function to an organization—the *to what extent* question (Ehling, 1992a; L. Grunig et al., 1992). With measures of the effects and value of public relations in hand, we then conducted the quantitative and qualitative segments of our study to look for evidence that excellent public relations programs had these effects more than did less excellent functions.

The result was a comprehensive, general theory of public relations. That general theory began with a premise of why public relations has value to an organization. We could use that premise to identify and connect attributes of the public relations function and of the organization that logically would be most likely to make the organization effective. Then we could link the outcomes of communication programs that make organizations more effective to the characteristics of a public relations function that theoretically contributes the most to organizational effectiveness. After completing the conceptualization, we submitted the general theory and the several middle-range theories and variables incorporated into it to empirical test—our extensive quantitative study of 327 organizations in the United States, Canada, and the United Kingdom and our qualitative study of 25 of the organizations with the most and least excellent public relations departments emerging from our study.

The result of 10 years of literature review, theory construction, and empirical research is a benchmarking study that identifies and describes critical success factors and best practices in public relations. We go well beyond typical benchmarking studies, however, which usually are empirical but not explanatory. Typically, these studies identify organizations that are believed to be leaders in an area of practice and then describe how they practice public relations or some other management function. Such studies answer the *how* question (how do the benchmarked companies practice public relations?), but not the *why* or *to what extent* questions. In his book on public affairs benchmarking, Fleisher (1995) said that it is important to measure what public relations units do, but that "It is just as important to discover the qualitative factors—the how's and why's behind the numbers—associated with the attainment of the numbers" (p. 15).

Our study provides a theoretical profile, a theoretical benchmark, of critical success factors and best practices in public relations. It is a profile that we initially constructed from past research and by theoretical logic. In addition, we gathered empirical evidence from organizations to confirm that this theoretical profile explains best actual practice as well as best practice in theory. The theoretical and empirical benchmark provided by the Excellence study makes it possible for public relations units to compare themselves with what Fleisher (1995) called "higher performing and world-class units in order to generate knowledge and action about public affairs roles, processes, practice, products/services, or strategic issues which will lead to performance improvement" (p. 4).

In most benchmarking studies, communication units compare themselves with similar units in their industry or with similar functional units inside the organization. The Excellence study, by contrast, is an example of what Fleisher (1995) called "generic benchmarking"—identifying critical success factors across different types of organizations. Generic benchmarking is most valuable theoretically, because it is unlikely that one organization will be "a world-class performer across the board" (p. 29). In the Excellence study, a few organizations exemplified all of the best practices, many organizations exemplified some of them, and others exemplified few of the practices—that is, the theoretical benchmark was normally distributed in the population of organizations.

The empirical results of the Excellence study provide strong and consistent support for the theory that guided the study. As also occurs in most research, however, the results suggest how to improve and revise our theoretical formulation of best practice, which we do at appropriate points in the book.

A theoretical benchmark does not provide an exact formula or detailed description of practices that a public relations unit can copy in order to be excellent. Rather, it provides a set of principles that such units can use to generate ideas for specific practices in their own organizations. As a comprehensive model of excellence in public relations, therefore, this theoretical and empirical benchmark provides a model:

- For auditing and evaluating public relations departments.
- For explaining to dominant coalitions why their organizations depend on public relations, how much value communication has to their organization, and how to organize and manage the function to achieve the greatest value from it.
- For the teaching of public relations to both beginners and experienced practitioners.

In his chapter on "How Communication Managers Can Apply the Theories of Excellence and Effectiveness" in *Excellence in Public Relations and Communication Management*, Repper (1992), the practitioner member of the Excellence team, reached two conclusions that identified the first two of the uses listed. First, he suggested the theory of excellence could be used to audit communication programs:

> One thing communicators never have been able to do is to compare our communication programs with a program that is considered the best and most effective. However, the normative theory provided in the book gives us an opportunity to measure the effectiveness of our communication programs against that of an ideal program. This comparison is the how to part of the book that each practitioner can use in planning his or her next communication program. (p. 112)[2]

Second, he explained the value of the theoretical benchmark for CEOs and other senior managers:

> The CEO also needs a yardstick to measure how well communication employees are doing their jobs. The CEO, therefore, will have a vested interest in the results of this study because we are trying to determine what public relations contributes to organizational effec-

---

[2]This quotation is presented in italics because it is a conclusion from *Excellence in Public Relations and Communication Management*. We follow the same procedure throughout this book whenever we provide a theoretical proposition or conclusion from *Excellence* that we used to link the theory and literature from the first book to the analysis of data presented in this book.

tiveness and also provide the yardstick for measuring excellence in communication. Thus, I believe this book will be as interesting and valuable to the CEO and organizational decision makers as to the professional communication practitioner. (pp. 113–114)

Similarly, Ehling (1992b), in his chapter on "Public Relations Education and Professionalism" in *Excellence,* concluded that public relations education needs more intellectual substance:

Problems are encountered in public relations education itself. Although three commissions on public relations education have recommended model curricula for both undergraduate and graduate public relations education, institutions of higher education do not feel compelled to adhere to such recommended models; there still is widespread evidence that various schools and departments, cashing in on the popularity of public relations among students, have added a course or two to existing sequences in journalism and advertise them as bone fide programs in public relations. (p. 457)

Even serious attempts to give public relations content that has intellectual substance, which can be defended ethically and made administratively viable, often have led to more difficulties than solutions. Efforts at defining publics have not as yet fully succeeded. Attempts to conceptualize public relations as some kind of socially oriented function frequently have resulted only in producing an outpouring of simple definitions that hardly get beyond that of slogans. . . . (p. 458)

We cannot and should not maintain that our general theory of excellence is the only intellectual framework for public relations education. However, we can maintain that it provides *an* overarching theory for the discipline and that the framework it provides satisfies one of the major criteria that must be met if public relations is to be a profession.

OVERVIEW OF THE EXCELLENCE THEORY

Excellence in Public Relations and Communication Management contained 23 chapters organized into five parts. Chapters in Part I, *The Basic Theory,* provided an integrating thread explaining why 14 characteristics of excellent public relations departments make organizations more effective. Part II, *The Program Level,* contained chapters describing how excellent public relations is planned, implemented, and evaluated at the level of individual communication programs aimed at such stakeholders as the media, employees, communities, customers, or investors. Part III, *The Departmental Level,* consisted of chapters describing how public relations departments are organized and managed. Part IV, *The Organizational Level,* contained chapters that described the organizational and environmental context most likely to nurture excellent public relations. Part V,

The Economic Level, described how the monetary value of public relations can be measured—the measures we used to estimate its value in the Excellence study.

Each of the 23 chapters listed from 1 to 15 theoretical propositions or conclusions that related the middle-range theories discussed in that chapter to the overall Excellence theory. We have used these propositions and conclusions in our analysis of the research presented in this book. For example, three of the propositions, from Repper (1992) and Ehling (1992b), were presented at the end of the previous section, when we discussed three applications of the theoretical benchmark provided by the Excellence study.

Table 1.1 of *Excellence in Public Relations and Communication Management* summarized 14 characteristics of excellent public relations programs and three effects of those programs. Table 1.1 of this book reproduces that table as a guide for the theoretical overview of this chapter. As we explicate each of these major concepts in the discussion that follows, we include the number of the concept from Table 1.1 in order to link this book to the previous one.

TABLE 1.1
Characteristics of Excellent Public Relations Programs

I. **Program Level.**
   1. Managed strategically.
II. **Departmental Level.**
   2. A single or integrated public relations department.
   3. Separate function from marketing.
   4. Direct reporting relationship to senior management.
   5. Two-way symmetrical model.
   6. Senior public relations person in the managerial role.
   7. Potential for excellent public relations, as indicated by:
      a. Knowledge of symmetrical model.
      b. Knowledge of managerial role.
      c. Academic training in public relations.
      d. Professionalism.
   8. Equal opportunity for men and women in public relations.
III. **Organizational Level.**
   9. Worldview for public relations in the organization reflects the two-way symmetrical model.
   10. Public relations director has power in or with the dominant coalition.
   11. Participative rather than authoritarian organizational culture.
   12. Symmetrical system of internal communication.
   13. Organic rather than mechanical organizational structure.
   14. Turbulent, complex environment with pressure from activist groups.
IV. **Effects of Excellent Public Relations.**
   15. Programs meet communication objectives.
   16. Reduces costs of regulation, pressure, and litigation.
   17. Job satisfaction is high among employees.

Note. From J. Grunig (1992a). Copyright 1992 by Lawrence Erlbaum Associates. Adapted by permission.

We begin the discussion of the Excellence theory by presenting a basic proposition about the value of public relations to an organization and to society. We relate this crucial element of the theory, in turn, to characteristics of the overall public relations department and to characteristics of communication programs for specific publics such as employees, customers, donors, or government. Finally, we examine characteristics of the environment and of the overall organization that provide the most nurturing context for an excellent public relations program.

Public Relations and Organizational Effectiveness: The Basic Premise of the Theory of Excellence

The Excellence theory is organized around the proposition that was presented at end of the chapter, "What Is an Effective Organization?" (L. Grunig et al., 1992). The proposition answers the Effectiveness Question by explaining *why* public relations contributes to organizational effectiveness and *to what extent* by asserting that public relations has monetary value to the organization:

> *Public relations contributes to organizational effectiveness when it helps reconcile the organization's goals with the expectations of its strategic constituencies. This contribution has monetary value to the organization. Public relations contributes to effectiveness by building quality, long-term relationships with strategic constituencies. Public relations is most likely to contribute to effectiveness when the senior public relations manager is a member of the dominant coalition where he or she is able to shape the organization's goals and to help determine which external publics are most strategic.* (p. 86)

Our review of the literature on organizational effectiveness showed that organizations are effective when they attain their goals. However, the review also showed that goals must be appropriate for the strategic constituencies that are found in the organization's environment, publics that have the power to constrain the ability of the organization to meet its goals and achieve its mission or that expect help from the organization in achieving their own goals.

Organizations strive for autonomy from their publics. Organizations also try to mobilize publics that support their goals and thus increase their autonomy. Having the autonomy to pursue their goals is important for organizations because effective organizations choose appropriate goals for their environmental and cultural context and then achieve those goals.

No organization ever achieves complete autonomy, although it may be an idealized goal. Organizations work toward this idealized goal by managing their interdependence with publics. Therefore, building relationships—managing interdependence—is the essence of public relations. Good relationships make organizations more effective because they allow organizations more freedom to achieve their missions. Ironically, however, organizations maximize their autonomy by giving up some of it to build relationships with publics.

Organizations plan public relations programs strategically at the level of the public relations department, therefore, when they identify the publics that are most likely to limit or enhance organizational autonomy. At the program level, excellent public relations departments design communication programs that manage conflict or potential conflict with these strategic publics, which helps organizations to build stable, open, and trusting relationships with them. As a result, the quality of relationships with strategic publics is a key indicator of the long-term contribution that public relations makes to organizational effectiveness.

Good relationships between organizations and their publics are two-way and symmetrical—that is, the relationships balance the interests of the organization with the interests of publics on which the organization has consequences and that have consequences on the organization. To build such relationships, organizations must fulfill the conclusion stated in the chapter of *Excellence* on "The Effect of Worldviews on Public Relations Theory and Practice" (J. Grunig & White, 1992) that: *"For public relations to be excellent, public relations must be viewed as symmetrical, idealistic and critical, and managerial"* (p. 31; Characteristic 9).

To be symmetrical means that organizations have the worldview that public relations practitioners serve the interests of both sides of relationships while still advocating the interests of the organizations that employ them. To be idealistic and critical means that public relations practitioners have the freedom to advocate the interests of publics to management and to criticize management decisions that affect publics adversely. To be managerial means that public relations fulfills the managerial role of negotiating and mediating the conflict that occurs between management and strategic publics.

When organizations define and organize their public relations function according to this worldview, public relations should serve the interests both of organizations and of society—which consists, for the most part, of publics. As a result, public relations has value both to organizations and to society. Most of the value of good relationships comes because both organizations and publics save the money they otherwise would spend on conflict—conflict that typically is manifested in *regulation, legislation, litigation, campaigns, and other forms of pressure from activist groups or regulatory bodies* (Characteristic 16 of Table 1.1). Inside the organization, excellent public relations *increases the level of satisfaction that employees have with the organization* (Characteristic 17), which, in turn, saves money that might be wasted on the consequences of bad relationships with employee publics—consequences such as strikes, absenteeism, low motivation, and turnover.

Our review of the literature on organizational effectiveness also identified the principle of requisite variety (Weick, 1979) as a defining characteristic of effective organizations. The principle of requisite variety states that there must be as much diversity inside the organization as in its environment for the organization to be able to build good relationships with all critical stakeholder publics.

For public relations, the principle of requisite variety means that practitioners from both genders (Characteristic 8) and from different racial, ethnic, and cultural backgrounds are needed in an excellent public relations department—not just for the benefit of these diverse practitioners but because they make the organization more effective.[3]

Excellent public relations departments do the actual work of building relationships with publics by planning, executing, and evaluating communication programs at the program level. Communication programs in excellent departments *are more likely to achieve their objectives* (Characteristic 15)—improved relational outcomes—than are the typical unplanned and unevaluated programs of less excellent departments. Excellent communication programs, to use Fleisher's (1995) term, are *efficient:* "They do the job right" (p. 79). Nevertheless, efficient programs will not contribute to organizational *effective*ness unless they are developed for publics for whom it is important—strategic—for the organization to build relationships (in Fleisher's language, they do not "do the right job" [p. 79]).

Chapter 4 of this book responds to the effectiveness research question. It explains the value of public relations to organizations in detail and analyzes evidence from the quantitative and qualitative parts of the study that test the basic premise of the Excellence theory.

Chapter 3 discusses how we constructed an overall index of public relations excellence—the Excellence factor. In that chapter, we also compare the scores on that factor for organizations in the three countries studied and for the four types of organizations. Finally, we examine the predicted relationship, from Table 1.1, of education in public relations and professionalism with the Excellence factor: *Academic training in public relations increases the potential for excellence in public relations* (Characteristic 7c). Communication departments have greater potential for excellence when they are staffed by professionals—people who have learned the body of knowledge in public relations and who are active in professional associations and read professional literature (Characteristic 7d).

Characteristics of Excellent Public Relations Departments

Chapters 5 through 8 begin the process of analyzing the Excellence question: What are the characteristics of public relations departments and programs and the internal and environmental context of the organization that increase the likelihood that the public relations function will have value both for the organization and for society? These are the critical middle-range theories that we inte-

---

[3]*Excellence in Public Relations and Communication Management* looked at requisite variety mostly from the perspective of gender. The quantitative study also included gender as a variable but not diversity in racial and cultural backgrounds of practitioners. In the qualitative study, however, we gathered information on racial and cultural diversity of communicators in the most and least excellent departments.

grated within the general theory of excellence in the first *Excellence* book. These four chapters begin this process of looking at middle-range theories by analyzing the data on characteristics of the overall public relations department. Later, we do the same for specific communication programs and for the environmental and organizational context of excellent public relations functions.

Table 1.1 contains seven characteristics of an excellent communication department. These characteristics can be placed into four categories that provide the themes for chapters 5–8 of this book:

1. *Empowerment of the Public Relations Function.* For public relations to contribute to organizational effectiveness as described by the basic theory of excellence, the organization must empower communication management as a critical management function. Chapter 5 reports data on the extent to which excellent public relations departments are empowered by their organizations. Empowerment of the public relations function subsumes four characteristics from Table 1.1. The first three consider the relationship of public relations to the overall management of the organization:

(a) *The senior public relations executive is involved with the strategic management processes of the organization, and communication programs are developed for strategic publics identified as a part of this strategic management process* (Characteristic 1). Public relations contributes to strategic management by scanning the environment to identify publics affected by the consequences of decisions or who might affect the outcome of decisions. An excellent public relations department communicates with these publics to bring their voices into strategic management, thus making it possible for stakeholder publics to participate in organizational decisions that affect them.

(b) *The senior public relations executive is a member of the dominant coalition of the organization* (Characteristic 10), or (c) *the senior public relations executive has a direct reporting relationship to senior managers who are part of the dominant coalition* (Characteristic 4). The public relations function seldom will be involved in strategic management nor will public relations have the power to affect key organizational decisions unless the senior public relations executive is part of or has access to the group of senior managers with the greatest power in the organization.

The fourth characteristic from Table 1.1 defines the extent to which practitioners who are not White men are empowered in the public relations function:

(d) *Diversity is embodied in all public relations roles* (Characteristic 8). The principle of requisite variety suggests that organizations need as much diversity inside as in their environment. Excellent public departments empower both men and women in all roles as well as practitioners of diverse racial, ethnic, and cultural backgrounds.

2. *Communicator Roles.* Public relations researchers have conducted extensive research on four major roles that communicators play in organizations—

the manager, senior adviser (also known as the communication liaison), technician, and media relations roles. The manager and technician roles are the most
common of the four. Communication technicians are essential to carry out
most of the day-to-day communication activities of public relations departments, and many practitioners play both manager and technician roles. In less
excellent departments, however, all of the communication practitioners—including the senior practitioner—are technicians. If the senior communicator is
not a manager, it is not possible for public relations to be empowered as a management function because there are no managers in the department.

Chapter 6 analyzes data on three characteristics from Table 1.1 related to the
managerial role:

(a) *The public relations unit is headed by a manager rather than a technician* (Characteristic 6). Excellent public relations units must have at least one senior communication manager who conceptualizes and directs public relations programs,
or this direction will be supplied by other members of the dominant coalition
who have little or no knowledge of communication management or of relationship building.

(b) *The senior public relations executive or others in the public relations unit must
have the knowledge needed for the manager role, or the communication function will not
have the potential to become a managerial function* (Characteristic 7b). Excellent
public relations programs are staffed by people who have gained the knowledge
needed to carry out the manager role through university education, continuing
education, or self-study.

(c) *Both men and women must have equal opportunity to occupy the managerial role
in an excellent department* (Characteristic 8). The majority of public relations professionals in the three countries studied are women. If women are excluded
from the managerial role, the communication function may be diminished because the majority of the most knowledgeable practitioners will be excluded
from that role. When that is the case, the senior position in the public relations
department typically is filled by a technician or by a practitioner from another
managerial function who has little knowledge of public relations.

3. *Organization of the Communication Function, Relationship to Other Functions,
and Use of Consulting Firms.* Many organizations have a single department devoted to all communication functions. Others have separate departments for
programs aimed at different publics such as employees, consumers, investors,
or donors. Still others place communication under another managerial function
such as marketing, human resources, legal, or finance. Many organizations also
contract with or consult with outside firms for all or some of their communication programs or for such communication techniques as annual reports or
newsletters. Chapter 7 analyzes data from the Excellence study on how organizations organize the public relations function.

For public relations to be managed strategically and to serve a role in the
overall strategic management of the organization, the Excellence theory states

that organizations must have an (a) *integrated communication function* (Characteristic 2). An excellent public relations function integrates all public relations programs into a single department or provides a mechanism for coordinating programs managed by different departments. Only in an integrated system is it possible for public relations to develop new communication programs for changing strategic publics and to move resources from outdated programs designed for formerly strategic publics to the new programs.

Even though the public relations function is integrated in an excellent organization, the function should not be integrated into another department whose primary responsibility is a management function other than communication. Therefore, the Excellence theory states that (b) *public relations should be a management function separate from other functions* (Characteristic 3). Many organizations splinter the public relations function by making communication a supporting tool for other departments. When the public relations function is sublimated to other functions, it cannot be managed strategically because it cannot move communication resources from one strategic public to another—as an integrated public relations function can.

When we wrote *Excellence in Public Relations and Communication Management*, little research was available on the role of public relations consulting firms in excellent organizations. Therefore, the Excellence theory made no predictions about the role of outside firms; but in the quantitative study we asked questions on how organizations use these firms in the communication function. Chapter 7 also reports these data.

4. *Models of Public Relations.* Public relations scholars have conducted extensive research on the extent to which organizations practice four models of public relations—four typical ways of conceptualizing and conducting the communication function—and to identify which of these models provides a normative framework for effective and ethical public relations. This research suggests that excellent departments design their communication programs on the two-way symmetrical model rather than the press agentry, public information, or two-way asymmetrical models.

Two-way symmetrical public relations attempts to balance the interests of the organization and its publics, is based on research, and uses communication to manage conflict with strategic publics. As a result, two-way symmetrical communication produces better long-term relationships with publics than do the other models of public relations. Symmetrical programs generally are conducted more ethically than are other models and produce effects that balance the interests of organizations and the publics in society. Symmetrical practitioners, therefore, have *mixed motives* (they are loyal both to their employers and to the publics of their organizations).

Chapter 8 analyzes data on four characteristics of Excellence from Table 1.1 related to models of public relations:

(a) *The public relations department and the dominant coalition share the worldview that the communication department should reflect the two-way symmetrical, or mixed-motive, model of public relations* (Characteristic 9).

(b) *Communication programs developed for specific publics are based on the two-way symmetrical, mixed-motive model* (Characteristic 5).

(c) *The senior public relations executive or others in the public relations unit must have the knowledge needed for the two-way symmetrical model, or the communication function will not have the potential to practice that excellent model* (Characteristic 7a).

The Excellence theory also states that organizations should have a (d) *symmetrical system of internal communication* (Characteristic 12). Data on the internal system of communication are analyzed along with other characteristics of the organization in chapter 11.

Characteristics of Excellent Communication Programs for Specific Publics

After analyzing these characteristics of the overall public relations department, we turned to a more microlevel analysis of programs developed for specific publics and the media: the media, employees, investors, the community, customers, government, members, and donors. Our theory, as summarized in Table 1.1, stated simply that communication programs organized by excellent departments should be *managed strategically* (Characteristic 1).

To be managed strategically means that these programs are based on research and environmental scanning, that varying rather than routine techniques are used when they are implemented, and that they are evaluated either formally or informally. In addition, we predicted that the communication professionals who participated in our research would have evidence to show that these programs had improved the relationships of the organization and its publics (Characteristics 16 and 17). Chapter 9 analyzes data on the origins and outcomes of communication programs in depth, and chapter 11 analyzes job satisfaction (Characteristic 17) as part of its analysis of internal characteristics of the organization.

Activism and the Environmental Context for Excellence

After examining the characteristics of excellent public relations departments and the programs they manage, we turned to the organizational context to determine whether communication Excellence can survive more or less on its own or whether it requires a nourishing external and internal context to flourish.

Externally, Table 1.1 predicts that *a turbulent, complex environment with pressure from activist groups* (Characteristic 14) stimulates organizations to develop an excellent public relations function. Previous research on activist groups shows that most organizations, at least in the United States, have experienced pressure from activism. In addition, research on power in organizations suggests that organizations are most likely to empower the public relations function when pressure from activists or crises produced by that pressure make public relations expertise valuable. Chapter 10 analyzes data on the extent to which organizations experience activism and on the relationship of this contextual variable to excellence in communication management.

The Organizational Context of Excellent Public Relations

Inside the organization, previous research by both organizational and public relations scholars has examined the extent to which the organizational characteristics of structure, culture, communication system, treatment of men and women, and power of the dominant coalition predict organizational behavior, in general, and public relations practice, in particular.

After reviewing this research in *Excellence in Public Relations and Communication Management,* we concluded that a power-control theory explains organizational and public relations behavior best. That is, organizations behave, in general, and practice public relations, in particular, as they do because the dominant coalition chooses to organize and manage in that way. That is why we predicted in Table 1.1 that the senior communicator in an excellent public relations function would have *power in or with the dominant coalition* (Characteristic 10), a characteristic that is analyzed in detail in chapter 5 on empowerment of the public relations function.

Nevertheless, previous research also suggests that the organizational context of a public relations function could nurture or impede excellent communication management, although to a lesser extent than it is shaped by the dominant coalition. Chapter 11 explores the internal context. In particular, it analyzes data on the extent to which organizations with excellent public relations have, as we predicted in Table 1.1:

- *Participative rather than authoritarian organizational cultures* (Characteristic 11).
- *A symmetrical system of internal communication* (Characteristic 12).
- *Organic rather than mechanical structures* (Characteristic 13).
- *Programs to equalize opportunities for men and women and minorities* (Characteristic 8).
- *High job satisfaction among employees* (Characteristic 17).

Chapter 11 analyzes the interaction among these internal characteristics of organizations to determine the extent to which internal communication and programs to enhance opportunities for women and minority employees help to provide a context that nurtures excellent public relations. The chapter asks, in other words, whether implementing some characteristics of excellence can, in turn, facilitate the development of the other characteristics of excellence.

WHAT CAUSES WHAT?

Since we wrote *Excellence in Public Relations and Communication Management*, members of the research team often have been asked where excellence in communication management begins: with the dominant coalition, the public relations department, organizational or societal culture, activist pressure, or what? Most theorists probably would develop a linear model of antecedents, processes, and outcomes of excellent public relations. It would be possible, for example, to specify that empowerment of public relations, activism in the environment, culture, structure, internal communication, and equal opportunity programs are antecedents to excellent public relations. Characteristics of public relations departments and programs could be specified as intermediary processes. The outcomes of public relations programs and the value assigned to public relations by the dominant coalition could be specified as outcomes.

We have resisted this linear type of thinking. It is possible to reverse many of the causal relationships just specified as a linear model. For example, an organization might develop an excellent public relations program because the dominant coalition valued public relations before the department became excellent. An excellent public relations department might help to create a participative culture, organic structure, symmetrical internal communication, or equal opportunity programs. Or the entire process might begin when a knowledgeable practitioner is employed by an organization that does not necessarily have a worldview that values public relations.

Figure 1.1, which is taken from chapter 1 of *Excellence in Public Relations and Communication Management,* models the interactive and systemic nature of excellent public relations and the organizational and environment context in which it is found. The model has the choice of publics and public relations models at its center because these choices are at the core of the strategic management of public relations and of the contribution of public relations to strategic management. At this time, we would replace the box labeled "Choice of PR Models as Strategies" with the broader set of variables that we used to describe strategically managed public relations programs in chapters 8 and 9—thus relabeling the box "Choice of PR Strategies."

The value of public relations to organizations—the contribution of communication management to organizational effectiveness—appears in the arrow that flows from the box now labeled "Choice of PR Strategies" to the box labeled "Environmental Interdependencies" because organizations that choose an excellent strategy will be more likely to manage conflict and, therefore, to manage critical environmental interdependencies and make the organization more effective.

The boxes at the outside of the model also make it clear that excellence can begin at one or more of four places: the dominant coalition, public relations potential, societal and organizational culture, or the environment. When we reported many of the results of the Excellence project in the *Manager's Guide to Excellence in Public Relations and Communication Management,* we organized the discussion into three categories: the Knowledge Base of the Communication Department (public relations potential in Fig. 1.1), Shared Expectations With the Dominant Coalition About Communication (worldview and the dominant coalition in Fig. 1.1), and the Character of Organizations (culture in Fig. 1.1).

The data reported in that book, which are discussed in greater depth in this book, show that excellence does not always begin in the same place in the model. In some organizations we studied, it began in one of the outside boxes in

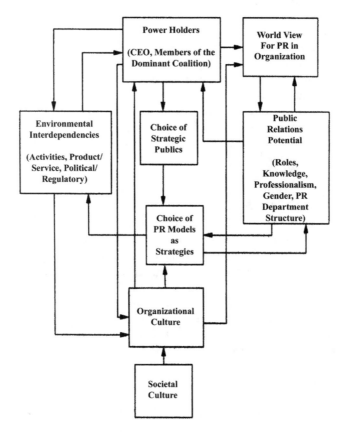

FIG. 1.1.   Factors influencing the choice of a model of public relations. Source: J. Grunig, 1992a, p. 23.

Fig. 1.1; in others, it began in a combination of boxes. There was no single pattern by which excellence emerged. These nonlinear origins and effects of excellence are particularly evident in the qualitative data we report in this book.

AN OVERVIEW OF THE EXCELLENCE RESULTS:
A GUIDE TO READING THE REST OF THE BOOK

Excellent Public Relations and Effective Organizations can be read in different ways. Some people will want to read the book from the first to the last chapter, in order to understand all of the details of our statistical and qualitative analysis as they unfold and the implications of these analyses for public relations theory. Others will prefer to begin by reading a summary of the results and then read only the chapters on specific middle-range theories of interest to them. In this final section of chapter 1, therefore, we highlight the results from each chapter and summarize how they confirm or expand the Excellence theory. This section also presents a concise summary of the results of the Excellence study, which should be a useful overview of the details that follow in each chapter.

Chapter 2, "The Methodology of the Excellence Study," explains the characteristics of our sample of organizations, our measures of concepts, and the quantitative and qualitative methods used to analyze the data. Readers who have only marginal interest in methods can skip this chapter: It is not necessary for understanding the remaining chapters. As scholars and researchers, however, we have an obligation to disclose the details of our methods for those who might want to conduct a similar study or who want to confirm the adequacy of our methods.

Chapter 3, "Isolating the Excellence Factor," takes a broad look at most of the data we collected at the departmental, organizational, environmental, and economic levels of analysis. We could not include the data on programs for specific publics in this chapter because not all organizations had programs for the same publics. We used factor analysis and canonical correlation to successfully isolate a single factor of excellence, showing that organizations with excellent public relations departments shared the same characteristics and that these characteristics correlated positively with the value attributed to public relations by the CEO. Some characteristics did not correlate so highly with the single factor of excellence as did others, so we left them out of our index of excellence and correlated them with the Excellence factor later. In subsequent chapters, we also correlated the characteristics of specific communication programs with the Excellence factor as well as other characteristics pertinent to the middle-range theories discussed in those chapters.

The Excellence factor we isolated strongly confirms the theory developed in *Excellence in Public Relations and Communication Management* and reviewed in chapter 1 of this book. We found that CEOs with excellent public relations departments valued the communication function almost twice as much as those with less excellent departments. CEOs who value public relations most believe it should be practiced essentially as spelled out by our theory of excellence. They also believe that public relations departments should be characterized by participation in strategic management, symmetrical communication combined judiciously with two-way asymmetrical communication, and leadership by strategic communication managers. Of these variables, participation in strategic management was the variable that most increased the value the dominant coalition assigned to public relations.

Heads of excellent public relations departments also reported that their units practice public relations according to these same principles of excellence. Of the variables that came from the top-communicator questionnaires, excellence in public relations was defined most by the knowledge that departments had to practice the managerial role and the two-way symmetrical and two-way asymmetrical models of public relations. Top communicators in excellent departments were somewhat more likely also to have studied public relations formally and to read professional publications about public relations. They were no more likely to participate in professional associations, however, than were practitioners in less excellent departments.

Chapter 3 also shows that the organizational and environmental context nurtured, but did not guarantee, excellent public relations. Organizations with excellent public relations were more likely to have participative cultures, organic structures, symmetrical communication systems, and high job satisfaction. They also fostered the careers of their female employees and were found in environments with more-than-average pressure from activist groups. Finally, chapter 3 shows that excellence in public relations seems to be generic to the three countries and the four types of organizations we found. Size of the organization also made no difference. And, heads of excellent departments came from all age groups and were equally likely to be women as men.

The index of excellence developed in chapter 3 contains variables that measured the value of public relations as well as key characteristics of public relations practice. Canonical correlation showed a strong relationship between excellent public relations and the value of public relations as determined by the CEO's estimated return on investment (ROI) from public relations.

Chapter 4, "The Value of Public Relations," analyzes the value of public relations in greater detail. It shows that the ROI on public relations, as estimated by the CEO, approached 225% under conditions of excellence. It was as low as 100 for the least excellent public relations departments. Even these estimates are averages over a number of years, however, because our respondents suggested that the ROI is lumpy, long-term, and often the result of something that does not happen. The major return from public relations may occur only once every 10 to 20 years, and that return may represent a problem that public relations prevented from happening—such as a strike, a crisis, litigation, a boycott, or regulation. In most cases, however, CEOs and communicators agreed that excellent public relations returns significantly more than it costs—and more than the typical department in their organization.

At the same time, chapter 4 provides evidence that public relations is one important factor—but by no means the only factor—that has an effect on the financial performance of organizations. However, we found little reason to believe that a single hard financial indicator could be found to measure the value of public relations. Rather, a softer indicator of the value of communication—compensating variation—allowed us to show that excellent public relations does contribute value both to the organization and to society. The public relations profession needs to identify a strong nonfinancial indicator of effective public relations, and the results of our qualitative interviews suggest that the concept of relationships would be the best such indicator—better than such nebulous and poorly defined concepts as reputation, image, goodwill, and brand that are popular buzzwords among public relations people today.

Chapter 4 also shows that the financial success that can be attributed to public relations does not come at the cost of social responsibility. The most effective organizations we studied relied on public relations to help determine which stakeholder groups were strategic for it and then to help develop credible, long-term relationships with those constituencies. Such high-quality relationships exist only when the organization acknowledges the legitimacy of the public, listens to its concerns, and deals with any negative consequences it may be having on that public.

Chapter 5, "Empowerment of the Public Relations Function," confirms that the public relations function must be empowered as a distinct and strategic managerial function if it is to play a role in making organizations effective. Our data show that the senior public relations officer in excellent departments played a role in making strategic organizational decisions, was a member of the dominant coalition or had access to this powerful group of organizational leaders, and had relative autonomy from excessive clearance rules to play this strategic role.

We learned that top communicators in excellent public relations departments had earned a close working relationship with their CEOs. That relationship seemed to result from extensive knowledge of the business or industry, a record of successful performance in the organization, expertise in strategic planning and managerial decision making that was not limited to communication, and a shared worldview of the value of two-way symmetrical public relations.

Finally, chapter 5 shows that departments are excellent as often when women are the senior communicator as when men are in that role. Likewise, increasing the number of women in the public relations department and in managerial roles had no effect on excellence. At the same time, however, we found that excellent public relations departments take active steps to include women in managerial roles and to promote them from inside rather than to bring in men from other managerial functions. Likewise, we found that excellent departments actively strive to increase racioethnic diversity in the function—pushing for more requisite variety in public relations.

Chapter 6, "Communicator Roles," confirms that excellent public relations departments have senior communicators who are managers rather than technicians. Most important, our results show that excellent departments have greater knowledge to perform a managerial role. Excellent departments also have higher levels of technical expertise than less excellent departments, although the data suggest that technical expertise has value only when it is accompanied by managerial expertise. Excellent public relations managers possess technical expertise or have it available to them—especially technical knowledge in media relations. However, expert technicians who have little managerial expertise or who are not supervised by expert managers add little value to the organization.

Our data also reveal more than one kind of managerial expertise. We found that excellent departments possess both strategic and administrative managerial expertise. Chapter 5 shows that strategic managers are essential to the functioning of an excellent public relations department. Chapter 6 shows, in addition, that public relations departments need administrative as well as strategic expertise. Like technical expertise, however, administrative expertise has little value without accompanying knowledge of how to practice strategic public relations.

Although the CEOs who completed our questionnaire viewed public relations roles in a more splintered and confusing way than did top communicators, CEOs of organizations with excellent public relations departments expected their top communicators to be managers. At the same time, they expected their top communicators to be experts in media relations—more strongly than did top communicators. In addition, our results suggest that CEOs often hire top communicators because of their technical expertise but then learn that technical expertise is insufficient when a crisis or major internal upheaval requires more strategic communication skills. When top communicators have managerial as well as technical knowledge, as our qualitative results show, they can meet such a challenge. When they have only technical expertise, they cannot.

We also found that gender makes little difference in the role enacted by top communicators in excellent departments, in the role expectations of CEOs, and in the expertise of the public relations department. Female PR heads are more likely to play dual manager–technician roles than are men—even in organizations with excellent public relations departments. Female top communicators also may have less opportunity than men to gain strategic expertise because of the time they must spend doing technical tasks. The gender of the top communicator, therefore, does not help or hinder communication Excellence, although female top communicators may have to work harder to develop strategic expertise.

Chapter 7, "Organization of the Communication Function, Relationship to Other Management Functions, and Use of Consulting Firms," addresses the question of how the communication function should be organized in organizations and what its relationship should be to other management functions, especially to marketing. Our data show that excellent communication functions rapidly are being integrated under the umbrella of public relations or corporate communication.

Organizations seem to be integrating communication activities through a central public relations department, or they have several specialized communication departments that are coordinated both formally and informally by a chief communication officer who usually holds the title of senior vice president or vice president of corporate communication. In addition to the coordinating role of this senior communication officer, organizations use a number of other ways to coordinate their activities, such as organization-wide meetings, communication policies, and unstructured interaction of communication professionals in different departments or business units.

These combinations of centralized or integrated specialized departments also generally have a matrix arrangement with other management functions—such as marketing, human resources, or finance. They work under an integrated philosophy of communication—a philosophy that is largely strategic and symmetrical. But the communication managers in these centralized and specialized departments work as peer professionals with their counterparts in other management functions. In excellent departments there is little conflict and competition with other management functions—including marketing. Inside excellent communication departments, professionals work as colleagues who are equally empowered.

Chapter 7 also shows that excellent communication departments seek support from outside public relations firms. All public relations departments in our sample purchased a substantial proportion of their technical publicity activities from outside firms, as well as a large proportion of their research support. Excellent public relations departments also sought strategic counseling from outside firms when they had difficulties with their publics, although most seem to possess the knowledge themselves to deal with these problems.

Although the marketing function in excellent organizations seldom dominates public relations, communication departments in less excellent organizations have a strong tendency to provide little more than technical support to the marketing function—technical support that most communication departments purchase from outside firms. A few of the excellent departments seem to have adopted marketing theory as the foundation for their communication programs—with its emphasis on customers, messages, and symbols. On the positive side, however, they also have adopted the strategic, two-way approach of contemporary marketing—although marketing theory has steered them toward an asymmetrical rather than a symmetrical approach to communication.

Chapter 8, "Models of Public Relations," assesses the extent to which excellent public relations departments base their practice on the concept of four models of public relations, which J. Grunig introduced in the 1970s as a way of understanding and explaining the behavior of public relations practitioners. These models are press agentry, public information, two-way asymmetrical, and two-way symmetrical. These public relations models have been researched and debated extensively. Do they describe actual public relations practice? Is the symmetrical model only an idealized, normative model? Is it unlikely that a large organization with more power than its publics would ever deliberately choose to practice symmetrical public relations?

The quantitative and qualitative data reported in chapter 8 provide the most comprehensive information ever collected on the models of public relations. As a result, those data suggest a significant reconceptualization of the models. We did find that the four models still provide an accurate and useful tool to describe public relations practice and worldview. Practitioners and CEOs do think about public relations in these ways, and the four models do describe the way communication programs are conducted for different types of publics. However, the differences among the two one-way and the two two-way models typically blur in the minds of CEOs and in the actual practice of some, but not all, programs. CEOs, in particular, view an excellent public relations function as including the two-way asymmetrical model as often as the two-way symmetrical model.

We found the answer to this joint preference of CEOs by isolating a two-way component of the two-way asymmetrical model. CEOs like the two-way asymmetrical model because they prefer the systematic use of research in that model. Most did not distinguish research conducted for symmetrical purposes from research conducted for asymmetrical purposes. Most CEOs do not want asymmetrical communication programs, although we did find exceptions in our detailed survey of cases. Organizations that define public relations as a marketing function, in particular, tend to see public relations only in asymmetrical or in one-way terms.

In chapter 8, we isolated three dimensions underlying the four models—one-way versus two-way, symmetry versus asymmetry, and mediated or interpersonal techniques. We also suggested further research on a fourth dimension, the ethics of communication. The overlapping concepts and practices of the models that we had found before—such as practicing the two-way symmetrical, two-way asymmetrical, and public-information models concurrently—now seem to have occurred because an organization had a symmetrical public relations worldview, favored extensive research, and practiced mediated as well as interpersonal communication.

Chapter 8 concludes, therefore, that excellent public relations can be described better in terms of these underlying dimensions than in terms of the four models themselves. Excellent public relations is research based (two-way), symmetrical (although organizations constantly struggle between symmetry and

asymmetry when they make decisions), and based on either mediated or interpersonal communication (depending on the situation and public). It also is
more ethical, although we did not measure ethics as a component of the models
in the Excellence study.

We also learned from both our quantitative and qualitative data that organizations typically turn to a symmetrical approach when activist pressure or a
crisis makes an asymmetrical approach too costly. Then, the CEO tends to
upgrade the communication function and hire a knowledgeable top communicator—although sometimes the top communicator comes first and convinces
the CEO of the need to enhance the communication function. By and large, organizations practice symmetrical public relations when the CEO understands
its value and *demands* it and the senior communicator and his or her communication staff have the knowledge to *supply* it. Much of that knowledge comes
from the ability to do research, to understand publics, and to collaborate and negotiate—skills that excellent communicators must have.

Chapter 9, "The Origins, Management, and Outcomes of Programs for Key
Publics," turns from analyzing the overall public relations department to an
analysis of programs for seven specific publics and the media: the media, employees, investors, the community, customers, government, and members. The
data show consistent support for the conclusion that organizations and public
relations departments that are excellent overall also have specific communication programs that are excellent.

Communication programs in excellent departments are more likely to have
strategic origins and less likely to have historicist origins. Excellent programs
also are based on environmental scanning research, and they are more likely to
be evaluated through all forms of evaluation (scientific, clip-file, and informal)
than are less excellent programs. Managers of excellent departments also are
more likely to report that evidence is available to show positive outcomes from
the programs, such as meeting their goals, change-of-relationship outcomes,
and avoidance of conflict.

These characteristics of excellent programs also are related to variables at the
departmental and environmental levels of analysis. Strategic origins for communication programs occur in organizations experiencing pressure from activist groups. When organizations experience activist pressure, they are likely to
use both formal and informal environmental scanning research. Programs are
more likely to have strategic origins if the communication department has the
expertise to enact the manager role and the top communicator enacts that role
frequently. Communication programs are more likely to be evaluated through
scientific, clip-file, and informal evaluation when activist pressure is high. Generally, organizations are more successful in dealing with activists when they
evaluate their communication programs. Formal and informal scanning and the
three forms of program evaluation all increase when the communication department has higher levels of managerial expertise and the top communicator

enacts that role frequently. Positive program outcomes also increase as a function of overall excellence, manager role expertise, and manager role enactment.

Chapter 10, "Activism and the Environment," relates the characteristics of communication Excellence with the nature of the organization's environment—especially the presence of activism. The chapter shows than an effective organization exists in an environment characterized more by dynamism and even hostility than by stability. We learned that activism pushes organizations toward excellence as they try to cope with the expectations of all their strategic constituencies. Excellent public relations departments respond to activists with two-way communication, symmetrical communication, involvement of activists in organizational decisions, and both formative and evaluative research on the activists. That pattern of results fits the Excellence theory: Excellent public relations departments scan the environment and continuously bring the voices of publics, especially activist publics, into decision making. Then, they develop programs to communicate symmetrically with activists and involve them with managers throughout the organization. Finally, they use both formative and evaluative research to manage their communication programs strategically.

The data on activism in chapter 10 firmly establish the two-way symmetrical approach to public relations as a positive or descriptive model as well as the ideal. We can make this assertion because we heard a great deal about symmetry in response to our questions about activism in the environment. For example, the head of public relations of an industry association scoring at the top of the Excellence scale described a community program he had developed that has won national prominence and acclaim. The program's first principle is listening and responding to the community's concerns. He emphasized that responsiveness may include change on the organization's part when pressure groups do not agree with it. Perhaps in no case was this more obvious than in a chemical corporation we studied. Crises and improving company performance both played a part in its overcoming what might have been crippling pressure from outside groups. As its vice president explained, since the catastrophe in Bhopal, his entire industry has become more willing to be open to the public.

Chapter 10 also shows that crises have the potential to enhance the career opportunities of public relations practitioners. Participants in only a handful of our two dozen qualitative cases failed to discuss at least one crisis situation that had resulted in a real shift both in their organization's culture and in its practice of public relations. More often, they spoke of increased appreciation for their function on the part of others in the organization; greater access to the dominant coalition as a result; more openness in communication; a new willingness to cooperate with pressure groups and the community at large; the concomitant likelihood of learning from these strategic constituencies; and greater support for or at least understanding of the organization from the community, the clients or customers, the media, and even government regulators.

Chapter 11, "Inside the Organization: Culture, Structure, Systems of Internal Communication, Gender, and Diversity," analyzes the internal organizational context in which excellent public relations is found. This chapter demonstrates conclusively that excellent public relations will thrive most in an organization with an organic structure, participative culture, and a symmetrical system of communication and in which opportunities exist for women and racioethnic minorities. Although these conditions alone cannot produce excellent public relations, they do provide a hospitable environment for excellent public relations.

Most important, these conditions provide a favorable context in which all employees work most effectively—but especially women and minorities. Within such an organization employees are empowered to participate in decision making. As a result, they are more satisfied with the organization and are more likely to support than to oppose the goals of the organization. In addition, employees who are empowered to participate in decision making and to engage in symmetrical internal communication are likely also to be effective symmetrical communicators with members of external publics as well as internal.

We also found that the effective organization provides a hospitable environment for its increasingly diverse workforce. The CEOs and employees we surveyed seemed to agree on all 22 aspects we measured on how women, in particular, are treated in their organizations. Although top management's perceptions were more optimistic, we were encouraged by the general correspondence among the responses from the CEOs, top communicators, and employees. All three groups of respondents clearly differentiated between areas in which women are most and least supported. The survey data suggest that equitable treatment of women, as evidenced primarily by economic equity, and programs to foster their careers (such as policies against sexual harassment and efforts to encourage women's leadership abilities) are an integral component of excellent organizations. Programs that provide a supportive work environment correlate especially highly with the other conditions found in excellent organizations. Likewise, excellent organizations are beginning to branch out and offer some proactive mentoring and advancement programs for women.

Our data show that when the public relations function was given the power to implement symmetrical programs of communication, the result was a more participative culture and greater employee satisfaction with the organization. However, we also found that symmetrical communication is not likely in an organization with a mechanical structure and authoritarian culture. Organic structure and symmetrical communication interact to produce a participative culture, and participative culture contributes strongly to employee satisfaction with the organization.

An organic structure seems to be the key to an effective organization—triggering changes in culture, communication, and satisfaction. Symmetrical communication has a strong role in creating and implementing organic structure, but a communicator cannot step into any organization alone and implement an organic structure or symmetrical system of communication. The top communicator must work with the dominant coalition to develop an organic structure for the organization while he or she is developing a system of symmetrical communication. Chapter 11, therefore, supports not only the need for symmetrical communication in an effective organization but also the need for the public relations function to be represented in the dominant coalition to create the organic structural context that is necessary to create a participative culture and subsequent employee satisfaction.

Chapters 3–11 of the book provide a clear portrait of excellent public relations and the environmental and organizational context in which it found. The final chapter, chapter 12, however, acknowledges that the Excellence study suggests new questions for research as well as providing answers to existing research questions. We identify four important areas for future research triggered by the results of the Excellence study: (a) the globalization of public relations, (b) strategic management and the nature of relationships, (c) ethics, and (d) the role of public relations in change.

For the globalization of public relations, chapter 12 points out that the absence of significant differences among the three Anglo countries in the Excellence study and the isolation of the same Excellence factor in subsequent research in Slovenia suggests that excellent public relations is likely to be similar in different national contexts. We then describe new research on *generic principles* of public relations Excellence and the need for *specific applications* when cultural, media, political, and economic systems are different.

The Excellence study confirmed the critical importance of involving public relations in strategic management and of the importance of relationships in determining the value of public relations. Nevertheless, public relations practitioners need better tools for strategic management, especially for environmental scanning and scenario building. They also need measurable indicators of the quality of long-term relationships to evaluate the success of communication programs and the overall performance of the department. Research is beginning in these areas, which we describe.

Although we did not specifically measure the role of ethics in public relations in the Excellence study, its importance emerged again and again in the results. Subsequent research on communication Excellence in Slovenia suggested that we add ethics as a generic principle of excellence to those already discussed in this chapter. We believe that public relations departments should provide ethics officers for their organizations. Research has begun to develop a philosophical theory of public relations ethics, but much more work is needed to refine such a theory.

Finally, chapter 12 points out that change is a permanent condition for organizations and that public relations should occupy a major role in helping organizations, their employees, and their publics cope with change. We list four areas of change that are particularly important for public relations: globalization;

feminization; new technology; and downsizing, mergers, and acquisitions. We suggest chaos theory as a promising way of understanding change and conclude that public relations practitioners should work toward a role as in-house activists who push the organization toward needed change.

REFERENCES

Dozier, D. M., with Grunig, L. A., & Grunig, J. E. (1995). *Manager's guide to excellence in public relations and communication management.* Hillsdale, NJ: Lawrence Erlbaum Associates.

Ehling, W. P. (1992a). Estimating the value of public relations and communication to an organization. In J. E. Grunig (Ed.), *Excellence in public relations and communication management* (pp. 617–638). Hillsdale, NJ: Lawrence Erlbaum Associates.

Ehling, W. P. (1992b). Public relations education and professionalism. In J. E. Grunig (Ed.), *Excellence in public relations and communication management* (pp. 439–464). Hillsdale, NJ: Lawrence Erlbaum Associates.

Fleisher, C. S. (1995). *Public affairs benchmarking.* Washington, DC: Public Affairs Council.

Grunig, J. E. (1992a). Communication, public relations, and effective organizations: An overview of the book. In J. E. Grunig (Ed.), *Excellence in public relations and communication management* (pp. 1–28). Hillsdale, NJ: Lawrence Erlbaum Associates.

Grunig, J. E. (Ed.). (1992b). *Excellence in public relations and communication management.* Hillsdale, NJ: Lawrence Erlbaum Associates.

Grunig, J. E. (1992c). What is excellence in management? In J. E. Grunig (Ed.), *Excellence in public relations and communication management* (pp. 219–250). Hillsdale, NJ: Lawrence Erlbaum Associates.

Grunig, J. E., Grunig, L. A., Dozier, D. M., Ehling, W. P., Repper, F. C., & White, J. (1991). *Excellence in public relations and communication management: Initial data report and practical guide.* San Francisco: IABC Research Foundation.

Grunig, J. E., & Repper, F. C. (1992). Strategic management, publics, and issues. In J. E. Grunig (Ed.), *Excellence in public relations and communication management* (pp. 117–158). Hillsdale, NJ: Lawrence Erlbaum Associates.

Grunig, J. E., & White, J. (1992). The effect of worldviews on public relations theory and practice. In J. E. Grunig (Ed.), *Excellence in public relations and communication management* (pp. 31–64). Hillsdale, NJ: Lawrence Erlbaum Associates.

Grunig, L. A., Dozier, D. M., & Grunig, J. E. (1994, December). *IABC excellence in public relations and communication management, Phase 2: Qualitative study, initial analysis: Cases of excellence.* San Francisco: IABC Research Foundation.

Grunig, L. A., Grunig, J. E., & Ehling, W. P. (1992). What is an effective organization? In J. E. Grunig (Ed.), *Excellence in public relations and communication management* (pp. 65–90). Hillsdale, NJ: Lawrence Erlbaum Associates.

Hammer, M., & Champy, J. (1993). *Reengineering the corporation.* New York: HarperCollins.

Mintzberg, H. (1983). *Power in and around organizations.* Englewood Cliffs, NJ: Prentice-Hall.

Peters, T. J., & Waterman, R. H., Jr. (1982). *In search of excellence.* New York: Warner.

Repper, F. C. (1992). How communication managers can apply the theories of excellence and effectiveness. In J. E. Grunig (Ed.), *Excellence in public relations and communication management* (pp. 109–114). Hillsdale, NJ: Lawrence Erlbaum Associates.

Weick, K. E. (1979). *The social psychology of organizing* (2nd ed.). Reading, MA: Addison-Wesley.

Who's excellent now? (1984, November 5). *Businessweek,* pp. 76–87.

CHAPTER TWO

Methodology of the Excellence Study

In 1985, the International Association of Business Communicators Research Foundation funded the Excellence study, the most comprehensive study ever undertaken of the communication profession. Ten years elapsed between that time and commercial publication of the first results (Dozier with L. Grunig & J. Grunig, 1995). This chapter explains the decade-long methodological approach we adopted.

Only by working as a team could the six investigators—together with graduate assistants, faculty colleagues, and members of the board of the IABC Research Foundation—plan and implement a study extensive enough to approach the answers to the research questions described in chapter 1. Our research design hinged on multiple methods, both qualitative and quantitative.

The study began with a thorough review of previous research, summarized in the first of the Excellence study books (see J. Grunig, 1992). In 1991, data collection began with a quantitative survey, using data generated by mailed questionnaires sent to multiple respondents in each participating organization. In 1994, the mail survey was followed by intensive observation of 25 organizations drawn from the original group of organizations. This ordering of data gathering, with the quantitative phase first, is somewhat atypical when qualitative and quantitative methods are combined in a single study (Broom & Dozier, 1990). However, we favored this because of the large body of research that preceded the Excellence study.

A BRIEF HISTORY OF RESEARCH ON PUBLIC RELATIONS AND COMMUNICATION MANAGEMENT

Research about public relations and communication management has improved significantly in recent decades. The early "case studies" in public relations, which resembled anecdotal "war stories" more than methodologically rigorous analyses, gave way to an influx of quantitative methods from the social sciences. Communication and public relations scholars turned increasingly to large-sample surveys and, to a lesser degree, to lab experiments. More recently, the resurgence of qualitative research in the social sciences has brought such tools as focus groups, long interviews, participant observation, and true case study research to the discipline.

At the same time, theoretical understanding of managed communication in organizations grew. With this growth, our research team came to understand that we could not study communication management and public relations in isolation from other functions in the organization, or from the organization's culture and structure (J. Grunig, 1992). Communication and public relations practitioners are constrained, researchers had learned, by what senior management wants from the public relations department and how much management supports those communication efforts.

Scholars and practitioners also discovered they could not measure outcomes or the impact of communication programs in isolation from organizational opportunities and constraints. Such opportunities and constraints may come from the communicator's relationship with key members of the dominant coalition. For example, the organization's CEO may block the top communicator's participation in strategic planning because the CEO fails to see the linkage between communication and strategic planning. Constraints also may come from the more diffuse influence of organizational culture. For example, a communicator's efforts to scan the organization's environment, to learn "what's going on out there," might meet with managerial indifference if the organization's culture is "closed" to the outside world.

PHASE 1: MAIL SURVEY

The overall research design of the Excellence study is displayed in Fig. 2.1. Because the Excellence team could draw on a number of important research streams, previous research provided many of the concepts examined in the study. Indeed, many operational measures of these key concepts were adapted from prior research, thus providing indexes and scales with documented reliability and validity. The Excellence study, therefore, was in no way exploratory. Phase 1, which involved a set of mailed questionnaires, linked a wide range of concepts and theories from previous studies. Notable among these was the research on models of public relations practice, organizational roles of practitioners, environmental scanning, program evaluation of public relations, women in organizations, internal communication, organizational structure, organizational culture, and activism.

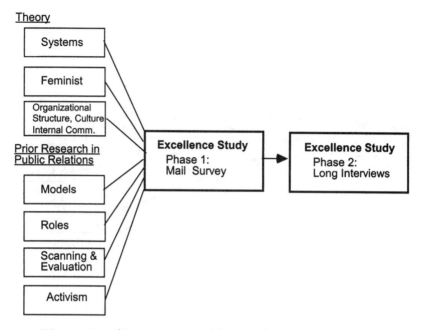

FIG. 2.1.   A graphic representation of the research design of the Excellence study.

Data Collection Strategy

The Excellence study used data collected from several vantage points in the participating organizations. This approach is illustrated in Fig. 2.2. Data collection was orchestrated by graduate assistants JoNell Mettinen, then at San Diego State University, and K. Sriramesh and Linda Childers Hon, both formerly at the University of Maryland. The first step in data collection involved soliciting an organization's participation through a mailed inquiry to a communicator in the organization, supported by a brochure extolling the virtues of the Excellence study and participation in it. If we received a positive response, a research team member worked with the responding communicator by telephone to identify all the communication units in the organization, the names and titles of top communicators, the reporting relationships, and the names and titles of the CEO and other members of the dominant coalition. The research team member and the contact person in the organization also devised a strategy for conducting a minisurvey of other employees in the organization.

The questionnaire for top communicators was a lengthy instrument completed by the highest ranking public relations practitioner in each organization. (The questionnaire is included in Appendix A.) If the organization had multiple departments responsible for different aspects of the function, then the head of

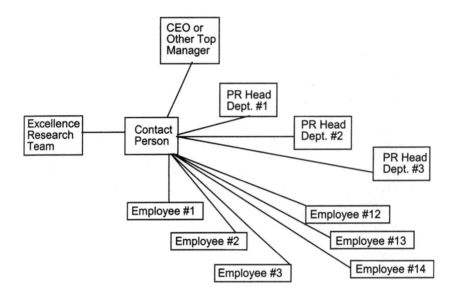

FIG. 2.2.   Data collection strategy for organizations participating in Phase 1 of Excellence study.

each department completed a top-communicator questionnaire. Most participating organizations (274 or 87%) had only one public relations or communication management department. About 7% ($N = 21$) had two public relations departments, and 4% ($N = 13$) had three public relations departments. Only 2% ($N = 5$) had four such departments. One organization had five separate departments responsible for some aspect of communication, and two organizations had eight departments for communication. In these organizations, the head of each department or unit responsible for public relations or communication management (or both) completed a top-communicator questionnaire.

The questionnaire for CEOs was shorter than the one for PR heads (Appendix B). It included most of the same questions asked the PR head, such as questions about participation in strategic managements, roles expected of the top communicator, public relations models, support for communication by the dominant coalition, membership in the dominant coalition, public relations models, activism, and support for women in the organization.

In addition, a brief employee questionnaire (Appendix C) was distributed to up to 20 employees in the organization. This questionnaire measured aspects of communication and organizational culture. In conjunction with the contact person in the organization, we on the research team devised a purposive sample of employees in various departments of the organization, representing different levels of responsibility in the organizational structure. On average, 14 people completed an employee questionnaire in each organization. In organizations with fewer than 20 employees, everyone in the organization except the CEO and top communicator completed these questionnaires.

A nonprobability, multistage sampling strategy was employed for the mailed survey. In the first stage, we relied on dimensional sampling to specify sampling elements across two dimensions: nationality and organizational type. By 1987, we had specified an initial sample of 300. It was constructed to include 200 organizations with headquarters in the United States and 50 organizations each in Canada and the United Kingdom. One hundred corporations were slated for study, along with 75 not-for-profit organizations, 75 government agencies, and 50 trade or professional associations. The breakdown of the original dimensional sample, with quotas for each cell, is provided in Table 2.1.

Corporations included utilities, consumer products, high-tech, energy, industrial manufacturers, banks and financial services, insurance, transportation, health, real estate development, media/publishing, entertainment, retail, food, and pharmaceuticals. The corporate category also included conglomerates, transnational corporations, and government-owned businesses. Not-for-profit organizations included colleges and universities, school systems, nonprofit hospitals, churches, charitable organizations, and public interest groups. Targets for these organizations were split proportionately among the three nations. Government agencies included federal, regional, state-provincial, local, and political agencies. Associations included both professional and trade types.

Within each cell of the dimensional sample, we used purposive sampling to maximize the variance of attributes of excellence within each cell. Purposive sampling is a nonprobability sampling technique used in this project to include organizations that have special characteristics important to the study of communication Excellence. On the one hand, organizations were included (in their appropriate cells of the table) that books and publications had identified as "excellent" according to some overall standard. On the other hand, organizations that recently experienced communication crises and substantial negative publicity also were included. Such a purposive sampling strategy increased the likelihood that subsamples within each cell of the table would include organizations with both excellent and less-than-excellent communication programs.

TABLE 2.1
Target Sample for the Excellence Survey by Nation and Type of Organization

| Type of Organization | Nation of Organization (Headquarters) | | | |
	United States	Canada	United Kingdom	TOTALS
Corporations	66	17	17	100
Not-for-Profits	50	13	12	75
Government Agencies	50	12	13	75
Associations	34	8	8	50
TOTALS	200	50	50	300

In addition to nationality, organizational type, and degree of excellence, we also sought variance in organizational size. Our sample included a range from very small (fewer than 20 employees) to very large (several thousand employees).

Final Sample

Table 2.2 shows the final sample of organizations that participated in the 1991–1992 Excellence survey. A total of 327 organizations provided at least one of the questionnaires requested. Three hundred sixteen organizations provided at least one top-communicator questionnaire, 292 provided a CEO questionnaire, and 281 provided a purposive employee sample. There were a total of 4,631 employees surveyed in the 281 organizations that returned the employee questionnaires. Four hundred seven top communicators completed questionnaires in the 316 organizations that returned at least one PR head questionnaire.

Breaking down the final sample by nation, organizational targets for both Canada and the United States were reached. However, participation from the United Kingdom fell short of target, with only 33 organizations—17 fewer than originally projected—included in the final sample. Regarding types of organizations, the final sample included 65 more corporations than the 100 originally projected. Not-for-profits fell 11 organizations short of the projected 75 organizations in the final sample. The final sample of government agencies fared a little worse, with 59 of 75 projected agencies included in the final sample. The final sample included 36 associations, 14 short of the projected 50 in the original target.

Response Rate

High response rates are not so critical to nonprobability sampling strategies as they are to probability sampling strategies that make statistical inferences from samples to populations. After Yin (1989), the Excellence study sought *analytical*

TABLE 2.2

Final Sample for the Excellence Survey by Nation and Type of Organization

| Type of Organization | Nation of Organization (Headquarters) | | | |
	United States	Canada	United Kingdom	TOTALS
Corporations	131	24	13	168
Not-for-Profits	41	12	11	64
Government Agencies	38	14	7	59
Associations	27	7	2	36
TOTALS	**237**	**57**	**33**	**327**

rather than *statistical* generalizations from the multiple ($N = 327$) case studies of participating organizations. That is, "previously developed theory is used as a template with which to compare the empirical results" (p. 38) of the study. As such, participating organizations in the Excellence study "should be considered like multiple experiments (or multiple surveys)" (p. 38).

To understand the response rate in the Excellence study, one must consider the pragmatic constraints in the data-collection process. Top communicators received a 21-page questionnaire; CEOs received a 7-page questionnaire. A seven-page questionnaire also was completed by up to 20 regular employees (14 was the average), sampled from the larger employee pool. The typical participating organization provided 1,700 variables of data; we received 100 pages of questionnaires from the typical organization. Operationally speaking, the Excellence survey proved extremely challenging to execute. Collecting survey information required the cooperation of each organization's top communicator. In addition to completing the top-communicator questionnaire, this person often served as *internal advocate* for that organization's participation, convincing the CEO or another member of the dominant coalition to fill out the CEO questionnaire. Typically, top communicators also helped administer the employee questionnaire to the sample of other employees.

Despite a stated desire to participate, many organizations balked at participation, once the bundle of questionnaires arrived by mail. Of those maintaining their original commitment, some could not orchestrate the CEO's continued support and participation in the end. In all, 12% of the organizations initially solicited through the mail returned a complete set of questionnaires.

Representativeness of the Phase 1 Sampling Strategy

The Excellence study sampled four types of organizations in Canada, the United Kingdom, and the United States for purposes of *extrapolation* (analytic generalization). The sample was not representative for purposes of statistical generalization. The nature of our research questions required the intensive study of a large number of organizations. Because of the sheer volume of information sought and the large number of organizational members providing information, the survey required a major commitment of organizational resources to participate.

Arguably, the Excellence study's sample is representative of organizations with 16 employees—ranging from the organization's top manager to regular employees—willing to fill out about 100 pages of questionnaires. Typically, the communication departments in such organizations are more powerful than in organizations that did not participate. Communicators provided the research team its entree into organizations.

We offered participating organizations an individual report of findings at project's end, identifying and comparing communication Excellence in each organization to others in the study. An interest in research is one attribute of communication Excellence. Power in the communication department is another attribute of communication Excellence. If the top communicator valued the research the Excellence study would provide and also possessed sufficient organizational power to convince the CEO to participate, then that organization joined the other 315 in the study.

Suppose the top communicator fell short in either area. In the end, his or her organization would drop out, not providing the necessary data to be included in the final sample. Because several organizations were unable to provide complete data after agreeing to participate, we theorize that even "less-than-excellent" organizations in the database are likely to be more excellent than organizations not participating. For these reasons, the participating organizations probably manifested higher levels of communication Excellence than those that did not participate. (On average, CEOs in organizations with the least excellent communication programs placed their return on investment in communication at 140%.)

In summary, the Excellence study Phase 1 survey sampled a sufficient number of the four types of organizations in three nations to permit extrapolation of findings to other corporations, not-for-profits, government agencies, and associations in Canada, the United Kingdom, and the United States. Statistical inferences and generalizations, on the other hand, are inappropriate.

Fractionation Scales

Questionnaires in the Excellence study made use of a state-of-the-art measurement tool called a "fractionation scale." Fractionation scales ask participants completing questionnaires to report how much of a particular characteristic they (or their organizations) possess and to compare it to a common standard for all questions. In the Excellence study, we asked the respondents to compare their response on each item to an average response to all questions in the questionnaire. If the participant in the survey thought that his or her organization possessed a characteristic that would be average for all questions in the questionnaire, he or she wrote down a score of 100. If the amount of that characteristic were "half the average," a score of 50 would be given to it. If twice average, a score of 200 would be assigned.

For example, the questionnaire asked top communicators to "describe the extent to which your public relations department makes a contribution to . . . strategic planning" using the fractionation scale. A score of 0 means the department makes no contribution; a score of 100 means that the department's contribution is about an "average" response for a typical item in the questionnaire. A score of 200 means the department's contribution is twice the "average" response. The person completing the questionnaire could assign as high a score as he or she wished. These responses do not mean that a department is average or above or below average for each question. In fact, a participant could believe that all public relations departments are below average on strategic planning, for example. He or she might believe the average for all organizations on this variable is 50 and that his or her organization is average on participation in strategic planning and thus assign his or her organization a score of 50.

A few top communicators declined to participate, once they saw how data were collected. However, most participants became rather facile with the fractionation scale. Overall, fractionation scales have many valuable properties that make them ideal for statistical analysis. As a pragmatic issue, however, fractionation scales complicate data collection.

Data Reduction and Analysis

Data from the Phase 1 survey were organized into three separate computer files that were then merged into a single, unified file. With more than 4,600 respondents, the employee data file was organized by individual respondents who were grouped together by organization. All variables from the employee questionnaires were aggregated, using the mean of each variable as an attribute of the organization. These aggregated data (means) then were merged with data from each top communicator. In organizations with more than one public relations or communication department, the aggregated employee data were appended to each top-communicator questionnaire. In addition, data from the CEO questionnaire were appended to each top-communicator questionnaire in the organization. The relationship between the three types of questionnaires and the resulting data structure for a single organization is illustrated in Fig. 2.3.

The final data file was organized by public relations departments, with the aggregated employee data and CEO data attached to top-communicator data in a redundant manner. For each organization, the primary public relations or communication department was designated by a dichotomous code, determined by the percentage of the overall budget allocated to the department. Unless otherwise indicated, the primary public relations or communication department ($N = 316$) was used in all analyses reported in this book.

Of the 316 organizations completing a CEO questionnaire and at least one top-communicator and employee questionnaire, 46 contributed insufficient data to permit computation of an Excellence score for the organization. We were able to increase the number of organizations with sufficient data to compute an Excellence score by computing the missing values for missing Excellence variables. We did so by using multiple regression analysis to compute the missing variables from the other Excellence variables—unless too many variables were missing to justify the estimation of missing values. In all, 270 organizations provided sufficient data to permit their inclusion in all areas of subsequent data analysis. For this reason, the number of organizations used in the analyses varies according to the set of variables involved.

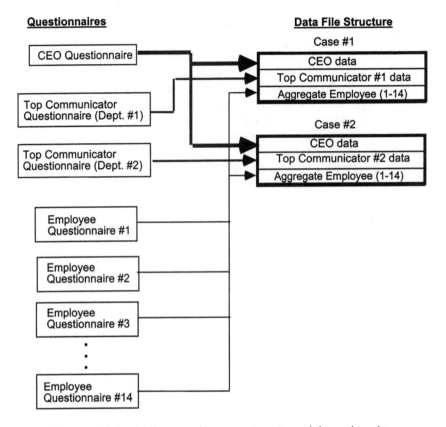

FIG. 2.3.   Relationship between Phase 1 questionnaires and the resulting data file structure for one organization with two communication departments.

PHASE 2: CASE STUDIES USING LONG INTERVIEWS

In 1994, some 3 years after completion of the mail survey, researchers at the University of Maryland and San Diego State University conducted case studies of 25 organizations from the original group of more than 300. We chose some cases because they exemplified communication Excellence in a variety of organizational types. We selected other cases because they seemed to have few characteristics of communication Excellence. We on the research team studied cases in all three nations, although the bulk of these case study organizations came from the United States.

The large-sample survey provided a detailed "snapshot" of each participating organization at one point in time. The case studies allowed for exploration, in an open-end fashion, of the organizational history of the communication function and the origins of excellence. Further, the passage of time since the original survey allowed us to examine the evolution of communication Excellence since the original survey. We also could determine whether intervention, in the form of results of the survey research, had an effect on the degree of excellence in each organization.

This methodological strategy allowed the Excellence study to play on the strengths of two different methodological approaches. The large sample provided the diversity of organizations to allow researchers and practitioners to extrapolate or make analytical generalizations from organizations in the study to other organizations throughout the three nations studied. The multiple questionnaires completed in each organization allowed the team to compare communicators' perspectives with those of the dominant coalition. The survey of employees provided broad measures of communication within organizations, as well as measures of organizational cultures and structures. The goal of these research activities was the construction of a nomothetic model of explanation, a general explanatory model applicable across organizational types and nations that accounts for the major sources of variation in the excellence of public relations and communication management programs.

The case studies took full advantage of research findings from the initial survey. We had closely analyzed each organization selected for case study. The team not only knew each organization's overall Excellence score from the Excellence factor (see chap. 3), but each investigator could compare top-communicators' perspectives with the dominant coalition's perspectives. We examined an overall measure of organizational culture provided by employees throughout each organization.

The qualitative research sought to measure the economic value of excellent and less-than-excellent public relations departments to their organizations. A second goal was to fill in gaps of understanding left by the survey research. In particular, we investigated the roles and status of practitioners of different races and ethnic groups, the seeming inconsistency between what CEOs reported as the value of public relations and the support they accorded it, and the historical factors that led—at least in part—to the development of programs deemed "excellent."

Cross-Cultural Issues

Considerations of time, cooperation, cost, and language constrained the cross-cultural range of the research encounter to three English-speaking countries. However, after Phase 1 of the Excellence study began, other scholars working under the direction of members of the Excellence research team applied the survey instrument to several additional cultural contexts. Parallel to Phase 1 of the Excellence study, graduate students at the University of Maryland investigated the practice of excellence in public relations in southern India (Sriramesh, 1991), Greece (Lyra, 1991), and Taiwan (Huang, 1990). As this book goes to press, other scholars are using modified versions of the Excellence questionnaires in different cultural contexts around the world.

In particular, findings of the Sriramesh, Lyra, and Huang studies convinced the Excellence research team that the cross-cultural nature of our research would be denied if we relied solely on quantitative methods. In all three cases, researchers relied on a face-to-face, qualitative approach—modifying the survey instruments as necessary to convey the *sense* of the questions to the practitioners whose language, customs, beliefs, values, and norms all differed from those of the people who developed that questionnaire.

The Excellence study gathered data in a single language: English. However, the Excellence team included one member who speaks the British form of this language—a man who had lived and worked in both Canada and the United Kingdom. Despite the risk and danger of field study, which is inherently sloppy (Blythin, 1985), the Excellence study fostered the kind of interaction implied by the term *cross-cultural*.

The cross-cultural nature of the study was only one rationale for combining qualitative and quantitative methodologies. The Phase 1 survey used relatively unambiguous concepts, scales, and indicators with known levels of reliability and validity. But these seemingly unambiguous measures generated anomalies during the quantitative data analysis. In Phase 2, the research team explored concepts that remained ambiguous or unclear—especially in those cases where we suspected that *context* was an important determinant. Thus, in Phase 2, our purpose shifted away from testing prior theory to discovering new relationships and building new theory. In this regard, the research team relied more on words than numbers.

Objectivity and Subjectivity in the Excellence Study

Gould (1981) contended that because numbers enjoy a special status, the mystique of science has deemed them the ultimate test of objectivity. Objectivity, in our view, is largely a mythical property of science. Quantitative methods, perhaps best exemplified by the laboratory experiment, can specify the conditions under which data are collected and analyzed. As such, research protocols can be replicated. However, the ability to replicate does not constitute objectivity. The process of selecting interesting research questions, the construction of theory, and the economic/political/institutional context in which these choices are made mitigate against the legitimate use of the term *objectivity*.

Perhaps a more biting condemnation of the myth of objectivity comes from feminist scholars, who argue that objectification inherently privileges those who do the research over those who participate in the research. As Muto (1988) put it: "The process of objectification requires privileging. I have to be above, or at least separate from, that of which I speak" (p. 20). Another feminist scholar, Kauffman (1992), explained that privileging may be by virtue of class, race, or gender. To make our knowledge more complete, she advocated developing approaches to research that value historically oppressed groups. Her message is especially persuasive to those of us engaged in cross-cultural study. A third feminist scholar, Keller (1985), invited the "demythification" of all science—not just its enduring claim of objectivity: "The survival of mythlike beliefs in our thinking about science, the very archetype of antimyth, ought, it would seem, to invite our curiosity and demand investigation" (p. 76). Our comparative approach privileged neither the quantitative nor the qualitative, neither the researcher nor the researched.

The review of related literature (J. Grunig, 1992) that provided the theoretical foundation for Phase 1 served as the conceptualization of Phase 2 as well. As a result, the qualitative research focused on what this approach could contribute to our emerging theory of excellence in public relations and communication management. From this rationale, the research team derived research questions for Phase 2 detailed later. Our line of inquiry was directed toward suspected alternatives, inspired by anomalies exposed by the quantitative analysis in Phase 1.

The research team's conceptualization of excellence was merely a focusing and bounding device. As Miles and Huberman (1984) reminded us, it need not serve as blinders or a straitjacket. That is, Phase 2 was not simply an unfocused exploration of seemingly interesting areas; this phase sought to balance the need to explain anomalies and answer research questions not fully addressed in Phase 1 with an openness to *serendipity*—the discovery of the unexpected. Thus, we were willing to be surprised in the second phase and attempted to maximize opportunities for the unexpected to occur.

The overarching goal of the case studies was to bring the survey results to life, to put flesh on the bones of the quantitative data. We sought to discover new insights by immersing the research team members (if even briefly) in organizations and to experience those organizations through the eyes and in the words of the communication managers and CEOs we interviewed. By studying internal dynamics in this way, we sought to contextualize the stark findings of the quantitative phase of the study.

Research Questions

A major goal of the qualitative phase of the Excellence study was to add context to the picture first painted through the survey data. In addition, we explored questions we did not pose in the initial quantitative phase. For instance, audience members hearing reports of Phase 1 findings have asked why we did not include the role of race and ethnicity in communication Excellence, along with gender. Using feedback from early reports of Phase 1 findings, we pared the "ideal" list of Phase 2 research questions and topic probes rather brutally into four major areas.

CEOs.   The first group of questions dealt with perceptions of the chief executive officers, in large part because of their role as cultural leaders within the organization. Further, the power-control perspective suggests that members of the dominant coalition tend to determine the models of public relations practiced, the extent to which this function is empowered, and the structure and culture of the organization.

Diversity.   A second group of questions addressed the growing diversity of the field of public relations and of the workforce in general. Such queries were appropriate for male as well as female participants. One goal was to elicit helpful suggestions or remedies for discrimination that disadvantaged groups often encounter at work. Research on women in public relations (e.g., Hon, 1992) suggested that we gear our inquiry toward organizational—rather than individual—solutions. Conceptually, we framed our consideration of these issues as matters of multicultural diversity.

The Public Relations Function.   A third group of questions dealt specifically with public relations. Questions about history, strategic management, career planning, and quality were asked of the department head or heads, as well as any others in the department who were willing to participate.

Monetary Value.   The final set of questions was of great importance to "consumers" of the research results. These questions probed the monetary contribution of excellent public relations and communication management to the organization. As detailed in chapter 4, monetary return on investment is but one way to conceptualize that contribution of communication Excellence to the "bottom line." In the Phase 1 survey, CEOs were asked to estimate their return on investment from capital resources dedicated to the public relations and communication management function. In Phase 2, members of the organization's dominant coalition were asked to estimate the contribution and worth of communication Excellence, a technique called compensating variation, and to explain why they assigned the values to public relations that they did.

The Qualitative Design of Phase 2

The research design of the second stage of the Excellence study served three purposes. First, it provided for communication among the members of the research team and various stakeholders in the Excellence study. Second, it set forth a plan of action when we headed into the field. Finally, the research plan served as a contract between the Excellence research team and the sponsoring foundation.

The research team opted for a comprehensive research design in order to reduce the onerous task of preparing final reports of the study's findings and conclusions. Along the way, the research plan provided a framework for interpreting with dispatch the results of the study. The research design sought to ameliorate a constellation of anticipated frustrations. These included:

- The long-distance relationship of members of the research team.
- The different values and experiences of research team members with qualitative methodology.
- Cross-cultural complications inherent in this three-nation project.
- The ambiguous procedures and standards for qualitative research.
- The flexibility and creativity qualitative research requires.
- The ubiquitous constraints of time, money, and energy.

The tidy, linear process implicit in the *Manager's Guide* and this book is actually a *reconstructed logic* (Kaplan, 1964). The *logic in use,* however, was more accurately typified by fits, starts, sidesteps, and backtracking, which typifies qualitative research designs as they are actually implemented. Indeed, most research designs—whether quantitative or qualitative—are more accurately described through their *logic in use.* Qualitative inquiry has achieved credibility as a methodological approach only recently in the social sciences. Few qualitative procedures are rigorously defined, as they are still evolving. For this reason, we take great care here to explain the logic of our choices and the nature of our constraints. The Phase 2 research design addressed six issues: (a) selection of the sample, (b) development of the interview protocol and approach to asking the questions, (c) procedures for recording the data, (d) explanation of the scheme for analyzing the data, (e) discussion of ethics and contingencies, and (f) preparation of the written report.

Claims and Standards for Qualitative Research

We make no inappropriate claims about *statistical* generalizability from the Phase 2 data. The value of qualitative research lies more in its potential to discover patterns that can be *extrapolated* from the organizations sampled to other organizations. The goal is to develop and elaborate the theory of communication Excellence first posited in the conceptualization for the Phase 1 survey (J. Grunig, 1992). Likewise, we make no claims of *objectivity* as the term is typically misused in the social sciences.

Qualitative research is subjected to different standards of quality than quantitative research. These standards are no less rigorous; they are simply better suited to the purpose and methods used. Together, our adherence to these standards attests to the soundness of our research design.

Lincoln and Guba (1985) provided four criteria that serve as alternatives to the traditional (quantitative) standards of validity and reliability. They are (a) dependability, or the assurance that appropriate adaptations to the situation under investigation have been made; (b) credibility, in that subjects are adequately portrayed so that the final portrait seems to have "truth value";[1] (c) confirmability, or enough objectivity (by which we mean intersubjective agreement) in the data analysis that a second researcher would be likely to come to the same conclusions; and (d) transferability, or the ability to transpose this set of findings to a relevant new situation. (The burden of transferability lies with the person who makes the transfer, rather than with the initial researcher. However, that researcher is obliged to make the context clear to other scholars.)

The Long Interview

Long personal interviews with organizational elites were used to collect the bulk of the data in Phase 2. Primary participants in this phase of the study were top communicators from selected organizations who agreed to participate. Shorter interviews also were conducted with a smaller sample of CEOs or other members of dominant coalitions with whom these practitioners work. The team also interviewed other members of the public relations department in selected organizations, because these lower level employees sometimes have a more critical perspective on communication and less of a vested interest in their organization.

Follow-up interviews with members of the dominant coalition and others in public relations were conducted most frequently over the telephone. However, more than one individual was queried because multiple perspectives were essential to the research design. Understanding of communication Excellence increased when we as the researchers drew on several perceptions of the same organizational process.

The long interview offered several advantages over other forms of data collection. The pluses include context, accuracy, comprehensiveness, and appropriateness. Long interviews expose the contexts of people's behavior, providing researchers with an understanding of the meaning of those behaviors (Seidman, 1991). *Context* is especially important in a cross-cultural study of this nature. Downs, Smeyak, and Martin (1980) argued that the long personal interview generates data that are both accurate and complete. D. Nachmias and C. Nachmias (1981) emphasized the method's inherent flexibility, which allows for open-end probes, flexibility regarding the order in which questions are asked, and the ability to clarify complex or unclear information. Dexter (1970) considered the face-to-face interview imperative when studying elites—the "important or exposed" people in an organization.

---

[1]Lincoln and Guba (1985) emphasized the importance of credibility to the constructors of the original reality—in other words, to the participants themselves. We take this to mean that interviewees should be able to recognize themselves and their situation in the final analysis of the data.

The long interview employs a predetermined but flexible structure of open-end questions. As McCracken (1988) explained, such preparation helps streamline the process of analyzing the resultant data. Data collection in the second phase actually constituted an adaptation of the McCracken technique. For each organization, he suggested three interviews of approximately $1\frac{1}{2}$ hours with each participant. In her landmark study of women in public relations, Hon (1992), however, found that a single lengthy interview was as likely to generate the insights necessary for our purposes. Kauffman (1992) learned that an hour and a half was as much time as she could responsibly ask from busy interviewees.

In Phase 2 of the Excellence study, a log was kept of all contacts with interviews and potential interviews. Members of the research team kept records of all calls made and received, letters sent and received, acceptances, and rejections. Perhaps most important, members of the research team also recorded the reasons, either stated or implied, for participating and not participating in the study.

Determining the Sample

Qualitative research design typically represents a compromise between the ideal and the realistic. Our desire to be comprehensive was tempered by limitations of time and money. In all, 25 organizations were studied via multiple long interviews in each participating organization. Most of the organizations in the final sample for Phase 2 were among the most excellent organizations in one or more areas. Several posted overall Excellence scores (see chap. 3) in the midrange. About six posted Excellence scores among the least excellent organizations participating in the Phase 1 survey.

In addition, we solicited organizations in all three nations, as well as different types of organizations (corporations, not-for-profits, government agencies, and trade or professional associations). However, in the final count, 22 of the organizations in the Phase 2 case studies were headquartered in the United States. One organization was headquartered in Canada and two were headquartered in the United Kingdom. The final Phase 2 sample included a chemical company, a blood bank, a cosmetics company, a medical association, two oil companies, a state lottery, a metal manufacturer, a steel manufacturer, two public utilities, an arts organization, a health organization, a medical products manufacturer, a financial services company, a hotel chain, three insurance companies, an aerospace corporation, an economic development agency, a hospital association, a federal agency, a university, and a disabled services organization. We did not seek a sample representative in the statistical sense, but a sample that maximized opportunities for contrast and serendipity across a wide range of contexts. This goal was achieved. Another key variable for inclusion in the sample was the organization's willingness to participate. We sought "quality" time with participants, as well as a willingness to be completely candid, even about sensitive issues.

Securing Cooperation

Before data collection for Phase 2, we on the research team developed a "script" of model responses when soliciting individuals and organizations for participation. The script was developed in conjunction with working practitioners on the board of the sponsoring foundation, people who could anticipate the kinds of questions and objections that their colleagues might pose. Here is an abbreviated script of responses to six typical questions or objections that occurred during solicitation of participants for this stage.

1. **Question or objection:** "We don't have time for this," or "We're not interested." **Possible response:** *I realize how busy you are. However, we really need you to help others understand what it takes to develop an excellent communication [or public relations] program. At the same time, you may find that when you read the book that results, you may learn from your peers as well. As far as we know, this project represents the first time that CEOs have discussed communication right along with top public relations practitioners.*

2. **Question or objection:** "Why me?" or "Why was my organization selected?" **Possible response:** *We scientifically selected your organization because of its pattern of high excellence and not-so-high excellence in various areas of communication management. It's extremely important for you to participate because of your organization's unique pattern of communication Excellence. We really need your help.*

3. **Question or objection:** "But our situation has changed since you did that first study. We have a different CEO now and he [or she] doesn't value public relations as much," or "I'm new here. I didn't take part in the survey." **Possible response:** *We realize that times change and that personnel change. It's not so important that we talk with the very same people in this second stage of our research. The organization itself is the most important factor. That's why we don't feel we can just substitute one organization for another. Your organization—rather than its CEO or the communication manager there—is the critical part.*

4. **Question or objection:** "How long will this take?" **Possible response:** *Again, I realize how busy you are. However, we can set up the interview whenever it's most convenient for you. It should take about an hour.* (In reality, 90 minutes were frequently needed to complete these interviews.)

5. **Question or objection:** "How will you use the results?" **Possible response:** *The ground rules are clear. We want an open, candid conversation with you. So, your identity and that of your organization will remain strictly confidential. We're looking more for patterns of communication practice than for any individual information. That's why it's so important that as many people as possible like yourself agree to be interviewed.*

6. **Question or objection:** "When will we get the results?" **Possible response:** *We hope to have the results available in June 1994.*

Conducting the Long Interview

Some interviews were conducted in person and on site. The value of such direct observation is obvious. A less apparent advantage of traveling to the workplace of participants was that this helped balance the power between interviewer and interviewee (Kauffman, 1992). Because of time and financial constraints, however, many of the long interviews were conducted by phone. Although the telephone interview is not the ideal modality for long interviews, the phone permitted qualitative case studies across a wider range of organizational settings by reducing the impact of geographical location on the collection of data.

Asking the Questions

The protocol for the long interviews is included as Appendix D. The protocol includes an introductory script, a list of questions to be asked, and a strategy for conducting additional long interviews with other members of the organization (subsequent to the initial interview in the public relations department). Every member of the Excellence research team was either an experienced interviewer or received intensive training in interviewing before conducting interviews. For example, one cohort of interviewers learned how to do long interviews by observing a senior member of the Excellence research team conduct multiple interviews with members of the same organization in a seminar-like setting.

The Phase 2 interviewers were instructed to employ "small talk" at the outset of the interview to put the participant at ease. Small talk also helped the interviewers find a common ground with the participant, which helped establish rapport. The easiest questions were asked first, helping to "warm up" the participant and build trust for the more difficult questions posed later on. Throughout the interview, team members were encouraged to probe and to follow up, adopting a *semistructured* approach. In many cases, questions were not asked in the order specified by the interview protocol. Instead, interviewers listened carefully to what they were told, modifying the question guide as needed. Interviewers concluded with a statement of thanks and a request: "May I call you back later on if I find I need to clarify something you said?"

Often, participants shared some of their most important and revealing observations at the very end of the interview, after the notebook was closed and the tape recorder turned off. Under such circumstances, team members were instructed to listen carefully and then write down those last-minute insights as soon as they left the office. A brief note of thanks was sent to all participating individuals and organizations.

Recording Responses

Field notes are, in short, the record of qualitative results. Tape recordings may augment note taking, but the notes themselves were critical. Tapes are particularly useful in capturing and preserving accurately the direct quotations that enliven the reports of findings. However, taking notes forces the interviewer to listen carefully for key points or patterns. Jotting down those impressions at the moment assisted the research team during subsequent analysis to "see the forest for the trees." Permission to record was obtained from all participants before the interview.

Analyzing the Data

Analysis of the Phase 2 qualitative data consisted of two main processes: data reduction and data interpretation. Data reduction of Phase 2 interviews began by listening carefully to the recordings—usually several times—and noting locations of key quotes. Handwritten notes taken during the interviews helped with this process. Key passages were flagged for verbatim inclusion in research reports. Some verbatim statements were so telling that they directly answered our research questions. Others were revealing because they typified statements made by other interviewees. Finally, some verbatim statements were important because they were strikingly idiosyncratic. The research team opted not to transcribe the entire interviews, because most of the interview statements could be tersely summarized in a few sentences.

Individual interviewers initiated the first phase of interpretation. The interviewer's first task was to clearly understand what the participant was saying. The second task was to integrate the information obtained from each of the participants within a single organization to construct a composite picture of the organization. The third task was to synthesize patterns that emerged across several organizations. Interviewers were urged not to force patterns or ignore interesting information simply because it did not "fit." The final task consisted of integrating the findings of the qualitative phase with what was already known from the Phase 1 survey.

Writing the Report

Reports of findings began with field notes and tapes. A separate "minireport" was written for each participating organization. Once the minireports were completed, Larissa Grunig (1994) authored a preliminary report, which integrated findings across all 25 participating organizations. Those findings also were integrated into the *Manager's Guide* and into the findings of this book.

We acknowledge that aspects of our own cultural and individual identities intruded into the writing process. The ultimate test of adequacy for the Phase 2 findings is whether we bridged the gap (even imperfectly) between our own cultures and those cultures we explored. The reader alone must render this final judgment. The bridge, of course, is always shaky. Geertz (1988) explained its tenuousness as "at one and the same time an intimate view and a cool assessment" (p. 10). Through our qualitative research, we hoped to get close to our participants and the context in which they work. As scientists, however, we sought to maintain our own standpoint somewhat apart from organizational contexts as we assessed and ultimately reported our findings.

The Values and Complications of Teamwork

The Phase 2 research team included the original six members of the grant team, as well as three graduate students at the University of Maryland and eight graduate students at San Diego State University. Graduate students at the University of Maryland included Judith Meyer and Kenneth Plowman; faculty colleague Linda Hon assisted as well. Graduate students at San Diego State University included Troy Anderson, Valerie Barker, Brian Ferrario, Danielle Hauck, Susie Maguire, Jim Ritchey, Natalie Walsh, and Kimberly White. John M. Blamphin of Rapier Marketing in London conducted the case study interviews in the United Kingdom. In addition, trustees of the IABC Research Foundation and individual IABC chapter members helped develop research questions. The synergism of such a group process enhanced the quality of the research design and execution. At the same time, teamwork complicated the process.

Despite the flexibility inherent in qualitative research design, we standardized our process to enhance comparability across investigators. Still, perfect overlap in outcomes and understandings did not result from the work of different team members. As Clifford (1986) warned, one should be suspicious of "any overly confident and consistent ethnographic voice" (p. 14) because of the inevitability of incomplete knowledge.

Collaboration between researcher and participant helped to crack the code of organizational cultures. In Phase 2, we discovered what respondents meant when they marked a certain number on the survey questionnaires. This search for meanings seemed especially important, given the cross-cultural nature of the research.

Ethical Concerns

Like much qualitative research, Phase 2 of the Excellence study relied on people's words as the primary data (Marshall & Rossman, 1989). As an ethical concern, we considered it incumbent upon us to value those people and those words. One way to *devalue* participants is to question the validity of self-reports. At the same time, the meaning of self-reports is established *reflexively* through the evaluation of multiple interviews from the same organization and of our earlier interpretations of those self-reports. In addition, our theorizing about communication Excellence (J. Grunig, 1992) and the Phase 1 survey data helped validate the self-reports. Standardization of the interview protocol permitted valid comparisons among responses of the participants.

Without devaluing self-reports, then, we sought to control for problems that Tan (1985) listed as inherent in the method. For example, interviewees may not be willing to tell "the truth" to interviewers they have not met before. Certain responses are viewed by participants as more socially acceptable than others. Other responses—such as describing oneself as a member of the dominant coalition—enhance the participants' prestige. We mitigated these problems by establishing rapport, creating trust, and probing, while assuring confidentiality. Another problem with self-reports, according to Tan, is that interviewees may not be aware of their feelings when first asked about an issue. In this regard, we took hesitations in the interview response as reassurances that the answers ultimately offered were thoughtful comments that approximated true internal states.

One ethical issue considered before data collection was the researcher's position and status relative to participants. Like Kauffman (1992), we believe that the relationship between researcher and researched shapes the ultimate analysis. Thus, we belabored our research design—believing, like Kauffman, that the process is part of the data. Other ethical considerations included our commitment to minimal investigator influence and no prior restraints on what the outcomes of our research would be. Throughout the processes of data gathering and analysis we were committed to in-depth, holistic descriptions and explanations in our participants' own words. By using open-end rather than closed-end questions, we maximized opportunities for participants to answer in forms and language they preferred (Wimmer & Dominick, 1987).

A final ethical issue involved the contributions of our participants. They gave of themselves by arranging schedules, spending time, and opening their lives to our inquiries. Marshall and Rossman (1989) suggested the need for reciprocity—giving back through "time, feedback, coffee, attention, flattery, tutoring, or some other appropriate gift" (p. 69). The form of such reciprocity, of course, must not violate personal ethics. One form of such reciprocity was the creation of opportunities for participants to mull over and express their attitudes and understandings verbally.

Conclusions

The Excellence study consciously selected two distinctive methodological approaches and combined the findings from the first phase of quantitative data collection to inform data collection during the second, qualitative phase of the study. Considered reflexively, this choice was appropriate. From the massive array of data from the mail survey conducted during Phase 1, a powerful nomothetic model of communication Excellence was developed (see chap. 3). This model, the Excellence factor, is grounded in earlier theorizing and research; however, the model could not have been constructed if the quantitative phase of the study had not sought data from multiple vantage points in the organizations studied. In Phase 2, the long interviews with participants in 25 organizations allowed the research team to put meat on the bones of the skeletal structure generated in Phase 1. Anomalies from the survey data were resolved. The snapshot of each organization generated by the cross-sectional survey was converted into a moving picture through the long interviews. The quantitative findings of Phase 1 were placed in the organization's historical perspective; the path of organizational evolution could be traced. Finally, the Phase 2 case studies helped clarify the contributions of communication Excellence to an organization's "bottom line."

USING OUR INSTRUMENTS

As mentioned earlier, we have included all of the instruments used in the Excellence study in the appendixes to this book. The three quantitative questionnaires include coding to indicate the concept that each question or set of questions measures. Most of the questions also appear in tables throughout the book, and the indicators in these tables can be traced to the questionnaires using the coding there.

Scholars can use our measures to replicate the Excellence study or parts of it. They also can use indicators for specific concepts of interest to them. Public relations professionals often ask if it is possible to use our instruments to audit their organizations. They can, although they would have to compare the scores of their organizations with the means and other statistical measures reported throughout the book.

The top-communicator questionnaire is the longest questionnaire and may be unwieldy for auditing purposes because it contains many questions about the planning and evaluation of specific programs that were not included in the overall index of excellence. For this reason, Appendix B also contains a shorter version of the PR head questionnaire that is comparable to the CEO questionnaire. It consists mostly of Part II of the original questionnaire and is most useful for those who might want to do an audit of a public relations department emphasizing only the variables included in the index of overall Excellence and variables closely related to the index (membership in the dominant coalition, relation to marketing, activism, and professional education and activities). The shortened questionnaire also substitutes for the measures of the model of public relations for specific programs with an overall measure of the models practiced in the department.

REFERENCES

Blythin, E. (1985, October). *Problems and solutions in the process and study of intercultural communication*. Paper presented at the Latin American Communication Panel, Pacific Coast Council on Latin American Studies, Las Vegas.

Broom, G. M., & Dozier, D. M. (1990). *Using research in public relations: Applications to program management*. Englewood Cliffs, NJ: Prentice-Hall.

Clifford, J. (1986). Introduction: Partial truths. In J. Clifford & G. E. Marcus (Eds.), *Writing culture: The poetics and politics of ethnography* (pp. 1–26). Berkeley: University of California Press.

Dexter, L. A. (1970). *Elite and specialized interviewing*. Evanston, IL: Northwestern University Press.

Downs, C. W., Smeyak, G. P., & Martin, E. (1980). *Professional interviewing*. New York: Harper & Row.

Dozier, D. M., with Grunig, L. A., & Grunig, J. E. (1995). *Manager's guide to excellence in public relations and communication management*. Hillsdale, NJ: Lawrence Erlbaum Associates.

Geertz, C. (1988). *Works and lives: The anthropologist as author*. Stanford, CA: Stanford University Press.

Gould, S. J. (1981). *The mismeasure of man*. New York: Norton.

Grunig, J. E. (Ed.). (1992). *Excellence in public relations and communication management*. Hillsdale, NJ: Lawrence Erlbaum Associates.

Grunig, L. A. (1994). *Phase II qualitative study: Initial analysis, interim report: Cases of excellence*. San Francisco: International Association of Business Communicators Research Foundation.

Hon, L. C. (1992). *Toward a feminist theory of public relations*. Unpublished doctoral dissertation, University of Maryland, College Park.

Huang, Y. (1990). *Risk communication, models of public relations and anti-nuclear activism: A case study of a nuclear power plant in Taiwan*. Unpublished master's thesis, University of Maryland, College Park.

Kaplan, A. (1964). *The conduct of inquiry: Methodology for the behavioral sciences*. Chicago: University of Chicago Press.

Kauffman, B. J. (1992). Feminist facts: Interview strategies and political subjects in ethnography. *Communication Theory, 2*(3): 187–206.

Keller, E. F. (1985). *Reflections on gender and science*. New Haven, CT: Yale University Press.

Lincoln, Y. S., & Guba, E. G. (1985). *Naturalistic inquiry*. Beverly Hills, CA: Sage.

Lyra, A. (1991). *Public relations in Greece: Models, roles and gender*. Unpublished master's thesis, University of Maryland, College Park.

Marshall, C., & Rossman, G. B. (1989). *Designing qualitative research*. Newbury Park, CA: Sage.

McCracken, G. (1988). *The long interview*. Newbury Park, CA: Sage.

Miles, M. B., & Huberman, A. M. (1984). *Qualitative data analysis: A sourcebook of new methods*. Newbury Park, CA: Sage.

Muto, J. (1988, Spring). If I'm reading this, I must not be by the pool. *Women's Studies in Communication, 11,* 20–21.

Nachmias, D., & Nachmias, C. (1981). *Research methods in the social sciences* (2nd ed.). New York: St. Martin's Press.

Seidman, I. E. (1991). *Interviewing as qualitative research*. New York: Teachers College Press.

Sriramesh, K. (1991). *The impact of societal culture on public relations: An ethnographic study of South Indian organizations*. Unpublished doctoral dissertation, University of Maryland, College Park.

Tan, A. S. (1985). *Mass communication theories and research* (2nd ed.). New York: Wiley.

Wimmer, R., & Dominick, J. R. (1987). *Mass media research: An introduction* (2nd ed.). Belmont, CA: Wadsworth.

Yin, R. K. (1989). *Case study research: Design and methods*. Newbury Park, CA: Sage.

CHAPTER THREE

Isolating the Excellence Factor

We began our analysis of the quantitative data from the Excellence study by attempting to reduce as much of the data as possible into a single index of excellence in communication management. This was necessary because both the Excellence theory and the data gathered in the study are complex. The theory consists of relationships among variables from such subtheories as public relations roles, participation in strategic management, and models of communication. The causal relationships among these subtheories could begin at different points for different organizations. The subtheories were operationalized into some 1,700 questions on three questionnaires administered to one or more heads of communication, the CEO or other executive manager, and an average of 14 employees in each of the 327 organizations we studied.

We tried to reduce these variables to a single index after first combining a number of indicators of variables into indexes or by using factor analysis to produce broader variables for related variables. We then factor analyzed these indexes or factors to isolate a single factor of excellence, which we then used to calculate an overall index of excellence in public relations. Factor analysis looks for clusters of variables to which people respond with similar answers when they complete a questionnaire. In the case of communication Excellence, our theory suggested that most of the characteristics of excellence would cluster together, as would the characteristics of less excellent programs. The most excellent public relations departments should possess most of the characteristics of excellence. The least excellent organizations should possess few of the characteristics of excellence and most of the characteristics of less excellent public relations. The majority of organizations, which fall in the middle of a normal distribution of excellence, should have midrange scores for most characteristics of both excellent and less excellent public relations or should possess some but not all of both sets of characteristics.

The factors produced by factor analysis represent underlying variables that are broader than the original variables analyzed. In this study, we expected that a factor would define an underlying variable of excellence in communication management, which would subsume the variables of the subtheories. It is important to point out that it is not possible to determine causal relationships among variables grouped on a factor-by-factor analysis. That limitation was not a problem in the Excellence study, however, because we had theorized that causation might run in different directions and start at different points for different organizations.

Factor analysis did allow us to determine if all of the characteristics of excellence clustered as we predicted so that we could use the underlying factor to identify the most and least excellent communication departments as well as average ones. We then used this index to choose organizations for the qualitative research, and the qualitative information provided insights on how excellent public relations came about in different organizations as well as detail on the outcomes produced by excellence. We also could use the Excellence factor to determine if other characteristics we measured would correlate with the index—thus providing additional detail on conditions related to excellent public relations. For example, we had no theoretical reason to include the use of outside consulting firms for different purposes as a part of the theory of excellence; but we could correlate the index of excellence with uses of consulting firms—thus determining if excellent departments use outside firms differently than do less excellent departments.

We began the search for a single Excellence factor with the goal of including as much of the information from the three survey questionnaires as possible in the index. We could not include variables for which we did not have information for every organization, however. Therefore, we could not include the variables from the first part of the questionnaire completed by the senior communicator, which asked eight and a half pages of questions about how the organization identified publics and how it planned, executed, and evaluated communication programs for those publics. (See Part I of the questionnaire for heads of public relations on pp. 564–573 in Appendix A.) Top communicators answered this set of questions for the three publics they chose as receiving most time and resources for public relations programs. Top communicators chose from a list of 17 stakeholder groups, but they chose only 8 groups often enough to provide sufficient data for analysis.

Because top communicators chose different publics, the same data were not available for all organizations. Therefore, we could not include the data on programs for different publics in the Excellence factor without eliminating many organizations from the analysis. As a result, we built the Excellence factor from the rest of the three questionnaires and later correlated the data from Part I of the public relations questionnaires with the Excellence factor public by public for organizations that had programs for each of the eight publics.

There also were several questions on the top communicator's and CEO's questionnaires that produced categorical data that could not be correlated with other variables. These questions asked about power of the public relations department, membership in the dominant coalition, organizational responses to activism, relationship to marketing and other managerial functions, gender of the top communicator, and country and type of organization. We analyzed these variables later by comparing mean scores on the Excellence factor and its component variables for the categories of the categorical variables.

Chapters 4 through 11 contain mean scores, analyses of reliability, and factor analysis of variables that went into the Excellence factor. Those data are presented in chapters following this one so that data related to the same subtheories can be analyzed together. These chapters also include statistical analyses of the relationship between the Excellence factor and the variables of the subtheory not included in that index, as well as data from the qualitative study. It is necessary to present an overview of the preliminary analyses of the subtheories in this chapter, however, to fully understand the characteristics of the Excellence factor.

OVERVIEW OF VARIABLES IN THE EXCELLENCE FACTOR

The Value of Communication

The major premise of the Excellence theory states that communication has value to an organization because it helps to build good long-term relationships with strategic publics, so measures of the value of public relations were perhaps the most important variables to be included in the Excellence factor. We measured the value of communication through the method of compensating variation, by which we asked the CEO to estimate the value of public relations in comparison to other management functions and to estimate the rate of return to communication. We also asked the top communicator to make similar estimates and to predict the estimates that the dominant coalition would make on the same variables. Finally, we asked both the CEO and the top communicator to estimate the extent to which the dominant coalition supports the communication function.

The CEOs and top communicators estimated the return on public relations almost equally—186% and 197%, respectively. The heads of public relations underestimated the CEO's estimate, however: 131%. Results were similar on the question that asked the CEOs and public relations heads to compare the value of the public relations department with the typical organizational department. Respondents were told that 100 was the value of a typical department. CEOs provided a mean score of 159 as the value of the public relations department. Heads of public relations departments rated the value of public relations even higher than did the CEOs—a mean of 189. As they did for the rate of return, however, the PR heads underestimated the value that the CEO would assign to the department (138), but not by so large a margin.

Contribution to Strategic Organizational Functions

Involvement in strategic planning is the major way in which excellent public relations departments identify publics with whom the organization needs to build relationships in order to be effective. We included the responses to four questions that asked CEOs and heads of public relations units the extent to which public relations contributes to four strategic functions: strategic planning, response to major social issues, major initiatives such as acquisitions or new products and programs, and routine operations such as employee communication or media relations.

For the overall sample, we found that public relations units most often contribute to routine operations and in response to major social issues. They are less likely to participate in major initiatives and, especially, in strategic planning. We also asked what public relations units do to contribute to strategic management when they are involved in the process. The departments not involved in strategic planning did not respond to these questions. The responses showed that communication units that participate in strategic planning most often do so through informal approaches, contacts with influential people outside the organization, and judgment based on experience. Public relations less often conducts research or uses other formal approaches to gathering information for strategic planning—an indication that many communication units are not qualified to make a full contribution to strategic planning.

The results for the CEOs and the heads of public relations units were similar. The only exception was for participation in strategic planning, for which public relations heads estimated the participation to be greater than did the CEOs. As a general picture, then, these results show that most public relations practitioners are not strategic managers. However, this picture changed dramatically when we looked at the departments that were most valued by their CEOs and that conform most to our criteria for excellence.

Public Relations Roles

It is difficult, if not impossible, for a public relations unit to be involved in strategic management if the top communicator mostly plays a technical rather than managerial role. Therefore, the extent to which the top communicator occupied four major roles—the manager, senior adviser, technician, and media relations roles—were major variables considered for inclusion in the Excellence factor.

We asked the CEOs four questions to measure the extent to which they believed the senior practitioner in their public relations department should occupy each of these four roles. Again, the results confirmed our theory of excellence—with only a few wrinkles. CEOs do not believe the senior person in the department should be a technician. They prefer the manager or communication liaison role, with media relations a close third. The difference between the manager and senior adviser role seems to reflect the difference in power that senior practitioners have in organizations. Managers have more responsibility than senior advisers. Thus, some CEOs seem to want a powerful, strategic manager in the senior position in communication; others want a less powerful communication adviser.

The strength of the media relations role demonstrates the preoccupation that CEOs have with the media. However, CEOs who valued public relations most ascribed only modest importance to media relations whereas those who value the function less assign great importance to that role.

When we compared the actual roles played by the heads of public relations units with those preferred by the CEO, the communication heads occupied the manager and technician roles essentially to the extent preferred by the CEOs. Both sets of data indicate that the technician role is least important for the head of a communication unit and the manager role most important. CEOs, however, prefer the less powerful senior adviser role equally with the manager role; whereas the communication heads reported a lower score for the extent to which they believe they occupy the senior adviser role. The difference seems to reflect a difference in power among communication heads.

The CEOs also prefer the media relations role to a greater extent than the communication heads reported playing that role. In particular, the CEOs prefer having the senior public relations person maintain media contacts more than the communication heads reported doing that activity. This difference, again, indicates the preoccupation of many CEOs with media relations.

Models of Public Relations

The four models of public relations (press agentry, public information, two-way asymmetrical, and two-way symmetrical) occupy a critical place in the theory of excellence. We asked the top communicators to respond to scales consisting of four questions each to estimate which of these models were used in communication programs for the organization's three most important publics. These responses could not be used to calculate the Excellence factor, however, because not all organizations had programs for the same three publics. However, we did use both the top communicator's and the CEO's estimate of which of these models represent the schema, or worldview, that defines the way the dominant coalition understood public relations.

In the CEO questionnaire, first, we asked the respondents to indicate the extent to which the four questions for each model describe the way they think public relations should be practiced. CEOs rated the press agentry and public information models low and the two-way symmetrical and asymmetrical models high. In line with our theory of excellence, they rated the two-way symmetrical model most highly. The CEOs rated the two-way asymmetrical model nearly as highly, but mostly because of items suggesting that research should be an integral part of public relations. They did not agree with the most telling statement about asymmetrical public relations, that its "broad goal is to persuade publics to behave as the organization wants them to behave."

Heads of communication units, however, underestimated the extent to which the dominant coalition values the excellent models of public relations. Communication heads overestimated the extent to which CEOs value the press agentry and public information models—especially the press agentry model—and underestimated the extent to which they value the two-way symmetrical and asymmetrical models. Actually, then, we found the schema for public relations to be more favorable in the average organization than what the heads of public relations units believe.

Potential of the Communication Unit

The dominant coalition of an organization may prefer a certain model of public relations for the organization and a certain role for its senior communication practitioner. The communication practitioners in the same organization, likewise, may prefer to practice a certain model—or believe that they practice that model or role. What generally determines the models and roles actually practiced by communication units, however, is the knowledge available in the unit to practice them. Knowledge to practice the managerial role and the two-way models are two characteristics included under the broad category of the "potential of the public relations department" in Fig. 1.1. The potential of the department also includes the professionalism of the practitioners working in the department. In constructing the Excellence factor, therefore, we examined items making up scales to measure the knowledge available in the communication units studied to practice each of the four models of public relations and the manager and technician roles as well two measures of professionalism.

We found that, on the average, communication units have more potential to practice the one-way, less excellent models of public relations than the more excellent, two-way models. The lowest mean was for the two-way asymmetrical model; the next lowest was for the two-way symmetrical model. Heads of communication units seem to believe their departments have the potential to achieve the objectives of the two-way models; but they also believe their units lack the theoretical knowledge necessary to achieve them. These results, then, suggest that communication units generally have less potential for excellence than for mediocrity. The means for the measures of knowledge for the excellent models were high enough, however, to suggest that many departments do indeed have potential for excellence.

For the communication roles, we found that the average department has about average ability to practice both the managerial and the technical roles. The mean was somewhat higher for the managerial role than for the technician role. However, we also found that the typical department has greater expertise in the more general managerial functions—such as managing people, developing a budget, and setting goals and objectives—than in the more strategic management functions. These strategic functions are evaluation research, environmental scanning, and research to segment publics. In short, the data suggest that communication managers are more likely to be technical supervisors than strategic managers.

Activist Pressure on the Organization

The extent to which organizations are exposed to pressure from activist groups was the primary variable we used to operationalize the effect of an organization's environment on the excellence of its public relations function. Pressure from activist groups, according to our theory, makes an organization ripe for public relations activities to communicate with the activists. We found that most organizations in our sample faced pressure from activist groups—an average score of 149 when 100 represented the pressure felt by the typical organization. Sixty percent of the CEOs said their organization faces the typical level of activism or more. The median score was 100, however, suggesting that a few organizations face extreme activist pressure but that the typical CEO thought that his or her organization faces average pressure.

The heads of public relations units rated activist pressure somewhat lower than did the CEOs, 117, but their median score was 100—like that of the CEOs. When asked how successful the organization had been in dealing with activist groups and how successful the activist group had been in dealing with the organization, both CEOs and PR heads rated the organization as more successful. CEOs rated the organization as being more successful than did the PR heads. The PR heads thought the activist groups were more successful than did the CEOs.

Employee Variables

For the initial analysis of the employee data, we put all of the data from the employee questionnaires into a single data file and analyzed them with the employee as the unit of analysis rather than the organization. Then, we averaged the data from employees in each organization—a value that we assigned to each organization for each employee variable. Aggregation in that way made it possible to correlate the employee data with the data from the CEOs and public relations directors, which was necessary to be able to include the employee variables in the Excellence factor.

For the first of the employee variables, organizational culture, we conducted an exploratory factor analysis of 45 statements about different characteristics of culture that we derived from the literature on organizational culture. We found two dominant factors. One can be described as a participative factor and the other as an authoritarian factor. All but 7 of the 45 variables included in the analysis loaded clearly on one of the factors.

After developing these measures of participative and authoritarian cultures, we correlated the factor scores for each organization with indexes of several other characteristics of excellent organizations that the Excellence theory suggested would facilitate excellent public relations. We found a strong intercorrelation among participative culture, organic structure, symmetrical internal communication, and job satisfaction (both with one's individual job and with the organization in which an employee works). In contrast, authoritarian cultures correlated strongly with mechanical structures, asymmetrical systems of internal communication, and low job satisfaction.

The Status of Women

The questionnaires for the CEO, head of public relations, and employees each contained 22 questions about the treatment of and opportunities for women in the respondent's organization. In our theorizing about excellence in public relations, we maintained that excellent public relations requires diversity in race and gender if an organization is to understand adequately the diversity outside the organization. In addition, organizations that value diversity provide hospitable environments for the majority of women who now make up the public relations profession.

To determine the relationship of diversity to other characteristics, the 22 questions asked about the treatment of women in the questionnaires completed by CEOs, employees, and heads of communication units were factor analyzed. We wanted to find out whether there were major dimensions that characterized the treatment of women. In each case, a one-factor solution was most satisfactory. That means that organizations that treat women well tend to treat them better than organizations that treat women poorly on all 22 attributes. The correlations of this factor—as computed for the responses of the CEOs, employees, and PR heads—with the other characteristics of excellent organizations measured in the employee questionnaire confirmed that excellent treatment of women is a characteristic of excellent organizations. The "treatment of women" factor that resulted from the estimates of employees, however, correlated more highly with the other variables from the employee sample than did the "treatment of women" factors that resulted from the estimates of CEOs and top communicators.

Although the one-factor solution was most satisfactory for determining the relationship of the gender variables to the Excellence factor, the factor analysis did suggest three subdimensions of the treatment of women—nondiscrimination policies, providing a supportive work environment, and mentoring and advancement programs. Chapter 11 discusses these subdimensions and their relationship to excellence in public relations in detail.

CONSTRUCTION OF AN INDEX OF EXCELLENCE IN PUBLIC RELATIONS

After we had constructed appropriate indexes or measures for each of these sets of variables and after we had completed the preliminary analysis described, we began to sort through the variables statistically to determine the best combination of variables to measure the overall excellence of public relations in the organizations we studied. We analyzed the CEO variables first, and then added the characteristics measured by the data from public relations directors and employees. The final product was an index of excellence. We used the index to assign an Excellence score to each organization that could be used to correlate with other characteristics of public relations departments and programs and with the characteristics of organizations.

The CEO's View of Excellence in Communication

To develop a preliminary and relatively simple picture of how CEOs view excellent public relations, we placed organizations into three categories based on responses to the item that asked respondents to compare the value of public relations with the average department in the organization. Most (212) of the responses fell into the category between 100 and 200, which is labeled "medium value" in Table 3.1. We compared the responses of the CEOs in this category with those of CEOs who rated public relations below 100 (38 respondents) and those who rated it above 200 (34 respondents).

Table 3.1 shows that CEOs who value public relations most think their department should practice the two-way symmetrical model and that their senior practitioner should be a communication manager or senior adviser. However, the media relations role is a close third. Participation of public relations in critical organizational functions, especially in strategic planning, most distinguishes the perceptions of CEOs who assigned these three levels of value to public relations. Likewise, Table 3.1 shows that valued departments have support from the dominant coalition and that the CEO assigns a return on investment in public relations about twice as high as for the low-valued departments.

TABLE 3.1

Characteristics of Public Relations in
Departments Valued Differently by CEOs

Variable	Low Value (n = 38)	Medium Value (n = 212)	High Value (n = 34)	F
Models of Public Relations				
Press agentry scale	7.36	7.97	8.31	0.97
Public information scale	6.84	6.63	5.52	2.29
Two-way asymmetrical scale	7.98	9.50	10.23	7.33**
Two-way symmetrical scale	8.55	9.91	10.83	6.68**
Public Relations Roles				
Technician scale	6.74	6.56	6.68	.05
Media relations scale	10.05	10.60	12.09	5.45**
Managerial scale	10.24	11.16	13.45	12.11**
Senior adviser scale	10.45	11.37	13.28	14.15**
Contribution to Organizational Functions				
Strategic planning	6.56	8.89	13.04	21.96**
Response to major social issues	8.78	11.95	14.27	22.57**
Major initiatives	8.24	10.90	14.20	30.06**
Routine operations	10.09	12.71	15.17	26.98**
Contribution to Strategic Management (if any)				
Regular research activities	5.05	8.29	11.07	15.86**
Research for specific questions	6.76	9.56	11.88	15.74**
Other formal approaches	6.11	9.12	11.72	18.22**
Informal approaches	7.74	10.54	14.21	33.18**
Contacts with knowledgeable people outside organization	8.88	11.32	15.55	32.52**
Judgment based on experience	8.89	11.38	14.45	19.37**
Other Variables				
Support for public relations by the dominant coalition	10.33	12.39	15.64	28.71**
Percentage return on public relations	126%	178%	265%	9.36**
				14.83**a
Activist pressure	7.63	10.41	10.97	2.98*
Success of activist groups	7.30	7.75	7.21	.32
Success of organization with activist groups	9.82	11.54	12.06	1.69
Percentage of time CEO spends on internal communication	22%	27%	28%	.99
Percentage of time CEO spends on external communication	15%	22%	25%	2.91*
CEO's estimate of the importance of communicating with external groups	12.72	14.09	17.24	14.58**

Note. Except for the percentages, the numbers in this table are based on an open-end, "fractionation scale." Scores are the square roots of responses on the scale for which respondents are told that 100 is a typical response on all of the items in the questionnaire. Thus, in this table a mean of 10—the square root of 100—represents this typical response.

aCalculated after scores were transformed to a square root to reduce skew.

*p < .05. **p < .01.

The CEOs with highly valued departments reported more activist pressure than did those with the less valued departments, but the difference was barely statistically significant. There was no significant difference in the reported success of activist groups or in the organization's success in dealing with them, although organizations in the highly valued group reported slightly more success dealing with activists. These results suggest that all organizations face activism but that activism does not produce excellence in public relations unless the public relations department has the requisite knowledge and professionalism and the support of the dominant coalition that are necessary to respond successfully to activists.

Finally, the CEOs who value public relations most spend more time in external communication themselves and value communication with external groups more than do CEOs who value public relations less. CEOs who most value communication also report spending a larger percentage of their time in internal communication than those who value it less, but the difference is not statistically significant.

After getting this overall feel for what matters to CEOs, we factor analyzed the CEO variables that we considered the best candidates for the Excellence factor and those that would be likely to load on a mediocrity factor. We also added the variable of the senior public relations person being named by the CEO as a member of the dominant coalition to the best predictors in Table 3.1. Table 3.2 shows that the first factor analysis produced two factors, which we have labeled "excellence" and "mediocrity." Table 3.2 confirms the differences in variables for CEOs who value public relations at the three different levels reported in Table 3.1. For some variables, the factor analysis shows the importance of the Excellence attributes even more strongly than did the comparison of three groups in Table 3.1.

According to the CEO data, excellent departments practice the two-way models of public relations—especially the two-way symmetrical model. Mediocre departments practice press agentry and public information and the two-way asymmetrical model to a slight extent. Excellent departments have managers or senior advisers in the senior position. Mediocre departments have technicians. In both kinds of departments, the senior person also handles media relations; but the excellent departments stress that role less than do the mediocre departments.

Excellent departments participate in strategic management and other vital functions of the organization. Mediocre departments do not. Excellent departments also are valued by the dominant coalition and the CEO. Mediocre departments are not. The senior person in public relations is a part of the dominant coalition in organizations with excellent public relations. He or she is not in the dominant coalition when public relations is mediocre. CEOs with excellent departments also believe it is more important to communicate with external groups than do CEOs with mediocre departments.

TABLE 3.2
Factor Analysis of Excellence and Mediocrity
in Public Relations as Seen by CEOs

Variable	Communality	Excellence Factor	Mediocrity Factor
Models of Public Relations			
Press agentry scale	.35	−.04	.59
Public information scale	.39	−.15	.61
Two-way asymmetrical scale	.27	.46	.25
Two-way symmetrical scale	.33	.55	.14
Public Relations Roles			
Technician scale	.50	−.06	.71
Media relations scale	.34	.23	.53
Manager scale	.31	.55	.10
Senior adviser scale	.44	.65	.11
Contribution to Organizational Functions			
Strategic planning	.32	.56	−.09
Response to major social issues	.49	.64	−.24
Major initiatives	.36	.60	−.03
Routine operations	.34	.58	−.06
Support for Public Relations			
Public relations in dominant coalition	.18	.42	−.04
Support for public relations by the dominant coalition	.53	.72	−.08
Value of public relations department	.47	.68	.01
Percentage return to public relations	.17	.40	−.12
CEO's estimate of the importance of communication with external groups	.38	.61	.06
Eigenvalue		5.08	2.31
Percentage of variance explained		**30%**	**14%**

Note.   The factor analysis reported in this table was based on the principal axis method.

An Index of Excellence Based on the Combined Data Sets

The CEOs who most valued public relations in our sample seem to prefer communication departments with the attributes described by our theory of excellence and to have senior communication managers who participate in the strategic management of the organization. Next, then, we asked whether these same organizations actually would have communication units performing according to our standards of excellence. Finally, we wanted to know whether these excellent communication units would be found in excellent organizations—those with participative cultures, organic structures, symmetrical systems of internal communication, and high levels of job satisfaction.

We addressed these questions by performing a factor analysis on a combined data set of variables from the CEO, PR heads, and employee samples. Most of the same variables included in the factor analysis for CEOs also were included in the questionnaire completed by heads of communication units. For the models of public relations, we asked questions about the models communication heads thought the dominant coalition prefers—the schema or worldview for public relations held by the dominant coalition.

We also asked the communication heads what role they actually play. We asked them how much knowledge was available in their department that is necessary to practice each of the models of public relations and to fill the manager and technician roles. We asked them the extent to which they participate in strategic management and other major organizational functions. And we asked the PR heads to estimate the level of support of the dominant coalition for public relations and the value and rate of return that the dominant coalition would ascribe to public relations. Finally, we included all of the aggregated characteristics of an excellent organization and less excellent organization in the factor analysis that we measured in the employee questionnaire.

In the first factor analysis of these combined variables, we attempted to reproduce the Excellence and mediocrity factors found with the CEOs alone. We were unsuccessful. One factor contained the Excellence variables from the CEO sample and the other Excellence variables from the sample of communication heads. The mediocrity variables and the characteristics of organizational Excellence did not load on either factor, or they had low loadings on both of these factors. As a result, these variables had a low communality. The implication of those results is that CEOs who prefer excellent public relations do not always have excellent public relations departments, and excellent communication departments are not always in organizations whose CEOs prefer excellent public relations. One could also say—in terms of simple economic theory—that the demand for excellent communication (from CEOs) and its supply (potential of the communication unit) often are not in equilibrium in the same organization.

We then performed a factor analysis with four factors to see if we could find separate excellence and mediocrity factors for CEOs and for heads of communication units. We could not. The result was a CEO Excellence factor, a PR head Excellence factor, and a single mediocrity factor combining the characteristics of mediocrity from both samples. The fourth factor contained the characteristics of excellent organizations, which had low loadings on the other factors.

The characteristics of excellent organizations, in other words, seem to exist independently of the characteristics of excellent public relations. Factor analysis tends to isolate variables in this way unless the computer is forced to associate variables by limiting the number of factors or by using a different type of rotation. Thus, we conducted a third factor analysis with three factors. An oblique rotation produced a solution that allowed us to examine the relationship among all of the variables most clearly.[1]

Table 3.3 shows the results of this analysis with three factors and an oblique rotation. The first factor has the highest loadings for the characteristics of excellence as described by the heads of communication units. However, the Excellence characteristics as measured in the CEO sample also generally had moderate loadings on this underlying dimension of excellence of the communication unit. The major surprises found on this factor is that communication heads reported practicing the technician and media relations roles as well as the manager and senior adviser roles—although the loadings for the two technical roles are smaller. The communication heads also reported high levels of knowledge for all of the roles and all of the models in their departments. This would suggest that all communication units have the knowledge needed to practice the press agentry and public information models and the technician and media relations role but that only excellent departments have the knowledge needed to practice the two-way models and the managerial roles.

For the models, however, the heads of excellent public relations units predicted that the dominant coalition would prefer the two-way symmetrical model. That model did not rate so highly with their CEOs as the two-way asymmetrical model, a preference that communication heads of excellent units apparently are not aware of.

Finally, we found a moderate loading for having formal university training in public relations with an excellent communication unit but no loading for participation in professional associations. The result seems to have occurred because many university programs in public relations provide training only for the technician role and not for the managerial roles or the two-way models. The loading is still positive, however, because several programs do provide such training;

---

[1]Rotation of factors is a fairly complex aspect of factor analysis, but it can be understood in reasonably simple terms. The factors produced by factor analysis are like the axes of a graph. For example, if one were to plot the relationship between age and salary for a group of people on a graph, he or she would plot the age and salary of each person in the group on two axes—one for age and one for salary. Factor analysis takes a set of relationships among pairs of variables and tries to determine a set of axes on which those pairs could be plotted so that they have the highest value or "loading"—first on one axis and then on a second or third until all of the variation in the pairs of variables is used up. The computer tries to place all of the variation on a single factor. As a result, the initial factor loadings are not pure. That is, most of the variables load highly on the first factor; and many variables load equally on more than one factor or axis. To make the loadings pure, the computer can rotate the axes so that variables load only on one axis, if the data make it possible. Axes normally are at right angles to each other—they are "orthogonal" or uncorrelated. If instructed to do so, the computer can rotate the axes to an oblique angle; and the rotated factors then are correlated. The researcher must exercise judgment to determine which solution explains the data best—that is, makes the most sense. All of the factor analyses in this report were based on orthogonal rotations, except for the one reported in Table 3.3—for which an oblique rotation seemed to explain the data best.

TABLE 3.3
Factor Analysis of Excellence and Mediocrity in Public Relations
Based on CEO, PR Head, and Employee Variables

Variable	Communality	PR Head Excellence Factor	Overall Mediocrity/CEO Excellence Factor	Culture Factor
Models of Public Relations Preferred by CEO				
Press agentry scale	.05	.11	.08	−.18
Public information scale	.07	.12	.21	−.08
Two-way asymmetrical scale	.22	.20	−.43	−.04
Two-way symmetrical scale	.27	.04	−.53	−.04
Models of Public Relations PR Director Believes the Dominant Coalition Prefers				
Press agentry scale	.10	.15	.24	−.14
Public information scale	.05	.06	.22	−.05
Two-way asymmetrical scale	.20	.44	−.08	−.03
Two-way symmetrical scale	.30	.55	−.09	−.07
Public Relations Roles Preferred by CEO				
Technician scale	.02	.01	.12	−.05
Media relations scale	.02	.06	−.13	−.01
Manager scale	.32	.10	−.56	.11
Senior adviser scale	.38	.07	−.61	.05
Public Relations Roles Practiced by PR Head				
Technician scale	.09	.29	.28	−.01
Media relations scale	.21	.42	.12	−.01
Manager scale	.47	.68	−.13	−.01
Senior adviser scale	.36	.58	−.03	.11
Contribution to Organizational Functions as Seen by CEO				
Strategic planning	.36	.04	−.60	.05
Response to major social issues	.45	.15	−.67	.05
Major initiatives	.37	.04	−.61	.02
Routine operations	.35	.17	−.58	.06
Contribution to Organizational Functions as Seen by PR Head				
Strategic planning	.34	.51	−.35	.02
Response to major social issues	.31	.51	−.24	.10
Major initiatives	.25	.47	−.20	.09
Routine operations	.34	.58	−.06	−.01
Support for Public Relations as Seen by CEO				
Public relations in dominant coalition	.21	.08	−.45	.08
Support for public relations by the dominant coalition	.49	.12	−.69	.15
Value of public relations department	.46	.06	−.67	.05
Percentage return to public relations	.16	.07	−.40	.07
CEO's estimate of the importance of communication with external groups	.27	.16	−.49	−.07

(Continued)

TABLE 3.3

(Continued)

Variable	Communality	PR Head Excellence Factor	Overall Mediocrity/CEO Excellence Factor	Culture Factor
Support for Public Relations as Seen by PR Head				
Public relations in dominant coalition	.07	.06	−.26	−.01
Support for public relations by the dominant coalition	.37	.52	−.36	−.02
Management clearance required for PR	.02	.10	.01	−.09
Value of public relations department	.25	.48	−.17	−.08
Prediction for value of PR department given by dominant coalition	.37	.57	−.27	.03
Percentage return to public relations	.13	.35	.07	−.06
Prediction for percentage return to PR given by dominant coalition	.13	.36	.02	−.06
Knowledge Available in PR Department as Reported by PR Head				
Press agentry model	.44	.66	−.07	−.05
Public information model	.53	.72	−.01	−.05
Two-way asymmetrical model	.47	.68	−.15	−.02
Two-way symmetrical model	.47	.68	−.14	.04
Technician role	.46	.67	−.01	−.13
Manager role	.66	.81	−.16	.01
Training and Professional Activity of PR Head				
Education in public relations	.04	.20	.05	−.03
Participation in professional associations	.01	.06	−.03	.05
Employee Perceptions of Organization				
Asymmetrical internal communication	.24	.15	.05	−.48
Symmetrical internal communication	.75	.00	−.08	.86
Organic structure	.41	.03	.01	.63
Mechanical structure	.30	.05	.03	−.55
Individual job satisfaction	.39	.08	−.06	.62
Organizational job satisfaction	.47	.07	−.05	.73
Participative culture	.48	.14	−.04	.67
Authoritarian culture	.23	.16	.05	−.46
Conditions for Women in Organization				
Employee perception factor	.18	.09	−.10	.41
CEO perception factor	.13	.10	−.39	.11
PR head perception factor	.25	.48	−.12	.11
Correlations Among Factors Resulting From Oblique Rotation				
Excellence factor		1.00		
Mediocrity factor		−.09	1.00	
Culture factor		−.04	.12	1.00
Eigenvalue		8.54	5.05	4.10
Percentage of variance explained		16%	9%	8%

Note. The factor analysis in this table is based on principal axis factoring and oblique rotation. The loadings reported in this table are from the factor structure matrix, which represents the correlation of the variables with the factor without controlling for the correlation of the factor with other factors.

and the knowledge for those roles and models can be found in several public relations textbooks.

The second factor can be called either the mediocrity factor or the CEO Excellence factor, depending on how one reads the signs of the variables. When a factor has both high positive and high negative loadings, it describes opposite ends of a continuum. One can look at that continuum from either direction. He or she can change the direction of looking at the factor by converting all of the negative signs to positive and all of the positive signs to negative. This is called "reflecting" the factor.

If the signs are left as they are for the second factor in Table 3.3, all of the characteristics of mediocre public relations have high positive loadings—characteristics such as the press agentry and public information models and the technician and media relations roles. All of the characteristics of excellence have high negative loadings on this factor—especially the CEO variables. If all of the signs are changed, however, this factor duplicates the CEO Excellence factor almost perfectly—the variables with high negative loadings on this second factor in Table 3.3 had high positive loadings on the Excellence factor in Table 3.2.

At the same time, the Excellence characteristics from the sample of communication heads had small to moderately negative loadings on this factor, suggesting at least a partial equilibrium between CEO demand for excellence and the actual excellence supplied by the communication unit. The consistent loadings on the first factor also suggest such a partial correspondence between supply and demand. The fact that the loadings for communication department variables are higher on the PR head Excellence factor and for the CEO on the CEO factor, however, shows that the correspondence is not perfect.

As in the other factor analyses, the characteristics of excellent organizations had their highest loadings on the third factor—which we have called the "culture factor." The characteristics of excellent organizations—participative culture, organic structure, symmetrical internal communication, and individual and organizational job satisfaction—have high positive loadings on this factor. The opposite characteristics—authoritarian culture, asymmetrical internal communication, and mechanical structure—have high negative loadings on the same factor. These loadings, of course, support our theory of organizational Excellence perfectly.

What, then, of the relationship between organizational and public relations Excellence? Two variables, participative organizational culture and asymmetrical internal communication, had small positive loadings on the Excellence factor for PR heads but not on the CEO Excellence factor. The loading of asymmetrical internal communication is difficult to explain. However, the secondary loading for culture suggests that a participative culture creates a favorable context for an excellent public relations department but that culture alone is not enough to bring about an excellent department and is not the major reason why CEOs see a need for excellent public relations.

We might ask, then, what does produce an excellent public relations department if the demand for it by the CEO and the dominant coalition and participative culture are not sufficient? The answer seems to lie in the senior public relations person being in the dominant coalition and his or her participation in the organization's strategic management. This explanation is what we called the power-control theory in *Excellence in Public Relations and Communication Management*. Public relations is excellent, that is, when the senior manager is empowered enough to implement it.

But, we should ask next, why are some senior communication managers empowered and others not? The results in Table 3.3 suggest that knowledge of strategic management, the two-way symmetrical and asymmetrical models, and the managerial role are the answer—although only the strategic management aspects of the managerial role. In the qualitative interviews of people in the excellent departments, we sought confirmation of this relationship between knowledge and empowerment.

The last significant piece of information in Table 3.3 is about the relationship of the conditions for women with the Excellence factors. The loadings do show a consistent pattern of association: Favorable conditions for women as seen by PR heads load on the PR Excellence factor. Favorable conditions as seen by CEOs load on the CEO factor. Favorable conditions as seen by employees load on the culture factor. The perceptions of employees and heads of communication units load positively with other characteristics of an excellent organization, but the perceptions of CEOs do not load at all. CEOs do not seem to be a good source for information on the treatment of women in their organizations.

A Final Index of Excellence in Communication Management

After completing this extensive factor analysis of most of the variables that we considered candidates for an index of excellence in public relations and communication management, we selected the variables that had the strongest relationship with each other and, therefore, the underlying variable of excellence. Although the three factors produced by the last factor analysis have great value in explaining the conditions that affect public relations in an organization, none of them is pure enough to produce a single index of excellence. To produce such an index, therefore, we put the characteristics of communication Excellence with the highest loadings on the PR head and CEO Excellence factor, the "training in public relations variable," all of the characteristics of organizational Excellence from the third factor, and the three "treatment of women" scales into a factor analysis limited to only one factor. A single factor would force the characteristics into a single index—if indeed the data allow the computer to do so.

Table 3.4 shows that this strategy was successful. The first 18 characteristics in Table 3.4—the Excellence characteristics from both the PR heads and the CEOs—load positively and highly on the same factor. In addition, loadings on

TABLE 3.4
Factor Analysis to Produce a Single Scale
of Excellence in Public Relations

Variable	Communality	Excellence Factor
CEO Variables		
PR in strategic planning	.08	.28
Support for PR by dominant coalition	.17	.41
Value of PR department	.11	.32
Importance of communication with external groups	.11	.34
Preference for two-way asymmetrical model	.15	.39
Preference for two-way symmetrical model	.11	.33
Preference for managerial role	.13	.36
Preference for senior adviser role	.12	.35
Public Relations Head Variables		
PR in strategic planning	.31	.56
Perceived support for public relations by dominant coalition	.32	.57
Estimate of the value dominant coalition would assign to PR	.33	.57
Estimate of preference for the two-way asymmetrical model by the dominant coalition	.23	.48
Estimate of preference for the two-way symmetrical model by the dominant coalition	.31	.55
PR head in manager role	.31	.56
PR head in senior adviser role	.24	.49
Knowledge of two-way asymmetrical model in public relations department	.41	.64
Knowledge of two-way symmetrical model in public relations department	.44	.67
Knowledge of managerial role in public relations department	.52	.72
Formal education in public relations	.02	.14
Characteristics of Organizational Excellence		
Participative culture	.06	.24
Symmetrical system of internal communication	.03	.19
Organic structure	.01	.12
Individual job satisfaction	.03	.16
Organizational job satisfaction	.04	.19
Treatment of women—employees	.05	.23
Treatment of women—CEOs	.10	.32
Treatment of women—PR heads	.25	.50
Eigenvalue		5.71
Percentage of variance explained		21%

Note. The factor analysis in this table was based on the principal axis method.

that factor show that excellence in public relations also correlates with a senior practitioner who has formal education in public relations, a participative culture, an organic structure, a symmetrical system of internal communication, individual and organizational job satisfaction, and favorable treatment of women. These last loadings are lower than the loadings of the variables for public relations Excellence, however—showing once again that education in public relations, culture, structure, and internal communication facilitate excellence in public relations but do not ensure it. Overall, the single factor in Table 3.4 puts numbers on the variables in our theory of excellence—numbers that provide strong support for the theory.

To produce a final scale of excellence in public relations that could be used to compare organizations, we used all of the CEO and PR head variables from Table 3.4, except for formal education in public relations; the best indicator of organizational Excellence, participative culture; and the best measure of treatment of women, from the PR Head questionnaire, and added them into a index of excellent public relations. Table 3.5 shows the results of an analysis of the reliability of this scale. The data in Table 3.5 show that the Excellence scale is highly reliable: It has a Cronbach's alpha of .84, and the Cronbach's alpha would not increase if any variable were eliminated.[2] Participative culture, however, does have low correlations with the rest of the scale.

We used this scale to provide a rating for each organization in our sample that each of these organizations used to audit their public relations units, that was used to identify the organizations with the most excellent public relations departments, and that we used to make further comparisons between the excellent organizations and the less-than-excellent organizations.

Canonical Correlations of Characteristics of Public Relations With Value of Communication

After constructing this scale of excellence in communication management, we conducted an additional analysis to determine the correlation of all of the characteristics of public relations in the Excellence scale as one set of variables with all of the estimates of the value of public relations as another set of variables. Our general theory of public relations states that the dominant coalition would support and assign greater value to public relations when the department and organization have the characteristics specified in the theory. Critics of our

---

[2]This reliability analysis was performed after we had estimated missing values for each of the Excellence variables, as explained in chapter 2. Estimating missing values made it possible to maintain the largest possible sample size for this and other analyses based on the Excellence variables and the index of Excellence. As we explained in chapter 2, also, many organizations reported data for more than one communication department. There were a total of 407 departments in the 316 organizations studied. It was possible to calculate total Excellence scores for the 270 organizations for which complete data were available from PR heads, CEOs, and employees. The reliability reported in Table 3.5 was for the 270 organizations for which complete data were available. We also calculated reliability with the public relations department as the unit of analysis ($n = 316$) with data available also from the CEO and employees in that organization), and Cronbach's alpha rose slightly to .85. The analysis by department should be treated with caution, however, because departments in the same organization had the same data for CEOs and employees and, therefore, were not completely independent of one another.

TABLE 3.5
Reliability Analysis of Excellence Scale

Variable	Item–Total Correlation	Squared Mult. Corr.	Alpha If Item Deleted
CEO Variables			
PR in strategic planning	.37	.37	.85
Support for PR by dominant coalition	.48	.45	.85
Value of PR department	.38	.38	.85
Importance of communication with external groups	.37	.39	.85
Preference for two-way asymmetrical model	.47	.53	.85
Preference for two-way symmetrical model	.39	.55	.85
Preference for managerial role	.42	.38	.85
Preference for senior adviser role	.41	.52	.85
Public Relations Head Variables			
PR in strategic planning	.51	.43	.84
Perceived support for public relations by dominant coalition	.53	.57	.84
Estimate of the value dominant coalition would assign to PR	.51	.51	.84
Estimate of preference for the two-way asymmetrical model by the dominant coalition	.45	.55	.85
Estimate of preference for the two-way symmetrical model by the dominant coalition	.48	.59	.85
PR head in manager role	.45	.45	.85
PR head in senior adviser role	.41	.44	.85
Knowledge of two-way asymmetrical model in public relations department	.57	.68	.84
Knowledge of two-way symmetrical model in public relations department	.55	.64	.84
Knowledge of managerial role in public relations department	.61	.71	.84
Estimate of support for women in the organization	.33	.22	.84
Participative organizational culture	.14	.15	.85
Cronbach's alpha = .85			

Note. The key statistic in Table 3.5 is Cronbach's alpha—an overall measure of the reliability of an index. Alpha represents the extent to which another scale measuring the same concept—in this case excellence in public relations—would correlate with this scale. A scale with an alpha approaching .90 is highly reliable. The table also contains three sets of statistics that analyze the reliability of each item in the scale. The item–total correlation is the correlation of each item with the sum of the other items. The squared multiple correlation is the percentage of variation in each item that can be explained by the other items. "Alpha if item deleted" shows whether the scale would be more or less reliable without each item.

method might argue that by putting both estimates of the support and value of public relations into the same index as the characteristics of public relations and the organization makes it impossible to demonstrate that characteristics of the public relations function specified by the Excellence theory increase the likelihood that the dominant coalition will support and value public relations. As we said in chapter 1, however, it also is possible that a dominant coalition that supports and values public relations will develop a public relations department with the characteristics of excellence—that is, cause and effect could run in the opposite direction.

Regardless of the direction of causation between excellent public relations and valued public relations, however, it is possible to use the statistical technique of canonical correlation to determine if there is a relationship between the two sets of variables. Canonical correlation works much like factor analysis, but the technique makes it possible to determine if two groups of variables correlate with each other simultaneously—in this case excellence of public relations and value of public relations. Canonical correlation produces "canonical variates" that are much like factors except that it separates the blocks of variables. The correlations of each variable with the underlying variate also indicate the strength of the relationship of each variable with the underlying variate.

Table 3.6 shows the result of a canonical correlation of the questions measuring the support and value of public relations by the dominant coalition and the rest of the Excellence variables. In contrast to factor analysis, canonical correlation indicates the number of underlying variates that can be extracted that are statistically significant. The first variate maximizes the correlation of all of the variables, and the second attempts to explain any remaining correlation between some or all of the variables that is not explained by the first variate. In this case, there were two significant variates.

As Table 3.6 shows, the first variate essentially reproduces the Excellence factor from the factor analysis in Table 3.4 and the index of excellence constructed in Table 3.5. All of the variables have high correlations with the underlying variate, with the exception of participative organizational culture, which has a positive but low correlation. The canonical correlation between the public relations and organizational variables and the value variables is high. This high correlation supports the theoretical soundness of the Excellence theory: Excellent public relations and an excellent context for public relations strongly related to the value assigned to the function by the dominant coalition.

In addition, the size of the correlations suggests which characteristics are most related to the perceived value of public relations most. Table 3.6 suggests that involvement of public relations in strategic management and the CEO's preference that the senior public relations person be a manager or senior adviser are most related to the perceived value of public relations. In other words, the

TABLE 3.6
Canonical Correlation of Variables Measuring Value
of Public Relations With Other Excellence Variables

Variable	Overall Variate	PR Head/ CEO Variate
Characteristics of Public Relations and Organization		
(Variable Group 1)		
CEO Variables		
PR in strategic planning	.64	.39
Importance of communication with external groups	.47	.32
Preference for two-way asymmetrical model	.51	.32
Preference for two-way symmetrical model	.42	.41
Preference for managerial role	.58	.24
Preference for senior adviser role	.56	.44
Public Relations Head Variables		
PR in strategic planning	.64	−.42
Estimate of preference for the two-way asymmetrical model by the dominant coalition	.34	−.22
Estimate of preference for the two-way symmetrical model by the dominant coalition	.44	−.49
PR head in manager role	.38	−.48
PR head in senior adviser role	.26	−.32
Knowledge of two-way asymmetrical model in public relations department	.43	−.26
Knowledge of two-way symmetrical model in public relations department	.39	−.26
Knowledge of managerial role in public relations department	.45	−.32
Estimate of support for women in organization	.43	−.41
Participative organizational culture	.11	.00
Value of Public Relations (Variable Group 2)		
CEO Variables		
Support for PR by dominant coalition	.37	.60
Value of PR department	.38	.37
Public Relations Head Variables		
Perceived support for public relations by dominant coalition	.41	−.56
Estimate of the value dominant coalition would assign to PR	.23	−.41
Canonical Correlation	.70**	.63**

*$p < .05.$ **$p < .01.$

CEOs seem to believe that public relations has its greatest value when it fulfills the managerial role specified in the Excellence theory.

The second variate in Table 3.6 illustrates another interpretation of the data already presented in this chapter. In a canonical correlation, variables with the same sign in each block of variables have a positive relationship with each other. For the second variate in Table 3.6, all of the variables that came out of the CEO questionnaire have a positive sign, and all of the variables from the public relations questionnaire have a negative sign. Participative culture has no correlation with the second variate, most likely because it came from the questionnaire completed by employees. Both sets of CEO variables correlate positively with each other, in other words; and both sets of senior communicator variables correlate positive with each other. The covariation between the two sets of variables that was not explained by the first variate, therefore, seems to reflect the difference between the supply of excellent public relations from the public relations heads and the demand for excellent public relations from the dominant coalition. The second variate provides additional evidence that supply of and demand for excellence are not always in equilibrium in the same organization.

Relationship of Excellence to Other Variables

We attempted to determine whether this index of communication Excellence has any relationship with variables we had considered but eliminated from the index by correlating it with these variables. We also correlated the index with several demographic characteristics of the communication department, the senior communicator, and the organization to see if excellence occurs more often in any of the categories.

Important to note, the presence of the top communicator in the dominant coalition, as our theory predicted, correlates moderately with the Excellence scale, especially when the CEO indicated who was in the dominant coalition (Tau[3] = .25, $p < .01$). When the PR head chose the members of the dominant coalition, the correlation was lower (Tau = .15, $p < .01$), although it was highly significant statistically. The CEO is most likely to know who is in the dominant coalition, so his or her choice of the members of the dominant coalition is the more important of the two variables. When the CEO said the PR head is a member of that power elite, the public relations department is more likely to be excellent—a fact that lends significant support to our theoretical proposition that in excellent departments the senior communicator is a member of or has access to the most powerful decision makers in the organization.

The Excellence scale also correlates at $r = .24$[4] with the extent of activist pressure reported by the CEO and .38 with the pressure reported by the head of the

---

[3]Tau refers to Kendall's Tau, which is a nonparametric correlation coefficient. A correlation coefficient is a measure of the extent to which two variables are related to each other. In the social and behavioral sciences, a correlation of .10 is low, .30 moderate, and .50 high. A nonparametric coefficient is appropriate for variables on a scale where the difference between numbers is not equal. For an either–or variable such as whether the PR head is or is not in the dominant coalition (a dichotomous variable), a nonparametric correlation is more appropriate than a parametric coefficient such as Pearson's r.

[4]r refers to the Pearson correlation coefficient—a measure of the extent to which two variables are related to each other. In the social and behavioral sciences, a correlation of .10 is low, .30 moderate, and .50 high.

communication unit. Both correlations are significant at the .01 level. These correlations, although moderate, support our theory that activist pressure in the organization's environment fosters excellence in public relations. In addition, the Excellence scale correlates positively with the success of the organization in dealing with activist groups as reported by the CEO ($r = .17, p < .05$) and by the communication head ($r = .29, p < .01$). The success of the activist group as reported by either the CEO or PR head does not correlate significantly with the Excellence scale, although there is a small positive correlation for the PR head ($r = .10$). There were no significant correlations between the percentage of time the CEO reported spending in either external or internal communication activities and the Excellence scale.

The overall education of the senior communicator has no relationship to excellence ($r = .02$), although having taken courses in public relations has a small positive correlation ($r = .12, p < .05$). The top communicator's membership in professional associations has no relationship to excellence ($r = .02$), but readership of professional publications has a small to moderate correlation ($r = .21, p < .01$). That correlation suggests that reading professional publications is important because it adds to the knowledge base of the practitioner, which is a major component of the Excellence factor. Specifically, readership of publications correlates at $r = .21$ ($p < .01$) with managerial knowledge in the public relations department, at $r = .13$ ($p < .05$) with knowledge of two-way symmetrical practices, and at $r = .21$ ($p < .01$) with knowledge of two-way asymmetrical practices.

The age of the senior communicator makes no difference in excellence ($r = .04$). The gender of the senior communicator also has no effect (Tau $= -.07$, where a high score indicates a female practitioner). In addition, the percentage of female employees in the public relations department has no relationship with excellence ($r = -.01$), nor does the percentage of female practitioners in the communication technician role ($r = .03$) and the percentage of women in the managerial role ($r = .01$).

Finally, the size of the organization does not correlate significantly with excellence in public relations ($r = .001$), although the number of practitioners in the public relations department has a small positive correlation with excellence ($r = .12, p < .05$). We interpret this difference as showing that an organization does not have to be large to have excellent public relations, but that an excellent public relations department typically has a few more employees than does a mediocre one.

In summary, these correlations suggest that a turbulent environment provides a context that demands excellent public relations; but that a public relations department cannot respond to that environment unless it possesses the knowledge to practice excellent public relations. Education in public relations helps build this knowledge base, but continuing study is necessary to add to that base. Neither men nor women have a monopoly on excellence. The same is true for large and small organizations.

National Differences in Excellence

Once we had determined the variables in the Excellence scale and had calculated a score for each organization on this scale, it was possible to compare the
average scores of organizations in the three countries studied—the United
States, Canada, and the United Kingdom. Table 3.7 compares the three countries on the 20 variables that make up the Excellence scale, as well as on selected
nonexcellent variables that could be used for comparison and several of the
variables related to excellence that were not included in the overall scale of excellence. Table 3.7 shows that there are virtually no differences among the three
countries in the overall level of excellence. The United Kingdom has a slightly
higher Excellence score than the United States and Canada, but the difference is
not statistically significant.

Statistically significant differences do appear among countries for four of the
variables that make up the Excellence scale. CEOs in Canada assigned a lower
value to the public relations department than did the CEOs in the United States.
Similarly, the senior communicators in the United Kingdom estimated that the
dominant coalition would assign a higher value to public relations than did the
top communicators in the other countries, especially Canadian communicators.
However, comparison of these two means in the United Kingdom suggests that
the top communicators there overestimated the value that the dominant coalition actually assigned to the function. The Canadian top communicators estimated that the dominant coalition would value public relations less than in the
other countries, which the comparison of means suggests is a realistic assessment. Third, top communicators in the United Kingdom estimated that the
dominant coalition would prefer the two-way symmetrical and two-way asymmetrical models more than did their counterparts in the other countries. The
difference is not statistically significant for the two-way asymmetrical model,
however.

In addition, comparison of these means with those of the CEOs in the United
Kingdom suggests that the difference among countries occurs mostly because
the top communicators overestimated the preferences of the dominant coalition for these two excellent models. At the same time, the British CEOs preferred the press agentry model more than did CEOs in the United States and
Canada—at a statistically significant level higher than the Canadians. The British top communicators, however, did not predict this preference of their CEOs
for press agentry accurately.

Perhaps related to the British CEOs' preference for press agentry is the fact
that top communicators in the United Kingdom reported significantly higher
levels of knowledge to practice both the press agentry and the public information models than did their counterparts in the United States and Canada. UK
practitioners also reported significantly less education in public relations than

TABLE 3.7
Comparison of Means for Excellence Variables for the
United States, Canada, and the United Kingdom

	United States	Canada	United Kingdom	F
		(z Scores)[a]		
Number	189	49	32	
Overall Index of Excellence	.02	−.02	.02	0.28
Variable *(Non-Excellence Variables in Italics)*				
CEO Variables				
PR in strategic planning	.03	.10	−.10	0.42
Support for PR by dominant coalition	.04	−.06	−.15	0.62
Value of PR department	.08	−.44	−.12	3.71*[b]
Importance of communication with external groups	.06	−.07	−.15	0.75
Preference for two-way asymmetrical model	.01	−.02	−.10	0.18
Preference for two-way symmetrical model	.05	−.15	−.21	1.27
Preference for press agentry model	.07	−.38	.19	4.84**[c]
Preference for public information model	.08	−.25	−.06	2.31
Preference for managerial role	.08	−.21	−.21	2.44
Preference for senior adviser role	.06	−.06	−.21	1.24
Preference for technician role	.06	−.09	−.20	1.20
Preference for media relations role	.04	−.09	−.11	0.58
Public Relations Head Variables				
PR in strategic planning	−.05	.08	.21	1.38
Perceived support for public relations by dominant coalition	.01	−.17	.19	1.61
Estimate of the value dominant coalition would assign to PR	.00	−.29	.22	3.23*[d]
Estimate of preference for the two-way asymmetrical model by the dominant coalition	−.12	.08	.19	1.88
Estimate of preference for the two-way symmetrical model by the dominant coalition	−.08	.08	.39	3.38*[e]
Estimate of preference for the press agentry model by the dominant coalition	.07	−.21	−.04	1.46
Estimate of preference for the public information model by the dominant coalition	.06	.07	−.16	0.69
PR head in manager role	.09	.14	.02	0.13
PR head in senior adviser role	−.04	.18	.14	1.12
PR head in technician role	.01	.01	.00	0.00
PR head in media relations role	.06	.12	.29	0.80
Knowledge of two-way asymmetrical model in public relations department	−.02	.15	.03	0.57
Knowledge of two-way symmetrical model in public relations department	−.01	−.05	.25	1.04
Knowledge of press agentry model in public relations department	.01	−.12	.47	4.11*[f]

(Continued)

TABLE 3.7
(Continued)

	United States	Canada	United Kingdom	F
	(z Scores)[a]			
Knowledge of public information model in public relations department	.05	−.03	.56	4.07*[f]
Knowledge of managerial role in public relations department	−.11	.17	.16	1.96
Knowledge of technician role in public relations department	.02	.16	.14	0.54
Estimate of support for women in the organization	.05	−.19	−.03	1.43
Employee Variables				
Participative organizational culture	.05	.02	−.41	3.03*[e]
Authoritarian organizational culture	.00	−.07	−.12	0.96
Variables Related to Excellence Not in Excellence Factor				
Education in public relations	.18	.02	−.37	4.41*[e]
Communication head in dominant coalition, seen by CEO	−.06	.15	.11	1.12
Communication head in dominant coalition, seen by head	−.01	.14	.11	0.56
Symmetrical internal communication	.06	−.06	−.29	1.86
Asymmetrical internal communication	.02	−.01	−.21	0.72
Support for women, seen by employees	.01	.04	−.40	9.23**[f]

[a]The scales for all of the variables in this table were converted to standardized z scores. Z scores have a mean of 0 and a standard deviation of 1. In a normal distribution, 68% of the population will have a z score between −1 and 1, 95% between −2 and 2, and 99% between −3 and 3. [b]The Tukey-HSD Multiple Range Test for differences among means shows a significant difference ($p < .05$) between the United States and Canada. [c]Canada significantly different from the United States and the United Kingdom. [d]Canada significantly different from the United Kingdom. [e]United States significantly different from the United Kingdom. [f]United Kingdom significantly different from the United States and Canada.

*$p < .05$. **$p < .01$.

did U.S. practitioners, perhaps explaining why they believe their knowledge of the one-way models is highest.

There were no differences among the three countries, though, in any of the roles variables—in the knowledge for these roles, the preferences of the CEOs, and the extent to which the top communicators said they practiced the roles. There also were no differences in the extent to which top communicators are in the dominant coalition in the three countries.

There were some interesting indications of cultural differences in British organizations compared to the United States and Canada. The United Kingdom had the lowest score on participative culture, which was significantly lower than the average for U.S. organizations. It also had the lowest average for authoritarian culture, however, although the differences among countries were not significant. These differences for the United Kingdom were mirrored in the scores for internal communication. Means for both symmetrical and asymmetrical internal communication were lower than for the United States and Canada, although the differences were not significant statistically. Perhaps reflecting the lack of participative culture in British organizations was a score significantly lower than for the United States and Canada on the support for women that employees in the United Kingdom reported. There were no differences in the report of this variable by PR heads, however.

We probably should not read too much into the differences in Table 3.7. The sample for the Excellence study was purposive, and it was small for Canada and the United Kingdom. The few significant differences in the table could have occurred by chance. However, the cultures of the three countries, although different to the casual observer, are among the most similar cultures in the world.[5] Therefore, we should not expect great differences. Our major conclusion should be that excellent public relations, as defined by our index of excellence, has equal validity at least in the three countries we studied.

However, we do find some interesting hints in Table 3.7 that British practitioners have less public relations education, that their CEOs value public relations in general less and press agentry more, and that British organizations are less participative and less conducive to women in comparison with the United States and Canada.

Difference in Excellence by Type of Organization

Table 3.8 compares scores on the overall index of excellence and the individual variables that make up the index by type of organization for the four types of organizations. In addition, it again compares selected nonexcellent variables that are related to the Excellence variables and several variables related to excellence but not included in the index of excellence. Table 3.8 shows that there are virtually no differences in overall excellence among the four types and for all but two of the component variables.

The public relations department in associations and nonprofit organizations is significantly more likely to participate in strategic management than those in corporations—as reported both by the CEO and head of public relations. Government agencies have average scores on participation in strategic

---

[5]For example, Hofstede's (1980) study comparing organizational cultures in 39 countries showed the United States, Canada, and the United Kingdom to have close scores on individualism, power distance, uncertainty avoidance, and masculinity. See also Sriramesh and White (1992) for a discussion of national cultures.

TABLE 3.8
Comparison of Means for Excellence Variables for Corporations,
Government Agencies, Associations, and Nonprofit Organizations

	Corporations	Gov't Agencies	Associations	Not-for-Profits	F
		(z scores)[a]			
Number	122	54	35	59	
Overall Index of Excellence	−.01	−.03	.01	.110	0.28
Variable *(Non-Excellence Variables in Italics)*					
CEO Variables					
PR in strategic planning	−.21	−.01	.53	.25	6.93**[b]
Support for PR by dominant coalition	−.01	−.04	.08	.01	.11
Value of PR department	−.19	−.05	−.04	.27	1.90
Importance of communication with external groups	−.11	.11	.05	.16	1.25
Preference for two-way asymmetrical model	−.07	−.12	.01	.23	1.46
Preference for two-way symmetrical model	.01	.02	−.12	−.06	.20
Preference for press agentry model	−.23	.15	.21	.26	4.81**[c]
Preference for public information model	−.22	.08	.31	.22	4.59**[d]
Preference for managerial role	−.04	−.12	−.08	.22	1.39
Preference for senior adviser role	.03	.06	−.17	.02	.47
Preference for technician role	−.22	.26	.39	.05	5.51**[e]
Preference for media relations role	−.21	.10	.20	.26	4.04**[c]
Public Relations Head Variables					
PR in strategic planning	−.17	.00	.38	.20	4.93**[d]
Perceived support for public relations by dominant coalition	−.04	−.12	.27	.05	1.42
Estimate of the value dominant coalition would assign to PR	−.11	−.04	.10	.12	1.12
Estimate of preference for the two-way asymmetrical model by the dominant coalition	−.04	−.14	−.07	.00	.22
Estimate of preference for the two-way symmetrical model by the dominant coalition	.02	−.04	−.04	.00	.06
Estimate of preference for the press agentry model by the dominant coalition	−.11	.20	−.07	.13	1.82
Estimate of preference for the public information model by the dominant coalition	−.06	.18	−.17	.07	1.21
PR head in manager role	.05	.04	.26	.15	.54
PR head in senior adviser role	−.05	.09	−.13	.18	1.03

(Continued)

TABLE 3.8
(Continued)

	Corporations	Gov't Agencies	Associations	Not-for-Profits	F
		(z scores)[a]			
PR head in technician role	−.21	.33	.16	.10	4.81**[f]
PR head in media relations role	−.19	.24	.21	.12	3.78**[f]
Knowledge of two-way asymmetrical model in public relations department	.02	.05	−.17	.09	.58
Knowledge of two-way symmetrical model in public relations department	.08	.09	−.18	−.11	1.14
Knowledge of press agentry model in public relations department	−.02	.06	−.21	.12	.92
Knowledge of public information model in public relations department	−.01	.02	−.07	.06	.13
Knowledge of managerial role in public relations department	.03	−.16	−.08	−.02	.42
Knowledge of technician role in public relations department	−.07	.07	.03	.08	.42
Estimate of support for women in the organization	−.01	.08	−.17	.04	.54
Employee Variables					
Participative organizational culture	.12	−.22	−.25	.00	2.43
Authoritarian organizational culture	.08	−.03	−.26	−.21	10.57**[d]
Variables Related to Excellence Not in Excellence Factor					
Education in public relations	−.05	.13	−.02	.02	.44
Communication head in dominant coalition, seen by CEO	−.17	−.05	.18	.32	4.11**[c]
Communication head in dominant coalition, seen by head	−.15	−.09	.27	.30	4.10**[c]
Symmetrical internal communication	.08	−.20	−.20	.09	1.78
Asymmetrical internal communication	.13	.21	−.42	−.26	5.52**[g]
Support for women, seen by employees	.01	.19	−.38	−.12	9.96**[h]

[a]The scales for all of the variables in this table were converted to standardized z scores. Z scores have a mean of 0 and a standard deviation of 1. In a normal distribution, 68% of the population will have a z score between −1 and 1, 95% between −2 and 2, and 99% between −3 and 3. [b]The Tukey-HSD Multiple Range Test for difference among means showed a significant difference ($p < .05$) between corporations and associations and not-for-profits and between government and associations. [c]Corporations significantly different from not-for-profits. [d]Corporations significantly different from associations and not-for-profits. [e]Corporations significantly different from government and associations. [f]Corporations significantly different from government. [g]Corporations and government significantly different from associations and not-for-profits. [h]Corporations and government significantly different from associations, government from not-for-profits.

*$p < .05$. **$p < .01$.

management. The same pattern can be seen at the bottom of Table 3.8 for the perception that the head of communication is a member of the dominant coalition—a variable that is related to excellence but not included in the index of excellence.

In general, nonprofit organizations and, to a lesser extent, associations have slightly higher means on several of the Excellence variables; and corporations are close to the mean on nearly all of the variables. There is a larger number of corporations in the sample than of the other types of organizations, however, so it is likely that the phenomenon of regression to the mean occurred. That is, the larger a sample the more likely that the sample mean will approach the true mean. Because of the smaller number of other organizations, it is possible that the sample included relatively more excellent departments than there are in the true populations of these types of organizations. It is possible that with a larger sample of all organizations these differences would disappear.

Nevertheless, these data suggest that it is not necessary to have the large, complex public relations departments that most corporations have for the communication function to be excellent. Nonprofit organizations, which generally are smaller, had more excellent departments on several specific criteria—probably because of closer interaction among all members of the organization, including those in the public relations department.

Although there are few differences among types of organizations in the Excellence variables, differences can be found among these four types of organizations in the nonexcellent variables in Table 3.8. For the managerial and technical roles, corporate CEOs and PR heads see a clear distinction in the role of the senior public relations person: He or she has a managerial and not a technical role. In nonprofits, the public relations head occupies both roles—indeed, he or she often may be the only public relations staff member. In associations, the head of public relations is more likely to be in a technician or media relations role, although the PR head is more likely to see his or her role also to be that of a manager than is the CEO.

The senior public relations person in government agencies is more likely to report being in a technician or media relations role than in the other types of organizations—especially in comparison with corporations. However, he or she is about average for the managerial role, participation in strategic management, and being in the dominant coalition. Such a combination of roles suggests that the historical public information or public affairs definition lives on in government—of disseminating information to the general population directly or through the media. At the same time, the data suggest that government agencies are moving toward a more managerial and strategic role.

The data for the nonexcellent models of public relations seem to confirm this pattern. Although there are no differences among organizations in the two excellent models of public relations, the two-way symmetrical and two-way asymmetrical, the CEOs in corporations are less likely to prefer the press agentry and public information models than are those in the other types of organizations. The data suggest that CEOs in corporations are less likely to see public relations as a one-way function than are CEOs of other organizations. For government agencies, the CEOs are in the middle in preferring these nonexcellent models; and the means are not significantly different from those for corporations. At the same time, the communication heads estimate that their CEOs prefer these two nonexcellent models more than do the PR heads in other types of organizations—although the differences are not significant.

The difference in the practice of managerial roles and two-way models does not seem to be a function of differences in the knowledge needed to practice them across the four types of organizations. Table 3.8 shows no significant difference in knowledge to practice any of the roles or models nor any difference in education in public relations for the four types of organizations.

The means for symmetrical and asymmetrical systems of employee communication in Table 3.8 seem to mirror the pattern for culture. Although there are no significant differences in the extent to which these organizations have symmetrical systems of internal communication, corporations and government agencies are significantly more likely to have asymmetrical internal communication than are associations and not-for-profits. Corporations combine symmetrical and asymmetrical communication, government agencies are more likely to have asymmetrical than symmetrical systems, associations seem to have neither, and nonprofits are more likely to be symmetrical than asymmetrical. The same combinations appear for participative and authoritarian cultures, suggesting that internal communication is closely aligned with organizational culture.

All things considered, Table 3.8 suggests that the characteristics of excellence are generic for all types of organizations. However, we must add that excellence is not the sole property of large corporate public relations departments. Smaller nonprofit organizations seem to be just as excellent and to provide conditions most conducive to excellence in public relations. At the same time, corporations seem to have moved their senior public relations officers away from the technician and media relations roles and the press agentry and public information models more than have the other types of organizations. In nonprofits in particular and in associations to a lesser extent, the public relations head is both a technician and a manager and does press agentry and public information as much as two-way communication. Government agencies seem to be moving toward a strategic, managerial, and symmetrical role; but they are not quite there yet.

SUMMARY AND CONCLUSIONS

The initial results presented in this chapter are striking and strongly confirming of the theory we developed in our first book on excellent public relations. Our results confirm that excellent organizations have participative cultures, organic structures, symmetrical communication systems, and high job satisfaction. Excellent organizations also take steps to foster the careers of their female employees—making maximum use of their human resources. Nevertheless, the results show that these characteristics, except to some extent participative culture, have only a limited direct effect on the excellence of the public relations function. They do, however, have a strong effect on the symmetry of the internal communication system.

Organizations with excellent public relations departments also tend to be found in environments with more-than-average pressure from activist groups. Most of the organizations we studied have experienced activism, however, so activism alone does not produce excellent communication management. These conditions in and around organizations create a nurturing environment for excellent public relations, although they do not ensure excellence.

We found that CEOs value public relations highly and that those with excellent public relations departments value the communication function almost twice as highly as those with less excellent departments. We found that CEOs who value public relations most believe that it should be practiced essentially as spelled out by our theory of excellence. They believe that public relations departments should be characterized by participation in strategic management, symmetrical communication combined judiciously with two-way asymmetrical communication, and leadership by strategic communication managers. Of these variables, participation in strategic management seems to be the one variable that most increases the value the dominant coalition assigns to public relations.

Heads of excellent public relations departments also reported that their units practice public relations according to these same principles of excellence. Especially important is the knowledge that the top communicators reported that their departments have to practice the managerial role and the two-way symmetrical and two-way asymmetrical models of public relations. Top communicators in excellent departments are somewhat more likely also to have studied public relations formally and to read professional publications about public relations. They are no more likely to participate in professional associations, however, than are practitioners in less excellent departments.

Excellent public relations departments often are found in organizations whose CEOs do not value public relations. In addition, CEOs who value excellent public relations often do not have excellent departments in the organization they head. In excellent organizations, the senior public relations person is part of or has access to the dominant coalition; and the CEO and other members of that dominant group of decision makers value public relations highly. This power-control theory seems to explain best why some public relations units are excellent and the conditions that are present when the CEO's demand for excellence in communication is in equilibrium with excellent public relations activities supplied by the public relations department.

Finally, we found that excellence in public relations seems to be generic to the three countries and the four types of organizations we studied. Size of the organization makes no difference. Heads of excellent departments come from all age groups and are equally likely to be women as men.

REFERENCES

Hofstede, G. (1980). *Culture's consequences*. Beverly Hills, CA: Sage.

Sriramesh, K., & White, J. (1992). Societal culture and public relations. In J. E. Grunig (Ed.), *Excellence in public relations and communication management* (pp. 597–614). Hillsdale, NJ: Lawrence Erlbaum Associates.

CHAPTER FOUR

The Value of Public Relations

This chapter speaks to one of the two major research questions of the Excellence study. In fact, the elusive goal of determining the value of public relations was a major reason why the IABC Research Foundation requested proposals for this ambitious study. In its proposal to the foundation, the research team that ultimately received the grant added a second question to this so-called "bottom line" query—an elaboration of the request to explain *how* and *why* communication contributes to the bottom line. We understood that only excellent public relations departments or communication managers with certain attributes could or would help make their organizations effective. So, we on the team asked about characteristics of excellence. The main issue for IABC's leadership, however, was this: *How does public relations make an organization more effective, and what is that contribution worth?*

The question of the value of public relations has been of great concern to professional communicators for many years because of the perception among both communicators and other managers that public relations is an intangible management function in comparison with other functions whose value can be described, measured, and evaluated through systematic research. Because of its intangibility, public relations often has been believed to suffer at budget time, and particularly during financial crises, because there is no way to demonstrate its worth.

For at least 25 years, therefore, public relations professionals and researchers have struggled to develop measures that would establish that public relations is effective or adds value. Among other measures, they have attempted to determine the advertising value of press clippings, to establish the readership of publications, or to do surveys or experiments to determine if communication campaigns or programs have had measurable effects on cognitions, attitudes, or behaviors. Many professional communicators have successfully demonstrated the effects of individual communication programs in one or more of these ways. Nevertheless, evaluation of communication programs falls short of demonstrating that the overall management function of public relations has value to an organization or to society.

Recently, public relations practitioners and firms have been on a quest to develop a single indicator[1] of the value of organizational reputation that they believe will establish that communication has a measurable monetary return that can be attributed to the public relations function (e.g., Fombrun, 1996; Jeffries-Fox Associates, 2000a). Many commercial research firms have developed a series of evaluative, attitudinal questions to measure reputation (Jeffries-Fox Associates, 2000b). As our interviews with organizations with excellent public relations functions show in this chapter, this quest for a magic number to demonstrate the overall value of public relations by estimating the value of reputation is fraught with difficulty and is not likely to provide a valid and reliable measure of the value of public relations.

These many forays into estimating the value of public relations have not been successful at least in part because of confusion over the organizational level at which public relations has value. We must recognize at the beginning of this chapter, therefore, that the value of communication can be determined at least at four levels.[2] These four levels provided the framework for organizing *Excellence in Public Relations and Communication Management:*

1. *Program level.* Individual communication programs such as media relations, community relations, or customer relations are successful when they affect the cognitions, attitudes, and behaviors of both publics and members of the organization—that is, the cognitive, attitudinal, and behavioral relationships among organizations and their publics. The program level has been the traditional focus of evaluative research in public relations. However, effective communication programs may or may not contribute to organizational effectiveness; many operate independently of the organization's mission and goals.

2. *Functional level.* The public relations or communication function as a whole can be audited by comparing the structure and processes of the department or departments that implement the function with the best practices of the

---

[1]Patrick Jackson, who before he died in 2001 was president of the Jackson, Jackson, & Wagner public relations firm in Exeter, New Hampshire, called this the quest for the "silver bullet" at the Conference on Corporate Communication held at Notre Dame University, November 17–18, 2000.

[2]It is also possible to evaluate public relations at a lower level than the four described next—the level of the individual message or publication such as an annual report or a brochure. We have not addressed the individual level of evaluation in the Excellence study because the purpose of the study was to determine how the public relations function and its component programs contribute to organizational effectiveness. In general, though, evaluation can be done at the individual level using similar concepts to those used at the program level.

public relations function in other organizations or with theoretical principles derived from scholarly research. Evaluation at this level can be called theoretical or practical benchmarking, as described in chapter 1. Although the value of public relations at the program and functional level is different, public relations departments that meet evaluative criteria at the functional level should be more likely to develop communication programs that meet their objectives more often than functions that do not meet these criteria.

3. *Organizational level.* For many years, organizational scholars have debated the question of what makes an organization effective. To show that public relations has value to the organization, we must be able to show that effective communication programs and functions contribute to organizational effectiveness.

4. *Societal level.* Organizations have an impact beyond their own bottom line. They also affect other organizations, individuals, and publics in society. As a result, organizations cannot be said to be effective unless they also are socially responsible; and public relations can be said to have value when it contributes to the social responsibility of organizations.

The initial request for proposals from the IABC Research Foundation focused on the organizational level of value. The research team added the second question, the Excellence question, because we believed public relations functions must be organized according to certain theoretical criteria before they would contribute value at the organizational level. In addition, as we explain further in this chapter, we must address the societal level as well if we are to determine the value of public relations.

In our review of relevant literature, conducted at the outset of this decade-long research, we began with the organizational level to develop a definition of organizational effectiveness. We reasoned that only by defining what we mean by an "effective" organization could we then determine the contribution that communication makes, or could make under conditions of excellent practice. This chapter begins with a brief recap of the literature of organizational effectiveness. It continues with a report of the data, both quantitative and qualitative, that relate to the value of public relations. It concludes with a discussion of the implications of these findings for public relations practice and education.

WHAT DO WE MEAN BY EFFECTIVENESS?

Sociologists, students of business management, social psychologists, marketing experts, and public relations theorists alike have studied the relationship between management practices and organizational effectiveness. Because of diverse disciplinary perspectives, their definitions of "effectiveness" diverge. So, too, does their reasoning lead to different conclusions for public relations scholars attempting to explain the correlation of communication with effectiveness.

Despite their differences, the work of organizational scholars leads to the conclusion that public relations has the potential to help make organizations effective. But what is the logic that makes it possible to arrive at this conclusion? And how, in turn, did we on the Excellence team integrate these divergent theories into a logical (and measurable) understanding of effectiveness that would allow us to determine the contribution of managed communication to effectiveness?

Four main schools of thought on effectiveness, emanating primarily from organizational sociology and business management, guided our initial conceptualization of the project. These perspectives were systems, competing values, strategic constituencies, and goal attainment. We synthesized these approaches, culling the concepts within each one that offered the most promise in explaining the relationship between effectiveness and communication.

The *systems* perspective emphasizes the interdependence of organizations with their environments, or the system with its suprasystem. Interdependence comes from mutual need. Presumably, organizations need resources from their environment—raw materials, a source of employees, clients or customers for the services or products they produce, and so forth. The environment, too, needs the organization for its products or services.

Systems theory also teases out the interfaces among subsystems within the organizational system. Students of systems theory come to understand that changes in any subsystem result in changes of the organizational whole. As the vice president of the economic development agency interviewed during the qualitative phase of the Excellence project explained it in lay terms: "We look at communication as being a critical component of the system. If you pull one chunk of it out, the system doesn't function properly."

Similarly, changes in the environment affect the organization—and vice versa. Thus, in the open system, management relies on boundary spanners such as public relations professionals to scan the environment. Specialists in communication act as the eyes and ears of the organization. They contribute to organizational effectiveness in at least two main ways: monitoring the environment to show top management what the situation is and helping top management decide how the organization should operate, contingent on its external context. Many public relations researchers, such as J. Grunig and Hunt (1984), Cutlip, Center, and Broom (1985), and Pavlik (1987), have built their theories on this open-systems concept as it was first described by social psychologists Katz and Kahn (1978).

Angelopulo (1990) applied the systems perspective to determine the potential effectiveness of organizations. He described the effective organization as one able to obtain desired responses from units of the environment through exchange relationships. He characterized the degree of openness of organizational members as "active outward orientation." He theorized that the greater the degree of active outward orientation, the greater the organization's potential effectiveness would be. Active outward orientation, consistent with open-systems theory, is a set of basic assumptions that results in the group's predisposition to behave as:

- An interacting, interrelated whole.
- An entity striving to maintain an awareness of the nature and potential of its relationship with the environment.
- An entity permeating all relevant subsystems with relevant information about the environment and the organization.
- An entity existing proactively within its environment.

Managers in a closed system, by contrast, operate as if they were autonomous from their suprasystem—unconstrained or unaffected by the forces in the environment that are acknowledged in the open system. Likewise, departments or subsystems of the closed organizational system operate with less coordination and interaction than in the open system—thus denying the mutual influence of each subsystem or functional area on the other. In the closed system, then, we would expect to find a less central, more marginal role for formal communication programs.

The literature extant at the time of our conceptualization showed that the predicted relationship between environment and communication function in the typical organization was only rarely realized. In other words, systems theory provided a more normative than descriptive explanation for organizational effectiveness. The literature showed that managers typically have a narrowly focused or inaccurate perception of the organization's environment. Even in cases where a dynamic or hostile environment existed, organizations often exhibited a closed-system mind-set that failed, then, to value the kind of strategic public relations that would help them cope with that turbulence. Because we believe that managed communication can, indeed, contribute substantially to organizational effectiveness, we looked beyond the systems perspective.

The *competing values* approach, like systems theory, provides an integrative framework in which to study effectiveness. Rather than emphasizing the ways in which organizations receive vital resources from their environments, however, it focuses on both means and ends. Measures of effectiveness are juxtaposed, as in Hage's (1980) typology that contrasts the value of efficiency with innovation and the value of quality with quantity.

Put simplistically, effectiveness becomes achievement vis-à-vis priorities. But how simple is too simple? Does a two-cell typology of dimensions of effectiveness overgeneralize? Or does a factor analytic study resulting in some 30 criteria (J. P. Campbell, 1977) make the determination of effectiveness more complex than necessary?

Despite these fundamental challenges, the competing values perspective, we argued in 1992, may offer special promise for organizations in transition because it can help top management get clear on the direction the organization should take. Nevertheless, we also looked beyond competing values in our search for an adequate definition of organizational effectiveness.

The *strategic constituencies* perspective, like systems theory, acknowledges interdependencies within the organization and, especially, between the organization and its environment. However, it focuses on those elements of the environment most critical to the organization. These aspects of the environment can be considered "strategic publics," or the groups most able to constrain or to help the organization.

This notion of specificity within the organization's environmental niche points to the value of public relations. As boundary spanners, managers of communication help the dominant coalition determine which elements of their domain are most important to reach. Organizational effectiveness is determined in part, then, by identifying those key publics. In fact, proponents of the population ecology approach to strategic constituencies (e.g., Denison, 1990; Hannan & Freeman, 1977; McKelvey, 1979) have argued that the environment determines which organizations will survive almost irrespective of actions of the organizations themselves. Thus we turn from this somewhat reactive perspective to one final school of thought on organizational effectiveness.

The *goal attainment* perspective proposes that the effective organization realizes its goals (Robbins, 1990). The emphasis is on ends, rather than any balance between means and ends as we have seen in the preceding approaches. Its attraction is the acknowledgment of purposeful action.

However, the power-control perspective forces us to question whose goals are being met. The self-interest of top managers, in particular, helps explain the irrationality of many decisions in the typical organization. In other words, those with the power to make decisions may make those decisions with personal—rather than organizational—goals in mind.

All four of these mainstream definitions of organizational effectiveness (and undoubtedly many more not reviewed here) help to explain why some operations are considered successful and thrive, whereas others are seen as ineffective and ultimately even may go out of business. Taken together, all four perspectives also help explain the value of excellent public relations. For example, we can glean from this brief review that managed communication helps the organization enact or understand its environment—the suprasystem with which it is mutually dependent. Significantly, boundary spanners such as public relations professionals may be responsible for determining which elements of that environment are strategic for the organization—which publics are most supportive or most adversarial and those most able to constrain or strengthen the organization's ability to meet its goals. We also know that departments of public relations can develop programs that build high-quality relationships with these strategic constituencies.

Relationships help the organization manage its interdependence with the environment. Of course, communication alone does not create and maintain these relationships; but communication plays a vital role. Then, too, relationships may not be entirely beneficial to the organization. They have the capacity to both limit and enhance the organization's autonomy within its environment. Nevertheless, the notion of relationships is so central to the literature of organizational sociology, business management, and—of course—public relations that at least two scholars defined "business" as "a connected set of relationships among stakeholders where the emphasis is on the connectedness" (Freeman & Gilbert, 1992, p. 12).

An interesting critique of the nature of relationships between the typical organization and its stakeholders was published at about the same time as the Excellence theory book (J. Grunig, 1992). This introspective piece, coauthored by R. Edward Freeman, helps explicate the complex connection between ethics and effectiveness. Freeman and his colleague Daniel R. Gilbert, Jr. (1992) set aside the earlier notion of stakeholder management as what amounts to a contest of autonomy:

> That is, stakeholders were clearly defined "names and faces" who were to be managed. If managers were to achieve their objectives, then they had to pay attention to stakeholders, regardless of their so-called "legitimacy." Stakeholder management was to be seen as understanding the rules of business. Caring had nothing to do with stakeholders and in fact Freeman argued that it didn't matter if managers cared about stakeholders or not. If managers wanted to stay in control, achieve their objectives, then stakeholders had to be managed. (p. 14)

The alternative, more contemporary, interpretation of the ethical and effective relationship between organizations and their strategic constituencies, Freeman and Gilbert (1992) proposed, is more blurred, more ambiguous. The key point, they reiterated, is the relationship. As they explained, "Managers who are effective define their very sense of self in terms of these discrete relationships, and focus on caring for and maintaining these relationships" (p. 12). The only risk they predicted in such a justice-oriented organization was the nurturance of existing relationships at the expense of innovation or the protection of the status quo at the expense of heroic action.

HOW PUBLIC RELATIONS CONTRIBUTES TO ORGANIZATIONAL EFFECTIVENESS

Integrating the relevant constructs within each of the four main perspectives on organizational effectiveness—systems theory, competing values, goal attainment, and strategic constituencies—results in the following definition: The effective organization balances its goals with the expectations of its strategic constituencies. This definition, in turn, led us to propose that:

*Public relations contributes to organizational effectiveness when it helps reconcile the or-
ganization's goals with the expectations of its strategic constituencies. This contribution
has monetary value to the organization. Public relations contributes to effectiveness by
building quality, long-term relationships with strategic constituencies. Public relations is
most likely to contribute to effectiveness when the senior public relations manager is a
member of the dominant coalition where he or she is able to shape the organization's goals
and to help determine which external publics are most strategic.*

The next chapter in this book explores the role of the top public relations person in the dominant coalition of the organization. Thus the data that follow are
organized around the other major aspect of this proposition: the value of identifying strategic publics and developing relationships with them.

Reading this far into the chapter should result in the understanding that communication managers are enormously valuable when they identify and work to
develop relationships with the groups most vital to the organization that employs them. Determination of so-called "target publics" is not so simple as it
may seem. But knowing which constituencies are strategic to the organization
also gets to the heart of the question of value, monetary and otherwise.

The astute practitioner of public relations acknowledges the importance of
what Mau and Dennis (1994) called "shadow" constituencies as well as the more
obvious, traditional stakeholders. Shadow publics are groups that do not affect
the organization's bottom line immediately or directly. They are critical because they can influence public perception of the organization. Emerging activist groups can be considered shadow constituencies. Failing to communicate
openly and symmetrically with such publics may send the message that they do
not matter to the organization.

The advantage in reaching out to these less obvious elements of the environment can be enormous. In fact, our data show that dealing with activism in the
environment actually propels the organization toward effectiveness. Despite
the time (and often frustration) involved in such interaction, it may result in
fresh perspectives and solutions to problems the organization—working in isolation or only with its most obvious publics—might not have considered.

THE TOTAL CONCEPT OF "VALUE"

So, we begin this presentation of results related to the value of public relations
with an explanation of the *totality* of the concept of "value." In doing so, we attempt to integrate the value of public relations to an organization with its value
to society. We reject any simplistic notion that the only relevant contribution
public relations makes is a monetary one, directly to the bottom line. We consider this kind of cause–effect, linear thinking to be overly narrow.

We prefer what may seem like a departure from traditional social scientific
theory and research, in the sense that we have collected and analyzed our data

more contextually and with greater integration than traditionally has been undertaken in our field. Otherwise, we feared, the actual contributions public relations can make to organizational effectiveness may be minimized in this project. Any analysis that looks only to the financial value of public relations and neglects its responsibility to society or at least the significant elements within that environment subordinates long-term viability to short-term success.

For just one example of this short- versus long-range thinking, consider the recent work of Wright, Ferris, Hiller, and Kroll (1995) on the financial impact of diversity. Their event study seemed to link affirmative action with economic benefit. They found that stock value in companies receiving the U.S. Labor Department's annual affirmative action award between 1982 and 1986 increased 90 days after the award. By contrast, stock prices of companies settling discrimination lawsuits declined during a comparable period following the announcement of the settlement of the suit. Thus the economists argued that they had provided empirical evidence of the benefit of diversity management. However, as Sha (1995) pointed out in her study of diversity management and public relations, "The implications of these findings were limited [in part because] stock price fluctuations did not necessarily reflect changes in relationships with publics, such as employees, suppliers, or advocacy groups, whose actions had the potential to affect" the company (p. 27).

One strategic constituency heretofore in the shadows for at least a number of American corporations is the gay and lesbian community. A cover story in *The Advocate* illustrates how pressure groups have attempted to influence the organizations they oppose by hitting them in the pocketbook. For example, the Wall Street Project, an organization of lesbian and gay shareholder activists, worked to make the restaurant Cracker Barrel Old Country Store Inc. drop what the Project considered an antigay stance. The activists' strategy was "to keep shareholder dissent growing and in the public eye in order to embarrass management while keeping pressure on through a consumer boycott" (Mickens, 1994, p. 42). Diane Bratcher, vice-chair of the Wall Street Project, acknowledged the long-term nature of this campaign for social responsibility: "I'm optimistic that the campaign will work, but it may take years" (as quoted in Mickens, 1994, p. 42).

Rather than relying on the political arena alone to effect change for gays, the Wall Street Project turned to economic leverage. It garnered 15.6% of the vote among shareholders to adopt a nondiscrimination policy and thus reinstate fired lesbian and gay workers (or those perceived to be homosexual) at Cracker Barrel. Although too small to carry the vote, this percentage exceeds the 11% margin that *The Advocate* article argued has persuaded other companies to approve, for example, antiapartheid policies. Because a vote of only 3% guarantees the inclusion of the measure on the ballot at the next year's shareholder meeting, lesbian and gay activists are convinced that their coordination of the vote ultimately will be effective. They also credited Cracker Barrel's own short-sightedness with helping them achieve their objectives:

Cracker Barrel underestimated the degree of concern among its shareholders, and anyone who discounts the importance of that doesn't understand the economics of the restaurant business. Their profitability depends on an ability to expand into new areas with new restaurants. They depend on investors, especially the pension funds, for the capital to expand. And the hostility in markets outside their Southern base will further undermine investor confidence. (Bratcher, as quoted in Mickens, 1994, p. 42)

To sustain this economic campaign against Cracker Barrel, the gay community urged shareholders to stay involved with the company and press for the antidiscrimination resolution. Activists in the Wall Street Project recommended against avoiding discriminatory companies or selling off their stocks. This advice is consistent with the philosophy of the Franklin Research and Development Corp., North America's largest investment firm to specialize in responsible investment. Following its "unified field theory of activism," the firm manages money with what *The Advocate* called "a double bottom line: to produce a profitable return as well as to reflect its clients' values and social concerns" (Mickens, 1994, p. 44).

This dual notion of profitability and responsibility, along with a long-term mentality, may be more critical in some situations than in others. Marketing guru Kotler (1988) developed a formula for calculating return on investment of public relations dollars. His model works well with communicative efforts in the area of new-product launches, for one. However, it is impractical to calculate in situations such as corporate takeovers, downsizing, or other crises. In those cases, we must look less to financial analysis and more toward a gauge of corporate social responsibility.[3]

Bryant (1989) described the factors that better test a company's performance than any single financial calculation. He argued that:

Return on capital employed, earnings per share, dividend policy and gearing structure may be of interest to the city and lenders of capital, but they indicate nothing about the efforts of the many employees involved, about the relative dependence and control between the firm and its suppliers, and about the long-term future of the firm in terms of the organization, people and machines it requires to meet its mission of supplying goods and services to the market. (p. 34)

Speaking from a professional, rather than scholarly, perspective, Kekst and Freitag (1991) made much the same point. They described what they termed the "public scrutiny test" essential for survival in this global age. Because of the potential for instant mobilization of public opinion, companies cannot afford to fail that test. The implications of the possibility of having the organization's actions instantly dissected by the media and judged, in turn, by the public are as

---

[3]For a review of the literature of social responsibility on a global scale, see Amba-Rao (1990).

follows: ". . . a company and its management will be measured by its financial performance, as it always has been. But it also means that a company will be measured by additional—and more intangible—yardsticks, such as management's 'vision,' 'depth,' 'culture,' and 'social responsibility quotient' " (p. 7).

The possibility of being judged and found wanting is especially great, in Kekst and Freitag's (1991) opinion, in times of crisis: industrial accidents, product recalls, or labor disputes. Surviving such disasters hinges on the strength of relationships the company has with its constituency groups. In their checklist of what to do in good times to engender continuing support in tough times, these two associates of the New York public relations firm Kekst and Co. suggested:

- Making communication a strategic business function, to be conducted at the highest level of the organization.
- Identifying individuals or groups that will determine the company's success or failure.
- Building relationships with those stakeholders.
- Regularly soliciting input from them, to isolate key issues they are concerned with.
- Adopting a long-term approach to communication programs.
- Training people to deal with crises.
- Making sure that all communication is as direct, factual, thorough, and honest as possible.

The Search for Nonfinancial Indicators

One way to estimate this total value of public relations is to determine the ways in which the function benefits an organization or society and then develop measurable nonfinancial indicators of these benefits. Patrick Jackson (2000), who was a principal owner of the public relations firm of Jackson, Jackson, & Wagner until he died in 2001, was a long-term advocate of measuring such indicators of the value of public relations. At a conference on reputation management at Notre Dame University, Jackson described how he and colleagues pressed financial accountants to identify ways in which they agreed public relations adds value to an organization. Jackson believed that these nonfinancial indicators of value added by public relations eventually contributed to the bottom line, although the actual return on each investment would be difficult to identify.

The discussion between Jackson and his colleague and accountants identified nine public relations strategies that have the following outcomes of value to an organization:

1. *Awareness and information.* Pave the way for sales, fund raising, stock offerings, and so forth.

2. *Organizational motivation.* Build morale, teamwork, productivity, corporate culture; work toward One Clear Voice outreach.
3. *Issue anticipation.* Give early warning of issues, social-political change, and constituency unrest.
4. *Opportunity identification.* Discover new markets, services, products, methods, allies, and positive issues.
5. *Crisis management.* Protect position, retain allies and constituents, and keep normal operations going despite battles.
6. *Overcoming executive isolation.* Make realistic, competitive, enlightened decisions; use knowledge of the human climate.
7. *Change agentry.* Ease resistance to change, promote smooth transition, and reassure affected constituencies.
8. *Social responsibility.* Create reputation, enhance economic success through "double bottom line," earn trust, attract like-minded supporters and customers.
9. *Public policy activities.* Elicit public consent to activities, products, policies, and removal of political barriers.

Both Kekst and Co. and Jackson, Jackson, & Wagner attributed value to the public relations function when public relations participates in the strategic management of organizations by identifying strategic constituencies in the environment of the organization and by using communication to build and maintain relationships with these strategic publics. Public relations professionals tend to use the term "reputation" as a surrogate for what we have called "relationships" in the Excellence study. The research firm Jeffries-Fox Associates (2000b), in a study for the Council of Public Relations Firms, identified the following sources of value for a corporate reputation (what we would call good relationships with strategic constituencies) in the business, public relations, and marketing literature:

- Increasing market share.
- Lowering market costs.
- Lowering distribution costs.
- Being able to charge a premium
- Avoiding overregulation.
- Being able to weather bad times.
- Greater employee alignment and productivity.
- Being able to attract and retain talent.
- Being able to attract investors.
- Being able to gain access to new global markets.
- Gaining more favorable media coverage. (p. 4)

From all of these discussions on how to determine the "value" of public relations, we concluded that there is some incongruence in trying to measure the "bottom line" in terms of the impact of public relations on the organization. "Bottom line" typically refers to dollars and cents and the monetary return on investment given back to a firm's shareholders. It is clear from our review of relevant literature, though, that public relations professionals view the bottom line in those terms and also beyond those terms. That is, they see their impact both in financial terms and in terms of long-term, credible relationships with key publics. Most, however, do not believe that money invested in public relations can be linked to a consistent, yearly monetary return on that investment.

Many chief executive officers link public relations with outcomes that supersede the monetary alone. C. B. Campbell (1992) interviewed 18 CEOs at considerable length and found that the majority believed managed communication does affect the bottom line. However, few of her interviewees consciously had linked public relations with bottom-line impact. Some actually rejected the notion, and for good reason. As one executive put it: "I just don't know how you can tie public relations to the bottom line. They'll just end up as mercenaries and the company will get nothing out of it, or it will get a one-time return and its benefit to the company will be over" (as quoted in C. B. Campbell, 1993, p. 16).

Others participating in Campbell's (1992) research explained that public relations is *a* contributing factor, rather than *the* determinant of organizational effectiveness. They spoke of team efforts, of weaving all aspects of their operation together, and of public relations being an integral part of running the business. In essence, these CEOs were agreeing that divorcing the contribution of public relations from the bottom line would be unwise; but isolating its impact alone would be difficult, if not impossible.

In addition to being part of the larger organizational system, and thus making its individual influence difficult to tease out and apart from the impact of other subsystems, public relations may make an *indirect* contribution to organizational effectiveness. To the extent that this function serves as the "conscience of the corporation," it emphasizes social responsibility. Preston (1981) reviewed studies of the relationship between socially relevant behaviors of corporations and their economic performance. He found little evidence of strong association between social responsibility and "the usual indicators of economic success" (p. 9). Instead, he concluded that responsible behavior affects performance indirectly. He explained that organizations typically engage in externally oriented activity to maintain their sociopolitical status quo—with the goal of preserving an environment in which to operate.

Verčič (2000) reached the same conclusion when he analyzed time-series data on three British organizations—British Airways, Shell, and the Post Office—to test the hypothesis that trust (an attitudinal evaluation of each public's relationship with an organization) explains the financial performance of a corporation. He found that "trust has no direct, functional relationship to organizational performance, but it determines [the organization's] contextual performance" (p. 343). He concluded that "the problem for organizations in not on the positive, but on the 'negative' side of trust" (p. 346). That is, organizations that develop nontrusting relationships with their publics find that their environmental context interferes with their ability to perform financially.

Similarly, Tuleja (1985) argued that ethical behavior helps corporations enhance their bottom line indirectly by developing more productive employees and avoiding excessive governmental and nongovernmental regulation.[4] Spending on good works may not result in profits, he explained, but it does help secure market advantage because of the long-term goodwill of strategic constituencies.

The absence of goodwill takes the heavy monetary toll of activism, regulation, or litigation. Poor relationships with strategic publics can cost a great deal, although credible relationships may not necessarily make money for the organization. Good relationships contribute, over the long haul and more indirectly than directly, to such bottom-line factors as employee productivity, customer satisfaction, and stockholder investment.

Further, as Francis (1990) said, business backs itself into a corner when it fails to attend properly to what lies *beneath* the bottom line. Why? The production of faulty products, environmental devastation, and executive crime all can contribute to financial risks created in any given quarter but capable of surfacing in the next quarter or the next decade.

The Value of Public Relations Is in Relationships

As a result, throughout our study we have looked at the bottom line in this way: *a combination of traditional financial return and the risks associated with the organization's long-term relationships.* There is precedent for this approach, in at least one major study of public relations and organizational effectiveness (C. B. Campbell, 1992). Corporate social responsiveness, in particular, transcends both the business and public relations arenas. To consider business ethics, public responsibility, or old-fashioned morality as an add-on, something supplementary to an organization's financial performance, is to misunderstand the history of public relations and the contribution this managed communication function continues to make in contemporary society.

Of course, to some corporate types, to some economists, and even to some ethicists, the economically appropriate action in itself is ethically desirable as such (Ulrich & Thielemann, 1993). They believe that moral demands must not jeopardize a company's continued economic success, a situation that Ulrich and Thielemann considered "heroic idealism" (p. 880). Their reasoning is that the company incapable of satisfying the demands of its market soon fails, thus facing such ethical dilemmas as finding staff redundant. They advocate reconciling the tension between ethical and economic viability for sustainable success.

---

[4]For a comprehensive review of the costs of governmental regulation, see Buchholz (1989).

We on the Excellence research team, too, struggled to achieve equilibrium between these two dimensions. Rather than merely critiquing economism,[5] our thinking led us to resolve (at least for the purposes of this book) these two fundamental dimensions of the business-ethical perspective posed by Peter Ulrich, director of the Institute for Business Ethics at the University of St. Gallen in Switzerland (Ulrich & Thielemann, 1993). First, we rejected the argument that the relationship between ethics and financial success is inherently conflictual. Instead, we assumed that harmony between these two goals is possible. Second, we rejected the perception that the organization is an autonomous system, one that follows its own functional logic to adapt to the market's competitive conditions. Instead, we perceived the organization as an integral part of the culture in which it operates.

Understanding that fully two thirds of U.S. society distrusts business as an institution (Freeman & Gilbert, 1992) suggests the importance of this harmonized, cultural view of organizations. In fact, since the days of Andrew Carnegie in the 19th century, American business has occupied this moral low ground in the eyes of its stakeholders. To the theorist of strategic management, R. Edward Freeman (1984), and his colleagues, the need to theorize about the legitimacy of business will prevail as long as this dominant view of business as a purely economic activity prevails.

Rather than endlessly debating whether economic performance or social goals should be the organization's priority, recall that Freeman and Gilbert (1992) saw business "as a connected set of relationships among stakeholders where the emphasis is on the connectedness" (p. 12). They explained: "We need to understand that stakeholders are in it together, rather than competing for limited and scarce resources, and that the fundamental reason that organizations as connected networks are effective is that they are built on the principles of cooperation and caring. Each stakeholder is 'adding to the value' of others, creating a good deal for all" (p. 12).

To reduce this understanding of the importance of relationships to economics alone is, in Freeman and Gilbert's (1992) opinion, "just silly" (p. 12). They advocated, instead, "stories about the kinds of companies we can build, the kinds of connected networks that are possible, and narratives about successes and failures" (p. 12).

Many public relations professionals and researchers insist that we must be able to measure an exact monetary value for the relationships created through the work of the public relations function. We explored this possibility when we conceptualized the Excellence study and rejected it as impossible for the following reasons flowing from the literature we reviewed in the first *Excellence* book and thus far in this chapter:

---

[5]Like Ulrich and Thielemann (1993), we take care not to equate "economism" with "unethical," ethically uninterested, opportunistic, or even cynical. It is one of several identifiable (and legitimate) thinking patterns among managers in our postmodern, pluralistic society.

- Relationships (and their product reputation) provide a context for behavior by consumers, investors, employees, government, the community, the media, and other strategic constituencies—but they do not determine this behavior alone. The behavior of these constituencies affects financial performance; but many other factors, such as competition and the economic environment, also affect that performance.
- Relationships save money by preventing costly issues, crises, regulation, litigation, and bad publicity. It is not possible, however, to determine the cost of something that *did not happen* or even to know that the negative event or behavior *would have happened* in the absence of excellent public relations.
- The return on relationships is delayed. Organizations spend money on relationships for years to prevent events or behaviors such as crises, boycotts, or litigation that *might* happen many years down the road.
- The return on relationships usually is lumpy. Good relationships with some constituencies such as consumers may produce a continuing stream of revenue, but for the most part the return comes all at once—for example, when crises, strikes, boycotts, regulation, litigation, or bad publicity are avoided or mitigated. Similarly, relationships with potential donors must be cultivated for years before a donor makes a major gift. As a result, it is difficult to prorate the delayed returns on public relations to the monies invested in the function each year.

As a result, we concluded that the technique of compensating variation provides the best method known to date to estimate the value of relationships cultivated by public relations to the organization. Ehling (1992) developed the rationale for using this technique in the first Excellence book. What follows is a compendium of narratives from the long interviews conducted for the Excellence study, along with the stories told by the statistical data, that show the value of compensating variation as a method of calculating the return on the communication function and the correlation of the characteristics of excellent public relations with that estimate. After analyzing these quantitative and qualitative stories, however, we return to the question of financial return by examining a study of the financial performance of eight electrical utilities included in the Excellence study sample.

RESULTS RELATED TO THE VALUE OF PUBLIC RELATIONS AND COMMUNICATION MANAGEMENT

We entered the data-gathering phase of the Excellence project with the understanding that public relations contributes both to the organization and to society and that its value lies in the value of relationships between the organization and publics in the internal and external environment of the organization. Public relations departments contribute this value at the organizational and societal levels, described at the beginning of this chapter, through excellent practice at the functional and program levels. Public relations programs, for example, are effective when they accomplish objectives that help to build successful relationships with publics that have strategic value to the organization.

In our research, then, we attempted to measure the value of relationships as a means of estimating the value of public relations. After reviewing the literature on cost–benefit analysis, we identified a method for estimating the value of public relations and comparing it with the costs. Cost–benefit analysis of public relations is difficult, however, because of the intangibility of the benefit—the value of relationships. One method we identified in the literature, "compensating variation," offered promise.

Compensating variation, as economists term this process, provides a way of transforming nonmonetary values, such as the benefit of good relationships to the organization and to society, into monetary values. The idea behind the method is simple. You ask people how much they would be willing to pay to have something. For public relations you ask members of the dominant coalition or public relations managers how much public relations is worth to them on either a monetary or nonmonetary scale.

The Excellence team—assisted by graduate students and other colleagues— helped both our survey respondents and participants in the qualitative study assign monetary values to communication benefits. We had proposed that:

> With quantification of public relations' primary end state—the maximization through communication of the difference between cooperation and conflict such that cooperation becomes the prime benefit—the methods and techniques of benefit–cost analysis can be brought to the evaluation of all public relations programs. To be public relations programs, their principal aim must be to attain, maintain, or enhance accord (cooperation, agreement, consensus) between an organization and its environment.

The end states of attaining, maintaining, or enhancing accord can be evaluated by assigning utilities to the degrees of achievement and by converting these utilities to monetary equivalents. Compensating variation provides a methodology that establishes and measures such equivalents. A compensating variation is:

- The amount of money a beneficiary of a program (such as the dominant coalition) would be willing to pay for a program (such as public relations) so that he or she would be equally well off with the program or the payment he or she is willing to make for it.
- Or the amount an entity (such as the dominant coalition) that is worse off because of the effects of a program (such as opposition from activists)

would be willing to pay to eliminate the effects, so that the entity is equally well off without the program or the payment.

Our method was limited by the fact that we asked only one party to the relationships between organizations and publics to estimate the value of the relationship—the organization's side. Ideally, we also would have asked representatives of publics, such as leaders of activist groups, to estimate the value of each relationship. With a survey sample of more than 300 organizations and a set of 25 qualitative cases, the cost in time and money of interviewing representatives of publics was prohibitive. Researchers in the future should extend our analysis by choosing a smaller number of participating organizations and interviewing both sides of relationships.

Quantitative Results Related to Value

In the survey research, we asked both the senior public relations executives and the CEOs who completed questionnaires to answer two questions based on the method of compensating variation. One of these questions asked both the CEO and the top communicator to provide a nonmonetary value for public relations in comparison with a typical department in the same organization. They assigned a value on the fractionation scale in which they were told that 100 would be the value of a typical department. In addition, the top communicator and the CEO were asked to assign a cost–benefit ratio to public relations—essentially a monetary value. The top communicators also were asked to predict how they thought members of the dominant coalition would respond to these same two questions.

The first column in Table 4.1 shows the results of these questions. Table 4.1 contains both the raw scores on the fractionation scale and the transformed values—the square roots of the responses—that we calculated to reduce the impact of a skew to the upper end of the scale. Table 4.1 also reports median and modal scores to reduce the impact of extreme scores given by a few respondents. The transformed values especially are useful in comparing scores among groups, although they lack the simplicity of a simple cost–benefit ratio or scale compared to 100.

In addition, Table 4.1 compares the scores on these variables across three levels of the scale of overall public relations Excellence. The Excellence scale was standardized into z scores, scores for which the mean is zero and the standard deviation (the average amount by which an organization varies from the mean) is 1. Thus, in Table 4.1, organizations with low levels of excellence were those with scores one standard deviation or more below the mean and organizations with high levels of excellence were those with scores one standard deviation or more above the mean. In a normal distribution, 68% of a sam-

TABLE 4.1
Estimated Value of and Return on Investment in Public Relations at Three
Levels of Excellence

		Level of Excellence			
	Total	Low (z < −1)	Medium (z = −1 − +1)	High (z > +1)	F
N	329	42 (13%)	246 (75%)	41 (12%)	
Value of PR					
Raw Value					
CEO Estimate	158.66[a]	109.09	155.90	231.50	13.31**
PR Estimate for Dominant Coalition	138.23[b]	93.69	131.85	223.75	40.96**
PR Estimate	189.15[c]	157.93	184.36	248.78	11.56**
Transformed Value					
CEO Estimate	12.15	10.13	12.12	14.54	15.41**
PR Estimate for Dominant Coalition	11.38	9.26	11.22	14.59	43.64**
PR Estimate	13.37	12.12	13.22	15.47	12.60**
Percent Return to PR					
Raw Value					
CEO Estimate	186.45[d]	139.59	189.11	224.64	2.65
PR Estimate for Dominant Coalition	130.84[e]	104.17	132.33	150.26	4.47*
PR Estimate	196.50[f]	158.81	197.68	228.17	2.59
Transformed Value					
CEO Estimate	13.04	11.34	13.16	14.22	4.36*
PR Estimate for Dominant Coalition	11.10	10.00	11.14	12.01	5.60**
PR Estimate	13.46	12.30	13.49	14.46	3.19*

[a]Median = 150, mode = 100 and 150 (25% and 24% in modal categories. [b]Median = 100, mode = 100 (29% in modal category). [c]Median = 200, mode = 200 (31% in modal category). [d]Median = 150, mode = 200 (24% in modal category). [e]Median = 100, mode = 100 (39% in modal category). [f]Median = 150, mode = 200 (20% in modal category).

*$p < .05$. **$p < .01$.

ple falls within a standard deviation of the mean. In our sample, 75% fell into this middle category. The analysis of variance (F statistic) in Table 4.1, therefore, shows whether the difference among these three levels of excellence is statistically significant. For this purpose, the transformed values are most important because they correct for the skew in the data, which can throw off the test of significance.

Table 4.1 shows that communication is a highly valued function in the typical organization we studied. CEOs and their heads of public relations rated the contribution of communication about equally in our survey research. As Table 4.1 shows, both groups of participants told us that public relations returns more than it costs to implement—on average, about 186% return on investment (ROI). This means that for every dollar spent on public relations, the organization gets back $1.86 in value. Even executives in organizations with the least excellent communication programs reported an average 140% ROI.

Survey respondents with excellent public relations programs cited an even higher ROI—about 225%. Whereas only 5% of our sample of CEOs said public relations returns less than what it costs, a full 40% credited communication with returning at least twice the cost.

A few CEOs and heads of public relations reported extremely high returns for communication. In four cases, figures cited were 1,000% and 1,500%. Such responses can skew an average, so we also reported the median (the number at which half the sample has a higher score and half a lower score) and the mode (the most frequent response) in Table 4.1 for the raw data. This table also shows the common misperception of our survey respondents in public relations. They did not seem to realize that their CEOs value communication so highly. They predicted that CEOs would estimate a return of 131%.

On the question that asked CEOs and top communicators to compare the value of public relations with the "typical" organizational department, only 12% said public relations adds less value than the typical department. More than one third, 36%, said it was twice as valuable or more. Not surprisingly, heads of public relations departments rated the value of public relations even higher than did the CEOs—a mean of 189 and a median of 200. As they did for the rate of return on investment, these top communicators underestimated the value that the CEO would assign to their department (but not by so large a margin).

Table 4.1, finally, shows a strong, consistent, and statistically significant relationship between the excellence of public relations and the value and rate of return assigned to it. The results for the comparative value question, however, shows a stronger difference than the return on investment question—suggesting this question may be the better estimate of value for future research. Two of the three comparisons of the raw data for return on investment were not statistically significant, but when the data were transformed all three differences were significant.

Table 4.2 explores the relationship between excellence in public relations and the value assigned to it by CEOs and top communicators more thoroughly by providing Pearson correlation coefficients between these measures of value, the total score on the Excellence scale, and scores on the components of the Excellence scale that measure the manager role, participation in strategic management, and the practice of two-way models of public relations. This table includes a third measure of value—taken from a question that asked the CEO and the top communicator to estimate the level of support that the dominant coalition gives to public relations. Because the variables measuring support of public relations by the dominant coalition and the value assigned to public relations were components of the overall Excellence scale, Table 4.2 also reports the cor-

TABLE 4.2

Pearson Correlations of Total Excellence Score and Selected Excellence Variables With Value of and Support for Public Relations by the Dominant Coalition

	Support for PR in DC as Estimated by		Value of PR as Estimated by			% Return on PR as Estimated by		
	Dom. Coal.	PR	Dom. Coal.	PR for DC	PR	Dom. Coal.	PR for DC	PR
Manager Role								
Knowledge	.14*	.30**	.07	.30**	.28**	.05	.17**	.19**
Reported by PR	.07	.33**	.08	.38**	.33**	.10	.32**	.29**
CEO Expectation	.35**	.21**	.36**	.24**	.17**	.21**	-.05	-.01
Strat. Management								
Reported by PR	.24**	.44**	.20**	.36**	.24**	.02	.23**	.11*
Reported by CEO	.39**	.23**	.48**	.14**	.11*	.29**	.03	-.01
Model of PR								
2S Knowledge	.12*	.25**	.02	.27**	.19**	.02	.19**	.20**
2A Knowledge	.11	.22**	.08	.28**	.20**	.01	.18**	.15**
PR Predicts CEO Prefers 2S	.05	.40**	-.01	.34**	.18**	.04	.25**	.15**
PR Predicts CEO Prefers 2A	.06	.22**	.00	.19**	.08	.03	.10*	.08
CEO Prefers 2S	.33**	.14*	.22**	.05	.07	.05	-.07	.01
CEO Prefers 2A	.31**	.21**	.19**	.15*	.14*	.05	.01	.02
Total Exc. Score	.46**	.59**	.37**	.58**	.38**	.22**	.21**	.28**
Exc. Score Without Value & Support	.41**	.45**	.32**	.43**	.32**	.21**	.19**	.18

Note. 2S = Two-way symmetrical model, 2A = Two-way asymmetrical model.

*p < .05. **p < .01.

relations between the three measures of value and the Excellence scale with these variables removed.

Table 4.2 provides reasonably strong and consistent support for the major proposition of the Excellence study—that excellent public relations provides value for the organization, at least as that value is estimated by the CEO and the top communicators in the organization. The correlations between the total and partial Excellence scales are particularly strong, although they are lower for the questions on rate of return than for the nonmonetary measures of value. The correlations of the value questions and the components of excellence in Table 4.2 also show a pattern of support for the fact that each of these indicators of excellence adds value to public relations. In general, the correlations are higher when both variables came from either the CEO or the top-communicator questionnaire. And, again, the relationships are weaker for the ROI variables than for the nonmonetary value questions.

Finally, Table 4.2 shows that perhaps the most consistent pattern of correlations is with the variables measuring the extent to which public relations is involved in strategic management. As we said in our conceptualization, involvement in strategic management provides a critical link between public relations and organizational effectiveness. Both CEOs and top communicators seem to attach more value to public relations when this linkage is present.

Table 4.3 provides the final set of results relevant to the value of public relations from the quantitative study. Table 4.3 reports correlations of the outcomes of specific communication programs—the program level—with the overall level of excellence in public relations. The heads of public relations who responded to our questionnaire were asked to answer eight and a half pages of questions about the research, planning, processes, models of public relations, means of evaluation, and outcomes of communication programs for the three most important publics of their organization. The complete analysis of these data is presented in chapter 9, but the results reported for outcomes of programs are relevant in this chapter because they provide evidence of the extent to which an excellent public relations function develops effective programs to communicate with strategic publics.

In our conceptualization, we explained that excellent public programs have three effects. They (a) meet communication objectives, (b) reduce the costs of regulation, pressure, and litigation, and (c) increase job satisfaction among employees. The first two of these categories of effects were measured through 19 questions that top communicators answered for the three most important communication programs in their organizations. The third effect was measured with a set of items about job satisfaction administered to employees sampled in each organization. The measure of job satisfaction is discussed in detail in chapter 11.

The heads of public relations in the organizations we sampled reported most often that the organizations had seven communication programs: for employ-

TABLE 4.3

Correlation of Overall Excellence With Outcomes of Seven Communication Programs

Communication Outcome	Employees	Media	Community	Investors	Customers	Government	Members
Organizational Satisfaction	.17**[a]						
Change in Relationship Scale	.36**	.32**	.36**	.50**	.41**	.02	.48**
Conflict Avoidance Scale	.32**	.29**	.34**	.56**	.44**	-.03	.25
Positive Media Coverage	.05	.21**	.24**	.11	.13	-.09	.14
Message Accuracy	.18*	.21**	.30**	.29	.31**	.01	.05
Increase in Sales	.13	.04	.13	.15	-.01	-.26	.37**
Achieve Goals	.22**	.36**	.39**	.46**	.33**	.22	.60**
Make Money	.11	.07	.16	.23	.06	-.17	-.04
Save Money	.25**	.10	.29**	.32*	.03	.05	.15
% of Organizations With Program	67	93	52	19	36	19	21

[a]Correlation between organizational job satisfaction aggregated for all employees in each organization and the total Excellence score. Organizational job satisfaction also correlated .67 with participative culture ($p < .01$). Participative culture, in turn correlated at .26 ($p < .01$) with the Excellence scale, which suggests that culture provides the primary linkage between excellence and job satisfaction.

*$p < .05$. **$p < .01$.

ees, the media, the community, investors, customers, government, and members of associations. Each top communicator was asked to estimate "the extent to which you believe observable evidence shows that [each of three programs] had one of the [19] effects listed below." A factor analysis, the data from which are presented in chapter 9, showed that 13 of the effects clustered on two factors. We called one of these factors the "change of relationship factor"[6] and the other the "conflict avoidance factor."[7] These two factors are particularly relevant to the question of value of public relations because they operationalize good relationships as objectives at the program level.

Six other items did not load highly on the two factors, so they are included as separate variables in Table 4.3. They are "positive media coverage resulted," "our message was received accurately," and "product sales or use of the organization's services increased." In addition, three items related directly to our conceptualization of organizational effectiveness are included as separate variables: "The program helped the organization meet its goals," "the program helped the organization make money," and "the program saved money for the organization."

With the exception of communication programs with government, Table 4.3 shows a consistent and strong pattern of correlation between the overall Excellence scale and the change in relationship scale, the conflict avoidance scale, and the achievement of organizational goals—the three variables most closely related to our conceptualization of organizational effectiveness. The correlation between the Excellence scale and the conflict avoidance scale for member publics, although moderate in size, was not statistically significant because of the small number of these programs. As is discussed in chapter 9, government relations programs typically do not correlate with Excellence in the same way that characteristics of other programs do—because, we think, these programs frequently are carried out by lawyers and others not experienced in public relations.

Receiving messages accurately correlated positively and significantly with the Excellence scale for employee, media, community, and customer programs but not for investor, government, and member programs. Positive media coverage correlated significantly with Excellence only for media and community

---

[6]The items loading on this factor were "attitudes of publics changed in support of our position," "the quality of communication with the relevant public improved," "there was greater cooperation between my organization and the relevant public," "the relevant public changed its behavior in the way my organization wanted," "understanding improved between my organization and the relevant public," and "a stable longer-term relationship was developed with the relevant public."

[7]Items loading on this factor were "litigation was avoided," "a strike or boycott was averted," "complaints from publics were reduced," "there were fewer disagreements and disputes with the relevant public," "there was less interference by government in the management of the organization," "activist groups were willing to negotiate with the organization," and "desirable legislation was passed or undesirable legislation was defeated."

programs. It is interesting also that increases in sales had the lowest correlation with Excellence for customer programs and a significant positive correlation only for member programs. Consistent with our conceptualization, saving money was more likely to correlate positively with Excellence than was making money, for which there were no statistically significant correlations. Saving money, however, correlated positively with Excellence only for employee, community, and investor programs.

The correlation between employee satisfaction with the organization and Excellence is reported in the employee column. This correlation is significant but relatively small. As the footnote to Table 4.3 points out, employee satisfaction correlated highly with participative culture ($r = .67$), and participative culture correlated moderately with Excellence ($r = .26$). This suggests that the outcome of employee satisfaction traveled from overall Excellence through the path of participative culture, which is part of the Excellence scale. This relationship is examined in more detail in chapter 11.

The results of our survey research, therefore, provide moderate to strong evidence that public relations has value to an organization because it builds relationships with strategic publics and that communication programs designed for these publics are effective when they have outcomes that contribute to the building of positive relationships. The survey results also provide moderate to strong evidence that public relations functions that we describe as excellent have greater value than less excellent programs and are more likely to have effects at the program level that improve relationships among organizations and publics.

Qualitative Results Related to Value

In our series of in-depth case studies, then, we asked CEOs, senior public relations executives, and other communicators in 25 organizations at the top and the bottom of the Excellence scale to help us understand these survey results. The principal question became why? Why is managed communication valued so highly? What, exactly, is its worth?

The answer lies primarily with activism. As you will read in chapter 10, most organizations are pressured by activist groups. Most included in our survey considered themselves more beset than "the typical organization." Public relations was credited with helping the organization deal with major social issues—but only if the head of public relations was in a strategic management role. In such cases, we learned, the benefits of avoiding crises may be expressed in concrete financial terms.

Why CEOs Value Public Relations.   Before attempting to attach a monetary value to public relations, we explored in considerable depth why some CEOs value communication so highly. We knew that the entire explanation does not lie in the degree of excellence of the public relations department. Some departments ranking high on the Excellence factor were devalued by the members of the dominant coalition we interviewed in our survey of cases. In addition, CEOs who value public relations often did not have excellent departments in the organizations they head—in large part because of a shortage of knowledgeable, strategic public relations managers and an oversupply of public relations technicians.

Two main answers to the question of why some CEOs value public relations so highly emerged from the long interviews. Those who most appreciated public relations credit it with:

- *Providing a broad perspective both inside and outside of the organization.*
- *Dealing with crises or the activist groups that often prompt those predicaments.*

A vice president of strategic planning in the chemical company described the valuable perspective public relations can provide in terms of "sharing the thoughts from all directions." One direction he stressed was from employees, and he tied Weick's (1979) notion of requisite variety into his conversation:

> If you have a communication function that represents the points of view of only parts of the employee population, then you have a hell of a time making sure we're addressing the sensitivities of all the people in the employee population. If I have a communication department that is made up of all White, male Pulitzer Prize–winning people off the *New York Times,* I might have some great writers but I'll probably have a tough time making sure all points of view are reflected.

A second top manager echoed this sentiment. The deputy director of the engineering research agency said: "We don't worry as much about the numbers we have of women, Blacks, and Hispanics. The main thing is in the process of making decisions, that we get the opinion of people and staff with different backgrounds. That way we come up with better solutions."

At least one top communicator spoke to the outlook he contributes as well. This agency head described his relationship with the CEO of the client firm as follows:

> I believe he trusts my opinion and judgment; and he knows above all that I won't bullshit him, that I'll tell him what the truth is. . . . I still maintain that the PR guy has got to bring to the table the outside perspective that is by definition lacking by those inside the organization. Otherwise, the outside perspective is not going to be at the table when decisions are made. . . . My CEO is smart enough to know that I'm not telling him that out of any vested self-interest, that I'm looking out for his interest and the company's interest. I'm certainly not saying it to make the meeting run longer.

Despite his 36 years in the association business, the CEO of another organization explained that his head of public relations contributes the perspective of both employees and clients that he himself, the CEO, may not have. Public relations is essential because, in his words: "Those of us who think lawyer-like, those of us who think CEO-like, those of us who think technical-like don't always take the big picture. And that's what the public relations/communication expert's forte is: to take that big picture, to place it in the instant context, and to make sure that the system responds to what the real issues are in a real-world kind of way." Help in times of crisis was mentioned as well, although one vice president of public relations explained that if you are not "a player" in noncrisis times, people in senior management will not think to call on you when trouble comes.

Senior management of one of the top-ranked organizations we studied did seem to value the contributions of public relations in dealing especially with activist groups. The CEO explained his top communicator's influence within the organization as a result of his training all members of the management staff in what he, the CEO, called "symmetrical negotiations or communication." That training has resulted in an approach to communication that the CEO considered "uniform" and described as "an open, discussed decision that we will engage in discussions no matter how frustrating, no matter how unnerving, no matter how ignorant they [the activist publics] are." But why be willing to talk with groups that often don't have the facts, don't trust the facts, or don't care about the facts? In his words, "Because you will never move the ball unless you engage in that discussion."

This same CEO told us that although some other senior executives in his industry may not value this kind of sophisticated public relations, many do. Their understanding of two-way communication, in particular, has served them well. He attributed their leadership roles in groups such as the U.S. Chamber of Commerce, the National Association of Manufacturers, and the Business Roundtable to their knowledge of and involvement with bilateral communication.

We heard from only one top communicator who believed CEOs come to value public relations for the personal recognition it can achieve for them. This was most likely, he believed, when the founder remained at the organizational helm. He considered this kind of ego boosting less-than-excellent public relations, however, and he predicted that "a really good CEO cannot get by without excellent communication. He may in the short term; but in the long term, it won't ever work." This consultant added that "CEOs are arriving somewhat begrudgingly—but arriving—at an awareness of the importance of the function."

Measures of Compensating Variation in the Qualitative Results. Compensating variation begins by isolating public relations as the primary cause (or at least an important contributing factor) of a beneficial outcome. This first step is not so easy as it may seem. We found that the very nature of public relations complicates the determination of what it causes to happen. Much of what public relations professionals do, in their capacity as boundary spanners between the organization and its strategic constituencies, involves "partnering," or the collaboration that characterizes two-way approaches to the field. How much credit, then, can a practitioner claim for the outcome of a program involving partnerships with individuals or groups within or beyond the confines of the organization?

For example, both the vice president and top communicator in an economic development agency had a difficult time in placing a monetary value on their communication department. Of course, the agency does not look for direct return because of its nonprofit nature. Still, as the vice president explained: "Like most economic development agencies, if you can crank a business up that employs 20 people . . . and they all pay taxes and the company pays taxes . . . there's been numerous models where multipliers have been everywhere from 3 to 7.5 times the original investment that gets returned to the state."

This member of the dominant coalition went on to describe the connection between the quality of his agency's communication and the quality of the businesses that are its customers. He simply found it impossible to separate out what public relations alone had contributed to these businesses' vitality.

In a second example of effective partnering, the oil company headquartered in the United States described the following scenario. Acting in concert with oil and gas industry corporations and other groups to achieve its legislative goals, the company (and the entire industry) realized significant savings. In 1993, the company estimated its savings from favorable tax legislation at approximately U.S. $20 million. In the state where the oil company has its corporate headquarters and many processing plants, three issues involving refining regulations were managed successfully through lobbying; this effort saved the oil company and its subsidiaries more than U.S. $260 million. Lobbying on one environmental issue resulted in a savings of U.S. $10 million; on a second environmental case, U.S. $100 million; and on a third such instance, a whopping U.S. $0.5 billion to $1.5 billion. All of these returns are examples of what we called lumpy returns earlier in this chapter. Nevertheless, attaching a portion of this dollar value to the communicative efforts of the company's public affairs office, undertaken in conjunction with counterparts in this turbulent industry, was impossible for our respondents.

Yet another example of successful collaboration came from the metal-manufacturing company. It worked with a diverse coalition of metal manufacturers, related heavy industries, and trade unions to lobby the federal government for more thorough application of trade laws. The coalition sought to restrict unfair trading practices in the United States by other countries. Its campaign resulted in favorable regulatory decisions: Countries violating antidumping laws would suffer penalty tariffs on their products. The value of 1992 imports covered by these trade regulations was U.S. $43.5 million. Steel imports declined, from more than 26% in 1984 to 20% in 1993. While using public affairs to help reduce unfair trading, the company also slashed capacity and employment but increased shipments by 11%. This overshadowed other U.S. metal producers, and the chairman and his top communicator both credited communication with playing a significant part.

In a final example of partnering, the senior vice president of a midwestern gas and electric company described his utility's role in conservation efforts with community-based organizations. One major communication initiative promoted energy efficiency in low-income housing. As a result of cooperating with neighborhood and social-service agencies in such visible campaigns, the company developed an effective public platform for rebutting groups that protest proposed rate increases. The vice president described representatives from community groups who had attended open meetings of the rate commission to speak about some of the good things the utility was doing. This top manager believed that their testimony helped counter the strident rhetoric of activist groups and brought balance to the hearings. He found it impossible to sort out the contributions of his company's communication department from the support that came from many other constituencies—but he was clear on the positive impact of these well-developed partnerships.

Of course, not all communication *does* contribute positively to organizational effectiveness. One strategic manager in a chemical company told us that funding for public relations can be like "throwing money in a hole." A concrete instance came from a not-for-profit organization specializing in services for the disabled. It involved a kind of internal partnering, and it illustrates both the complexity and importance of coordinating public relations efforts.

Each fund-raising program in this nonprofit had a web of linkages to the agency's departments. Many of those units depend on volunteers. One overzealous volunteer successfully approached a foundation for a U.S. $15,000 donation. She did not realize that the organization had a grant proposal in to the foundation for U.S. $100,000. The foundation considered its $15,000 donation the extent of its obligation and thus denied the larger request. Our participants from this organization told us that the lack of a department head to oversee internal communication about its development efforts cost it U.S. $85,000. We were reassured when the executive director indicated that the director of communications would coordinate these situations in future. Nevertheless, we emerged with a case study of poor internal communication costing an organization U.S. $85,000 in donations.

Thus, and to reiterate, we looked most carefully at the public relations departments deemed "excellent" because, presumably, excellence in practice can make a positive difference.

The most difficult part of the process of compensating variation comes at the end, when participants must judge what that positive outcome is worth in pounds or dollars. Compensating variation may be especially problematic when assessing the value of public relations. The director of corporate communication for a chemical company considered this function "too far from the bottom line to be able to relate it."

The top communicator in a development company offered another explanation: "Our business is not a science, and it isn't measured totally in dollars. You have to take risks. And you want to win more than you lose." However, like her counterpart in the utility company and several others we spoke with, she sensed the growing importance of quantifying the value of public relations for an upper-management team that is increasingly numbers oriented. She had attempted to measure press coverage through a formula that took into the account the number of column inches of positive press and added value for front-page placement. She concluded, "One can create these systems to try to quantify public relations; but in the final analysis, it's a leap of faith."

Rather than relying on faith to convince top management of what communication programs actually contribute to organizational effectiveness, compensating variation consists of a series of steps, all designed to conduct a kind of cost–benefit analysis. The break-even point, where return and investment are equal, is the compensating variation. The essence of this process is determining the amount of money an organization would be willing to spend to keep the communication program, given its effects.

Our participants, CEOs and heads of public relations alike, were very specific when discussing the effects of their communicative efforts. The typical outcomes they listed include:

1. Rooting out waste in work through employee communication programs.
2. Turning around declining stock prices through financial relations or media relations (or both).
3. Raising the national ranking of the operation primarily through media relations.
4. Unblocking overseas markets formerly frozen because of insensitive intercultural communication.
5. Averting lawsuits or restrictive legislation (or both) through good relationships with activists and regulators.
6. Gaining acceptance for rate hikes through customer relations.
7. Increasing contributions through donor and community relations.
8. Surviving crises of confidence through long-term relationships with all stakeholders.
9. Simply outlasting tough economic conditions that doomed competitors with less effective communication programs.

These benefits (explored in greater depth later in this chapter) are, in some cases, mushy. How much, exactly, is employee productivity (or job satisfaction) worth? How much, exactly, does the organization save by avoiding conflicts with strategic constituencies—conflicts that could lead to governmental regulation or legal action?

Moving up in a national rating system, as the engineering research station did, can be considered mushy because its value is difficult to quantify. Nevertheless, this high standing is vitally important to members of the dominant coalition there. (In fact, the manager of communication considered her CEO "obsessed" with rankings.) A second instance of a mushy outcome is so called because public relations is only one of a myriad factors that led to the outcome. It is doubtful that anyone could determine the role of communication alone, in this instance, in greater stock value.

Other outcomes on our list are tangible and measurable, such as the green light for the utility company's proposed rate hike. Even in these seemingly concrete cases, determining the extent of long-term benefits—especially of socially responsible programs—is difficult.

Whether the outcome is firm or intangible, recall that the second major aspect of compensating variation is assessing the monetary value of the outcome. Many participants in the case study research were unable or unwilling to do so. This was true of most communicators and most members of dominant coalitions we interviewed at length. In many cases, their difficulty or reluctance reflected philosophical objections as much as operational difficulties.

When asked to determine the monetary value of averting lawsuits, restrictive legislation or regulation, consumer boycotts, strikes, or other kinds of problems they mentioned that had been solved in whole or part by excellent communication, most of the people we talked with seemed to demur in principle. Some cited the not-for-profit status of their organizations as a reason for considering advantageous outcomes in nonmonetary terms. At least one top communicator was reluctant to link dollar figures to public relations efforts because she feared the numbers would seem almost unbelievably high.

Several other participants argued simply that the benefits of communication are inherently intangible. The top communicator in the oil company affiliate, for example, said: "You can't [prove] the value of public affairs. The chairman knows because he's got a feel. The chairman is a very experienced line manager, and he knows." Despite this confidence in his boss to appreciate public relations, the head of communication in the oil company affiliate nevertheless had a system for arguing for more programs and bigger budgets. Rather than offering proof of his contribution to the bottom line, he proposed negative scenarios such as, "If you don't do this, then that is not going to happen." His specific objection to proving the value of public relations using numbers is that in such cases: "The disaster has happened. You can say, 'That has cost us too much.' " He preferred what he considered a more proactive approach, halting the development of the crisis by pointing out, "If you go ahead on this course, there will be a downside even if I can't tell you how much it will be."

Still other participants believed that matching dollar spent with dollar re-turned was unnecessary. Some did not see a compelling need to measure their contributions because they had what we determined was a confidence born of a history of success. They knew they added value, so they did not perceive a need to justify their existence in monetary terms. And, as the senior vice president of a midwestern utility told us, this exercise could be replaced by intuition: "I don't think you can link the dollars you spend on public relations to every bottom line. If you believe that it is there; if you value [public relations]; if you have an intuitive sense that it is there, then you will devote human and capital resources to it. If you don't, you won't."

By contrast, a few of our participants had little difficulty in converting ob-servable effects of communication programs into money saved or money earned. This ability was only one of several key discriminators between excel-lent and not-so-excellent organizations. Participants in organizations at the top of the Excellence scale had a clearer idea of the value public relations adds. In the mediocre organizations, the cost of *not* having effective communication was more obvious. For example, we heard about the time, energy, and negative publicity that resulted from reacting to crises rather than anticipating those con-flicts or, through long-term relationships, avoiding them in the first place.

Also, the "excellently challenged" organizations were less likely to provide fi-nancial support to do any kind of evaluation research in public relations. Chap-ters 8 and 9 reveal more data about the relationship between evaluative re-search and models of public relations and outcomes of communication programs, respectively.

Perhaps the most dramatic instance of an organization ready to respond to the question of how much good relationships with strategic publics are worth came from the chemical association. There, the CEO and head of public rela-tions both attested to the value of public relations well beyond what we might have imagined. When asked just what communication is worth in dollars and cents, they answered that it can be worth everything, especially in times of cri-sis. To the CEO, effective communication could save the organization. In his terms, "You're betting the ranch." This came from the leader of an industry that had experienced a crisis of such global proportions that his assertion carried great weight.

Public Relations in Times of Crisis.   Less sensational yet equally important answers came from a number of other organizations included in our in-depth look at most and least excellent operations. Like the chemical association, most involved crises. Credible, positive relationships may serve as a buffer between the organization and its key constituencies in times of crisis. Our participants questioned how such dimensions could be measured. They believed the integra-tion of responsibility and profitability makes such a determination nearly impossible. Thus they tended to describe their "for instances" in vague, rather than concrete, financial terms.

For example, the head of public relations in a development company offered several such instances without attaching a dollars-and-cents value to the ways in which communication had helped her organization cope. She explained that with every successful resolution of a crisis, the CEO was proud of the way her department had operated. Surely the confidence of the organization's top management has value, but what is a CEO's pride worth?

In addition, this company's top communicator made the compelling argument that although turning around a crisis does not necessarily generate sales, it does generate goodwill. She believed that this would benefit the company in the long run. The evidence on which she based this assertion was the fact that her company had emerged from a 5-year period of conservative, no-growth behavior as a result of the U.S. economy. Many of the company's competitors had not survived these tough economic conditions. Now that her company not only is surviving but becoming more active, "We're ready to jump back in," this knowledgeable and highly professional woman said. However, she considered the challenge of attaching a price tag to the benefits of survival or weathering crises over the long haul impossible. More interestingly, she was unwilling to try. Why? "I think we would undervalue it; but, on the other hand, the number we might come up with would be so staggering, it probably wouldn't be believed."

The top communicator in a real estate company perhaps best articulated one common explanation for the difficulty or even undesirability of attributing money made or saved to public relations efforts. Much of her work involves forestalling crises. This kind of help, she reminded us, is rarely acknowledged or appreciated because it is largely invisible. Best practices in public relations may prevent situations from degenerating into crises in the first place—what we called a delayed return earlier in this chapter. To use an unfortunately trendy term, excellent public relations is "proactive," rather than "reactive."

Relationships With Strategic Publics. Many communicators and their CEOs valued public relations not because they perceived it to have a specific monetary return on their investment in communication but because they understand that communication works with other management functions to build good long-term relationships with stakeholders. These strategic publics typically include employees, investors, customers, the media, government regulatory bodies, donors, and communities. In fact, the greatest contribution that CEOs, in particular, acknowledged for public relations was help in providing a perspective or broad picture of both the internal and external landscape of the organization. This perspective becomes critically important as the organization faces pressure from activist groups. In fact, our findings in this area lead us to assert that activism or other crises help push the organization toward excellence.

Practitioners and CEOs alike credited open communication—explaining one's position, listening to others, and making adjustments in response to what one is hearing—with helping improve the overall functioning of their organizations. They considered this kind of interactive communication, which we would call two-way symmetrical public relations, not preferable but essential for survival in this dynamic era.

Research is an integral part of any two-way communication program. Payoffs can be enormous, as we learned from an arts organization. For more than a decade, funding had remained flat. Historically, the amount of money sought never was obtained. Such failure was accepted, even expected, by the organization's leadership. It always settled for a percentage of the total amount deemed available. As the top communicator told us, "If you asked for [U.S.] $350,000, you usually got $150,000."

Then, the director of public relations worked with senior management to conduct research and make its case to state legislators for increased funding and additional grants. The director pushed message points stressing the impact of the arts on local economies, the importance of art to local communities, and the positive role the arts play in the social development of at-risk youth in those communities. Such presentations, based on targeted research, garnered the full U.S. $350,000 grant sought—the first total success in the organization's history. The message about how youth can be influenced positively exerted such an impact that the state legislature granted an additional U.S. $25,000 for a year-long study to evaluate the effect of a U.S. $1 million grant to start arts programs for at-risk young people.

This top communicator told us of another potential opportunity that resulted from its presentations to the legislature. The state was hoping to convince the International Olympic Committee to hold the winter games there. The state was looking to the arts organization to provide information and entertainment to help overcome the impression that the state is a "dry, boring place" and that people attending the games would have little else to do. We came away from interviews with this organization convinced that its head of public relations has helped the department become more proactive and strategic. It involves itself in decision making about issues as they emerge, rather than after they "explode," in his words. Its score on the Excellence factor at the time of our survey research had been only in the 21st percentile.

Despite such positive outcomes, our participants were not naive or Pollyannas about the likelihood of their establishing positive relationships with *all* the strategic publics that may oppose them. However, interviewees in the most excellent organizations acknowledged the value of simply having those activists "suspend disbelief" about their operations—at least long enough to give them a chance to, in one's words, "deliver the goods." That same top communicator agreed with his president that "there are a number of [activists] who are never going to change and they are going to be in opposition to us. They call themselves environmental groups, but really they're political change groups—and that's the way life is."

Despite this note of reality, almost cynicism with the way the world works, this sophisticated professional said: "It's useful to find ways to talk with each other and listen to each other. In some cases, we're really gonna gain some help and some converts; and in some cases people will at least suspend disbelief and give us a chance to change and improve."

Public Relations and the Amorphous Concept of Goodwill.   The most common sentiment expressed among participants unable or unwilling to engage in the process of compensating variation was that "it's hard to reduce goodwill to a number." Other participants used terms such as a "good image" and "reputation" to describe this amorphous concept. Although "goodwill," "good image," and a "positive reputation" are not precise, public relations practitioners typically use such terms as indicators of a positive relationship. In *Excellence in Public Relations and Communication Management* we used reciprocity, trust, credibility, mutual legitimacy, openness, mutual satisfaction, and mutual understanding to describe the same concept. It was striking, therefore, when participants used some of these same terms to describe the amorphous concept of a good relationship.

Although participants often were able to calculate just what engendering this good cost them, rarely could they say what they reaped in return. For example, the top communicator in a hospital association located in the Pacific Northwest described the strategic counsel that had benefited members of the association tangibly. Her advice was based on a sophisticated understanding of shifting public opinion regarding health care issues. Her counsel was born of two-way communication—the ability to anticipate trends through environmental scanning. Specifically, she advised the association to sever its ties with businesses and insurers held in low regard by the public. The dominant coalition agreed. The association's break with insurance companies, in particular, helped secure passage of legislation that benefited the association's hospital members. The governor of Washington cited this organization's role as instrumental in the legislation. The public affairs director, herself a member of the dominant coalition, explained her inability to complete the process of compensating variation as follows: "As far as costs go, you could say it cost [U.S.] $100,000 in public opinion research, another [U.S.] $100,000 to participate in the political campaign, plus my salary; but you can't put a price tag on the years of *goodwill* [emphasis added] this legislation will buy us with the governor, the legislature, and the public."

Not surprisingly, her CEO quarreled with the basic notion of placing a monetary value on the benefits of communication to organizations such as his hospital association. Not-for-profit organizations, he argued, do not measure the "bottom line" in terms of profit-and-loss.

We also heard with disappointing frequency that public relations adds value because "we make them look good"—and there is no way to quantify that. In addition, we heard much about the importance of credibility—and the concomitant impossibility of measuring its worth. At least for the chemical corporation included in our survey of cases, credibility was the essence of employee communication. The communication director there explained that the value of communication comes from gaining credibility, which he defined as "a level of trust among employees and how they view senior management." He elaborated: "Credibility is the issue. That is the sole measure of everything we do. Is it credible? Is it believable? If I can say 'yes,' then regardless of how much it costs, I know the corporation is getting value for what it is paying for."

We probed, then, as part of the process of compensating variation to ask the director if he could put a dollar value on credibility. He answered in two ways. First: "If it's on next year's budget, if it survived another bloodletting, it has value." In a sense, this is consistent with compensating variation. If management is willing to fund a communication program, it must believe the value of the program exceeds its cost. Second, the director answered that a communication program has value if the public for whom it is intended is willing to pay for it, just as people pay to see a movie. He said most employee publications contain "bs," "baloney and sweetness": "How much would employees pay for that? Not much. Today, I believe our employees would pay 15 to 25 cents for our employee publication." We followed up yet again, asking him how much it is worth to management to have employees willing to pay for a publication. He responded in terms of desired behavioral outcomes: "You want them to be committed to the corporation, to the business strategy, to do the job safely, in our case, in a low-cost fashion. The business strategy has to be directly related to what you want the employees to do or else you waste money."

We concluded that this chemical company believes firmly that communication contributes value that exceeds its cost. Participants there helped confirm the theory that explains the contribution of public relations to organizations: Communication has value because it improves the organization's behavioral relationships—the behavioral outcomes—with strategic publics such as employees. The relationship has value, but neither interviewee from this company believed it is possible to quantify its value.

Similarly, several public relations directors spoke of "image" or "image enhancement." One had a hard time pinning down a dollar figure for the contributions of communication at her utility. However, she described an 8-year image campaign designed to show how the organization was doing. Senior executives used the evaluation data from the campaign as an indicator of overall company performance. In this way, they were beginning to link public relations efforts to larger corporate goals. The company's recognition of bottom-line contributions is, in her opinion, indirect at this time. Thus, despite a growing appreciation for managed communication, she contended that increasingly public relations must prove its worth. Although she did not relate any instances of direct pressure or threats to her budget, she mentioned a "gut feeling" that told her, "Boy, we've got to make them understand how important this stuff is."

At least one participant in the case study research did manage to estimate the return on his agency's investment in public relations for purposes of reputation management. This senior manager of the engineering experiment station gauged the ROI by a factor of 8 to 10. With an annual department budget of a half-million dollars, that meant communication services were worth U.S. $5 million yearly. However, the manager of communication there denied that a dollar value could be attached to what she called "image" value. She brought up the correlation of high standing in national rankings with good image, saying that top management may not realize that status and claims of greatness, reflected in those rankings, must be accompanied by substance.

More often, the experience of a public utility in the South seemed typical. Its communication department responded expertly during a natural disaster. It maintained constant contact with the media and community leadership. Thus the community was continuously informed of the progress of the company's repair efforts during the ice storm. The president told us only that "we came out of it with a very white cap."

In another instance of natural disaster, this time a hurricane, we heard more about the perceived connection between image and ultimate success for the organization. The CEO of a Fortune 500 company explained that link as follows: "The image of an industry affects the laws that are written, the ability to raise capital funds, and the recruiting of talented employees. One way or another, it does affect the bottom line."

This metal-manufacturing operation, with sales of more than U.S. $4 billion and a market share of 11%, nevertheless had suffered over the last decade from the economic recession and a loss of market share to international imports. In 1994, the company made a conscious decision to maximize its position—in part through the use of more progressive public relations techniques. The CEO believed that these two-way approaches would improve the company's image. He cited the effect of donating materials to rebuild homes in sections of Florida devastated by Hurricane Andrew. As a result, needy people received help and the company promoted its products—and its reputation as a good corporate citizen.

When asked to calculate just what communication had contributed to the company's bottom line, the manager of public relations at the metal manufacturer offered a different example—this one from the 1970s, at the peak of the energy crisis. At that time, the company operated mining interests. In one of its mining communities, the decision to increase production by introducing above-ground mining generated considerable opposition from local people and environmental groups. Activists threatened legislation to prevent the proposed surface mining. Effective communication, involving demonstrations of damage control and attractive landscaping, convinced citizens of the community and other interested parties that the company would be environmentally responsible. In addition, the company invited reporters to visit its mining operation. It encouraged interviews with miners, their supervisors, and townspeople.

The manager of public relations (himself a former journalist) told us that, in general, journalists left with a favorable impression. "They must have," he said. "Eventually, [the media] stopped calling us and called other companies instead." He and the CEO agreed that if activist opposition had succeeded in blocking the new mining operation, the company would have lost "millions of dollars."

Public Relations and Prices. Even some of the top communicators who argued against the desirability of assigning a monetary value to the contributions of public relations offered instances in which communication enhanced their bottom line. A member of the dominant coalition in the midwestern utility, for example, talked about price increases. He explained that although no customer likes to pay more, effective communication helped people understand the reason for rate hikes. He added: "It's not easy to connect—the budget dollars on public relations to what might have been a more favorable leaning from a regulatory commission on a rate request—but we think it's there."

A second, related case came from the senior vice president of a chemical company. He and his director of corporate communication both were unwilling to relate public relations in dollar terms to a bottom-line issue. However, they explained that over the last 10 years, the company averaged an 8% return on capital. During the best year of that decade, it returned 25%; the worst year, nothing. The last year was a bad year for the corporation but it still returned 8% on capital—the average of the last 10 years. They agreed that public relations had played a large part in this major turnaround. As the vice president said:

> Now, do I believe we accomplished that without the benefit of communication? No, of course not, communication in every respect . . . in causing the underlying performance, in getting out there and making sure that the investment community knew what we were doing. But for those two things, our stock would not be at an all-time high today. The value of [the corporation] was $150 million higher in the hands of shareholders today than when they went to sleep last night. Now, do I believe that today somehow we got some leverage from the few million dollars we spend on communication each year? Damn right, I do!

Similarly, the top communicator in an aerospace corporation described the relationship between media relations and stock prices there. Her communication department traditionally has relied on asymmetrical programs. This approach paid off when the financial media helped build the value of its stock. In 1992, when the company's new management took over, stock value hovered at U.S. $19 per share. By 1994, the stock had risen to about U.S. $92. This growth in stock prices generated millions of dollars for shareholders over a mere 3-year period. The head of public affairs said that although the processes of liquidation, consolidation, and mergers fueled these economic gains, success hinged on the positive response of the financial community to her department's program of media relations.

Public Relations and Unblocking Markets.   The experiences of an equipment manufacturer headquartered in the United States may provide ideas for communicators unfamiliar with making a monetary assessment of what communication actually is worth to their organization. This company credited public relations with helping avoid lawsuits and a freeze on access to a large Asian market.

The lawsuit involved an equipment failure in a foreign subsidiary, resulting in loss of lives. The U.S. operation was able to contain the public relations problem to the European country where the incident happened, through the use of a public relations firm in that country. All media inquiries about the incident were referred to the European public relations firm, even if the inquiry had originated in the United States. The second incident involved bribery in a market in the Far East. The American company severed its relationship with its business partner in that market and publicly apologized for the incident. Its strategy was based on an understanding of the importance of honor and saving face in that culture. The firm was able to reenter the market after a relatively short hiatus. Our respondents from this equipment manufacturer estimated the value of their successful containment strategies in Europe and Asia in excess of U.S. $100 million.

Communication Can Mean Life Itself.   One not-for-profit organization collaborated with the Excellence team to develop monetary estimates of the benefit communication offered both the organization and its clients. This blood bank was able to avoid a significant drop in blood donations at the peak of the AIDS crisis in the United States in the 1980s. Many people had developed the irrational fear that donating blood might increase their risk of contracting the HIV virus. Both communicators and members of the dominant coalition we interviewed credited effective media relations, in particular, with minimizing the drop to about 3% (about 2,700 units of blood) during the worst year of the scare. Blood banks in a comparable city experienced a 15% drop. Some cities lost up to 25% of their donations at that time. Using the unit price of blood in 1994, when we conducted our survey of cases, the blood bank saved U.S. $986,000 in retained donations when compared with the worst-case scenario of a possible 25% drop.

In another program where success was credited to excellent communication, the same blood bank organized a bone-marrow-testing campaign to help a young boy with leukemia. Bone-marrow transplants work only when a match can be found between the potential donor and the patient with leukemia. The drive to find a compatible donor for this child netted 30 donations of bone marrow for people with leukemia and other related diseases. You may wonder, and we asked, what is the value of saving up to 30 lives? One indicator is the cost of the bone-marrow-transplant procedure itself, placed at U.S. $100,000. The monetary value to leukemia patients of the campaign for bone-marrow donations can thus be placed at U.S. $3 million.

We heard similar instances from the heart health organization included in our survey of cases. Changing lifestyles tops this organization's agenda. Unhealthy dietary habits represent a major target for change. It aims to achieve this and other transformations in lifestyles through education and increased funding for research.

Over the past decade, the average amount of fat consumed as a percentage of diet has declined significantly. The link between consumption of fat and heart disease is well known. With this decrease in consumption of fat comes huge savings, both human and financial. At present, our participants in the heart health organization assured us, the dollar savings is incalculable because such benefits will be realized only (and perhaps tabulated) years hence—another example of what we called a delayed return.

The vice president of communication said she firmly believes the change is mainly a product of the organization's communication program. Her organization had scored in the 99th percentile in the quantitative phase of the Excellence study. Her CEO also credited public relations with the move toward healthy lifestyles among the organization's strategic constituencies. He asked, "What else could it be?"

This CEO was more skeptical about communication's direct contributions to research funding and donations, although he expressed the hope that providing educational materials might inspire more generous contributions and higher levels of federal funding. His top communicator offered an encouraging example. Before 1989, women's heart health rarely received attention. That year, her organization developed a program to increase awareness of the issue. Over the subsequent years, media interest in the subject grew significantly. More important, and more relevant to this discussion, research funding and actual research in the pharmaceutical industry targeted at women's heart health both increased dramatically. The human benefits are obvious.

Saving Money and Making Money.   Throughout the Excellence project, we on the research team have asserted that public relations contributes primarily by saving money, rather than making money. This latter function we assign more to marketing. The assistant executive director of public affairs of a Canadian medical association seemed to agree. In her organization, membership marketing is the area where communication and making money can be linked most logically. She told us that effective marketing translates into more members and thus more money for the association.

However, through our long interviews with elite participants in all kinds of organizations, we have arrived at a better understanding of the complex relationship between making and saving money. In essence, that relationship may be reciprocal. The strategic manager in a chemical company we studied expressed this interconnection most forcefully. He used the realm of human resources to illustrate:

> To the extent that we're getting all of our employees, through employee communication, oriented around our strategy, which is, number one, to root out work that we do that wastes money, by definition communication is saving us money. It's saving us money by better enabling people who should be saving us money to go out there and get the job done. Ultimately, that loops around and helps us make money. So, employee communication today is saving us money and making us money.

A second, similar instance of public relations both saving and making money came from the state lottery. It relates to an external, rather than internal, public. Also, the benefits of communication in this "neo-business, neo-government" agency were rooted in traditional models of public information and publicity rather than the two-way models in evidence at the chemical company. The manager of business and planning at the state lottery explained that press coverage increased awareness of her agency. Clever media slants, she contended, led to larger, rapidly growing jackpots. Good publicity, in turn, helped reduce spending on advertising. As she explained the interrelationship: "Good communication is based on making and saving money by pumping out a variety of new angles to get press coverage. Millions of dollars are made from good public relations in this respect and it saves hundreds of thousands of dollars each year."

When Communication Neither Makes nor Saves Money—And That's Okay. A participant from the medical association described a scenario in which the role of public relations could not be linked to positive bottom-line, financial effects. He equated public affairs with trying to further good public policy, irrespective of dollars. His example was serving as an advocate of seat belt legislation. This advocacy actually hurt his members' bottom line, at least in the short run, because fewer accident victims meant fewer patients for doctors to treat.

A second, less dramatic but equally instructive example came from the gas and electric company included in our survey of cases. The public relations manager pointed out that even when her CEO takes public relations seriously, others within the dominant coalition may not. She mentioned marketing, in particular. She explained that although the two departments do many similar things, marketing has an easier time than public relations in demonstrating its impact. As a result, the potential for subjugation exists. So far, public relations has been able to maintain its critical role in the arena of customer service because utilities increasingly are adopting a demand-size philosophy. She called this "demarketing," or trying to give customers what they want while pushing for energy conservation.

The Correspondence Between Budgets and Effects of Managed Communication. In this, the final section of our findings about the value of public relations, we revisit the notion of return on investment in communication. We began with tables of survey data showing how CEOs and their top communicators perceive the relationship between money spent on public relations and money either saved or earned as a result. We conclude with what we learned about this cost–benefit ratio from the long interviews with participants in two dozen organizations.

Looking at the tables alone in chapter 4 might suggest that, because respondents credited managed communication with returning, on average, a value of about one and a half times what it costs, bigger budgets for public relations would result in correspondingly greater effects. Analyzing interview responses suggests that that assumption would be false.

Money may be a necessary but not sufficient condition for excellence in public relations. As the top communicator in the medical products company put it: "You can have a large department and do nothing more than slightly value-added activities and various audiences will wonder what good it is. Or you can have a small department with a few great people and have a very high value to the organization."

Predictably, given the economic recession that was the context of our research in the field, we heard much about downsizing, "right" sizing, people being found redundant, and doing more with less. This kind of budget cutting is not restricted to public relations. All departments of the typical organization may suffer cutbacks. In the southern public utility, for example, the senior communication specialist told us that because of centralization, all departments have smaller budgets today than they did when we completed the survey research. However, he pointed out that this does not mean that departments are valued less than before. Nor does it mean they necessarily accomplish less. As he said, "We may have fewer dollars now, but we do a better job with it." We determined that a change in leadership of the utility, along with major corporate restructuring, actually strengthened what already was an excellent communication department—one that had scored in the 99th percentile in the quantitative phase of this project.

Paradoxically, hard times for its industry and the corporation itself also resulted in positive reforms for communication at the metal manufacturer we studied. *Forbes* magazine had documented the industry's new lease on life and featured the company and its chairman in that article. It likened the industry to a patient recovering from a long-term, debilitating disease and the company itself as part of the lean, muscular body now able to hold its own in global competition. Likewise, we determined that the manufacturer's public relations department could hold *its* own in the strategic management of the corporation.

The top communicator in the medical association also rejected the link between modest budgets or downsizing and how people are valued. He argued that downsizing actually amplified the role of communication because his department, public affairs, must deal with the fallout in the media. Likewise, communication in human resources must deal with outplacement issues. So, although his budget has suffered by U.S. $600,000, he did not believe his role had been diminished.

Two of the people we interviewed in the chemical company agreed that budget cuts might not mean disaster for public relations. They have sacrificed quantity but never quality. The company spent U.S. $1.2 million on its shareholder report 4 years before the qualitative phase of our research. That year, it spent less than $300,000. The vice president told us he considered the lower priced report better. Indeed, it won an award. In a similar vein, the company's communication director told us that more money does not necessarily mean the department will be proportionately more effective: "If I had [U.S.] $10 million rather than $1 million, I would be more effective but not 10 times more effective."

The Efficacy of Compensating Variation

The interview guide for our case study protocol provided a series of probes to help the Excellence team help communicators and others work through the process of assigning monetary value to communication benefits. Based on our experience, it seems that many organizations could assess the value of communication Excellence in monetary terms if they could first learn the techniques of compensating variation. Although the term is intimidating, the procedure is not.

However, we found only limited support for our proposition that *all* public relations programs could be evaluated using this cost–benefit measure. The proposition, as worded, overstates the current capability and willingness of too many of the professionals we interviewed. Participants in our case study research agreed that the end states they were after were exactly what we had proposed: achieving, maintaining, and even enhancing accord with their publics. They believed that communication, indeed, often made the difference between cooperation and conflict with their strategic constituencies. However, for a host of reasons summarized later in this section, more often than not they were unable or unwilling to speculate on how much cooperation was worth to their organizations.

Undaunted, we continue to believe working with this process may help public relations professionals see that the benefits of at least some of their programs are not so intangible as they thought. To assign monetary value, the communicator needs to isolate communication as a primary cause of a beneficial outcome. Second, he or she might work with other managers to assess, collectively, the monetary value of that outcome. The process of collectively assessing money value of an effect reaps additional rewards for the communication department. If other members of the dominant coalition work with communicators to determine the value of desired outcomes, in lieu of undesirable outcomes, an intersubjective reliability can be built around the estimate. That is, the monetary value attached to an outcome represents the best thinking of those who run the organization—even if that value is "mushy" and something less than truly "objective." Further, this process of collaboration may help develop a peer professional relationship between heads of public relations and their counterparts in other subsystems of the organization.[8]

Professional associations such as IABC and the Public Relations Society of America (PRSA) tend to emphasize the need to attach a financial value to public relations. However, most of the people we talked with were not thinking in this way. Instead, CEOs and their top communicators alike were thinking about how public relations fits into the big picture of the organization. That picture includes, but is not limited to, bottom-line profitability. Long-term relationships with strategic publics and a sense of responsibility to those stakeholders seemed equally important. Further, our participants were unwilling or unable to separate out the discrete contribution of public relations when it operated in concert with other groups. We heard a great deal more about the benefits of partnering, collaboration, and coalition building than we had anticipated, based on the literature we reviewed.

When participants in the qualitative research did talk about the value of public relations in dollar or pound amounts, the numbers were high. Readers may quibble with the millions of dollars supposedly saved in fending off a lawsuit or the entire company saved by the successful handling of a crisis. You may find yourself uncomfortable crediting communicative efforts with saving human lives, at a cost savings of U.S. $100,000 each. However soft you consider these figures to be, keep in mind that we were addressing our questions related to financial value to the people with the greatest expertise in organizations: CEOs or other members of the dominant coalition in addition to their managers of public relations.

FINANCIAL PERFORMANCE REVISITED: A STUDY OF EIGHT ELECTRIC COMPANIES IN THE EXCELLENCE SAMPLE

As we have said several times in this chapter, we did not attempt to establish a direct connection between the excellence of the public relations function and the financial performance of the organizations we studied. For the government

---

[8]Chapter 5, which deals with empowerment of the public relations function, goes into considerable detail about the critical importance of working together and on a par with other managers.

agencies, not-for-profit organizations, and associations in the sample, the link to financial performance might not be so critical as it would be for the corporations. In addition, the quality of the public relations function would be only one of many variables that could affect the financial performance of a corporation—and it would not be possible to identify, let alone control statistically, all of the other variables that affect performance to isolate the impact of public relations. Nevertheless, Hoxie (1992) did do a study to compare the excellence of public relations with the financial performance of eight electric companies that were included in our sample to make a rough analysis of the relationship between the two.

Hoxie (1992) found that the eight utilities had public relations departments whose scores on the Excellence scale covered the full range of organizations in the Excellence study, although their mean score on excellence was slightly higher than the mean for the entire sample—that is, the public relations functions for these utilities were generally more excellent than for the other organizations. Hoxie isolated the two utilities with the highest Excellence scores and the two with the lowest Excellence scores. The two utilities with the highest Excellence scores also were among the highest-scoring organizations in the total Excellence sample—with scores in the 99th and 94th percentiles. Hoxie then made detailed financial comparisons between the two companies with the most excellent communication functions and those with the least excellent functions for a 3-year period. She included measures of percentage change in sales, profits, change in profits, return on invested capital, return on common equity, share price as a percentage of book value, price–earnings ratio, dividend yield, dividend payout, dividend total return, and earnings per share.

Both companies with high scores on communication Excellence had outstanding financial performance during the period studied. Of the two companies with low Excellence scores, one had poor financial performance and the other mixed performance on the different indicators—generally supporting Hoxie's (1992) hypothesis that excellence in public relations would correspond with strong financial performance. She explained, "It does appear that public relations excellence is *a factor* [emphasis added] in each utility's financial performance" (p. 447).

At the same time, our two compensating variation measures of the value of public relations did not correspond perfectly with overall excellence or with financial performance. Both the CEO and the PR head did assign high values to the communication function in the utility with the highest Excellence score, and the CEOs and PR heads assigned average to low values in the two companies with low Excellence scores. However, both the PR head and the CEO in the second utility with a high Excellence score assigned slightly below average scores to the value of public relations. This lack of correspondence could suggest that the CEO of the second utility did not appreciate the quality of his or her communication function (which essentially would be error variance when only a few organizations made up the sample) or it could suggest, as we have said, that excellent public relations alone does not account for outstanding financial performance.

Hoxie (1992) pointed out that all of the utilities in the Excellence sample faced a similar environment of financial difficulty and activist pressure:

> It should be pointed out that the general time period which was under study (1987 through 1990) followed closely on the heels of a recessionary time in the United States and was a time when most utilities were struggling to diversify their fuel mixes to avoid further problems caused by unstable, often costly world oil prices. In addition, all four utilities faced strong activist pressure while trying to build nuclear power facilities. However, the outcome and effects of that activism on each utility varied. (pp. 448–449)

Hoxie (1992) concluded that although the utilities shared these environmental problems, the two utilities with excellent public relations functions *"consistently* managed to do well in their financial performance, while two other utilities . . . struggled with numerous costly problems and remained mired in costly litigation and entangled in regulatory politics" (p. 449). She proposed two possible explanations of her finding that excellence in public relations corresponded with strong financial performance:

> *Scenario 1.* Utilities with effective public relations staff and programs save money for the organization and gain benefits that make the utility financially successful. These utilities show outstanding financial performance and high Excellence scores.
> *Scenario 2.* Utilities that are financially successful, to start with, have good financial performance and can afford to hire effective public relations staff, who in turn, exhibit PR Excellence when tested. (p. 449)

Hoxie (1992) believed that the results of her study could be interpreted in either way. However, she reasoned that the conceptualization behind the Excellence study supported the first scenario more than the second. She explained:

> What the findings for this study seemed to imply is that the extent of public relations effectiveness is an important *factor* in overall organizational effectiveness, which, in turn, affects the organization's financial performance. While organization effectiveness is not the *only* factor that affects financial performance, it is a strategic factor and is closely related to overall effectiveness of public relations. (p. 452)

Hoxie's (1992) study, therefore, supported our conceptualization in this chapter and in the first *Excellence* book: The excellence of the public relations function is *one* important factor in determining organizational effectiveness and subsequent financial performance, but it is not the only factor. Other factors may overwhelm public relations in determining organizational performance; therefore, it is theoretically questionable, if not dangerous, for the public relations profession, to search for a silver bullet that uses a *single* financial or even nonfinancial indicator to measure the value contributed by public relations both to organizations and to society.

SUMMARY AND CONCLUSIONS

The data reported in this chapter support the proposition about the contribution excellent public relations can make to organizational effectiveness. Organizations strive for good relationships with the publics in their internal and external environment that limit their ability to pursue their goals. Organizations also try to cultivate relationships with publics that support their goals. Building and maintaining good relationships with these strategic constituencies maximize the organization's autonomy to achieve its goals. This is important, because the literature shows that effective organizations are those that choose appropriate goals—given the expectations of their stakeholders. Stakeholder publics may be of obvious importance, such as employees. They also may be shadowy constituencies, such as *prospective* employees of diverse backgrounds and concerns.

When public relations helps the organization develop relationships with publics deemed "strategic" for it, the organization *saves* big money by reducing the costs of litigation, regulation, legislation, or pressure campaigns that result from bad relationships with publics—especially activist groups. We heard of small financial savings that come through careful targeting of the message to appropriate publics. In earlier years the economic development agency, for example, had distributed its publications to about 2,000 clients—regardless of the clients' business or the publication's contents. By devising a system for matching publications to clients, the top communicator saved her agency considerable money in printing and postage costs. We even heard of saved *lives* that resulted at least in large part from educational and media campaigns devised by astute communicators in the medical association, the blood bank, and the heart health organization.

Expertly managed communication also helps the organization *make* money by cultivating relationships with donors, employees, consumers or clients, shareholders, the trade press, the community, and legislators or other regulatory bodies. In some cases, the organization actually collaborates with these other groups through coalition building or shared investments in campaigns of mutual concern. Determining the return on communication's investment in this joint process turned out to be nearly impossible. However, partnering can be spectacularly successful, both in concrete and immediate financial terms and in the more nebulous and long-term sense of what our participants called "image," "goodwill," "public visibility," and "reputation."

All of this is likely to happen when the head of public relations is a part of the organization's top management. There, through the process of shared decision making, CEOs, their top communicator, and other members of the dominant coalition are most likely to get top dollar back from their investment in public relations. This ROI is likely to approach 225% under conditions of excellence. It may be as low as 100 for the least excellent public relations departments. Even these estimates are averages over a number of years, however, because our respondents suggested that the ROI is lumpy, long term, and often the result of something that does not happen. That is, the major return from public relations may occur only once every 10 to 20 years; and that return may represent a problem that public relations prevented from happening—such as a strike, a crisis, litigation, a boycott, or regulation. In most cases, however, CEOs and communicators alike agree that public relations returns significantly more than it costs—and more than the typical department in their organization.

At the same time, we found evidence that public relations is one important factor—but by no means the only factor—that has an effect on the financial performance of organizations. However, we found little reason to believe that a single hard financial indicator could be found to measure the value of public relations. Rather, a softer indicator of the value of communication—compensating variation—allowed us to show that excellent public relations does contribute value both to the organization and to society. The public relations profession needs to identify a strong nonfinancial indicator of effective public relations, and both our conceptualization and the results of our qualitative interviews suggest that the concept of relationships would be the best such indicator—better than such nebulous and poorly defined concepts as reputation, image, goodwill, and brand that are popular buzzwords among public relations people. Indeed, in research subsequent to the Excellence study J. Grunig and Huang (2000) and Hon and J. Grunig (1999) developed indicators of relationships to serve as metrics for measuring the success of public relations. We discuss that emerging program of research more in the concluding chapter of this book.

Encouragingly, we also found that none of the financial success that can be attributed to public relations must come at the cost of social responsibility. The most effective organizations we studied rely on public relations to help determine which stakeholder groups were strategic for it and then to help develop credible, long-term relationships with those constituencies. Such high-quality relationships exist only when the organization acknowledges the legitimacy of the public, listens to its concerns, and deals with any negative consequences it may be having on that public.

Undeniable evidence came from the chemical association. There, the head of public relations is credited with developing a program of citizen advisory panels that has changed his entire industry's way of operating and, concomitantly, its reputation. This program of social responsibility reflects the vice president's belief in the legitimacy of the public interest. His accompanying public relations efforts have been characterized in the trade press as "sophisticated," "very aggressive," "skilled," "more open," "responsive," and "more effective." He himself believes the program is helping his industry change in ways that respond to citizens' concerns about health, safety, and the environment. As he was quoted as saying in a weekly trade publication, "Changing one's own performance, not 'educating' the public, is the only successful strategy" (as quoted in Begley, 1993, p. 23). In the next chapter, we see how effective communicators have managed to develop as professionals who are capable of such high-level, effective performance.

REFERENCES

Amba-Rao, S. C. (1990, November). *Multinational corporate social responsibility, ethics, and the third world governments: Agenda for the 1990s.* Paper presented at the meeting of the Association for the Advancement of Policy, Research, and Development in the Third World, Mexico City.

Angelopulo, G. C. (1990). The active outward orientation of the organisation. *Communicare, 9*(1), 5–20.

Begley, R. (1993, December 8). Selling responsible care to a critical public: CMA takes its message to the airwaves. *Chemical Week,* p. 23.

Bryant, J. (1989). Assessing company strength using added value. *Long Range Planning, 22,* 34–44.

Buchholz, R. A. (1989). *Business environment and public policy* (3rd ed.). Englewood Cliffs, NJ: Prentice-Hall.

Campbell, C. B. (1992). *Assessing the bottom-line impact of effective public relations programs from a CEO's perspective.* Unpublished master's thesis, University of Maryland, College Park.

Campbell, C. B. (1993). Does public relations affect the bottom line? Study shows CEOs think so. *Public Relations Journal, 49*(10), 14–17.

Campbell, J. P. (1977). On the nature of organizational effectiveness. In P. S. Goodman & J. M. Pennings (Eds.), *New perspectives on organizational effectiveness* (pp. 13–55). San Francisco: Jossey-Bass.

Cutlip, S. M., Center, A. H., & Broom, G. M. (1985). *Effective public relations* (6th ed.). Englewood Cliffs, NJ: Prentice-Hall.

Denison, D. R. (1990). *Corporate culture and organizational effectiveness.* New York: Wiley.

Ehling, W. P. (1992). Estimating the value of public relations and communication to an organization. In J. E. Grunig (Ed.), *Excellence in public relations and communication management* (pp. 617–638). Hillsdale, NJ: Lawrence Erlbaum Associates.

Fombrun, C. J. (1996). *Reputation: Realizing value from the corporate image.* Boston: Harvard Business School Press.

Francis, J. D. (1990). A look beneath the bottom line. *Public Relations Journal, 46,* 16–17, 32.

Freeman, R. E. (1984). *Strategic management: A stakeholder approach.* Boston: Pitman.

Freeman, R. E., & Gilbert, D. R., Jr. (1992, Spring). Business, ethics and society: A critical agenda. *Business and Society,* pp. 9–17.

Grunig, J. E. (Ed.). (1992). *Excellence in public relations and communication management.* Hillsdale, NJ: Lawrence Erlbaum Associates.

Grunig, J. E., & Huang, Y. H. (2000). From organizational effectiveness to relationship indicators: Antecedents of relationships, public relations strategies, and relationship outcomes. In J. A. Ledingham & S. D. Bruning (Eds.), *Public relations as relationship management: A relational approach to the study and practice of public relations* (pp. 23–53). Mahwah, NJ: Lawrence Erlbaum Associates.

Grunig, J. E., & Hunt, T. (1984). *Managing public relations*. New York: Holt, Rinehart & Winston.

Hage, J. (1980). *Theories of organizations: Form, process, and transformation*. New York: Wiley.

Hannan, M., & Freeman, J. (1977). The population ecology of organizations. *American Journal of Sociology, 82*, 929–964.

Hon, L. C., & Grunig, J. E. (1999). *Guidelines for measuring relationships in public relations*. Gainesville, FL: The Institute for Public Relations, Commission on PR Measurement and Evaluation.

Hoxie, R. C. (1992). *Cost/benefit effects and the role of excellent public relations for electric utilities faced with environmental or consumer activist situations: An analysis of the public relations programs in eight electric utilities that faced activist situations*. Unpublished master's thesis, University of Maryland, College Park.

Jackson, P. (2000, November 17). *Reputation: Assessing nonfinancial measures*. Presentation at The Conference on Corporate Communication, University of Notre Dame, South Bend, IN.

Jeffries-Fox Associates (2000a, March 3). *Toward a shared understanding of corporate reputation and related concepts: Phase I: Content analysis*. Basking Ridge, NJ: Report Prepared for the Council of Public Relations Firms.

Jeffries-Fox Associates (2000b, March 24). *Toward a shared understanding of corporate reputation and related concepts: Phase II: Measurement systems analysis*. Basking Ridge, NJ: Report Prepared for the Council of Public Relations Firms.

Katz, D., & Kahn, R. L. (1978). *The social psychology of organizations* (2nd ed.). New York: Wiley.

Kekst, G., & Freitag, M. (1991). Passing the "Public Scrutiny Test." *Public Relations Quarterly, 36*(3), 7–8.

Kotler, P. (1988). *Marketing management: Analysis, planning, implementation, and control*. Englewood Cliffs, NJ: Prentice-Hall.

Mau, R. R., & Dennis, L. B. (1994). Companies ignore shadow constituencies at their peril. *Public Relations Journal, 50*(5), 10–11.

McKelvey, B. (1979). Comment on the biological analog in organizational science, on the occasion of Van de Ven's review of Aldrich. *Administrative Science Quarterly, 21*, 212–226.

Mickens, E. (1994, April 19). Waging war on Wall Street. *The Advocate*, pp. 40–45.

Pavlik, J. V. (1987). *Public relations: What research tells us*. Newbury Park, CA: Sage.

Preston, L. E. (1981). Corporate power and social performance: Approaches to positive analysis. *Research in Corporate Social Performance and Policy: A Research Annual, 3*, 1–16.

Robbins, S. P. (1990). *Organization theory: Structure, design, and application* (3rd ed.). Englewood Cliffs, NJ: Prentice-Hall.

Sha, B. L. (1995). *Intercultural public relations: Exploring cultural identity as a means of segmenting publics*. Unpublished master's thesis, University of Maryland, College Park.

Tuleja, T. (1985). *Beyond the bottom line*. New York: Facts on File.

Ulrich, P., & Thielemann, U. (1993). How do managers think about market economies and morality? Empirical enquiries into business-ethical thinking patterns. *Journal of Business Ethics, 12*, 879–898.

Verčič, D. (2000). *Trust in organizations: A study of the relations between media coverage, public perceptions and profitability*. Unpublished doctoral dissertation, The London School of Economics and Political Science, University of London, London.

Weick, K. E. (1979). *The social psychology of organizing* (2nd ed.). Reading, MA: Addison-Wesley.

Wright, P., Ferris, S. P., Hiller, J., & Kroll, M. (1995). Competitiveness through management of diversity: Effects on stock price valuation. *Academy of Management Journal, 38*, 272–287.

CHAPTER FIVE

Empowerment of the Public Relations Function

The essence of the Excellence theory is that effective communication helps manage an organization's interdependencies with its strategic constituencies—the publics that either support or constrain organizations through their activism, litigation, or pressuring for government regulation. This chapter explores in depth several aspects of this notion, especially the role of public relations in strategic management. To be involved in strategic management, public relations must be represented among the organization's top-level decision makers. Thus we analyze the role of public relations in the dominant coalition. As a part of that analysis, we depict the typical relationships between heads of public relations and their counterparts in other functional areas. We also differentiate between the typical reporting relationship and the ideal connection between the communication manager and his or her CEO.

Central to this chapter is the question of how the public relations function and individual practitioners become empowered to play this senior role. To answer, we delve into the history of excellent programs included in our survey of 25 cases. We also offer a prognosis for the women who increasingly are attracted to this career field. Empowerment of women in public relations may predict the centrality or the marginalization of the function for everyone in future.

THEORETICAL BACKGROUND

Empowerment Within the Dominant Coalition

More specifically, we are interested in perceptions of chief executive officers, in large part because of their role as cultural leaders within the organization and also because the power-control perspective suggests that members of the dominant coalition determine the approach to public relations practiced. Adherents to power-control theory question the rationality of organizations. They deny that organizations operate much as machines do, trying to optimize responses to their environment. Instead, the power-control perspective argues that people in organizations form coalitions with others to enhance their power base. The most powerful of such coalitions is the dominant coalition.

Cyert and March (1963) were the first to focus on this aspect of organizational power. A decade into their program of research, they (1973) determined that an organization's behavior is determined by the values of its dominant coalition. Rather than acting to maximize organizational effectiveness vis-à-vis the environment, the dominant coalition acts both to serve organizational purposes and to maintain its personal power (Robbins, 1990). Similarly, Mintzberg (1983) concluded that members of the power elite willingly exploit their discretion to attain their own goals.

Only within the last two decades has a comprehensive and theoretically pleasing definition of what Thompson (1967) simply called the "inner circle" emerged. Our conceptual definition of the dominant coalition, from Stevenson, Pearce, and Porter (1985), is: "an interacting group of individuals, deliberately constructed, independent of the formal structure, lacking its own internal formal structure, consisting of mutually perceived membership, issue oriented, focused on a goal or goals external to the coalition, and requiring concerted member action" (p. 251).

In essence, the dominant coalition is the group of individuals within the organization who have the power to determine its mission and goals. They are the top managers who "run" the organization. In the process, they often make decisions that are good enough to allow the organization to survive but designed primarily to maintain the status quo and keep the current dominant coalition in power. Thus Allen (1979) believed that the dominant coalition dictates organizational action to a far greater degree than does the environment. And, because our review of relevant literature from sociology, political science, public policy, psychology, public relations, and business management supported this conclusion, we dedicate this chapter to the question of empowering communicators to function within or with the dominant coalition.

Much of the literature on organizational power has defined the concept in terms of being able to *control the behavior of others* or the ability of those in power to secure their own interests. The thrust of the Excellence theory, however, is the *empowerment* both of public relations and of publics affected by organizational decisions. Pieczka (1996) suggested that these two perspectives are incompatible. She said that:

> [They] lead to internal tension within the resultant theory. For example, how can
> it be possible to talk about decentralization, empowerment and trust, and at the
> same time claim that to be effective public relations needs to be in the dominant
> coalition. In other words, no matter how strongly one believes that organizations

should be diffused and autonomous in relation to their employees, there is still a centre of power and to make a difference one has to be in this center. (p. 154)

The Excellence theory would not appear to be internally inconsistent if one is aware that our concept of empowerment is not the same as the traditional concept of power, defined as the ability to control others. In *Excellence in Public Relations and Communication Management*, we distinguished between the perspectives of holding *power over others* versus *empowerment* of everyone in the organization. J. Grunig (1992a) called this the difference between asymmetrical and symmetrical concepts of power: "People in organizations use power asymmetrically when they try to control and make others dependent on them. . . . The symmetrical concept of power, in contrast, can be described as *empowerment*—of collaborating to increase the power of everyone in the organization, to the benefit of everyone in the organization" (p. 564). He quoted Frost (1987), who said:

Current writings and research on empowerment . . . treat . . . empowerment as the use of power to create opportunities and conditions through which actors can gain power, can make decisions, can use and expand their abilities and skills, can create and accomplish organizational work in ways that are meaningful to them. . . . (p. 539)

L. Grunig (1992) cited Kanter (1979), who also defined power as empowerment:

She studied both powerfulness and powerlessness. The latter, she contended, breeds bossiness—one main reason for empowering any bosses in organizations, including the head of the public relations department. She also linked powerlessness with job dissatisfaction, explaining that accountability without power (responsibility for results without the resources to get them) creates frustration or failure or both. Think instead of the advantages to sharing power Kanter (1979) cited. Her revelation is that organizational power can grow—rather than shrink—by being shared. (p. 492)

Finally, J. Grunig (1992b) cited Kanter's (1983) distinction between integrated and segmented organizational structures and cultures. Segmented companies wall off departments in narrow compartments, whereas integrated companies "ensure that multiple perspectives will be taken into account in decisions" (p. 28).

The Excellence theory emphasizes the empowerment of public relations in the dominant coalition, not because that would allow public relations to help dictate organizational decisions but because empowerment allows the organization to benefit from the expertise of the public relations profession—something that is most likely to happen when the public relations function is in-volved in the strategic management of the organization.

Empowerment in Strategic Management

The importance of empowering public relations is clear if we look at strategic management as the arena in which important organizational problems are iden-tified and decisions are made about how to address those problems. Mintzberg (1994), for example, emphasized the process of strategic management more than the specific plans that result from the process. He defined planning as "a formalized procedure to produce articulated result, in the form of an integrated system of decisions" (p. 31); and he defined strategic as "an adjective to mean relatively consequential" (p. 27).

Our view of the empowerment of public relations also fits well with Knights and Morgan's (1991) and Knights' (1992) postmodern view of strategic manage-ment as a subjective process in which the participants from different manage-ment disciplines (such as marketing, finance, law, human resources, or public relations) assert their disciplinary identities. Public relations has value in this perspective because it brings a different set of problems and possible solutions into the strategic management arena. In particular, it brings the problems of stakeholder publics into decision making—publics who make up the environ-ment of the organization.

The environment, however, is not an objective reality that all managers will see in the same way. Weick (1979) pointed out that managers enact their envi-ronment; therefore, excellent public relations has value in strategic manage-ment because it enables the organization to enact those parts of the environ-ment that representatives from other management disciplines are unlikely to recognize and by helping strategic decision makers determine which stake-holder publics are "relatively consequential" to the decisions, to use Mintz-berg's (1994, p. 27) terms.

In some organizations, the head of public relations is empowered: He or she is a member of the power elite or has access to it. However, only practition-ers who know how to manage the function strategically have the necessary expertise to participate in the policy process of their organizations. Such com-municators, we establish herein, are empowered to act independently—as true professionals—while still cooperating with their peers who head the other departments of the organization. Maples (1981) found that managers value or-ganizational roles that demand autonomous decision making. The greater the autonomy, the greater the value that managers should hold for both the func-tion and for public relations practitioners.

In conceptualizing the relationship between public relations and strategic management in the first *Excellence* book, J. Grunig and Repper (1992) main-tained that public relations must be part of the overall strategic management process of an organization and that public relations itself must be managed strategically. At the organizational level, J. Grunig and Repper's model stated that the senior public relations practitioner should identify stakeholders, publics, and issues that arise around the consequences of organizational decisions. At the functional level of the public relations department, then, the model stated that communication programs should be developed for strategic publics identified at the organizational level. To be strategic, communication programs then should be planned, managed by objectives, and evaluated.

Figure 5.1 presents an improved model developed from J. Grunig and Repper's (1992) conceptualization of the role of public relations in the overall strategic management process of an organization and the nature of strategic management of public relations programs.[1] The central concepts in this model are Management Decisions at the top, Stakeholders and Publics at the right, and Relationship Outcomes at the left. Connecting management and publics are the consequences that the behavior of each has on the other—the interdependence between an organization and its environment that creates the need for a public relations function.

When strategic decision makers of an organization make decisions, they must interact with publics through the public relations function because their decisions will have consequences on publics or because the organization needs supportive relationships with publics in order to implement decisions and achieve organizational goals. Publics also might seek a relationship with an organization in order to seek a consequence from the organization—such as AIDS activists who try to get a pharmaceutical company to produce an orphan drug or an environmental group that seeks a reduction in pollution. Thus the consequences of organizational decisions (and behaviors resulting from those decisions) define who the publics of an organization are and, therefore, the publics with whom the organization needs a relationship.

J. Grunig and Repper (1992) described the role of public relations in the overall strategic management of an organization in terms of three stages: the stakeholder, publics, and issues stages. These stages can be seen on the right side of Fig. 5.1. When a strategic public relations practitioner (or practitioners) participates in strategic management, his or her major role is to scan the environment of organizational stakeholders to identify potential publics who might be affected by the consequences of decisions or who might be attempting to set the agenda for an organizational decision by seeking consequences from an organization. The double arrow labeled "consequences" in the upper-right corner of Fig. 5.1 shows this mutual influence of management and publics on each other.

J. Grunig and Repper (1992) viewed stakeholders as broad categories of people who might be affected by management decisions—such as employees, con-

---

[1]We acknowledge the contribution of Danny Moss of Manchester Metropolitan University in the United Kingdom and Chun-ju Hung of the University of Maryland in developing this model.

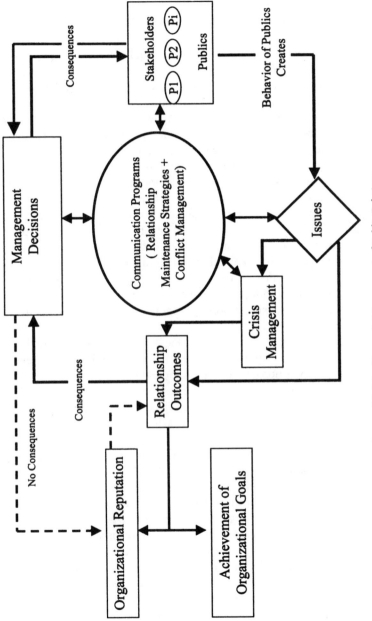

FIG. 5.1. Model of Strategic Management of Public Relations.

sumers, investors, or community residents. When a strategic public relations manager scans the environment, therefore, his or her first step should be to think broadly in terms of stakeholder categories. Then he or she should use a theory of publics, such as J. Grunig's (1997) situational theory of publics, to identify and segment active, passive, and latent publics from the nonpublics that might also be present in the stakeholder category.

It is important to segment active publics, because active publics typically behave in a way that makes issues out of the consequences of organizational decisions. This behavior may be individual or it may be collective—when members of publics organize into activist groups. Sometimes publics react negatively to harmful consequences of an organization's behaviors—such as pollution or discrimination. At other times, they act positively to try to secure a behavior from an organization that has useful consequences for them. At other times, publics collaborate with organizations to secure consequences of benefit to both.

Figure 5.1 then shows that publics that cannot stop the consequences that harm them or secure the consequences that benefit them generally make issues out of the consequences. Issues, in turn, can become crises if they are not handled well. When issues or potential issues are discussed and negotiated with publics, the result is improved relationships with publics. And, as we saw in chapter 4, relationships with publics have a crucial role in achieving organizational goals and in producing a positive reputation for the organization. The major role of public relations in strategic management, therefore, is encompassed in the inner loop of connections in Fig. 5.1—a process based on building relationship with strategic publics. Those relationships affect the achievement of goals and the reputation of the organization at the outer left of the figure— but they are not the only factors that have an effect on those two variables. The behavior of management, the economic environment, and the contribution of other management functions also affect the achievement of goals and organizational reputation.

At the center of the strategic processes described in Fig. 5.1 is the oval representing communication programs—programs to build and maintain relationships with publics and to manage conflict with publics. As originally stated by J. Grunig and Repper (1992), communication with potential publics is needed before decisions are made by strategic decision makers, when publics have formed but not created issues or crises, and during issue and crisis stages. Communication programs at the latter two stages are generally termed issues management and crisis communication by public relations practitioners. What Fig. 5.1 attempts to demonstrate, however, is that communication with publics before decisions are made is most effective in resolving issues and crises because it helps managers to make decisions that are less likely to produce consequences that publics make into issues and crises. If a public relations function does not communicate with publics until an issue or crisis occurs, the chance of resolving the conflict is difficult.

The center oval in Fig. 5.1 contains what J. Grunig and Repper (1992) called the strategic management of public relations programs themselves—as opposed to the participation of public relations in the overall strategic management of the organization. They stated that such programs should begin with formative research, then develop achievable and measurable objectives, implement the program, and end with evaluation of whether the objectives have been met. The extent to which excellent public relations programs follow such a process is examined in chapter 9. In addition, J. Grunig and Repper said that communication programs would be more effective if they are symmetrical (attempting to balance the interests of organizations and their publics) rather than asymmetrical (concerned only about the interest of the organization). The extent to which excellent public relations functions have symmetrical rather than asymmetrical objectives is examined in chapter 8.

The final path in Fig. 5.1 is the dotted-line path from "Management Decisions" to "Organizational Reputation" to "Relationship Outcomes"—a path labeled "No Consequences." This path seems to capture the approach to public relations advocated by many rhetorical scholars of public relations, advocates of integrated marketing communication, and advocates of reputation management. Such scholars seem to believe that positive messages—mostly disseminated through the mass media—about management decisions can create a positive organizational reputation. Such a path would produce what we call a "reputational relationship"—a relationship based on limited involvement of an "audience" (but not a "public") with an organization. J. Grunig (1993) also called this a symbolic rather than a behavioral relationship between an organization and people outside the organization.

We believe that publicity about management decisions can create such a reputational relationship between an organization and the audience exposed to the messages. And, we believe that such a reputational relationship appears in many of the popular measures of reputation such as the *Fortune* magazine list of Most Admired Corporations. As Verčič (2000) showed, however, negative messages about bad behaviors of management are more likely to affect a reputational relationship than are "business as usual" messages (p. 123)—which are generally defined as "positive" messages in most commercially available analyses of media coverage. As a result, the positive publicity approach to public relations has little effect—or value.

We have labeled the dotted line "No Consequences" because we believe that organizations have reputational relationships only with people for whom the organization has no consequences. We have described such people as audiences rather than publics because they are not truly publics—groups of people who are affected by the consequences of organizational decisions and who organize to do something about the consequences (J. Grunig & Hunt, 1984). As such, these audiences have little importance to an organization because they have no consequences themselves on the organization. As soon as an organization or public has consequences on the other, they begin to develop an involving behavioral relationship rather than low-involvement reputational relationships. It is at that point that they become active and strategic publics rather than passive audiences.

In this chapter, we see that excellent practitioners of public relations, to a great extent, participate in a strategic management process like that described in the inner loop of Fig. 5.1. However, we also see that many practitioners equate participation in strategic management with producing messages for the dotted-line loop and that many still do not truly understand the role of public relations in strategic management.

Empowering Diverse Practitioners

In addition to the empowerment of public relations in the dominant coalition and in strategic management, we posed questions about gender because of the growing diversity of the field of public relations and of the workforce in general. These queries were appropriate for male as well as female participants in the research process; feminization of the field will affect everyone who practices public relations. One of our goals was to elicit helpful suggestions or remedies for the discrimination that disadvantaged groups often encounter at work. As a result of much recent research on women in public relations (e.g., Hon, 1992), our questions were geared more toward organizational—rather than individual—solutions.

We framed our discussion of these issues in the concept of multicultural diversity. We reasoned that the organization that discriminates against women or members of racioethnic minorities fails to capitalize on all its human resources. By contrast, the effective organization provides equal opportunities for men and women throughout the company. In public relations, avoiding sexism and other forms of oppression takes on special importance: The growing diversity of both the workforce and the environment means that the excellent public relations department must be equally diverse, an implication of Weick's (1979) principle of requisite variety. However, the work of Johnson and Acharya (1981) showed that gender is a significant determinant of public relations role and power in the organization.

Individual Characteristics Leading to Empowerment

As part of our exploration of empowerment, we posed a group of questions that dealt specifically with public relations—history of the department, expertise of the top communicator, career development, and participation in strategic management. Participation in strategic management allows public relations practitioners to evolve beyond the reactive style of traditional communicators who respond to an endless stream of crises. Strategic communication programs, we demonstrate in this chapter, are proactive. They anticipate areas of potential conflict with key publics and move to reduce emergent conflicts before hard-and-fast positions on such issues have been taken by either activists or the organization's dominant coalition. As a result, they help avoid expensive government regulation, litigation, or pressure from dissatisfied employees or outside groups.

We know from the literature of dispute resolution that win–win solutions to potential conflicts are best negotiated in the early stages of conflict, before the parties involved take rigid public positions. We also understand, from theories of publics, that public relations practitioners who are strategic help the organization determine which parties in its environment are most critical to it at the time.

But what qualifies some communicators to play this strategic role? The literature establishes that characteristics of practitioners themselves are a significant predictor of exclusion from the dominant coalition. These factors include lack of business expertise (Lesly, 1981; Lindenmann & Lapetina, 1981); passivity (Anshen, 1974); naivete about organizational politics (Nowlan & Shayon, 1984); and inadequate education, experience, or organizational status (Anshen, 1974). We were interested in determining the opposite side of this coin—factors that predict *inclusion* in the powerful group of top managers that shape the organization's ideology.

RESULTS PERTAINING TO STRATEGIC MANAGEMENT AND PUBLIC RELATIONS

In the theoretical conceptualization of the Excellence study, we predicted that communication departments cannot make organizations more effective unless public relations functions as an integral part of management. We further suggested that the senior public relations practitioner must be part of the dominant coalition, function at a high level of decision making, and participate in strategic management if public relations is to be excellent and is to make the organization more effective.

More specifically, the proposition tested in this section of the chapter about empowerment of public relations is as follows: *Public relations is most likely to be excellent—to contribute to organizational effectiveness—when it is an integral part of an organization's strategic management process and when public relations itself is managed strategically.*

The arena of strategic management may represent the greatest difference between excellence and mediocrity in public relations. In the least excellent organizations, communication played virtually no part in strategic decision making. In most organizations that scored high in overall Excellence, members of the public relations department described their vital role in strategic management.

Quantitative Results Relating to Strategic Management

This chapter addresses the question of whether excellent public relations departments are represented in strategic decision making at the organizational level, because that relationship with top management is a major indicator of the empowerment of public relations. In addition, we address the strategic management of specific public relations programs in chapter 9, which presents results on the origins and outcomes of public relations programs.

Both the questionnaire for the head of public relations and for the CEO asked two questions about the relationship of public relations to the organization's strategic planning. The first question asked the top communicator and the CEO to "describe the extent to which your public relations department makes a contribution to each of the following functions of your organization: (a) strategic planning, (b) response to major social issues, (c) major initiatives [e.g., acquisitions, major new programs, movements into new markets, launches of new products or services], and (d) routine operations [e.g., development and maintenance of employee communication, community relations, or media relations programs]." The first three of these alternatives indicate the involvement of public relations in overall management; the fourth indicates the contribution of public relations only at the functional level.

The second question asked the PR heads and CEOs who said that public relations makes some contribution to "strategic planning and decision making" to estimate the extent to which public relations contributes to strategic processes in six ways: "(a) regularly conducted and routine research activities, (b) specific research conducted to answer specific questions, (c) formal approaches to gathering information for use in decision making other than research, (d) informal approaches to gathering information, (e) contacts with knowledgeable people outside the organization, and (f) judgement based on experience."

Table 5.1 first reports the mean responses to these questions. That table also includes the correlation of the responses to these questions with the overall index of excellence and three of the variables related to the managerial role that were part of the index: the extent to which the top communicator estimated that her or his role is that of the manager and senior adviser, the extent to which the CEO thought the top communicator should enact one or both of these managerial roles, and the knowledge that the top communicator estimated was available in the public relations department to enact a managerial role.

The mean scores in Table 5.1 generally are close to the hypothetical average answer of 10 on the transformed fractionation scale. The means also differ little for the top communicators and the CEOs, although the top communicators were somewhat more likely to say they are part of strategic planning than were the CEOs. Both PR heads and CEOs gave higher scores for the involvement of public relations in routine operations than in the more strategic organizational functions—suggesting that public relations more often is routine than strategic in the organizations sampled.

TABLE 5.1
Pearson Correlations of Strategic Public Relations Variables
With Index of Excellence and Managerial Variables

	N	Mean[a]	Excellence Index	Manager Role	Senior Adviser Role	Knowl. Man. Role
Contribution to Organizational Functions						
Strategic Planning						
PR Head	375	10.09	.51**[b]	.29**	.27**	.38**
CEO	288	9.07	.32**[b]	.26**	.23**	.13*
Response to Major Social Issues						
PR Head	377	11.68	.44**	.31**	.29**	.42**
CEO	287	11.79	.41**	.34**	.38**	.26**
Major Initiatives						
PR Head	376	11.20	.45**	.31**	.24**	.34**
CEO	290	10.93	.28**	.36**	.32**	.07
Routine Operations						
PR Head	376	12.83	.43**	.47**	.34**	.41**
CEO	290	12.66	.38**	.33**	.37**	.18**
Contribution to Strategic Planning						
Regular Research						
PR Head	329	7.68	.54**	.20**	.25**	.47**
CEO	246	8.30	.30**	.37**	.29**	.08
Specific Research						
PR Head	331	8.89	.49**	.21**	.21**	.43**
CEO	247	9.55	.27**	.31**	.23**	.05
Formal Approaches to Gathering Information						
PR Head	331	8.64	.58**	.28**	.28**	.47**
CEO	243	9.14	.27**	.32**	.28**	.04
Informal Approaches to Gathering Information						
PR Head	333	11.28	.22**	.13*	.12*	.18*
CEO	248	10.71	.34**	.37**	.31**	.09
Contacts Outside Organization						
PR Head	334	11.62	.38**	.28**	.32**	.32**
CEO	247	11.63	.30**	.40**	.39**	.00
Judgment Based on Experience						
PR Head	319	11.60	.47**	.27**	.24**	.30**
CEO	172	11.56	.35**	.33**	.36**	.09

[a]The means reported in this column are the square-root transformation of the open-end fractionation scale. A score of 10 on the transformed scale is equivalent to the typical response of 100 on the original scale.
[b]The correlation of the Excellence scale with the PR head's estimation of his or her participation in strategic management and the CEO's estimation of that participation were calculated with the Excellence scale with that variable removed because the variable was part of the Excellence scale, and autocorrelations otherwise would result.
$*p < .05.$ $**p < .01.$

Both PR heads and CEOs also were less likely to say that public relations contributes to strategic planning through formal research (either regular or for specific questions) or through formal approaches than they were to say that it contributes through informal approaches to gathering information, contacts with knowledgeable people, and judgment based on experience. The latter differences indicate that informal methods of environmental scanning are more common than formal methods in these organizations.

The correlations with the Excellence index are moderate (about .30) to high (about .50) for all of the strategic variables in Table 5.1. The high correlation of public relations involvement in strategic planning resulted even though the PR head's estimation of his or her contribution and the CEO's estimate were removed from the Excellence scale to avoid autocorrelation—the correlation of a variable at least in part with itself because of its inclusion in the scale. The CEO's estimate of participation, however, correlated lower than did the top communicator's estimate.

The other strategic variables in Table 5.1 were not included in the Excellence index, however. Their correlations with excellence are almost as high, in general, as the correlation of involvement in strategic management. As with the correlations of involvement in strategic management, the variables as estimated by the top communicator generally were high and the estimates of the CEOs moderate. These differences could mean that the PR head knows better what his or her involvement is, or it could mean that PR heads were optimistic in estimating their contributions. The higher correlations with the estimates of the PR heads, however, suggest that the first explanation is more likely.

Two other patterns stand out in the correlations with the Excellence index. First, the correlations of "routine operations" with excellence are about as high as the correlations of the more strategic variables. This suggests that excellent departments are more active in *both* strategic and routine operations than are less excellent departments. Second, the correlations of regular and specific research and formal approaches to information gathering are higher for the PR heads than are informal approaches and outside contacts. "Judgment based on experience," however, correlates as highly as research and formal methods. These correlations show that excellent departments combine formal research and methods of environmental scanning with the experience of the top communicator when they contribute to strategic processes, although they do not ignore the traditional informal methods. The correlations for the CEOs are similar across both the formal and informal methods, however, suggesting they might not be fully aware of the extent of formal environmental scanning activities that even excellent public relations departments conduct.

The correlations of all of the strategic variables with the manager and senior advisor roles are moderate and similar for both roles and for both top communicators and CEOs. The similarity of the correlations for the more powerful managerial role and the less powerful senior advisor role suggests that top communicators, even in excellent departments, probably play both roles to some extent (see chap. 6 for more discussion of these roles). Both also were included in the Excellence index for this reason. The lower correlations of the strategic variables with these roles in contrast with the correlations with overall Excellence, however, provide evidence that not all public relations managers are *strategic* managers. Many probably supervise the routine operations of the public relations department more than they participate in strategic management of the organization. This difference suggests that future research on public relations roles should develop more categories of managerial roles.

For the CEOs, the correlations of the managerial role with all of the contributions to strategic planning are higher than for the PR heads, in contrast to the pattern in the rest of the table. These higher correlations seem to indicate that CEOs who think their top communicators should be managers also perceive that their PR heads are doing both formal and informal environmental scanning—an indicator that CEOs of excellent organizations do see the importance of environmental scanning by their public relations department for strategic decision processes.

The final column in Table 5.1 shows the correlation of our index of knowledge needed for the managerial role with the strategic variables. As we saw in chapter 3, the index of managerial knowledge was the strongest of all 20 indicators in the Excellence index. These correlations for the top communicators are consistently high, although as expected they are lower for the informal methods of contributing to strategic management. The higher correlations of this index of managerial knowledge than of the two managerial role enactment scales most likely occurred because the knowledge scale contained more items about knowledge needed for strategic management than for routine management. The strategic items in the index of managerial knowledge were "conduct evaluation research, provide objective information about your organization, develop goals and objectives for your department, perform environmental scanning, develop strategies for solving public relations and communication problems, use research to segment publics, and manage the organization's response to issues." Only "managing people" and "preparing a departmental budget" were more routine than strategic. The high correlations of this index with the strategic variables, therefore, show that excellent public relations departments have the knowledge to participate in strategic management and that they actually put that knowledge to use.

Table 5.1 shows that the correlations for the strategic variables estimated by the CEOs with this index of knowledge are not so high, however. The correlations with the contributions to strategic planning are not significant. In part, this lack of correlation could have occurred because the index of knowledge was estimated by the top communicator and the other variables by the CEO; and variables correlate less when the scores come from different people. Still, we expected the correlations to be higher. The low correlations probably mean that

CEOs do not fully recognize the capability of their public relations department, even in excellent organizations, or they are not fully aware of the contributions their communication departments make to strategic processes.

Qualitative Results Related to Strategic Management

In spite of the strong support we found in the quantitative results for involvement of public relations in strategic management, we discovered in our long interviews that strategic management and strategic planning both have myriad meanings. To the real estate development company, strategic planning is done strictly on a financial basis. It is no more than numbers crunching. As a result, public relations is out of the planning loop. To the oil company affiliate, which also was ranked toward the top in overall Excellence, strategic management in public affairs refers almost exclusively to media relations. One of its top communicators explained his principal role as "to represent the company in its interface with the media and other influential audiences." We can sum up the situation there as strategy flowing down, techniques flowing up and across.

In other organizations, strategic planning is an integral part of the public relations function. For example, in the excellent gas and electric company we studied, the manager of public affairs is part of a strategy team. Thus he is directly involved in the ongoing strategic management of the organization. The senior vice president there offered this evidence of his influence. Immediately following a merger, a communication issues team was set up. The manager of public affairs was paired with his counterpart at the other utility. Joining this team were representatives from internal communication, the rate division, and shareholder relations. The team developed the strategy that guided all of the organization's postmerger actions. Thus we see how merging with another public utility led to more recognition of communication's role in the strategic management of this company.

To the real estate development company alluded to earlier, however, communication does not enter into the CEO's worldview related to strategic planning. According to his top communicator, the CEO's overriding focus is on financial planning. Despite the expertise in his public relations department, he sees that function primarily as taking care of problems when they develop.

The medical association we studied provides an example of a public relations department involved in strategic planning *despite* what two of its top communicators described as the president's "lukewarm support" for public affairs. In this case, the association's board of directors has pushed the importance of communication. The support of this influential *group* seemingly outweighs the lack of interest on the part of the CEO. There, the assistant executive director for public affairs considered himself active in setting the "strategic agenda" for the whole organization. He gives advice to the board about the association's mission—extending far beyond communication goals.

A second communicator in the same organization saw the interplay between the communication function and strategic management differently. She considered her counterpart in public affairs *too* involved in strategy. She believed the public affairs function had taken over the strategic agenda of the entire association. As a consequence, she predicted a power struggle between the new president, who values participation, and the head of public affairs, whom she characterized as a "one-person kingdom."

Without question, the director of corporate communications plays an integral role in the overall strategic management of his chemical company. He provided a worst-case scenario as his illustration: the issue of environmental equity or environmental racism in areas where chemical plants are built. He said he is involved in planning for this concern right along with people from health, safety, and the environment; legal; and business. As he put it, "We're not just waiting for it to hit the fan." He added that some of this strategic planning is accomplished over lunch rather than as a more formal responsibility.

The vice president of strategic planning to whom the top communicator reports in this company explained the relationship between public affairs and strategic planning as follows:

> Most people perceive strategic planning over here at this end of the corporation and if you get through R&D, marketing, and manufacturing and all these things somewhere at the other end you have someone worrying about public affairs and public relations. My answer is that they have a linear view of a corporation. If you view a corporation as being a [cyclical] work process . . . then you take that linear view of the corporation and bend it around into a circle. Then it's funny, what comes together in the circle—strategic planning and public affairs.

He went on to say that everything in a company has to do with relations with the outside world. He also explained public affairs as more a two-way than a transmittal process. Thus, in his opinion, "It's perfectly logical for the public relations function to be directly tied to the strategic function."

The director of corporate communication in this company used a copyrighted flow chart to explain how members of his department have "moved from being order takers to strategic planners." This approach was characterized by an employee communication specialist we interviewed in the same company as "a methodical, planned way to do work that is tied into the business side of things." In a nutshell, the director said, it subjects any request for communication to an "alignment check." That is, it determines whether the request fits the company's overall strategic goals before committing resources to the project.

To summarize, relating public relations to strategic management may be the key to empowering the department from serving only a technical role to being regarded as a critical management function. However, our in-depth interviews showed that this concept means different things to different people. To some, such as the oil company affiliate, strategic management is sophisticated media relations. To others, it means managing the entire public relations department. To still others—such as the top communicators in the utility company, the industry association, and the chemical corporation—strategic management is not limited to communication with the media or supervision of one's own department. Instead, it extends throughout the organization and embodies that process defined by J. Grunig and Repper (1992) in the first *Excellence* book.

Public relations professionals in this role go beyond their traditional communication function to serve as counselors and strategic planners. They are involved in every dimension of the organization, largely through their collaboration with peers in other departments and within the dominant coalition. We saw such a relationship in the medical association. These relationships allow for access to the dominant coalition, even when the top communicator is not a regular member of that power elite and even when the CEO does not adequately value the function or that communicator's potential to help resolve confrontations.

The importance of managing conflict with strategic publics, in particular, is that it reduces the potential costs associated with their dissatisfaction. Participation in strategic management also elevates public relations from its traditional reactive style of responding to communication crises to a proactive, responsive style of anticipating and then helping reduce emerging conflicts.

By contrast, we found that the operation of average departments can be explained as more "historicist." They do what they do because they always have done so. The American arts organization, for example, was ranked in the 21st percentile in the quantitative phase of the Excellence study. The top communicator there fell in the 5th percentile regarding departmental knowledge and ability to enact the communication manager's role. Not surprisingly, the organization itself was disappointed with the "flat" performance of this department and the status quo of funding levels it had achieved for the last decade.[2] Managers of this kind of static program fail to conduct the research or engage in the environmental scanning necessary to identify emerging publics that could prove vital to their organization's long-term viability. They may manage their own departments adequately. However, they fail to tie in their departmental objectives with the larger goals of the organization. As a result, their contribution to overall organizational effectiveness is minimal.

In summary, therefore, we found strong support for the proposition linking excellent public relations with strategic management in both the qualitative and quantitative data amassed in this study. Excellent departments in our study were linked to strategic decision processes in almost exactly the way described

---

[2]Since then, top management made a conscious decision to hire a practitioner with appropriate skills in public relations. The organization seems to be evolving into a truly excellent one, thanks in part to this senior communicator, who is able to plan and execute a sophisticated public relations program.

in the J. Grunig and Repper (1992) model. They scanned the environment, especially through formal research, although they also used informal methods and their judgment based on experience. They provided the outside perspective needed by other participants in strategic decision making. However, we also found that not all CEOs, even in some organizations with excellent departments, fully understood what a strong public relations department can do for the organization or sometimes even what their department does. Some public relations heads also saw their involvement in strategic management in limited terms, such as only in media relations.

In general, however, we found that involvement in strategic management and knowledge of how to do environmental scanning and strategic thinking about public relations are probably the strongest attributes of excellent public relations departments. We also found a profile in our case studies of how the best public relations departments actually practice such strategic public relations.

RESULTS PERTAINING TO PUBLIC RELATIONS IN THE DOMINANT COALITION

The backgrounds of members of the research team in organizational sociology may have predisposed us to devalue the importance of any individual in today's complex corporation or government agency. Thus we put forth this proposition about the *group* that determines organizational policy: *To be an excellent department, public relations must be included within the dominant coalition.*

However, we came to acknowledge that individuals—through both their worldviews and their skills—actually do transform organizational processes. One of the most undeniable illustrations came from the industry association we studied. There, the head of public relations is credited with developing a program of citizen advisory panels that has changed his entire industry's way of operating and, concomitantly, its reputation.

A second case supports this argument for the potential influence of a single person. This case involves not an individual communicator but a top manager. It profiles an organization that is moving closer to excellence from its previous rank (higher than three fourths of the organizations surveyed but not at the top). After our initial survey research, the communication department in this chemical corporation began to report to a new vice president of strategic planning, investor relations, and public affairs. His background was in strategic planning. He recognized and made use of the knowledge of two senior communicators, one in corporate communication and the other in marketing communication. Today, the public relations function is part of strategic management.

Nevertheless, the policy of most organizations is determined not by an individual but by a group of powerful decision makers: the dominant coalition.

Thus we proposed that public relations cannot fulfill its potential unless the top communicator is included in the dominant coalition.

Quantitative Results Related to the Dominant Coalition

The questionnaires for both the senior communicator and the CEO included a question asking the respondents to indicate who they believed were members of the dominant coalition in their organization. The question began with a description of the dominant coalition: "Today's organizations are so complex that many of them require more than a single leader to operate effectively. Instead of a single powerful person, then, many organizations are controlled by a *group* of powerful people—often called the 'dominant coalition.' In your organization, who is represented in this power elite?"

The PR heads and CEOs first were asked to indicate whether each of four specific senior managers were part of the dominant coalition: "the chief executive officer; the chief financial officer; the chief operating officer; and the head of public relations, public affairs, or communication." This list made it possible for us to compare the frequency of membership of public relations with three other officers who typically are members of the dominant coalition. Both respondents then were asked to list any other top managers they believed were members of the dominant coalition.

In addition to these internal members of the dominant coalition, we also asked whether the dominant coalition might contain members from outside the organization—following the suggestion of Mintzberg (1983), who had conceptualized a number of coalitions of external groups with internal coalitions. Therefore, we asked the two respondents if representatives of specific external groups also were part of the dominant coalition. Because these groups represented external constituencies with whom public relations departments typically build relationships, we expected they would be represented more often in organizations with high scores on the Excellence factor. Respondents were asked to indicate if six specific groups were represented in the dominant coalition: "owners/stockholders, employee associations, clients, suppliers, competitors, and activist groups." They then were asked again to list any other external groups they considered to be members of the dominant coalition.

Table 5.2 reports the results for the four top managers listed on the questionnaire. It shows the percentage of respondents in all organizations who indicated that each top manager was in the dominant coalition and compares it with the percentage in the organizations with the most excellent public relations function—those with a z score on the Excellence factor greater than 1.0, which roughly represented the top 10% of public relations departments. Not surprisingly, the senior public relations officer was least likely of the four top managers

TABLE 5.2
Frequency of Membership of Internal Managers in Dominant Coalition
and Comparison of Public Relations Excellence by Membership

Member of DC	N	%	% z > 1.0[a]	Excellence Score (z Scores)		T
				In DC	Not in DC	
	(Multiple Responses)					
CEO						
CEO Report	281	98	97	.01	.10	0.33
PR Report	359	97	97	−.01	.49	2.05**
Chief Financial Officer						
CEO Report	226	79	72	.03	−.05	0.62
PR Report	254	67	71	.05	−.05	0.92
Chief Operating Officer						
CEO Report	193	68	59	.02	.00	0.20
PR Report	233	63	58	.05	−.04	0.80
Public Relations						
CEO Report	123	43	73	.34	−.22	5.44**
PR Report	174	47	61	.19	−.12	3.07**

[a]N (CEOs) = 29; N (PR heads) = 38.
*$p < .05$. **$p < .01$.

to be chosen as a member of the dominant coalition. Still, nearly half of the CEOs and PR heads chose public relations. In organizations with the most excellent public relations functions, this percentage rose dramatically to 61% reported by the PR head and 73% reported by the CEO. In those organizations, public relations was represented in the dominant coalition as frequently as the chief financial officer and the chief operating officer.

The importance of representation in the dominant coalition also can be seen in the last three columns of Table 5.2, which compare the mean scores on the Excellence factor for organizations in which each of these top managers is part of the dominant coalition with those for which he or she is not a part. With one exception, there was no significant difference for the top managers other than public relations. For public relations, there was a highly significant difference in excellence when public relations was reported to be in the dominant coalition compared to when the senior communicator was not included—especially when the membership was reported by the CEO. Interestingly, excellence was greater when the PR head reported that the CEO was *not* in the dominant coalition, but the number in this category was too low to make much sense of that difference.

In summary, Table 5.2 provides strong confirmation for our major proposition about the participation of public relations in the dominant coalition: Public relations is more excellent when the top communicator is a part of the dominant coalition, especially when the CEO recognizes his or her participation in that power elite.

Table 5.3 lists other internal members of the dominant coalition who were volunteered by either the PR head or CEO in an open-end question and compares the percentage of respondents overall who listed each category with the percentage of respondents in organizations with excellent public relations departments. The major pattern in this table is that most groups are mentioned more frequently by respondents in excellent organizations than in the overall sample. In particular, the percentage of "managers germane to communication" increased in organizations with excellent public relations departments compared to the average whereas the percentage of "managers outside communication" decreased. Likewise, the percentage of CEOs who mentioned managers of "environmental/external affairs" nearly tripled in organizations with excellent public relations.

Other categories suggest that organizations that include managers from outside the very top of the hierarchy in the dominant coalition are more likely to have excellent public relations—indicated by the higher percentage of "heads of operating units," "department directors," and "administrative officers." The latter is especially interesting because public relations often reports to an administrative officer when it does not report directly to the CEO. At the same time, organizations with excellent public relations were somewhat less likely to report

TABLE 5.3

Frequency of Membership of Other Internal Managers in Dominant Coalition of All Organizations and Organizations With Excellent Public Relations

Member of DC	PR Head			CEO		
	N	%	% z > 1.0 (N = 38)	N	%	% z > 1.0 (N = 29)
		(Multiple Responses)				
Other Senior Executive	271	84	79			
Legal Officer	47	15	18	49	19	24
Head Operating Unit	77	24	42	63	24	24
Technical/Research Head	28	9	16	26	10	21
Manager Germane to Communication	15	5	13			
Managers Outside Communication	88	27	13			
Corporate Secretary	4	1	8	8	3	10
Division Directors	52	16	0			
Department Director	88	27	34			
Board of Directors	8	2	0			
Executive Committee	4	1	0			
Board President	1	0	0			
Planning Officer				35	13	14
Human Resources				43	16	3
Marketing/Sales				73	28	34
Administrative Officer				21	8	17
Environmental/External Affairs				33	13	31
Others	119	37	42			

additional officers at the top of the hierarchy in the dominant coalition—"other senior executives" and "division directors."

Somewhat surprisingly, CEOs with excellent public relations departments less often reported the senior human relations officers to be a member of the dominant coalition. The percentage of marketing heads in the dominant coalition, however, increased slightly in the excellent organizations. Interestingly, heads of technical or research functions were reported to be in the dominant coalition more often in the organizations with excellent public relations.

Overall, therefore, Table 5.3 suggests that public relations is empowered more in organizations with flat structures than in organizations with tall structures—that is, in organizations that empower managers throughout the organization, not just those at the very top of the hierarchy.

Table 5.4 switches the focus to the six external groups listed in the questionnaire. Comparing the percentage of respondents overall who reported each group with the percentage of respondents in organizations with excellent public relations shows a tendency to list more external groups in the dominant coalitions of excellent organizations—as we expected. In addition, the heads of public relations were more likely to suggest additional external groups than

TABLE 5.4

Frequency of Membership of External Groups in Dominant Coalition
and Comparison of Public Relations Excellence by Membership

				Excellence Score (z Scores)		
Member of DC	N	%	% z > 1.0^a	In DC	Not in DC	T
	(Multiple Responses)					
Owners/Stockholders						
CEO Report	62	24	24	.05	.00	0.35
PR Report	80	25	32	.14	−.02	1.35
Employee Associations						
CEO Report	24	9	14	.28	−.05	1.51
PR Report	35	11	18	.36	−.05	2.31**
Clients						
CEO Report	37	14	17	.07	.01	0.36
PR Report	45	14	21	.35	−.03	2.50**
Suppliers						
CEO Report	13	5	3	−.12	.02	0.54
PR Report	18	6	13	.34	.00	1.57
Competitors						
CEO Report	9	3	7	.61	.00	2.11*
PR Report	15	5	11	.76	−.02	3.29**
Activist Groups						
CEO Report	13	5	0	−.26	.03	1.14
PR Report	18	6	13	.62	−.02	2.84**

^{a}N (CEOs) = 29; N (PR heads) = 38.
*p < .05. **p < .01.

were the CEOs. The greatest difference between PR heads and CEOs was for activists.

The last three columns of the table, then, compare the average score on the Excellence factor of organizations that mentioned each group with those that did not mention them. These columns show that excellence is higher when the top communicator reports that four of the six groups are represented in the dominant coalition—"employee associations," "clients," "competitors," and "activists." Although the differences were not significant, the Excellence scores also were higher when the PR head chose "owners/stockholders" and "suppliers" as part of the dominant coalition. In contrast, the difference in excellence was significant for the CEOs only when they included "competitors" in the dominant coalition; and this difference was significant only at the .05 level.

Table 5.5, finally, lists the responses to the open-end question that asked respondents to suggest other external members of the dominant coalition. These responses generally were widely scattered and in small numbers, and they showed few differences between the average and excellent organizations. The two most frequent suggestions were "boards of directors" and "government." For "boards of directors," the percentage of responses did not differ between average organizations and those with excellent public relations. The percentage mentioning government more than doubled in excellent organizations, however; and more top communicators mentioned it than did CEOs.

TABLE 5.5
Frequency of Membership of Other External Groups
in Dominant Coalition of All Organizations and
Organizations With Excellent Public Relations

	PR Head			CEO		
Member of DC	N	%	% z > 1.0 (N = 38)	N	%	% z > 1.0 (N = 29)
			(Multiple Responses)			
Government	27	8	18	12	5	13
Members, Customers, Financial Supporters, Directors	10	3	0	11	4	3
Committee Chairs	5	2	0	6	2	3
Outside Board	1	0	0	2	1	0
Financial Advisers	2	1	0	2	1	0
Executive Committee	5	2	5	3	1	3
General Counsel	5	2	0			
Volunteers	6	2	0	5	2	0
Board of Directors	32	10	8	18	7	7
Legislative Affairs	2	1	0			
Alumni	2	1	0	2	1	7
Others	59	18	21			

In short, PR heads were more likely than CEOs to name outside groups as members of the dominant coalition; but they did so only in organizations with excellent public relations departments. Tables 5.4 and 5.5, therefore, provide additional evidence of the role of excellent public relations in strategic management. Top communicators in those organizations seem to recognize outside groups more than do CEOs as members of the organization's dominant coalition—suggesting that they are the managers in the organization most likely to understand and recognize the power of these groups to affect organizational decisions.

Because the data on the relationship of excellence in public relations and membership in the dominant coalition suggest that organizations that empower more people in general tend also to empower public relations, we calculated a new variable, "size of the dominant coalition," and correlated it with the Excellence factor. To calculate the size of the dominant coalition, we added all the managers cited by the CEOs and PR heads to both the closed- and open-end questions about internal and external members of the dominant coalition. The results showed that PR heads, in general, named one more member of the dominant coalition than did CEOs. The mean number named by top communicators is 5.77 members of the dominant coalition (standard deviation of 2.56). The mean named by CEOs is 4.78 (standard deviation of 2.05).

Correlational statistics showed that the larger the dominant coalition, the greater the excellence of public relations in the organization. The correlation is largest when the CEO named a larger dominant coalition: For PR heads, the correlation is .14 ($p < .05$); for CEOs, the correlation is .26 ($p < .01$).

We then compared the size of the dominant coalition by type of organization and size of organization and found no significant differences between any two types or sizes of organizations. Corporations, government agencies, associations, and nonprofit organizations generally had about the same number of members in the dominant coalition. Likewise organizations with more than 50,000 employees had only one more member of the dominant coalition as reported by the top communicator (mean of 6.68, standard deviation of 2.78) than organizations with fewer than 500 employees (mean of 5.51, standard deviation of 2.48). When reported by the CEO, the difference was even smaller: mean of 4.91 (standard deviation of 1.45) for large organizations versus a mean of 4.60 (standard deviation of 2.03) for small organizations.

We can conclude from these data on the dominant coalition that organizations that empower their employees in general are most likely to empower public relations. These empowering organizations can be large or small. They are equally likely to be corporate, governmental, association, and nonprofit organizations. The organizations, in turn, that empower public relations are more likely to have excellent public relations functions. In organizations with excellent public relations, external groups are more likely to be empowered in management decisions than they are in organizations with less excellent public relations.

In the quantitative analysis, we also examined data related to our second proposition about the participation of public relations in this powerful group of decision makers: *To increase their access to the dominant coalition, public relations practitioners should increase their own expertise via education, experience, and professionalism.* To test this proposition quantitatively, we compared the mean scores on six variables related to knowledge and education in public relations for organizations in which the top communicator or the CEO reported that the head of public relations is a member of the dominant coalition with organizations in which the top communicator is not a member. These variables included academic training in public relations, readership of professional publications, membership in professional associations, and the indexes of knowledge in the public relations department to practice the managerial role, the two-way symmetrical model, and the two-way asymmetrical model.

These comparisons provided only limited support for the proposition. Mean scores on education in public relations, readership of publications, and membership in professional associations were almost identical regardless of whether the PR head was in the dominant coalition, as reported by both the top communicator and the CEO. Knowledge to practice the two-way symmetrical and two-way asymmetrical models was slightly higher when the PR head was in the dominant coalition, but the difference was not statistically significant. The only significant difference occurred for knowledge to practice the managerial role, both as reported by the top communicator ($t = 2.09$, $p < .05$) and the CEO ($t = 2.51$, $p < .05$).

It seems, therefore, that managerial knowledge affects whether other top managers include the top communicator in the power elite but that understanding of other aspects of excellent public relations has little effect. To understand the subtleties of how PR heads get into the dominant coalition, we need the more in-depth insights provided by our qualitative results.

Qualitative Results Related to the Dominant Coalition

The cases we explored in depth also provided partial support for the proposition that public relations is more likely to be excellent when the function is part of or close to the dominant coalition. We begin with the engineering experiment station. Although the top communicator is not yet a regular participant within the dominant coalition, she expressed confidence in approaching those who are. She said: "You need to feel comfortable to walk into his [the CEO's] office and say, 'Hello, what's going on?' If that atmosphere doesn't exist, there is nothing you an do to make it be that way." A second instance comes from the cosmetics company, where the top communicator consults regularly with the CEO on most strategic matters, even those outside his area of expertise. As the head of the public relations firm representing the company, however, he does not participate in daily decisions made by members of the dominant coalition. Both of these top communicators have access to the dominant coalition, rather than actually belonging to that powerful group.

The head of public affairs for the medical association contended that communicators must participate in strategic management of the overall organization to be a true part of the dominant coalition. In his view, thinking strategically *as a communicator* will not lead necessarily to the senior management role. He emphasized that communicators must make a contribution beyond their specialized area. We found that in most organizations deemed excellent, the real reason top communicators and their CEOs value communication is because they understand that communication works with other managerial functions to build quality, long-term relationships with all strategic publics. Public relations professionals who do so have managed to surpass their traditional communicative role to function as counselors, negotiators, and strategic planners. They are involved in every dimension of the organization—and especially with the dominant coalition.

The nature of some organizations seems to preclude this advisory role. The chairman of the oil company affiliate we studied limits the communicative function to media relations largely because this affiliate rarely has a fundamental effect on the parent company. The extent of public affairs, then, is to provide what one of its top communicators called "input": "For example, if I detect that something the marketers are doing is not going to be very well received by customers or public at large, then I can go along—either directly to the line manager concerned or to [the public affairs manager] who raises it with the chairman."

Regardless of the nature of the industry or the organization's culture, CEOs tend not, as one president himself put it, to "enshrine the PR function." Instead, they simply expect good work and believe that good pay for it is adequate reward.

Part of this lack of recognition for what public relations can accomplish at the highest level stems from a phenomenon that may be peculiar to CEOs: their belief that once they have experienced something, they are expert in it. As an industry association CEO said: "If they go into an advertising program, they immediately become expert copywriters. If they have a successful public relations effort, they immediately become public relations counselors. If they made a suggestion in a piece of litigation, then they immediately become more capable in handling the legal problems, government relations on the Hill, state affairs. . . ." He considered this "a terrible mistake." Just because a CEO gains experience in an aspect of communication does not mean that he or she garners the proficiency of the staff experts.

A second, related problem involving CEOs may be the nature of their education. The top communicator at the disabled services agency believed that the only way for public relations ultimately to be considered part of the dominant coalition is to include the public relations curriculum in schools of business. She reasoned: "Business schools are where our future CEOs are being trained. They will only consider important that which they, too, have had to master." With the current situation, she contended, MBAs are taught to discount public relations because it will not lead to a top-management track.

At least one association head we talked with agreed about the importance of including the head of public relations in the dominant coalition and empowering that person to take risks. But how does a public relations practitioner become a member of the dominant coalition? To answer that question, we return to our second proposition related to the participation of public relations in this powerful group of decision makers: *To increase their access to the dominant coalition, public relations practitioners should increase their own expertise via education, experience, and professionalism.*

Excellent public relations programs require expert practitioners. Not every communicator knows how to manage the department strategically and symmetrically. We learned from our long interviews that practitioners might acquire mastery of the rapidly expanding theoretical body of knowledge in this field from several sources. Many of the professionals we talked with had gained their understanding from college coursework in public relations, and we predict that their number will increase exponentially. (University programs are beginning to go beyond technical training to emphasize the managerial role and two-way models of public relations.) Other participants in our research, however, have relied on experience, self-study, and professional development courses to gain a toehold with the dominant coalition.

Before elaborating on these findings, we must point out that participants agreed that many organizations—excellent and mediocre—do not include their top communicators in the power elite. Even the vice president and director of corporate affairs at an organization ranked in the 99th percentile of overall Excellence is not a member of the dominant coalition in her development and management company.

Second, we would add the word *slowly* to the process of gaining access to top management. Only over time does even the most expert communicator become a true part of this influential group. As the manager of communication at the engineering experiment station put it, she takes one step at a time to offer her counsel. She said: "You have to build . . . You can't press it [becoming part of the dominant coalition] on people . . . especially in what has traditionally been a very hierarchical society [the academy]."

Similarly, a manager of communication in an industry association believed that, regardless of one's position description, "You have to earn your stripes." One CEO explained that his top communicator had the confidence of only one or two other vice presidents initially. Because of the communicator's substantial contributions and concomitant change in culture, however, he came to be accepted within the circle of top decision makers. According to the CEO, his acceptance took "a lot of knocking and arguing and cajoling and seminaring and mentoring."

Beyond longevity, what efforts have individuals in public relations made to gain the expertise, especially in communication management, that would empower them to join the dominant coalition? One senior vice president at a utility company considered his lack of formal education in public relations an asset. Because of his initial naivete about communication, he entered the field "unencumbered with any bias or prejudice as to how to best practice." Working together with a public relations firm, he has managed to develop the strategic nature of public relations in his organization. However, this communication department has been downsized since the original survey. No one today is strictly involved in managerial activities.

More of the cases we studied established education as pivotal. Of course, we wondered why education was so much more important to some practitioners than to others. Apparently this value is instilled early on. As one interviewee, who has a graduate degree in journalism, explained, his midwestern upbringing led him to appreciate continuing education—whether formal or informal. He said he had learned as much on the job and through mentors as in college.

This vice president considers himself still in the learning stage, despite years of experience in both association and corporate public relations as well as in community journalism. At the time of our interviews, he had been nominated for *Public Relations Quarterly*'s "Corporate PR Superstar." Among the countless reasons cited for this honor, he was credited with "transforming what was a staid, archaic, largely ineffective association PR department into a modern, highly effective and respected operation" (Bishop, 1993, p. 3).

During the course of our interview with this top communicator, we learned that he continues to study the professional literature of public relations. He alluded to having read recent research results that talked about "obtaining behaviors from the target publics" and "building an interest in one's organization." He brought his years of experience to bear in thinking about that survey:

> It reminds me of other thoughts I constantly have and do battle with. "Communication," "outreach," "education"—all of those are good words, but the way we think of them, and sometimes use them as something to educate other people so they will begin thinking our way—I think if we go down that track, we're in for nothing but trouble . . . as opposed to encouraging a process that listens, that responds, that changes, that improves.

The vice president called his appreciation for this kind of two-way balanced communication "an important lesson we have been learning"—and something that distinguishes contemporary public relations from the profession 30 years ago.

Many practitioners in this qualitative study were also journalism majors. Others had studied communication, anthropology, history, educational administration, English, and economics. Quite a few had master's degrees. More, such as the manager of communication and the publication editor at the engineering and technology research agency, said they had learned by "trial and error." (Although this organization scored in the 97th percentile 3 years ago in overall Excellence, its top communicator ranked the department at about the midpoint in terms of expertise available there to play the managerial role and even lower in expertise in two-way public relations.)

This approach to learning is what the director of sales at a direct-marketing company called "hands on." She also learned by what she called "osmosis" from the past president. She said she "listened to him on the phone and listened to him talk to people. He was a great trainer and a great leader." She considered him "always the marketer."

To that experience and role modeling, two midlevel communicators we interviewed added extensive involvement with IABC. Their manager pays for them to attend frequent conferences and workshops. She herself recently studied for the ABC accreditation exam and completed her master's degree with an emphasis on public relations.

Again and again, we heard similar stories about the importance of self-education. One head of public affairs, for example, attributed his expertise in enacting the senior management role to buying and reading major texts in public relations. He also participates actively in IABC. To this self-study and professional involvement, he added his former work as an aide to a Cabinet minister and as a reporter. (Predictably, many of our participants had experience in journalism.)

One senior communicator alluded to his knowledge both of communication and of the chemical industry. He gained the latter primarily through helping the company deal with its crises. During downsizing, for example, he learned he had to be a businessperson as well as a professional communicator. His cutting-edge knowledge of communication came not through a degree in that field but, beyond experience, through regular reading of professional publications and research journals. He listed *Communication Research* and *Journal of Communication* specifically. A specialist in employee communication in his office mentioned learning from her internship experience and reading about employee communication in publications of Hewitt Associates.

The next chapter goes into considerable depth on how education and other factors already alluded to here help ambitious practitioners make the transition from technician to manager. In so doing, they qualify themselves for inclusion in the dominant coalition. Among the key attributes explored in chapter 6 are expertise in the industry, important external contacts (both people and information), longevity with the company, expertise in strategic planning and two-way symmetrical communication, envisioning oneself as a manager, and thinking like a CEO.

We conclude our answer to the question of potential for public relations in the dominant coalition with a contrary yet dramatic example. The practice of the oil company affiliate we studied was to hire a non-public-affairs person to administer the department. That person typically was a line manager or some other long-time employee who needed the public affairs experience to advance. The affiliate's philosophy was that you can teach public relations techniques, but you cannot teach the company's culture and industry. As one communicator there described the manager of public affairs, "[He] runs the department; but if it came to what's the difference between [gasoline] and diesel, he really doesn't have a clue."

In summary, we did find support for the proposition that public relations professionals will increase their access to the dominant coalition through education, experience, and professionalism. However, we found no single route to this knowledge and experience. Mostly, we can say that practitioners who have access to the dominant coalition are knowledgeable—both about public relations and the organization for which they work—and experienced. However, they have gained that knowledge in a number of different ways.

Related to this proposition is another one we proposed that refers to how members of the dominant coalition think about public relations. Throughout this chapter, we explore the question of empowerment—how some public relations practitioners manage to reach high-level positions where they are able to make their greatest contributions to the organizations that employ them. We know that the answer undoubtedly lies in part with those astute and ambitious communicators. Another critical factor, of course, is the worldview that members of the dominant coalition have for their function. Thus we proposed: *Members of dominant coalitions in excellent organizations will come to value public relations as a critical managerial—rather than merely technical—organizational function.*

Public relations becomes less excellent when top management demands only technical tasks of its communication department rather than demanding the managerial role from its top communicator. Scholars have called this kind of expectation a "worldview." Practitioners may describe it much as John Budd, Jr. (1995), CEO of The Omega Group, did in a column for the trade press. His premise was that public relations is a practical, hands-on business rather than a theoretical one. Thus he reasoned that the most experienced people in public relations are the best. He questioned, then, why these seasoned pros are being downgraded or eliminated. His explanation came as much from top management as from public relations people themselves. If a public affairs executive earns a six-figure salary for taking charge of the transmission of paperwork, his or her CEO may well ask why someone lower in the hierarchy could not accomplish as much for substantial cost savings. To Budd: "That CEO *should* be saying, 'I need him or her [the public relations professional] to tell me when I'm wrong. To tell me what I'm not thinking of. To remind me that facts are not important but the perception of facts is.' If a CEO were looking at pr with that in mind, you wouldn't see senior people being dismissed or diminished" (p. 2).

The state lottery in our sample provided a convincing exemplar of the difference the mind-set of top management makes. This organization posted a 99th percentile Excellence score overall in 1991. A new CEO took over in 1993, implementing large-scale changes in public relations. This new CEO regarded communication solely as marketing communication. He demoted the top communicator who completed the questionnaire in 1991, moving her into a subordinate role in marketing and removing her from the dominant coalition. The CEO decided to make the communication department a technical support unit for marketing and other organizational units. He canceled the agency's relationship with a public relations firm that provided technical and production services under the old structure. This technical mandate became the new mission of the communication unit.

The consequences for communication Excellence are just what one would expect from an understanding of the Excellence factor. Now, the top communicator is a member of the dominant coalition in name only. Communication makes little or no contribution to strategic planning. The public relations staff consists largely of "journalists in residence," trained and experienced in writing and other technical functions but inexperienced in strategic management, planning, and decision making.

By contrast, gaining access to the group of powerful people who make policy for the organization hinges on several factors. These factors include past successes in public relations (especially in times of crisis) and respect on the part of its top management. As with strategic planning, access may be on a more informal than formal basis. Although the senior communicator in a top-ranked real estate development company is not part of the management team, she does confer with the CEO on important issues related to communication with both internal and external publics. Apparently this informal access has come about as a result of her expertise in the two-way public relations her CEO appreciates (her communication department scored in the 99th percentile in terms of its knowledge base). Because the CEO is not focused on publicity or promotion, he values her ability so solve communication problems and, even more, to anticipate potential problems.

A second dramatic example of an organization in transition came from the insurance company in our study—and it hinges on a top communicator with the expertise necessary to serve at the highest level yet shut out of the dominant coalition. Why? He perceived the senior management in place at the time of our survey research as failing to support the communication department—despite his expertise. Now, however, with the recent retirement of his group vice president and the earlier retirement of the CEO, he reports directly to a new CEO. He said that in a 2-week period, he had spent more time on the phone with the current CEO than he did in his first 7 or 8 years with the previous president: "He's [the current CEO] a very direct guy. He'll pick up the telephone and call me and I'll do the same with him." We consider it reasonable to speculate that this director of communication soon may find himself within the power elite. This organization had been ranked in the 15th percentile in overall Excellence.

To summarize, members of the dominant coalition are not inclined to include communication at that level. These powerful individuals typically do not see public relations as a key player in the organization. They may call on public relations for help in times of crisis, but even that is unlikely if they do not already consider communication vitally important. Thus our participants emphasized the need to educate their CEOs and others in top management about the potential for public relations. This process of education was constant, they explained, because of the constantly changing cast of characters in the typical organization. However, to some, such as the vice president for communication in an industry association, the need for this kind of education is a plus. It keeps him in business. His expertise makes him indispensable.

That said, we conclude that our evidence provides considerable support for both propositions included in this section. Public relations cannot make its maximum contribution to strategic management of the organization if it is not a part of the organization's dominant coalition. However, there are excellent departments whose head is not a regular member of this decision-making group. Thus we found that membership in the dominant coalition is an important characteristic of excellence, but it is not a mandatory requirement.

We can say with a degree of certainty that public relations becomes involved in overall strategic management only when members of the dominant coalition consider it a managerial—rather than technical support—function. However, we also found something of a chicken-and-egg situation here. In some cases, the top communicator became a part of the dominant coalition after demonstrating success in strategic management. In others, the public relations head was empowered to carry out the strategic planning process only after he or she managed to enter or gain access to the dominant coalition.

A new generation of top management may be more receptive to public relations at the highest level. For just one example, we point to the head of public relations in the insurance company who described her new CEO as "very much interested in the medium and the messages and how messages are framed and our input on other cares and concerns of the corporation." However, we know that a change in CEO does not necessarily mean new or renewed support for the public relations function, as we saw in the state lottery.

Most important, as the previous chapter showed, excellent departments are valued by the dominant coalition and mediocre departments are not. Members of the power elite are more likely to include the senior public relations person in organizations with excellent communication initiatives than in those with more average programs.

REPORTING RELATIONSHIPS BETWEEN THE HEAD
OF PUBLIC RELATIONS AND TOP MANAGEMENT

Our literature review led us to hypothesize that *public relations in centralized structures should be located at the top of the organizational hierarchy.* Only there would the function enjoy the power necessary for influencing the organization's strategic direction. We explored this proposition in considerable depth in our questionnaires and during our survey of cases. Our reasoning was that for the perspectives of the organization's diverse strategic publics to be factored into organizational policy, the head of public relations must be involved with the dominant coalition. He or she must have a direct reporting relationship that guarantees ready access to the organization's powerful decision makers.

Recall that including public relations in the dominant coalition is an important characteristic of excellence but that it is not necessary in all cases. This finding is fortunate, because we learned that many organizations—regardless of their placement on the Excellence scale—do not include their top communicators in the power elite. Excellent organizations do so to a considerably greater extent than do the least excellent operations. Even in the most effective organizations within our sample of almost 300, apparently, the decision to include public relations at the highest level came gradually. Only slowly, over time, does even the most accomplished communicator become a true part of this influential group. This part of our chapter on empowerment delves more deeply into the relationship between members of the dominant coalition and their direct reports in public relations.

Quantitative Results Related to Reporting Relationships

We began by surveying both CEOs and PR heads about the reporting relationship of top communicators to senior management. We asked first if the head of public relations reports directly to the most senior manager in the company. If he or she did not, we asked if the reporting relationship was at least an indirect relationship to the CEO. If the answer to both questions was no, we asked if there were one of two two-step reporting relationships: either a relationship in which the head of public relations reports to another senior manager who, in turn, reports to the CEO, or a relationship in which he or she reports to a more junior level of management.

Table 5.6 shows first that most top communicators report directly to the CEO—about 57% based on the questionnaires completed by both the PR head and the CEO. Another 27% report indirectly to the CEO according to both questionnaires, so that about 85% of all top communicators report at least indirectly to the CEO. To a great extent, however, this reporting relationship did not distinguish excellent from less excellent public relations departments—at least as defined by the overall Excellence score. Important differences did ap-

TABLE 5.6

Mean Z Scores on Selected Excellence Variables for Reporting
Relationships of the Head of Public Relations to Senior Management

PR Head Reports:	N	%	Participation in Strategic Management, According to CEO	Participation in Strategic Management, According to PR Head	PR Head in Manager Role	PR Head in Senior Adviser Role	Overall Excellence Score
Directly to CEO							
PR Head Report	183	55	.22	.18	.12	.11	.08
CEO Report	154	58	.26	.15	.13	.14	.07
Indirectly to CEO							
PR Head Report	95	29	−.29	−.24	−.10	−.06	−.08
CEO Report	68	26	−.23	−.20	.00	−.11	−.01
To Senior Manager Who Reports to the CEO							
PR Head Report	45	14	−.14	−.09	−.27	−.36	−.07
CEO Report	38	14	−.33	−.24	.09	−.02	−.20
To a Junior Level of Management							
PR Head Report	5	2	−.22	−1.14	.42	−.26	−.08
CEO Report	5	2	−.88	−.12	.46	.27	.10
F							
PR Head Report			6.30**[a]	7.47**[b]	3.13*[c]	3.33*[c]	0.84
CEO Report			8.31**[d]	3.47**[a]	0.50	1.06	1.03

[a]The Tukey-HSD Multiple Range Test shows the difference between the PR head reporting directly and indirectly to the CEO to be significant at the .05 level.
[b]The Tukey-HSD Multiple Range Test shows the difference between the PR head reporting directly to the CEO to be significantly different at the .05 level from reporting indirectly to the CEO and to reporting to a junior level of management. [c]The Tukey-HSD Multiple Range Test shows the difference between the PR head reporting directly to the CEO to be significantly different at the .05 level from reporting to a senior manager who reports to the CEO. [d]The Tukey-HSD Multiple Range Test shows the difference between the PR head reporting directly to the CEO and all other reporting arrangements to be significant at the .05 level.

*p < .05. **p < .01.

pear, however, in the key managerial variables, especially in participation in strategic management.

As Table 5.6 shows, top communicators who report directly to their CEO are in departments that have slightly higher overall Excellence scores than do their counterparts who report to the CEO through a longer chain of command. The difference, however, is not statistically significant. When we compared the means on each for the component variables of the Excellence scale by different reporting arrangements, significant differences did appear in the extent to which the top communicator reported playing a managerial or senior adviser role and, especially, in the extent to which both the CEO and the top communicator reported that public relations participates in strategic management at the organizational level.

First, based on the questionnaire completed by the PR head, top communicators who report directly to the CEO were more likely to say they play either the managerial or senior advisor role. Not all of the individual comparisons were statistically significant, however, in large part because of small numbers of respondents in the lesser reporting roles. When the CEO reported the relationship, the top communicator also generally had higher scores on these two managerial roles, although the differences were not statistically significant. To a large extent, the lack of significance can be attributed to the fact that the five top communicators who report to a junior level of management had the highest scores on these two variables—a finding that has little meaning because of the small number of such top communicators.

The most important effect of the reporting relationship is the access that a direct relationship to the CEO provides the top communicator to strategic management processes of the organization. Important to note, the effect is greatest when the CEO reported both the reporting relationship and the participation of public relations in strategic management. In short, a direct reporting relationship appears to be a necessary, if not a sufficient, condition for participation in strategic management, which is one of the most critical components of excellent public relations.

In addition to asking these questions about reporting relationships, we also probed the empowerment of the public relations function by asking the top communicator three questions about the nature and extent of clearance procedures required of communication activities in his or her organization. First, we asked a general question requesting the top communicator to estimate how extensive the clearance process is in his or her organization. There was no significant correlation with the index of excellence ($r = .00$) or with any of its constituent variables. Then, we asked the top communicator to check any of nine descriptive statements that described the nature of the clearance process in his or her organization (Table 5.7). Finally, we asked him or her to check each of 10 statements about the types of communication activities that must be cleared by senior managers outside the public relations unit (Table 5.8).

TABLE 5.7
The Clearance Process for Public Relations by Senior Management,
as Described by Top Communicators

Reason for Clearance (Multiple Responses)	N	%	Excellence Score When a Reason	Excellence Score When Not a Reason	T
I believe I can make final decisions fairly autonomously.	220	59	.14	−.16	3.00**
I usually seek informal approval for a project because I believe that is prudent operating procedure in this organization.	289	78	.05	−.11	1.36
I voluntarily submit my writing to a clearance process to avoid mistakes.	182	49	.05	−.01	0.57
I voluntarily submit my activities to a clearance process as a courtesy.	157	42	.17	−.09	2.49*
I voluntarily submit my activities to a clearance process as a way of keeping top management informed.	283	76	.07	−.17	2.06*
Some decisions are autonomous but most decisions are taken to the boss for his or her OK.	132	36	−.13	.09	2.06*
Although my press releases and projects do not require formal clearance, anyone up the ladder can change them or say "no way."	93	25	−.07	.04	0.94
Most of what I write has to be cleared.	99	27	−.09	.05	1.20
The clearance process here depends on who is in power at the time; some top administrators require more clearance than others.	89	24	−.11	.06	1.43
Number of respondents.	371				

*$p < .05$. **$p < .01$.

Although the first general question suggests that excellent departments are not free from clearance procedures, these two tables provide modest support for the idea that excellent public relations departments have somewhat more autonomy than do less excellent ones. In addition, they show that clearance procedures seem to be a fact of life for all communication departments, including excellent ones. First, Table 5.7 shows that heads of excellent public relations functions are significantly more likely than heads of less excellent functions to say they "can make final decisions fairly autonomously" and less likely to say that "some decisions are autonomous but most decisions are taken to the boss for his or her OK." At the same time, the heads of excellent units are more likely to say they "voluntarily submit my activities to a clearance process as a way of keeping top management informed."

TABLE 5.8
Communication Activities That Must Be Cleared by Senior Managers Outside
the Public Relations Unit

Activities Requiring Clearance (Multiple Responses)	N	%	Excellence Score When Required	Excellence Score When Not Required	T
New projects.	175	49	−.03	.05	0.87
Projects requiring major expenditure.	284	79	−.04	.22	2.32*
Oral or written statements that involve numbers.	166	46	.11	−.06	1.65
Financial information.	249	69	.05	−.05	0.90
Crisis communications.	238	66	.06	−.06	1.13
Statements with direct quotes.	196	54	.03	.00	0.38
Specialized content.	168	47	.06	−.02	0.73
Statements with political ramifications.	239	66	.06	−.06	1.15
Sensitive information.	279	78	.02	.01	0.02
Statements about top administrators.	198	55	.06	−.04	0.92
Number of respondents.	360				

*$p < .05$. **$p < .01$.

However, most heads of both excellent and less excellent units (78%) said they usually seek informal approval for projects because "that is prudent operating procedure in this organization." Only a quarter of all heads agreed that "anyone up the ladder can change press releases or say 'no way,'" that "most of what I write has to be cleared," or that "the clearance process depends on who is in power at the time." In short, Table 5.7 suggests that most public relations departments are not burdened with excessive clearance but that excellent departments have somewhat more autonomy than do less excellent ones.

Likewise, Table 5.8 shows that heads of excellent public relations departments are significantly less likely to say that clearance is required for "projects requiring major expenditure." Otherwise, there were no differences between excellent and less excellent departments in the types of communication activities for which clearance is required. Nearly 80% are required to clear "projects requiring major expenditure" and that contain "sensitive information." Two thirds of all departments must clear "financial information," "crisis communications," and "statements with political ramifications." More than half must clear "statements about top administrators" and "statements with direct quotes." Slightly less than half of the departments must clear "new projects," "oral or written statements that involve numbers," and "specialized content."

In summary, most public relations heads in our survey seemed to experience reasonable clearance procedures, being required to clear activities at times where the input of top management is needed to ensure the accuracy or involvement of management and not being required to clear more routine activities for which the involvement of management is not necessary. At the same time, these data support the proposition that excellent departments are more empowered than less excellent departments as evidenced by slightly less rigid and extensive clearance procedures.

Qualitative Results Related to Reporting Relationships

A remarkable number of personnel changes characterized the years between the survey and the long interviews. In the case of an insurance company, within the 2-week period between the first and second qualitative interview, the communication group vice president took early retirement. At the time of the in-depth interview, the head of public relations reported directly to the president. It was too soon to assess the effects of this change in the organization chart, but it does underscore the dynamism that is possible.

Both CEOs and their top communicators came and went. Some retired, some were fired, some were promoted, some were hired away by other companies, and others died. One entire communication department was wiped out between the initial and follow-up research. We tried to interview the same people who had filled out the questionnaires. Often, that was not possible. That, of course, was the downside. The upside was that we could begin to assess the difference the CEO makes—or the knowledgeable (rather than merely experienced) public relations professional. We also could explore the changing nature of the critical relationship between senior management and top communicators.

Titles of our participants told us less about their part—if any—in the strategic management of their organization than did their descriptions of what they did and, in particular, to whom they had direct access. Job descriptions, we heard, actually limited what some of our interviewees were able to do. Regardless of title or salary, the top communicator who does not have access to top management is constrained in his or her practice of public relations. On the other hand, CEOs who valued and understood public relations tended to ask for the opinion and advice of their top communicators on matters far afield from communication.

Ideally, there is both formal and informal communication between the head of public relations and members of the dominant coalition. More important than any formal title, formal reporting relationship, or formal channel of communication is the extent of communication they experience. Even if the top communicator does not sit with the power elite regularly, he or she still can be effective if the organization allows for informal opportunities to share intelligence and to offer counsel.

Gaining the trust of senior management depends in large part on knowing the business or industry as well as public relations—and then speaking the language of that enterprise. Our participants from the chemical corporation made this case eloquently. Knowing the business also suggests knowing the people in that business who provide useful contacts that help, in turn, to elevate the status of the practitioner.

A long-term relationship between the head of public relations and the CEO also leads to a direct reporting relationship. At times, the relationship can be characterized as "peer professional," or on an equal level. For example, the communication manager who has worked for the same president, as had been the case of the cosmetics company, had credibility with that CEO. Because of his longevity, the head of public relations also had numerous contacts considered vital to the organization.

This aggregation of more specific qualitative findings starts with a discussion of what we learned about chief executive officers' perceptions of public relations. Analysis of the survey data had told us that top management's understanding of and support for public relations in large part determines how public relations is practiced. (The relationship seems almost reciprocal. *Top Dog* [Pincus & DeBonis, 1994], the part novel, part business how-to book,[3] established that the CEO's expertise with communication is the major link to his or her leadership competence.)

At this point, then, we were especially interested in learning how a close relationship of credibility and trust developed between members of the dominant coalition and their top communicators in the departments ranked "excellent." To a lesser extent, we were interested to know what kept such a relationship from developing in less excellent operations—especially those with a strong knowledge base in public relations or those with high expectations for public relations on the part of the CEO, but not both.

We organize our analysis of these qualitative findings around several subquestions, beginning with why some CEOs value communication so highly. We offer only the same caveat that one of our participants suggested: "Characterizing CEOs is like beginning a sentence with, 'All women.' CEOs are individuals; they all have different motivations."

1. Why do some CEOs value public relations so highly?

Perhaps the number-one reason cited was that good, professional public relations counsel helps top management deal with the many problems it faces. But how does public relations help? Two main answers emerged: *providing a broad perspective both inside and outside of the organization and dealing with crises* or the activist groups that often prompt those predicaments. These responses are described in detail in the previous chapter. A brief review provides the following insights.

A vice president of strategic planning in the chemical company described the valuable perspective public relations can provide in terms of "the sharing of thoughts from all directions," including but not limited to employees. Thus he

---

[3]Initial findings of the Excellence project were juxtaposed against research conducted for *Top Dog* in an article (Pincus, 1994) published in *IABC Communication World*.

echoed Weick's (1979) notion of requisite variety, explaining that if the communication department represented the perspective of only some of the company's workforce, it would be difficult to address all employees' concerns. The deputy director of the engineering research agency agreed that the opinion of diverse staff members should be included in the process of making decisions to solve tough problems.

Many CEOs we interviewed mentioned that public relations is essential in times of crisis. Other senior managers valued the contributions of two-way symmetrical public relations especially in dealing with activist groups. Only one top communicator we talked with said he believed CEOs come to value public relations for the personal recognition it can bring them.

As indicated earlier in this section, change is pervasive at least in the organizations we studied. A new CEO can increase the value and support given to the communication department by the entire dominant coalition. At the same time, a change in CEO in organizations with excellent communication departments quickly can unravel those outstanding programs. Public relations becomes less excellent when top management demands only technical tasks of its communication department rather than demanding the managerial role from its top communicator, as we saw in the case of the state lottery.

From these cases we can determine that the most effective programs are characterized by a state of equilibrium between top management's expectations for public relations and the potential of that department. If the head of public relations does not understand the demands or perceptions of the dominant coalition, frustration and miscommunication are likely. Excellent communication is unlikely.

The essence of the answer to this question, then, is that CEOs in effective organizations have a worldview for public relations that is exactly what the Excellence theory suggests: two-way and symmetrical. They are determined that the senior person in public relations be a strategic manager. All of this sounds promising, until we remember that the potential for public relations, graphically depicted in the next chapter, is on average low to moderate. Thus what the CEO wants and what she or he is able to hire may be vastly different. The next subquestion explores this common gap in expectations.

2. Which came first—good public relations or value and support for public relations that led, in turn, to the hiring of an expert practitioner?

Answers to this chicken-or-egg question provided a mixed picture. Some of our participants even seemed to contradict themselves, as in the case of the industry association CEO. He told us first that he had gone looking for an expert communicator and hired one. He went on to explain, however, that because he was not expert in communication himself, he could not judge precisely who would have the necessary skills.

Typically, we heard that having a skillful communication manager on board led to increasing value and support for the function. At the chemical company, for example, an astute vice president recognized the expertise yet frustration that existed in his communication departments, both corporate and marketing. By encouraging those communicators, he helped propel the function toward excellence. As he put it: "[Excellence in public relations] started with the fact we had some good people. If I hadn't had a couple of talented communication managers, I couldn't have done anything. You can't make a silk purse out of a sow's ear." Not surprisingly, he considered himself a "zealot" in his appreciation for the criticality of public relations. He also acknowledged the support for strategic communication on the part of both the chairman and the COO.

The top communicator in this organization agreed in principle with this description of the factors leading to excellence. He emphasized, however, that it was not solely a top-down change. He added the significant factors of a crisis, the improving performance of the company, and communication initiatives within the company's industry association to his own expertise and the predisposition of senior management.

The midwestern utility we studied is equally illustrative. The leadership of the management team is credited with moving this organization from reactive to proactive. The CEO was singled out during our interview with a director of communication services as having revolutionized the company's philosophy of communication. She characterized the new model as "more open, up front, and honest than the company has known before." However, the public relations department contributed to this transformation as well: It paired operational expertise (primarily in electrical engineering) with expert public relations counsel. These factors—support from the top and expertise in communication—combined with several serious and embarrassingly visible crises to strengthen the contributions this public relations department makes to overall organizational effectiveness.

One top communicator with high rankings on all aspects of effectiveness measured in the survey research described the chasm he had seen between CEOs who take the lead in encouraging two-way communication, who believe in and champion public outreach, and those who do not. He did not consider the latter "a failure" but, instead, job security. He called them "somebody to work on." And he saw a need for educating CEOs worldwide, citing German companies as specific examples.

Education takes time. The communication manager in the chemical company said that although he had made "tremendous strides" in this direction, senior management retains "its fundamentally conservative mind-set." He agreed that changing the worldview of management is at best incremental. He continued to consider senior management an audience like any other, one whose perceptions he might want to change.

3. If CEOs truly value public relations to the extent they indicated in our survey, then why the modest budgets for the function and even the downsizing of public rela-

tions in the typical organization? In other words, are CEOs paying lip service to a notion they have been counseled to say they consider important?

We found that some CEOs may express a favorable attitude toward public relations in principle. Until they have experienced firsthand what it can do for them, they may not be true believers. Perhaps an industry association CEO said it best when describing how CEOs within his member companies came to appreciate public relations. He talked about sending those top managers to Capitol Hill along with experts in government relations.

The CEOs got "hooked" when they were successful. Good experience with sophisticated public relations, then, led to an understanding of its value because public relations came alive for the CEOs. He explained, "Once they see it pay off, then it becomes a substantive reality to them." (We heard from his counterpart in a public relations agency an inverse relationship: "Once a CEO has gotten burned by his failure to effectively communicate, he begins to understand how important public relations is.")

However, the same industry association CEO argued somewhat with an underlying premise of the initial question—that public relations somehow takes more "hits" than other functions in the typical organization. Although he acknowledged that it is always easier to make cuts in some parts of the company than others, he contended that all departments get cut sooner or later.

This CEO went on to describe what he had experienced as a cycle or series of iterations that begins when public relations and advertising are cut back. This typically happens, he said, because top management does not understand how these communication functions contribute directly to the productive capacity or profitability of the company. What happens next, he explained, is that the people laid off are "farmed over to an agency" where they capture a share of the organization's outside budget. Then, when a few years go by and business picks up, these same communicators are hired back. Why? According to the CEO: "We're all control freaks. You want them [the public relations practitioners] talking about *your* product and *your* price and *your* policy. The agency thing— it's all squeaky wheel." He also alluded to the time and money spent orienting the agency staff to the client's business.

One top communicator in a medical association concurred that public relations may not be inordinately targeted for cuts. He rejected the link between modest budgets or downsizing and how people are valued. He argued instead that downsizing actually has magnified the importance of public affairs because it must deal with the ensuing media coverage. In the same way, communicators in human resources enlarge their responsibility to deal with outplacement issues.

Two of the people we interviewed in the chemical corporation agreed that "a reasonable share" of money has been taken from *every* corporate function in recent years and also that budget cuts may not mean disaster for public relations. Several other interviewees alluded to downsizing. Like the communicators in the chemical corporation and in the association, they claimed, at the same time, that their department's effectiveness had not been compromised. Those remaining in the public relations department simply had to "pull together more" and work at a "maximum pace," according to a director of communication in a midwestern utility. Her organization, ranked among the most excellent in our survey, has dealt with the seeming discrepancy between its expressed support for public relations and cutbacks there by providing assistance in communication from the department of human resources.

Another organization we studied, the engineering experiment station, relied on the principles of Total Quality Management to help its communication staffers work more efficiently with the many projects they are expected to juggle. Again, they have not compromised the caliber of their performance. As the deputy director in this agency said, "It is an impressive volume of work done with a quality result." As a result, the members of the communication division have become what the publication editor called "evangelists on TQM."

One company we studied dissolved its entire corporate communication department between the time of the initial survey and this follow-up research. Now, its public relations is handled by an outside firm. As the commentary of the CEO of the chemical association suggested earlier on in this section, however, the company was not about to give up control of the public relations function. It has become the majority owner of the agency; the agency head serves as a *de facto* member of the cosmetics company's senior management team. In fact, the public relations agency reports directly to the CEO whereas the other departments (such as sales and marketing) report through vice presidents.

Taken together, the answers to these questions and the survey data both provide qualified support for the contention that excellence hinges in part on a direct reporting relationship between the head of public relations and senior management. Some of our participants, especially those in the most outstanding public relations departments, did report directly to the CEO. They were integral to the management of the total organization. More often the top communicator was not a formal member of the dominant coalition, but at least that person had the ear of the top policymakers. In such departments, budgets were not cut inordinately although no department of today's organization, we heard, is immune from downsizing. Sharing expectations of two-way symmetrical communication with the power elite, having the expertise to conduct such sophisticated public relations, and establishing a reputation for credibility and business acumen all helped secure adequate funding—and a direct reporting relationship.

EMPOWERING WOMEN AND RACIOETHNIC MINORITIES

Feminization of the field of public relations is a relatively new phenomenon. Women have represented the majority of practitioners only since the mid-1980s. They reached numerical parity with men in 1982, up from only 25% of the field two decades earlier (Smith, 1968). One of the dramatic shifts we observed during the decade of the Excellence research was the rapid switch from a male to female majority in public relations practice. Although public relations cannot be considered "female dominated," because relatively few women hold top-level positions, it clearly has become "female intensive." Women are not represented in managerial roles to the extent that their numbers would suggest, as chapter 6 makes clear.

However, women constitute about 60% of the practice (U.S. Department of Labor, 1995[4]) and about 80% of the student population in the United States. The situation in Canada is similar. A 1991 national census there showed that 62% of all Canadian practitioners of communication and public relations were female.[5] IABC's *Profile 2000* showed that 71% of its members were female. In the United Kingdom, surveys done of the membership of the Institute for Public Relations showed that in 1998 48% of the membership was female, compared with 21% in 1987. Of members under 30, 75% were women. Sixty-two percent of members in their 30s were women, compared to 47% in their 40s, and 19% over 50.[6]

In our chapter in the first *Excellence* book on the status of women in public relations (Hon, L. Grunig, & Dozier, 1992), we did not develop any formal propositions about the impact of gender on the practice of excellent public relations. However, we concluded that, to date, gender research and discussion in public relations too often have failed to recognize that if feminization brings deflating salaries and status, the real problem lies in society's devaluation of women and the feminine—not in women themselves. Thus, suggestions for salvaging the stature of public relations merely by training women to ascend within a male-dominated management structure miss the point. Worse, such recommendations further exacerbate the underlying obstacle—sexist judgments that privilege men and penalize women.

With that perspective, we posed the following research question: *Will the continuation of a masculine mind-set lead to the feminine qualities of consensus building and listening characteristic of the two-way symmetrical model?* When we wrote the theory book, we said that the obvious answer was "no." With time, and the growing percentage of women both in the public relations office and in the

---

[4]The U.S. Department of Labor's (1995) Bureau of Labor Statistics, which conducts monthly surveys of employed people in the United States, lists detailed occupational categories. Communicators are labeled as "public relations specialists."

[5]These statistics on the Canadian labor force were provided to the research team courtesy of the Labour Market Information Unit, Metro Vancouver, Canada Employment Centre, Vancouver, B.C. In Canada, public relations practitioners are included under the category "Professional Occupations in Public Relations and Communication." Changes in Canadian occupational coding precluded making comparisons over time, as we were able to do with U.S. statistics, but communication professionals there indicate that much of the gender shift has occurred in the last few decades. Our thanks go to Robert Mattiole, labor market information analyst, for his assistance.

[6]These data were supplied by John White of the City University of London who, along with Andrew Myers of the Cranfield School of Management, conducted the 1998 survey.

classroom, this issue grows in significance. Many scholars and practitioners have argued that the increased efficacy and professionalism of public relations are linked to practicing this kind of dialogic communication.

We explored the impact of gender on public relations in both the quantitative and qualitative phases of our research. In this chapter, we look for any differences in excellence in public relations that may be associated with the gender of the top communicator and with the relative numbers of women in the technician and managerial roles. Chapter 6 explores roles in more depth. Then, in chapter 11, we look at the overall situation for women in the organizations we studied—both in the public relations department and throughout the organization—and correlate that situation with measures of internal communication, organizational structure, organizational culture, and satisfaction with the organization. We did not include any questions related to racioethnic characteristics in the quantitative portion of the study, but we did explore the question of diversity in depth in the qualitative portion of the study.

Quantitative Results Related to Gender

The quantitative data, first, showed few demographic differences between male and female heads of public relations who responded to our survey. We had virtually the same number of men and women in our sample who were top communicators—both in the sample of top communicators in primary public relations departments and the heads of all communication departments in the sample. (Remember that many organizations had several secondary communication departments.) Top communicators who were men were somewhat older than the women (45 years vs. 39 years). They had roughly equal levels of education, both generally and in public relations. Women at the time of our survey research were more likely than men to be members of IABC (52% vs. 26%). Women supervised smaller departments than did men: On average, women oversaw departments with 8 staff members, compared with the 19 employees men typically managed.

Some differences among countries emerged in this data analysis. Slightly more than half (51%) of the department heads we surveyed from the United States were female. Women headed somewhat more (61%) of departments we studied in Canada. In the United Kingdom, men headed communication departments by an almost equally large margin (60%).

We did not include questions about salary, for several reasons. Most important, we wanted to stay focused on organizational rather than individual characteristics. Further, members of the Excellence team and other colleagues have studied the wage gap in a number of previous studies (e.g., Broom, 1982; Cline et al., 1986; Dozier, 1987, 1989; Dozier & Broom, 1995; Dozier, Chapo, & Sullivan, 1983; Toth & Cline, 1989; Wright, L. Grunig, Springston, & Toth,

1991). This research has established that women earn less than men. Age, experience, contributions to management decision making, and role all contribute to this differential. When these influences were controlled, women in 1979 earned 79 cents for every dollar men earned. In 1991, women earned 95 cents for every dollar men earned.

Thus the pay gap seems to be narrowing. Dozier and Broom (1995) found that in 1991, women with sufficient professional experience were playing an expanded role in managerial decision making, compared with 1979. Without controlling for the powerful forces of managerial role and experience, the divergence between men's and women's salaries in public relations seems staggering: In 1991, women earned 74 cents for every dollar their male colleagues made.

The overall communication Excellence of both the primary public relations department in an organization and all of the communication departments in the sample was virtually identical regardless of whether the department was headed by a man (z score slightly above the mean of zero [.06] for all departments) or a woman (z score $= -.03$) ($t = 0.88$, n.s.). Women headed 51% of the public relations departments in organizations ranked in the top 10% of the Excellence scale. Women headed 69% of the departments ranked at the bottom. Men tended to cluster toward the center.

There also were no significant differences between men and women on all but 1 of the 20 variables that made up the overall scale of excellence. The significant difference was in the top communicator's estimate of the support that women receive in the organization. As might be expected, female top communicators rated the support lower ($z = -.19$) than did men ($z = .16$) ($t = 3.44$, $p < .01$).

In addition to comparing the excellence of departments headed by men and women, we also correlated the overall Excellence scale and each of its component variables with the responses to three questions answered by the top communicator about percentages of women in the public relations department and in different roles. The PR head estimated the percentage of female employees in the department, the percentage of members of the department who occupy technician roles who are women, and the percentage who occupy managerial roles who are women. On average, the percentage of women in the departments studied was 64%. The percentage of employees in technical roles who were women was 60%; the percentage of those in managerial roles who were women was 50%.

The correlation coefficients essentially were zero for all of these variables with the overall scale of excellence and with each of the component variables, with the exception of three low, but statistically significant correlations. There were low to moderate correlations of participative culture with the percentage of women in the technical role ($r = .20$, $p < .01$) and the managerial role ($r = .21$, $p < .01$). These correlations suggest that participative culture increases the number of women in all public relations roles, regardless of whether they are managerial or technical roles. The other small correlation was a negative correlation between the percentage of women in managerial roles and the CEO's expectation that the top communicator be in the managerial role ($r = -.11$, $p < .05$)—suggesting a slight tendency for the CEO not to expect his or her top communicator to be a manager when there are more women in managerial roles.

In addition to these three questions about the percentages of women in the public relations department, we also asked the top communicator two more judgmental questions about the promotion of women in the public relations department. The first question asked the respondents to estimate the extent to which the communication department has included women in all communication roles—managerial as well as technical. The second question asked whether the department has "promoted women from within the department rather than hired men from outside communication or public relations to manage the function"—essentially the extent to which men from other functions have been allowed to encroach on the public relations function rather than promoting women into managerial roles.

Both of these questions correlated moderately to highly with the scale of overall Excellence: $r = .42$ ($p < .01$) for inclusion of women in all roles and $r = .37$ ($p < .01$) for promotion of women from within rather than encroachment of men from outside. Both of these variables also correlated with nearly all of the component variables of the scale, although the correlations were highest with the Excellence variables that came from the top communicator rather than from the CEO. Most likely, as in previous analyses, the correlations were higher for the top-communicator variables because all responses came from the same person.

In summary, the quantitative analyses show that public relations departments headed by women are as excellent as those headed by men and that the relative number of men and women in the department and in managerial and technical roles have no effect on excellence. Women, nevertheless, manage smaller departments and perceive less support for women in the organization than men. CEOs also seem to have lower expectations that the head of public relations be a manager when there are more women in managerial roles. However, public relations tends to be more excellent when organizational culture is participative and the organization actively promotes women into managerial roles in public relations rather than excluding them in favor of men encroaching on the function from outside.

Qualitative Results Related to Gender and Racioethnic Diversity

In the qualitative stage of the research, we did not deal so much with numbers as with the qualities of the people, the organizations, and the processes we studied. Thus we cannot say how many more women or people of color may be practicing public relations now than when we conceptualized the research.[7] Nor have we established what proportion is breaking the glass ceiling to advance into the ranks of top management.

We *did* find evidence to support what both the trade and scholarly press in public relations have described as a trend toward increasing multiculturalism and feminization of the field. Women and minorities are getting in. They are entering the paid labor force in unprecedented numbers. Whether they are getting *on* remains to be seen. We found little evidence of women or people of color in senior management slots. We heard much concern over the issue of the glass ceiling, however, and we did learn what the more excellent organizations were trying to do to overcome any lingering discrimination. We also have come to understand *why* the effective CEOs and their communication staffs appreciate the potential these employees offer.

We found, for example, that the gender of the practitioner may affect his or her approach to public relations. In the medical association whose top communicator ranked it only in the 12th percentile in support for women employees at the time of the survey research, the new president—a woman—is credited with pushing for more participative management. Another senior woman we interviewed in the organization, the manager of communication, is working toward more symmetrical public relations. She stresses listening and trying to improve her department's service to members. The assistant executive director of corporate affairs there linked positive changes in the association with these new roles for women. Women's emergence at the highest levels, then, may be playing a part in some underlying transformations occurring in both communication and organizational culture.

Even at lower levels and in more traditional roles, women in public relations represent a bargain for the organization that employs them. From our long interviews comes at least one poignant description of the dual-role fulfillment of the typical female practitioner. In this case, however, the dual roles are that of technician and staff support rather than technician and manager. The top communicator at the economic development agency said that in her organization, "Females are expected to not only write the press releases but type the envelopes [and] get the stamps, when we could be spending our time doing management work." This agency, located in a southern American city, was ranked in the 4th percentile at the time of the survey. Although it is moving rapidly toward excellence in public relations, with new hires in the communication de-

---

[7]Interestingly, we found anecdotal support for the theoretical understanding that men, in particular, tend to overestimate the number of women who have come into their field (and especially their office). In the engineering experiment station, for example, the publication editor differed with a member of the dominant coalition on the number of women working there. She said it is not 50/50, as the deputy director contended. She did acknowledge that women have held positions as high as second to the CEO in this organization. She also pointed out that, traditionally, engineering has not empowered women and that there are few women and minorities to draw from the employment pool.

partment and greater expectations on the part of top management, change will come slowly for women. The vice president told us that women there are moving beyond the technician's role in public relations roles by developing managerial skills. However, he pointed out that the larger societal culture of the South challenges women: Women have to prove their abilities while not offending the traditionally male dominant coalition.

Most people we spoke with framed their responses to questions about the value of diversity in terms of hiring and retaining the best people—regardless of their race, ethnicity, or gender. They considered the treatment of women and minorities in public relations more a business issue than an ethical one. Some emphasized a need to empower *everyone*, suggesting that they might be reluctant to single out any group for seemingly special treatment.

Our participants also told us that when given an opportunity to perform at the managerial level, women were effective. Success comes with the price of being ever vigilant, however. As the top communicator in the state arts organization put it, "Women must tread the line of being very confident and able to express their views, but avoid the 'bitch' label." Participants described these effectual women alternately as "winners" and "bulldogs." The latter label, like "bitch" in our view, bespeaks a stereotyping that time and women's successful experiences may help overcome. CEOs (most of whom were men) and their top communicators (many of whom also were men) seemed surprised that women could be both tough and effective. Although they espoused support for their female employees, the case of the chemical company was instructive: At the time of our survey research, 15% of its communication staff was female and all women there were in the technician role. At the time of the long interviews, 20% of the staff was female and one woman in public relations was in a managerial position. The woman we interviewed in this corporation emphasized the importance of having such a role model: "It makes me aspire to be like her. It really inspires me when I see a woman who is really competent."

However, this Hispanic woman was unwilling to suggest that senior women automatically would support the careers of other women. Instead, she described what feminist scholars have called the "Queen Bee Syndrome": "Sometimes women in high places feel they've done it the way men want them to. Once they've gotten there, they almost can't relate to women." She spoke of finding few women to talk with in her company and being surprised to see how many women actually are in the field when she attends IABC meetings.

At least one participant believed that women in public relations may crack the glass ceiling more easily than in other functional areas. The top communicator in the medical products company contended that most women are hired to fill unstated quotas. He said that the best way for people—women and men alike—to succeed there, once hired, is to "have the ability to talk through issues and discuss problems exceptionally well . . . when you do that well, you earn the respect of everyone."

A number of participants, especially those in the average and less-than-average organizations, cited men's longevity in the typical organization as an advantage over women at promotion time. As one female director of public relations explained, women who might be in their second or third decade of employment stopped out of the workforce to raise their families. They are now re-entering the public sphere; but few in this generation come back in at the top. At the hotel chain, ranked in the 18th percentile on the Excellence scale, promotions are based on seniority. Although the company employs a substantial number of women in managerial positions, there are no women in top communication jobs. Minorities are significantly underrepresented at all levels. No recruitment programs designed to prepare women and racioethnic minorities for senior slots were reported.

Other participants alluded to certain industries—such as engineering, medicine, and auto insurance—as traditionally less hospitable to women and minorities in management roles. These fields may not be attractive to women, either. However, there may be room for optimism. As the top communicator at the aerospace corporation explained: "In our field, top management is culled out of the engineering departments, which is an area traditionally not popular with women. This is changing. There is no real fast track to the top. You just need to have perseverance. I don't really believe that a 'glass ceiling' is being actively imposed."

Many of our participants looked forward to the process they called "attrition," wherein they believed women would rise inexorably to positions of top management as older men in those slots now retire. The head of public relations in the aerospace company believed that the glass ceiling exists because of history and, as a result, "It will not always be there."

Taken together, the remarks of most participants confirmed the need to welcome nontraditional employees, especially in communication, for much the same reason Weick (1979) proposed in his theory of requisite variety. To reiterate, an organization is more likely to be successful if it has as much diversity inside the organization as in its environment. Public relations, of course, serves as a boundary-spanning function between the organization and that milieu. One corporate vice president translated this academic lingo into what he saw as the practical significance for his chemical company:

> It's very important for us to have a diverse workforce because the population out of which you hire the best and brightest people is diverse. If we don't have a diverse workforce, then we are only going to effectively hire out of some fraction of the population and gradually the quality of our workforce relative to our competitors is going to degrade. So, we want to be an organization in which people of all backgrounds—ethnic, gender, race, religious, whatever—feel comfortable.

Similarly, the top communicator at the financial services corporation told us that the payback for the aggressive recruitment and equal treatment of women and ethnic minorities is evident: Diversity expands corporate thinking.

In sum, the feminization of the public relations profession will limit the potential of a public relations department if the organization discriminates against women—who often play the dual role of manager and technician and for slightly less pay than their male counterparts who typically engage in a purer set of managerial activities. Excellent public relations departments and effective organizations have developed mechanisms to help women gain the power they need to advance from the technician to the management role and to implement their understanding of two-way symmetrical public relations.

HOW COMMUNICATION DEPARTMENTS BECOME EXCELLENT

The question of how communication departments become excellent was one of the most difficult to answer definitively. We *can* say that excellence develops incrementally, over time—just as earlier sections of this chapter established that a close relationship between the top communicator and his or her CEO develops only glacially. Our evidence suggested that improvement in the public relations function is more a process of evolution than overnight success—even in the instances of crisis, changing personnel, or the popular initiatives such as quality management, reengineering, and diversity we heard so much about.

Public relations departments in the most excellent organizations are headed by people with tremendous knowledge of communication. On the one hand, their expertise allows them to operate almost independently—as professionals typically do. Some management structures also lead to this kind of free rein. For example, the matrix design in place at the industry association and a development company we studied requires each director to manage his or her department autonomously on communication-related issues yet integrate the operation with the organization's overall mission through cooperation with peers in other departments.

Being most effective also requires the support of the dominant coalition. One vice president of communication who oversees a staff of 25 in his full-service department explained that the CEO, in particular, plays a strong role in the department's efficacy. That leader must, first, acknowledge that public relations is important and, second, provide the necessary budget. He elaborated on the need for resources: to do research, to hire good staff, and to retain that staff. His CEO agreed that "you can't sell from an empty wagon."

What we heard from the midwestern utility company was virtually identical. There, too, the leadership consistently has supported excellence in public relations. Both interviewees described their CEO as advocating a proactive, open, honest, and two-way model of public relations. The senior vice president explained that allocation of resources is the determining factor—especially when funds are limited. As he put it, "What you value is where the money goes." In large part because of the crises his organization had experienced, it had come to value good communication.

Thus we concluded, as had the senior communicator in the chemical company, that the communicator's knowledge of strategic management is a necessary but not sufficient condition for excellence in public relations. In his case, there was a "confluence of forces" pushing his organization from a moderate ranking in excellence toward the top of the scale. His own role as a talented communicator and expert in the business was significant. However, it took crises that sensitized top management to the importance of public relations and a mediating vice president who understood public relations and had strong connections with that senior management to effect real change.

Finally, the company's performance is a factor in achieving excellent public relations. As the chemical corporation's vice president explained: "The job of the communication function is to get you the reputation you deserve. Until not too long ago, we probably were getting the reputation we deserved; and everyone wanted to blame the communication function for it. One of the things that's helped is that we've had a good message to deliver: The company has been performing better."

SUMMARY AND CONCLUSIONS

The overarching theory tested in this chapter was the idea that the public relations function must be empowered as a distinctive and strategic managerial function if it is to play a role in making organizations more effective. The senior public relations officer must be a part of the senior management team, play a role in making strategic organizational decisions, be a member of the dominant coalition or have access to this powerful group of organizational leaders, and have relative autonomy from excessive clearance rules to play this strategic role. In addition, the growth in the number of female practitioners should not hinder this empowerment of the public relations function; indeed the growth should be valued for the diversity it brings to public relations. In addition, excellent departments should seek more of the scarce supply of minority practitioners to add to their ability to understand the environments faced by their organizations.

To a great extent, this chapter has provided sound empirical support for this overarching theory. Many organizations, including some of the excellent ones, have not fully empowered their public relations professionals. But in excellent public relations departments, by and large, public relations professionals are involved in strategic management. In particular, their role is as environmental scanners, providing information needed about strategic publics affected by managerial decisions. They get this information through formal research and various informal methods of gaining information about organizational constituencies.

Although not all of the managers of excellent communication functions were in the dominant coalition, nearly two thirds of top communicators in the top 10% of our organizations were in that powerful group, compared to about 45% in the overall sample. When public relations was in the dominant coalition, that elite group also tended to include more representatives of outside constituencies. The larger the dominant coalition, the more likely it was that the top communicator was a member. That result suggests that the more an organization empowers most of its employees and outside constituents, the more likely it is also to empower public relations.

We found that the knowledge base of public relations practitioners increased their chance of being involved in strategic management and being accepted by the dominant coalition. Public relations practitioners in excellent organizations had more expertise in public relations. They did not all have college degrees in the field, although several did. Instead, they seemed to be self-educated; at least one participant in the qualitative research alluded to enhancing his practice after reading and studying the *Excellence* theory book. Others emphasized what they had learned from mentors.

Excellent communicators are more likely to be team players than independent operators. They cultivate relationships not only with members of their external publics but also with their counterparts inside the organization. They promote teamwork within their own departments as well, empowering middle managers there to develop and work toward achieving a vision. In particular, these effective communicators have earned a close working relationship with their CEO. This relationship is characterized by credibility. It tends to result from extensive knowledge of the business or industry; longevity plus a track record of successful performance in the organization; expertise in strategic planning and managerial decision making that is not limited to communication; and a shared worldview of the value of two-way symmetrical public relations, in particular.

Having such an expert communicator in place tended to lead to high value for public relations, rather than having a CEO who valued public relations in the first place seeking and hiring someone with that expertise. However, there were many significant exceptions to this pattern. Several senior executives in our study seemed determined to hire and support the best communicator they could find. To them, that meant a person capable of going beyond functions typically associated with public relations. It also meant a person whose expertise in public relations extended well beyond publicity, promotion, or media relations to encompass conflict resolution, environmental scanning, and dialogue with key publics.

Most of the top communicators in our survey reported directly to the CEO or indirectly through another senior manager. Such a reporting relationship does not ensure excellence, but we found that without such a clear path to the CEO public relations cannot contribute much to organizational effectiveness. A direct relationship with the CEO provides the top communicator access to strategic management processes of the organization. A direct reporting relationship, therefore, appears to be a necessary, if not a sufficient, condition for participation in strategic management, which is one of the most critical components of excellent public relations.

The need to be team players also showed up in our data on clearance procedures. Most public relations heads in our survey cannot act unilaterally. They are required to clear their activities at times where the input of top management is needed to ensure the accuracy or involvement of management. They are not required to clear more routine activities. At the same time, we found that excellent departments are more empowered than less excellent departments, as evidenced by having somewhat more autonomy to make major decisions without interference from top management.

Finally, we found that departments are excellent as often when women are the senior communicator as when men are in that role. Likewise, increasing the number of women in the public relations department and in managerial roles had no effect on excellence. At the same time, however, we found that excellent public relations departments take active steps to include women in managerial roles and to promote them from inside rather than to bring in men from other managerial functions. Likewise, we found that excellent departments actively strive to increase racioethnic diversity in the function—pushing for more requisite variety in public relations.

In short, excellent public relations departments are interesting and challenging places for capable and knowledgeable professionals to work. In these departments, public relations people are empowered, they play an active strategic role, their expertise in communication and environmental scanning is valued, and they are valued when they bring gender and racioethnic diversity into the function.

REFERENCES

Allen, T. J. (1979). *Managing the flow of technology: Technology transfer and the dissemination of technological information within the research and development organization.* Cambridge, MA: MIT Press.

Anshen, M. (Ed.). (1974). *Managing the socially responsible corporation.* New York: Macmillan.

Bishop, D. R. (1993, Summer). J-- H-------, PR superstar. *Public Relations Quarterly,* pp. 3–4.

Broom, G. M. (1982). A comparison of sex roles in public relations. *Public Relations Review, 8(3),* 17–22.

Budd, J., Jr. (1995, May 22). Is disturbing trend an early-warning signal for profession? *pr reporter, tips & tactics,* pp. 1–2.

Cline, C. G., Masel-Walters, L., Toth, E. L., Turk, J. V., Smith, H. T., & Johnson, N. (1986). *The velvet ghetto: The impact of the increasing percentage of women in public relations and organizational communication.* San Francisco: IABC Foundation.

Cyert, R. M., & March, J. G. (1963). *A behavioral theory of the firm.* Englewood Cliffs, NJ: Prentice-Hall.

Cyert, R. M., & March, J. G. (1973). *A behavioral theory of the firm* (2nd ed.). Englewood Cliffs, NJ: Prentice-Hall.

Dozier, D. M. (1987, May). *Gender, environmental scanning, and participation in management decision making.* Paper presented at the meeting of the Public Relations Interest Group, International Communication Association, Montreal.

Dozier, D. M. (1989). Breaking the "glass ceiling." *Public Relations Review, 4*(4), 6–14.

Dozier, D. M., & Broom, G. M. (1995). Evolution of the manager role in public relations practices. *Journal of Public Relations Research, 7*(1), 3–26.

Dozier, D. M., Chapo, S., & Sullivan, B. (1983, August). *Sex and the bottom line: Income differences between men and women in public relations.* Paper presented at the meeting of the Public Relations Division, Association for Education in Journalism and Mass Communication, Corvallis, OR.

Frost, P. J. (1987). Power, politics, and influence. In F. M. Jablin, L. L. Putnam, K. H. Roberts, & L. W. Porter (Eds.), *Handbook of organizational communication: An interdisciplinary perspective* (pp. 503–548). Newbury Park, CA: Sage.

Grunig, J. E. (1992a). Symmetrical systems of internal communication. In J. E. Grunig (Ed.), *Excellence in public relations and communication management* (pp. 531–576). Hillsdale, NJ: Lawrence Erlbaum Associates.

Grunig, J. E. (1992b). What is excellence in management? In J. E. Grunig (Ed.), *Excellence in public relations and communication management* (pp. 219–250). Hillsdale, NJ: Lawrence Erlbaum Associates.

Grunig, J. E. (1993). Image and substance: From symbolic to behavioral relationships. *Public Relations Review, 19*(2), 121–139.

Grunig, J. E. (1997). A situational theory of publics: Conceptual history, recent challenges and new research. In D. Moss, T. MacManus, & D. Verčič (Eds.), *Public relations research: An international perspective* (pp. 3–46). London: International Thomson Business Press.

Grunig, J. E., & Hunt, T. (1984). *Managing public relations.* New York: Holt, Rinehart & Winston.

Grunig, J. E., & Repper, F. C. (1992). Strategic management, publics, and issues. In J. E. Grunig (Ed.), *Excellence in public relations and communication management* (pp. 117–158). Hillsdale, NJ: Lawrence Erlbaum Associates.

Grunig, L. A. (1992). Power in the public relations department. In J. E. Grunig (Ed.), *Excellence in public relations and communication management* (pp. 483–502). Hillsdale, NJ: Lawrence Erlbaum Associates.

Hon, L. C. (1992). *Toward a feminist theory of public relations.* Unpublished doctoral dissertation, University of Maryland, College Park.

Hon, L. C., Grunig, L. A., & Dozier, D. M. (1992). Women in public relations: Problems and opportunities. In J. E. Grunig (Ed.), *Excellence in public relations and communication management* (pp. 419–438). Hillsdale, NJ: Lawrence Erlbaum Associates.

International Association of Business Communicators. (2000). Profile 2000: A survey of the profession. *Communication World, 17*(4), 21–52.

Johnson, D. J., & Acharya, L. (1981, August). *Organizational decision making and public relations roles.* Paper presented at the meeting of the Association for Education in Journalism, Athens, OH.

Kanter, R. M. (1979, July–August). Power failure in management circuits. *Harvard Business Review,* pp. 65–75.

Kanter, R. M. (1983). *The change masters.* New York: Simon & Schuster.

Knights, D. (1992). Changing spaces: The disruptive impact of a new epistemological location for the study of management. *Academy of Management Review, 17,* 514–536.

Knights, D., & Morgan, G. (1991). Corporate strategy, organizations, and subjectivity: A critique. *Organisation Studies, 12,* 251–273.

Lesly, P. (1981). The status and role of public relations. *Public Relations Journal, 37,* 14–17.

Lindenmann, W., & Lapetina, A. (1981). Management's view of the future of public relations. *Public Relations Review, 7*(3), 3–13.

Maples, S. F. (1981). *Relationship of organizational structure to public relations decision-making.* Unpublished master's thesis, California State University, Fullerton.

Mintzberg, H. (1983). *Power in and around organizations.* Englewood Cliffs, NJ: Prentice-Hall.

Mintzberg, H. (1994). *The rise and fall of strategic planning.* New York: The Free Press.

Nowlan, S. E., & Shayon, D. R. (1984). Reviewing your relationship with executive management. *Public Relations Quarterly, 39*(1), 5–11.

Pieczka, M. (1996). Paradigms, systems theory and public relations. In J. L'Etang & M. Pieczka (Eds.), *Critical perspectives in public relations* (pp. 124–156). London: International Thomson Business Press.

Pincus, J. D. (1994, May). Top Dog meets Excellence. *IABC Communication World,* pp. 26–29.

Pincus, J. D., & DeBonis, J. N. (1994). *Top dog.* Hightstown, NJ: McGraw-Hill.

Robbins, S. P. (1990). *Organization theory: Structure, design, and applications* (3rd ed.). Englewood Cliffs, NJ: Prentice-Hall.

Smith, R. W. (1968, October). Women in public relations. *Public Relations Journal,* pp. 26–27.

Stevenson, W. B., Pearce, J. L., & Porter, L. W. (1985). The concept of "coalition" in organization theory and research. *Academy of Management Review, 10*(2), 256–268.

Thompson, J. D. (1967). *Organizations in action.* New York: McGraw-Hill.

Toth, E. L., & Cline, C. G. (Eds.). (1989). *Beyond the velvet ghetto.* San Francisco: IABC Research Foundation.

U.S. Department of Labor. (1995). *Employment and earnings,* Table 22, *41*(1), 206.

Verčič, D. (2000). *Trust in organizations: A study of the relations between media coverage, public perceptions and profitability.* Unpublished doctoral dissertation, The London School of Economics and Political Science, University of London, London.

Weick, K. E. (1979). *The social psychology of organizing* (2nd ed.). Reading, MA: Addison-Wesley.

Wright, D. K., Grunig, L. A., Springston, J. K., & Toth, E. L. (1991, November). *Under the glass ceiling: An analysis of gender issues in American public relations, 1*(2). New York: Foundation for Public Relations Research Monograph.

CHAPTER SIX

Communicator Roles

The extensive and lengthy analysis of practitioner roles in this chapter is driven by three factors. First, this constitutes the only extensive review of previous roles research in more than a dozen years (see Dozier, 1992). Second, the Excellence study examined practitioner roles at several levels of analysis. Roles were measured in terms of departmental expertise or knowledge to enact various roles, the actual roles enacted by each department's top communicator, and the role expectations of the organization's CEO (or other senior-ranking executive). To make sense of findings at these multiple levels of analysis requires considerable deconstruction. Third, practitioner roles play a central role in the overall Excellence of communication departments and organizations.

Roles are abstractions about the patterned behaviors of individuals in organizations, a way of classifying and summarizing the myriad activities that an individual might perform as a member of an organization. By playing roles, individuals mesh activities, yielding predictable outcomes. Arguably, organizations are defined as systems of roles. In public relations, the concept of practitioner role has been systematically studied for about 25 years; such research places practitioner roles at the nexus of a network of important antecedent concepts and professional consequences. In the Excellence study, new role measures were developed and used to expand this important theoretical area.

THE CONCEPT OF ORGANIZATIONAL ROLE

In their early conceptual work, Daniel Katz and Robert Kahn (1966, 1978) sought to bridge the gap between sociology and psychology by assigning a central place to roles enacted by individuals in organizations. Building on the work of Linton (1936), Newcomb (1951), T. Parsons (1951), and Merton (1957), Katz and Kahn argued that formal organizations are contrivances best understood as open systems made up of acts and events involving people linked together through sets of ongoing relationships and behaviors. An individual in an organization occupies an *office*, such as vice president for corporate communication, which is a point in organizational space defined by its relationships to other offices and the organization as a whole. Each office has an associated set of behaviors that the occupant of that office is expected to enact.

Whereas office is defined by such relatively static indicators as job title and job description, organizational *role* is defined as "recurring actions of an individual, appropriately interrelated with the repetitive activities of others so as to yield a predictable outcome" (Katz & Kahn, 1978, p. 189). Roles, then, are measured by what individuals do repetitively in their day-to-day work. Related concepts include role sending, role expectations, and role receiving. *Role sending* is the social process whereby relevant officeholders in an organization prescribe and proscribe the behaviors that define role expectations for an individual officeholder. With particular regard to roles of communicators, relevant officeholders include members of the dominant coalition. *Role expectations*, the aggregate of the activities and behaviors expected of the officeholder, are especially important when those of the top communicator do not mesh with those of the dominant coalition. Role expectations generally reflect conceptions of the role held by others, modified by "impressions of the abilities and personality of the officeholder" (Katz & Kahn, 1978, p. 190). Such modification is especially relevant when core competencies of the communication department are considered.

The top communicator, defined in the Excellence study as the senior administrative or management officeholder in the communication or public relations department, plays a key role as both transmitter and interpreter of expectations about communication originating with the dominant coalition, regarding communication's role and function in the organization. The *role received* by top communicators is subjective, constructed from role-sending messages from the dominant coalition, but also learned by top communicators through formal education and previous work experiences. The top communicator's role is also affected by what subordinates in the communication department communicate about their expectations, as well as the material conditions of their work. Role sending and role receiving rarely occur through an epiphany; rather, a feedback loop permits the ongoing modification of the role sent and received. The concept of feedback loop plays a crucial role in the demand–delivery loop, a concept developed to help explain the findings of the Excellence study.

Organizational Roles in Public Relations

Launched by Glen Broom in the 1970s (Broom & Smith, 1978, 1979), roles research in public relations sought to abstract distinct roles from the day-to-day activities of public relations professionals. Broom conceived of practitioners as consultants to dominant coalitions, with each role providing a distinct form of assistance. Initially, five roles were explicated; however, pretesting led Broom to reduce the number of roles to four.

The *expert prescriber* was identified in the literature as the organization's acknowledged expert on all matters relating to public relations (Broom, 1982; Broom & Smith, 1978, 1979; Cutlip & Center, 1971; Newsom & Scott, 1976). Much like the traditional doctor–patient relationship, the expert prescriber makes recommendations and the dominant coalition complies. Broom drew from the consulting literature (Kurpius & Brubaker, 1976; Walton, 1969) to conceptualize the *communication facilitator* role. Acting as a "go-between," the communication facilitator is deeply involved in process, attending to the quality and quantity of information flowing between the dominant coalition and key publics. Broom conceptualized the *problem-solving process facilitator* as a practitioner assisting a dominant coalition to think systematically and solve public relations problems for the organization. The elements of this role were drawn from organization theory and development (Baker & Schaffer, 1969; Schein, 1969). The fourth role that Broom conceptualized was that of *communication technician*. In this role, the practitioner acts as a technical services provider, generating the collateral materials needed to implement a communication or public relations program planned through another communication role. That is, the communication technician was conceptualized as implementing communication programs planned by others in the organization. Broom regarded practitioners enacting this role predominantly as "journalists-in-residence," hired away from news organizations for their media relations and production skills.

OPERATIONAL ISSUES

Following an early experiment with consulting roles, Broom (1982) operationalized six behavioral measures for each of the four roles he conceptualized (Broom, 1982), using a 1–7 scale that ranged from *never* to *always*. Survey respondents were told that the statements described different aspects of what public relations practitioners do. If the statement described something that never occurred in the practitioner's work, the respondent was instructed to circle 1 (never). If it always occurred, circle 7 (always). If that aspect happened occasionally, the respondent was instructed to circle the number that best described his or her work.

In the initial use of the 24-item battery of role measures, Broom conducted a survey of a systematic sample of current members of the Public Relations Society of America (PRSA). The role measures proved generally reliable, with Cronbach alpha coefficients as follows: expert prescriber, .93; communication facilitator, .79; problem-solving process facilitator, .90; and communication technician, .84 (Broom, 1982). This 24-item set has been used extensively in public relations roles research over the last 20 years.

The Manager–Technician Dichotomy

In analyzing the initial survey data, Broom (1982) discovered three roles that he had conceptualized as distinct were, at the operational level, highly inter-correlated. The expert prescriber, the communication facilitator, and the problem-solving process facilitator are all conceptually distinct roles that practitioners enact simultaneously in their actual, day-to-day work. However, all three conceptual roles are not correlated with the communication technician role. The rotated factor matrix of the item set from the 1979 survey, as well as a follow-up study of the same population (PRSA members) in 1991, are provided in Dozier and Broom (1995) for the manager role and the technician role.

Broom's finding prompted Dozier (1983, 1984c) to conduct exploratory factor analysis on data from three practitioner surveys, from which he inductively generated the *communication manager* role. The communication manager enacts aspects of the expert prescriber, problem-solving process facilitator, and communication facilitator roles. Those enacting the communication manager role make communication policy decisions and are held accountable—by themselves and by others—for the success or failure of communication programs. The communication manager role involves the dominant coalition in a systematic planning process and serves as a catalyst for decision making. Such practitioners also facilitate communication between the dominant coalition and publics by informing management of public reactions to organizational policies, procedures, or actions—or all three.

Minor Roles

In analyzing the data, Dozier (1983) found that several minor roles emerged, in addition to the manager and technician roles. These minor roles included the *communication liaison* role, which he argued was similar to the manager role but thwarted by organizational constraints from policymaking authority. In the Excellence study, this minor role was conceptualized and operationalized as the *senior adviser* role. In addition, Dozier (1983, 1984c) identified a *media relations specialist* role, which he argued was a variation on the communication technician role, specializing in external or public media rather than internal communication. However, these minor roles have proved relatively unstable across surveys. The manager and technician roles, however, have remained remarkably stable from survey to survey, as indicated by factor analytic solutions and reliability coefficients.

Dominant Role

For certain analytic purposes, communicators' scores on the manager and technician scales can be compared and communicators classified as either predominantly managers or predominantly technicians, depending on the higher score.

Dominant role is an operational indicator that a communicator is either a manager or a technician, based on role activities most frequently enacted. Dominant role can be determined by comparing the means of items that make up the manager and technician roles and then assigning dominant role status to the higher of the two means. A second approach is to compare factor scores for the two roles, which are first normalized. The dominant role is assigned to the higher of the two factor scores.

However dominant role is operationalized, this statistical artifact allows the communicator's role status to be treated as dichotomous, as either/or. This variable is useful for certain statistical analyses (e.g., chi-square, t test, F test). However, use of dominant role involves the ultimate of simplifications because it dichotomizes the rich nuances captured by the original 24-item role set. Every communicator enacts aspects of the manager and technician roles, as well as all four of the original conceptual roles. Further, the role set itself is a simplification of the fluid and complex organizational activities that professional communicators and public relations practitioners enact each day. This compression of practitioner roles into this simply dichotomy has been criticized strongly by a number of public relations scholars (e.g., Creedon, 1991; Toth & L. Grunig, 1993; Toth, Serini, Wright, & Emig, 1998)—primarily because they believe the dichotomy disguises the nature of work done by female practitioners.

Creedon (1991), in particular, considered the idea of separate roles to be a false dichotomy. She said that emphasis on two discrete roles has led to a "hierarchy of two seemingly dissimilar roles—the manager who decides policy and the technician who implements 'his' policies" (p. 79). She offered a counter-perspective: "Some technicians process information, some produce creative products, and some manage the process as well as produce the product" (p. 78). She cited research suggesting an overlap between roles: Women participate in decision making, considered a managerial activity, but at a lower level than do men. She also summarized research indicating that decision-making activity exists in other "apparently nonmanagerial categories, variously described as linking, liaison, or information-processor role" (p. 71).

Whereas Creedon revisioned the technician role to demonstrate that female technicians actually perform a number of managerial activities, Toth and L. Grunig (1993) focused on "the devaluation of women who perform managerial tasks similar to those performed by men" (p. 173). Toth and L. Grunig conducted separate factor analyses for men and women of a set of managerial activities and another set of technical activities. After comparing the profiles, they concluded that "The managerial activities of the men were more 'managerial' in nature, involving the counseling and policy-making role and then evaluating and supervising the work of others" (p. 170). Women performed a wider range of managerial activities than men, especially middle-management activities. These middle-management activities included such tasks as supervising the work of others, meeting with clients and executives, meeting with peers, conducting research, implementing new programs and events, making media contacts, and handling correspondence and telephone calls.

The rationale for the oversimplification of practitioner behavior is rooted in a set of nomothetic presuppositions. The goal of using abstractions like organizational roles is to provide a partial description and explanation of practitioner behavior across a wide range of organizational settings, as well as to test relationships between role indicators and the hypothesized antecedents and consequences of role enactment. The utility of such oversimplifications is best judged by their contributions to the theory and practice of public relations. In some research, the simplifications have been useful, but in the case of roles of women a simple dichotomy seems to have disguised the true roles of women in public relations.

Role Ambiguity

Katz and Kahn (1978) noted that officeholders are not simply passive recipients of roles sent but actively construct their roles from the myriad messages and consequences about what is expected or proper for an office. *Role ambiguity* is the degree to which these signals and consequences are unclear or inconsistent. Ahlwardt (1984) provided evidence that communicators in organizations are subject to high levels of role ambiguity, because the role sent by the dominant coalition and immediate supervisor may be at odds with the communicator's professional role expectations learned through formal education or communicated by the professional associations (Dozier, 1992). Indeed, top communicators in the Excellence study used no less than 15 different job titles to describe the office of top communicator.

On the other hand, role ambiguity provides communicators with the wiggle room needed to enact role behaviors in a strategic and proactive manner, a process called "role taking." *Role taking* is a concept similar to role received, except that it places greater emphasis on the officeholder as an active, reflexive agent (rather than passive recipient of role messages), able to enact role behaviors outside those assumed by dominant coalitions. Culbertson (1991), for example, argued that the technician role is "highly codified and repetitive," whereas the process facilitation aspects of manager role enactment allow "subtle role taking" by communicators (p. 54). This, in turn, allows communicators to use role enactment as a means of defining or redefining the communication function as excellent.

RESEARCH ON THE ORGANIZATIONAL ROLES OF COMMUNICATORS

In the last decade, the organizational role of communicators has been one of the most extensively studied concepts in public relations research. In a review of the most frequently cited works in the area of public relations (including the *Journal of Public Relations Research, Public Relations Review, Public Relations Research Annual,* and *Journalism and Mass Communication Quarterly*) from 1990 to 1995, Pasadeos, Renfro, and Hanily (1999) found that the two most frequently cited journal articles were Broom's (1982) publication of gender differences in role playing and Broom and Dozier's (1986) first published explication of the manager–technician dichotomy. This citation network study led Pasadeos et al. to conclude that public relations roles was "the largest category of most cited works" (p. 39).

Such interest in the concept is due, in part, to the number of professional issues that are linked to communicator roles. Antecedent to role enactment are concepts of gender and professional experience. Linked to role enactment is the degree to which the communicator uses research to scan the organization's environment and to evaluate the effectiveness of communication programs. Several studies have used roles to help explain the use of new media technology in public relations. Role enactment has also been linked to participation in management decision making, strategic planning, participation in issues management, and encroachment on the public relations function. Role enactment has been tied to salaries paid to communicators and the satisfaction they report from their work. In addition to the Excellence study, roles research has been conducted in other nations and cultures.

Gender, Professional Experience, and Roles

One of the most hotly debated issues regarding roles research has been the issue of gender, professional experience, and roles. Broom (1982) first noted that women tended to cluster in the communication technician role; men tended to play the conceptual components of the manager role (e.g., expert prescriber, problem-solving process facilitator, and communication facilitator) more frequently. In subsequent research, Dozier, Chapo, and Sullivan (1983) argued that role segregation by gender helped explain income disparities between male and female communicators of equal professional experience. Broom and Dozier (1986) noted that their panel study of PRSA members indicated that women performed manager role activities less frequently than men, but not significantly so. However, women performed technician role activities significantly more frequently than men. This finding was true for both the 1979 survey and the 1985 survey. Toth and L. Grunig (1993) found a similar relationship in their survey of 1,003 PRSA members in 1991, using a more parsimonious set of role measures. On the other hand, Zoch, Patterson, and Olson (1997) conducted a survey of 44 public relations practitioners working for the 91 school districts in South Carolina and found that men performed manager role activities significantly more often than did women. Men were especially active with regard to strategic planning and policy decision making.

Gender discrimination plays an important role in this process of role segregation. Hon (1995) provided a detailed feminist critique of a wide range of factors and conditions that affect women in public relations. One popular rival explanation is that women in public relations play the manager role less frequently because they have fewer years of professional experience. An important stream of research regarding roles and gender are the three surveys of public relations practitioners in 1979, 1985, and 1991, under the direction of Broom (1982; Broom & Dozier, 1986; Dozier & Broom, 1995). By comparing manager and technician role enactment by men and women, while controlling for professional experience, data from the 1979 survey showed that men enacted the manager role more frequently, even after controlling for years of professional experience in public relations and length of employment with current employer. However, the same analysis of the 1991 data set indicated that, although women enacted the manager role less frequently than men, the difference had more to do with years of professional experience and length of employment with their current employer than with gender per se (Dozier & Broom, 1995). More significantly, the antecedent variables that Dozier and Broom analyzed from the 1979 and 1991 surveys (education, number of communicators in department, years of professional experience, length of employment with current employer, and gender) accounted for less than a third of the variance in manager role enactment.

The conventional wisdom holds that an entry-level communicator enters the practice with the expectation that he or she will enact the technician role predominantly. With more professional experience, practitioners move from the technical role to management responsibilities. However, a panel study by Broom and Dozier (1986) of 206 communicators who completed questionnaires in 1979 and 1985 showed that the process of increased enactment of the manager role and decreased enactment of the technician role did not follow this progression for all practitioners. Although manager role scores increased and technician role scores decreased from 1979 to 1985, this pattern was more pronounced for men than for women.

Professional experience is, indeed, positively related to enacting the manager role. However, the explained variance in manager role enactment accounted for by years of professional experience is small. In a 1979 survey of PRSA members, years of professional experience in public relations accounted for 7% of the variance in manager role enactment. In a follow-up survey of the same respondents in 1985, a more mature sample of communicators indicated that years of professional experience accounted for less than 1% of the explained variance in manager role enactment. Similarly, in a 1991 survey of PRSA and IABC members, a systematic sample indicated that years of professional experience in public relations work accounted for only 1% of the variance in manager role enactment. Clearly, role enactment makes a key contribution to understanding public relations and communication management precisely because years of professional experience and job titles do not illuminate relationships with other concepts important to excellence in public relations and communication management.

L. Grunig, Toth, and Hon (2001) reviewed this program of research by Broom, Dozier, and their colleagues as well as research they had conducted in two Glass Ceiling studies commissioned by PRSA in 1990 and 1995. After analyzing the 1990 data set, Toth and L. Grunig (1993) had concluded "that the failure to promote women derives not only from gender and years of professional experience, but from differences in the on-the-job experience in public relations. Although female managers in public relations perform managerial tasks, they continue to perform the technical tasks, too. In a sense, women are 'doing it all' " (L. Grunig et al., 2001, p. 224).

L. Grunig et al. (2001) analyzed the role profiles of men and women produced by the 1990 and 1995 surveys. We discussed the 1990 profiles earlier when we pointed out that dichotomizing measures of roles disguises the fact that women combine technical and managerial activities more than men. Toth and L. Grunig (1993) also found that women engage in more middle-management activities and men in more top-management activities.

When L. Grunig et al. (2001) compared the 1995 factor profiles for men and women with the 1990 profiles, they found that both men and women concentrated more on middle-management activities in 1995. They interpreted this change as a loss in status of the public relations function, for both men and women. They concluded that this change resulted from the "economic downsizing of the early 1990s, when there were many reports of senior public relations managers losing their jobs" (p. 247). Nevertheless, the 1995 profile showed that men did not lose as much ground as women: "Women lost ground in the range of activities that could have helped their professional advancement. In other words, the picture that emerges between 1990 and 1995 suggests that *women are farther from, rather than closer to, breaking through the glass ceiling in publics relations*" (p. 248).

L. Grunig et al. (2001) concluded that professional experience does not produce a change from a technical role to a managerial role for women as much as it does for men. Focus group data from the 1991 and 1995 Glass Ceiling studies provided details about these differences in the experiences of men and women. First, women in the focus groups said they were more willing than men to do technical work as well as managerial work, to accept a dual manager–technician role, and "to help out wherever needed" because it was not "beneath them" (p. 243). One women who participated in a focus group explained it this way:

> Are we undermining ourselves when they come to me and say, "How come you haven't had time to do these strategic-level things?" and it's because I've been taking care of the technical things that need to be done. I think we are doers. We'll do whatever needs to be done without regard for whether this is beneath me or

not. But in the grand scheme of things, does that work against us in the perception of others . . . when they see us typing labels?

Second, participants in the focus groups suggested that women play a dual role more than men because they are less likely to delegate work. "This is how one man explained what he has experienced. Technical work such as answering phones, running the copy machine, and stacking envelopes is included as part of female management's 'daily repertoire.' However, he said, 'The male managers that I know seem to delegate that' " (p. 245). Third, female managers in the focus groups talked more about "people" concerns whereas men focused on the strategic aspects of management. "Women said they felt pressured to *do* more, rather than to *strategize* more" (p. 250).

L. Grunig et al. (2001) also identified a third factor in the 1990 and 1995 Glass Ceiling data that they called the "agency factor," a factor that described the roles of men and women working in public relations firms. Broom, Dozier, and their colleagues had excluded public relations practitioners in firms from their analyses because they had found that the roles are different from those of in-house practitioners and because agency personnel perform different roles for different clients. L. Grunig et al. said that economic downsizing in the 1990s resulted in many men starting their own firms after they lost their in-house jobs. Furthermore, they said:

> [The agency profile reflects] the expert prescriber role introduced by Broom and Smith in 1979; but it also included the skills of handling correspondence, making telephone calls, and making media contacts. As such we also can link it to the role of communication liaison. In this factor—more collaborative and research-based than the two major roles—we see such additional activities as meeting with clients, executives, and peers; counseling management; and doing research. (p. 246)

The agency profile, however, included more activities for men than it did for women. In particular, "Men in this role do more work associated with the managerial role than do women" (p. 246).

Research on gender differences in the roles of men and women in public relations, in summary, has played a valuable role in understanding the differing experiences of men and women in the profession. In a broad sense, the research shows that men are more likely to be managers and women to be technicians. However, this broad difference conceals a great deal of difference in the experiences of women in public relations. Both male and female technicians typically do managerial work as well as technical work. Because there are more women in the technical role, however, this fact disguises the extent to which women engage in managerial activities. When women do managerial work, they tend to do it as middle managers rather than top managers, which is more the province of men. Because of the willingness to nurture others, to not delegate work, and to "do it all," women also have fewer professional experiences that prepare them for top management in comparison with men.

Roles and Organizational Environments

An organization's perceived environment can be, among other descriptors, simple or complicated, placid or turbulent (Duncan, 1972; Emery & Trist, 1965; Terreberry, 1968; Thompson, 1967). Pearce and Robinson (1982) defined an organization's *environment* as all conditions and forces that affect the organization's strategic options but are beyond the organization's control. Dozier (1992) argued that manager role enactment should increase as an organization's environment becomes more complicated or more turbulent.

However, dominant coalitions do not respond to an objective organizational environment. Rather, dominant coalitions respond to *representations* (or enactments), subjective sets of shared perceptions of the organization and its environment that members use to make decisions (White & Dozier, 1992). Indeed, the boundary between the organization and its environment is perceptual and fuzzy, described as "an arbitrary invention of the organization itself" (Starbuck, 1976, p. 1078). The communicator's organizational role becomes crucial in the construction and modification of such representations, because communicators serve as *boundary spanners* (see Aldrich & Herker, 1977), organizational members who frequently interact with the organization's environment and who gather, synthesize, and relay information about the environment on to the dominant coalition and others inside the organization (White & Dozier, 1992).

Organizations and communicators can engage in boundary-spanning activities with varying degrees of formality and sophistication. Organizations can formalize management information systems (MIS) to collect and organize information in forms suitable to different points and levels in the decision-making process (Humphreys, 1985). Theoretically, dominant coalitions pay greater attention to information from boundary spanners under conditions of environmental turbulence (Emery & Trist, 1965; White & Dozier, 1992).

However, organizations and, particularly, dominant coalitions anticipate and respond to environments of their own creation. Although a material reality does exist beyond the arbitrary boundaries of the organization, meaning attached to representations of that environment is best regarded as an artifact of organizational culture (White & Dozier, 1992). Organizations have cultures with their own implicit, unstated, and frequently invisible presuppositions about the organization itself, its environment, and the connection between the two. Like a tourist visiting another nation and culture, the boundary spanner has opportunities to see the organization from the outside and can develop sensitivities to how others regard the organization.

From the power-control perspective (see chap. 5 and L. Grunig, 1992), representations of organizational environments become chips in the game of organizational politics. When dominant coalitions make strategic decisions, they use representations of organizational environments as part of a complicated drama, "which involves power, influence, negotiation, game playing, organizational politics, complex social relationships with real people, not merely office holders" (Eden & Sims, 1979, p. 120).

With specific regard to public relations, Broom (1986; Broom & Dozier, 1990) suggested that organizations could be viewed along an open–closed systems continuum. In a closed-system organization, public relations planning and decision making follow a historicist causal model; what communicators implement during the current budget cycle is driven substantially by what they implemented last year, modified by whims of powerful people inside the organization. In an open-systems organization, representations of the organizational environment are constantly updated through feedback loops, information flowing into the organization about how constituencies in the environment are responding to organizational behaviors and to issues important to the organization.

Perceived complexity and turbulence in the organizational environment ought to increase manager role enactment among top communicators because dominant coalitions sense an increased need for information from boundary spanners, in order to make decisions that *satisfice*—the term used to describe a decision that is good enough although not necessarily the best possible decision. Vari and Vecsenyi (1984) described five distinct roles in management decision making: decision makers, proposers, experts, consultants, and facilitators. White and Dozier (1992) suggested that communicators play their most important role when they serve as consultants who advise on methods of problem representation:

> As generalists, (communication) practitioners must strive to provide fuller representations of the environment to decision makers. Communication managers are uniquely positioned to ensure that decision makers have adequate (rather than idiosyncratic) language / code systems and appropriate (rather than local) conceptual frameworks for representing the decision problem in a form that permits a solution that satisfices. (p. 105)

At the same time, communicators find it difficult to resolve conflicts with publics when they could have been avoided through more informed decision making. The practitioners' lament is often that they are not included in decision making but are asked to repair the damage once it "hits the fan."

D. J. Johnson and Acharya (1982) and Acharya (1983) identified 16 attributes of organizational environments and then asked a systematic sample of 229

PRSA members to evaluate each element with regard to complexity and variability to generate the following typology: nonthreatening/static, nonthreatening/dynamic, threatening/static, and threatening/dynamic. Technician role enactment was predominant in organizations with nonthreatening/static environments only. Components of manager role enactment were associated with the other three environments. Manager role enactment (especially the expert prescription and problem-solving process facilitation aspects of that role) were especially pronounced in environments that communicators described as both dynamic and threatening.

In a related manner, Lauzen and Dozier (1992) found that manager role enactment increased among corporate communicators studied as a function of environmental pressure and instability. In 1989, Lauzen (1991, 1992) conducted a survey of 168 communicators systematically sampled from *O'Dwyer's Directory of Corporate Communications*. Lauzen adapted Duncan's (1972) 10-item index to measure how important communicators regarded a list of strategic publics. The number or range of publics regarded as important to the organization was taken as an operational indicator of environmental pressure on the organization. Lauzen also adapted Duncan's scale to measure environmental instability, operationalized as how often the attitudes or behaviors of key publics change. Manager role enactment increased significantly as a function of both the range of publics as salient or exerting pressure ($r = .20$, $p < .01$) and the perceived instability of their attitudes and behaviors ($r = .16$, $p < .05$).

Emerging technologies like the Internet permit communication practitioners to play expanded boundary-spanning roles. M. A. Johnson (1997) argued that use of two-way communication technologies like the Internet engenders an audience or public orientation among communicators, rather than an orientation toward the organization's dominant coalition. This becomes a key orientation in helping dominant coalitions construct representations of environments that satisfice.

Roles and Program Research

For public relations practitioners and communication managers to serve as effective boundary spanners, they must act as the eyes and ears of organizations, as well as spokespersons. That is, communication practitioners must supplement the traditional crafts of one-way communication (such as organizing press conferences, writing news releases, and producing public relations materials) with competencies that permit them to enact two-way communication. Public relations practitioners have always performed this two-way communication function informally, by talking to media contacts, handling complaints from publics, and the like. However, boundary-spanning communicators can perform a two-way communication function more effectively if they understand and use program research.

Program research is information gathering and analysis conducted (or subcontracted) by communicators to scan the organization's environment and to evaluate the effectiveness of communication programs. Use of program research among communicators has been studied extensively, especially as such program research relates to role enactment (Dozier, 1990). Although informal gathering of information is a natural extension of the knowledge base of the "journalist-in-residence" (Broom & Smith, 1978, 1979), the use of focus groups, representative sampling, survey methodology, and quantitative data analysis are all properly regarded as innovations in public relations and communication management. As a technology cluster, the innovation of public relations research is expected to follow the S-curve of adoption, with a few innovators using program research in the beginning, followed by a midpoint of fairly rapid adoption, and then a slowing of rate of adoption (Rogers, 1983).

Central to excellence in public relations and communication management is the knowledge base to use the two-way models (see chap. 8; see also Dozier with L. Grunig & J. Grunig, 1995), both symmetrical and asymmetrical. Both two-way models rest on the need for communicators to act as eyes and ears for their organizations, keeping the dominant coalition informed as to how strategic publics react to organizations and issues important to them.

Dozier (1984a, 1984b, 1986, 1987, 1988a, 1988b, 1988c) conducted a number of studies of practitioner use of evaluation methods and environmental scanning techniques, which were later summarized (Dozier, 1990). The distinction between scanning research and evaluation research, as originally conceptualized, proved less useful when the behavior of communicators was studied inductively. Using factor analysis, Dozier identified three approaches to program research. The *scientific approach* uses formal research techniques to survey publics and track reactions to the organization, conduct public relations audits, subscribe to public opinion research services, use demographic data for decision making, conduct focus group message tests, and review published public opinion surveys. Implicit in the scientific approach is the knowledge base to make sense of such information. The *mixed approach* consists of some formal techniques (such as content analysis of clip files and quantitative analysis of complaints by phone or letter) blended with seat-of-the-pants techniques (such as attending meetings and conferences and monitoring placements through close media contacts). The *informal approach* consists entirely of essentially informal, oral communication between the communicator and members of key publics. This approach uses phone calls to members of target publics, calling back attendees of special events, conducting long interviews with publics, and talking with field personnel.

No approach is inherently superior, because such choices are driven by many contextual factors. These include time frame, budget, communicator relationships with the dominant coalition, and whether findings are likely to be challenged or not (Broom & Dozier, 1990; Dozier, 1990). However, the approaches do differ in the degree to which a specialized knowledge base is required, with the scientific approach requiring the most specialized knowledge and the informal approach requiring the least. This can be seen in the relative frequency with which the different approaches are used. In Dozier's 1987 study of IABC members (Dozier, 1988c, 1990), the informal approach was used most frequently. On a 7-point scale ranging from never (1) to always (7), the informal approach posted a mean of 4.3, significantly higher than the 4.1 mean for the mixed approach. The scientific approach posted a mean of 2.9 on the same scale, significantly less than both the informal and mixed approaches.

Hon (1998) conducted long interviews with a nonprobability sample of 32 communicators and 10 other executives to determine how public relations programs were evaluated. As in previous research, communicators used a number of evaluation tools, ranging from informal to scientific. As in Dozier's (1988c, 1990) IABC survey in 1987, Hon found little formal research. She concluded, "Only two practitioners described evaluation scenarios that seem pretty close to ideal" (p. 130), with one communicator using research to plan and evaluate communication programs and another reporting that formal evaluation was built into each of the agency's programs.

In Dozier's 1987 survey of IABC members (Dozier, 1988c, 1990), use of the mixed approach was the most highly correlated with enactment of the manager role ($r = .42, N = 200, p < .01$), followed by use of the scientific approach ($r = .28, N = 198, p < .01$) and the informal approach ($r = .19, N = 202, p < .01$). That is, enacting the communication manager role is positively related to using all three approaches to program research. Enacting the communication technician role, on the other hand, is negatively related to using the scientific approach, but not significantly so ($r = -.03, N = 201, p = .36$). Technician role enactment is not significantly related to the informal approach ($r = .04, N = 205, p = .25$). Only the mixed research approach, with its emphasis on seat-of-the-pants and clip-file evaluation, posted a significant correlation with technician role enactment ($r = .12, N = 204, p = .04$).

Regarding evaluation alone, Broom and Dozier's (1986) 6-year panel study of PRSA members in 1979 and 1985 permitted an analysis of evaluation activities in 1985 as a function of change in manager role scores since the 1979 survey. Practitioners who increased their manager role scores from 1979 to 1985 posted higher evaluation scores than did practitioners whose manager role enactment scores remained unchanged or decreased (Dozier, 1990).

Role enactment and program research interact differently for men and women. Based on surveys of communicators in 1985 and 1987, Dozier (1990) argued that program research plays a larger role in career advancement of women than it does for men. For men, manager role enactment is somewhat more important. Dozier argued (1989, 1990) that the use of program research provided female communicators with a mechanism for career advancement.

Roles and the Dominant Coalition

Implicit in the manager–technician dichotomy is an assumption about the communicator's relationship with the dominant coalition. Concern about management participation is closely tied to normative definitions of public relations as an emerging profession. Arguably, public relations is a management function that is effective only when top communicators have access to management and strategic decision making, either as formal members of dominant coalitions or as informal advisers privy to such decision making on a regular basis (see J. Grunig, 1992a).

Broom (1982) used a 5-point, five-item index to operationalize the concept of participation in management decision making. Communicators were asked how often they participated in decisions on adopting new policies, meetings with management to discuss major problems, meetings regarding the adoption of new programs or procedures (or both), meetings to evaluate and discuss the results of new programs, and meetings on how to implement new programs. The index had a Cronbach's alpha of .92 in the 1979, 1985, and 1991 surveys.

As expected, enactment of the manager role is significantly and positively correlated with participation in management decision making. Dozier and Broom (1995) confirmed the relationship in the 1979, 1985, and 1991 surveys. In 1979, the Pearson correlation coefficient between manager role enactment and decision-making participation was .66 ($N = 438$, $p < .001$). In the 1985 follow-up survey of the same respondents, the correlation was .65 ($N = 208$, $p < .001$). In the 1991 survey, the correlation between manager role enactment and decision-making participation was .66 ($N = 197$, $p < .001$).

In a 1995 national survey of communicators working for hospitals, Gordon and Kelly (1999) found strong relationships between reported manager role competencies in the communication department, departmental expertise to participate in strategic planning with the dominant coalition, and the overall effectiveness of the hospital. They used four indicators of hospital effectiveness: meeting its budget, reaching short-term goals in the strategic plan, making progress or reaching long-term goals, and advancing the hospital's mission. Overall hospital effectiveness was strongly related to manager role competencies in the communication department ($r = .65$, $p < .01$) and departmental competencies to participate in strategic planning ($r = .64$, $p < .01$).

Enactment of the communication technician role, on the other hand, is not associated with participation in management decision making. In Broom's (1982) survey of PRSA members in 1979, technician role enactment was not significantly related to participation in management decision making ($r = .07$, $N = 438$, $p = .16$). When the components of the index were tested separately, only participation in meetings on how to *implement* programs was significantly correlated with participation ($r = .15$, $N = 439$, $p < .01$). In a retest of the same relationships with a subset of the same respondents in 1985, the overall correlation was not significant ($r = .06$, $N = 208$, $p = .37$). When the components of the index were tested separately, none of the relationships was statistically significant. In 1991, the relationship was tested again with the same results. No significant relationship was found between technician role enactment and participation in management decision making ($r = .07$, $N = 202$, $p = .33$). When tested individually, none of the components of the index was correlated with technician role enactment.

Issues Management. Issues management is one area in which communicators typically work with dominant coalitions and participate in decision making. Issues management is the "proactive process of anticipating, identifying, evaluating, and responding to public policy issues that affect organizations and their publics" (Cutlip, Center, & Broom, 1994, p. 16). Numerous scholars and practitioners have examined issues management in the context of public relations (Crable & Vibbert, 1985; Dyer, 1996; Gaunt & Ollenberger, 1995; Hainsworth & Meng, 1988; Heath, 1998; Heath & Cousino, 1990; Heath & Nelson, 1986; Jones & Chase, 1979; Lauzen, 1994, 1997; Trumbo, 1995).

Of particular relevance to manager role enactment is Lauzen and Dozier's (1994) study of 182 senior-level communicators sampled from the 1991 *O'Dwyer Directory of Corporate Communications*. Lauzen introduced the concept of outer-directed issues management practices, defined as an orientation toward the organizational environment that is symmetrical, open, and proactive, using information from the environment in an instrumental (rather than symbolic) way to align and adapt to the environment. Using a measure of outer-directed issues management practices, Lauzen and Dozier tested a model that posited that perceived environmental complexity and turbulence would cause the dominant coalition to seek greater manager role enactment and decision-making participation from their top communicators. Such demand, however, is mediated by the degree to which the organizational culture is participative and the issues management system is outer directed. In testing their model, Lauzen and Dozier found that perceived environmental complexity was positively correlated with participative culture ($r = .36$, $p < .01$) and outer-directed issues management practices ($r = .45$, $p < .01$). Communicator participation in management decision making was also positively correlated with participative organizational culture ($r = .44$, $p < .01$) and outer-directed issues management practices ($r = .52$, $p < .01$). Participation in decision making was strongly correlated with manager role enactment ($r = .52$). However, manager role enactment and decision-making participation were not related to environmental complexity, once the influence of participative culture and outer-directed issues management practices were controlled.

Encroachment.   Manager role enactment and participation in management decision making are related to the concept of encroachment. Encroachment is the assignment of nonpublic relations professionals to manage the public relations function (Dozier, 1988a; Lesly, 1981). In 1989, Lauzen (1991, 1992) conducted a survey of 168 communicators systematically sampled from *O'Dwyer's Directory of Corporate Communications.* Her study used the concept of *marketing imperialism* to hypothesize that less powerful communication departments would experience imperialism from several other departments, in addition to marketing (Lauzen, 1991).

Lauzen developed a model predicting reduced encroachment as a function of manager role enactment and *powerful public relations schema.* She adapted powerful schema from J. Grunig and White (1991), who conceptualized communicators' schema as abstract knowledge structures used to organize knowledge and behavior regarding the communication function in organizations. Such schema may be powerful if communicators see themselves as nonsubstitutable; no other individuals or units in the organization can adequately perform the public relations and communication management function.

Lauzen argued such schema are based on formal training and specialized expertise. She (1991) found that manager role enactment and powerful schema both contributed to reducing encroachment into the public relations domain by other departments in the organizations studied. In a 1990 study of 262 communicators also systematically sampled from *O'Dwyer's Directory of Corporate Communications,* Lauzen (1993; Lauzen & Dozier, 1992) found that manager role enactment by the top communicators played a key role in reducing encroachment by the organization's marketing department into the management of areas (e.g., public affairs, employee communication, and media relations) traditionally regarded as in the public relations domain.

Kelly (1993) studied encroachment among communicators who work for fund-raising organizations. She conducted telephone interviews with a purposive sample of 19 communicators in organizations that included educational institutions, human service organizations, health organizations, and organizations devoted to the arts, culture, and humanities. Based on her research, Kelly adapted Lauzen's model that linked encroachment to manager role enactment of the top communicator. Role enactment was driven by communicator aspirations and competencies, the role sent by the dominant coalition, and the perception of public relations as a primary or secondary function in the organization. In addition, she posited that environmental turbulence and dependency on fund-raising contributed to encroachment.

Gender and Management Decision Making.   Women communicators participate significantly less in management decision making than do their male colleagues. This finding was confirmed in the 1979 survey of PRSA members

(Broom, 1982), the 1995 follow-up with a subsample of the same respondents (Broom & Dozier, 1986), and the survey of PRSA and IABC members in 1991 (Dozier & Broom, 1995). In all three surveys, however, these differences disappeared when the influence of manager role enactment was controlled. Logically, the path to greater participation in management decision making is through communication manager role enactment.

One strategy for women pursuing career advancement is to develop mentoring relationships with other, senior members of the organization. The literature suggests that advancement in organizations often occurs when a senior member of the organization treats an entry-employee as an *informal assistant,* teaching the junior colleague the ropes and thus helping the new employee learn how things get done in the organization. Mentoring, then, provides one mechanism for career advancement.

However, a study of 190 practitioners sampled from the IABC and PRSA directories indicated no direct relationship between the protégé's management participation and decision making, on the one hand, and quality of mentoring on the other (Tam, Dozier, Lauzen, & Real, 1995). Key to deconstructing the findings was an examination of the gender attributes of mentor–protégé pairings. Better mentoring (measured as giving advice, providing information, and demonstrating concern about the protégé's advancement) is provided in same-gender pairs (e.g., female–female), when compared to cross-gender pairs (e.g., male–female).

Among the four possible combinations of gender pairings, female mentors provided the highest quality of mentoring to female protégés. However, with regard to manager role enactment, protégés in female–female pairings posted the lowest career advancement scores. Strength of the relationship was reduced when age of protégés was controlled (Tam et al., 1995). The authors theorized that mentoring was superior in same-gender pairings and especially from female mentors; management role enactment of the mentor is positively related to how helpful a mentor can be in a protégé's career advancement: "Regardless of their gender, practitioners with male superiors had more chances to enact the manager role. Technician role enactment, on the other hand, is more influenced by the subordinate's gender. Female subordinates tend to enact the technician role with significantly greater frequency than male subordinates, regardless of their supervisors' gender" (p. 269). Management role enactment of superiors, then, can either enhance or limit the career advancement opportunities of all their subordinates, when advancement is defined as management role enactment and participation in management decision making.

Role Enactment and Income

A sensitive area of scholarship in public relations and communication management is the link between manager role enactment and income. In the published research on role enactment and income, the empirical findings are largely irrefutable. Communicators playing the manager role predominantly earn higher salaries than practitioners playing the technician role predominantly. For instance, in the 1979 survey of PRSA members, communicators playing the manager role predominantly earned $39,364 annually, compared to $24,406 for technicians (Broom, 1982). That is, technicians earned 62% of what managers earned in 1979. In the 1985 follow-up with a subsample of the same communicators, managers earned $61,753. Those enacting the technician role predominantly earned $40,564, or 66% of what managers earned (Broom & Dozier, 1986). In a 1991 survey of PRSA and IABC members, communicators enacting the manager role predominantly earned $67,803. Technicians, on the other hand, earned $44,932 annually, or again 66% of what managers earned that year (Dozier & Broom, 1995).

The empirical evidence is definitive that salary differences in the incomes of managers and technicians are not due to differences in professional experience. For example, in the 1979 survey of PRSA members, the adjusted income of those enacting the manager role predominantly (after controlling for the influence of years of professional experience in public relations) equaled $37,300. The adjusted income for technicians in 1979 was $28,740, or 77% of what managers with equal experience were earning (Broom, 1982). In the 1985 follow-up, the adjusted income of those enacting the manager role predominantly was $61,120. Among technicians in the 1985 follow-up survey, adjusted income was $42,210, or 69% of what managers with equivalent professional experience were earning (Broom & Dozier, 1986). In the 1991 survey of PRSA and IABC members, the adjusted income of those enacting the manager role predominantly equaled $62,710. Among technicians in the 1991 survey, the adjusted income was $51,560, or 82% of what managers with equal professional experience were making. In all three studies, professional experience was a significant predictor of manager role enactment and also a significant predictor of income. However, in those three studies, manager role enactment remained a significant predictor of income, even after communicators had been equalized in terms of professional experience.

Role enactment and income are related in complex ways. Dozier and Broom (1995) proposed a model that attempted to integrate prior theorizing and research findings and then tested it on two independent samples of PRSA members collected 12 years apart. Enactment of the manager role predominantly was placed at the center. The model posited gender as antecedent to all other variables in the model. Men were hypothesized to have more years of professional experience and to have been employed by their current employer (tenure) for a longer period of time. Overall professional experience and tenure were hypothesized to contribute positively to manager role enactment.

Dozier and Broom (1995) also theorized that gender discrimination contributed to higher incidences of men enacting the manager role predominantly, after removing the effects of professional experience and tenure. Enacting the manager role predominantly was posited as positively correlated with participation in management decision making. Such participation was, in turn, hypothesized as positively correlated with income. Additional variance in income was hypothesized between men and women, once participation in decision making and manager role enactment were removed.

Using 440 completed questionnaires from the 1979 survey, the model just described was confirmed. However, using 203 completed questionnaires from the 1991 survey, the residual variance between gender and enacting the manager role predominantly had declined dramatically, with the beta coefficient dropping from .19 in 1979 to .08 in 1991. That is, men in the 1991 survey were more likely to enact the manager role predominantly; but men having more professional experience and tenure substantially accounted for such enactment. In addition, the residual variance between gender and income also declined dramatically, from a beta weight of .25 in 1979 to a beta weight of .03 in 1991. That is, men earned higher incomes than women in 1991; but that income difference was substantially accounted for by the intervening variables of professional experience, manager role enactment, and participation in decision making.

Dozier and Broom (1995) were quick to point out that their findings were tentative, due in part to a smaller sample size in the 1991 survey. However, the findings do show some progress in reducing the more blatant forms of gender discrimination with regard to role enactment and income. More germane to the issue at hand, enactment of the manager role predominantly serves as a key intervening variable in explaining income differences between men and women.

Roles and New Technology

New communication technologies are transforming mediated communication in the 21st century, placing demands on public relations practitioners and communication managers to adopt such technologies. Role enactment provides a useful theoretical framework for thinking about communication and technology. Dozier (1989) argued that new technologies can be divided into those that enhance what communicators already do and those that allow the communicator "to do something completely new and different, to play a different role in the organization" (p. 4). He asserted that every technological innovation should be evaluated with regard to its role appropriateness. Technologies, which were innovative at the time, included desktop publishing and internal e-mail distribution lists; these technologies enhance enactment of the technician role. Other innovations, like statistical application software for personal computers, enhance the enactment of the manager role, because such applications "provide a tool for analyzing data collected by scanning the environment and detecting public relations problems or opportunities" (p. 5). Technologies that help disseminate messages enhance technician role enactment; technologies that help solve strategic problems enhance manager role enactment.

Anderson and Reagan (1992) conducted a survey of public relations practitioners in the state of Washington to assess the relationship between role enactment and use of new technologies. They computed correlations between manager and technician role enactment and 20 technologies previously identified as relevant to public relations (Druck, Fiur, & Bates, 1986). Findings indicate that managers and technicians use different technologies and in different ways. Manager role enactment was significantly correlated with the use of technology for strategic planning purposes such as public affairs policy planning, issues management, media monitoring, market and demographic planning, and budgeting. Technician role enactment was not correlated with these applications.

In a series of case studies with 17 communicators in 12 American corporations, Thomsen (1995) found evidence of further relevance of new technology to manager role enactment. Through a semistructured interview protocol, Thomsen found communicators using commercial online databases to participate in environmental scanning, allowing managers to identify emerging issues earlier in the issue cycle, and helping their organizations become more proactive in their responses.

M. A. Johnson (1997) conducted a qualitative study of 17 communicators in an American city in the Southeast, permitting in-depth exploration of uses of new communication technologies. Her findings suggested that the availability of online research services through the Internet could accelerate the adoption of research tools advocated in the professional literature (e.g, Broom & Dozier, 1990).

Satisfaction and the Subjectivity of Role Enactment

Enormous normative value is placed on the importance of manager role enactment in the professional literature (Cutlip et al., 1994; J. Grunig & Hunt, 1984). Manager role enactment permits the communication department to counsel decision makers in dominant coalitions, in order to practice the two-way symmetrical model (see chap. 8 and Dozier et al., 1995). One might expect that manager role enactment would be positively correlated with job satisfaction among communicators.

In their 1991 survey of PRSA members, however, Dozier and Broom (1995) found that enacting the manager role predominantly was not significantly correlated with job satisfaction, once the influence of decision-making participation was removed (beta = .03). They found a higher beta weight (beta = .11) when they conducted a similar analysis from a comparable survey of PRSA members in 1979, but the residual correlation was small compared with the direct contribution of decision-making participation on job satisfaction (beta = .48).

In analyzing data from a panel study of 206 PRSA members from 1979 to 1985, Broom and Dozier (1986) found that practitioners who enacted the manager role predominantly in 1979 posted higher job satisfaction scores than did practitioners enacting the technician role predominantly. However, 6 years later, job satisfaction among managers had declined and satisfaction among technicians had increased; managers and technicians did not differ significantly with regard to job satisfaction in the 1985 survey. Using dominant role enactment from the 1979 and 1985 data, Broom and Dozier developed a four-way typology of career paths: technician-to-manager, technician-to-technician, manager-to-technician, and manager-to-manager. They then analyzed change in job satisfaction for each career path. Technicians who stayed in the technical role increased most on the job satisfaction index, up .53 on a 5-point scale. Technicians who became managers over the 6 years posted an increase of .23, less than half the gain of technicians who remained technicians. Job satisfaction among managers who stayed in that role for the 6 years dropped slightly (Broom & Dozier, 1986).

Some evidence (Broom & Dozier, 1986; Dozier & Broom, 1995) suggests that if communicators could participate in management decision making, they would otherwise prefer to enact the technician role. For example, McGoon (1993) reported the results of an informal fax poll conducted by *Communication World*. Most of the 170 communicators responding indicated that they preferred writing, editing, producing publications, and other activities of technical role enactment. Only 18 of the 170 said they liked managing the activities in the public relations or communication department. Four of the 170 said they liked working with top management as their preferred work activity. When asked what they would like to be doing in 10 years, responses included: "writer collecting royalties on a runaway best-seller children's book," "living in Italy writing books," "on a beach," "owning my own greenhouse," and "in France working as an English professor." Zoch et al. (1997) surveyed communicators for all 91 school districts in South Carolina and found that creativity, which generally is associated with the technician role, was one of five factors rated higher than salary in contributing to communicator job satisfaction.

A more systematic analysis of the subjective dimensions of role enactment was conducted by Dozier and Gottesman (1982) of communicators in the San Diego area. Using Q-methodology (Broom & Dozier, 1990; McKeown & Thomas, 1988) in conjunction with large-sample survey methods, Dozier and Gottesman relied on intensive data collection from a few respondents to construct models of communicator belief systems about their roles and their work. They found one belief system highly correlated with enactment of the technician role in the survey portion of the study. Labeled *creative artistic* practitioners, communicators highly loaded on this factor indicated that they preferred the spontaneous, intuitive, and creative aspects of their work.

If the creative artistic practitioner seeks opportunities to enact activities defining the technician role, the Q-study sheds light on Broom and Dozier's (1986) finding from their panel study that technicians who remained technicians over the 6-year period posted the largest increase in job satisfaction. Dozier and Gottesman (1982) reported that although creative artistic practitioners said they served in top- and middle-management positions, as well as staff positions, they seemed to avoid activities associated with manager role enactment. Creative artistic practitioners, Dozier and Gottesman reported, wanted "more say in organizational decisions" but remained "distrustful of changes implied by climbing the organizational ladder to decision-making levels" (p. 26). This finding helps explain Dozier and Broom's (1995) finding from the 1991 survey of PRSA members that manager role enactment is not correlated with job satisfaction, once participation in decision making is controlled.

As noted by Creedon (1991), the manager–technician dichotomy is problematic for a number of reasons. With regard to the creative activities associated with technician role enactment, she cited Parsons' finding that college students majoring in public relations who were surveyed at four American universities expressed little ambition to do creative work. P. R. Parsons (1989) found that "One of the most dramatic and surprising findings of the study was the degree to which public relations students disliked all the proffered forms of creative work" (p. 165). Whether emphasis on manager role enactment plays a role in the way college students select their majors is unclear. However, emphasis on manager role enactment in public relations textbooks (e.g., Cutlip et al., 1994; J. Grunig & Hunt, 1984) may influence future communicators to regard manager role enactment as "preferable" (Creedon, 1991, p. 76).

Despite such notable research on communicator job satisfaction as the 1990 and 1995 PRSA studies (Serini, Toth, Wright, & Emig, 1997), the interface of role enactment, job satisfaction, and communicator belief systems has not been adequately investigated. Indeed, the normative demands for manager role enactment are at least paradoxical, given what working communicators report about their job satisfaction, their ambitions, and belief systems about their work. As discussed later, some of the paradox is caused by a certain slipperiness in past roles research with regard to whether the individual communicator or the communication department served as the unit of analysis.

Use of Role Measures Outside the United States

Most roles research has been conducted in the United States (Acharya, 1983; Broom, 1982; Broom & Dozier, 1985, 1986; Broom & Smith, 1978, 1979; Dozier, 1981, 1983, 1984a, 1984c, 1986, 1987, 1988c, 1989, 1990; Dozier & Broom, 1995; Dozier & Gottesman, 1982; D. J. Johnson & Acharya, 1982; Lauzen, 1991, 1992; Lauzen & Dozier, 1992; Sullivan, Dozier, & Hellweg, 1984, 1985). However, before the Excellence study, some roles research had been conducted outside the United States.

Piekos and Einsiedel (1990) explored the relationship between role enactment and evaluation methods among Canadian communicators using membership lists of the Canadian Public Relations Society (CPRS) and the International Association of Business Communicators. They received 309 questionnaires by mail. As in earlier U.S. studies, Piekos and Einsiedel found that components of the manager role (expert prescriber, problem-solving process facilitator, and communication facilitator) correlated positively and significantly with evaluation methods, both scientific and intuitive. However, technician role scores also correlated with both scientific and intuitive evaluation research. They speculated that greater specialization and larger communication departments in the United States might account for the difference. In Canada, a large number of department heads enact the technician role predominantly.

Later, Coombs, Holladay, Hasenauer, and Signitzer (1994) conducted a comparative analysis by surveying communication professionals in Austria, Norway, and the United States. After dichotomizing respondents as either managers or technicians using an eight-item subset of Broom's role measures, they found that practitioners played the manager role predominantly in Austria (75%) and the United States (70%), whereas a minority of Norwegian communicators (41%) enacted the manager role predominantly. Coombs and his colleagues cited differences in educational systems as contributing to this difference.

The factor structure of role items appeared very robust in a 1994 survey of 127 communicators and public relations practitioners in Bangkok, Thailand (Ekachai, 1995). Ekachai subjected the 24 items to exploratory factor analysis, which would permit the greatest opportunity for the Thai factor analysis to deviate from factor analysis conducted on U.S. samples. In the Thai factor analysis, 10 items loaded heavily on the first factor, which Ekachai interpreted as the manager role factor. Nine of the 10 items on her manager role factor also loaded heavily on the Dozier and Broom (1995) manager factor found for American communicators in 1979 and 1991. (Dozier and Broom used confirmatory factor analysis, which forced a two-factor solution, based on earlier research demonstrating the utility of that dichotomy.)

Ekachai (1995) found that technician role activities, as isolated in the 1979 and 1991 surveys of U.S. communicators (Dozier & Broom, 1995), were split across two factors in the Thai sample. She interpreted these as a media relations specialist factor and a graphic technician factor; all six items from Ekachai's media relations specialist and graphics technician factors were the items that also loaded on Dozier and Broom's technician factor. In addition, Ekachai reported a separate factor for enactment of the communication liaison role, which likely would have merged with the manager factor, had confirmatory factor analysis (specifying a two-factor solution) been employed.

Different Role Measurement Strategies

Much of the roles research in public relations and communication management has used Broom's 24-item set (Dozier & Broom, 1995) or a subset of it, combining items to form indexes of the four conceptual roles postulated by Broom

(Broom, 1982; Broom & Smith, 1979), the two-role dichotomy proposed by Dozier (1983), or both. However, several researchers have used different operationalizations of what practitioners do and the roles they play in organizations.

Ferguson (1979) constructed a universe of practitioner activities by combing the public relations literature and survey data from communicators. After eliminating duplications, she reduced the measures to a set of 45 items. Ferguson focused on identifying the role norms of communicators by asking "how appropriate or proper" each activity was for those participating in the survey (p. 3). After Katz and Kahn (1978), such activities might be described as the role received and the expectations of the office as understood by the communicator (not actual role behaviors enacted). Ferguson collected data from a national sample of PRSA members and subjected her item set to factor analysis. Eight interpretable factors emerged; two other factors were discarded because too few items loaded on those factors to permit interpretation. Ferguson named her factors as: problem-solver manager, staff manager, researcher, goodwill ambassador, meeting organizer, journalist-technical communicator, public community relations, and personnel-industrial relations.

More recently, Berkowitz and Hristodoulakis (1999) developed a 13-item set of norms or ideals applicable to public relations work, derived from a discussion of activities and functions of public relations in Cutlip et al. (1994). The item set was self-administered to a campus chapter of the Public Relations Student Society of America and mailed to a sample of PRSA members in a nearby city in the American Midwest. The resulting data were subjected to cluster analysis, specifying a two-cluster solution. The first cluster was interpreted as a management orientation, with high value placed on counseling management in decision making. The second cluster was interpreted as a technician orientation, with high value placed on being a "people person" and regarding public relations primarily as a creative activity.

Guth (1995) developed a 10-item set that measured the technician role, with some items similar to Broom's technician items (e.g., write news releases and serve as photographer) and others quite different (e.g., take dictation and cannot be fired except for policy violation). Guth also developed a 20-item manager role index. Some items were similar to Broom's expert prescriber (e.g., develop organizational policy), problem-solving process facilitator (e.g., counsel others on public relations concerns), and communication facilitator (e.g., serve as organizational spokesperson). Other items were strikingly different (e.g., serve at the pleasure of the CEO, have private office, and have 4-year college degree).

Wright (1995) conducted intensive observations with 148 executives who were members of the Arthur Page Society, a professional organization of senior-level communicators. He used a one-page questionnaire (returned by fax machine), conversational (long) interviews, and two focus groups at a meeting of the Arthur Page Society to collect data. Based on his research, Wright advocated a "third major role for public relations—communication executive, comprised mainly of corporate senior vice presidents who report directly to CEOs" (p. 181).

Morton (1996) triangulated on the manager and technician roles by using a variety of proxy measures associated with different levels of role enactment, as well as a more direct measure of "primary activities" reported by respondents (p. 365). She used years of professional experience, salary, number of others that the respondent supervised, education, and organizational type to discriminate between managers and technicians via these correlates. More directly, respondents were further differentiated by indicating the following as primary activities: writing, developing campaigns, producing publications, supervising others, advising management, and coordinating events.

Leichty and Springston (1996) combined Broom's (1982) 24-item set with 14 additional items they adapted from the organizational boundary-spanning literature. Their questionnaire was completed by 137 members of the Public Relations Council of Alabama. When subjected to exploratory factor analysis, eight factors with eigenvalues greater than 1.0 emerged. Two factors, however, consisted of only two items, making them somewhat difficult to interpret. Factor 2 consisted of four items associated with the manager role factor (see Dozier & Broom, 1995); none of 14 boundary-spanning items loaded heavily on this factor. Factor 6 consisted of four technician role measures from the Broom set, with no heavy loadings for any of the 14 additional boundary-spanning activities. Factor scores were generated for each respondent for each of the eight factors. Next, factor scores were subjected to a series of cluster analyses. A five-cluster solution was deemed superior to other solutions and interpreted as internals, generalists, externals, traditional managers, and outliers.

Wright, L. Grunig, Springston, and Toth (1991) and Toth, Serini, Wright, and Emig (1998) conducted surveys of PRSA members in 1990 ($N = 1,027$) and in 1995 ($N = 678$). A 17-item role set developed at Boston University was used in each survey, including items the same as (or similar to) Broom's original, four-role typology: expert prescriber (e.g., making communication policy decisions), problem-solving process facilitator (e.g., counseling management), and communication facilitator (e.g., meeting with clients and executives) roles, as well as measures of the communication technician (e.g., writing, editing, and producing messages). Data for women and men were factor analyzed separately for both surveys. The 1990 exploratory factor analysis yielded two factors for both men and women; the two factors closely parallel the manager and technician role factors. In 1995, however, the factors became less distinguishable, with many items posting lower factor loadings than in 1990. Moreover, the exploratory factor analysis revealed a third factor in 1995 that Toth and her colleagues (1998) interpreted as the *agency profile*. Items with high factor loadings included meeting with peers, meeting with clients and executives, evaluating program results, handling correspondence, and making phone calls.

Given the diversity of approaches to measuring practitioner roles, which way is best? The simple answer is: It depends. As noted in a previous review of roles research (Dozier, 1992), roles are abstractions of the myriad activities of communicators in their day-to-day work. As such, conceptualizing and measuring roles is inherently problematic. Roles research in public relations and communication management has used quantitative methods extensively, drawing items from a review of the literature (e.g., hypothetical-deductive approach) to construct a nomothetic model of explanation. These presuppositions are built into much of the roles research in public relations. Within those assumptions, the use of factor analysis or cluster analysis as data reduction tools adds additional wrinkles. In exploratory factor analysis, the number of factors increases as a function of the number of items analyzed. In confirmatory factor analysis and cluster analysis, data reduction is forced. As such, there is no one right number of roles or one right way to measure them.

However, several issues ought to be weighed when selecting role measures. At an operational level, how reliable have role measures proven in past research? Many reports of role studies do not provide reliability coefficients. Using role measures from prior research permits direct comparison of findings from one study to the next.

Perhaps the most important consideration, however, should be the theoretical utility of the measure. How has a particular approach to role measurement contributed to our understanding of public relations? Clearly, Broom's 24-item role set and the manager–technician dichotomy have contributed the lion's share of new understanding about how roles relate to a myriad interesting professional and social issues. At the same time, the evolution of communication as a profession suggests that the original 24-item role set needs constant reinvention through intensive observation of what communicators do. A recommended strategy is to conduct data collection and analysis in parallel, treating new measures as separate from the original item set. In this manner, we may be able to reduce the number of new factors that are "discovered" every time the item set is modified by additional items.

Criticisms of Roles Research

Criticisms of roles research in public relations ranges from the methodological to the ideological. Starting with the narrowest methodological criticism, some have argued (Leichty & Springston, 1996; Toth & L. Grunig, 1993; Toth et al., 1998) that the manager–technician role dichotomy oversimplifies the complexities of role enactment. Corrective strategies have included using Broom's original four-way typology and expanding the number of items (Leichty & Springston, 1996), as well as attending to cross-loadings and factor analyzing women and men communicators separately (Toth & L. Grunig, 1993; Toth et al., 1998). Culbertson (1991) recommended further research into the process of role received and role taking, rather than focusing exclusively on role enactment.

A broader critique of roles research is embedded in radical and, to some degree, liberal feminist theory. Creedon (1991) provided the first comprehensive critique of roles research from this perspective. Other scholars such as Toth and L. Grunig (1993), Hon (1995), and Toth et al. (1998) have contributed to and provided further elaboration of this critique. This critique has a number of important elements.

First, the gender of researchers and worldviews embedded in their socialization as either men or women affects what research questions they consider important and how they go about studying them. This perspective is not uniquely feminist; rather, it reflects presuppositions that favor intensive observation, idiographic modeling, and reflexivity found in ethnomethodology (Fetterman, 1998; Rossman & Rallis, 1998).

Second, and somewhat as a consequence of the first, men and women studying roles look for different things, find different information in the data, and make sense of what they do find in different ways. Dozier's manager and technician role typology, for example, "homogenized and dichotomized the meaning of work in the field" (Creedon, 1991, p. 78). Creedon argued that women who study roles found liaison and decision-making activities among technicians, activities that male researchers had treated as part of the manager role.

Third, much roles research places greater normative value on the manager role than the technician role, devaluing the work that most women do in public relations. Such preference for the manager role emanates from male socialization to favor hierarchy and categorization, as well as open-systems theory, in which theories of organizational roles are embedded. The feminist critique challenges both justifications for manager role preference.

Fourth, strategies for reducing gender discrimination against women communicators (e.g., Dozier, 1988a) often treat organizational biases as a constant and suggest women change their behaviors (e.g., do more research and enact the manager role) to overcome institutionalized mechanisms of gender discrimination. A radical feminist critique of such liberal incrementalism is that the "victim is blamed" (Creedon, 1991, p. 73) for her condition. In addition, women are urged to enact the manager role within the existing discriminatory structures by "aligning themselves with the masculine stereotype (power and control)" (Hon, 1995, p. 33).

Fifth, liberal incrementalism that underlies much roles research never challenges the patterns of privilege and marginalization inherent in presuppositions of the open-systems model of organizations or the liberal pluralistic model of society as a whole (Hon, L. Grunig, & Dozier, 1992). At core is the manifest unequal distribution of power in organizations and in society. Moreover, according to this critique, the solution to power inequities in organizations and in society is not simply to redistribute power. As L. Grunig (1992) argued, *empowerment* is a more useful concept, wherein power is shared (a positive-sum game) rather than accumulated or lost (zero-sum game) in a hierarchical manner. Hon (1995) provided a plan for empowering women in public relations by fusing liberal feminist tactics with a radical feminist strategy for changing organizations and social systems.

CONTRIBUTION OF THE EXCELLENCE STUDY TO ROLES RESEARCH

Despite the large body of research in this area (Pasadeos et al., 1999), the Excellence study makes a unique contribution to our understanding of practitioner roles. One difficulty with previous roles research is the blurring of the level of analysis. Typically, data about role enactment have been provided from individual practitioners through cross-sectional surveys. Except for such gross measures as departmental size and reporting relationships, the role of the individual respondent has been examined independently of the context of the communication department. This is especially problematic because manager role enactment involves a wide range of competencies, all of which may not reside in a single individual but may be spread among a number of communicators. Along these lines, the present study systematically analyzed these competencies as separate variables at the departmental (rather than individual) level of analysis. A second difficulty with roles research is a preoccupation with role enactment, without regard to the role sent or the role received. The Excellence study charted new territory by asking top communicators what role they actually enact, as well as the role expectations they have received from the dominant coalition. Finally, the Excellence study asked CEOs (or other top managers of organizations) what they expect from their top communicators, what role their top communicator *should* play.

In each chapter of this book, we have related our original propositions from the theory book that guided the Excellence study to the results of the study. In the theory book, Dozier (1992) reviewed the extensive literature on roles at that time and derived 15 propositions that summarized extant research. This chapter focuses on Dozier's first proposition, that *variance in practitioner role activities can be parsimoniously accounted for through two basic organizational roles: managers and technicians.* Most of the other 14 propositions specify that the managerial role will be associated with other variables included in the Excellence scale or with variables that are, in turn, associated with these characteristics of excellence. These variables are the two-way symmetrical and asymmetrical models, involvement in strategic decision making, environment scanning, program planning and evaluation, openness of management to the environment, and a threatening environment. As a result, we have collapsed Dozier's other 14 propositions into a single proposition: *The managerial role will be associated with the other characteristics of an excellent public relations function.*

QUANTITATIVE RESULTS RELATED TO ROLES

Results of the Excellence study regarding communicator roles in organizations involve (a) the expertise available in the department to engage in various role enactments, (b) the actual enactment of various role activities by the top communicator in the department, and (c) the expectations of the dominant coalition with regard to role enactment by the top communicator. Each aspect of organizational role is linked to other characteristics of excellence in organizations, as well as with overall Excellence.

Role Expertise in the Department

One area of roles research that has received scant attention in prior studies is expertise to enact various role activities. In the Excellence study, we decided to treat such expertise as an attribute of the communication or public relations *department,* rather than an attribute of the individual respondent. Earlier research (Broom & Dozier, 1986; Dozier & Broom, 1995) indicated that formal education or training are poor predictors (at best) of role enactment. We therefore decided to construct indexes deductively from previously established measures of communicator role enactment, logically generating a series of tasks requiring specialized departmental expertise consistent with the enactment of communicator roles.

A set of 16 tasks was included in the questionnaire completed by the top communicator or public relations head.[1] Top communicators were asked to use the fractionation scale to describe "the extent to which your department or someone in your department has the expertise or knowledge to perform" these tasks. The tasks, as described in the top-communicator questionnaire, are summarized in Table 6.1. Eight tasks were operationalized as measures of manager role expertise; they appear in rank order at the top of Table 6.1, based on the amount of such expertise in the communication department, as reported by top communicators ($N = 270$). As indicated, the highest level of departmental expertise was reported for developing departmental goals and objectives. This kind of expertise was followed by the expertise to develop strategies to solve public relations problems, prepare departmental budgets, manage organizational responses to issues, and manage people. For these five items, raw means

---

[1]Top communicator and PR head are used interchangeably to designate the senior-ranking communicator in the organization's primary communication department who completed the top-communicator questionnaire.

TABLE 6.1
Departmental Expertise to Enact Communicator Roles

Departmental Expertise to Enact Manager Role	Raw Means	Transformed Means
Develop goals & objectives for department	167.5	12.5
Develop strategies to solve PR problems	158.7	12.2
Prepare departmental budget	148.4	11.6
Manage organization's response to issues	146.6	11.0
Manage people	129.9	10.9
Conduct evaluation research	83.7	8.2
Use research to segment publics	80.3	7.7
Perform environmental scanning	64.6	6.1
Mean	123.3	11.1
Pearson Correlation With Overall Excellence		+.60*
Cronbach's Alpha		.83

Departmental Expertise to Enact Technician Role	Raw Means	Transformed Means
Produce publications	167.6	12.3
Write news releases & features	157.0	12.0
Coordinate press conference or event coverage	149.4	11.7
Write speeches	124.6	10.3
Produce audiovisual materials	122.7	10.1
Write an advertisement	97.1	8.6
Take photos	91.2	8.3
Create & manage a speakers' bureau	79.6	7.3
Mean	123.3	11.1
Pearson Correlation With Overall Excellence		+.42**
Cronbach's Alpha		.80

*$p < .001$, with manager role department expertise removed from Excellence scale. **$p < .001$.

and transformed means (mean of the square roots of the raw scores on each measure) are all above 100 and 10, respectively. This means that all are above what top communicators regard as an average response for all items in the questionnaire.

The next three items involved specialized expertise that few communication departments have in abundance. These include the expertise to conduct evaluation research, to use research to segment publics, and to perform environmental scanning. Each of these items has a mean that is below average, compared to the other measures of expertise. Naturally, scores on the manager role expertise index (created by computing the average of all eight transformed items) are highly correlated with overall Excellence scores (see chap. 3). The manager role expertise index has a Cronbach's alpha reliability coefficient of .83, meaning that it is a reliable measure for purposes of testing relationships with other variables.

Eight items were operationalized from technician role enactment measures used in previous research. Top communicators were asked to assess the department's expertise to conduct eight tasks associated with technician role enactment. These items from the top-communicator questionnaire also are summarized in Table 6.1. The highest level was reported for producing publications, followed by expertise to write news releases and features, coordinate press conferences or coverage of events, write speeches, and produce audiovisual materials. On average, top communicators reported higher-than-average expertise to perform these tasks.

On the other hand, top communicators reported below-average expertise in their departments to write an advertisement, take photos, and create and manage a speakers' bureau. These items posted means below 100 and 10, respectively, for the raw and transformed scores. The Cronbach's alpha reliability coefficient for the technician role expertise scale (mean of all eight transformed technician role expertise items) is .80, meaning that it is sufficiently reliable for testing relationships with other variables.

To better understand the underlying structure of the role expertise items, separate factor analyses were conducted on the manager expertise items and the technician expertise items. Because this item set had never been used in previous studies, exploratory factor analysis (principal component factor extraction rotated to a varimax solution; cross-loadings below .20 not reported) was employed (see Table 6.2). The manager item set represents two empirical and conceptually distinct aspects of manager expertise. One form of manager expertise can be interpreted as *administrative manager* expertise (Factor 1). Items for the administrative manager expertise factor are organized in descending order by factor loadings, with items most central to the underlying construct at the top of the list. This ranking by factor centrality closely parallels the ranking by the amount of role expertise in the department, reported in Table 6.1. Factor 2 can be interpreted as *strategic manager* expertise. Whereas administrative expertise involves the day-to-day operations of a well-run department (regardless of the four public relations model used), strategic expertise is closely tied to a set of strategic tools a communication department needs to use the two-way models (both symmetrical and asymmetrical) and contribute to the organization's strategic planning process.

Technician role expertise is also made up of two empirically and conceptually distinct components (see Table 6.2). The first factor can be interpreted as *internal technician* expertise. This expertise involves the technical production of photos, advertisements, audiovisual materials, publications, and running a speakers' bureau. The second factor can be interpreted as *media relations* expertise. This involves such competencies as coordinating a press conference or media coverage of an event, writing news releases and features, and writing speeches. Taken together, these items denote the cluster of competencies needed for maintaining good relations with the media whereas items denoting internal technician expertise are largely preoccupied with production, without regard to distribution or publics (e.g., the media).

TABLE 6.2
Factor Analysis of Manager and Technician Role Expertise
in the Communication Department

Components of Manager Role Expertise	Factor Loadings	
	Administrative Manager (F1)	Strategic Manager (F2)
Develop goals & objectives for department	.89	
Prepare departmental budget	.82	
Develop strategies to solve PR problems	.81	.26
Manage organization's response to issues	.74	
Manage people	.63	.30
Conduct evaluation research		.86
Use research to segment publics	.30	.79
Perform environmental scanning	.28	.61

Components of Technician Role Expertise	Factor Loadings	
	Internal Technician (F1)	Media Relations (F2)
Take photos	.84	
Write an advertisement	.71	
Produce audiovisual materials	.68	.38
Create & manage a speakers' bureau	.54	.28
Produce publications	.51	.48
Coordinate press conference or event coverage		.83
Write news releases & features	.27	.80
Write speeches		.67

Note. Principal components extraction with all factors with eigenvalues greater than 1.0 rotated to the varimax solution displayed herein.

The manager and technician role expertise indexes displayed in Table 6.1 were used intact for further analysis, recognizing that both indexes have meaningful subcomponents.[2] Table 6.3 displays relations between manager role expertise and technician role expertise with each of the characteristics of excellence. Regarding manager role expertise, we expected and found strong correlations with other departmental competencies to use the two-way models of public relations, both symmetrical ($r = .72$, $p < .01$) and asymmetrical ($r = .72$, $p < .01$). We also expected and found strong correlations for the value ($r = .31$, $p < .01$) and support ($r = .29$, $p < .01$) provided to the communication department

[2]Separate correlations were calculated for the combined variables in the strategic manager and administrative manager factors with the overall index of excellence (with the managerial expertise variable removed). Both correlations were high and roughly the same (.49 for the strategic expertise and .54 for administrative expertise), which suggests that excellent public relations departments need both types of managerial expertise.

TABLE 6.3

Correlations of Manager and Technician Role Expertise
in Department With Other Characteristics of Excellence

Other Characteristics of Excellence	Manager Role Expertise	Technician Role Expertise
Expertise to Use Two-Way Symmetrical Model[a]	.72**	.46**
Expertise to Use Two-Way Asymmetrical Model[a]	.72**	.48**
Value Dominant Coalition Places on PR[a]	.31**	.20**
Support Dominant Coalition Gives to PR[a]	.29**	.13*
PR's Contribution to Strategic Planning[a]	.35**	.22**
Manager Role Enactment by PR Head[a]	.57**	.38**
Senior Adviser Role Enactment by PR Head[a]	.47**	.35**
Dominant Coalition Expects Two-Way Symmetrical Model Used[a]	.38**	.20**
Dominant Coalition Expects Two-Way Asymmetrical Model Used[a]	.42**	.19**
Support for Women Employees[a]	.31**	.11*
Support Dominant Coalition Gives to PR[b]	.13*	.02
Value Dominant Coalition Places on PR[b]	.07	.02
Importance of Knowledge/Communication With Outside Groups[b]	.13*	.17**
Dominant Coalition Expects Two-Way Asymmetrical Model Used[b]	.18**	.11*
Dominant Coalition Expects Two-Way Symmetrical Model Used[b]	.09	.04
Dominant Coalition Expects PR Head to Enact Manager Role[b]	.13*	.08
Dominant Coalition Expects PR Head to Enact Senior Adviser Role[b]	.10*	.11
PR's Contribution to Strategic Planning[b]	.10*	.05
Participative Organizational Culture[c]	.14**	.07
Overall Excellence Score	**.60**	**.41**

[a]From PR head (top-communicator) questionnaire. [b]From CEO questionnaire. [c]From employee questionnaire (data aggregated for all employees in the organization surveyed).

*$p < .05$. **$p < .01$.

by the organization's dominant coalition, as reported by the top communicator. The CEOs reported a weaker but significant correlation between manager role expertise and support given to the communication department by the dominant coalition ($r = .13, p < .05$) but not for value ($r = .07, p > .05$). Top communicators reported that manager role expertise in their departments was strongly correlated with communication's contribution to strategic planning in the organization ($r = .35, p < .01$).

According to top communicators, department expertise to enact the manager role is strongly correlated with the actual enactment of the manager role ($r = .57, p < .01$) and a variation on manager role enactment called "senior adviser" role enactment ($r = .47, p < .01$) by top communicators. Likewise, CEOs reported that their dominant coalitions expect higher levels of manager ($r = .13, p < .05$) and senior adviser ($r = .10, p < .05$) role enactment from their top communicators in organizations with communication departments with higher levels of manager role expertise. In organizations with higher departmental manager expertise, expectations that communicators use the two-way models of public relations, both symmetrical and asymmetrical, are significantly higher. These higher expectations were reported by both top communicators and CEOs (see Table 6.3). In addition, manager role expertise is positively correlated with the importance that CEOs place on communication and knowledge regarding external publics ($r = .13$, $p < .05$). Manager role expertise is also positively correlated with two aspects of organizational culture: organizational support for female employees ($r = .31$, $p < .01$) as reported by top communicators and the overall participative nature of the culture ($r = .14$, $p < .01$) as reported by a sample of regular employees. As expected, the correlation of manager role expertise (with manager expertise removed from the Excellence scale to prevent autocorrelation) with the overall Excellence score is .60 ($p < .01$), accounting for over a third of the variance in the 20-item Excellence factor.

More intriguing and less expected was the strong correlation of technician role expertise with many characteristics of excellence. Previous research suggests that technical role *enactment* is unrelated to indicators of excellence, such as participation in management decision making and strategic planning. However, as indicated in Table 6.3, top communicators reported that their departments' technician expertise is positively correlated with expertise to use the two-way models of public relations, the value and support given the communication department by the dominant coalitions, communication's contribution to strategic planning, and actual enactment of both the manager and technician roles by the top communicator. Relationships between technician role expertise and variables provided by CEOs, however, are generally weak and insignificant. Nevertheless, CEOs did report significant, positive correlations between technician role expertise and the importance they place on communication with outside publics ($r = .17$, $p < .01$) and dominant coalition expectations that the two-way asymmetrical model be used ($r = .11$, $p < .05$). The correlation between technician role expertise and overall Excellence scores is .41 ($p < .01$).

As detailed in the qualitative section of this chapter and elsewhere (Dozier with L. Grunig & J. Grunig, 1995), the seeming importance of technician role expertise to excellence can be understood only through the symbiosis of both manager and technician competencies within the same excellent department. When excellent communication departments are examined over time, problems or opportunities (such as a crisis, merger, or change in CEOs or dominant coalitions) occur that provide communicators a chance to *deliver* excellent work. This alters the dominant coalition's expectations of the communication department, leading the coalition to *demand* such communication excellence in the future. This demand–delivery loop (Dozier with L. Grunig & J. Grunig, 1995) provides excellent communication departments with the power to demand scarce resources (e.g, staff and budget). However, excellent communication programs depend on excellent execution, meaning that communication departments need the traditional craft skills embodied in departmental technician expertise. In this framework, departmental expertise to enact the technical role is a necessary but not a sufficient condition for excellence.

Empirically, this symbiosis between manager and technician role expertise in the department is shown in the strong, positive correlation between manager role expertise and technician role expertise ($r = .57$, $p < .01$). Table 6.4 displays the relationships between technician role expertise and other characteristics of excellence, after controlling for the influence of manager role expertise. Ten of the 21 relationships in Table 6.4 are negative, although none of these is statistically significant. Only three relationships in Table 6.4 are statistically significant. Expertise to use the two-way asymmetrical model posts a significant, positive partial correlation (*partial r* = .11, $p < .05$) with technician role expertise. Actual enactment of the senior adviser role by the top communicator shows a significant, positive partial correlation (*partial r* = .11, $p < .05$) with technician role expertise. CEOs report a significant, positive partial correlation (*partial r* = .11, $p <$

TABLE 6.4
Partial Correlations of Technician Role Expertise
in Department With Other Characteristics of Excellence
After Controlling for Manager Role Expertise

Other Characteristics of Excellence	Technician Role Expertise (Partial r)
Manager Role Expertise in Department[a] (zero-order correlation, not partial)	**.57****
Expertise to Use Two-Way Symmetrical Model[a]	.09
Expertise to Use Two-Way Asymmetrical Model[a]	.11*
Value Dominant Coalition Places on PR[a]	.03
Support Dominant Coalition Gives to PR[a]	−.05
PR's Contribution to Strategic Planning[a]	.03
Manager Role Enactment by PR Head[a]	.08
Senior Adviser Role Enactment by PR Head[a]	.11*
Dominant Coalition Expects Two-Way Symmetrical Model Used[a]	−.02
Dominant Coalition Expects Two-Way Asymmetrical Model Used[a]	−.07
Support for Women Employees[a]	−.08
Support Dominant Coalition Gives to PR[b]	−.06
Value Dominant Coalition Places on PR[b]	−.02
Importance of Knowledge/Communication With Outside Groups[b]	.11*
Dominant Coalition Expects Two-Way Asymmetrical Model Used[b]	.01
Dominant Coalition Expects Two-Way Symmetrical Model Used[b]	−.01
Dominant Coalition Expects PR Head to Enact Manager Role[b]	.01
Dominant Coalition Expects PR Head to Enact Senior Adviser Role[b]	.07
PR's Contribution to Strategic Planning[b]	−.01
Participative Organizational Culture[c]	−.02
Overall Excellence Score	**−.01**

[a]From PR head (top-communicator) questionnaire. [b]From CEO questionnaire. [c]From employee questionnaire (data aggregated for all employees in the organization surveyed).
*$p < .05$. **$p < .01$.

.05) between the importance they place on communication with outside publics and technician role expertise in their communication departments (as reported by top communicators). However, the partial correlation between overall Excellence and technician role expertise in the communication department is −.01.

Tables 6.3 and 6.4, along with chapter 3, underscore three important findings about organizational roles. First, departmental knowledge or expertise to enact the manager role is the single most important attribute of an excellent communication department. Second, a strong symbiotic relationship exists between manager and technician role expertise in excellent communication departments. Third, technician role expertise is of no consequence to communication Excellence without the manager role expertise within the department to put those technical resources to appropriate, strategic uses.

Role Enactment by the Top Communicator

Sixteen items were derived from previous studies of role enactment and used to operationalize four distinct organizational roles of communication managers and public relations practitioners. These included the manager role, the senior adviser role, the media relations role, and the technician role. Top communicators were asked to choose a number on the fractionation scale that "indicates how well each of the following items describes the work that *you* do as a public relations practitioner."

As displayed in Table 6.5, manager role enactment was measured by four activities that top communicators were asked to use to describe their own work as department heads. These items closely parallel the *expert prescriber* role as first conceptualized by Broom (Broom, 1982; Broom & Smith, 1978, 1979). The manager role enactment item that top communicators reported best described their work was being the organization's expert at solving public relations problems. This item was followed by taking responsibility for the success or failure of public relations programs, being held accountable by others in the organization for the success or failure of the public relations program, and making communication policy decisions. Means for both the raw and transformed scores were above the average. After manager role enactment was removed from the overall Excellence scale, the manager role enactment index posted a strong correlation with overall Excellence ($r = .58$, $p < .01$). The manager role enactment index also posted a solid reliability coefficient (Cronbach's alpha $= .89$).

Related to the manager role enactment is the role of senior adviser. Based on research and analysis conducted prior to developing questionnaires for the Excellence study (e.g., Broom & Dozier, 1986), some senior practitioners enacted a role as informal managers, providing guidance and counseling to the dominant coalition in solving public relations problems; but they were not vested with formal policymaking authority. In the Excellence study, manager and senior adviser role enactment were very highly correlated ($r = .76$, $p < .01$). The

TABLE 6.5
Levels of Manager and Senior Adviser Role Enactments
by the Top Communicator in the Department

Manager Role Enactment	Raw Means	Transformed Means
I'm considered the expert at solving PR problems	162.1	12.5
I take responsibility for PR program success/failure	162.1	12.4
Others hold me accountable for PR program	154.8	12.4
I make communication policy decisions	145.2	12.0
Mean	156.2	12.2
Pearson Correlation With Overall Excellence		+.58**
Cronbach's Alpha		.89

Senior Adviser Role Enactment		
I am senior counsel to top decision makers	160.0	12.6
I create opportunities for management to hear publics	118.2	10.9
I represent my organization at events and meetings	115.0	10.7
I don't make PR policy but provide suggestions	77.4	8.8
Mean	116.8	10.6
Pearson Correlation With Overall Excellence		+.51**
Cronbach's Alpha		.54

*$p < .001$, after removing manager role enactment from Excellence scale. **$p < .001$, after removing senior adviser role enactment from Excellence scale.

senior adviser role enactment item that top communicators reported best described their work was serving as senior counsel to top decision makers when communication or public relations is involved. This was followed by creating opportunities for management to hear publics and representing their organizations at events and meetings. Top communicators reported above-average means for all three items. The fourth item, however, posted a significantly lower mean: "Although I don't make communication policy decisions, I provide decision makers with suggestions, recommendations, and plans." Although the senior adviser index posted a strong, positive correlation with overall Excellence ($r = .51$, $p < .01$) after senior adviser role enactment was removed from the Excellence scale, the reliability coefficient for this index was low (Cronbach's alpha = .54). The item above asserting that the top communicator does not make policy decisions was a major source of the unreliability of this measure.

Table 6.6 displays a breakdown of the indexes used to measure media relations and internal technician role enactment by top communicators. The media relations role was first identified by Dozier (1983) as an offshoot of the technician role because of its isolation from policymaking. In the Excellence study, this link between media relations and internal technician role enactment was strongly confirmed. Media relations and internal technician role enactment

TABLE 6.6

Levels of Media Relations and Internal Technician Role
Enactments by the Top Communicator in the Department

Media Relations Specialist Role Enactment	Raw Means	Transformed Means
I use my journalistic skills to find newsworthy material	145.1	12.0
I keep others informed of media coverage	143.5	12.0
I maintain media contacts for my organization	115.1	10.7
I am responsible for placing news releases	80.5	9.0
Mean	121.1	10.9
Pearson Correlation With Overall Excellence		+.58**
Partial Correlation With Excellence (manager enactment controlled)	+.02	
Cronbach's Alpha		.87
Internal Technician Role Enactment		
I edit for grammar and spelling the writing of others	89.3	9.4
I am the one who writes communication materials	87.1	9.3
I produce brochures, pamphlets, and other materials	82.6	9.1
I do photos and graphics for PR materials	30.1	5.5
Mean	72.1	8.3
Pearson Correlation With Overall Excellence		+.04
Partial Correlation With Excellence (manager enactment controlled)	−.09	
Cronbach's Alpha		.81

**p < .001 for zero-order Pearson correlation coefficient.

posted a strong, positive correlation among top communicators describing their own work ($r = .62$, $p < .01$). The media relations enactment measure that best described the work of top communicators was using their journalistic skills to figure out what the media will consider newsworthy about their organizations. This item was followed by keeping others in the organization informed of what the media report about their organization, maintaining media contacts, and placing news releases. Media relations role enactment was highly correlated with overall Excellence ($r = .58$, $p < .01$); however, media relations enactment also was correlated highly with manager role enactment ($r = .49$). Apparently, media relations is one of the things that top communicators do in their role as managers. Once the influence of manager role enactment is controlled, the relationship between media relations role enactment and overall Excellence disappears (*partial r* = .02, $p > .05$). The media relations enactment index posted a solid reliability coefficient (Cronbach's alpha = .87).

Internal technician role enactment is derived from Broom's original conceptualization of the role typology (Broom, 1982; Broom & Smith, 1978, 1979). As shown in Table 6.6, the technician role enactment item that top communicators reported as best describing their work was editing the writing of others in their organizations for grammar and spelling. However, even as the most highly scored item, the mean for this item was below average for both the raw and transformed scores. This item was followed by writing communication materials; producing brochures, pamphlets, and other materials; and doing photos and graphics for public relations materials. Although the internal technician enactment index posted a low average among top communicators (mean = 8.3 where 10.0 is average), the index is reliable (Cronbach's alpha = .81). Internal technician role enactment is not correlated with overall Excellence ($r = .04$, $p > .05$).

Because of the poor reliability of the senior adviser index, the high correlation between manager and senior adviser indexes, and the high correlation between media relations and internal technician indexes, factor analysis was conducted on items measuring the manager and senior adviser enactment items as one set and the media relations and internal technician items as another set. The principal components method was used to extract the factors, and factors with eigenvalues greater than 1.0 were rotated to a varimax solution. The results are displayed in Table 6.7. It turns out that the manager/senior adviser distinction does not help to illuminate the underlying structure of the manager role. Indeed, seven of the eight items loaded heavily on the first factor. This parallels the manager role as first inductively generated through factor analysis (Broom, 1982; Broom & Dozier, 1986; Dozier, 1983; Dozier & Broom, 1995), consisting of items first developed by Broom to measure the expert prescriber, communication facilitator, and problem-solving process facilitator. Factor 2 is not interpretable, consisting of a single item that does not belong with the other measures: "Although I don't make communication policy decisions, I provide decision makers with suggestions, recommendations, and plans."

Factor analysis of the combined media relations and internal technician enactment items is also displayed in Table 6.7. After using the principal component method to extract the factors and then rotating those with eigenvalues greater than 1.0 to a varimax solution, the original delineation of the media relations and internal technician roles were replicated. That is, media relations and internal technician seem to be empirically and conceptually distinct. However, three of the four media relations items were heavily cross-loaded with the internal technician factor. By the same token, three of the four internal technician items were heavily cross-loaded with the media relations factor.

Because one purpose of scale construction and factor analysis is parsimony, the 16-item role enactment set was subjected to factor analysis as one set. Again, the principal component method was used to extract the factors, and those with eigenvalues greater than 1.0 were rotated to a varimax solution. The results are displayed in Table 6.8. Nine items loaded most heavily on Factor 1, which can be interpreted as the manager factor. Unlike the original manager factor operationalized deductively, this factor was generated inductively from patterns in the data provided by top communicators when they described their work. This empirically derived role enactment includes making communication policy decisions and taking responsibility (and being held ac-

TABLE 6.7
Factor Analysis of Manager, Senior Adviser, Media Relations Specialist, and
Internal Technician Role Enactment by the
Top Communicator in the Department

| | Factor Loadings | |
	Manager (F1)	Senior Adviser (F2)
Components of Manager Role Expertise		
I am senior counsel to top decision makers	.86	
I take responsibility for PR program success/failure	.84	
Others hold me accountable for PR program	.84	
I make communication policy decisions	.83	
I'm considered the expert at solving PR problems	.82	
I represent my organization at events and meetings	.62	
I create opportunities for management to hear publics	.61	.33
I don't make PR policy but provide suggestions		.96

| | Factor Loadings | |
	Media Relations Specialist (F1)	Internal Technician (F2)
Components of Technician Role Expertise		
I keep others informed of media coverage	.86	
I use my journalistic skills to find newsworthy material	.84	.25
I maintain media contacts for my organization	.81	.33
I am responsible for placing news releases	.64	.58
I do photos and graphics for PR materials		.80
I produce brochures, pamphlets, and other materials	.25	.79
I am the one who writes communication materials	.38	.77
I edit for grammar and spelling the writing of others	.39	.64

Note. Principal components extraction with all factors with eigenvalues greater than 1.0 rotated to the varimax solution displayed herein. Factor analysis was conducted separately on the manager/senior adviser items and on the media relations/technician items.

countable) for the success or failure of public relations programs. But the role also involves facilitating communication between publics and the dominant coalition, as well as facilitating problem solving. Of the nine items, the top eight items in Table 6.8 were used to create a manager role enactment index. The item with the lowest factor loading on Factor 1 ("I use my journalistic skills to figure out what the media will consider interesting about our organization") was deleted from the new manager enactment index because it reduced the index's reliability and because it was heavily cross-loaded with Factor 2. The manager enactment index from factor analysis subsumed both the old manager and senior adviser items, but it deletes the problematic item: "Although I don't make communication policy decisions, I provide decision makers with suggestions, recommendations, and plans." The reliability of the new

TABLE 6.8

Factor Analysis of Manager and Technician Role Enactment
by the Top Communicator in the Department

	Factor Loadings	
Components of Manager Role Expertise	Manager (F1)	Technician (F2)
I am senior counsel to top decision makers	.87	
I make communication policy decisions	.83	
Others hold me accountable for PR program	.83	
I take responsibility for PR program success/failure	.82	
I'm considered the expert at solving PR problems	.80	
I keep others informed of media coverage	.69	
I create opportunities for management to hear publics	.62	
I represent my organization at events and meetings	.61	
I use my journalistic skills to find newsworthy material[a]	.60	.58
I am responsible for placing news releases		.84
I am the one who writes communication materials		.83
I produce brochures, pamphlets, and other materials		.77
I do photos and graphics for PR materials		.72
I edit for grammar and spelling the writing of others		.71
I maintain media contacts for my organization	.38	.69
I don't make PR policy but provide suggestions[a]		.50
Cronbach's Alpha	**.91**	**.87**

Note. Principal components extraction with all factors with eigenvalues greater than 1.0 rotated to the varimax solution displayed herein. All 16 role enactment items included in the analysis.

[a]Not included in scales or in computing reliability, because of improved reliability by deleting item.

index is .91. The new index is highly correlated with overall Excellence ($r = .47$, $p < .01$), after the manager and senior adviser enactment measures were removed.

Seven items loaded heavily on Factor 2, which can be interpreted as the technician factor. This factor subsumes the measures of media relations and internal technician. It does not include the item heavily cross-loaded with Factor 1 ("I use my journalistic skills to figure out what the media will consider interesting about our organization"), but it does include the problematic item from the original senior adviser index ("Although I don't make communication policy decisions, I provide decision makers with suggestions, recommendations, and plans"). When reliability of the technician enactment index was computed, deletion of this latter item improved the reliability of the technician enactment index. The top six items for Factor 2 were used to compute the final index, which has a reliability coefficient of .87. The technician enactment index is not correlated with overall Excellence ($r = -.01$, $p > .05$).

Table 6.9 displays the relationship between manager role enactment, technician role enactment, and the other characteristics of excellence. Note that these are the new indexes derived from a single factor analysis of all 16 items.

Manager role enactment by the top communicator is highly correlated with departmental expertise to do so (enact the manager role), as well as the expertise to use the two-way models. According to top communicators, such manager role enactment is positively and significantly correlated with the value and support that the dominant coalition gives the communication department, the contribution public relations makes to strategic planning, and the expectations of the dominant coalition that the communication department use the two-way models (both symmetrical and asymmetrical). Manager role enactment is also correlated with management support for women employees and employee's perception that the organization's culture is participative.

Based on the CEO data, manager role enactment by the top communicator was not nearly so strongly linked to excellence. These lower correlations probably resulted in part because the variables of the Excellence index taken from the CEO questionnaire did not correlate so highly with variables taken from the PR

TABLE 6.9
Correlation of Manager and Technician Role Enactment
of the Top Communicator in the Department With
Other Characteristics of Excellence

Other Characteristics of Excellence	Manager Role Enactment	Technician Role Enactment
Expertise to Enact Manager Role[a]	.55**	.04
Expertise to Use Two-Way Symmetrical Model[a]	.48**	.05
Expertise to Use Two-Way Asymmetrical Model[a]	.38**	.07
Value Dominant Coalition Places on PR[a]	.42**	.10*
Support Dominant Coalition Gives to PR[a]	.39**	−.02
PR's Contribution to Strategic Planning[a]	.34**	.08
Manager Role Enactment by PR Head[a]	—	.29**
Dominant Coalition Expects Two-Way Symmetrical Model Used[a]	.35**	−.02
Dominant Coalition Expects Two-Way Asymmetrical Model Used[a]	.28**	.01
Support for Women Employees[a]	.30**	−.09
Support Dominant Coalition Gives to PR[b]	.11*	−.03
Value Dominant Coalition Places on PR[b]	.03	−.05
Importance of Knowledge/Communication With Outside Groups[b]	.17**	.08
Dominant Coalition Expects Two-Way Asymmetrical Model Used[b]	.15**	−.04
Dominant Coalition Expects Two-Way Symmetrical Model Used[b]	.05	−.12*
Dominant Coalition Expects PR Head to Enact Manager Role[b]	.11*	−.16**
Dominant Coalition Expects PR Head to Enact Senior Adviser Role[b]	.09	−.11*
PR's Contribution to Strategic Planning[b]	.12*	−.11*
Participative Organizational Culture[c]	.10*	−.01
Overall Excellence Score (manager/senior adviser enactment items removed)	**.47***	**−.01**

[a]From PR head (top communicator) questionnaire. [b]From CEO questionnaire. [c]From employee questionnaire (data aggregated for all employees surveyed in the organization).
*p < .05 for zero-order Pearson correlation coefficients. **p < .01 for zero-order Pearson correlation coefficients.

head questionnaires as with other CEO variables—a trend discussed in chapter 3 and reported in several chapters of this book. Variables whose measures came from different respondents did not correlate so highly as variables whose measures came from the same respondents.

CEOs reported higher levels of dominant coalition support for the communication department when their top communicators reported higher levels of manager role enactment ($r = .11, p < .05$). However, the value of communication to the dominant coalition is not related to the level of manager role enactment of top communicators ($r = .03, p > .05$). The expectations of the dominant coalition that the two-way asymmetrical model be used are positively and significantly correlated to manager role enactment ($r = .15, p < .01$); however, no significant correlation was detected for dominant coalition expectations for use of the two-way symmetrical model and manager role enactment ($r = .05, p > .05$). Manager role enactment by the top communicator is positively and significantly correlated with expectations of the dominant coalition that the top communicator enact that role ($r = .11, p < .05$). However, manager role enactment is not correlated significantly with the dominant coalition's expectation that the senior adviser role be enacted ($r = .09, p > .05$). In part, this may be due to the low reliability of the senior adviser index. According to CEOs, manager role enactment by the top communicator is positively and significantly correlated with the importance placed on communication with outside publics ($r = .17, p < .01$) and public relations' contribution to strategic planning ($r = .12 p < .05$).

Technician role enactment by top communicators, on the other hand, is generally unrelated to characteristics of excellence. The correlation between technician role enactment and those characteristics are displayed in Table 6.9. The strongest correlation is between technician and manager role enactment ($r = .29, p < .01$). The only other positive relationship between technician role enactment and excellence is a significant, positive correlation between the value the dominant coalition places on the communication function and technician role enactment ($r = .10, p < .05$). However, this relationship disappears when the influence of manager role enactment is controlled (*partial r* $= -.02, p > .05$). CEOs generally report negative relationships between technician role enactment by their top communicators and characteristics of excellence. Overall, there is no correlation between technician role enactment by top communicators and overall Excellence ($r = -.01$).

The findings regarding role enactment by top communicators support five conclusions. First, manager role enactment is an amalgam of expert prescription, communication facilitation, and problem-solving process facilitation, replicating previous research. Excellent top communicators even use their journalistic skills to figure out what the media will find interesting about their organizations (see the cross-loading in Table 6.8.). However, the basic manager–technician distinction remains a fundamentally reliable and powerful theoretical and empirical distinction to describe and explain what practitioners do in organizations. Second, manager role enactment by the top communicator is positively and significantly correlated with overall communication Excellence, as well as with most of the characteristics that make up the Excellence factor. Third, actual manager role enactment is dependent on the expertise—either personal or elsewhere within the department—to enact that role. Fourth, whereas communication *departments* must have high levels of managerial and technical expertise to become truly excellent, top communicators build excellent departments only by enacting the manager role predominantly. Fifth, excellent top communicators are activists who enact higher-than-average levels of both the manager and technician roles; however, it is manager role enactment that counts toward excellence. The only positive relationship between technician role enactment and the 21 characteristics of excellence is its relationship to manager role enactment.

Role Expectations of the Dominant Coalition

In the CEO questionnaire, participants were asked to use the fractionation scale to indicate "how well each of the following items describes the work that *you* think the *head of the public relations or communication department* should do." Because the CEO is the most powerful member of the organization's dominant coalition, these items reflect strong *role sent* expectations of the dominant coalition. The item set consisted of 16 measures adapted directly from the set of items measuring actual role enactment by top communicators. Whereas role enactment measures completed by top communicators reflect the degree to which items reflect the communicators' actual work, role expectation measures reflect what a powerful member of the dominant coalition thinks the organization's top communicator *should* be doing.

Table 6.10 provides a breakdown of manager and senior adviser role expectations as originally conceptualized. All four measures of manager role expectations posted above-average means. The item with the highest expectation was that the top communicator should serve as the organization's expert in solving public relations problems. This item was followed by the expectation that the top communicator take responsibility for the success or failure of the public relations program, that he or she should be held accountable by others in the organization (for the communication programs), and that the top communicator should make communication policy decisions. As expected, manager role expectations were positively and significantly correlated with overall Excellence ($r = .34$, $p < .01$), even after manager role expectation items were removed from the Excellence scale. However, the reliability of the manager role expectation index was low (Cronbach's alpha = .61), meaning that the items making up the manager role expectation index did not covary consistently with each other, perhaps indicating that the separate items measured something other than a single, unified construct.

TABLE 6.10
Manager and Senior Adviser Role Expectations of the
Dominant Coalition as Reported by the CEO

Manager Role Expectations (Top communicator should . . .)	Raw Means	Transformed Means
be the organization's expert in solving PR problems	188.5	12.5
take responsibility for success/failure of PR program	162.1	11.8
be held accountable for success/failure of PR program	154.8	11.2
make communication policy decisions	145.2	9.9
Mean	162.7	11.3
Pearson Correlation With Overall Excellence		+.34**
Cronbach's Alpha		.61
Senior Adviser Role Expectations (Top communicator should . . .)		
be senior counsel to top decision makers	182.7	13.1
not make PR policy but provide suggestions	151.2	11.6
create opportunities for management to hear publics	139.5	11.4
represent organization at events and meetings	119.6	9.9
Mean	148.3	11.5
Pearson Correlation With Overall Excellence		+.36**
Cronbach's Alpha		.45

**p < .001, after removing manager and senior adviser role expectations from Excellence scale.

Senior adviser role expectations also posted above-average means for all four items (see Table 6.10). The highest expectation of CEOs was that their top communicators should serve as senior counsel to top decision makers when communication or public relations issues are involved. This item was followed by the expectation that top communicators should not make communication policy decisions—that he or she should provide decision makers with suggestions, recommendations, and plans. Top communicators should also create opportunities for management to hear publics and represent the organization at events and meetings. As expected, the senior adviser role expectation index correlated positively and significantly with overall Excellence ($r = .36$, $p < .01$), even after senior adviser role expectations were removed from the Excellence scale. As with the manager role expectation index, however, the reliability of the index was low (Cronbach's alpha = .45), indicating that the index does not measure a single, unified construct in a reliable manner.

Table 6.11 displays the four items measuring media relations role expectations of CEOs. The highest expectation with regard to this role is that their top communicators should keep others in the organization informed of what the media are saying about the organization and issues important to the organization. The next highest expectation is that top communicators should use journalistic skills to figure out what the media will consider newsworthy about their organizations, followed by the expectation that top communicators should

TABLE 6.11
Media Relations Specialist and Internal Technician Role Expectations
of the Dominant Coalition as Reported by the CEO

Media Relations Expectations (Top communicator should . . .)	Raw Means	Transformed Means
keep others informed of media coverage	145.6	11.6
use journalistic skills to find newsworthy material	136.9	11.2
maintain media contacts for the organization	136.1	11.2
be responsible for placing news releases	110.0	8.8
Mean	132.2	10.7
Pearson Correlation With Overall Excellence		+.11*
Partial Correlation With Excellence (manager expectations controlled)		+.01
Cronbach's Alpha		.65
Internal Technician Expectations (Top communicator should . . .)		
be the one who writes communication materials	71.5	7.5
edit for grammar and spelling the writing of others	69.9	7.1
produce brochures, pamphlets, and other materials	65.8	6.9
do photos and graphics for PR materials	42.7	4.8
Mean	62.5	6.6
Pearson Correlation With Overall Excellence		+.04
Cronbach's Alpha		.84

*$p < .05$ for zero-order Pearson correlation coefficient.

maintain media contacts for their organizations and be responsible for placing news releases. The media relations role expectation index correlated positively and significantly with overall Excellence ($r = .11, p < .05$). However, media relations role expectations are also positively correlated with manager role expectations ($r = .25, p < .01$). Once the influence of manager role expectations are controlled, the partial correlation between media relations role expectations and overall Excellence disappears (*partial r* $= .01, p > .05$). More problematic is the low reliability coefficient for the media relations role expectation index (Cronbach's alpha $= .65$), which again indicates that the index does not measure a single, unified construct reliably.

Regarding internal technician role expectations of top communicators, all four items posted lower-than-average means. With a transformed mean of 7.5 (where 10 is average), the CEOs' highest internal technician expectation was that top communicators should be the ones who write communication materials, followed by editing for grammar and spelling the writing of others in the organization; producing brochures, pamphlets, and other materials; and doing photos and graphics for public relations materials. The internal technician expectation index posted an insignificant correlation with overall Excellence ($r = .04, p > .05$). Of the four measures of role expectations for top communicators, only the internal technician expectation is highly reliable for testing relations with other variables

(Cronbach's alpha = .84). As originally operationalized, the indexes for manager, senior adviser, and media relations expectations are unreliable.

Theoretically speaking, one might expect CEOs to organize their conceptualization of the top-communicator role in a manner somewhat different from how communication managers and public relations practitioners would. Empirically, the a priori operationalization of role expectations, deduced from earlier research on communicators, did not yield reliable indexes of role expectations. Therefore, exploratory factor analysis was utilized on all 16 items in the role expectation set to determine inductively how CEOs structure their role expectations for top communicators. The principal component method of factor extraction was employed, with all factors with eigenvalues greater than 1.0 rotated to a varimax solution.

The rotated factor matrix for CEO role expectations appears in Table 6.12. By comparing this table with a similar factor analysis of role enactment items from the top-communicator questionnaire in Table 6.8, some key differences emerge. Top-communicator role enactment items (as reported by those top communicators) split quite nicely into two factors with few cross-loadings. The manager factor, as defined by the role enactment of top communicators, is rich and detailed. Nine items are most heavily loaded on the manager factor (Factor 1) in Table 6.8. The manager factor consists of expert prescription, communication facilitation, and problem-solving process facilitation. Manager role expectations of CEOs (Factor 2 in Table 6.12), however, are less detailed—a condensed amalgam of expert prescription, communication facilitation, and problem-solving process facilitation. Technician role enactment, as reported by top communicators (refer back to Table 6.8), consists of seven items that meld both internal technician and media relations role enactment items. The technician role expectations of CEOs, on the other hand, are entirely internal technician expectations (see Factor 1 in Table 6.12).

For CEOs, media relations items are important expectations of top communicators (see Table 6.11). Media relations expectations of CEOs appear as Factor 3 in Table 6.12. Media relations expectations include the item: "Although he or she should not make policy decisions, he or she should provide decision makers with suggestions, recommendations, and plans." The other three expectations are consistent with the media relations expectations as originally conceptualized and operationalized.

Factor 4 in Table 6.12 represents a set of unified expectations (among CEOs) that have no equivalency when role enactment is measured among top communicators. This role expectation can be interpreted as senior media manager role expectations. According to these expectations, senior media managers should take responsibility for the organization's communication or public relations programs. Because of his or her experience and training, others should consider the top communicator in this role as the organization's expert at solving public relations problems. At the same time, top communicators in this role should be

TABLE 6.12
Exploratory Factor Analysis of the Role Expectations
of the Dominant Coalition as Reported by the CEO

Technician Expectations (TEC)	TEC	MGR	MRS	SMM	REP
Top communicator should . . .					
produce brochures, pamphlets, and other materials	.86				
be the one who writes communication materials	.84				
do photos and graphics for PR materials	.77				
edit for grammar and spelling the writing of others	.72		.29		
Cronbach's Alpha = .84					

Manager Expectations (MGR)	TEC	MGR	MRS	SMM	REP
Top communicator should . . .					
be held accountable for success/failure of PR program		.82			
create opportunities for management to hear publics		.77			
make communication policy decisions		.75			.20
be senior counsel to top decision makers		.72	.44		
Cronbach's Alpha = .80					

Media Relations Expectations (MRS)	TEC	MGR	MRS	SMM	REP
Top communicator should . . .					
use journalistic skills to find newsworthy material	.24		.78		
maintain media contacts for the organization	.41		.70		
keep others informed of media coverage		.49	.65		
not make PR policy but provide suggestions			.61		−.36
Cronbach's Alpha = .73					

Senior Media Manager Expectations (SMM)	TEC	MGR	MRS	SMM	REP
Top communicator should . . .					
take responsibility for success/failure of PR program		.29		.90	
be the organization's expert in solving PR problems				.72	.59
be responsible for placing news releases	.52	−.28		.69	
Cronbach's Alpha = .69					

Representative Expectations (REP)	TEC	MGR	MRS	SMM	REP
Top communicator should . . .					
represent organization at events and meetings					.91

Note. Principal components extraction with all factors with eigenvalues greater than 1.0 rotated to the varimax solution displayed herein. All 16 role expectation items from the CEO questionnaire were included in the analysis.

responsible for placing news releases. This item is heavily cross-loaded with the technician expectations factor but not the media relations factor. Although this factor is difficult to interpret without additional items, the role expectation seems to be one of a senior communicator running a public relations program along traditional lines: Public relations equals publicity. The public relations programs managed by top communicators in this role would be largely media-based programs. Factor 5 consists of a single item, the expectation that the top communicator should represent the organization at events and meetings.

The five factors indicate a more fragmented view of role expectations among CEOs, when compared with the actual role enactments of top communicators. Among CEOs, both manager and technician role expectations are truncated and short on detail. Among top communicators, manager and technician role enactments are expansive and detailed. Despite these differences, Table 6.12 indicates that the factor analysis yields reliable indexes for manager and technician role expectations; although the item set is smaller than the one used to operationalize role enactment among top communicators. The CEO manager role expectation index, as derived from the factor analysis, is reliable (Cronbach's alpha = .80); the technician index (identical to the one in Table 6.12) is also reliable (Cronbach's alpha = .84).

Table 6.13 displays the correlation coefficients between manager and technician role expectations of CEOs and the various characteristics of communication Excellence. Manager role expectations (as reported by the CEOs) are positively and significantly correlated with the communication department's expertise (as reported by top communicators) to enact the manager role and use the two-way models of public relations. The CEO's manager role expectations are also positively and significantly correlated with the value and support that the dominant coalition provides to public relations, as reported by top communicators. When CEOs report high manager role expectations of their top communicators, their top communicators report enacting that role more frequently.

High CEO expectations of manager role enactment are tightly linked to a number of important indicators of communication Excellence. If CEOs think their top communicators should enact the manager role frequently, they also report high support for the communication department ($r = .45$, $p < .01$) and value placed on communication by the dominant coalition ($r = .36$, $p < .01$). These same CEOs report that they want the two-way models to be used, both symmetrical ($r = .29$, $p < .01$) and asymmetrical ($r = .45$, $p < .01$). They report high contributions from their communication departments to strategic planning ($r = .30$, $p < .01$) and place great importance on knowledge about and communication with outside groups ($r = .44$, $p < .01$).

Whereas CEOs who report high manager role expectations say they want their communicators to use the two-way models, apparently the message is not

TABLE 6.13
Correlation of Manager and Technician Role Expectations
of the Dominant Coalition With Other Characteristics of Excellence

	Manager Role	Technician Role
Other Characteristics of Excellence Expectations	Expectations	
Expertise to Enact Manager Role	.13*	−.16**
Expertise to Use Two-Way Symmetrical Model[a]	.11*	−.17**
Expertise to Use Two-Way Asymmetrical Model[a]	.11*	−.11*
Value Dominant Coalition Places on PR[a]	.23**	.05
Support Dominant Coalition Gives to PR[a]	.22**	−.03
PR's Contribution to Strategic Planning[a]	.14*	.01
Manager Role Enactment by PR Head[a]	.12*	.04
Senior Adviser Role Enactment by PR Head[a]	.03	.06
Dominant Coalition Expects Two-Way Symmetrical Model Used[a]	.07	.02
Dominant Coalition Expects Two-Way Asymmetrical Model Used[a]	.06	−.05
Support for Women Employees[a]	.09	−.07
Support Dominant Coalition Gives to PR[b]	.45**	−.10
Value Dominant Coalition Places on PR[b]	.36**	−.01
Importance of Knowledge/Communication With Outside Groups[b]	.44**	.01
Dominant Coalition Expects Two-Way Asymmetrical Model Used[b]	.29**	−.04
Dominant Coalition Expects Two-Way Symmetrical Model Used[b]	.45**	.02
PR's Contribution to Strategic Planning[b]	.30**	−.01
Participative Organizational Culture[c]	.11*	−.07
Overall Excellence Score (manager/senior adviser enactment items removed)	**.44**	**−.07**

[a]From PR head (top-communicator) questionnaire. [b]From CEO questionnaire. [c]From employee questionnaire (data aggregated for all employees surveyed in the organization; avg. $N = 12$).

*$p < .05$ for zero-order Pearson correlation coefficients. **$p < .01$ for zero-order Pearson correlation coefficients.

getting through to top communicators. There is no significant correlation between CEOs' reports of high manager role expectations and what their top communicators say the dominant coalition wants with regard to using the two-way models, both symmetrical ($r = .07$, $p > .05$) and asymmetrical ($r = .06$, $p > .05$). Whereas expectations are clear in the minds of CEOs responding to the survey, those same expectations are not so clearly understood by top communicators who must implement those expectations. Overall, manager role expectations of CEOs are positively and significantly correlated with overall Excellence ($r = .44$, $p < .01$), even after manager and senior adviser items (as originally delineated) were removed from the Excellence scale.

On the other hand, technician role expectations of top communicators by their CEOs indicate no significant, positive correlations with the characteristics of communication Excellence. The only significant relationships are negative. CEOs expect their top communicators to enact the technician role in communication departments with low expertise to enact the manager role ($r = -.16, p < .01$) and low expertise to use the two-way symmetrical model ($r = -.17, p < .01$) and the two-way asymmetrical model ($r = -.11, p < .05$). The correlation between technician role expectations of the CEO and support given to the communication function (according to the CEO) is also negative, but not statistically significant ($r = -.10, p > .05$). CEOs' expectations of technician role enactment of their top communicators is negatively correlated with overall Excellence, but the relationship is not statistically significant ($r = -.07, p > .05$).

Five conclusions can be drawn from the quantitative findings regarding role expectations of the dominant coalition (as reported by the CEO) and characteristics of excellence. First, CEOs conceptualize the role of communicators in a fragmented manner. As a consequence, their role expectations are highly truncated, splintered, and confusing to top communicators who must act on them. Stated positively, communication Excellence occurs when CEOs demand excellence, top communicators understand that expectation unequivocally, and communication departments have the expertise to deliver excellence.

Second, CEOs have manager and technician role expectations for their top communicators. Generally, CEOs post higher-than-average manager role expectations for their top communicators and lower-than-average technician role expectations. Third, high CEO manager role expectations are associated with high overall Excellence of the organization's communication program, as well as with communication's contribution to strategic planning, value and support given to public relations, and manager role enactment by top communicators. That is, manager role expectations are clustered together with other expectations of excellence among CEOs.

Fourth, CEOs' technician role expectations of their top communicators have no significant positive association with overall Excellence or its components. Whereas technical expertise is critical to program execution—and excellent communication departments are superior with regard to the technical execution of programs—technician role expectations of the top communicator are not associated with excellence in any way.

Fifth, lower levels of departmental expertise to enact the manager role or use either of the two-way models of public relations are significantly associated with higher levels of technician role expectations from the CEO. We suspect that this is a push–pull relationship, replicated over time. Dominant coalitions hire communicators consistent with their technical role expectations. Because these technicians lack the expertise to enact the manager role, the dominant coalition's role expectations focus on what its communicators can do—until such time that an environmental crisis or major internal upheaval precipitates a change in the communication department.

Gender and Roles

As our literature review in this chapter revealed, scholars who have studied the effects of gender on public relations practice have devoted a great deal of attention to the roles of men and women in the field. The literature suggests that men are more likely to be communication managers and women to be technicians. If the top communicator is limited to the technician role, which may be more common for women than men, then the department will be less likely to be excellent than if the top communicator is a manager. Women who are managers, however, tend to "do it all," enacting a dual role of technician and manager.

We saw earlier in this chapter that the overall support for women in an organization correlates positively with the managerial role. In this section, we look more directly at the roles of male and female top communicators in our sample. Table 6.14 compares the means for men and women on all of the original roles scales as well as the new scales that we created after factor analyzing the original role items.

That table shows, first, that our top communicators—regardless of their gender—consistently had higher scores for enacting the manager role in comparison with the technician role. Our CEOs also consistently preferred that both male and female top communicators be managers more than technicians. *T* tests show that all of these comparisons are significantly different at the .01 level. Expertise, however, is relatively equal for most of the roles for departments headed by both men and women. Unfortunately for excellence in public relations, the critical knowledge for strategic management is the lowest of the types of expertise for both men and women. The greatest expertise, in contrast, is for administrative management and media relations.

Table 6.14 shows that there is no significant difference in the extent to which male and female top communicators enact the manager role and in the extent to which CEOs expect the manager role for their top communicator. This is true for both the original scales and the new scales developed from factor analysis. On the other hand, female top communicators are significantly more likely than males to also enact the technician role on both sets of measures. CEOs also are significantly more likely to expect their female top communicators to enact both a technician and manager role than they are to expect male top communicators to enact that dual role. Expertise was almost identical for all roles in departments headed by men and women, with the possible exception of expertise in strategic management and media relations—where men had a slight advantage. These two differences were significant at the .10 level but not at the .05 level.

These data, then, support the conclusion that female PR heads are more likely to play dual manager–technician roles than are men—even in organizations with excellent public relations departments. As our literature review concluded, these data also suggest that women may have less opportunity

TABLE 6.14
Comparison of the Roles of Male and Female Top Communicators

Role Enacted	Male PR Heads	Female PR Heads	T
	Transformed Means		
Manager	11.87	11.65	0.72
Senior Adviser	9.71	9.92	0.80
Technician	6.16	7.56	3.76**
Media Relations	9.27	9.56	0.68
Combined Management Factor	11.32	11.25	0.29
Combined Technician Factor	7.47	8.24	2.19*
Role Expectation of CEO			
Manager	11.47	11.17	0.81
Senior Adviser	11.44	11.54	0.38
Technician	5.94	7.16	2.90**
Media Relations	10.27	11.03	2.19*
New Management Factor	11.46	11.30	0.49
New Technician Factor	5.94	7.16	2.90**
Role Expertise			
Manager	10.09	10.02	0.23
Technician	9.89	9.89	0.02
Administrative Management Factor	11.47	11.71	0.79
Strategic Management Factor	7.74	7.07	1.75[a]
Internal Technician Factor	9.04	9.38	0.97
Media Relations Factor	11.46	10.91	1.67[a]

Note. There were 191 male top communicators and 181 female top communicators in the sample of all departments, although the numbers varied slightly in different cells because of missing data. There were 129 males and 144 females in the data on the role expectation of the CEO, which were limited to the primary PR department of the organization.

[a]Although not significant at the .05 level, these differences were significant at the .10 level.
*$p < .05$. **$p < .01$.

than men to gain strategic expertise because of the time they must spend doing technical tasks. The gender of the top communicator, therefore, does not help or hinder communication Excellence. Female top communicators may have to work harder to develop strategic expertise, which is necessary for excellence, at the same time that they engage in technical activities that are not expected of men.

QUALITATIVE RESULTS RELATED TO ROLES

Our in-depth interview studies help to flesh out the stark numeric skeleton of the linkages among role expertise, role enactment, role expectations, and communication Excellence. We asked CEOs, top communicators, and others in 25 organizations to respond to a schedule of open-end probes about public relations in their organizations. In this way, we were able to take the cross-sectional data from the quantitative survey and supplement it with organizational histories or biographies that permitted a richer theoretical understanding of excellence as a process occurring over time, rather than as a fixed attribute of organizations.

Manager Role Competencies in the Department

Theoretically, one should not be surprised to discover that departmental expertise to enact the manager role is the single best indicator of communication Excellence in organizations. After all, manager role enactment by the top communicator is predicated on the knowledge base to do so. High manager role expectations of the dominant coalition cannot translate into excellent communication programs without the knowledge base to do so. As the CEO of a major chemical-manufacturing company put it: "If I hadn't had a couple of talented communication managers, I couldn't have done anything. You can't make a silk purse out of a sow's ear."

A statewide organization that provided fund raising for arts organizations was selected for an in-depth case study because it had a low score on the Excellence scale. At the time of the survey, the communication program was under the direction of someone with no communication or public relations experience and training. A turning point for this arts organization, we learned in our interviews, was the hiring of a new CEO. Located in a politically and socially conservative state, the new CEO wanted an innovative approach to communication and public relations. The state legislature provided major funding for the arts program, but most legislators (and perhaps their constituents as well) generally disapproved of lifestyles and values associated with the creative or artistic communities. A new public relations director was hired, bringing a set of sophisticated manager role skills to the department and the organization. Using research, the new top communicator—in conjunction with other top managers—demonstrated that young people at risk of delinquency could find more socially constructive avenues for their energies through the arts. Funding for the arts was recast as a delinquency prevention strategy. The state legislature gave the arts organization its full budget request (a first), plus additional funding to better document teen participation in the arts. None of these changes would have occurred without the expertise to enact the manager role.

Manager role expertise is most usefully conceptualized as an attribute of a department, rather than an individual attribute (e.g., the top communicator). Furthermore, the manager–technician dichotomy plays a useful role as a data-analytic strategy; but our qualitative research indicates a powerful synergism when managerial and technical expertise are seen as complementary, such that the whole is greater than the sum of parts. For example, a blood bank on the West Coast of the United States was selected for case study because of its high

Excellence score on the quantitative portion of the study. During the long interviews, it became apparent that the public relations director had emerged as a
member of the dominant coalition during the peak of the AIDS epidemic, when
many people refused to donate blood, based on the fear that giving blood was
dangerous. At that time, the top communicator had been hired for her strong
journalistic and media relations skills.

Through a masterful media relations campaign, this blood bank was able to
hold the drop in blood donations to about 3%. At the same time, other cities on
the West Coast experienced 15% to 25% drops in donations. By responding to
this crisis through traditional public relations expertise, the top communicator
was able to hire a younger assistant with strong research and planning skills.
These two communicators reported working together to provide the expertise—both managerial and technical—that the dominant coalition required to
plan and execute excellent communication programs. The CEO indicated that
it mattered little who provided the expertise. The CEO needed both types of expertise and the communication department was able to provide it.

Manager Role Enactment by the Top Communicator

Manager role expertise is a necessary but not sufficient condition for communication Excellence. Specifically, top communicators need to enact manager role
behavior, often in an organizational setting where others neither understand
nor appreciate a strategic approach to public relations and communication
management.

For example, one public utility company in the U.S. Midwest spans four
states; it scored near the top in overall Excellence at the time of the 1990–1991
survey. At the time of the case study in 1994, the top communicator supervised
a staff of eight. Her expertise as a manager came, in part, from her formal education (bachelor's degree in public relations), but also from in-house training provided by the company and her own work experience. In addition, she reported
that a mentoring relationship with a senior member of the dominant coalition
had helped her build her manager role expertise.

As a result of her expertise and mentoring, the top communicator recognized that she needed to participate in strategic planning, to deal with the organization's relationships in a proactive manner. "Part of the problem that public
relations has had in the past," she told an interviewer for the Excellence study,
"is that they are the people that you bring in on the tail end to make things look
better, or polish over something that's not quite right." Instead, the top communicator took it upon herself to be the "eyes and ears" of the organization, a
description of her role confirmed in a separate interview with her supervisor.
This expertise allowed her to carve out a role as a manager who helps solve
problems, sometimes nipping them in the bud so that they never become issues. "Top management comes to accept you when they see work coming out

of the department that meets their strategic objectives," she said of her role as a communication manager. "You've got to be adding value in their eyes. Then you get a place at the table. You've got to start thinking in strategic planning terms."

Viewing public relations as proactive rather than reactive (brought in at the "tail end to make things look better") is an important attribute of manager role enactment. The top communicator for a state hospital association with high overall Excellence scores put this managerial orientation succinctly: "One must watch issues emerge, understand demographics, and be able to project into the future. If you want to move beyond [traditional reactive public relations], you really need to be able to watch the outside world and be able to anticipate what it is going to do."

Manager Role Expectations From CEOs

The case studies indicate a complex and triangulated relationship between CEO and dominant coalition expectations of manager role enactment, actual manager role enactment by the top communicator, and the departmental expertise to enact the manager role. The state hospital association mentioned earlier, for example, followed a traditional approach to public relations and organizational communication in the 1970s and 1980s. The main function of the communication department was to publish the association newsletter. As increased competition and managed care brought hospitals into increasing turmoil, the CEO of this hospital association realized he needed to make some changes: "Our whole mission changed. I realized the importance of communication with the public. I insisted on hiring new people with strong skills, both in writing and speaking and in management."

The CEO of a major American metal manufacturer did not need a crisis to know he wanted managers—not technicians—running his communication department. Originally selected because of the organization's low scores on the Excellence scale in the 1990–1991 survey, the interviewer for the Excellence study was initially perplexed when she discovered through case study interviews that the manufacturer appeared to have an excellent communication program. Two events had occurred between 1990 and 1994 to radically transform the organization. First, the chairman of the board and CEO was replaced by a new executive. This executive had once been in charge of corporate communication during his climb up the corporate ladder. At the same time, the top communicator who had completed the questionnaire in 1990 had retired. A new person now headed the communication department; the interaction was synergistic. The new top communicator (a vice president) played a strong manager role because of the importance the CEO placed on communication. The vice president for corporate communication described the CEO as a "great communicator" who speaks "with conviction" about corporate images that reflect the substantive reality of the organization's actual relationships with constituents. Addressing an industry conference of heavy-manufacturing companies, the CEO said: "An image should be a reflection of reality—a mirror of an industry's strengths and importance. Be assured that if we don't take action to shape the image of our company and our industry, others will do it for us—and that image may be as distorted as a fun-house mirror."

On the other hand, what CEOs demand in terms of communication Excellence also can be taken away. A state lottery in the western United States was originally selected for a case study because of its near-perfect score on the Excellence scale. Since the 1990–1991 survey, however, the top managers of the state lottery organization (a hybrid public–private entity established to raise funds for the government through gambling) had changed. With the new dominant coalition came a new set of perceptions about the role of communication. The two-way models of communication so heavily used at the time of the survey were largely replaced with traditional one-way models of publicity and public information.

Although the new top communicator meets frequently with the CEO, others we interviewed in the organization indicated that these meetings are largely times for the CEO to give orders to the top communicator and exchange information. The meetings do not involve strategic decision making. Use of research also had declined dramatically. Technical functions of the communication department were subcontracted to outside firms in 1990–1991. In 1994, these technical functions had been brought back in house. According to several communicators interviewed, the role of communication in strategic planning has been drastically reduced, reflecting the prevailing philosophy of the dominant coalition that the purpose of the communication department is to implement the strategic decisions made by others. As one staffer who has weathered the transition concluded, "There is a new CEO who has a different concept of the public relations role in an organization."

Sometimes, however, organizations evolve; and temporary shifts in perspective become institutionalized. A crisis or internal change may bring about a change in the manager role expectations and enactment of top communicators. The AIDS crisis at the blood bank described earlier is a case in point. A traditional top communicator, hired for her journalistic and media relations expertise, helped the organization avert a disaster. As a consequence, the communication department had won enough power in the organization to build up its management role expertise. This expertise, in turn, provided the communication department the capacity to enact the manager role on a continuing basis.

How permanent is this change in the role of the top communicator? We asked the CEO of the blood bank if the role of the top communicator would go back to what it had been before the AIDS crisis, should the current person leave. The CEO admitted that it would be hard to replace his current top communicator, "but the [manager] perspective would not vary. We would look for another like [the current top communicator]. That would take some effort. Others have tried and failed. But we wouldn't change our perspective."

SUMMARY AND CONCLUSIONS

The results of the Excellence study solidly support our proposition that the distinction between the manager and technician role for the senior communicator in a public relations department is a core factor distinguishing excellent from less excellent departments. However, the results also show the vital supporting role of technical expertise to the management role. More than any other variable, the availability of knowledge to perform a managerial role distinguishes excellent departments from less excellent ones. Excellent departments also have higher levels of technical expertise than do less excellent departments. Nevertheless, technical expertise has value only when it is accompanied by managerial expertise. Public relations managers are most effective when they also possess technical expertise or have it available to them—especially technical knowledge in media relations. Expert technicians who have little managerial expertise or who are not supervised by expert managers have little value to the organization.

Our data also revealed more than one kind of managerial expertise. Public relations departments can possess strategic managerial expertise, administrative managerial expertise, or both. We found that excellent departments possess both kinds of expertise. In chapter 5, we showed that strategic managers are most essential to the functioning of an excellent public relations department. This chapter established, in addition, that public relations departments need administrative as well as strategic expertise. Like technical expertise, however, administrative expertise has little value without accompanying knowledge of how to practice strategic public relations. At the same time, our data show that communication departments possess less strategic knowledge than knowledge needed to practice any of the other roles.

The managerial role is equally important for public relations when the perspective of the dominant coalition is taken into account. Although CEOs view public relations roles in a more splintered and confusing way than do top communicators, the CEOs of organizations with excellent public relations departments expect their top communicators to be managers. The greater importance assigned to communication with outside groups by the dominant coalition, in addition, the stronger its expectation will be that the top communicator should be a manager rather than a technician.

CEOs also expect top communicators to be expert in media relations—more strongly than do top communicators. In addition, our results suggested that CEOs often hire top communicators because of their technical expertise but then learn that technical expertise is insufficient when a crisis or major internal upheaval requires more strategic communication skills. When top communicators have managerial as well as technical knowledge, as our qualitative results showed, they can meet such a challenge. When they have only technical expertise, they cannot.

We also found that gender makes little difference in the role enacted by top communicators, in the role expectations of CEOs, and in the expertise of the public relations department. However, we found that female PR heads are more likely to play dual manager–technician roles than are men—even in organizations with excellent public relations departments. We also found that women may have less opportunity than men to gain strategic expertise because of the time they must spend doing technical tasks. The gender of the top communicator, therefore, does not help or hinder communication Excellence; but female top communicators may have to work harder to develop strategic expertise while they must engage in technical activities that are not expected of men.

REFERENCES

Acharya, L. (1983, August). *Practitioner representations of environmental uncertainty: An application of discriminant analysis.* Paper presented at the meeting of the Public Relations Division, Association for Education in Journalism and Mass Communication, Corvallis, OR.

Ahlwardt, E. (1984). *Coorientational states as predictors of organizational role ambiguity and conflict: An analysis of U.S. Navy commanding officer and public affairs officer dyads.* Unpublished master's thesis, San Diego State University, San Diego.

Aldrich, H., & Herker, D. (1977). Boundary spanning roles and organizational structure. *Academy of Management Review, 2,* 217–230.

Anderson, R., & Reagan, J. (1992). Practitioner roles and uses of new technologies. *Journalism Quarterly, 69,* 156–165.

Anderson, R., Reagan, J., Sumner, J., & Hill, S. (1989). A factor analysis of Broom and Smith's public relations roles scale. *Public Relations Review, 15*(3), 54.

Baker, J. K., & Schaffer, R. H. (1969). Making staff consulting more effective. *Harvard Business Review, 47*(1), 68.

Berkowitz, D., & Hristodoulakis, I. (1999). Practitioner roles, public relations education, and professional socialization: An exploratory study. *Journal of Public Relations Research, 11,* 91–103.

Broom, G. M. (1982). A comparison of sex roles in public relations. *Public Relations Review, 8*(3), 17–22.

Broom, G. M. (1986, May). *Public relations roles and systems theory: Functional and historicist causal models.* Paper presented at the meeting of the Public Relations Interest Group, International Communication Association, Chicago.

Broom, G. M., & Dozier, D. M. (1985, August). *Determinants and consequences of public relations roles.* Paper presented at the meeting of the Public Relations Division, Association for Education in Journalism and Mass Communication, Memphis, TN.

Broom, G. M., & Dozier, D. M. (1986). Advancement for public relations role models. *Public Relations Review, 12*(1), 37–56.

Broom, G. M., & Dozier, D. M. (1990). *Using research in public relations: Applications to program management.* Englewood Cliffs, NJ: Prentice-Hall.

Broom, G. M., & Smith, G. D. (1978, August). *Toward an understanding of public relations roles: An empirical test of five role models' impact on clients.* Paper presented at the meeting of the Public Relations Division, Association for Education in Journalism, Seattle, WA.

Broom, G. M., & Smith, G. D. (1979). Testing the practitioner's impact on clients. *Public Relations Review, 5*(3), 47–59.

Coombs, W. T., Holladay, S., Hasenauer, G., & Signitzer, B. (1994). A comparative analysis of international public relations: Identification and interpretation of similarities and differences between professionalization in Austria, Norway, and the United States. *Journal of Public Relations Research, 6,* 23–39.

Crable, R. E., & Vibbert, S. L. (1985). Managing issues and influencing public policy. *Public Relations Review, 11*(2), 3–16.

Creedon, P. J. (1991). Public relations and "women's work": Toward a feminist analysis of public relations roles. In J. E. Grunig & L. A. Grunig (Eds.), *Public relations research annual* (Vol. 3, pp. 67–84). Hillsdale, NJ: Lawrence Erlbaum Associates.

Culbertson, H. M. (1991). Role taking and sensitivity: Keys to playing and making public relations roles. In J. E. Grunig & L. A. Grunig (Eds.), *Public relations research annual* (Vol. 3, pp. 37–65). Hillsdale, NJ: Lawrence Erlbaum Associates.

Cutlip, S. M., & Center, A. H. (1971). *Effective public relations* (4th ed.). Englewood Cliffs, NJ: Prentice-Hall.

Cutlip, S. M., Center, A. H., & Broom, G. M. (1994). *Effective public relations* (7th ed.). Englewood Cliffs, NJ: Prentice-Hall.

Dozier, D. M. (1981, August). *The diffusion of evaluation methods among public relations practitioners.* Paper presented at the meeting of the Public Relations Division, Association for Education in Journalism, East Lansing, MI.

Dozier, D. M. (1983, November). *Toward a reconciliation of "role conflict" in public relations research.* Paper presented at the meeting of the Western Communication Educators Conference, Fullerton, CA.

Dozier, D. M. (1984a, June). *The evolution of evaluation methods among public relations practitioners.* Paper presented at the meeting of Educator Academy, International Association of Business Communicators, Montreal, Canada.

Dozier, D. M. (1984b, August). *Priority research issues in public relations.* Paper presented at the meeting of the Foundation for Public Relations Research and Education, Gainesville, FL.

Dozier, D. M. (1984c). Program evaluation and roles of practitioners. *Public Relations Review, 10*(2), 13–21.

Dozier, D. M. (1986, August). *The environmental scanning function of public relations practitioners and participation in management decision-making.* Paper presented at the meeting of the Public Relations Division, Association for Education in Journalism and Mass Communication, Norman, OK.

Dozier, D. M. (1987, May). *Gender, environmental scanning, and participation in management decision-making.* Paper presented at the meeting of the Public Relations Interest Group, International Communication Association, Montreal, Canada.

Dozier, D. M. (1988a). Breaking public relations' glass ceiling. *Public Relations Review, 14*(3), 6–14.

Dozier, D. M. (1988b, May). *The vertical location of the public relations function in organizations.* Paper presented at the meeting of the Public Relations Interest Group, International Communication Association, New Orleans, LA.

Dozier, D. M. (1988c, July). *Organic structure and managerial environmental sensitivity as predictors of practitioner membership in the dominant coalition.* Paper presented at the meeting of the Association for Education in Journalism and Mass Communication, Portland, OR.

Dozier, D. M. (1989, May). *Implementing public relations strategies and theories with high technology.* Paper presented at the meeting of the Public Relations Interest Group, International Communication Association, San Francisco.

Dozier, D. M. (1990). The innovation of research in public relations practice: Review of a program of studies. In J. E. Grunig & L. A. Grunig (Eds.), *Public relations research annual* (Vol. 2, pp. 3–28). Hillsdale, NJ: Lawrence Erlbaum Associates.

Dozier, D. M. (1992). The organizational roles of communications and public relations practitioners. In J. E. Grunig (Ed.), *Excellence in public relations and communication management* (pp. 327–356). Hillsdale, NJ: Lawrence Erlbaum Associates.

Dozier, D. M., & Broom, G. M. (1995). Evolution of the manager role in public relations practice. *Journal of Public Relations Research, 7,* 3–26.

Dozier, D. M., Chapo, S., & Sullivan, B. (1983, August). *Sex and the bottom line: Income differences between women and men in public relations.* Paper presented at the meeting of the Public Relations Division, Association for Education in Journalism and Mass Communication, Corvallis, OR.

Dozier, D. M., & Gottesman, M. (1982, July). *Subjective dimensions of organizational roles among public relations practitioners.* Paper presented at the meeting of the Public Relations Division, Association for Education in Journalism, Athens, OH.

Dozier, D. M., with Grunig, L. A., & Grunig, J. E. (1995). *Manager's guide to excellence in public relations and communication management.* Hillsdale, NJ: Lawrence Erlbaum Associates.

Druck, K. B., Fiur, M., & Bates, D. (1986). *Public relations and new technology.* New York: Foundation for Public Relations Research and Education.

Duncan, R. B. (1972). Characteristics of organizational environments and perceived environmental uncertainty. *Administrative Science Quarterly, 17,* 313–327.

Dyer, S. C. (1996). Descriptive modeling for public relations environmental scanning: A practitioner's perspective. *Journal of Public Relations Research, 8,* 137–150.

Eden, C., & Sims, D. (1979). On the nature of problems in consulting practice. *Omega, 7,* 21–32.

Ekachai, D. G. (1995). Applying Broom's role scales to Thai public relations practitioners. *Public Relations Review, 21*(4), 325–336.

Emery, F. E., & Trist, E. (1965). The causal texture of organizational environments. *Human Relations, 18,* 21–31.

Ferguson, M. A. (1979). *Role norms, implicit relationship attributions and organizational communication: A study of public relations practitioners.* Unpublished master's thesis, University of Wisconsin, Madison.

Fetterman, D. M. (1998). *Ethnography: Step by step* (2nd ed.). Thousand Oaks, CA: Sage.

Gaunt, P., & Ollenberger, J. (1995). Issues management revisited: A tool that deserves another look. *Public Relations Review, 21*(3), 199–210.

Gordon, C. G., & Kelly, K. S. (1999). Public relations expertise and organizational effectiveness: A study of U.S. hospitals. *Journal of Public Relations Research, 11,* 143–166.

Grunig, J. E. (1992a). Communication, public relations, and effective organizations: An overview of the book. In J. E. Grunig (Ed.), *Excellence in public relations and communication management* (pp. 1–28). Hillsdale, NJ: Lawrence Erlbaum Associates.

Grunig, J. E. (Ed.). (1992b). *Excellence in public relations and communication management.* Hillsdale, NJ: Lawrence Erlbaum Associates.

Grunig, J. E., & Hunt, T. (1984). *Managing public relations.* New York: Holt, Rinehart & Winston.

Grunig, J. E., & White, J. (1991, August). *The effect of worldview on public relations theory and practice.* Paper presented at the meeting of the Public Relations Division, Association for Education in Journalism and Mass Communication, Boston.

Grunig, L. A. (1992). Power in the public relations department. In J. E. Grunig (Ed.), *Excellence in public relations and communication management* (pp. 483–501). Hillsdale, NJ: Lawrence Erlbaum Associates.

Grunig, L. A., Toth, E. L., & Hon, L. C. (2001). *Women in public relations: How gender influences practice.* New York: Guilford.

Guth, D. W. (1995). Organizational crisis experience and public relations roles. *Public Relations Review, 21*(2), 123–136.

Hainsworth, B., & Meng, M. (1988). How corporations define issues management. *Public Relations Review, 14*(4), 18–30.

Heath, R. L. (1998). New communication technologies: An issues management point of view. *Public Relations Review, 24*(3), 273–288.

Heath, R. L., & Cousino, K. R. (1990). Issues management: End of first decade progress report. *Public Relations Review, 16*(1), 6–18.

Heath, R. L., & Nelson, R. A. (1986). *Issues management: Corporate public policymaking in an information society.* Beverly Hills, CA: Sage.

Hon, L. C. (1995). Toward a feminist theory of public relations. *Journal of Public Relations Research, 7,* 27–88.

Hon, L. C. (1998). Demonstrating effectiveness in public relations: Goals, objectives, and evaluation. *Journal of Public Relations Research, 10,* 103–135.

Hon, L. C., Grunig, L. A., & Dozier, D. M. (1992). Women in public relations: Problems and opportunities. In J. E. Grunig (Ed.), *Excellence in public relations and communication management* (pp. 419–438). Hillsdale, NJ: Lawrence Erlbaum Associates.

Humphreys, P. C. (1985). *Intelligence in decision support.* Paper presented at the meeting of the 10th Research Conference on Subjective Probability, Utility, and Decision-Making, Helsinki, Finland.

Johnson, D. J., & Acharya, L. (1982, July). *Organizational decision-making and public relations roles.* Paper presented at the meeting of the Public Relations Division, Association for Education in Journalism, Athens, OH.

Johnson, M. A. (1997). Public relations and technology: Practitioner perspectives. *Journal of Public Relations Research, 9,* 213–236.

Jones, B. L., & Chase, W. H. (1979). Managing public policy issues. *Public Relations Review, 5*(2), 3–23.

Katz, D., & Kahn, R. L. (1966). *The social psychology of organizations.* New York: Wiley.

Katz, D., & Kahn, R. L. (1978). *The social psychology of organizations* (Rev. ed.). New York: Wiley.

Kelly, K. S. (1993). Public relations and fund-raising encroachment: Losing control in the non-profit sector. *Public Relations Review, 19*(4), 349–365.

Kurpius, D. J., & Brubaker, J. C. (1976). *Psychoeducational consultation: Definition, functions, and preparation.* Bloomington: Indiana University Press.

Lauzen, M. M. (1991, August). *When marketing imperialism matters: An examination of marketing imperialism at the managerial level.* Paper presented at the meeting of the Public Relations Division, Association for Education in Journalism and Mass Communication, Boston.

Lauzen, M. M. (1992). Public relations roles, intraorganizational power, and encroachment. *Journal of Public Relations Research, 4,* 61–80.

Lauzen, M. M. (1993). When marketing involvement matters at the manager level. *Public Relations Review, 19*(3), 247–259.

Lauzen, M. M. (1994). Public relations practitioner role enactment in issues management. *Journalism Quarterly, 71,* 356–368.

Lauzen, M. M. (1997). Understanding the relation between public relations and issues management. *Journal of Public Relations Research, 9,* 65–82.

Lauzen, M. M., & Dozier, D. M. (1992). The missing link: The public relations manager role as mediator of organizational environments and power consequences for the function. *Journal of Public Relations Research, 4,* 205–220.

Lauzen, M. M., & Dozier, D. M. (1994). Issues management mediation of linkages between environmental complexity and management of the public relations function. *Journal of Public Relations Research, 6,* 163–184.

Leichty, G., & Springston, J. (1996). Elaborating public relations roles. *Journalism & Mass Cmmunication Quarterly, 73,* 467–477.

Lesly, P. (1981). The stature and role of public relations. *Public Relations Journal, 37*(1), 14–17.

Linton, R. (1936). *The study of man.* New York: Appleton–Century.

McGoon, C. (1993). Life's a beach, for communicators. *Communication World, 10*(1), 12–15.

McKeown, B., & Thomas, D. (1988). *Q methodology*. Newbury Park, CA: Sage.

Merton, R. K. (1957). *Social theory and social structure* (Rev. ed.). New York: The Free Press.

Morton, L. P. (1996). Do public relations managers and technicians value news releases differently? *Public Relations Review, 22*(4), 355–368.

Newcomb, T. M. (1951). *Social psychology*. New York: Dryden.

Newsom, D. A., & Scott, A. (1976). *This is PR: The realities of public relations*. Belmont, CA: Wadsworth.

Parsons, P. R. (1989). Values of communication studies and professional self-selection. *Journalism Quarterly, 66*, 161–168.

Parsons, T. (1951). *The social system*. New York: The Free Press.

Pasadeos, Y., Renfro, R. B., & Hanily, M. L. (1999). Influential authors and works of the public relations scholarly literature: A network of recent research. *Journal of Public Relations Research, 11*, 29–52.

Pearce, A. J., II, & Robinson, R. B., Jr. (1982). *Strategic management: Strategy formation and implementation*. Homewood, IL: Irwin.

Piekos, J. M., & Einsiedel, E. F. (1990). Roles and program evaluation techniques among Canadian public relations practitioners. In L. A. Grunig & J. E. Grunig (Eds.), *Public relations research annual* (Vol. 2, pp. 95–113). Hillsdale, NJ: Lawrence Erlbaum Associates.

Rogers, E. M. (1983). *Diffusion of innovations* (3rd eds.). New York: The Free Press.

Rossman, G. B., & Rallis, S. F. (1998). *Learning in the field: An introduction to qualitative research*. Thousand Oaks, CA: Sage.

Schein, E. H. (1969). *Process consultation: Its role in organizational development*. Reading, MA: Addison-Wesley.

Serini, S. A., Toth, E., Wright, D. K., & Emig, A. G. (1997). Watch for falling glass . . . women, men, and job satisfaction in public relations: A preliminary analysis. *Journal of Public Relations Research, 9*, 99–118.

Starbuck, W. H. (1976). Organizations and their environments. In M. D. Dunnette (Ed.), *Handbook of industrial and organizational psychology* (pp. 1069–1124). Chicago: Rand McNally.

Sullivan, B. S., Dozier, D. M., & Hellweg, S. A. (1984, August). *A test of organizational role hierarchy among public relations practitioners*. Paper presented at the meeting of the Public Relations Division, Association for Education in Journalism and Mass Communication, Gainesville, FL.

Sullivan, B. S., Dozier, D. M., & Hellweg, S. A. (1985). Practitioner pursuit of the ideal role. *International Public Relations Review, 9*(2), 14–18.

Tam, S. Y., Dozier, D. M., Lauzen, M. M., & Real, M. R. (1995). The impact of superior–subordinate gender on the career advancement of public relations practitioners. *Journal of Public Relations Research, 7*, 259–272.

Terreberry, S. (1968). The evolution of organizational environments. *Administrative Science Quarterly, 12*, 377–396.

Thompson, J. D. (1967). *Organizations in action*. New York: McGraw-Hill.

Thomsen, S. R. (1995). Using online databases in corporate issues management. *Public Relations Review, 21*(2), 103–122.

Toth, E. L., & Grunig, L. A. (1993). The missing story of women in public relations. *Journal of Public Relations Research, 5*, 153–175.

Toth, E. L., Serini, S. S., Wright, D. K., & Emig, A. G. (1998). Trends in public relations roles: 1990–1995. *Public Relations Review, 24*(2), 145–163.

Trumbo, C. (1995). Longitudinal modeling of public issues: An application of the agenda-setting process to the issue of global warming. *Journalism & Mass Communication Monographs, 152*.

Vari, A., & Vecsenyi, J. V. (1984). Selecting decision support methods in organizations. *Journal of Applied Systems Analysis, 11*, 23–36.

Walton, R. E. (1969). *Interpersonal peacemaking: Confrontations and third party consultation*. Reading, MA: Addison-Wesley.

White, J., & Dozier, D. M. (1992). Public relations and management decision making. In J. E. Grunig (Ed.), *Excellence in public relations and communication management* (pp. 91–108). Hillsdale, NJ: Lawrence Erlbaum Associates.

Wright, D. K. (1979). Some ways to measure public relations. *Public Relations Journal, 36*(7), 17.

Wright, D. K. (1995). The role of corporate public relations executives in the future of employee communications. *Public Relations Review, 21*(3), 181–198.

Wright, D. K., Grunig, L. A., Springston, J. K., & Toth, E. L. (1991). *Under the glass ceiling: An analysis of gender issues in American public relations* (PRSA Foundation Monograph Series, Vol. 1, No. 2). New York: Public Relations Society of America.

Zoch, L. M., Patterson, B. S., & Olson, D. L. (1997). The status of the school public relations practitioner: A statewide exploration. *Public Relations Review, 23*(4), 361–375.

CHAPTER SEVEN

Organization of the Communication Function, Relationship to Other Management Functions, and Use of Consulting Firms

At this point in our analysis of the Excellence data, we believe we have shown convincingly that public relations is a vital management function for all organizations. Public relations provides more than a technical support role to other management functions such as marketing, human resources, or finance. Senior public relations officers are managers rather than—or as well as—technicians who, when empowered by the dominant coalition, provide an essential role in the strategic management of the organization.

In this chapter we move from the roles played by public relations practitioners to the organizational structures in which the public relations function is housed. Organizations call their public relations function many different names, such as public relations, corporate communication, communication, public affairs, external affairs, or community relations. Sometimes those names suggest different emphases for the public relations function; sometimes they are merely euphemisms for the name "public relations."

Some organizations develop separate departments for specialized communication programs such as marketing communication, employee communication, investor relations, or government relations. Other organizations place the communication function in one or more departments that house other management functions, such as marketing, human resources, or finance. Still other organizations contract with outside public relations firms for their entire public relations function or for specialized services such as research, media relations, publications, or special events. In this chapter, we address the question of whether these structural differences enhance or detract from communication excellence.

INTEGRATION VERSUS SUBLIMATION
OF THE PUBLIC RELATIONS FUNCTION

In the first *Excellence* book, the research team proposed that integrating all communication functions through a single public relations department would enhance the ability of the communication function to participate in strategic management. With such integration, public relations departments are arranged into horizontal structures that reflect the strategic publics or stakeholders of the organizations. The managers of these subfunctions—such as employee relations, marketing communication, investor relations, or community relations—have a matrix relationship with both the public relations department and the functional department they serve (see also Tierney, 1993). However, the decision of which publics are most strategic at a particular time is made by the senior public relations officer in collaboration with the CEO and other members of the organization's dominant coalition; and resources are moved from program to program depending on which publics are most strategic in different situations. With such integration, marketing communication reports to public relations but serves marketing, employee communication reports to public relations but serves human resources, and so forth.

Specifically, Dozier and L. Grunig (1992) stated the following proposition in describing the implications of the literature they reviewed in their chapter on "The Organization of the Public Relations Function":

> To summarize, open-systems theory suggests that the public relations unit should be unified within a single department rather than fragmented and distributed as a technical support function among several organizational units. Further, the public relations unit should be placed high in the organizational hierarchy. That is because public relations, as part of the adaptive subsystem, must exchange information with the managerial subsystem, must participate in strategic decision making that affects the organization's relations with internal and external publics. Regarding horizontal structure, the unit should be flexible and decentralized. As a boundary-spanning function within organizations, the public relations unit should change its structure and processes in response to environmental pressures.

We have not been alone in advocating the concept of integrated communication in the time since the first *Excellence* book was published. In particular, proponents of the concept of integrated marketing communication (IMC) have advocated the integration of all marketing communication functions, such as advertising, product public relations, and promotion, under the roof of a marketing department or, at least, a marketing communication department.

Most IMC theorists and practitioners now have dropped the "M" from IMC to call this idea "integrated communication" (IC) rather than "integrated marketing communication" (e.g., Duncan & Moriarty, 1997; Gronstedt, 2000). One prominent early advocate of IMC, Caywood (1997), has begun to use the terms "public relations" and "integrated communication" synonymously (see the discussion by Hunter, 1999a). However, most theorists of integrated communication still come from an advertising or marketing perspective and still see the customer as the focus of communication efforts even though they emphasize the importance of other stakeholders and recommend the integration of all communication programs for different stakeholders.

Duncan and Moriarty (1997) called their new integrated model "integrated marketing," which they defined as a "cross-functional process for managing profitable brand relationships" (p. 9). After reviewing the recent literature on integrated communication, Hunter (1999a) concluded that the concept of brand is at the center of thinking about IC and recommended that public relations and marketing be integrated into a single function.

In contrast, we have included the overarching premise in our theory of communication excellence that *the organization is best served by the inherent diversity of perspectives provided by marketing and public relations when those functions remain distinct, coordinated yet not integrated.* We also have believed that the concept of relationships with publics is a more fruitful way of understanding the outcome and value of communication programs than is the concept of brand (or image or reputation). Duncan and Moriarty (1997) said much the same thing when they wrote, "In essence brand equity is determined by the quality of a brand's relationships with its customers and other key stakeholders" (pp. xii–xiii). However, we believe that a brand is a cognition that people develop about a product (although some extend the concept from the product to the organization). A brand cannot have a relationship with a stakeholder; only an organization can have such a relationship. Therefore, we prefer to limit the meaning of the concept of brand to the cognitions that customers have of products and to use the more useful term of "relationships" to understand the value of communication programs.

Major changes have occurred in the thinking of scholars of integrated communication since Ehling, White, and J. Grunig (1992) addressed the question of the relationship of public relations to marketing in the first *Excellence* book. The question of the relationship of public relations and marketing remains, however, because integrated communication scholars still focus on customers and place the marketing concept of brand at the center of their thinking. Ehling, White, and J. Grunig addressed the relationship of public relations and marketing with this proposition: *The public relations function of excellent organizations exists separately from the marketing function, and excellent public relations departments are not subsumed into the marketing function.*

The logic of this proposition is that public relations is a distinct management function from marketing and, therefore, that it should not be sublimated to marketing. The same logic applies to the sublimation of public relations to human resources, finance, or any other management function. There is much more literature on the relationship between public relations and marketing, however, than on the relationship of public relations to other management functions. Nevertheless, public relations must work with and support all other management functions to improve their communication with publics so we do not view public relations, marketing, human relations, or other management functions as rival or adversarial functions.

The Excellence theory, as summarized in chapter 1, specified two principles that are relevant to this chapter: Organizations should have (a) *an integrated communication function,* but (b) *public relations should be a management function separate from other management functions.* These principles can be elaborated by the following more specific principles about the relationship of public relations to strategic management and to other management functions such as marketing:

1. The public relations function should be located in the organizational structure so that it has ready access to the key decision makers of the organization—the dominant coalition—and so that it can contribute to the strategic management processes of the organization.
2. All communication programs should be integrated into or coordinated by the public relations department or a senior executive with a public relations title, such as senior vice president of corporate communication.
3. Public relations should not be subordinated to other departments such as marketing, human resources, or finance.
4. Public relations departments should be structured horizontally to reflect strategic publics and so that it is possible to reassign people and resources to new programs as new strategic publics emerge and other publics cease to be strategic.

USE OF PUBLIC RELATIONS FIRMS

In this chapter, we also examine the extent to which the organizations we surveyed used outside public relations firms and the ways in which they used those firms. In the theory book, Dozier and Repper (1992) reviewed literature related to one kind of service provided by outside firms: research. That review produced the following proposition:

> *Research is an essential component of strategic public relations, but few communication managers are trained as researchers. Most practitioners, therefore, buy much of their research from commercial firms. Communication managers should not buy research "off the shelf" from these firms, however, unless that research provides the information needed at a particular stage of strategic public relations—especially when needed for environmental scanning and evaluation of programs.*

This proposition followed the logic of our principle of integration of the public relations function. If organizations buy research from an outside firm, we believed, the research methods used should flow from the logic of the strategic management process of the organization and public relations' role in it. Research should not be done for its own sake, and many research strategies and methods may not be appropriate for the strategic process of public relations in a particular organization.

The same logic would apply to other services purchased from outside firms, whether those services are managerial or technical. A strategic communication manager must find a means of integrating all of the public relations activities of an organization. That strategic manager could be housed in an outside firm or in an in-house department. Or, an in-house strategic manager could purchase strategic counsel from an outside firm as well as technical services or research support. Duncan and Moriarty (1997) also emphasized integration in choosing an outside firm by advocating the use of firms that offer integrated communication services. Gronstedt (2000), similarly, suggested using a single outside firm worldwide to integrate communication services; but he also acknowledged that "few communications suppliers can offer first-class service in all disciplines and in every part of the world" (p. 201).

Before the survey, we had no idea how excellent public relations departments would use outside firms, other than our belief that both internal and external public relations activities should be integrated. In the survey, therefore, we asked top communicators whether their organizations used the services of outside firms and, if they did, whether those services included technical support, strategic counsel, or research.

CONCEPTUALIZATION OF INTEGRATED COMMUNICATION[1]

Since the publication of our theory book, as mentioned previously, additional literature has been developed on the concepts of integrated communication and integrated marketing communication. Before presenting relevant results from the Excellence study, we review that literature to provide conceptual background for our data.

In the United States and throughout the world, the discussion of integrating communication programs began with the question of whether public relations, advertising, and sales promotion should be integrated through a mechanism called "integrated marketing communication." IMC consists of integrating what Harris (1991) called "marketing public relations" with advertising. In Harris' terms, "corporate public relations" would remain a separate function and would not be placed under the marketing function. This concept of integrated

---

[1]Portions of this section were published previously in J. Grunig and L. Grunig (1998).

marketing communication fits the definition of the American Association of Advertising Agencies (AAAA):

> A concept of marketing communications planning that recognizes the added value of a comprehensive plan that evaluates the strategic role of a variety of disciplines—general advertising, direct response, sales promotion, and public relations—and combines these disciplines to provide clarity, consistency and maximum communication impact. (as quoted in Duncan and Caywood, 1996, p. 18)

Although there have been exceptions, IMC generally has been supported by advertising and marketing communication scholars and professionals and resisted by their counterparts in public relations. At first, the debate centered on the question of whether the role of public relations is to support marketing or whether it serves a broader social and political function. Later, advocates of IMC accepted the premise that public relations has a broader function than supporting marketing; but they generally seemed to have believed that theories of marketing and marketing communication could be used for this social-political function as well as for the marketing of products and services.

The Relationship Between Public Relations and Marketing

The question of the relationship between public relations and marketing may seem like a new question, but it has at least a 100-year history. Tedlow (1979) studied the history of corporate public relations from 1900 to 1950 and concluded that the public relations function survived during that half century because it fulfilled the broader social-political function:

> Public relations has promised two benefits to business: increased sales and protection from unpopularity which could lead to detrimental governmental or regulatory agency activity. . . . It is not as a sales device, however, but as a method for protection against the political consequences of a hostile public opinion that corporate public relations has been most influential. If it had been restricted to sales promotion, public relations might have been absorbed by advertising departments and could have been dismissed as a footnote to business history. Instead, it grew into a tool for dealing with many publics, including residents of plant communities, employees, suppliers and dealers, and politicians as well as customers. (pp. 193, 196)

The debate has continued, however, as both scholars and practitioners have questioned the relationship of public relations to the concepts of integrated marketing communication (IMC) and integrated communication (IC). White and Mazur (1995) captured this debate when they described three possible "futures" for public relations:

There are a number of possible futures for public relations. In the first scenario, it becomes largely a technical practice, using communication techniques to support marketing activities and is involved in work on product and corporate branding, corporate reputation, market penetration and development.

In the second, public relations will increasingly become a social practice, helping organizations fit into their social environments, and working on relationships between groups to help bring about social and economic development, and to help in completing social tasks.

These futures are not mutually exclusive. Public relations is a strategic and enabling practice. To progress, it will need to mark out its agenda, and to invest in a programme of research and development to do this. (p. 266)

Kotler and Mindak (1978) were among the first to address the relationship between public relations and marketing when they outlined five alternative arrangements: (a) separate but equal functions (marketing and public relations have different functions, perspectives, and capabilities), (b) equal but overlapping functions (both are important and separate functions but they share some terrain, especially product publicity and customer relations; in addition, public relations serves as a "watchdog" on the social responsibility of marketing), (c) marketing as the dominant function (marketing manages the relationship with all publics in the same way as the relationship with customers—"megamarketing"), (d) public relations as the dominant function (if public relations builds relationships with all key publics of the organization, then programs to build relationships with customers—i.e., marketing—would be a subset of public relations), and (e) marketing and public relations as the same function (public relations and marketing converge in concepts and methodologies, and a single department manages the external affairs of the company).

Hallahan (1992) modified Kotler and Mindak's (1978) typology to include six arrangements: (a) celibate (only one of the functions exists), (b) coexistent (the two functions operate independently), (c) combative (the two functions are at odds), (d) cooptive (one function usurps the other), (e) coordinated (the two functions are independent but work closely together), or (f) combined (the two functions operate within a single unit).

Public relations scholars and professionals have expressed fear of arrangements in which marketing dominates public relations or when the two are combined into a single unit—arrangements that Lauzen (1991, 1992) has called "marketing imperialism" and "encroachment" on public relations territory. In a book on hospital public relations, for example, Lewton (1991) described the problems of either a dominant or combined structure:

Obviously, when the issue is one of merging both functions, and either public relations being "under marketing," or marketing being "under public relations," some concerns are inevitable, just as there would be concerns if a hospital were going to have the human resources department report to finance, or medical staff relations report to the legal department. In a public relations–marketing merger, the PR professionals wonder why their discipline is seen as a subset of marketing (which it isn't), and wonder what marketing number-crunchers know about media and stakeholder relations. They're concerned that other noncustomer audiences will be ignored. If marketing is placed under public relations, marketers wonder how a PR vice president can make decisions on pricing or set up an effective sales rep program. They're concerned that their customers—who are their universe—will get lost in the midst of "all those audiences." (p. 51)

Integrating Communication: From IMC to IC

One can hardly deny the merits of integrating all marketing communication functions (see, e.g., Hunt & J. Grunig, 1994). However, until recently the view of public relations held by most adherents of IMC has been extremely narrow, as several studies (e. g., Canonico, 1994; Hunter, 1997; Tierney, 1993; Tillery, 1995) have documented. Most adherents of IMC have seen public relations as a technical support function and not as a management function, considered public relations to be press agentry or product publicity alone, and focused solely on customer publics. In addition, most interest in IMC seemed to come from advertising professionals and agencies (Hunter, 1997; Tierney, 1993); and most studies that showed support for IMC from the profession have been studies of marketing managers that have been sponsored by advertising associations (see Duncan & Caywood, 1996).

To overcome the objections to IMC from public relations scholars and professionals, adherents of the concept began to use the term "integrated communication" (IC) in place of IMC (Duncan, Caywood, & Newsom, 1993; Newson & Carroll, 1992). Dropping the "M" from "IMC" expanded the definition to include stakeholders other than consumers and dropped the inference that public relations was a marketing function.

Duncan and Caywood (1996) proposed seven stages through which communication programs can be integrated: awareness, image integration, functional integration, coordinated integration, consumer-based integration, stakeholder-based integration, and relationship management integration. Their last two stages closely resemble the integration of communication through the public relations function that we have included in our Excellence theory. Indeed, Duncan and Caywood stated that public relations will come to the fore in the last two stages of integration, while pointing out the first five stages emphasize marketing communication and customer relations only:

Although the full role of public relations may have seemingly been limited in the first five stages to the promotional aspects of marketing public relations, the sixth stage demands a fully integrated corporate communications function. Communication at the corporate stage of integration must include employees, the media, community leaders, investors, vendors, suppliers, competitors, government at all stages, and so on. (pp. 31–32)[2]

Gronstedt (1996) proposed a similar "stakeholder relations model" that included 11 stakeholder groups, only 1 of which is consumers. He described several "receiving tools," "interactive tools," and "sending tools" that come from the tool bags of public relations, marketing, and advertising. Nevertheless, Gronstedt placed consumers at the center of his stakeholder diagram in the belief that the consumer always is the most strategic stakeholder.

We disagree with that fundamental premise. One can make an equally good case that employees or investors are the most strategic public. In reality, however, different publics are more or less strategic for different kinds of organizations; and which public is most strategic changes as situations change. For example, investors may be most strategic during a takeover attempt; employees may be most strategic following downsizing; and donors generally will be most strategic for nonprofit organizations.

The integration of communication functions that we have proposed, therefore, incorporates these higher levels of integration proposed by IMC theorists. The major difference is that we do not propose moving integration upward through the marketing communication function. Rather we propose beginning at the highest level of integration and then pulling marketing communication and communication programs for other stakeholders into the public relations function. Drobis (1997–1998), the chairman of Ketchum Public Relations Worldwide, took the same position when he declared that "integrated marketing communication is dead":

It died because we never could decide if it was a tool to help sell advertising and public relations agency services or if it was a true, complete communications discipline. As a result, the term "integrated marketing communications" was frequently abbreviated to "integrated communications" and came to stand for many things, but nothing in particular. Admittedly, integrated marketing communications as it was originally conceived seemed to stand for the blending of multiple forms of marketing communications. Still, given its potential for greatness, the discipline withered under the chronic stress of being misunderstood by public relations professionals, many of whom consider the role of public relations in "integrated marketing communications" too narrow. Let's just call its cause of death "unknown." (p. 6)

---

[2]Caywood (1997) presented a slightly different version of these stages—dropping two stages and adding a new one. The revised stages were awareness, image integration, functional integration, consumer-based integration, stakeholder integration, and utopian integration. Utopian integration largely consisted of integration based on an "advanced, information-based, and probably digital system" (p. xxiii). These revised stages do not seem to affect the conclusions we have made about the implications of these stages. We still believe that integration should begin at the stakeholder stage. The utopian stage seems to be an elaboration of the stakeholder stage using new technology.

Drobis went on to say that "integrated communication" must "go beyond marketing to encompass employee and labor relations, investor relations, government affairs, crisis and risk management, community affairs, customer service and just about any other facet of management where effective communications is a critical success factor" (p. 7). He concluded: "Public relations practitioners are in the best position to manage the integrated communications process because, unlike other communications disciplines, they are involved in every facet of the organization. It is their job to listen and respond to the full range of important stakeholders" (p. 9).

Pettegrew (2000–2001) posed the question, "If IMC is so good, why isn't it being implemented?" Pettegrew maintained that "most American coporations have yet to fully implement the foundational ideas contained in IMC" (p. 29), mostly because CEOs have not supported these ideas and because they do not fit with the "marketing culture" of the organization. Pettegrew's definition of IMC seems to be a combination of IMC and IC thinking. On the IMC side, most of eight conditions he listed for IMC practice involved speaking with one voice, consumers, and brands. However, on the IC side, he also emphasized the importance of "two-way dialogue" (albeit only with consumers) and, most important, emphasized that organizations must not place excellent marketing ahead of corporate reputation.

Pettegrew (2000–2001) described Nike and Procter & Gamble, two companies generally used as examples in the IMC literature as champions of the concept. According to Pettegrew:

> Both companies are very strong in marketing, but remain weak in public relations, employee communication, or both . . . Both Nike and Procter & Gamble are marketing organizations, organized around product marketing . . . Staff communication functions such as investor relations, public affairs, and human resources have traditionally played support roles. (p. 33)

Pettegrew (2000–2001) concluded, "While Nike and Procter & Gamble do an excellent job with the marketing side of marketing communications without integrating their public and employee relations, their corporate reputations have suffered" (p. 33). As examples of damage to corporate reputation, he described poor handling of issues such as "child-labor sweatshops in Asia" for Nike (p. 32) and "phone-tapping of three employees suspected of leaking company information" and "a botched job of dealing with some of the physiological effects of its new fat substitute, Olestra" (p. 32) for Procter & Gamble.

Mirroring our concern about the sublimation of public relations to marketing under the pure IMC concept, Pettegrew (2000–2001) warned, "Beware of companies with strong marketing cultures, because issues like corporate reputation will take a back seat to the provincialism of brand management" (p. 30).

In practice, communication professionals who provide marketing communication skills (both advertising and marketing public relations) have different technical expertise than do other specialized public relations people (Spicer, 1991). Therefore, marketing communication programs often are housed in separate departments from other public relations functions even though they practice IMC—usually in business units rather than at headquarters (Hunter, 1997). Or, marketing communication programs are located in marketing departments (Hunter, 1999a).

IMC scholars, however, have begun to recognize the limitations of integrating only the marketing aspects of communication and are turning to a concept of integrated communication that closely resembles our view of integration of the communication function (Caywood, 1997; Duncan & Moriarty, 1997; Gronstedt, 2000). In addition, Hunter's (1999a) study of 76 Fortune 500 companies showed that public relations, employee communication, marketing communication, and advertising are being integrated in practice through a vice president or senior vice president of corporate communication or through the public relations department—although a few companies still have separate departments for each of these communication programs. Although Hunter did not present data on the disciplinary backgrounds of these vice presidents of corporate communication, we believe most have a background in public relations or in public relations combined with one of the other communication disciplines.

Hunter (1999a) noted that Caywood (1997), in his revised version of the Duncan and Caywood (1996) model of stages of integration, used "the terms 'Integrated Communications' and 'Public Relations' synonymously" (p. 133). Hunter said that Caywood did not explicitly explain the reason for the shift in terminology but that in a personal e-mail Caywood told him "that he uses the term 'public relations' to refer to the profession of communication management, whilst he would rather use the term 'integrated communications' to refer to an overall management process for a company, its corporate and product brands, and its life-time customer and stakeholder relationships" (pp. 133–134).

Duncan and Moriarty (1997) also expanded their concept of IMC from earlier works to what they most recently have called "integrated marketing" (IM). Although customers and marketing remain at the center of Duncan and Moriarty's theory, their revised theory emphasizes communicating with all stakeholders and not just customers, the importance of "quality, long-term brand relationships" (p. xiv), and the importance of interactive communication:

> The difference between IMC and IM is like the difference between cosmetics and character building. Cosmetics can make most people look better and more attractive; however, if their behavior and character are not consistent, those who have been attracted will soon end the relationships. In other words, integrating the marketing communications is futile *if contrary, more powerful messages are being sent by other actions of the company.* (p. xv)

They added: "Over the last decade companies and agencies thought they could end all these mixed messages and build better relationships by merely making sure their marketing communications had 'one voice, one look.' Unfortunately, building long-term profitable brand relationships requires much more" (p. xiii).

Duncan and Moriarty (1997) seem to have extended the concept of integrated communication to all of marketing. They pointed out that the traditional 4-Ps "have become a millstone around the necks of companies. Marketing was never meant to be just about product, pricing, place, and promotion but, rather, about creating brand relationships—long-lasting profitable relationships" (p. 5). Duncan and Moriarty also appeared to make no distinction between the disciplines of marketing and communication: "The fuel that drives any relationship—personal or commercial—is communication. There is no way to have a relationship without some form of communication. For this reason, communication is the lifeblood of integrated marketing. And real communication means listening as well as speaking" (p. 9).

Nevertheless, Duncan and Moriarty (1997) pointed out that marketing communications such as advertising and product publicity "play only a part—and often only a small part—in determining the quantity and quality of brand relationships" (p. xiv). In addition to getting information from these planned communications, customers and other stakeholders get messages from using products themselves, from service, and from unplanned sources such as "news stories, employee gossip, actions of special interest groups, comments by the trade and by competitors, findings by government agencies or research institutions, and the proverbial word-of-mouth that one hopes will confirm the other brand messages" (pp. 86–87).

Duncan and Moriarty (1997) said that their integrated concept of marketing and communication should not be located in a specific department such as marketing or communication. Rather, "it requires a cross-functional process that has a corporate focus, a new type of compensations system, core competencies, a database management system that tracks customer interactions, strategic consistency in all brand messages, marketing of the company's mission, and zero-based marketing planning" (p. xiv).

Although Duncan and Moriarty (1997) emphasized customers throughout their book, they said that their IM strategy "can also be used to manage relationships with other stakeholders besides customers—employees, shareholders, government regulators, the media, suppliers, community" (p. xii). In addition, they pointed out that their central concept of brand equity actually "is determined by the quality of a brand's relationships with its customers and other key stakeholders" (p. xiii).

We think, therefore, that it is a misnomer to call this process of symmetrical communication and relationship building "marketing" alone. Rather, we believe that Duncan and Moriarity (1997) chose most of the key concepts of excellent public relations that we have identified in the Excellence study—such as symmetrical communication, relationship building, involvement in strategic management, and recognition of communication as a critical management function that supports all other management functions. Because of their backgrounds in advertising, however, Duncan and Moriarty seemed to understand these concepts best when they were applied to relationships with customers. At the same time, however, we believe that there is more to marketing than communication and that communication and marketing should not be equated.

Gronstedt (2000) came even closer to our theory of excellent public relations in his study of how world-class companies use integrated communication. He expanded on his earlier theory of stakeholder integration to focus on integration in a broad sense. He pointed out that integration is "commonly defined as the process of achieving unity of effort in various organizational subsystems. Ergo *integrated communications* is the stuff that profitable relationships are built on in the Customer Century" (pp. 7–8).

Gronstedt (2000), like us, emphasized that integrated communication is a strategic management process: "Note that it's a 'strategic management process' that must permeate through entire organizations, rather than a quick-fix crash program or campaign from the marketing or communications departments. It goes beyond customers to involve other 'stakeholders' as well, which includes every group or individual with a stake in the company's success" (p. 8).

Gronstedt (2000) also used clear and colorful language to distinguish integrated communication from integrated marketing communication:

> Don't mistake this definition of integrated communications for a warmed-up version of the cries in the early 1990s for "integrated marketing communications" (IMC), the catalyst for a myriad of conferences, articles, books, and classes. IMC has been an important step in the direction of integrated communications, but an insufficient one, motivated in large part by communications agencies' appetite for more business. The supply-driven fad of IMC represented a Production Century view of packaging and transmitting marketing communications messages that speak with one voice. The difference between the conventional version of IMC and the strategic approach to integrated communications described in this book is the difference between chicken manure and chicken salad. Instead of a skin-deep integration of messages and creative execution, this book defines integrated communications as a process of adding value and cultivating relationships with key customers and stakeholders. (pp. 8–9)

In addition to his emphasis on relationships, Gronstedt (2000) discussed the importance of listening and dialogue, of involving everyone in the organization in communication, and of communication managers acquiring a seat at the management table—all essentially the same as some of our principles of excellence. With regard to a seat at the management table, Gronstedt explained:

> Communications professionals need to rise to the occasion and assume a more strategic role. They need to integrate the various marketing and communications support functions, which are increasingly handled by outside specialists. But

more importantly, they need to bring thoughtfully conceived agendas to the senior management table that address the strategic issues of business planning, re-
source allocation, priorities, and direction of the firm. (p. 203)

To explain integrated communication, Gronstedt (2000) presented what he
called a 3-D model. The three dimensions in the model are *external* ("involving
everyone in the organization in both inbound and outbound communications
with customers and stakeholders" [p. 17]), *vertical* ("opening up forthright, frequent, and two-way communications among senior management, middle management, and employees" [p. 17]), and *horizontal* ("integrates communication
among people working at different business units, departments, and countries"
[p. 17]). We show the importance of essentially these same principles in chapter
8 (on the models of public relations) for the external dimension and in chapter
11 (internal communication, structure, and culture) for the vertical and horizontal dimensions.

Although Gronstedt (2000) repeatedly emphasized that stakeholders other
than customers are equally important, his models (e.g., on p. 8) and discussion
separated customers from other stakeholder groups. Like Duncan and Moriarty, this emphasis probably reflects Gronstedt's background in advertising.
Nevertheless, the principles in Gronstedt's book can be seen as affirmation of
our Excellence principles with particular application to the marketing communication component of the public relations function.

In addition to emphasizing the value of integrating communication within
an organization and with its stakeholders, other writers have extended the concept of integration to integrating the organization with society—in much the
same way that we explained the value of public relations at the societal level in
chapter 4. For example, Caywood (1997) said that "public relations managers
will lead their organizations' relationships with society. From the micro relationships built with many stakeholder groups, the corporate and organizational
public relations professional will guide the corporate values that permit organizations to operate in society at a macro level" (p. xiii).

The German scholar Zerfass (1996) also included society in his concept of integration. As translated and explained by Hunter (1999a), "The particularly
noteworthy elements of this model is Zerfass' attempt to combine public relations and communication management theory with general management theory and view the whole process in a broader, socio-political context" (p. 148).

Empirical Studies of Integrated Communication

Gronstedt's (2000) theory of integrated communication was derived to a large
extent from his extensive interviews and observations in 14 "world class" companies. From the United States, these companies were Allen-Bradley (now a division of Rockwell Automation), Eastman Chemical Company, Federal Ex-

press, Hewlett-Packard, Motorola, Saturn, and Xerox. From Europe, they were ABB, Danfoss, Design to Distribution (D2D, now Celestica), Ericsson, ISS, Philips, and Rank-Xerox.

Gronstedt (2000) pointed out that these companies came from "all walks of business life" (p. 11), making different products and having been in business for different amounts of time. However, he said that all had one thing in common, "an obsessive customer focus" (p. 11). He added that they applied the same rigor "to communication with other key stakeholders, including investors, news media, and the local community" (p. 11). He said, "What gives these companies the world-class epithet is their ability to successfully integrate all three dimensions" (p. 11)—external, vertical, and horizontal. Throughout the book, Gronstedt presented examples and quotes supporting his conclusion that these successful companies integrate all of their communication activities throughout these dimensions.

Hunter (1997, 1999a) conducted two studies of the extent to which U.S. Fortune 500 companies integrated their communication activities—for a master's thesis and doctoral dissertation at the University of Salzburg in Austria. In his master's thesis, Hunter (1997, 1999b) found that public relations and marketing most commonly were separate but equal management partners in a representative sample of 75 of the 300 largest U.S. corporations—in contrast to the frequent discussion in the theoretical literature about subservient relationships between public relations and marketing. Of these corporations, 81% had separate public relations and marketing departments. In two thirds of the cases the two departments were on the same level; and when one was above the other, public relations was as likely to be above marketing as below.

About a third of the public relations departments reported directly to the CEO and a third to a vice president of corporate communication. The other third reported to other vice presidents or lower level managers. Few public relations departments reported to or were integrated into a marketing department in these companies. As might be expected, Hunter (1997) also found that marketing was more likely to be dominant in consumer product companies, for whom the consumer stakeholder is most important. Public relations, however, dominated in utilities, which are regulated and for which government and other stakeholders are crucial.

Hunter followed up his survey with qualitative interviews with public relations executives in six companies. In contrast to discussions in the literature of conflict between public relations and marketing, he found that these executives described their relationships with marketing as positive. Marketing and public relations departments cooperated as equal partners who respected the contributions of the other. The situation that Hunter found in the United States suggests that we should examine not whether public relations and marketing should be integrated or merged but how they work together most fruitfully in successful, well-managed organizations.

For his doctoral dissertation, Hunter (1999a) conducted a similar empirical study and received responses from 76 of 300 Fortune 500 companies he contacted. In this survey, 80% of the participants reported that they practiced some form of integrated communication. Of those who reported that they did not practice integrated communication, one third said that they planned to do so in the future. However, 85% of the companies that said they practiced integrated communication said they did so by combining all communication functions in a communication department. Only 10% integrated all communication programs through the marketing department, and only 5% combined the marketing and communication departments into a single department.

Hunter (1999a) asked the participating organizations how they organized their public relations, advertising, marketing communication, sales promotion, direct marketing, and internal communication activities. Participants reported that public relations functions most often were organized into a separate department or that they reported to a vice president or senior vice president of corporate communication. Marketing communication and advertising generally reported to marketing or were organized into separate departments. The pattern was the same for direct marketing and sales promotion, although they tended to report to marketing more than did marketing communication and advertising. Sixteen percent of the time, in addition, both marketing communication and advertising reported to corporate communication. That was less true for direct marketing and sales promotion.

For employee communication, the pattern was similar to that of public relations. Employee communication reported to corporate communication in 33% of the cases and to public relations in 26% of the cases. Twenty-nine percent of the organizations placed employee communication in a separate department. Only 9% reported to human resources and 4% to marketing.

Hunter's studies, therefore, show a pattern emerging in the organization of the communication function in U.S. corporations. Corporations are adopting an integrated structure in which specialized communication functions either are organized into separate departments or are part of the public relations department. When they are separate departments, they often report to a vice president of corporate communication. Only marketing communication functions report at times to marketing, but they are equally likely to report to a vice president of corporate communication.

Structural Mechanisms for Integrating the Communication Function

Consistent with our Excellence principle of the need to integrate the communication function in an organization, the literature on integrated marketing communication and integrated communication consistently advocates some form of structure for integrating communication activities within an organization and with activities provided by outside firms.

Schultz, Tannenbaum, and Lauterborn (1993), in the first major book on integrated marketing communication, called for centralizing the communication function and heading it with a "communications czar"—"consolidation of the communication function into one person or group" (p. 168). Like us (see chap. 11), they recognized the value of decentralization of organizational structures in general: "The idea of centralized control would appear to be in direct conflict with today's management concept that attempts to push decision making as far down as possible in the organization and closer to the customer" (p. 165). Nevertheless, they added, "While this is a sound and needed management concept, problems occur when the communication function is broadly distributed throughout the organization" (p. 165). They did not recommend changing the decentralized structure of the overall organization but "simply a consolidation of the communications function into one person or group" (p. 168).

Gronstedt (2000) called for a more informal and spiritual leader to integrate the communication function—a pope rather than a czar. In the "world-class" companies he studied, he found that communication heads functioned more as leaders and facilitators of collaboration than as authority figures. "They need to counsel, mediate, support, network, act as change agents, and add value to communications professionals in the business units" (p. 188), Gronstedt said. In contrast to an "authoritative 'communications czar' to integrate communications, which is sometimes suggested, . . . the communications leaders of these world-class companies are better described as 'communications popes,' who provide spiritual leadership without the formal authority of a virtual organization of communications professionals around the world" (pp. 189–190).

In addition to the communication pope, Gronstedt (2000) also suggested several informal mechanisms for coordinating communication activities. These were "big-tent meetings" (p. 185) of the public relations staffs from throughout a global company, the use of "Intranets and other forms of internal computer networks," and a "communications guideline book" (p. 187).

In his book on reputation, Fombrun (1996) suggested a chief reputation officer to oversee what he called six staff groups—customer service relations, investor relations, employee relations, community relations, government relations, and public relations: "If we examine existing practice, in most companies the activities of these six groups are typically isolated within business units, with disparate reporting lines and involvement in corporate-level decision making. What this says is that in terms of reputation management, no one is really minding the shop" (p. 196).

Fombrun (1996) then described the role of this chief reputation officer in almost the same language we have used to describe the management role of the chief public relations officer in the Excellence study:

> The CRO could be made to join the executive suite as a full partner, complementing the more traditional chief executive, financial, operating, and informa-

tion roles. The CRO would recognize the different tasks that a company must undertake to build, sustain, and defend its reputational capital. In all aspects, however, it's a role that emphasizes close coordination—a matrix arrangement—with the traditional functions of marketing, finance, human resources, and operations. (pp. 197–198)

Van Riel (1995) listed five mechanisms that organizations typically use to coordinate communication activities—mechanisms that seem to subsume those already described by other authors. They range from formal coordination by one person to more informal methods:

1. Coordination by one person, solely in charge of all communication departments. This type of coordination will occur especially in small organizations with a limited number of communication departments.
2. Coordination by a steering committee in which representatives of all communication departments participate, sometimes extended with representatives of managers with a commercial line function. Coordination is based on the guidelines of a common communication policy.
3. Coordination by ad hoc meetings. Meetings are only organized in situations where problems arise that need to be solved collectively.
4. Coordination by grouping several communication managers together in one location, so they will be "forced" to interact frequently, both privately and professionally.
5. Combination of 1, 2, 3, and 4. (p. 163)

All in all, there seems to be agreement in the literature with our principle of the need for either or both formal or informal integration of the public relations function in organizations. As we see in the Excellence data, our excellent public relations functions practiced most of the methods of integration suggested by these authors.

From Structure to Differences in Public Relations and Marketing Communication Theory

Public relations theorists and marketing communication theorists—especially advertising scholars—traditionally have conceptualized communication in very different ways—although in recent years marketing communication scholars such as Caywood (1997), Duncan and Moriarty (1997), and Gronstedt (2000) seem to have moved closer to public relations theory in their thinking. Many integrated communication programs, however, continue to apply marketing communication theory rather than public relations theory to communication management in ways that we believe are detrimental to the public relations function. If integrated communication programs are to be most effective, we believe they should be based on public relations theories rather than marketing communication theories.

The following characteristics of marketing communication theory, in particular, differ from our public relations approach:

1. *The recurring ideas that all publics can be treated as though they are consumers and that consumers are the most important publics.* Consumers may be the most important public for consumer product companies and in some situations for other organizations. However, publics become more or less strategic to an organization as situations change. Thus, it is important to view all stakeholders as important and to recognize that strategic publics will not be the same for all organizations or at all times.

2. *A tendency to overgeneralize the importance of marketing or of communication,* with statements such as "everything is marketing and marketing is everything" or "all communication is marketing and all marketing is communication" (Schultz et al., 1993, p. 45). Philosophers of science say that if something is everything, one cannot distinguish it from anything else and, therefore, it also is nothing. We believe there is more to marketing than communication and to communication than marketing.

3. *"Speaking with one voice" as an advantage touted for integrating the communication functions of the organization.* The concept also goes by the terms "orchestration," "consistent voice," and "seamless communication" (Duncan & Everett, 1993). Newsom and Carroll (1992) decried what they considered the "Tower of Babel" that results from people in public relations and marketing communicating with different voices. Moriarty (1996) called for a "synergy of persuasive messages." We question, however, whether these catchy phrases mean that dialogue, interaction, learning, and innovation—the essence of what we call two-way symmetrical communication—are to be discouraged. We believe all members of organizations should be encouraged to speak *and listen* to many members of publics and markets in many voices so that they get new ideas and innovate. The organization may gain an advantage in speaking with one voice; it suffers the disadvantage of listening with one ear.

4. *Defining two-way communication as a response to a message rather than a reciprocal and continuous process of listening and dialogue* (e.g., Schultz et al., 1993). In our strategic theory, public relations is an ongoing process built into the organizational structure in which the ideas of publics are brought into the decision-making processes of management and in which affecting the behavior of management is just as important as affecting the behavior of publics.

5. *Overemphasis on the behavior of publics and underemphasis on the behavior of management.* It is much easier to control one's own behavior than that of others. Thus, the purpose of public relations is to contribute to organizational decision making so that the organization behaves in ways that publics are willing to support rather than in ways that publics oppose with their own behaviors.

6. *An emphasis on messages and symbols and their effects on the cognitions and atti-tudes of publics rather than on the behavioral relationships of organizations and publics* (see J. Grunig, 1993a, 1993b). Marketing communication concepts such as iden-tity, image, brand, and reputation (e.g., Rebel, 1997; Van Riel, 1995) suggest that the right message can implant the corporate "identity" into the public's "image" and, by implication, that one can manage reputation by managing the production and distribution of messages. In our view, the reputation of a corpo-ration consists of the behaviors of the corporation that publics recall cog-nitively. The value of a brand lies not just in the recognition of a name but in the trust people have in a company and its products. Thus, we believe the most ef-fective way to manage a reputation or brand image is by using two-way sym-metrical communication to help manage the organizational behaviors that pro-duce a bad reputation and to develop a trusting relationship with both consumer markets and publics.

As our update of the literature on integrated communication has shown, marketing communication theories seemed to be moving away from viewing communication in these ways. The Excellence data show, however, that practi-tioners at some organizations—especially the less excellent ones—still base their communication programs on these message-centered, asymmetrical, and customer-centered approaches. As we see when we analyze our data, however, the excellent public relations departments integrate their programs, do not sub-limate them to marketing or other organizational functions, and base their communication programs on strategic and symmetrical ideals rather than mes-sage-only, asymmetrical views of communication.

With the framework provided by this updated conceptualization of the inte-gration of communication functions in organizations and of their relationship to marketing and other management functions, we now turn to the results of the Excellence study to determine how the structure of the public relations function affects its excellence.

QUANTITATIVE RESULTS RELATED TO ORGANIZATION OF THE COMMUNICATION FUNCTION

We addressed three questions discussed in this chapter in the questionnaire completed by the head of each public relations unit included in our survey. First, we asked whether the departmental arrangement of the public relations function had an effect on excellence. Second, we asked whether the relative sup-port for marketing and public relations affected excellence. Third, we examined the extent to which and how excellent public relations departments used out-side firms in their public relations programs.

Organization of Public Relations Departments

Initially, we expected that organizations with excellent public relations functions would integrate or coordinate their communication activities through a central public relations department rather than having independent units for such communication programs as marketing communication, employee communication, investor relations, or media relations—either as stand-alone units or units that are subordinated to other functions such as marketing, human resources, or finance. Independent units challenge strategic public relations because it is difficult to shift resources from one set of stakeholder publics to another when those publics become more or less strategic to organizational interests.

Some of the organizations we studied had a single public relations department, some had one or more specialized departments, and some had public relations programs administered by non-public-relations departments. The latter were most likely to be programs for consumers (marketing; 13% of the programs) and members of associations (9% of the programs). However, even these latter programs were relatively rare. Most public relations functions were organized through either a central public relations department or one or more specialized departments—split evenly between these two types of arrangements (45% for central departments and 48% for specialized departments). Employee relations, investor relations, community relations, and member relations (when it was not in a non-PR department) were slightly more likely to be found in specialized departments. Media relations, government relations, donor relations, and customer relations (when it was not in a non-PR department) were more likely to be found in central departments.

As we explained in chapter 2, in some of the organizations surveyed the head of more than one communication department completed the top-communicator questionnaire. A total of 370 heads completed at least a portion of the questionnaire in 298 organizations in which at least one public relations head answered a portion of the questionnaire. In 70 organizations, additional PR heads completed at least part of the questionnaire. We compared the responses from heads of single and central departments with the responses from heads of secondary departments to analyze whether centralization of the public relations function increased its level of excellence.

We classified each communication department in two ways. First, we coded departments into two categories: (a) the department was the only communication department in the organization or was the highest level communication department in a multidepartment organization or (b) the department was a secondary department. We also analyzed the title of the communication heads and placed them into three categories that indicated whether their title suggested that they headed a (a) central public relations department, (b) a specialized communication department, or (c) a communication program in a non-public-

TABLE 7.1
Types of Public Relations Departments

Type of Title of PR Head	Single or Highest Department	Secondary Department	Total
Central Public Relations			
Number	155	11	166
Percentage	93	7	
Specialized Public Relations			
Number	134	42	176
Percentage	76	24	
Non-Public-Relations			
Number	9	19	28
Percentage	32	67	
Total	298	74	370

relations department. Table 7.1 presents a cross-tabulation of these two variables.

Table 7.1 shows that heads of public relations departments that were the only communication department or the highest public relations department in an organization overwhelmingly had a title suggesting that they had central, high-level responsibilities. However, a few secondary departments also had heads with high-level titles. Three fourths of the heads of single or central departments also had specialized titles, such as employee communication, community relations, or media relations. At the same time, three fourths of the top communicators with non-public-relations titles were found in secondary departments.

Table 7.2 compares the means on the overall index of excellence for the three departmental arrangements coded from the titles of communication heads. Excellence was slightly above average for centralized departments, about average for specialized departments, and below average for programs in non-PR departments. Table 7.2 also shows that the non-PR departments had the lowest maximum and minimum scores, meaning at least one was the poorest department and none was the highest. The differences were not significant, however.[3]

In short, the departmental arrangement seemed to make little difference, although these organizations rarely subordinated public relations to other functions. Central public relations departments were no higher in excellence than were specialized units, although these quantitative data cannot show what if any coordination occurred among the specialized units. We were able to find

---

[3]The same pattern was found for the individual Excellence variables. One of the differences was significant, however: the managerial role of the top communicator, which was lowest in non-PR departments.

TABLE 7.2
Comparison of Means on Overall Excellence by Type
of Communication Department

Department Type	Number	Mean	Standard Deviation	Minimum	Maximum
			(z Scores)		
Central PR	146	.06	.86	−1.93	3.05
Specialized PR	149	.01	.93	−1.98	3.55
Non-PR	26	−.16	1.14	−2.40	2.79

Note. $F = 0.64$, not significant.

more details about methods of coordination other than centralization in our qualitative data, which we analyze later.

Relative Support for Public Relations and Marketing

In the questionnaire completed by the heads of public relations departments, a series of three questions asked whether the organization had separate communication units for "marketing-related public relations" and another for "public affairs"—essentially the distinction that Harris (1991) and others have made between "marketing public relations" and "corporate public relations." A second question asked which unit had the larger budget. We then asked, "Regardless of whether you have separate units, which function—public affairs or marketing-related public relations—receives more support from senior administrators—the dominant coalition?"

The first two questions produced no significant differences in Excellence scores. Fifty-eight percent of the top communicators responded that their organizations did not have separate units for marketing-related and public affairs programs. Forty-two percent said they had separate programs. The z score for excellence was .11 for those with separate programs and −.03 for those with combined units. The difference was not significant ($F = 1.92$, $p < .17$). For those organizations with separate departments (the second question), excellence was lowest when the budget for marketing communication was greater ($z = −.22$), medium when the public affairs budget was greater ($z = .05$), and highest when the budgets were equal ($z = .12$). The differences were not significant, however ($F = 2.24$, $p < .11$).

We thought there might be a greater difference if we compared excellence for responses to these two questions for the corporations alone because they are more likely to have marketing functions than are government agencies, nonprofits, and associations. The difference was even smaller for the question of whether there are separate departments ($z = .03$ for separate departments and −.03 for joint departments, $F = .17$, $p < .68$). Excellence was highest ($z = .66$) when budgets of separate departments were equal, and it was higher for corporations than for all organizations. It was lowest when the public affairs budget was highest ($z = -.23$) and at the mean ($z = .07$) when marketing communication had the highest budget. The difference still was not significant, however ($F = 2.07$, $p < .13$)

The third question was most successful in showing the effect of support for marketing and public affairs communication programs on overall public relations Excellence. Table 7.3 shows the mean score for the overall index of excel-

TABLE 7.3

Comparison of Means on 20 Excellence Variables and Overall
Index of Excellence by PR Head's Perception of Support
for Public Relations and Marketing by Dominant Coalition

| | Support Is Greater for: | | | |
| | Marketing | PR | Equal | |
Characteristics of Public Relations and Organization	(n = 75)	(n = 104)	(n = 137)	F
	(z Scores)			
CEO Variables				
PR in strategic planning	−.16	.03	.14	2.49*
Importance of communication with external groups	−.19	.12	.09	2.54*
Preference for two-way asymmetrical model	−.29	.05	.21	6.62***
Preference for two-way symmetrical model	−.32	.13	.11	4.68***
Preference for managerial role	.01	.09	.07	0.14
Preference for senior adviser role	−.15	.16	.09	2.18
Public Relations Head Variables				
PR in strategic planning	−.17	−.07	.13	2.89**
Estimate of preference for the two-way asymmetrical model by the dominant coalition	−.05	−.05	.08	0.44
Estimate of preference for the two-way symmetrical model by the dominant coalition	−.17	.00	.11	2.31*
PR head in manager role	−.11	−.02	.09	1.13
PR head in senior adviser role	−.10	−.03	.04	0.51
Knowledge of two-way asymmetrical model	−.15	−.04	.07	1.28
Knowledge of two-way symmetrical model	−.15	.02	.04	1.12
Knowledge of managerial role	−.06	−.09	.02	0.33
Estimate of support for women in organization	−.31	.11	.05	5.47***
Participative organizational culture	.25	−.11	−.04	3.76**
Value of Public Relations				
CEO Variables				
Support for PR by dominant coalition	−.19	.21	.00	3.63**
Value of PR department	−.15	.19	−.03	2.27*
Public Relations Head Variables				
Perceived support for PR by dominant coalition	−.31	.08	.07	4.98***
Estimated value dominant coalition would assign to PR	−.12	.06	−.04	0.78
Overall Excellence Index	−.22	.05	.12	3.62**

Note. N = 316.
*p < .10. **p < .05. ***p < .01.

lence and each Excellence variable when support for marketing communication was higher, when support for public affairs was higher, and when the support was "approximately equal." On the overall index, excellence was below average when marketing received greater support, average when public affairs received greater support, and above average when the two received approximately equal support. The differences were statistically significant.

Table 7.3 shows essentially the same pattern for most of the individual Excellence variables, although some of the differences were not significant. In some cases, though, the mean for the variables was highest either when public affairs received greater support or when the support was even. Almost always, the mean was lower when marketing communication received greater support. The table indicates, however, that public relations was about equally likely to perform a managerial or senior adviser role with all three levels of support; and CEOs were equally likely to prefer such a managerial role. Levels of knowledge to perform a two-way symmetrical or asymmetrical model of public relations and the managerial role also were not significantly different.

However, CEOs valued and supported public relations significantly less when marketing communication received greater support and when the PR head estimated less support from the dominant coalition. Most important, CEOs were significantly less likely to see public relations as a strategic management function and as a two-way function when marketing communication received greater support from the dominant coalition. The same was true when the top communicator said he or she participated in strategic planning and when he or she estimated that the dominant coalition would prefer the two-way symmetrical model. Interestingly, the PR heads estimated that women received significantly less support in organizations where marketing communication dominated. In contrast to the pattern of Table 7.3, however, organizations that emphasized marketing communication over public affairs were most likely to have participative organizational cultures, in contrast to authoritarian cultures.

Overall, then, Table 7.3 supports that idea that public relations is most likely to be excellent when marketing communication does not dominate the communication function. Public relations has its greatest value when that function and the marketing function are treated as equal partners in management.

To summarize the data on the relationship between marketing communication and other public relations programs, it seems to make little difference whether marketing communication and other public relations programs are housed in the same or separate departments or, when they are in separate departments, whether one has a larger budget than the other. When marketing communication dominates how senior management thinks about and supports the public relations function, however, overall communication Excellence suffers.

Use of Outside Public Relations Firms

As we stated previously in this chapter, we had no expectations about how excellent public relations departments would use outside public relations firms. We did believe that any services purchased outside should be integrated with those used inside. In the questionnaire for the top communicators, we asked whether their department or someone else in the organization used the services of outside firms. If the answer was yes, we asked whether six different services were used, ranging from technical support to research and strategic counsel.

The data reported in Table 7.4 show that public relations departments that used outside firms had higher overall Excellence scores than those that did not. In addition, departments that used outside firms scored higher on several of the managerial and two-way communication variables in the Excellence index. Top communicators with greater knowledge for the managerial role, who are more likely to enact a manager role, and who report that they participate in strategic management are more likely to seek support from outside firms. In addition, they are more likely to have knowledge to practice the two-way symmetrical model; and they believe their CEOs expect them to practice both two-way models. Their CEOs, likewise, express a preference for the two-way asymmetrical model.

We also asked each top communicator to estimate the percentage of six types of public relations activities that typically can be purchased from outside firms. The mean percentages for all departments in the sample are reported in

TABLE 7.4

Significant Differences in Mean Z Scores of Excellence
Variables Between Communication Departments That
Use and Do Not Use Outside Firms

Excellence Variable	Use Outside Firms	Do Not Use Outside Firms	T
Overall Excellence Scale	.12	−.15	2.66**
Knowledge for Managerial Role	.12	−.30	3.60**
Knowledge for Two-Way Symmetrical Model	.12	−.23	3.30**
Participation in Strategic Management, Reported by PR Head	.14	−.21	3.36**
Manager Role Enactment	.09	−.14	2.10*
PR Head Prediction of Preference for the Two-Way Symmetrical Model by the Dominant Coalition	.13	−.19	3.02**
PR Head Prediction of Preference for the Two-Way Asymmetrical Model by the Dominant Coalition	.14	−.23	3.35**
CEO Preference for Two-Way Asymmetrical Model	.13	−.10	2.08*

Note. $N = 328$.
*$p < .05$. **$p < .01$.

Table 7.5. The most frequent service purchased was preparation and placement of publicity and advertising materials (34% of these activities), followed by research (26% of these activities). Other activities reported in Table 7.5 were purchased less often—from 10% for assistance in developing a department or auditing a current department to 16% for consulting about strategic problems.

We then correlated these percentages with the overall Excellence score of the departments that used outside firms. All but two of the correlations essentially were zero. Excellence correlated with using outside firms for consulting about top-level strategic problems at a level that was significant at the .10 but not at the .05 level ($r = .13, p < .07$). It also correlated negatively with using firms for the preparation of publications ($r = -.12, p < .08$), at a level that is significant only at .10.

Overall, then the departments in our sample used public relations firms mostly for the technical functions of publicity and advertising as well as for research to communicate in a two-way function. Excellent departments used outside firms significantly more than did less excellent departments, and they were somewhat more likely to use the firms for high-level strategic counseling than were less excellent departments—reinforcing their profile as departments involved in the strategic decision processes of organizations.

Overall, the quantitative results show that public relations activities in the organizations in our sample generally were located in either centralized or specialized public relations departments. Very few were located in marketing departments or other departments such as human relations or finance. These excellent public relations departments were not necessarily centralized. Both centralized and specialized departments could be equally excellent. However,

TABLE 7.5

Average Percentage of Six Public Relations Activities
Purchased From Outside Firms by All Departments
in the Excellence Sample That Use Outside Firms

Activity	Percentage
Preparation and placement of publicity and advertising materials	34
Preparation of publications directed to employees, stockholders, investors, and similar publics	13
Consulting about relations with the news media during periods of actual or potential controversy or disputes	16
Consulting about top-level strategic problems related to the relationship this organization has with outside organizations or groups	17
Research in support of the public relations function	26
Assistance in developing a public relations or communication department or doing a public relations audit of an existing program	10

Note. $N = 238$.

excellent departments received greater or equal support from their dominant coalitions than did marketing. Excellence declined when marketing dominated public relations. Excellent departments also were more likely to seek support from outside public relations firms. Like all public relations departments, they were most likely to use outside firms for publicity and for research. Excellent departments, however, were somewhat more likely than less excellent departments to seek strategic support from outside firms. The correlation was not high, most likely because excellent departments possess strategic knowledge themselves.

With these quantitative results in mind, we turn to the qualitative data to flesh out the picture of how excellent departments are organized. In particular, the qualitative results should add to our understanding of how organizations integrate communication in ways other than through a centralized department.

QUALITATIVE RESULTS RELATED TO ORGANIZATION OF THE COMMUNICATION FUNCTION

We used two central principles of our general theory of communication Excellence when we analyzed the quantitative data on the organization of the public relations function—that all communication functions should be integrated but that the public relations function should not be sublimated to other functions such as marketing, human resources, or finance. Those same two principles emerged in the qualitative results as well.

Throughout our case studies, we found evidence that an excellent public relations function either is organized into a centralized department, is coordinated through a senior vice president with a title such as vice president of corporate communication or public affairs, or is coordinated informally and integrated through the CEO or another senior manager—who was not a communicator—in the dominant coalition.

We also found very few instances in which public relations was sublimated to marketing, human resources, or other management functions. We found most of the examples of such sublimation in the organizations we interviewed because they scored at the bottom of the Excellence scale—and the consequences were bad for public relations. In a few of the excellent departments, we found evidence of marketing thinking like that described in the conceptual section of this chapter on differences between public relations and marketing theory. The public relations function was still excellent in spite of the marketing influence, but the emphasis of those departments mostly was on customers and on concepts such as sponsorships. These marketing-oriented departments also saw the purpose of communication to be more asymmetrical than symmetrical.

Integration and Coordination of the Communication Function

The first theme that emerged from our analysis of the interviews was the ways in which related communication functions were integrated or coordinated in the organization. We saw that theme first in a negative sense. One of the most highly challenged organizations in terms of excellence serves as an illustration of what happens when the public relations function is not integrated or coordinated.

The director of public relations in this insurance company reported to a group vice president. The four areas reporting to the group vice president were the actuary department, the legislative council, community relations, and communication. The marketing department reported to a different group vice president. This organizational structure presented many challenges to those in communication who wished to practice managerial as well as technical skills in public relations and who wanted to promote two-way symmetrical communication between the company and its publics. The director of public relations there believed communication might be improved if one group vice president were to oversee the areas of communication, community relations, and marketing.

We found a similar example of fragmented communication in the aerospace corporation that scored in the 12th percentile of the Excellence scale. Two to 3 years before we interviewed the top communicator, the company had a centralized department that controlled dissemination of information to the media for all of its three divisions (which was a much narrower definition of integration than what we mean by integration of the communication function). Since that time, the company granted each division authority to respond to media questions. However, there was no longer any integration of the communication function. At the time of the interview, each division was responsible for its own communication and public affairs, in part because of downsizing of the corporation. In contrast to these two negative cases, we found that most of the excellent public relations functions were integrated either formally through a single department or position or informally through top management.

Integration Through a Single Department or Position.   We found that having a single public relations department or a senior vice president responsible for all communication functions effectively integrates all public relations programs. The CEO of the disabled services organization, for example, planned to give his communication department a more influential status in the already top-ranked agency. Although he had not implemented this change at the time we interviewed him, he expressed the difficulty of channeling energy toward a collective goal when each department wanted to "do its own thing." Instead, he intended public relations to coordinate all contacts with the public (especially the volunteer-run auxiliary department).

Similarly, the senior communication specialist in an electrical utility told us that the pooling of resources in his company required the support of public relations that did not exist before restructuring. Previously, the communication departments within each state utility of the parent company had functioned independently. Reorganization resulted in a single, centralized communication unit at the corporate level, with "branches" in each of four states.

This organization had had an excellent communication department even before the restructuring, and it brought that expertise to the new configuration. However, the head of public relations explained the benefits of the corporate restructuring this way: "It has really allowed us to be more focused and our lines of communication are much better. We have been able to be more efficient. We have one focus, our goals are all the same, everybody's working toward those goals, and everybody knows who in the end is responsible for the actions of the department."

Others in the utility agreed that the new, centralized structure enhanced both the communication function and the overall organization. Centralization under the parent company enables its state utilities to operate more effectively. The senior communication specialist cited a recent natural disaster as an example of the advantages of the centralized structure: "When the biggest ice storm in our system's history hit us, we were able to mobilize 4,000 people in the field to work on it. A single utility just couldn't do it."

Restructuring also has meant the promotion of more women into management than in the past. Traditionally, women had not held high-level positions in utilities. The top communicator told us that empowering women to play senior management roles requires a combination of experience on the part of the women and the willingness of the organization to allow women to prove their worth.

Another utility in our sample, a stockholder-owned gas and electric company, integrated its public relations function through a senior vice president of customer and corporate affairs—who reported directly to the CEO. Reporting to this vice president was a manager of public affairs. Under the manager of public affairs were a director of communication services, a director of government affairs, and a director of community services.

The U.S. oil company had a carefully integrated public relations function, centered in a vice president for public affairs. The function was divided into four parts: state and local relations, federal relations, communications and programs, and corporate identity. State and local relations was responsible for communication at the state, regional, and local levels. Federal relations was divided into a lobbying group in Washington, DC, and an analytic group at corporate headquarters. The communications and programs division was responsible for employee communication, media relations, charitable contributions, general programs, public opinion research, and image advertising. Corporate identity was responsible for the oil company's logotype and for maintaining standards for the logo on letterhead, trucks, and service stations. Each division reported to the vice president of public affairs, who reported to the CEO.

The vice president of public affairs also participates in monthly meetings of the public affairs committee, along with the CEO, two vice-chairs of the board of directors, and the heads of other large operating or subsidiary companies. The vice president also is a member of the public policy committee, along with the CEO and the board of directors. The public policy committee meets three to four times a year to discuss public policy issues in a broader context than does the public affairs committee.

The blood bank, which scored in the 91st percentile of the Excellence scale, organized its communication function under the umbrella of community relations. The second-ranking communicator was the public affairs officer, who reported to the director of community relations. The director of community relations reported directly to the CEO.

A new public affairs department in the metal manufacturing company provided a similar example of integration through a high-level vice president of public affairs. We studied the organization because of its low Excellence score—in the 11th percentile. Previously, the public relations unit had largely been responsible for media relations and was staffed mostly by "journalists-in-residence," including the communication manager who headed the department. However, a new CEO, who understood the value of communication because of previous involvement with the function, created a new position of vice president of public affairs between the time of our quantitative and qualitative studies. The public affairs department, at the time of our in-depth interviews, served as a corporate umbrella for all communication functions, including media relations, community relations, public policy at the state and federal levels, and public information. As top communicator, the vice president for public affairs took part in strategic management and had a major role in establishing and accomplishing corporate objectives.

Integration of Multiple Communication Departments.   Not all of the excellent organizations we interviewed integrated their public relations function through a single public relations department or through an executive vice president with a communication-related title. Several organizations used less formal ways to coordinate the communication function.

The director of corporate communication at the chemical company agreed that it would be better to have all communication functions under one department. However, integration in his company was achieved, first, through a savvy vice president of strategic planning and, second, through informal collaboration among the communication functions. He considered the critical factor "not who you report to but rather whether you have access." As an illustration of his direct access to top management, he pointed to a recent meeting with analysts: "I was there with all of the officers of the company."

The cosmetics company had one of the most difficult problems of integration among our excellent organizations. At the time we administered the quantitative questionnaire, the head of an outside public relations firm had been providing strategic direction to the corporate communications staff. "But the staff was really too small to do the job. Everything they were doing was just putting out fires and they were getting nowhere," the agency head told us. "They were not strategically oriented at all.

"One day when we were together planning, they [the corporate communication staff] were dismissed as a group," he continued. "All of a sudden, I was told we were to take their responsibilities as an outside agency." This relationship later resulted in the cosmetics firm buying a majority interest in the public relations firm and becoming a limited partner.

At the time of our in-depth interview, there was no central communication function in the organization. Corporate communication was handled by the public relations firm, sales force communication by a sales force communication department, and marketing communication by the marketing department. The director of sales force communication and the marketing director said this decentralized arrangement did not cause problems of coordination, but the agency head acknowledged that the arrangement was still in flux and that a relationship among the three communication functions had not yet developed. The director of sales force communication said that the agency head was "tight with the CEO" and often did not respect her knowledge. Coordination was improving, she said, but she added that coordination was difficult because "the agency is just not there every day."

The agency head acknowledged the need to "be a little more astute than we are right now at deciding who is going to handle what." He insisted, though, that coordination was accomplished through top management: "This is strictly an operational issue, not a policy kind of thing. At a policy or strategic level it is always very clear who is doing what."

In the medical association, the communication function largely was housed in a department of public affairs, which was responsible for external relationships—especially communication with the government on behalf of members. A separate and much larger department of corporate affairs was responsible for member services and human resources. The two departments shared the internal communication program. Further integration of the two departments took place at the strategic management level, although not always successfully because the assistant executive director for corporate affairs said she believes public affairs dominates the association's strategic agenda.

The oil company affiliate, in contrast to most of our cases of excellence, had a fragmented communication function. The company had separate public affairs and marketing departments, which did not communicate systematically with each other. Public affairs was responsible for the in-house magazine yet there was an independent employee relations department. The marketing department managed marketing communication.

A hotel chain that we interviewed because of its low Excellence score—in the 18th percentile—provided an example of the negative consequences of a fragmented communication function on the managerial role of public relations. The company was split into several business groups, and the communication and public relations function was spread throughout the organizational structure.

The top communicator in corporate relations reported directly to the CEO. Duties of corporate relations included media relations, preparation of the annual report, and financial relations. Lodging's top communicator reported to the senior vice president of sales and marketing and was responsible for executive speech writing, special events, employee newsletters, media relations, and crisis communication. In the contract management division, the top communicator reported to the president of the division and was responsible for internal communication, sales support and marketing communication, and media relations.

A fourth group, employee communication, provided photographic services, audiovisual services, and management communication services such as brochures, pamphlets, and employee communication vehicles for the organization as a whole. Employee communication charged fees for the services it performed for other units in the corporation. Other communication groups within the organization, however, frequently elected to use outside vendors instead of purchasing services from employee communication. Employee communication reported to the senior vice president of human resources.

As a result of this fragmented public relations structure, top communicators in the lodging group, the contract management group, and the employee communication group contributed little to key decisions by the dominant coalition. Rather, communication and public relations were conceptualized largely as technical activities in support of marketing rather than as key contributors to management decision making. One top communicator in the company defended that role by saying public relations really is not so important that he should fight for an integrated structure that does more than support marketing:

> We are definitely in a phase where we are driven from the top right now, which is good. . . . PR in the [hotel chain] has always been a strong part of the marketing environment and there's always been an appreciation of its value. It's not a matter of the evolution of its value or its prestige. I'm not one of those people who have always tried to ward off being defensive about the area of public relations, which a lot of PR people spend a great deal of time on. So I don't spend a lot of time justifying our existence or defending the area. . . . It's not the most important thing the company does. . . . PR just fits in with a whole lot of other things and there are many more crucial issues in the business world.

Sublimation, or Lack of It, to Other Management Functions

The previous case of a hotel chain provided a clear case of the fragmentation of public relations and its sublimation to marketing, except perhaps for its employee communication function. In examining the case studies of excellence, however, we found very few found other examples of the sublimation of public relations to marketing, human resources, finance, or other functional areas of management. Nevertheless, we did find examples of public relations functions that were guided by marketing concepts—in much the same way that we described in the conceptual section of this chapter.

Before it encountered financial difficulty, an international insurance company, which scored in the 81st percentile of our Excellence scale, had its skilled top communicator, the head of corporate communication, report to the marketing department. In times of emergency, however, he had direct access to the CEO. After he played a critical role in the process of reconstruction and renewal after its financial crisis, the company was reorganized into five business units, which were supported by a smaller corporate center. Corporate communication became a part of that corporate center, and its head began to report directly to the CEO.

In the financial services company, we found evidence that both the dominant coalition and the public relations practitioners we interviewed considered public relations to be a marketing function—even though a vice president of corporate communication headed the function. That company scored in the 90th percentile of the Excellence scale, largely on the strength of its participation in strategic management. In explaining why the dominant coalition valued communication, the vice president equated public relations and marketing but said the company considers the joint function to be essential: "Marketing is very important. The company has always viewed public relations as very important since we are a very visible company." In the annual report, the company also emphasized the marketing concept of brand—"a collection of intangible assets, including quality customer service, security, recognition and tradition—that has been created over time and is now defined by our customer's perceptions."

The deputy director of the engineering research agency expressed strong support for both two-way symmetrical and asymmetrical communication but also saw the outcome of communication largely in marketing terms. His objective for communication was as an improvement in national rankings of engineering agencies and in "reputation management." He also referred to audiences as "customers." Likewise, the publications editor we interviewed talked about getting professors who participated in the agency's research to think more about "positioning." All of these terms reflect a marketing orientation to public relations.

The manager of communications in the engineering agency expressed reservations to us about this marketing approach: "The CEO is obsessed with improving our ranking and wants to involve public relations to help out." What the dominant coalition does not realize, according to the manager of communications, is that there has to be substance to back claims of greatness. "This stuff can't be made up; you have to base it on something," she said. The deputy director, however, said he believed the substance was there, that the school's reputation lags reality, and that public relations can close the gap.

In the oil company affiliate, the public affairs department was separate from marketing; but its primary activity was sponsorships, which has marketing overtones. "We tend to look to the popularity of a sponsorship amongst our marketers for feedback as to whether we are doing the right thing or not," according to the media relations manager we interviewed. At the same time, the public affairs department was distinctive from marketing in that it interacted with other "influential publics," including Members of Parliament and media and oil associations.

The oil company affiliate's manager of media relations described a case, however, in which the public affairs department worked with the marketing department to take a more symmetrical approach to customers—in a way that mirrors our view of an ideal relationship between public relations and marketing. The company wanted to stop supplying fuel oil to residential customers because the tanks were aging and most customers were moving to natural gas:

> So we wanted to get out of those systems. That produces all sorts of problems; like how are you going to encourage people, are you just going to tell them "sorry, we're not going to supply you anymore." Are you going to give them notice? How much notice are you going to give them? Are you going to give them some sort of incentive? You are going to cause them to expend money that they don't have to expend now to have their existing boiler converted or a new boiler put in. You are going to disrupt people's lives. So we said to our marketing department, "Well look, we understand the commercial drive to do this; but we think you ought to perhaps be a little more gentle in the way you're approaching customers and give them more time to make other arrangements." In fact, we eventually suggested they give a sum of money, about 500 pounds, to customers as a sort of loyalty bonus. And generally speaking it's been well received. In the initial stages they did get into some difficulties, and as typical they called us in once they got into difficulties. We weren't consulted right at the start; but once we saw the way things were headed, it was public affairs that got this policy amended and changed. So we do have an influence on the way marketers behave, and the way the company behaves.

The heart health agency, which used a combination of the two-way models but relied more on the asymmetrical than the symmetrical, also typically described its communication program in marketing terms. The association organized its communication program in a single department of communication rather than of marketing. However, the CEO described in detail the rationale behind the association's "market" targeting policy and its plan for communicating message points effectively. The top communicator described publics as "markets." She provided a detailed analysis in a video presentation of how the organization developed its logo and how the organization builds awareness of its goals among volunteers. An ongoing image survey provided further evidence of using research to tailor messages—in a way that is typical of the marketing approach based on the two-way asymmetrical model.

The state lottery, for which we conducted an in-depth interview because of an Excellence score in the 99th percentile, serves as an example of what happens to a communication function when it becomes subservient to the marketing department. In the 3 years between the completion of the quantitative questionnaires and the case study interview, a new CEO arrived who saw public relations largely as a technical support function for marketing. The public affairs department still was separate from marketing, but it served mostly to provide technical support to other divisions of the organization, especially marketing. The current CEO "describes the department's function as communication marketing," according to the current director of public affairs. (The previous director of public affairs lost organizational rank and was given technical tasks in the marketing department.)

At the time of our case study, the parts of the public affairs department had been revamped to serve as an in-house public relations firm. Public affairs then consisted of the new in-house agency, a news bureau, a speakers' bureau, and a unit responsible for all publications. Communicators had been assigned to more technical duties to save costs and create efficiency, according to the assistant director of public affairs. Coincidentally, the public affairs department lost its role in strategic management and turned from a two-way symmetrical model to one that is "primarily two-way asymmetrical, mixed with a lot of one-way communication," according to the director of marketing.

Essentially the same situation existed in an insurance company that rated at the bottom of the Excellence scale—the 6th percentile. In our in-depth interviews, the top communicator reported that the communication department "is part of the marketing department" and that the communication department exists as a service or support unit to marketing. As a result, communication was not viewed as a managerial function, it had no role in strategic management, and the model of public relations practiced was "pretty much one-way, unfortunately," according to the top communicator.

The only instance in our survey of cases in which public relations reported to a vice president of human resources was a medical products subsidiary of one of the largest corporations in the United States. Although the company scored in the 97th percentile of the Excellence scale and highly on the measures of the two-way models and managerial roles, the top communicator had virtually no role in strategic management (2nd percentile, according to the CEO). Access to the dominant coalition had to come through the top human resources officer. However, sublimation to human resources did not seem to result in an emphasis on asymmetrical communication in the same way that sublimation to marketing did in the previous cases.

Peer Relationships Between Public Relations and Other Functional Areas

Even though we have maintained throughout the analysis in this chapter that public relations should not be sublimated to other management functions, we learned from an association CEO, as early as the pilot testing of our interview protocol, about the importance of a "peer professional" relationship among directors of public relations and the heads of the other functional areas of the organization.

We posed no specific propositions about collaboration between top communicators and their colleagues in other departments. However, in studying *how public relations practitioners work together (or at cross-purposes) with their counterpart managers throughout the organization,* we came to believe that the ideal relationship is that of peer professionals. As a result, we learned a great deal—not about "turf battles" between public relations practitioners and their peers in other functions—but about how successful public relations professionals collaborate and build relationships with their peers.

This concept was emphasized in the interview conducted at the 1993 IABC conference. There, the CEO explained that professionals in public relations should be on a par (in terms of expertise, brains, respect, and salary) with their counterparts in science, law, lobbying, and so forth. When this is the case, public relations can become part of the management team that runs the organization. That association CEO offered the following evidence: "If I had five staff members and five CEOs [of member companies] standing in a room and I invited you to come in and listen to the discussion and then tell me which five were the CEOs and which five were the staff, you couldn't distinguish them because that's the relationship that exists intellectually and personally."

The association's director of communication did point out that the CEOs' suits were considerably more expensive than his, but seriously. . . . This top communicator added that his approach is to find ways to help his peers, along the lines suggested by TQM and also WIIFM: He demonstrates, over time, "what's in it for them."

The CEO also described the "grazing rights" that public relations people should have in all departments rather than being territorial and sticking strictly to their own department or to issues narrowly defined as communication. He explained: "You don't have lines and boxes, turf. What you have is grazing rights. So you have the opportunity to go over into the other guy's pasture, and that person has the opportunity to come over into yours. We share our problems and we share our conclusions."

Another part of this relationship equation has to do with the unique role of public relations. To some of our interviewees, the advice coming from the communication department balances counsel emanating from other quarters. The top communicator at the gas and electric company said: "You're going to find people in the organization—some of them at pretty senior levels—who are going to say, 'Don't talk; don't say a word. We might be sued or we're going to damage our market.' " He saw his role as countering that closed attitude. However, he reminded us that public relations practitioners must be at a level of responsibility and respect within their organizations to guarantee that their opinion carries equal weight.

Even relationships marked by what one member of senior management called "productive tension" can be healthy and constructive. He talked about how the manager of public affairs and his counterparts in other departments of this utility "push each other and push back."

We heard a lot about the need to "push." In an organization where communication is not highly valued by senior management, the director of public relations advised: "You have to be pushy sometimes—you really do have to step out of the square that you're in and make others aware of what can be done or should be done." This is how she operates: "[In a situation where a public relations presence is needed] we write a memo, make a call, try to insert ourselves. I think it's just a lot of pushing. And if you make one good connection, it's easier to make others." However, a public relations manager in the same gas and electric company pointed out that even when the CEO takes public relations seriously, others within the dominant coalition—especially marketing—may not.

The transition of the chemical corporation's communication department from being an "order taker" to strategic public relations has changed the nature of its relationship with other departments. At this point, communicators collaborate with and counsel those other units. One member of the dominant coalition described the reciprocal nature of the connection: "People on his [the director's] staff work with each business team to represent the [communication] function and to bring back their business guidance."

Such alliances with counterparts in the organization may be especially important for top communicators who are not a formal part of the dominant coalition. The director of corporate affairs for the real estate company suggested that the best way for the top communicator to succeed in an organization is through relationships. Because she is not actually part of the dominant coalition, she has had to create strong rapport with those who *are*: "I have to rely on maintaining *very good* relationships with those senior vice presidents and making myself invaluable to them and anticipating things that are coming up in order to say, for example, 'I heard about this and I'd love to get involved and here are some ideas I have.' "

This director stressed that the process is ongoing: "One clearly has to make the effort to maintain those relationships because you don't get the information any other way." Her job, as she described it, was to "ferret out" information that will help prevent the company from making bad mistakes. In her matrix organization, she must act as an internal boundary spanner—aware of issues at every level. She called herself "a pleasant snoop."

Such pushing for collaboration may be especially critical to the career success of women in public relations. Women tend not to be included automatically in the information and social networks of the organization, especially at the highest levels. Thus they would have little opportunity to meet and be mentored by those in a position to help promote them unless they made a determined effort. This effort can help the public relations function as well as the individual female practitioner.

The top communicator at the economic development agency explained that public relations has been undervalued by her dominant coalition because of the preponderance of women in the field. She contended that when women are employed as communicators, they are viewed as clerks. When men are employed as communicators, they are viewed as managers. However, her organization—ranked in the 4th percentile in overall Excellence—is poised to move beyond its traditional limitations. According to both the vice president and the head of public relations, the president is rethinking what the role of the communication department should be. Even now, according to the vice president: "We look at communication as being a critical component of the system. If you pull one chunk of it out, the system doesn't function properly."

One obvious internal connection within the organizational system is between public relations and human resources. Even communicators at the middle level of management can be expected to develop relationships with their counterparts in that department. The employee communication specialist with the chemical company traced her involvement with human resources back 6 or 7 years, when she heard about acting as a liaison with personnel at an IABC meeting. As a result, she called her counterpart to suggest they work more closely together. In particular, she has helped employees understand and value their benefits. She contrasted this stance with years ago, "when benefits were a secret."

Another organization that valued teamwork and interdependence was the medical products company. Its top communicator and director of human resources both touted the value of sharing information with internal counterparts along with clients and the parent corporation. Such sharing helps build organizational linkages and stronger communities. As the director of human resources explained the company's systems philosophy: "It would be hard for one component to succeed without communicating with others. We make it a point to empower our entire workforce with the information, tools, and resources to make better decisions. We'd rather have 15,000 minds engaged than just a few at the top." Examples of team building and sharing of information across departments and publics at this organization, ranked at the top of the Excellence scale, include:

- Global councils that meet regularly to talk about the corporation's operations around the world.

- Sales and service employees located next to each other so they can share ideas with teams of local customers, ensuring overlapping measurements and quality checks.
- A management policy declaring open and honest communication on internal issues from the outset, using the communication department to both "tell the story" and gather feedback.
- The top communicator contended, "We have many more internal mechanisms than most typical organizations to ensure positive things [such as morale] and minimize negative things [rumors]."

Despite its advantages, cultivating relationships among departments is a challenge in most organizations. Coordination is a particular problem—one made even more difficult when public relations is managed by an outside firm. The agency head counseling the cosmetics company, for example, used words like *flux* and *lag* to describe his relationship with other units there. He said, "We need to be a little more astute than we are right now at deciding who is going to handle what right off the bat."

Relationships Inside the Public Relations Department

At this point, we add a postscript about collegiality, relationships, and teamwork. We want to belabor what might be the obvious. We have written much about how communication managers interact with their peers in other departments, but we want to emphasize the importance of relationships *within* the department as well.

The ideal leader, we heard, is not a micromanager. At the engineering experiment station, the staff of the communication manager told us she stays away from the technical. She is there for consultation and "the big picture." She herself credited a mastery of TQM with being able to devote more and more of her time to management. That, in turn, has made the office "better off," in the words of the agency's publication editor. The teamwork inherent in this effective operation pays off as well; but as the editor astutely pointed out, "The leader has to be open to it." To reiterate, this leader is not characterized as autocratic. Her subordinates and superior alike praise her for working well with groups.

SUMMARY AND CONCLUSIONS

Starting at about the time we began work on the Excellence project in 1985, there has been extensive debate about how the communication function should be organized in organizations and what its relationship should be to other management functions, especially marketing. Numerous scholars and professionals have called for the integration of all communication activities in an organization into a single department or for communication to be coordinated in some way by a communication czar, pope, or chief reputation officer.

Advertising scholars and practitioners originally advocated the integration of these communication activities though the marketing function or, on a smaller scale, through a marketing communication department or executive. Public relations scholars and practitioners largely resisted this move, although some endorsed it as a way of empowering public relations through alignment with the more powerful marketing function. Public relations people pointed out that most communication activities other than marketing communication have long been integrated through the public relations function or through a chief public relations or communication officer. They feared that marketing encroachment or dominance of the public relations function would diminish the role of public relations in organizations.

By today, IMC scholars and practitioners have moved away from integrated *marketing* communication to what they now call integrated communication—although most still concentrate their attention on consumers and marketing communication programs. What they now call integrated communication differs little from our principle of integration of all communication activities under the public relations function that we proposed in the first *Excellence* book and tested in the Excellence study. Public relations scholars and practitioners, likewise, now seem to have embraced the idea of pulling marketing communication activities under the public relations umbrella—although data reported by Hunter (1999a) show that a large proportion of marketing communication programs still report to marketing rather than public relations.

Our data and those reported by Hunter (1997, 1999a) from surveys of Fortune 500 companies show that communication functions rapidly are being organized under the rubric of public relations or corporate communication. Organizations seem to be integrating communication activities through a central public relations department, or they have several specialized communication departments that are coordinated both formally and informally by a chief communication officer who usually holds the title of senior vice president or vice president of corporate communication. In addition to the coordinating role of this senior communication officer, organizations use a number of ways to coordinate their activities, such as organization-wide meetings, communication policies, and unstructured interaction of communication professionals in different departments or business units. Our data show that this integration has occurred most often in organizations that have excellent public relations functions, as we have defined excellence.

These combinations of centralized or integrated, specialized departments also tend to have a matrix arrangement with other management functions—such as marketing, human resources, or finance. They work under an integrated philosophy of communication—a philosophy that is largely strategic and symmetrical. But the communication managers in these centralized and specialized departments work as peer professionals with their counterparts in other management functions. They collaborate with their peers. In excellent departments there is little conflict and competition with other management functions—including marketing. Inside excellent communication departments, professionals work as colleagues who are equally empowered. As the field becomes female-intensive, the implications are clear: Women must be included in the organization's power and information networks.

Excellent communication departments also seek support from outside firms. All public relations departments in our sample purchased a substantial proportion of their technical publicity activities from outside firms, as well as a large proportion of their research support. Excellent public relations departments also sought strategic counseling from outside firms when they had difficulties with their publics, although most seem to possess the knowledge themselves to deal with these problems.

Although the marketing function in excellent organizations seldom dominates public relations, communication departments in less excellent organizations have a strong tendency to provide little more than technical support to the marketing function—technical support that most communication departments purchase from outside firms. A few of the excellent departments do seem to have adopted marketing theory as the foundation for their communication programs—with its emphasis on customers, messages, and symbols. On the positive side, however, they also have adopted the strategic, two-way approach of modern marketing—although marketing theory has steered them toward an asymmetrical rather than a symmetrical approach to communication.

The challenge for public relations theorists and practitioners, therefore, seems to be to persuade their counterparts in marketing to adopt a more symmetrical approach to communication. Recent books by Gronstedt (2000) and Duncan and Moriarty (1997) suggest that this conversion already may be occurring.

REFERENCES

Canonico, G. C. (1994). *Integrated marketing communications: Its role in public relations education.* Unpublished undergraduate honors thesis, Syracuse University, Syracuse, NY.

Caywood, C. L. (1997). Twenty-first century public relations: The strategic stages of integrated communications. In C. L. Caywood (Ed.), *The handbook of strategic public relations & integrated communications* (pp. xi–xxvi). New York: McGraw-Hill.

Dozier, D. M., & Grunig, L. A. (1992). The organization of the public relations function. In J. E. Grunig (Ed.), *Excellence in public relations and communication management* (pp. 395–418). Hillsdale, NJ: Lawrence Erlbaum Associates.

Dozier, D. M., & Repper, F. C. (1992). Research firms and public relations practices. In J. E. Grunig (Ed.), *Excellence in public relations and communication management* (pp. 185–215). Hillsdale, NJ: Lawrence Erlbaum Associates.

Drobis, D. R. (1997–1998). Integrated marketing communications redefined. *Journal of Integrated Communications, 8,* 6–10.

Duncan, T., & Caywood, C. (1996). The concept, process, and evolution of integrated marketing communication. In E. Thorson & J. Moore (Eds.), *Integrated communication: Synergy of persuasive voices* (pp. 13–34). Mahwah, NJ: Lawrence Erlbaum Associates.

Duncan, T., Caywood, C., & Newsom, D. (1993, December). *Preparing advertising and public relations students for the communications industry in the 21st century.* Report of the Task Force on Integrated Communications. Evanston, IL: Northwestern University Department of Integrated Marketing Communication.

Duncan, T., & Everett, S. (1993). Client perceptions of integrated marketing communications. *Journal of Advertising Research, 33*(3), 30–39.

Duncan, T., & Moriarty, S. (1997). *Driving brand value: Using integrated marketing to manage profitable stakeholder relationships.* New York: McGraw-Hill.

Ehling, W. P., White, J., & Grunig, J. E. (1992). Public relations and marketing practices. In J. E. Grunig (Ed.), *Excellence in public relations and communication management* (pp. 357–394). Hillsdale, NJ: Lawrence Erlbaum Associates.

Fombrun, C. J. (1996). *Reputation: Realizing value from the corporate image.* Boston: Harvard Business School Press.

Gronstedt, A. (1996). Integrating marketing communication and public relations: A stakeholder relations model. In E. Thorson & J. Moore (Eds.), *Integrated communication: Synergy of persuasive voices* (pp. 287–304). Mahwah, NJ: Lawrence Erlbaum Associates.

Gronstedt, A. (2000). *The customer century: Lessons from world-class companies in integrated marketing and communication.* New York: Routledge.

Grunig, J. E. (1993a). On the effects of marketing, media relations, and public relations: Images, agendas, and relationships. In W. Armbrecht, H. Avenarius, & U. Zabel (Eds.), *Image und PR (Image and PR)* (pp. 263–295). Opladen, Germany: Westdeutscher Verlag.

Grunig, J. E. (1993b). Image and substance: From symbolic to behavioral relationships. *Public Relations Review, 91*(2), 121–139.

Grunig, J. E., & Grunig, L. A. (1998). The relationship between public relations and marketing in excellent organizations: Evidence from the IABC study. *Journal of Marketing Communications, 4,* 141–162.

Hallahan, K. (1992, August). *A typology of organizational relationships between public relations and marketing.* Paper presented at the meeting of the Association for Education in Journalism and Mass Communication, Montreal.

Harris, T. L. (1991). *The marketer's guide to public relations.* New York: Wiley.

Hunt, T., & Grunig, J. E. (1994). *Public relations techniques.* Fort Worth, TX: Harcourt Brace.

Hunter, T. (1997). *The relationship of public relations and marketing against the background of integrated communications: A theoretical analysis and empirical study at US-American corporations.* Unpublished masters thesis, University of Salzburg, Salzburg, Austria.

Hunter, T. (1999a). *Integrated communications: Current and future developments in integrated communications and brand management, with a focus on direct communication and new information and communication technologies, such as the Internet and stakeholder databases.* Unpublished doctoral dissertation, University of Salzburg, Salzburg, Austria.

Hunter, T. (1999b). The relationship of public relations and marketing. *Integrated Marketing Communications Research Journal, 5*(1), 41–44.

Kotler, P., & Mindak, W. (1978). Marketing and public relations: Should they be partners or rivals. *Journal of Marketing, 42*(10), 13–20.

Lauzen, M. M. (1991). Imperialism and encroachment in public relations. *Public Relations Review, 17*(3), 245–256.

Lauzen, M. M. (1992). Public relations roles, intraorganizational power, and encroachment. *Journal of Public Relations Research, 4,* 61–80.

Lewton, K. L. (1991). *Public relations in heath care: A guide for professionals.* Chicago: American Hospital Publishing.

Moriarty, S. E. (1996). The circle of synergy: Theoretical perspectives and an evolving IMC research agenda. In E. Thorson & J. Moore (Eds.), *Integrated communication: Synergy of persuasive voices* (pp. 333–354). Mahwah, NJ: Lawrence Erlbaum Associates.

Newsom, D. A., & Carroll, B. J. (1992, August). *The tower of babel: A descriptive report on attitudes toward the idea of integrated communication programs.* Paper presented at the meeting of the Association for Education in Journalism and Mass Communication, Montreal.

Pettegrew, L. S. (2000–2001). If IMC is so good, why isn't it being implemented? Barriers to IMC adoption in corporate America. *Journal of Integrated Communications, 10,* 29–37.

Rebel, H. (1997). Towards a metaphorical theory of public relations. In D. Moss, T. MacManus, & D. Verčič (Eds.), *Public relations research: An international perspective* (pp. 333–354). London: International Thomson Business Press.

Schultz, D. E., Tannenbaum, S. I., & Lauterborn, R. E. (1993). *Integrated marketing communications.* Chicago: NTC Business Books.

Spicer, C. H. (1991). Communication functions performed by public relations and marketing practitioners. *Public Relations Review, 17,* 293–306.

Tedlow, R. S. (1979). *Keeping the corporate image: Public relations and business, 1900–1950.* Greenwich, CT: JAI.

Tierney, J. P. (1993). *The role of public relations in integrated marketing communications: A preliminary study.* Unpublished master's thesis, University of Maryland, College Park.

Tillery, R. (1995, April). *The organization of the public relations function: A literature review from 1991–1993.* Paper presented at the meeting of the Mid-Atlantic Graduate Communications Conference, University of Maryland, College Park.

Van Riel, C. B. M. (1995). *Principles of corporate communication.* London: Prentice-Hall.

White, J., & Mazur, L. (1995). *Strategic communications management: Making public relations work.* Wokingham, England: Addison-Wesley.

Zerfass, A. (1996). *Unternehmensführung und öffentlichkeitsarbeit: Grundlegung einer theorie der unternehmenskommunikation und public relations* [Corporate leadership and public relations: An outline of a theory of corporate communications and public relations]. Opladen, Germany: Westdeutscher Verlag.

CHAPTER EIGHT

Models of Public Relations

If we were to choose a few keywords to describe the Excellence theory developed in this book and previously in J. Grunig (1992a) and Dozier with L. Grunig and J. Grunig (1995), we would list five: Excellent public relations is *managerial, strategic, symmetrical, diverse,* and *ethical.*

As we have seen in previous chapters, the terms *managerial* and *strategic* are linked in our theory of public relations excellence. To be excellent, the public relations function must headed by a manager who is involved in the strategic decision processes of the organization. The remaining three terms—*symmetrical, diverse,* and *ethical*—also are linked by the first term—*symmetrical.* If the public relations function is to contribute value both to the organization and to society, the concept of symmetry suggests, the function must be based on values that reflect a moral obligation to balance the interests of an organization with the interests of publics with which it interacts in society (J. Grunig, 2000). When public relations practice is based on *symmetrical* values, it also brings both *diverse* perspectives and *ethical* considerations into organizational decisions and behavior.[1]

We can describe excellent public relations in its simplest expression, therefore, as strategic, symmetrical communication management. To this point in this book, we have emphasized the strategic, managerial side of excellence in public relations. In this chapter we turn to symmetry as a crucial characteristic of communication Excellence.

In two chapters of the theory book that guided the Excellence study (J. Grunig & L. Grunig, 1992; J. Grunig & White, 1992), we reviewed the extensive

---

[1]We did not study ethics explicitly in the Excellence study, although we discussed the topic in relation to the symmetrical model in J. Grunig and White (1992). In Verčič, L. Grunig, and J. Grunig (1996), we added ethics as a principle of excellent public relations. For additional discussion of the role of symmetry in ethical public relations, see J. Grunig and L. Grunig (1996).

literature and research on the four models of public relations (press agentry, public information, two-way asymmetrical, and two-way symmetrical) that were developed by J. Grunig in the early 1980s (J. Grunig, 1984; J. Grunig & Hunt, 1984). The concept of symmetrical communication also occupied a central, integrating role in the chapter on internal communication (J. Grunig, 1992b), which serves as the focus for chapter 11 of this book.

In the chapter of the *Excellence* book on the "Effect of Worldviews on Public Relations Theory and Practice" (J. Grunig & White, 1992), we put forth the proposition that *for public relations to be excellent, public relations must be viewed as symmetrical, idealistic and critical, and managerial*. In the chapter on models of public relations (J. Grunig & L. Grunig, 1992), we concluded with the following summary proposition:

> *The two-way symmetrical model of communication is a real as well as a normative model. It is a model that organizations can use but often do not use because an authoritarian dominant coalition sees the approach as a threat to its power. Two-way symmetrical public relations, however, epitomizes professional public relations and reflects the growing body of knowledge in the field. This ethical approach also contributes to organizational effectiveness more than other models of public relations. Practitioners of the two-way symmetrical model are not completely altruistic; they also want to defend the interests of their employers—they have mixed motives. A substantial body of knowledge exists that provides practitioners with advice both on how to collaborate interpersonally with publics and on how to use media symmetrically to communicate with them. The two-way symmetrical model, as refined in this chapter, therefore, is a major component of excellence in public relations and communication management.*

The four models of public relations, and especially the two-way symmetrical model, have been the most controversial and the most debated component of the Excellence theory since our theory book was published. Many authors (e.g., Yarbrough, Cameron, Sallot, & McWilliams, 1998) essentially have equated the entire Excellence theory with the two-way symmetrical model. The discussion and debate about the models of public relations have contributed to the further development of the symmetrical theory, but a number of critics have raised questions about the four models and about symmetry in public relations that we discuss and answer before interpreting the quantitative and qualitative results of the Excellence study pertaining to the models of public relations.

THE TWO-WAY SYMMETRICAL MODEL: HISTORY AND QUESTIONS[2]

Before the 1970s, public relations scholars seldom, if ever, did research to explain the behaviors of public relations practitioners. Until that time, scholars

---

[2]Portions of this section previously have been published in J. Grunig (2000) and J. Grunig (2001b).

typically accepted the behavior of practitioners as given and looked for ways to describe, evaluate, and improve whatever practitioners did in the name of public relations.

J. Grunig (1976) published the first of a large number of studies that began to look at public relations as a dependent variable to be explained rather than as an independent variable whose effects were to be described. In that study, J. Grunig identified two patterns of public relations practice that he described as *synchronic* and *diachronic* public relations, using Thayer's (1968) concepts of two types of communication. J. Grunig (1984) extended these two types of public relations into the concept of four models of public relations and developed an instrument to measure them.[3]

In their 1984 textbook, *Managing Public Relations*, J. Grunig and Hunt used the four models both to describe the historical development of public relations and as a set of ideal types that described typical ways in which contemporary public relations is practiced. These four models are called press agentry/publicity, public information, two-way symmetrical, and two-way asymmetrical. Press agentry/publicity and public information are both one-way models. Practitioners of press agentry seek attention for their organization in almost any way possible, whereas public information practitioners are journalists-in-residence who disseminate accurate, but usually only favorable, information about their organizations. With the two-way asymmetrical model, practitioners conduct scientific research to determine how to persuade publics to behave in the way the client organization wishes. With the two-way symmetrical model, practitioners use research and dialogue to bring about symbiotic changes in the ideas, attitudes, and behaviors of both the organization and its publics.

In *Managing Public Relations*, J. Grunig and Hunt (1984) speculated that a contingency theory would explain when and why organizations practice these models—that is, the different models of public relations could each be effective, depending on the structure of the organization and the nature of its environment. In later work, however (J. Grunig, 1989; J. Grunig & L. Grunig, 1989,

---

[3]Some explanation is necessary here to clarify our use of the terms *theory* and *model*. We use *model* to mean a simplified representation of reality (J. Grunig & L. Grunig, 1992)—in this case to refer to simplified representations of how practitioners think about and practice public relations. We use *theory* as conceptualized in Suppe's (1977) semantic conception of theories. In the semantic conception of theories, a theory is the abstract meaning, or the idea, in a scientist's mind. The scientist can express this *theory* only through different kinds of representations—such as through words, diagrams, mathematical equations, and other types of *models*. Therefore, the models of public relations are representations that we have used as part of an underlying general theory of public relations, which links the models to other components of the Excellence theory as well as to variables that explain why organizations practice different models of public relations—variables such as organizational structure, environments, culture, and power. As the underlying theory (our thinking) has developed, however, we have begun to see the symmetrical model in broader terms. The theory now goes beyond the description of one type of practice to a broader normative theory of how public relations should be practiced.

1992), we dropped this contingency approach. Both research and conceptual development of the theory suggested that organizations could practice each of the models under certain contingent conditions and contribute to organizational effectiveness. However, we also suggested that using the two-way symmetrical model or a combination of the two-way symmetrical and two-way asymmetrical models that we then called the *mixed-motive model* could almost always increase the contribution of public relations to organizational effectiveness.

Murphy (1991) developed the idea of a mixed-motive model, based on concepts from game theory. She equated the symmetrical model with games of pure cooperation, in which one side always tries to accommodate the interests of the other. In a mixed-motive model, by contrast, organizations try to satisfy their own interests while simultaneously trying to help a public satisfy its interests. We never have viewed the two-way symmetrical model as advocating pure cooperation or of total accommodation of a public's interest. We saw it as a way of reconciling the organization's and the public's interests. Therefore, Murphy's mixed-motive model accurately describes the two-way symmetrical model as we originally conceptualized it (see J. Grunig & L. Grunig, 1992).

For many reasons, the models of public relations and the two-way symmetrical model, in particular, have become popular theories and topics of research in public relations. J. Grunig and L. Grunig (1989, 1992) reviewed many of the studies published at the time. Since those two reviews the models have been the focus of numerous other studies, theses, and dissertations throughout the world.

Research on the models in other countries generally has confirmed that the models do describe the practice of public relations in many cultures and political systems; but it also has suggested variations in the models—in particular, patterns of practice that can be described as personal influence and cultural interpretation (J. Grunig, L. Grunig, Sriramesh, Huang, & Lyra, 1995). Research also has suggested that practitioners in countries such as Korea are most likely to practice the craft models of press agentry and public information, although they aspire to practice the two-way symmetrical and asymmetrical models (Kim & Hon, 1998).

Many scholars have embraced the models because they seem to fit well with reality and to describe the experience of practitioners. The models also have been useful teaching tools for distinguishing between the typical practice of public relations and more advanced practices. Finally, the models have become a useful research tool for analyzing public relations practice in numerous settings and for explaining why public relations is practiced in these different ways.

Whenever a theory becomes as widely discussed as the models of public relations have become, it also becomes the target of criticism by scholars who want to defend or develop a competing theory. It is not surprising, therefore, that the models have become the target of several critics. Many of these critics have focused on J. Grunig's (1989) and J. Grunig and L. Grunig's (1992) suggestion that the two-way symmetrical model provides the normative ideal for public relations under most situations and, therefore, on the central role of that model in our theory of excellence in communication management. Many, but not all, scholars of persuasion and rhetoric seem to feel that their approach to public relations, which we understand as pure advocacy of an organization's interests, is challenged by our suggestion that the symmetrical model is the most ethical and effective of the four models. Critical scholars, who seem to believe that public relations cannot be practiced in the socially constructive way described by the symmetrical model, have argued that the symmetrical model represents a utopian ideal that no large and powerful organization ever does or would use. We address four questions about symmetrical theory raised by these critics, beginning with the question of whether the symmetrical model is practiced at all in the real world.

Is the Two-Way Symmetrical Model Only a Normative Model?

We have distinguished between a positive and a normative theory many times in describing the models of public relations (e. g., J. Grunig & L. Grunig, 1992). A positive model is a theory that describes and explains how public relations *is* practiced. A normative model explains how public relations *should be* practiced. A normative theory also can describe positive practice, which adds support to the idea that it *can be* practiced. A number of critics, however, have interpreted our use of the term "normative theory" to conclude that we have said the symmetrical theory is normative only and not also a positive theory explaining how public relations actually is practiced.

For example, Leitch and Neilson (2001) stated: "In their extensive study of public relations practice within organizations, J. Grunig and L. Grunig (1989) were unable to find many instances of symmetrical public relations. Thus, despite their efforts to create a descriptive theory, J. Grunig and L. Grunig reluctantly acknowledged that the symmetrical model was primarily a normative theory" (p. 129).

In fact, we (J. Grunig & L. Grunig, 1989) reviewed a large number of studies of the models and concluded that all four models—including the two-way symmetrical model—are positive models that describe the actual practice of public relations: "In total, then, the data reported here do seem to provide evidence supporting the concurrent validity and empirical accuracy of the four models. They do exist in the real world, and they do seem to capture variations in public relations behavior better than any current theory" (p. 41).

Leitch and Neilson (2001) said that we were "unable to find many instances of symmetrical public relations," but they seem to have based that erroneous conclusion on our report of one study of how organizations communicated with activist groups in the Pacific Northwest (L. Grunig, 1986). We did conclude that "very few of the organizations used the two-way symmetrical model in their overall programs" (J. Grunig & L. Grunig, 1989, p. 59). However, this was only one of many studies that we reviewed in the chapter cited. All of the other studies provided evidence that all four models are both normative and positive.

Leitch and Neilson—and other writers before them—seem to believe that we had concluded the symmetrical theory is normative alone because research had never been able to show an expected theoretical and empirical link between several organizational and environmental variables and the practice of the four models. For example, we (J. Grunig & L. Grunig, 1989) concluded that "*the logical relationship between the models and the environment of an organization* functions as more of a normative theory than a positive theory of public relations" (italics added; p. 59). Note that we said the *relationship* between the models and several contingent conditions in the environment of the organization was normative and not that the models themselves were strictly normative.

In this extensive program of research, we examined several variables that might explain why organizations practice different models, including the product/service environment, the political/regulatory environment, organizational structure, and technology. Normatively, organizations *should have* practiced different models in different environmental contexts but because of lack of knowledge of the two-way models many practitioners continued to practice the press agentry and public information models even when, logically, the two-way models would have been more appropriate for the organizational context.

Such misinterpretation of our research is not uncommon in the literature. Our unsuccessful attempts to explain *why* different positive models are practiced have been interpreted as concluding that the models themselves are normative. In fact, we did find other positive variables to explain why the models were practiced: "That research identified organizational ideology and power of the public relations department vis-à-vis the dominant coalition as central concepts in the positive theory" (J. Grunig & L. Grunig, 1989, p. 59). Organizations often practice asymmetrical models because members of the dominant coalition perceive public relations as a way of exercising power and because of authoritarian organizational cultures.

There is a great deal of evidence, then, that all four models are actually practiced by organizations. But should the positive practice of symmetrical public relations also be the normative model of public relations—the best way to increase the contribution of public relations to organizational effectiveness?

Is the Two-Way Symmetrical Model the Normative Ideal for Public Relations Practice?

Many scholars have reacted negatively to our suggestion that the symmetrical model is normatively superior to the others because they believe that one or more of the other models represent acceptable public relations practice or because they believe that public relations always is asymmetrical. Most of them have been trained in the social science discipline of persuasion and social influence, in the humanistic tradition of rhetoric, or in the applied social science of marketing communication. These theorists see no problem with a public relations practitioner who represents only the interests of his or her employer or client without concern for the interests of publics.

Miller (1989), a social scientist, claimed that public relations and persuasion are "two Ps in a pod" (p. 45) and that public relations is by nature asymmetrical. Van der Meiden (1993), who took a marketing perspective, defended an asymmetrical approach to public relations by arguing that the symmetrical model means that organizations would have to abandon their self-interest, which he considered to be unrealistic as well as ill advised.

In contrast, we have stated consistently that the symmetrical model actually serves the self-interest of the organization better than an asymmetrical model because "organizations get more of what they want when they give up some of what they want" (J. Grunig & White, 1992, p. 39). In addition, J. Grunig and Hunt (1984) wrote that persuasion still is a relevant concept in the symmetrical model. The difference is that "If persuasion occurs, the public should be just as likely to persuade the organization's management to change attitudes or behavior as the organization is likely to change the public's attitudes or behavior" (p. 23).

Leichty and Springston (1993) were among the first to point out that most organizations practice a combination of the four models. They also maintained that our original contingency approach to the models is more realistic than our more recent recommendation that the symmetrical model is the best normative approach to public relations under most situations. Leichty (1997) added that there are limits to collaboration, especially when crises caused by activist opposition require a confrontational response or when opponents are unreasonable or unwilling to collaborate.

Murphy and Dee (1996) described such a case in a conflict between DuPont and Greenpeace, which they concluded would continue despite some agreement between the two on solutions to the issue. Murphy and Dee used multiple regression analysis to set up decision profiles that both DuPont and Greenpeace used to evaluate issues. They also asked both groups to estimate the profiles of the others. Although the actual profiles of both groups were closer than the profiles they projected for the other, the researchers could not get the two to agree on a compromise solution they constructed to represent the interests of both parties:

> Both corporate public relations practitioners and environmental activists doubtless want to enhance public awareness of their position on environmental issues. In taking its case to the public, DuPont could rightly emphasize the similarities between its position and those of environmental activists. However, Greenpeace would surely prefer to emphasize the differences rather than the similarities be-

tween its position and DuPont's. If DuPont aligns itself with environmental activism, Greenpeace loses the use of DuPont, an evil other, as a rallying point. (pp. 30–31)

Murphy and Dee's (1996) study does not call the value of the symmetrical model into question because we have never said that the symmetrical model *always* would be successful. Indeed, Leichty (1997) was correct when he pointed out that there are limits to collaboration. We acknowledged similar limits in J. Grunig and L. Grunig (1992) when we listed several reasons, identified by Gray (1989), why organizations often refuse to collaborate: ". . . institutional disincentives (such as environmental groups that do not want to dilute their advocacy of a cause), historical and ideological barriers, disparities in power, societal dynamics (such as individualism in the United States), differing perceptions of risk, technical complexity, and political and institutional cultures" (p. 319). Then, in support of the idea that symmetrical public relations is not inevitably successful, we quoted Gray, who said:

Clearly the record of collaborations to date is a checkered one. Many experiences contain aspects of both success and failure. While the evidence is not 100 percent favorable, it is heartening. For example, even when parties do not reach agreement, they frequently applaud the process. Moreover, the numbers of disputes and problems for which collaboration is a possible alternative is growing. Finally, as we learn more about what works and what does not, the number of successes should increase. (p. 260)

Susskind and Field's (1996) book, *Dealing With an Angry Public*, is, in essence, a manual on how to practice the two-way symmetrical model in conflict situations. In their chapter on conflicts based on differences in values, however, Susskind and Field acknowledged that such conflicts (e.g., the abortion conflict) are particularly difficult to resolve "because basic notions of self-worth are at stake" (p. 155). They explained that:

Debates involving values are not only about what we want, but also who we think we are and who we think "they" are in relation to us. Debates involving values upset our view of the world and ourselves. In value-laded debates, to compromise or to accommodate neither advances one's self-interest nor increases joint gains. Compromise, in its most pejorative sense, means abandoning deeply held beliefs, values, or ideas. To negotiate away values is to risk giving up one's identity. Thus, such conflicts are intense. (p. 155)

Nevertheless, Susskind and Field (1996) suggested a number of incremental steps that could be taken at least to defuse the conflict, get the parties to talk with one another, and achieve small areas of agreement. "First-level" changes can be accomplished, they said: ". . . the disputants may agree on peripheral

changes that do not eliminate the ongoing hostilities but alleviate specific problems" (p. 158). For example, after employees were killed at a Planned Parent-
hood clinic, the Catholic Church called for a moratorium on sidewalk demonstrations and asked protesters to move their vigils inside churches.

"*Second-level changes,*" Susskind and Field (1996) explained, "alter some aspects of the ongoing relationship, but fundamental values are not challenged or
transformed, at least in the short run" (p. 159). For example, groups opposing
each other on abortion: ". . . agreed to meet to discuss adoption, foster care, and
abstinence for teenagers. Surprisingly, these groups agreed to support legislation to pay for the treatment of pregnant drug addicts. They also established an
ongoing dialogue that transformed the way they dealt with each other. For instance, they began to meet individually, on a personal basis, to work on problems they had in common" (p. 159).

Susskind and Field (1996) added that "*third-level change* is far more difficult"
because it requires change "in the way people view themselves" (p. 159). They
explained that for individuals such change requires extensive therapy. As a result, they added, "In the practical world of day-to-day management, we do not
think it is likely that any one institution, be it a corporation or a government
agency, can bring changes at the third level" (p. 159)

In short, the two-way symmetrical model sometimes will be less effective
than at other times. The major question, then, is whether an asymmetrical approach will be more successful when a symmetrical approach is not completely
effective. That question has been the major focus of a program of research by
Cameron and his associates (Cameron, 1997; Cancel, Cameron, Sallot, & Mitrook, 1997; Cancel, Mitrook, & Cameron, 1999; Yarbrough et al., 1998). Like
others cited earlier, Cameron and his colleagues took issue with our conclusion
that the symmetrical model is the most effective normative model in most situations. In the first article in the series, Cancel et al. (1997) equated the symmetrical model with accommodation and the asymmetrical model with advocacy. In
its place, they developed a contingency theory defining 87 conditions that might
explain why public relations professionals decide whether to accommodate
publics or to engage in advocacy only for their organization.

However, the symmetrical model, as we have conceptualized it, cannot be
equated with accommodation. We never have defined the symmetrical model
as the accommodation of a public's interest at the expense of the organization's
self-interest. In fact, the concept of symmetry directly implies a balance of the
organization's and the public's interest. Total accommodation of the public's
interest would be as asymmetrical as unbridled advocacy of the organization's
interests.

In later publications, Cameron's research team softened its criticism of the
symmetrical model. For example, Yarbrough et al. (1998) said in a parenthetical
statement: "(the authors believe that some degree of accommodation or openness to accommodation is at the crux of two-way symmetrical communica-

tion)" (p. 40). Obviously, this is the case. Public relations could not be symmetrical without accommodation, but the essence of the symmetrical model is that *both* the organization and a public must be willing to accommodate the interests of the other.

Cameron and his colleagues have stated in each of their articles that they believe public relations professionals are least likely to practice symmetrical public relations when an organization considers the stance of a public to be morally repugnant. In such cases, they challenge our claim (J. Grunig & L. Grunig, 1996; J. Grunig & White, 1992) that the symmetrical model is inherently ethical: "For some issues, taking a moral stand means NOT engaging in two-way symmetrical communication because to do so would place communication *process* above ethical *principle*" (Cancel et al., 1999, p. 173). In short, they believe that *accommodating* a morally repugnant public ("the Hitlers of the world" [Yarbough et al., 1998, p. 40]) is morally wrong.

Again, however, the symmetrical model is not about accommodation alone. It may be unethical to accommodate a repugnant public; it is not unethical to talk with its representatives. And as Susskind and Field (1996) have shown in earlier quotes, there are examples in which competing parties have improved their relationship with groups they previously considered morally repugnant. In addition, organizations believe far too often that publics with which they are in conflict are morally repugnant and that the organization's stance is morally superior. The same is true of activist groups such as Greenpeace, which believe they have a moral duty to oppose evil corporations (as exemplified in Murphy and Dee, 1996).

Yarbrough et al. (1998) acknowledged the problem of believing one's position is morally superior to that of the opposition when they said, "Organizations necessarily weather charges of paternalism when members of the organization are convinced that they know more about the situation and are acting in the best interests of all parties or for a greater good" (pp. 40–41). J. Grunig (2001a) found the same when he reviewed the contribution of Edward L. Bernays to public relations theory and practice. On the one hand, J. Grunig said, "Bernays probably was the first public relations theorist; and because one of the most important criteria of a profession is that it be based on a theoretical body of knowledge, we can indeed find the origins of public relations as a profession in his writings" (p. 303).

But, J. Grunig (2001a) added that although Bernays was a liberal who was deeply concerned about society, he also was paternalistic in that he believed he knew what was best for others and that he could use propaganda to get people to behave in a way that was in their self-interest, even though they did not recognize that self-interest. Knowing what is best for others, J. Grunig said, often is clouded by one's self interest: "I believe that most practitioners have difficulty distinguishing between the interests of their clients and the interests of society. That is a decision I believe we can make more easily with the two-way symmet-

rical model of public relations than the two-way asymmetrical model that dominated the thinking of social scientists in the 1920s" (pp. 304–305).

There obviously are situations in which an organization, or a public, has a
more reasonable or moral position than the other. However, the point of the
symmetrical model is that neither side can really know the morality or reason-
ableness of the other side's interests without talking with its representatives either
interpersonally or through formal research. If, after dialogue, one side finds that it
cannot accommodate the other, then the symmetrical approach suggests that advocacy of its interests or withdrawal from the dialogue is ethically reasonable.

Cancel et al. (1999) added two additional reasons why collaboration is difficult or impossible: (a) when antitrust law prohibits collusion among competitors and (b) when "an organization faces two publics locked in intractable moral
conflict" (p. 173) such as a corporation that must deal both with Planned Parent-
hood and an antiabortion group. The first situation is not really a public relations situation; it describes organization-to-organization communication and
not organization-to-public communication. The second example is well known
in the conflict resolution literature and has been recognized by Verčič (1997) in
the public relations literature. Multiparty conflicts do not call the efficacy of the
symmetrical model into question; instead, they require more sophisticated
means of symmetrical communication and conflict resolution, methods that research is only beginning to identify.

In spite of these criticisms, however, the contingency theory proposed by
Cameron and his colleagues does not really challenge the symmetrical model.
Rather, we see their theory as an elaboration of the symmetrical model. Symmetry in public relations is really about balancing the interests of organizations
and publics, of balancing advocacy and accommodation. As their research
shows, the management of an organization is not always willing to accommodate publics. In some situations it is willing to accommodate; in others it is not.
In addition, their case studies illustrate well the interactions among public relations professionals, top management, and publics that characterize real-life application of the symmetrical model.

In light of these critiques of the two-way symmetrical model as the ideal,
normative model for public relations, we can return to the question that headed
this section: Is the two-way symmetrical model the normative ideal for public
relations practice? Our answer again is "yes," just as it was in the proposition
that ended the chapter on models of public relations in the first *Excellence* book.
The symmetrical model does not reject the notion of persuasion, which has
been the concern of many scholars of rhetoric and social influence. It does reject
the idea of asymmetrical persuasion in public relations, but it endorses the idea
of symmetrical persuasion. The symmetrical model also cannot be equated
with accommodation or seen as a polar opposite of advocacy.

Balancing self-interest with the interests of others is a give-and-take process
that can waver between advocacy and collaboration, or what Spicer (1997)

called *collaborative advocacy* and Raiffa (1982) called *cooperative antagonism* (see our application of this term in Dozier with L. Grunig & J. Grunig, 1995). Heath (1998) described the process in this way: "Enactment assumes that symmetry and asymmetry are more a matter of the dynamics between parties than something that one either thinks, does, or says independent of the other" (p. 17).

Mixed motives, collaborative advocacy, and cooperative antagonism all have the same meaning as symmetry. Symmetry means that communicators keep their eye on a broader professional perspective of balancing private and public interests. Their job, however, consists of more than simultaneous argumentation or "a wrangle in the marketplace" (Heath, 1992, p. 17). They must listen as well as argue. This does not mean that symmetrical practitioners should not argue or attempt to persuade. Rather they must consistently remind themselves and management that they may not be right and, indeed, that their organization may be better off if it listens to others.

Symmetry also means dialogue (Heath, 2001). Baxter (1994) used the theory of dialogism developed by the Russian rhetorical scholar Bakhtin to describe interpersonal relationships. We believe that the concept also can be used to describe symmetrical relationships between organizations and publics.

According to Baxter (1994), "The 'dialogue' is the centerpiece of dialogism. To Bakhtin, the essential quality of a dialogue was its simultaneous fusion or unity of multiple voices at the same time that each voice retained its differentiated uniqueness. This dynamic tension between fusion-with and differentiation-from the Other served for Bakhtin (1981, p. 272) as a general metaphor for all social processes" (pp. 234–235).

Baxter and Montgomery (1996) described this simultaneous fusion with the Other while retaining the uniqueness of one's self-interest as a dialectical perspective on social life, "a belief that social life is a dynamic knot of contradictions, a *ceaseless interplay* between contrary or opposing tendencies" (p. 3). The central theme of their dialectical approach to relationships mirrors the symmetrical model, "that of taking seriously the voice of the other—the voice of difference—in personal relationships" (p. xiii). This dialectical perspective on relationships, therefore, describes well the challenge of symmetrical public relations.

Is the Symmetrical Model Too Idealistic?

Although social science and rhetorical scholars of persuasion believe that public relations is a necessary part of a democratic society, critical scholars such as L'Etang (1996a), Kersten (1994), and Gandy (1982) typically have viewed public relations as "necessarily partisan and intrinsically undemocratic" (L'Etang, 1996a, p. 105). Thus, to them, the symmetrical model represents a utopian attempt to make an inherently evil practice look good:

There is, however, a problem in the attempt which some make to maintain the ideal of "symmetry" alongside the role of public relations as advocate. Surely, symmetry and advocacy are in opposition. The only way around this tension is to argue that public relations ensures that all views are held, i.e., that the playing field is level. Whether this sort of pandering to the liberal conscience is justifiable is a matter for debate: a debate which has yet to take place with public relations. (L'Etang, 1996a, pp. 96–97)

Pieczka (1996a) also objected to the use of the symmetrical model as a normative theory of how public relations should be practiced as well as a descriptive theory of how public relations is practiced. She said that using the symmetrical model as a normative ideal is a closed-minded attempt to impose a single point of view on others: "This is rather reminiscent of Victorian missionaries explaining savages' habits of walking about naked or praying to rain by their lack of civilization. It is not a bad explanation; but it is a good one only from a particular point of view" (p. 154).

In addition, Pieczka (1996a), like many critical scholars, expressed more interest in criticizing the symmetrical theory than in constructing a replacement: ". . . the author here is more interested in critiquing frameworks than in building them" (p. 126). Pieczka's view of criticism can be contrasted with Dozier and Lauzen's (2000) call for marrying public relations theory and critical theory for the betterment of public relations practice.

The view that the symmetrical model is utopian also can be found in critiques such as those of Kunczik (1994), Pieczka (1995), and L'Etang (1995), who argued that the symmetrical model is overly idealistic and is based on assumptions that seldom exist in reality. Their specific criticism, however, seems to have been more of Habermas' (1984) ideal communication situation or of Pearson's (1989) application of Habermas' theory to the symmetrical theory than of our formulation of the theory. In addition, these critics typically have ascribed theoretical assumptions to the symmetrical theory that are different from our presuppositions about the theory. In particular, they have argued that the theory assumes liberal pluralism (Coombs, 1993; Dozier & Lauzen, 1998), modernism (Pieczka, 1996a), functionalism (Pieczka, 1996a), or a shared desire for equilibrium and harmony in society (Pieczka, 1996a; Vasquez, 1996).

If all of these theoretical presuppositions were accurate, the theory of two-way symmetrical communication would envision public relations as a force that allows competing groups in a pluralist society equal access to decision makers, maintains functional equilibrium in society, and produces goodwill and harmony. In addition, all competing organizations, groups, and publics would enter into dialogue with the intent of achieving consensus. For example, Vasquez (1996) described the two-way symmetrical model in this way: "Namely, the two-way symmetrical model conceptualizes public relations as a negotiation situation in which parties hold or perceive they hold compatible, rather than incompatible, goals. Simply put, the compatible goal is a shared mission of social progress" (p. 65).

To this perceived assumption of a "a shared mission of social progress," Pieczka (1996b) added the equally naive assumption, which we already have discussed, that public relations always is successful: "The view of society that seems to be assumed is that in which various interest groups (and publics) are unavoidably pitched one against another but where conflict can always be resolved by the process of negotiation, which breeds at least as much mutual understanding as is necessary for compromise" (p. 64). Finally, L'Etang (1996a) finished this naive construction of the symmetrical theory by stating that the theory assumes all public relations is practiced in a utopian fashion: "What these arguments do is present public relations as being intrinsically moral in its peace-keeping function as well as in its promotion and support of democracy" (p. 96).

Moloney (1997) wrote that this naive utopian portrayal of the two-way symmetrical model has been adopted by public relations educators in the United Kingdom, in particular as a way of justifying the teaching of public relations when the popular perception of public relations is one of opprobrium:

> For university teachers seeking to found their work on an academically respectable basis, his [J. Grunig's] and Hunt's work were welcome to staff competing on campuses for resources against teachers of older and more established disciplines. The Grunigian paradigm gave them academic status. More emotionally, it met internalized needs of UK public relations teachers who had to convince themselves that they were worth a place on higher education campuses. Whatever the explanations, the outcome in the lecture theatre has too often been: "Public relations is a good thing called symmetrical communications" rather than "Maybe it should be that but the data seem not to fit." (p. 140)

Moloney (1997) went on to distinguish between positive and normative models. He added to this discussion, however, by pointing out that it is a mistake to believe that a normative theory describes *all* positive practice:

> Now the distortion by disciples enters in. Teachers (as well as trainers and articulate public relations professionals) do not adequately express this imbalance of types between majority "bad" practice and minority "good" practice. They over-emphasize the latter, forgetting its feeble grip on actual public relations behaviour in the UK, at least as witnessed by the public. In doing so, they laud the normative but minority practice so much so that the distinction between practice and norm is blurred to the point of erasure by frequent repetition. The normative aspect of symmetrical communication has, so to speak, been over-stamped on its minority existence. (p. 140)

Cheney and Christensen (2001) called our models of public relations "largely idealized models" and recommended "being very cautious" about the quantitative and qualitative data we have cited as evidence of the positive practice of the models, which they called "managerial accounts and self-reports." They suggested that, "In a society where the notions of dialogue, symmetry, and responsiveness have become almost sacred terms . . . it should be no surprise to find these notions often used and represented by decision makers in their descriptions of organizational practices" (p. 180).

Such a claim is the ultimate put-down of both quantitative and qualitative approaches to social science and, if accepted, would discredit all of the research evidence that we have painstakingly gathered and interpreted in this book. Cheney and Christensen (2001) would have us believe that the participants in our research either were deluding themselves or lying to us. We do not believe that was the case.

In support of the qualitative data we have collected, we refer to the ethics of qualitative research, which teach us the value of accepting self-reports at face value: Why ask people to participate in our research if we do not believe what they tell us? We addressed this ethical question in chapter 2 when we said:

> Like much qualitative research, Phase 2 of the Excellence study relied on people's words as the primary data (Marshall & Rossman, 1989). As an ethical concern, we considered it incumbent upon us to value those people and those words. One way to *devalue* participants is to question the validity of self-reports. At the same time, the meaning of self-reports is established *reflexively* through the evaluation of multiple interviews from the same organization and of our earlier interpretations of those self-reports.

In our qualitative research, we did not ask participants if they practiced "dialogue, symmetry, and responsiveness," to use Cheney and Christensen's (2001) words. We asked them to talk about their public relations practice in their own words. Sometimes respondents actually used the term symmetry, as was the case for the industry association that ranked at the top of our index of excellence. In most cases, however, we interpreted their nontheoretical—and nonsacred—words in our theoretical terms.

To support our quantitative data, the answer to Cheney and Christensen (2001) is even easier. First, we used operational definitions rather than the actual "sacred terms" in the questionnaire; and measures of the different models and other concepts were interspersed throughout the questionnaires to discourage a response set. Second, and most important, all participants would have given us the same responses and there would have been no variance in the data if the symmetrical model were a godlike concept. The fact that every study we have ever conducted of the models has produced normally distributed data clearly contradicts Cheney and Christensen's assertion.

Some disciples of the symmetrical theory and the critical scholars who debunk it, therefore, seem to have reconstructed the theory inaccurately in their minds. Their conceptualization of the theory has led some disciples to whitewash public relations practice or, for critical scholars, produced the belief that we have constructed an idealized, utopian conception of the role of public relations in society. In contrast, we have not conceptualized symmetrical public relations as taking place in an ideal situation where competing interests come together with goodwill to resolve their differences because they share a goal of social equilibrium and harmony. Rather we believe that symmetrical public relations occurs in situations where groups come together to protect and enhance their self-interest. Argumentation, debate, and persuasion take place. But dialogue, listening, understanding, and relationship building also happen because they are more effective in resolving conflict than are one-way attempts at compliance gaining.

Critical scholars often give the impression that we stand alone as idealists when we advocate basing the practice of public relations on the two-way symmetrical model. However, one can find similar and complementary approaches in the communication and social science literature. For example, Deetz (1992), a scholar of organizational communication, mirrored the symmetrical role for public relations practice when he criticized what he called self-serving managerialism and described a new role for management as one of coordinating the interests of owners and other stakeholders of an organization:

> In a capitalist society, private owners have the right to have their property and profit interests represented. But in a democratic society, we recognize that other groups and interests are equally invested in the corporation and have their own rights of representation. Management could be seen as a legitimate coordinating function whereby conflict among these various interests could be brought to the fore and innovative responses could be formulated. (pp. 4–5)

Following the lead of Kruckeberg and Starck (1988), a number of public relations scholars (Culbertson & Chen, 1997; Leeper, 2001; Starck & Kruckeberg, 2001; Wilson, 2001) have embraced the philosophy of the communitarian movement, which we believe shares the same presuppositions as the symmetrical model. Communitarians emphasize that community is more important than individualism. According to Wilson, "The philosophy of communitarianism does not advocate a communal society in its traditional sense. The philosophy celebrates individual rights but asserts that the provision of such rights requires responsibility on the parts of all members of the community. No participant (i.e., no profit-making organization) is sacrificed for the gain of the other participants, but all actors assume a share of responsibility" (p. 523).

Culbertson and Chen (1997) articulated six tenets of communitarianism that are relevant for public relations:

1. Whether a behavior is right or wrong depends in large part on its positive contribution to *commitment to and quality of relationships.*
2. Community requires a sense of interconnectedness and *social cohesion.*

3. Identification of—and humble but firm commitment to—*core values and beliefs* are essential to a sense of community.

4. People who claim *rights* must be willing to balance them with *responsibilities*.

5. Community requires that all citizens have a feeling of *empowerment*—of involvement in making and implementing decisions that bear on their lives.

6. Community requires a *broadening of one's social world*—one's array of significant others—so as to reduce fragmentation and enhance breadth of perspective. (pp. 37–40)

Leeper (2001) contrasted communitarianism with liberalism—the emphasis on individual rights and the neutrality of government vis-à-vis different interests. He concluded that there are strong parallels between the communitarian worldview and symmetrical public relations and between the liberal worldview and asymmetrical public relations: "The symmetrical models, like communitarianism, are based on an interactive epistemology, are based on actional theory as the correct ontological approach, define the public relations world as an interactive place, hold that theory is not value free, and hold that a function of theory is idealistic and change oriented" (p. 100).

J. Grunig (2000) articulated a symmetrical philosophy of public relations that embraces the values of the communitarian movement. He maintained that the public relations function should promote the value of *collectivism* in what typically are individualistic organizations—especially in countries with individualistic cultures like the United States (see, e.g., Hofstede, 1980). In addition, he argued that public relations should work to develop *communal relationships* (Clark & Mills, 1993) with publics rather than exchange relationships alone.

J. Grunig (2000) also said that public relations should help to build a democracy that is based on the principles of societal corporatism (Cawson, 1986; Charlton, 1986; Ziegler, 1988) rather than pluralism (which Leeper, 2001, called liberalism). In a pluralistic democracy, government remains neutral and independent from interest groups and promotes competition. In a democracy characterized by societal corporatism, government (and other organizations) build collaborative relationships with interest groups (publics) it affects or is affected by.

Societal corporatism is different from pure corporatism, where interest groups and government agencies have closely knit relationships that deny access to groups without such relationships (Coombs, 1993). Societal corporatism represents a middle ground between pluralism and corporatism, in which government builds relationships with relevant interest groups rather than remaining neutral and allowing them to compete as in the case of pluralism. Government and other organizations build those relationships openly in a societal corporatist system and encourage other interest groups to ask for relationships when they are affected by the actions of the organization.

Coombs (1993) rightly pointed out, we believe, that the rhetorical perspective to public relations—with its "free marketplace of ideas" and "wrangle in the marketplace"—assumes a pluralistic perspective. We think he is incorrect, however, when he asserted that our symmetrical, managerial perspective (which Coombs incorrectly called the systems perspective) also assumes a pluralistic system. J. Grunig (1989) and J. Grunig and White (1992) no doubt confused Coombs by embracing the concept of interest group liberalism as consistent with the symmetrical model. We agree that interest group liberalism, which "views the political system as a mechanism for open competition among interest or issue groups" (J. Grunig, 1989, p. 39), is a pluralistic concept; and we no longer see it as consistent with the symmetrical model.

Tying all of these values together is the value of *collaboration,* which J. Grunig (2000) said should be the core value of public relations professionals. Public relations people who use a symmetrical approach can facilitate collaborative processes because they are educated professionals who have expertise in working with others to facilitate dialogic communication and relationship building. To be successful, however, they must be able to convince their client organizations and their publics that a symmetrical approach will enhance their self-interest more than an asymmetrical approach and, at the same time, enhance their reputations as ethical, socially responsible organizations.

Even if critical scholars were to accept this philosophy of public relations as being possible, however, they generally question whether large, powerful organizations would embrace that philosophy when they have more power than the publics with which they interact. This is the next question that has been raised about symmetrical public relations.

Does Public Relations Help Only the Powerful?

Critical scholars who argue that organizations generally have greater power than their publics and have no reason to engage in symmetrical communication also argue that organizations can enhance their self-interest more easily by dominating their publics through asymmetrical communication (e.g., Dozier & Lauzen, 1998, 2000; Kersten, 1984). In L'Etang's (1996b) words, the symmetrical theory does not "explore the social or political contexts which allow certain interests an enhanced position in which they have more choice in the nature and type of communicative acts they carry out" (p. 122).

Several scholars have called attention to the fact that public relations theory and research have been developed more for use by powerful corporate and governmental organizations than by the organizations of publics—activist groups (Dozier & Lauzen, 1998; Karlberg, 1996; Rodino & DeLuca, 1999). These scholars have argued, first, that activist public relations is different because activists lack power. Second, they have argued that collaboration is bad because it means that activists must compromise their values with the values of what activists consider to be evil target organizations.

Leitch and Neilson (2001), for example, first restated the incorrect idealistic version of the symmetrical theory that we already have discussed, that "the model assumed that it was possible for an organization to meet its publics on equal terms and to rationally determine mutually beneficial outcomes" (p. 128). Then, they misconstrued our approach to segmenting publics to suggest that we believe a public is important only if an organization chooses to communicate with it—a misunderstanding repeated by Cheney and Christensen (2001, p. 181).[4] According to Leitch and Neilson, "publics have been viewed solely from the perspective of the organization and not from that of the publics themselves" (p. 127).

Consistently over the years, in contrast, J. Grunig has defined publics as groups of people that have consequences on organizations or on whom organizations have consequences (e.g., J. Grunig & Hunt, 1984). From the organizational perspective, publics are important if they have consequences on the organization. From the perspective of a public, the organization is important if it has consequences on it (see Fig. 5.1 and the discussion of it in chap. 5 of J. Grunig & Hunt). J. Grunig and Repper (1992) also said: "Important publics can be those that threaten the organization. They also can be publics on which the organization has negative consequences but that do not yet have the power to constrain the organization" (p. 123). J. Grunig's (1997) situational theory of publics—a key component of our theory of public relations and strategic management—segments publics based on *their* perceptions of a situation and subsequent behavior, not on the desire of an organization to have relationships with them.

Leitch and Neilson (2001) then used the statement from Cutlip, Center, and Broom (1994) that there is no such thing as a general public (we also consistently call the idea of a general public an oxymoron) to suggest that public relations scholars have "turned their backs on democracy" (p. 130). Cheney and Christensen (2001) similarly repeated the idea that segmenting publics means that a symmetrical public relations practitioner would not be concerned about the larger society.

We and most other public relations scholars have long used the idea of segmenting publics from the general population as a means of identifying those groups with which an organization truly needs relationships. We have done this

---

[4]Leitch and Neilson (2001) seemed to have reached this erroneous conclusion based on a statement by J. Grunig and Repper (1992), which they called an "organization-centered view of publics . . . taken to the extreme" (p. 129). J. Grunig and Repper said, "A public, a market, or any other segment of a population exists only because a researcher or practitioner uses a particular theoretical concept to identify it" (p. 129). Leitch and Neilson dropped the words "a researcher" from the quote, changing its meaning to make it sound more organization centered. J. Grunig and Repper were saying only that without a theoretical concept a researcher, a practitioner, or anyone else could not identify what to observe—a basic notion of both the philosophy of science and of cognitive psychology. The same would be true from the perspective of a public. A member of a public would not know that he or she is part of that public unless he or she had been introduced to a theoretical concept explaining the nature of a public.

to disabuse public relations practitioners of the idea that they can communicate with a mass audience and persuade an entire population to behave as the organization wants.

We believe that society consists of a pattern of relationships among organizations and publics (Leitch and Neilson [2001] used Habermas' notion of a lifeworld to describe this pattern of relationships). We believe that organizations need relationships with publics that can affect the organization—have consequences on it. We also believe that it is the social responsibility of organizations to develop relationships with publics on whom they have consequences (see, e.g., J. Grunig & Hunt, 1984, chap. 3, and J. Grunig & White, 1992), even if those publics have no power to affect the organization (see J. Grunig & L. Grunig, 1996).

Leitch and Neilson (2001), however, called this ethical view of public relations "simply absurd" because of differences in the power of organizations and publics:

> It is simply absurd to suggest that an interaction between, for example, a transnational corporation and a public consisting of unskilled workers in a developing country can be symmetrical just because the interaction is symmetrical in form. It is even more absurd to suggest the reverse—that the interaction between this worker public and the corporation can be symmetrical if the workers adopt the correct attitude and are willing to compromise. In practice, in cases where access to resources is so unequal, attempting to practice symmetrical public relations might constitute a self-destructive discourse strategy for the least powerful participant. (p. 129)

Cheney and Christensen (2001) echoed the same idea: "The full extent of corporate power in the world today needs to be acknowledged. For example, how is it today that relatively unorganized and resource-poor groups or individuals enter into even two-way symmetrical discussions?" (p. 181).

The question of unequal power between organizations and publics has been debated repeatedly in recent years in the public relations scholarly literature— especially in relationship to the feasibility of the symmetrical model when publics are relatively powerless.

On the one hand, we believe that critical scholars ignore the countervailing power that publics have when they organize into activist groups—or an activist group organizes them or works on their behalf (see, e.g., Anderson, 1992)—and use such tactics as media advocacy (Wallack, Dorfman, Jernigan, & Themba, 1993), litigation, legislation, and regulation (Mintzberg, 1983) to accomplish their goals. Indeed, many public relations practitioners believe their organizations have lost control to activist groups. Leitch and Neilson's (2001) example of unskilled workers in a developing country, for example, is directly contradicted by the experience of Nike and other apparel manufacturers who have been forced to make major changes in developing countries because of the "sweat shop" issue raised by activist groups working on behalf of just such low-income workers.

On the other hand, we readily acknowledge that many publics have less power than do many of today's large, multinational organizations. That is why J. Grunig originally developed the idea of the symmetrical model (for the intellectual and value origins of the model, see J. Grunig, in press). He believed that public relations could provide an institutionalized mechanism within organizations for empowering otherwise powerless publics and for incorporating considerations of ethics and social responsibility into management decision processes. Critical scholars deny that public relations can play such a role and argue that, in the end, powerful organizations give an *illusion of symmetry* only to achieve their own ends (e.g., Kersten, 1994; Stauber & Rampton, 1995, especially chap. 9).

J. Grunig (2000) maintained that the answer to the dilemma of how to practice symmetrical public relations in a situation of unequal power lies in the power of professionalism. A substantial body of knowledge on professionals developed in sociology in the 1950s and 1960s, and journalism and public relations researchers have applied the same measures to their disciplines. Scholars have used several approaches to determine the extent to which an occupation or individual practitioners in that occupation are professionalized. Until recently, the most popular method has been the *trait* method. With this method, researchers developed a list of theoretical characteristics of a profession and then applied it to an occupation such as public relations to determine the extent to which it is professionalized.

Although the lists of professional traits are not always the same, five traits appear on most of the lists. J. Grunig and Hunt (1984) listed five such traits: (a) a set of professional values, (b) strong professional organizations that socialize practitioners into these values, (c) professional norms, such as those provided by a code of ethics, that can be used to enforce values, (d) technical skills acquired through professional training, and (e) an intellectual tradition and an established body of knowledge. At the core of professionalism, therefore, are values and the specialized skills and knowledge needed to implement those values.

In addition to studying the traits of a profession, scholars recently have taken a power-control approach and defined a profession as one in which practitioners "control the substance, performance, and goals of their work" (Beam, 1990, p. 2). Pieczka and L'Etang (2001) reviewed the literature on this new perspective on professions and used it to analyze the development of public relations in the United Kingdom. In conclusion, they pointed out that their analysis should do the following:[5]

---

[5]Pieczka and L'Etang (2001) again dismissed our work and that of most other public relations scholars as "strongly anchored in the more idealistic, functionalist approach to professions" (p. 234). Apparently, they were unaware that we and other public relations scholars had incorporated the power-control perspective into our thinking about professionalism, as evidenced in Serini (1993) and J. Grunig (1998, 2000).

[It should] help practitioners to understand their own roles, not simply in terms of managerial/technical levels or organizational position but also in a much broader context in terms of the power of the occupational role in society. We suggest that further reflection on the nature of public relations expertise, particularly in view of its success in establishing itself as a distinct and commercially viable service, would be beneficial. (p. 234)

Professionals, in other words, have the power to carry out their work based on the knowledge and standards of their profession and their acceptance and respect in society. Nonprofessionals do not have that power. Instead, clients or superiors in the organization tell them what to do—and often those orders violate professional standards (J. Grunig, 1998). Society also does not respect the profession enough for public relations practitioners to rely on public and governmental respect for empowerment.

In the Excellence study, we used a power-control theory to explain why organizations practice public relations as they do. We said that members of the dominant coalition of the organization—the most powerful decision makers—ultimately decide how public relations is to be practiced. We showed in chapter 5 of this book that when the senior public relations executive is a member of that dominant coalition or has ready access to it, the organization is more likely to practice excellent public relations. We also found that senior practitioners who understand the professional body of knowledge in public relations are more likely to be part of the dominant coalition and therefore in a position where they can influence the choice of a public relations model.

Serini (1993) conducted a participant-observation study of how public relations people working in an anonymous high-tech firm defined professionalism and how they applied professional skills. The professionals she studied generally had limited autonomy to make decisions. They constantly had to negotiate with senior management to be able to do what they thought best. However, the more professional the practitioner, the more successful he or she was in these negotiations with non-public-relations superiors. Serini's research suggests that the traits of professionalism can help practitioners gain power to make decisions. Professionalism provides them with the credibility and respect necessary to negotiate for and eventually attain that power.

We found much the same thing in the detailed case studies reported in chapter 5. The crucial characteristic needed for the practice of excellent public relations was the knowledge necessary to practice strategic, symmetrical public relations. This means, then, that professionals must know, respect, and understand the body of knowledge in public relations. It also means that they must be skilled in negotiating with superiors and clients to implement that body of knowledge. If those conditions are present, public relations professionals can have considerable negotiating power when they work with client organizations and senior managers to apply their professional values.

The negotiating power of knowledgeable, professional practitioners, therefore, provides a possible solution to the problem of unequal power between organizations and their publics—if and when it exists. Public relations *professionals*, by definition, believe their role is to balance the interests of their clients with the interests of the publics that constitute society. In addition, and also by definition, public relations professionals have mastered a body of knowledge that nonprofessionals have not mastered, which helps them to implement their professional values effectively.

Related to professionalism is the concept of public relations as an in-house activist. Several critical scholars, such as Pieczka (1996a), have asserted that our theories of public relations are "modernist"—that is, based on a belief in rational, linear, and positivistic scientific thought. In contrast, we believe the symmetrical model and the theory of strategic management explored in chapter 5 are decidedly postmodern. Postmodernists emphasize that there is no single truth and that one should value and listen to multiple voices (for a discussion of modernism and postmodernism, see Holtzhausen, 2000). The postmodern concept of micropolitics—which emphasizes the role and impact of multiple interest groups in government and organizational decision making—fits squarely with our view of the role of public relations in the strategic management process and with our view of publics. We concur with Holtzhausen, therefore, who described the public relations *professional* as an in-house activist who brings the micropolitical process into management decision making and articulates and supports the interests of publics in that process.

The discussion of the role of power in public relations also has led many scholars to suggest that public relations theory and research should address the question of how to conduct public relations for activist groups. Dozier and Lauzen (2000), for example, suggested the need to "liberate the intellectual domain" (p. 3) of public relations theory and research to encourage scholars to examine the communication needs of activist groups rather than only the "invisible client" (p. 6)—large and powerful corporations and other organizations. As a result, public relations scholars have begun to debate whether public relations must be practiced differently for activist groups than for other organizations. Dozier and Lauzen (2000) and Rodino and DeLuca (1999) have argued that a different theory will be needed for activist groups.

Karlberg (1996) criticized us for applying the symmetrical theory only to corporations and government agencies, but he also suggested that activist organizations would benefit from using the symmetrical model. Kovacs (1998) found that to be true in her study of activist groups pressuring the British Broadcasting Corporation. The more they emphasized collaboration and relationship building, the more successful activist groups were in getting the BBC to listen and incorporate their needs into programming decisions.

Both Karlberg and Kovacs suggested that the symmetrical model is equally useful for activist groups as it is for other organizations. We agree, believing that the principles of excellent public relations are generic to all kinds of organizations, including activists. The idea is analogous to a global theory developed by Verčič et al. (1996); L. Grunig, J. Grunig, and Verčič (1998); and Wakefield (1997). These scholars developed a global theory consisting of "generic principles" and "specific applications" (see chap. 12). They then found evidence that the same broad, generic principles of public relations are normatively most effective throughout the world. However, they also said that these generic principles must be applied differently in different cultures and political and economic systems. J. Grunig and Jaatinen (1999) applied the same generic-specific approach to different types of organizations when they said that the principles of public relations are the same in government agencies as in corporations, nonprofit organizations, and associations. Nevertheless, they said, the generic principles must be applied differently in different types of organizations.

J. Grunig (2000) said he believes the same generic-specific approach applies to activist groups. The generic principles are the same, but a public relations practitioner must apply the principles differently when specific conditions are different. The most important specific condition occurs when an activist does indeed lack power vis-à-vis an organization. J. Grunig and L. Grunig (1997) developed a normative model for public relations that incorporates lack of power into the model and that includes more advocacy than found in other forms of symmetrical public relations. They theorized that activists initially should approach an organization using a collaborative approach. This makes the overall strategy more likely to be ethical. If the organization fails to respond to this offer of collaboration, then they recommended asymmetrical, advocacy strategies to make the activists' problem a problem for the other organization. These strategies include Wallack et al.'s (1993) media advocacy, community organizing, and coalition building.

J. Grunig (2000) reported that initial case study research by students in the graduate Seminar in Public Relations Publics at the University of Maryland showed that some activist groups do apply this normative model. Positive (descriptive) case studies showed that groups for which outside support and opposition is divided seemed most likely to follow the normative model. Groups for which support is nearly unanimous (such as Amnesty International or health organizations) generally used a public information model (in the form of media campaigns) to mobilize support for their popular cause. Groups with little or no support, such as radical activist groups, often resorted to varying degrees of terrorism, media advocacy, or other forms of direct action to embarrass target organizations.

Whether public relations for activist groups should be different than for other organizations is a question that we did not address in the Excellence study and that deserves much further research. However, we can answer our third question, whether public relations works only to the benefit of the most powerful groups, in the negative. We believe that both theoretical and empirical evidence supports the idea that symmetrical public relations can work in situations of unequal power—to the benefit of the least powerful. Professionalism based on knowledge and empowerment provides the key to breaking the dilemma of unequal power.

We conclude this review of the literature on the models of public relations published since the first *Excellence* book by reaffirming the proposition stated at the beginning of this chapter—that the two-way symmetrical model of public relations provides the normative ideal for excellent public relations. Nevertheless, we acknowledge that the questions asked about the symmetrical model confirm the need for constant reconceptualization of the theory.

When J. Grunig first developed the models of public relations, they were little more than what philosopher of science Dudley Shapere (1977) called an "initial vague idea" (p. 694)—a useful but undeveloped concept that stimulates additional research. Now the models have been researched and critiqued extensively, and the theory of symmetrical public relations has been developed into an improved theory. Nevertheless, further research remains necessary. As Suppe (1977) put it, a good theory is always underdetermined by data—meaning that good theories suggest more researchable ideas than scholars are able to test and support with data available at one time:

> Examination of successful, illuminating, products of science throughout its history reveals one pervasive characteristic—the most impressive achievements of science are the ones which are underdetermined by the available data. Characteristic of science is the acceptance and rejection of comprehensive theories on the basis of available data which, in principle, are insufficient to establish either the truth or falsity of these theories. (pp. 17–18).

We turn, then, to the quantitative and qualitative evidence gathered in the Excellence study to further support the symmetrical model or to suggest further reconceptualization of it.

QUANTITATIVE RESULTS RELATED TO MODELS OF PUBLIC RELATIONS

When we constructed the three questionnaires for the quantitative portion of the Excellence study, we measured the four models of public relations at three levels: (a) the worldview toward public relations of the dominant coalition (measured by the models preferred by the CEO and as predicted for the CEO by the head of public relations), (b) strategies used in communication programs for specific stakeholder publics, and (c) the knowledge available in the public relations department to practice each of the four models.

The first of these measures was based on J. Grunig and L. Grunig's (1992) review of the previous research on the models, which suggested first that the models described the organization's schema for understanding what public relations is (the worldview of the organization) more than they described the day-to-day practice of the overall public relations function. Measuring the models as worldview also was based on J. Grunig and L. Grunig's conclusion that the culture of the organization was a possible explanation of why organizations chose a model of public relations to practice.

J. Grunig and L. Grunig (1992) concluded from previous research that organizations typically practice different models for programs aimed at different publics. Therefore, we thought we could measure the actual practice of the models better by asking heads of public relations in our sample to estimate the extent to which the questions that we used to measure the models described communication programs for the three most important publics of their organization.

The measures of knowledge available to practice each of the four models was based on J. Grunig and L. Grunig's (1992) conclusion that knowledge available in a public relations department, along with culture, best explained why public relations departments practice the models that they do. They concluded, in essence, that practitioners do what they know how to do. Wetherell (1989) previously had tested and used these measures of knowledge.

These three measures of the models of public relations also mirror three characteristics of an excellent public relations department described in chapter 1 of both this book and the first *Excellence* book:

1. *The public relations department and the dominant coalition share the worldview that the communication department should reflect the two-way symmetrical model of public relations.*[6]
2. *Communication programs developed for specific publics are based on the two-way symmetrical model.*
3. *The senior public relations executive or others in the public relations unit must have the knowledge needed for the two-way symmetrical model, or the communication function will not have the potential to practice the excellent model.*

In the Excellence study, we measured the worldview of the dominant coalition toward public relations and the models used for specific communication

---

[6]In the first *Excellence* book and in chapter 1 of this book, we included the words "or the mixed-motive model" after the phrase "two-way symmetrical model." We have dropped the reference to the mixed-motive model here because of the recent conceptualization reported in this chapter that led to the conclusion that there is no difference between the two-way symmetrical and the mixed-motive models.

programs by using a 12-item scale that J. Grunig and a number of graduate students had developed at the University of Maryland—four items for each model (for details, see J. Grunig & L. Grunig, 1992). These four scales had known reliabilities, which were adequate but not high. The knowledge scales for each of the four models were developed by J. Grunig and Wetherell for use in Wetherell's (1989) thesis. These knowledge scales had higher reliabilities than the scales measuring the actual practice of the models.

After developing scales for the four models measured in these three ways, we correlated them with the scale of overall Excellence after removing all of the variables measuring the models from that scale. Recall that in chapter 3, the scales measuring both the two-way symmetrical and the two-way asymmetrical models were included in the Excellence scale—for models preferred by the CEO, models predicted by the PR head, and the knowledge in the public relations department. In this chapter, we report moderate to high correlations of all three measures of the two-way symmetrical and two-way asymmetrical models with the modified Excellence scale and no correlations or negative correlations with the press agentry and public information models.

After further analysis, however, we learned that the positive correlations of the two-way asymmetrical model with the Excellence scale largely resulted from the two-way nature of that model and not because of its asymmetrical nature. We then calculated scales for three dimensions of the models (one-way and two-way, asymmetrical and symmetrical, and mediated and interpersonal) and found that excellent public relations is characterized by two-way and symmetrical communication but not by one-way or asymmetrical communication. We also learned that excellent public relations can be either mediated or interpersonal—eliminating confusion between the press agentry and public information models and mediated communication suggested by the data.

The Worldview of the Dominant Coalition

We measured the worldview of the dominant coalition both in the CEO questionnaire and in the questionnaire completed by the head of public relations. The CEOs, or other senior managers who completed the CEO questionnaire, were presented the 12-item scale measuring the four models and were asked to estimate the extent to which each of the items described how they believed public relations should be practiced. The top communicators were asked to estimate the extent to which the same items described the way they believed the dominant coalition thought public relations should be practiced in that organization.

Table 8.1 contains the means of the resulting data and analyzes the reliability of the scales for the four models applied to the worldview of the dominant coalition—the preferences of the CEO and the predictions of the PR head for the

TABLE 8.1

Means and Reliability of the Models of Public Relations the Dominant Coalition Thinks the Organization Should Practice

Model and Question	Mean (Transformed Scale)		Item–Total Correlation		Alpha If Item Deleted	
	PR Head Predicted for CEO	CEO	PR Head Predicted for CEO	CEO	PR Head Predicted for CEO	CEO
Press Agentry Model						
The purpose of public relations is, quite simply, to get publicity for this organization.	8.73	7.63	.59	.53	.72	.61
In public relations, one mostly attempts to get favorable publicity into the media and to keep unfavorable publicity out.	10.51	9.97	.52	.43	.75	.68
The success of a public relations program can be determined from the number of people who attend an event or who use products and services.	9.22	8.20	.55	.47	.74	.65
For this organization, public relations and publicity mean essentially the same thing.	8.21	5.90	.66	.53	.67	.61
Scale Means and Cronbach's alpha	**9.17**	**7.92**			**.78**	**.70**
Public Information Model						
In public relations, nearly everyone is so busy writing news stories or producing publications that there is no time to do research.	6.90	7.68	.31	.46	.52	.62
In public relations, accurate information should be disseminated but unfavorable information should not be volunteered.	10.15	8.29	.26	.36	.55	.68
Keeping a clipping file is about the only way there is to determine the success of public relations.	5.59	4.63	.47	.54	.39	.67
Public relations is more of a neutral disseminator of information than an advocate for the organization or a mediator between management and publics.	6.76	5.53	.35	.50	.48	.59
Scale Means and Cronbach's alpha	**7.35**	**6.53**			**.56**	**.68**

(Continued)

TABLE 8.1
(Continued)

Model and Question	Mean (Transformed Scale)		Item–Total Correlation		Alpha If Item Deleted	
	PR Head Predicted for CEO	CEO	PR Head Predicted for CEO	CEO	PR Head Predicted for CEO	CEO
Two-Way Asymmetrical Model						
After completing a public relations program, research should be done to determine how effective this program has been in changing people's attitudes.	7.78	9.78	.59	.50	.57	.43
In public relations, the broad goal is to persuade publics to behave as the organization wants them to behave.	9.84	7.49	.07	.08	.85	.76
Before starting a public relations program, one should look at attitude surveys to make sure the organization and its policies are described in ways its publics would be most likely to accept.	8.12	9.95	.68	.49	.49	.42
Before beginning a public relations program, one should do research to determine public attitudes toward an organization and how they might be changed.	8.12	10.27	.68	.52	.49	.42
Scale Means and Cronbach's alpha	**8.46**	**9.37**			**.70**	**.59**
Two-Way Symmetrical Model						
The purpose of public relations is to develop mutual understanding between the management of an organization and publics the organization affects.	11.05	12.26	.51	.41	.67	.59
Before starting a public relations program, surveys or informal research should be done to find out how much management and our publics understand each other.	7.95	9.82	.48	.48	.68	.54
The purpose of public relations is to change the attitudes and behavior of management as much as it is to change the attitudes and behaviors of publics.	6.66	8.77	.55	.39	.64	.61
Public relations should provide mediation for the organization—to help management and publics negotiate conflict.	7.24	8.49	.53	.44	.66	.57
Scale Means and Cronbach's alpha	**8.23**	**9.83**			**.72**	**.65**

Note. N for the PR Head's Prediction for the CEO = 364. N for the CEOs = 280.

dominant coalition.[7] The means in Table 8.1 are generally below the hypothetical average score of 10 on the transformed scale for all items in the questionnaire. Means below 10 would suggest that neither the top communicators nor the CEOs believed these items described the public relations function in their organization as well as many other items in the questionnaires. However, the average for most items did not fall far below the hypothetical average of 10.

The reliabilities for the four scales applied to these two estimates of the worldview for public relations in the organization generally were moderately high—ranging from a low of .56 on the PR head's prediction for the public information model to .78 for the PR head's prediction for the press agentry model. Most of the reliabilities were in the .70s range. They were higher than the average reliabilities reported by J. Grunig and L. Grunig (1992) for seven studies at the University of Maryland in which the indexes were developed and about the same as reported by Wetherell (1989) in a study in which the fractionation scale also was used. (The fractionation scale improves the reliabilities of the scales.) The reliabilities of these scales were lower than for many of the other indexes developed in the Excellence study, but most of the other scales had more than four items in them and reliabilities increase as more items are added to a scale.

With the exception of one item used in the two-way asymmetrical scale, the reliability could not have been improved by removing one or more items from the scale. The exception was the second item used to measure the two-way asymmetrical model: "In public relations, the broad goal is to persuade publics to behave as the organization wants them to behave." Without this item, the alpha for the two-way asymmetrical model preferred by the CEO would have increased from .59 to .76. The top communicator's predicted preference for that same model by the dominant coalition would have increased from .70 to .85.

That item, however, represents what we believe is the truest description of an asymmetrical purpose in the two-way asymmetrical scale. The other three items measured the extent to *which formative or evaluative research* was used to achieve what we had believed to be asymmetrical objectives such as identifying attitudes of publics and determining how those attitudes might be changed. In retrospect, these other three items seem to measure the dominant coalition's preference for research in general rather than the use of research to accomplish asymmetrical objectives. Later we show that this scale measures a preference for *two-way* communication more than it measures a preference for two-way *asymmetrical* communication and that our research participants apparently did

---

[7]In Tables 8.1 to 8.3 and 8.5 to 8.7 we included all public relations heads in the analysis even if they were not the heads of a central public relations unit—a possible N of 407, although the number usually is lower because of missing data. In Table 8.4, we included only the heads of the central public relations department when we correlated the predictions of the PR head for the dominant coalition with the Excellence scale to avoid a problem of lack of independence. Data for programs for specific publics were based on all public relations heads in the sample.

not distinguish between the use of research for symmetrical and asymmetrical purposes.

Because the one item that lowered reliability was the best operational definition of asymmetrical communication as we understand the concept, we left that item in the initial scale of the two-way asymmetrical model. We did correlate that single item with the Excellence scale, however, to show the difference between two-way and asymmetrical communication.

The means for the overall scales in Table 8.1 show that in contrast to most of the previous studies of the actual practice of the models reported in J. Grunig and L. Grunig (1992), the CEOs in this research preferred the two-way models to the press agentry and public information models. The two-way symmetrical was the model most preferred by CEOs, followed closely by the two-way asymmetrical model. The means for the press agentry and especially for the public information model were considerably lower. In short, the CEOs in this study did not have a prevailing worldview that public relations should be one-way or asymmetrical, as J. Grunig (1989) had conjectured. Instead their worldview seemed to reflect a preference for two-way and symmetrical public relations.

The top communicators anticipated these preferences to a large extent. They were wrong when they predicted that the dominant coalition would most prefer the press agentry model, although the means for their predictions for the two-way models were not much lower. They also predicted that the CEOs would prefer the two-way asymmetrical model to the two-way symmetrical model, but the difference was slight. In general, the heads of public relations believed the dominant coalition wanted press agentry and asymmetrical communication more than the CEO actually preferred.

Knowledge to Practice the Four Models

Table 8.2 reports the means and the analysis of reliability for the four-item scales that we developed to measure the extent to which a public relations department had the knowledge to practice each of the four models of public relations. Overall, the means for these knowledge variables—especially for the press agentry and public information scales—were higher than the means of the worldview items. In addition, the knowledge scales were more reliable than were the worldview scales—with Cronbach's alphas of .83 for the press agentry, .75 for the public information, .70 for the two-way asymmetrical, and .75 for the two-way symmetrical model. Alpha could not be increased by eliminating any of the items.

The means for the press agentry and public information models were above the hypothetical average of 10; the means for the two-way models were below 10. In this sample, public relations departments reported more knowledge to practice the traditional models of public relations than to practice the two-way and research-based models.

TABLE 8.2

Means and Reliability of Knowledge to Practice the Models
of Public Relations in the Public Relations Department,
as Reported by the Head of Public Relations

Model and Question	Mean (Transformed Scale)	Item–Total Correlation	Alpha If Item Deleted
Please estimate the knowledge your department has to:			
Press Agentry Model			
Convince a reporter to publicize your organization.	10.93	.75	.77
Get your organization's name into the media.	11.70	.78	.75
Keep bad publicity out of the media.	8.93	.57	.85
Get maximum publicity for a staged event.	10.46	.62	.82
Scale Mean and Cronbach's alpha	**10.50**		**.84**
Public Information Model			
Provide objective information about your organization.	11.77	.44	.75
Understand the news values of journalists.	11.95	.67	.62
Prepare news stories that reporters will use.	11.07	.67	.61
Perform as journalists inside your organization.	10.77	.48	.75
Scale Mean and Cronbach's alpha	**11.39**		**.75**
Two-Way Asymmetrical Model			
Get publics to behave as your organization wants.	9.37	.44	.67
Use attitude theory in a campaign.	5.93	.55	.59
Manipulate publics scientifically.	5.02	.67	.51
Persuade a public that your organization is right on an issue.	10.63	.34	.74
Scale Mean and Cronbach's alpha	**7.74**		**.70**
Two-Way Symmetrical Model			
Determine how publics react to the organization.	9.97	.51	.71
Negotiate with an activist group.	7.04	.61	.65
Use theories of conflict resolution in dealing with publics.	7.23	.55	.68
Help management to understand the opinion of particular publics.	10.66	.52	.70
Scale Mean and Cronbach's alpha	**8.73**		**.75**

Note. N = 370.

Practice of the Four Models in Eight Communication Programs

Table 8.3 reports the means and Cronbach's alphas for the PR head's estimation of the extent to which his or her department practiced each of the four models in communication programs for eight of the major publics reported in the Excellence study. (In this table, we did not include the item–total correlations and the alphas if an item were removed in order to reduce its complexity.) In chapter 9, we analyzed the origins and outcomes of programs for the first seven of these publics. In this chapter, we also analyzed the eighth most important public, donors, because of the potential application of the models to that category of

TABLE 8.3

Means and Reliability of the Models of Public Relations Actually
Practiced in Eight Communication Programs for Specific Types
of Publics, as Reported by the Head of Public Relations

Communication Program (N)	Press Agentry Model	Public Information Model	Two-Way Asymmetrical Model	Two-Way Symmetrical Model
Means (Transformed Scale)				
Employees (184)	4.17	5.19	7.38	8.31
Media (247)	7.87	7.01	6.16	7.19
Investors (53)	4.72	4.75	6.73	7.30
Community (141)	8.00	5.98	7.11	7.70
Customers (97)	7.63	5.66	7.95	7.31
Government (55)	5.45	5.14	7.35	7.78
Members (56)	6.13	5.41	6.80	7.18
Donors (22)	8.43	7.36	6.61	7.51
Cronbach's alpha				
Employees (184)	.61	.27	.66	.58
Media (247)	.67	.58	.68	.45
Investors (53)	.59	.62	.79	.44
Community (141)	.62	.49	.78	.69
Customers (97)	.66	.48	.59	.36
Government (55)	.73	.50	.64	.48
Members (56)	.52	.47	.71	.55
Donors (22)	.33	.49	.23	.65

publics. The PR heads in our sample reported only 22 donor relations programs,
however, making analysis difficult.

Most of the alphas for these specific scales were comparable to those we reported for the preferences of the dominant coalition for the models of public relations, although a few of them are unacceptably low. In most cases, the low
alphas resulted because individual items did not fit well with a specific program.
Eliminating certain items would have increased the low aphas of the two-way
symmetrical model for investors, the public information and two-way symmetrical models for customers, and the press agentry model for donors to at least
.50 and generally to .60. For every public, eliminating the same item on the purpose of public relations in the two-way asymmetrical model that reduced reliability in the worldview questions also would have improved the alphas here.
The alphas of the public information model for employees and the two-way
symmetrical model for media could not be improved by eliminating items—
most likely because the wording of the items did not fit these programs well.

To maintain consistency in the scales, however, we decided to leave all of the
items in the scales because different items were problematic for different programs. We also wanted to keep the problematic item in the two-way asymmetrical scale, again, because of its value in describing an asymmetrical purpose of

public relations. The low reliabilities for some models for some programs should be kept in mind, however, when we analyze relationships with these models.

As with the worldview questions, the means for the models applied to these eight publics were all below the hypothetical average of 10. The lowest means generally were for the public information model, although the means for the press agentry model were particularly low for investors, government, and members.

In contrast to the claims in the literature that the two-way symmetrical model is only an idealistic, normative model, the means for that model in Table 8.3 were the highest or almost the highest for all eight of these programs. For the media, the community, customers, and donors the press agentry model had only a slightly higher mean than the two-way symmetrical model. For customers, the two-way asymmetrical model also was slightly higher—probably reflecting the marketing origin of that model.

This mixture of the press agentry model and the two-way symmetrical model for the media, the community, customers, and donors probably occurred because of the mediated nature of these programs. Respondents seemed to equate the press agentry model with mediated communication in these programs—a phenomenon we explore later by isolating mediated and interpersonal dimensions of the models.

Correlations With the Excellence Scale

Now that we have constructed the necessary scales to measure the four models of public relations in three ways, we can examine Table 8.4 for evidence to support our major proposition of this chapter—that the two-way symmetrical model will be a major component of excellence in public relations and communication management. Table 8.4 does provide a strong and, with a few exceptions, consistent pattern of support for the symmetrical proposition. It also shows, however, that the two-way asymmetrical model consistently correlates with excellence in a pattern almost identical to that of the two-way symmetrical model.

Table 8.4 shows that both two-way models, symmetrical and asymmetrical, correlate positively and significantly with the Excellence scale for the worldview of public relations preferred by the CEO and predicted by the PR head for the dominant coalition, for the knowledge to practice these two models in the department, and for the application of the models to five of the eight programs included in this analysis. The correlations of the two-way models for member programs and donor programs are positive but low. These low correlations are not statistically significant, however, most likely because of the small sample size for these two programs.

TABLE 8.4
Pearson Correlations of Models of Public Relations
With Excellence Scale With Models Removed

Application of Model (N)	Press Agentry Model	Public Information Model	Two-Way Asymmetrical Model	Two-Way Symmetrical Model
PR Head Predicted for CEO (294)	−.04	−.10	.28**	.37**
CEO (270)	−.01	−.09	.37**	.35**
Knowledge in PR Department (297)	.45**	.44**	.43**	.48**
Employees (184)	.06	−.02	.38**	.47**
Media (247)	−.12	−.12	.22**	.22**
Investors (53)	.01	.04	.36**	.32**
Community (141)	.02	−.09	.26**	.25**
Customers (97)	.01	.03	.44**	.37**
Government (55)	−.06	.07	.05	.09
Members (56)	−.18	−.16	.18	.15
Donors (22)	.16	.19	.10	.20

$*p < .05.$ $**p < .01.$

There are no positive correlations for these two models with the Excellence scale for government programs, however. The lack of correlation with government programs appears also for other variables in chapter 9, reflecting a pattern that we found throughout the results for specific programs. As explained in Dozier with L. Grunig and J. Grunig (1996), governmental relations programs often are run by lawyers or former politicians with limited knowledge of public relations and, probably for this reason, these programs do not follow the same patterns as other public relations programs.

At the same time, Table 8.4 shows a consistent pattern of no correlations or negative correlations of the press agentry and public information models with the Excellence scale. The exceptions are the high positive correlations of knowledge to practice all four models with the Excellence scale. Those correlations suggest that excellent departments possess more knowledge to practice all types of public relations than do less excellent departments. Not only do they know how to practice the two-way models better, they also know how to practice the traditional models better.

These correlational data strongly support the central proposition of this chapter—the primacy of the two-way symmetrical model in excellent public relations. However, they also suggest that the two-way asymmetrical model is equally important. Therefore, we tried to determine whether those correlations occurred because of the *asymmetrical* nature of the two-way asymmetrical model or because of its *two-way*, research-based nature. To do so, we correlated the one item in the two-way asymmetrical scale that describes an asymmetrical purpose for communication, but that was not a reliable indicator in the scale, with the Excellence scale with the models variables removed. Again, that item read, "In public relations, the broad goal is to persuade publics to behave as the organization wants them to behave."

When that item was used to measure the CEO's preference for models and the PR head's prediction of the models preferred by the CEO, it did have a small but significant correlation with the modified Excellence scale ($r = .17$, $p < .01$; $r = .16$, $p < .01$). These correlations were much smaller than the correlations of the overall two-way asymmetrical scale with that scale, however ($r = .28$ and $r = .37$). The correlations of this item with the modified Excellence scale when the head of public relations applied them to the eight specific programs were all negative or small and nonsignificant—with one exception.[8] For community relations programs, the item correlated at $r = .20$ ($p < .05$) with the modified scale. There seems to be no logical explanation of why this variable would correlate with excellence for community relations and not for the other programs. Most likely, the correlation occurred by chance.

These correlations do suggest that CEOs with excellent communication departments harbor a small interest in purely asymmetrical objectives for public relations and that their top communication executives recognize this preference. However, the public relations departments did not seem to apply a pure asymmetrical objective in specific programs. Rather than suggesting that organizations with excellent communication departments prefer and practice both the two-way asymmetrical and the two-way symmetrical model, though, they suggest that the dominant coalition prefers a two-way research-based communication program and that it prefers a symmetrical purpose for public relations to an asymmetrical purpose. In addition, the data show that the department applies two-way methods to specific programs within a framework of a symmetrical purpose.

Confirmatory Factor Analysis of the Four Models

In the Excellence study, as we have just seen, and in all of the other studies of the models reported in J. Grunig and L. Grunig (1992), researchers have found a positive correlation between the two two-way models and between the two one-way models. That pattern could indicate—empirically at least—that there are only two models of public relations rather than four. If the data were to show that there are only two models, we would be forced to retreat conceptually to J. Grunig's (1976) original notion that there are only two models—essentially one-way and two-way models—that do not distinguish between symmetrical and asymmetrical purposes of communication.

One way to test whether a theory of two models would fit the data better than a theory of four models would be to conduct an exploratory factor analysis

---

[8]The Pearson's correlation coefficients were as follows: employees ($r = .13$, n.s.), media ($r = .01$, n.s.), investors ($r = -.01$, n.s.), customers ($r = -.06$, n.s.), government ($r = -.20$, n.s.), members ($r = -.07$, n.s.), and donors ($r = .19$, n.s.).

of all 16 indicators and let the computer determine any patterns of relationships among the indicators. With exploratory factor analysis, a researcher essentially abandons the theory that guided the writing of the indicators and lets the computer determine whether a different theory is needed to explain the intercorrelations among the indicators.

In the first *Excellence* book, J. Grunig and L. Grunig (1992) reviewed several studies in which exploratory factor analyses were conducted on the indicators of the models. All of the studies produced a two-factor solution rather than a four-factor solution—supporting the idea that empirically there are only two models even though theory suggested that there are four. The new theory indicated by this empirical analysis would be that there are only two models of public relations explained by the indicators we have written and that the distinction between a symmetrical and an asymmetrical purpose is not relevant to understanding how public relations actually is practiced.

In the Excellence study, we did conduct an exploratory factor analysis of the indicators of the models preferred by the CEO, knowledge to practice the models, and the actual application of the models in programs for eight publics. As in previous studies, these exploratory factor analyses clustered the indicators into two factors; and a four-factor solution did not cluster the items into the four models they were supposed to measure.

J. Grunig and L. Grunig (1992), however, pointed out that a confirmatory factor analysis would provide a better test of our theory of four models than would an exploratory factor analysis. With exploratory factor analysis, the statistical program correlates and clusters items into empirical factors with no guidance from theory. In a real sense, we let the computer do our thinking for us. With confirmatory factor analysis, the researcher can specify which items theoretically should fit on each factor; the computer confirms whether the fit of the data to the theory is a good one. Confirmatory factor analysis also allows the researcher to compare alternative theoretical structures with the original one to see which theory fits the data best. With confirmatory factor analysis, the researcher does the thinking and the statistical program reveals how well each alternative theory explains the data.[9]

To test our four-model theory of public relations, we conducted a confirmatory factor analysis of the items used to measure the models preferred by the CEO, the models the PR head predicted the dominant coalition would prefer, the knowledge in the public relations department to practice the four models, and the actual practice of the models in media relations programs. We analyzed the models only for media relations programs because the sample size was larg-

---

[9]Exploratory factor analysis is done with a conventional factor analysis program in a statistical package such as SPSS. Confirmatory factor analysis is done with a program that does structural equation modeling such as EQS, LISREL, or AMOS. We used the EQS program for the analysis reported here.

est for that program. The sample size for the other programs was not large enough to produce a valid outcome.[10]

The first step in confirmatory factor analysis is a check on the reliability of the items used to measure each factor. If the reliability of an indicator is too low to allow an adequate fit of the data, that indicator is eliminated. For the two-way asymmetrical model, we had to remove the problematic indicator we have discussed previously from the analysis of the models predicted for the CEO, of the models preferred by the CEO, and of the models practiced in media relations programs. This item, which read, "In public relations, the broad goal is to persuade publics to behave as the organization wants them to behave," was the best pure descriptor of an asymmetrical intent for a program. Removing that item, therefore, transformed the two-way asymmetrical model into a two-way model characterized by using formative and evaluative research in public relations.

For the confirmatory factor analysis of the CEO's preferred models, one item also was removed from the public information factor: "In public relations, accurate information should be disseminated but unfavorable information should not be volunteered." This item also contributed little to alpha in Table 8.1, and eliminating it did not change the nature of the public information index.

Four items were removed for the confirmatory factor analysis of the items measuring knowledge to practice the four models. One item was removed from the press agentry factor: "Keep bad publicity out of the media." Two were removed from the public information factor: "Provide objective information about your organization" and "Perform as journalists inside your organization." One item was removed from the two-way asymmetrical factor: "Persuade a public that your organization is right on an issue." A review of Table 8.2 shows that these items had little effect on Cronbach's alpha. Removing them also did not change the theoretical meaning of the remaining four factors.

For the confirmatory factor analysis of the items measuring the practice of the four models in media relations programs, one item was removed from the press agentry factor: "We determined how successful this program was from the number of people who attended an event or who used our products or services." One item also was removed from the two-way symmetrical factor: "Before starting this program, we did surveys or informal research to find out how much management and our publics understood each other." Both of these items described a type of formative or evaluative research, which the PR heads participating in the survey apparently did not believe described their media relations programs. Removing either variable did not affect the nature of the theoretical model underlying the indicators.

---

[10]We acknowledge the assistance of Colin Elliot, a former graduate student at the University of Maryland, in conducting this confirmatory factor analysis.

For each of the four analyses, we compared the fit of four different solutions describing the relationships among the four models of public relations. These four solutions consisted of four independent factors, four separate factors that all were allowed to covary, two pairs of factors that were allowed to covary, and two independent factors. Error covariances were added when they improved the fit of the model to the data. Four independent factors would show that the four models are discrete and that they are seldom practiced or preferred together. Two independent factors would show that there are only two models and that they are not practiced or preferred together. The other solutions would show that there are four models but that they are practiced or preferred together at times.

Figures 8.1 to 8.4 display the final solutions that maximized the Comparative Fit Index (CFI) for each of the four applications of the models in the Excellence study. In none of these applications did a two-factor solution provide the best fit of the data—confirming J. Grunig and L. Grunig's (1992) prediction that the four models would hold up in a confirmatory factor analysis even though they could not be produced in an exploratory factor analysis. Beyond that result, each model is somewhat different and reflects varying application of the models or preferences for the models in these different applications.

For both applications of the models to the worldview of the dominant coalition, the optimal solution was two pairs of covarying factors. That is, the PR heads predicted that the CEOs would distinguish among the four models but that if they preferred one one-way or one two-way model they also would prefer the other (Fig. 8.1). The same was true for the actual preferences of the CEOs (Fig. 8.2). These solutions thus provide a satisfactory explanation of the correlations typically found between the two two-way models and the two one-way models: CEOs can distinguish among the four models, but they seem to think both two-way models should be practiced at the same time or both one-way models.

For the knowledge to practice the four models, the optimal solution was four covarying factors. This means that there are four discrete types of knowledge that mirror the models of public relations but that departments typically possess all four types of knowledge and do not possess knowledge of, say, two-way models to the exclusion of knowledge of one-way models. That solution explains the high correlations of all four types of knowledge with the Excellence scale that appeared previously in Table 8.4.

Finally, for the actual application of the four models to media relations programs, the optimal solution also was four covarying factors. That solution suggests that there are four discrete models practiced in media relations but that media relations programs tend to include all four—especially the two-way models and the public information model. The final model seems to confirm that our survey participants tended to confuse the one-way models with mediated forms of communication, as we have suggested previously. Mediated communication, of course, can be two-way and symmetrical, although most media re-

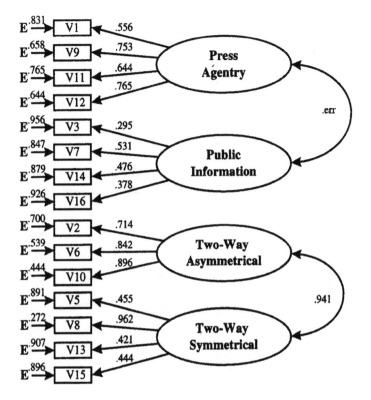

All paths are significant at .05 level.
CFI=.915
X²=261.747, 80 degrees of freedom

FIG. 8.1. Confirmatory factor analysis for models of public relations predicted by the public relations head for the CEO (two pairs of covarying factors).

lations programs probably are not based on research and mostly disseminate information without regard for the information needs of publics. Our analysis, though, suggests that excellent media relations programs combine elements of symmetrical and two-way communication with the traditional public information model used in media relations.

The confirmatory factor analysis, therefore, supports the usefulness of our original four-model theory of public relations purpose and behavior and helps to explain why certain models are preferred or practiced together. However, we must add that the CFIs show an adequate but not an excellent fit of the data. A CFI of .90 is considered the minimum acceptable level, and higher CFIs show progressively better fits. The best fits were for the knowledge to practice the

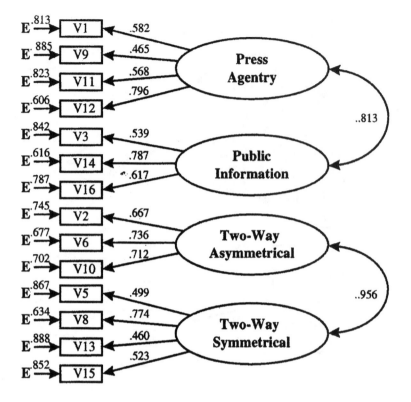

All paths are significant at .05 level.
CFI=.940
X²=129.775, 71 degrees of freedom

FIG. 8.2   Confirmatory factor analysis for models of public relations preferred by the CEO (two pairs of covarying factors).

models (CFI = .950) and the CEO's preference for models (CFI = .940). The worst fits were for the practice of the models in media relations programs (CFI = .916) and the PR heads' prediction for the dominant coalition (CFI = .915).

The measures of the knowledge needed to practice the four models provided the best fit in this confirmatory factor analysis. These indexes also had the highest Cronbach's alphas and the highest correlations with the Excellence scale—confirming that these relatively new measures of knowledge are the best indicators of the presence of the four models of public relations.

The confirmatory factor analysis as well as previous correlational analyses suggest, however, that there are dimensions underlying the four models, especially two-way communication and mediated communication, that could be measured both to improve our measures of the models of public relations and

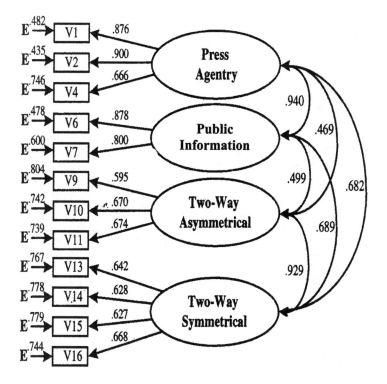

All paths are significant at .05 level.
CFI=.950
X²=151.445, 44 degrees of freedom

FIG. 8.3. Confirmatory factor analysis of knowledge to practice the models of public relations as reported by the public relations head (four covarying factors).

to refine the conceptualization of the theory itself. In our final quantitative analysis, we identify and measure those underlying dimensions and correlate them with the Excellence scale.

From Models to Dimensions of Public Relations Behavior

The four models of public relations began as a vague, general idea that has stimulated a great deal of positive, descriptive research on how public relations is practiced in many types of organizations and in many countries. The two-way symmetrical model also has focused attention on how to build a normative model of ethical and socially responsible public relations. As a result, the models have served a valuable function for the public relations discipline.

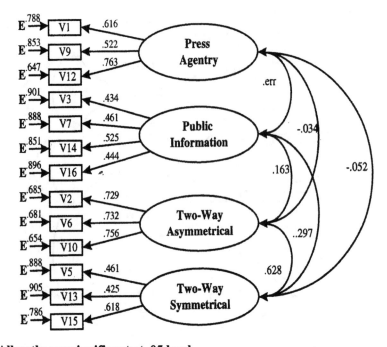

All paths are significant at .05 level.
CFI=.916
X^2=111.943, 58 degrees of freedom

FIG. 8.4. Confirmatory factor analysis of the models of public relations used in media relations programs (four covarying factors).

The analyses of the models we have reported thus far from the Excellence study suggest, however, that it is time to move on from the four, or more, models of public relations to develop a more comprehensive theory that goes beyond the typology represented by the four models. Typologies are a useful way to begin the development of a theory, but for science and scholarship to progress we need to move beyond typologies to conceptualize and measure the theoretical dimensions that underlie a typology.

To develop this more comprehensive theory, we can isolate four underlying variables that together define the models and that we have alluded to in analyzing the Excellence data thus far. The first set of these variables is *symmetry and asymmetry,* or the extent to which collaboration and advocacy describe public relations strategy or behavior. The second set of variables includes the extent to which public relations is *one-way or two-way.* These variables were part of J. Grunig's (1984) original conceptualization of the models.

In addition, the results from the Excellence study that we have analyzed thus far have suggested that direction of communication should be measured separately from symmetry and asymmetry. Three of the four indicators of the two-way asymmetrical model measured the extent to which organizations used asymmetrical forms of research in their public relations practice. These research-based variables were the most reliable of the four indicators and were the only variables that were reliable enough to use to measure the two-way asymmetrical model in the confirmatory factor analysis. The fourth indicator, which simply stated that the purpose of public relations was to persuade publics to behave as the organization wanted them to behave, has not correlated with the Excellence scale.

Those results, therefore, have suggested that the strong showing of the asymmetrical model in the Excellence factor resulted more from use of the research activities measured by the index than from the asymmetrical nature of that research. Research participants seem not to distinguish *asymmetrical* research from *symmetrical* research, or research in general.

The third set of variables is the use of *mediated and interpersonal forms of communication.* As we have seen, our survey participants seem to have equated the one-way models—especially the public information model—with mediated communication in describing the application of the models to programs for particular publics and especially to media relations.

J. Grunig et al. (1995) first called attention to interpersonal communication as an element of the models when they identified what they called a personal influence model of public relations in India, Taiwan, Greece, and the United States. They pointed out that this model is common in lobbying and in media relations, where public relations practitioners use interpersonal relationships and connections to facilitate relationships. In their research, J. Grunig and his colleagues found these interpersonal connections usually to be asymmetrical and manipulative; but they concluded that they could be symmetrical as well as asymmetrical.

We also have observed that participants in our research projects sometimes have equated the two-way models—especially the two-way symmetrical model—with interpersonal communication and the one-way models with mediated communication. In actuality, all four models could be practiced through mediated or interpersonal communication. However, the one-way models usually are implemented through mediated communication.

The fourth dimension is the extent to which public relations practice is *ethical.* Generally, we have said that the symmetrical model is inherently ethical and that the other models can be ethical, depending on the rules used to ensure ethical practice (J. Grunig & L. Grunig, 1996; J. Grunig & White, 1992).

Given these four dimensions, we can describe the original models as points on four continuous variables. The *press agentry model,* for example, is relatively one-way, asymmetrical, and unethical and characterized mostly by mediated communication. The *public information model* also is one-way and asymmetrical and characterized mostly by mediated communication, but it is generally more ethical than the press agentry model. The *two-way asymmetrical model* is two-way and asymmetrical and can be practiced either ethically or unethically and through either mediated or interpersonal communication. The *two-way symmetrical model* is two-way, symmetrical, and nearly always ethical; it can be implemented through either mediated or interpersonal communication.

We did not measure ethical communication in the Excellence study, but we have been able to develop scales for each of the other three dimensions underlying the models of public relations from the data collected in the study. To do so, we reconfigured the items used to measure the four models for specific communication programs such as media and employees according to the dimension that they logically seemed to fit best. We also used several items that we had developed for other purposes in the Excellence study—to measure whether research was used to develop the eight specific programs for different stakeholder publics and to determine whether different types of mediated and interpersonal communication activities had been used to implement the programs.

We tested the reliability of these new scales on the four most common communication programs, which had the largest sample sizes for analysis. These were programs for employees, the media, the community, and customers. Preliminary factor analysis confirmed that the items we chose loaded on single factors and, therefore, that we had chosen appropriate items for these new scales. We then conducted a reliability analysis of the new scales. We compared the reliability of a single direction scale (a continuum from one-way to two-way) and a single symmetry scale (a continuum from asymmetrical to symmetrical) with separate scales for one-way, two-way, symmetrical, and asymmetrical communication to determine whether to use combined or separate scales. The reliabilities for the separate two-way and symmetrical scales were higher than for the combined scales, so we have used separate scales in the analyses that follow. Because mediated and interpersonal communication never seemed to be mutually exclusive, we tested only separate scales for these two forms of communication.

Table 8.5 reports the results of the reliability analysis for the two-way and the one-way scales. Table 8.6 reports reliability results for the symmetrical and asymmetrical scales, and Table 8.7 reports results for the mediated and interpersonal scales. The two-way scale was especially reliable, with Cronbach's alphas in the general area of .80. Alphas for the one-way scale ranged from .51 for employees to .76 for media. Alphas for symmetrical communication ranged from .62 for employees to .72 for customers. The alphas for asymmetrical communication ranged from .51 to .58, but this scale had only three items—limiting the size of the alpha. The alphas for mediated communication all were in the .70 range. Those for interpersonal communication ranged from .57 for customers to .72 for employees. This scale contained only four items, however. For a few

TABLE 8.5

Reliability of One-Way and Two-Way Dimensions of Employee, Media, Community, and Customer Communication Programs

Dimension and Item	Item–Total Correlation				Alpha If Item Deleted			
	Employees	Media	Community	Customers	Employees	Media	Community	Customers
Two-Way Communication								
After completing a public relations program, research should be done to determine how effective this program has been in changing people's attitudes.	.58	.56	.74	.66	.74	.73	.82	.80
Before starting a public relations program, one should look at attitude surveys to make sure the organization and its policies are described in ways its publics would be most likely to accept.	.56	.51	.58	.64	.74	.74	.84	.80
Before starting a public relations program, surveys or informal research should be done to find out how much management and our publics understand each other.	.59	.58	.64	.56	.74	.72	.82	.81
Before beginning a public relations program, one should do research to determine public attitudes toward an organization and how they might be changed.	.57	.50	.75	.62	.74	.74	.84	.80
Techniques such as VALS or PRIZM are used to segment publics.	.12	.31	.39	.51	.81	.76	.86	.82
Focus groups are used to research the target public.	.59	.38	.59	.48	.74	.76	.84	.82
The actual communication program is based on research on the issue and public.	.59	.43	.74	.69	.74	.75	.82	.79
At budget time, funding depends on the demonstrated effectiveness of this program.	.28	.41	.38	.38	.78	.76	.86	.83
Public relations personnel provide management with information gained through this program.	.35	.40	.36	.33	.77	.76	.86	.83
Cronbach's alpha					**.78**	**.77**	**.86**	**.83**

(Continued)

TABLE 8.5
(Continued)

Dimension and Item	Item–Total Correlation				Alpha If Item Deleted			
	Employees	Media	Community	Customers	Employees	Media	Community	Customers
One-Way Communication								
The purpose of public relations, is, quite simply to get publicity for this organization.	.30	.53	.37	.44	.45	.71	.53	.64
In public relations, nearly everyone is so busy writing news stories or producing publications that there is no time to do research.	.14	.52	.33	.43	.56	.71	.55	.64
The success of a public relations program can be determined from the number of people who attend an event or who use products and services.	.25	.42	.28	.48	.47	.74	.57	.63
For this organization, public relations and publicity mean essentially the same thing.	.52	.59	.49	.41	.35	.69	.47	.64
Keeping a clipping file is about the only way there is to determine the success of public relations.	.34	.48	.39	.38	.45	.72	.52	.66
Public relations is more of a neutral disseminator of information than an advocate for the organization or a mediator between management and publics.	.19	.44	.13	.43	.50	.73	.63	.64
Cronbach's alpha					**.51**	**.76**	**.59**	**.68**
N	184	247	141	97				

TABLE 8.6

Reliability of Symmetrical and Asymmetrical Dimensions of Employee, Media, Community, and Customer Communication Programs

Dimension and Item	Item–Total Correlation				Alpha If Item Deleted			
	Employees	Media	Community	Customers	Employees	Media	Community	Customers
Symmetrical Communication								
The purpose of public relations is to develop mutual understanding between the management of an organization and publics the organization affects.	.39	.39	.45	.44	.56	.63	.62	.69
The purpose of public relations is to change the attitudes and behavior of management as much as it is to change the attitudes and behaviors of publics.	.25	.32	.53	.40	.65	.66	.58	.71
Public relations should provide mediation for the organization—to help management and publics negotiate conflict.	.40	.40	.43	.47	.55	.62	.63	.68
Reviewed management decisions to identify public relations problems.	.45	.49	.36	.56	.53	.59	.66	.65
Identified a public relations problem by reviewing the extent to which the organization has been socially responsible.	.46	.52	.41	.63	.51	.56	.64	.62
Cronbach's alpha					**.62**	**.67**	**.68**	**.72**
Asymmetrical Communication								
In public relations, the broad goal is to persuade publics to behave as the organization wants them to behave.	.21	.29	.26	.55	.58	.57	.62	.18
In public relations, accurate information should be disseminated but unfavorable information should not be volunteered.	.39	.40	.39	.09	.30	.39	.40	.79
In public relations, one mostly attempts to get favorable publicity into the media and to keep unfavorable publicity out.	.38	.40	.44	.60	.31	.39	.30	.09
Cronbach's alpha					**.51**	**.55**	**.55**	**.58**
N	184	247	141	97				

TABLE 8.7

Reliability of the Mediated and Interpersonal Dimensions of Employee, Media, Community, and Customer Communication Programs

Dimension and Item	Item–Total Correlation				Alpha If Item Deleted			
	Employees	Media	Community	Customers	Employees	Media	Community	Customers
Mediated Communication								
This program utilizes press releases, press conferences, or other contacts with the media.	.29	.39	.51	.30	.71	.70	.75	.70
Magazines, newsletters, brochures, or other publications are produced in this program.	.44	.56	.55	.33	.67	.65	.74	.70
This program uses special events, tours, or open houses.	.56	.59	.63	.60	.64	.65	.72	.62
This program uses tapes, films, or other AV materials.	.61	.36	.57	.67	.62	.71	.74	.60
This program uses advertising or other forms of paid space in the media.	.25	.28	.38	.28	.71	.72	.78	.71
Personnel in this program write speeches or position papers.	.50	.48	.44	.46	.66	.67	.76	.67
This program publicizes products or services.	.33	.39	.45	.29	.71	.70	.76	.71
Cronbach's alpha					**.71**	**.72**	**.78**	**.71**
Interpersonal Communication								
Contacts are made with government officials in this program.	.58	.33	.30	.34	.62	.57	.60	.51
Public relations personnel or senior managers meet personally with leaders of activist groups.	.63	.46	.47	.39	.59	.46	.56	.48
This program uses interpersonal negotiating techniques to resolve conflicts.	.67	.40	.44	.35	.55	.51	.49	.51
This program makes contact with financial analysts, specialized reporters, or other experts.	.20	.34	.33	.34	.80	.56	.58	.52
Cronbach's alpha					**.72**	**.60**	**.61**	**.57**
N	184	247	141	97				

variables for different programs, we could have increased alpha by deleting one item; but we chose to include the same items in the scales for all of the programs to maintain their consistency. These new scales either were more reliable than the scales we developed for the models themselves for the individual programs or were equally reliable as the scales that had high reliability in the original analyses of the four models.

Table 8.8 reports the correlations of these six new scales with the full Excellence scale and with the Excellence scale with all of the models variables removed. The results strongly support our revised conceptualization of the dimensions of public relations behavior and their role in communication Excellence. Both forms of the Excellence scale had moderate to high correlations with two-way communication, symmetrical communication, and both mediated and interpersonal communication—as we had expected. With one exception, the correlations with one-way communication and asymmetrical communication all are negative or nonsignificant. Asymmetrical communication did have a small but significant correlation with the full Excellence scale but not with that scale when the models variables were removed.

These final results, therefore, strongly confirm that symmetrical communication is a key determinant of excellent public relations and that asymmetrical communication is not. They also suggested, however, that two-way, research-based public relations programs are perhaps the most important component of excellent public relations programs—reinforcing the role of public relations in strategic management identified in chapters 5 and 7 and that is reconfirmed in chapter 9. These results also confirm the relevance of a new model of excellent two-way communication, practiced within a symmetrical worldview of relationships among organizations and publics, that first was reported in Dozier with L. Grunig and J. Grunig (1996).

A Model of Two-way Communication in a Symmetrical Framework

We have used the quantitative results of the Excellence study as the empirical basis for revising our theory of models of public relations into a new contingency model. That model includes both symmetrical and asymmetrical elements and assumes that excellent public relations is based on research, environmental scanning, and two-way communication programs. Rather than placing the two-way asymmetrical model at one end of a continuum and the two-way symmetrical model at the other end, as J. Grunig and L. Grunig (1992) did, Dozier with L. Grunig and J. Grunig (1995) introduced the model in Fig. 8.5, which depicts either end of the continuum as asymmetrical. A public relations strategy at either end would favor the interests of either the organization or the public to the exclusion of the other. The middle of the continuum contains a symmetrical, win–win zone where organizations and publics can engage in both negotiation and persuasion.

TABLE 8.8
Pearson's Correlations of the Mediated and Interpersonal Dimensions of Employee, Media, Community, and Customer Communication Programs With the Full Excellence Scale and the Excellence Scale With Models of Public Relations Removed

Scale and Program	Full Excellence Scale	Excellence Scale With Models Removed
Two-Way Communication		
Employees	.59**	.47**
Media	.50**	.36**
Community	.53**	.38**
Customers	.51**	.48**
One-Way Communication		
Employees	.01	−.03
Media	−.14*	−.18**
Community	−.01	−.03
Customers	−.08	−.04
Symmetrical Communication		
Employees	.52**	.41**
Media	.37**	.26**
Community	.36**	.24**
Customers	.44**	.41**
Asymmetrical Communication		
Employees	.13	.14
Media	.08	.05
Community	.19*	.10
Customers	.05	.06
Mediated Communication		
Employees	.43**	.36**
Media	.38**	.31**
Community	.40**	.27**
Customers	.31**	.33**
Interpersonal Communication		
Employees	.24**	.14*
Media	.39**	.27**
Community	.44**	.37**
Customers	.33**	.27**

Note. N = 184 for employees, 247 for media, 141 for community, and 97 for customers.
*p < .05. **p < .01.

With this new model of combined two-way public relations, the difference between the mixed-motive and the two-way symmetrical model disappears. In fact, describing the symmetrical model as a mixed-motive game resolves the criticism that the symmetrical model forces the organization to sacrifice its interests for those of the public.

In the model, organizations and publics are viewed as having separate and sometimes conflicting interests. Nevertheless, negotiation and collaboration

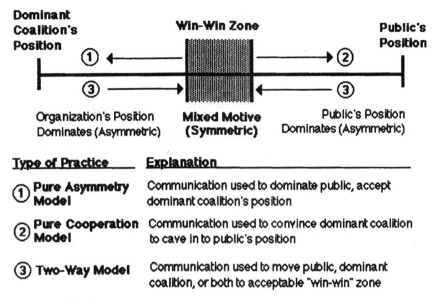

FIGURE 8.5   New model of symmetry and two-way communication.

make it possible for organizations and publics to find common ground in the
win–win zone. The model suggests that a number of outcomes are possible
within the win–win zone. Unsatisfactory and unstable relationships exist on either side of the win–win zone, with one party exploiting the other. To the left of
the win–win zone, the organization's position dominates to the public's disadvantage. To the right, the public's position dominates to the organization's disadvantage.

Communication can be used to manipulate or persuade publics to accept the
dominant coalition's position asymmetrically. This is indicated by Arrow 1 in
Fig. 8.5. Instead of negotiating for a relationship in the win–win zone, communicators try to take advantage of publics. Such practices are the zero-sum or
win–lose game played by communicators practicing pure two-way asymmetrical communication.

Communication can be used by publics to persuade the organization's dominant coalition to accept the public's position outside the win–win zone. When
communicators in the organization try to help publics to do so, they use the
pure cooperation model, which Murphy (1991) and Cancel et al. (1997), directly, and Van der Meiden (1993), indirectly, equated with the two-way symmetrical model. This practice is indicated by Arrow 2 in Fig. 8.5. As Van der
Meiden and others have pointed out, dominant coalitions are unlikely to appreciate public relations practitioners who try to persuade the organization they
work for to accept clearly undesirable positions that benefit publics at the expense of organizations.

Arrow 3 in Fig. 8.5 represents the two-way symmetrical model. Communicators negotiate with both publics and dominant coalitions to reach an outcome or relationship in the win–win zone. In communicating with publics, public relations practitioners may use research-based, two-way communication to try to persuade publics to move toward the organization's position. In communicating with dominant coalitions, they use research-based environmental scanning to try to persuade dominant coalitions to move toward the public's position. This new contingency model is a two-way, excellent, model of public relations that subsumes the symmetrical and two-way dimensions of the models of public relations. Although we found that pure asymmetry does not characterize excellent public relations (Arrow 1 in Fig. 8.5), persuasive tactics sometimes may be used to gain the best position for organizations within the win–win zone. Because such practices are bounded by a symmetrical worldview that respects the integrity of long-term relationships, the two-way model assumes that professional public relations is based on symmetrical, collaborative values (J. Grunig, 2000).[11] Practically speaking, the two-way model also means treating dominant coalitions as another public influenced by communication programs.

This new model of excellent, two-way public relations seems to provide an ideal combination of a positive and a normative theory. Positively, that is, descriptively, it offers a model of how excellent public relations departments balance the divided loyalties they encounter as they try to serve the interests of their client organization and the interests of the publics to which they have a social responsibility. Normatively, the new model specifies the ideal public relations situation in which organizations strive to reach the win–win zone as they build relationships with their publics. The characteristics of a relationship in the win–win zone also can provide criteria for evaluating the success of public relations. Finally, the model provides suggestions of strategies that public relations practitioners can use when they find the relationship tipped toward one or the other end of the continuum.

Why Do Organizations Practice Public Relations as They Do?

Throughout our program of research on the models of public relations, we have attempted to show that the models describe how public relations *is practiced* and how public relations *should be practiced*. As described in J. Grunig and L. Grunig (1992) and in the conceptual portion of this chapter, however, we also have tried to correlate the practice of or preference for the models with different organizational, environmental, and personal variables that might explain why organizations practice public relations as they do. J. Grunig and L. Grunig reported previous research had resulted in little success in connecting the mod-

---

[11]See also J. Grunig (1994) for a discussion of evidence that a symmetrical worldview has pervaded the thinking of public relations practitioners throughout history.

els to organizational structure, technology, or the product/service and political/regulatory environment of an organization, although J. Grunig (1976) found some evidence that professionalism of the practitioner predicted the use of two-way models.

Based on this research, J. Grunig and L. Grunig (1992) predicted that organizations choose a model of public relations based primarily on who holds power in the dominant coalition, pressure from activists, organizational culture, and the knowledge of the public relations department to practice different models. The effect of these variables on the choice of models also can be seen in Fig. 1.1, which was reproduced from chapter 1 of the first *Excellence* book (J. Grunig, 1992).

In the last quantitative analysis of the models data, therefore, we correlated these variables with the measures of the models that we used in the Excellence study and with the newly constructed dimensions underlying the models. We used two variables to measure the empowerment of the public relations function: the participation of the public relations head in strategic management and the membership of the top communicator in the dominant coalition. We also used the extent of activist pressure on the organization and the knowledge to practice the four models and correlated all of these variables with the models in the worldview of the CEO, in the knowledge of the public relations department to practice the programs, and in the extent to which the models and dimensions were applied to the four largest programs for publics. The most significant of these data are shown in Table 8.9.

None of these explanatory variables correlated significantly with the press agentry or public information models or with the one-way or asymmetrical dimensions, so we excluded them from Table 8.9. We also used the results from the top communicator's questionnaire, rather than the CEO's, to measure the participation of the PR head in the dominant coalition and the extent of activist pressure. The top communicator's estimates of those variables correlated positively with the models and dimensions, whereas the CEO's estimates generally did not correlate significantly or correlated lower than did the PR head's estimates. In contrast, though, the CEO's estimate that the top communicator was in the dominant coalition correlated more strongly with the models and dimensions. We surmise that these differences occurred because the top communicator has better knowledge than the CEO of activist pressure and of his or her participation in strategic management, whereas the CEO is in a better position to judge whether the top communicator is part of the dominant coalition.

Although some of the correlation coefficients in Table 8.9 are small or nonsignificant, they do show a pattern that explains a great deal about how organizations come to adopt two-way and symmetrical programs of public relations. First, it seems clear that possessing the knowledge to practice the two-way symmetrical and two-way asymmetrical models is the strongest predictor of whether those models actually are applied in programs to communicate with

TABLE 8.9
Pearson's Correlations of Factors That Predict the Two-Way
Models and Two-Way and Symmetrical Dimensions of These Models
With the Models and Dimensions

Model or Dimension and Specific Application	Participation in Strategic Management (PR Head's View)	Membership in the Dominant Coalition (CEO's View)[a]	Activist Pressure (PR Head's View)	Knowledge of Two-Way Asymmetrical Model	Knowledge of Two-Way Symmetrical Model
Two-Way Asymmetrical Model					
PR prediction for CEO	.30**	.11*	.11*	.40**	.33**
CEO preference	.25**	.17**	.21**	.23**	.17**
Knowledge in PR department	.32**	.05	.36**		
Employee programs	.45**	.10	.16*	.43**	.32**
Media programs	.23**	.09	.06	.34**	.30**
Community programs	.24**	.09	.17*	.38**	.33**
Customer programs	.36**	.22*	.10	.39**	.25*
Two-Way Symmetrical Model					
PR prediction for CEO	.32**	.09	.20**	.32**	.43**
CEO preference	.08	.21**	.18**	.11	.08
Knowledge in PR department	.33**	.07	.46**		
Employee programs	.36**	.10	.08	.35**	.37**
Media programs	.10	.06	.04	.28**	.35**
Community programs	.15	.09	.32**	.21*	.38**
Customer programs	.34**	.14	.05	.24**	.19
Two-Way Dimension					
Employee programs	.52**	.17*	.15*	.40**	.29**
Media programs	.25**	.11*	.06	.43**	.41**
Community programs	.32**	.16*	.19*	.51**	.48**
Customer programs	.45**	.19*	.13	.44**	.30**
Symmetrical Dimension					
Employee programs	.41**	.14*	.13	.40**	.34**
Media programs	.16*	.13*	.07	.27**	.40**
Community programs	.15	.13	.21*	.23**	.39**
Customer programs	.55**	.15	.04	.29**	.17

Note. $N = 364$ for the PR head's prediction for the CEO, 370 for knowledge in the PR department, 280 for CEO preferences, 184 for employee programs, 247 for media programs, 141 for community programs, and 97 for customer programs.
[a]Correlation coefficient is Kendall's Tau because the variable was dichotomous.
*$p < .05$. **$p < .01$.

specific publics. The major exception seems to be the application of the two-way symmetrical model to consumer relations. Here the predominant use of the two-way asymmetrical model in marketing seems to overwhelm the knowledge of the two-way symmetrical model in the public relations department.

Likewise, the greater the knowledge to practice both two-way models, the more likely it is that organizations will practice the two-way and the symmetrical dimensions of the models. Knowledge of the two-way asymmetrical model particularly predicts application of the two-way dimension, and knowledge of the two-way symmetrical model best predicts the application of the symmetrical dimension to communication programs.[12] Consumer programs again were the exception.

Activist pressure, in turn, helps to explain why some organizations develop knowledge to practice two-way asymmetrical and symmetrical communication. Activist pressure also helps to explain why some CEOs prefer the two-way models—especially the two-way symmetrical model. Finally, Table 8.9 shows that empowering the public relations department is particularly related to the two-way dimension of the models—the use of research to scan the environment and to plan and evaluate programs. Public relations is allowed to participate in strategic management and, to some extent, becomes a member of the dominant coalition when it has the knowledge to conduct research that brings information into the strategic management process.

The process of developing an excellent public relations program, therefore, seems to work like this. Activist pressure causes the dominant coalition to recognize the need for greater two-way and symmetrical expertise in the public relations department. Therefore, more knowledgeable practitioners are hired, people who use research and symmetrical communication in their public relations programs. Research, in particular, makes the top communicator useful in strategic planning—therefore gaining him or her a seat at the decision-making table and, occasionally, membership in the dominant coalition.

In addition to this pattern, we also correlated the mediated and interpersonal dimensions of the models with the knowledge to practice both the two-way asymmetrical and two-way symmetrical models. Knowledge to practice the press agentry and public information models did not correlate significantly with either the mediated or interpersonal dimensions. The correlations with both forms of two-way knowledge were mostly moderate with both dimensions for all four programs (in the .30 to .40 range), showing that knowledgeable departments communicate both through the media and interpersonally.

Finally, we constructed a single scale of organizational structure (ranging from mechanical to organic [see chap. 11]) and correlated it and the indexes of participative and authoritarian culture with the models and dimensions. None

---

[12]We also explored whether having had university courses in public relations, readership of trade and research publications, and membership and activity in professional associations were related to the knowledge needed to practice the two-way symmetrical and asymmetrical models. Having taken public relations courses correlated at a small but significant level with the knowledge to practice the two-way asymmetrical model ($r = .18$, $p < .01$) and the two-way symmetrical model ($r = .16$, $p < .01$). There also was a significant correlation with knowledge to practice the public information model ($r = .11$, $p < .05$) but not with the press agentry model. Readership of public relations publications correlated from $r = -.19$ to $r = .22$ for the knowledge to practice all models ($p < .01$ for all four). A scale of professional activity based on membership in and activity in professional public relations associations did not correlate significantly with the knowledge to practice any of the models.

of the correlations with structure was significant, confirming previous research. In addition, neither type of culture correlated significantly with any of the models or dimensions, with a few random exceptions, showing that culture does not have a direct effect on communication programs per se (see also Sriramesh, J. Grunig, & Dozier, 1996). As we see in chapter 11, however, both structure and culture are strongly related to the overall system of internal communication in an organization. Organic structures tend to produce symmetrical systems of internal communication, which in turn produce participative cultures.

The analysis of these relationships completes our analysis of the quantitative data on the models of public relations. These data have helped us to clarify the nature of models of public relations and have helped us to conceptualize an improved theory of symmetrical communication. In the qualitative portion of the Excellence study, we found additional evidence of the utility of the symmetrical theory and the revisions we have made to that theory.

QUALITATIVE RESULTS RELATED TO MODELS
OF PUBLIC RELATIONS

Like the quantitative results, the results of the qualitative research firmly established that the two-way symmetrical approach to public relations is a positive or descriptive model as well as the normative or ideal. We can make this assertion because we heard a great deal about symmetry in communication during our interviews with the most excellent operations—even though respondents used that term infrequently.

We also found evidence in our case studies of the organizations scoring the highest and lowest on the Excellence scale of why organizations change the focus of their public relations programs from the traditional, media-and-message approaches of press agentry and public information to the two-way models. The explanations suggested by the qualitative study mirror those from the survey research. In some cases, a new CEO came in with a new worldview of two-way and symmetrical communication—often triggered by an organizational crisis or activist pressure. In other cases, a knowledgeable practitioner was hired and he or she changed the view of the dominant coalition about the public relations function.

We found a great deal of evidence that the symmetrical model is becoming a professional ideal for public relations, but we also found evidence that organizations continue to practice a two-way asymmetrical model unless the symmetrical model becomes a strategic necessity when an asymmetrical approach is too risky. Most of our excellent departments that practiced the two-way asymmetrical model combined it with a symmetrical worldview, as described in Fig. 8.5. However, a few departments that conceptualized public relations as a marketing function practiced public relations mostly according to the two-way asymmetrical model. Most who practiced the two-way asymmetrical model, however, did so because of its emphasis on research. Many other research participants had a lot to say about research and two-way communication—symmetrical and asymmetrical—mirroring the two-way dimension of the models we identified in the quantitative data.

Symmetry in the Organization's Worldview

One concrete instance of a symmetrical worldview came from the industry association that scored in the 99th percentile of the Excellence scale. The head of public relations there described a community program he developed that has won national prominence and acclaim. The program's first principle was listening and responding to the community's concerns. He emphasized that responsiveness may include change on the organization's part when pressure groups do not agree with it. His CEO echoed the importance of two-way, responsive, and responsible communication: "If you can't deal with a bilateral communication relationship, or what you call 'symmetrical,' then find another job."

But why should communities or other groups that know little about the industry be allowed to "interfere" with the business? First, and perhaps most obvious, government regulation may mandate the publics' involvement. Second, cooperation with publics acknowledges their legitimacy. The association CEO explained, "We understand very clearly that the public is going to give us a franchise to operate and therefore they need to be involved in the process."

Less obvious but more important, in our view, is that coalitions initially hostile may become supporters when actively engaged with the organization. As the top communicator in the association explained: "You might not have the power or the position you feel you need to sell an idea, but if you've got a community advisory panel that is well selected and well balanced and *they* weigh in with an opinion, that's going to be the best friend you ever had."

Short of this kind of collaboration is the value of shared intelligence. Talking with and listening to outside groups enhances the organization's ability to contend with its turbulent environment. The industry association CEO was unequivocal on this point: "We're finding that we're making better decisions when they're [community groups] involved in our process. It's not like we're doing it for fun or to keep them quiet and off our backs. It's that we've learned a lot from them and we're making a lot of improvements because of public involvement."

The CEO and his top communicator agreed that their bias is "toward openness and toward dialogue." Communicating openly with activists and demonstrating a willingness to change the organization rather than trying to dominate those groups may result in an all-important credibility. The CEO called this "perception and reputation," and he credited his association's reputation for credibility and technical expertise with helping it deal with pressure groups over the long haul.

Other organizations also described crisis situations that led to a change in the organizational mind-set to one of symmetrical communication. The first example was provided by the gas and electric company, which scored in the 94th percentile of the Excellence scale. Both of the interviewees in that organization—the senior vice president for customer and corporate services and the director of communication services—attributed a symmetrical worldview to the vision of the CEO, who coincidentally scored in the 99th percentile in his expectations for both the two-way symmetrical and asymmetrical models. The communication director described the communication model in the utility as "more open, up front, and honest than the company has known before."

Both the vice president and the director attributed the origin of this symmetrical worldview to two critical events. According to the vice president, problems with the construction of a nuclear power plant in the late 1970s were a "rude" and expensive awakening for the utility. Before that event, the company focused on technology and engineering. The public relations problems with the nuclear plant, however, forced the company to make sure it "attended to perceptions of people" and to make sure those perceptions are "aligned with reality" and "not letting large differences occur."

The other wake-up call, described by the director, was a media report that the utility's repair personnel were sleeping in their trucks on the job. The reports were not true, according to the director, but the incident led to more open relationships with the media—updating the media every few hours during storms and training employees to respond to media inquiries.

In the real estate development company, the top communicator also described two crisis situations in which the company practiced symmetrical communication—reflecting a symmetrical worldview toward crisis communication, at least. This top communicator had scored in the 99th percentile on knowledge to practice both the two-way symmetrical model and the two-way asymmetrical model. When a shooting occurred on one of the company's properties, resulting in a number of injuries, the company immediately sent an emergency response team—including the top communicator—to the site. "We brought in doctors, we brought in counselors; anybody whom anybody wanted, we got—no questions asked," she said. "Nobody was billed for anything, and we just stayed with it."

In another case, a hurricane created a major payroll problem for company employees in Florida. Many banks were closed, and automatic teller machines had been devastated. As a result, employees could not cash their paychecks. According to the top communicator: "It dawned on us that the people down there were not going to get paid. How could they buy water? How could they buy food? We talked to the comptroller's division, and they immediately contacted a bank to obtain cash. Everybody on our payroll down there received cash."

The cosmetics company, which scored in the 82nd percentile on the Excellence scale, had dissolved its corporate communication department and invested that function in an outside public relations firm of which the company had become majority owner. The top communicator who completed the questionnaire was head of the outside firm. We interviewed him as well an in-house director of sales force communication. Both described a symmetrical worldview of communication in the organization and traced its origin to the dominant coalition.

The director of sales force communication said she learned a symmetrical worldview from a past president, who had started his career in journalism and advertising before coming to the company. She said she "listened to him on the phone and listened to him talk to people. He was a great trainer and a great leader." The agency head described this same symmetrical worldview that began with the current CEO: "I believe he trusts my opinion and judgment, and he knows above all that I won't bullshit him, that I'll tell him what the truth is. I still maintain that the PR guy has got to bring to the table the outside perspective that is by definition lacking by those inside the organization. Otherwise, the outside perspective is not going to be at the table when decisions are made."

In the engineering research agency, we found an example of an organization in which the deputy director we interviewed as a member of the dominant coalition expressed a strong preference for both two-way symmetrical and asymmetrical communication (96th and 84th percentile) but the top communicator estimated much lower support for those models by the dominant coalition (3rd and 1st percentile). The top communicator also estimated that knowledge available to practice these models at only the 56th and 17th percentiles.

Communication personnel did practice the two-way symmetrical model internally, especially through their zeal for total quality management. However, the deputy director had greater expectations for two-way communication with external "customers" to improve the ranking and reputation of the agency. Most of what the communication staff did externally, however, seemed to reflect the public information model—such as the preparation of brochures and publications and media relations—even though top management expressed a strong preference for both forms of two-way communication.

A major metal-manufacturing company provided an example of change toward a two-way model of communication when a new CEO replaced a retiring technician, who headed essentially a communication services unit, with a higher ranking strategic communicator. The company had scored in the 11th percentile of the Excellence scale and in the 9th and 14th percentiles of knowledge to practice the two-way symmetrical and asymmetrical models in the survey. Those results occurred because the former top communicator, who had the rank of manager rather than vice president, essentially worked as a journalist-in-residence—writing news releases, organizing press conferences, producing the annual report and internal publications, and supervising the technicians involved in these tasks. When this manager retired, a new CEO, who previously had played a role in the company's communication activities, promptly appointed a new vice president of public affairs, to whom the new communication manager then reported. Together, the CEO and the new vice president of public affairs transformed the communication function into a research-based strategic function.

Confirmation of the importance of a symmetrical worldview, in a negative sense, came from one of three insurance companies among the case studies. This one scored at the bottom of the Excellence scale—in the 15th percentile. Knowledge needed to perform the two-way symmetrical and asymmetrical models was at a similar low level—the 19th percentile for both. The top communicator attributed these low scores to the previous CEO, who she said had little interest in communication, and to an organizational structure in which the top communicator reported to a general group vice president rather than the CEO.

No mechanism appeared to be in place in this organization to bring information into the organization. According to the director of public relations, "I think we do a good job of telling associates what management wants. I'm not sure we do a good job of getting feedback." She believed, however, that a change in worldview would come with the new CEO. She said the new CEO "seems to have his ear closer to the rail than prior management. He seems more willing to listen to input with respect to effecting change relative to concerns from our external groups. . . . My guess is that there will be a dramatic shift in the manner in which we do things here."

In another case study of an organization low on the Excellence scale (the 12th percentile), the top communicator of the aerospace company also posted low scores on the knowledge to practice the two-way symmetrical (3rd percentile) and asymmetrical (14th percentile) models. The CEO's scores, however, showed a preference for both two-way models in the middle of the scale. The top communicator understood that preference, even overestimating that the dominant coalition would register preferences for these two-way models in the 94th and 87th percentile. The top communicator, who came into public relations with a background in art and editing, also scored low on the managerial scale and in participation in strategic management—even though the CEO estimated a higher participation in strategic management than did the top communicator herself. Clearly, the top communicator in this aerospace company lacked the skills to meet the CEO's expectations.

Public relations in this corporation consisted mostly of media relations, which the top communicator maintained has a clear impact on stock prices. She also maintained that as a government contractor, the company had little need for research-based communication because there were only 12 purchasers of its products. The top communicator said that informal telephone calls and personal one-on-one contacts provided all the information the company needed to make strategic decisions. The community relations program used one-way and asymmetrical techniques such as image advertising to publicize the corporate giving program. The company did emphasize internal communication, however, through a total quality management program.

This aerospace company probably practiced more symmetrical communication than its knowledge scores indicated, although it used interpersonal communication to do so rather than research. Nevertheless, this also seemed to be an organization where the demands for excellent communication by the dominant coalition were not being met by the knowledge of the senior practitioner.

A dramatic example of the importance of a CEO in establishing a worldview for the communication function came from the state lottery for which we conducted in-depth interviews because of an Excellence score in the 99th percentile. In the 3 years between the completion of the quantitative questionnaires and the case study interviews, however, a new CEO came in with a different concept of public relations. The former top communicator, the director of public affairs, was demoted to a technical support function in the marketing department—taking over technical duties previously handled by an outside public relations firm.

The new CEO, according to the director of marketing we interviewed, questioned whether communicators belong in strategic planning as a matter of philosophy. He believed that the communication (which was called public affairs) department should largely involve dissemination of information to the public, a one-way model of public relations practices. "Good communication is based on making and saving money by pumping out a variety of new angles to get press coverage," the former top communicator and now the business and planning manager said. "Millions of dollars are made from public relations in this respect and it saves hundreds of thousands of dollars each year." These benefits from communication, however, are rooted in the traditional models of public information and press agentry. Press coverage increases awareness of the lottery. Clever media angles, the business and planning manager said, lead to larger, rapidly growing jackpots. Good publicity, in turn, helps reduce advertising spending.

The current marketing director added, "The model here is primarily two-way asymmetrical with a lot of one-way communication added in." The current assistant director of public affairs described the two-way asymmetrical model perfectly: "We listen to the public and influence them." The former top communicator added, "The CEO does place some emphasis on internal communication, but then the previous CEO placed greater emphasis on it. The former CEO saw an important role for public relations in all aspects of policy making and planning. The current CEO sees the public relations practitioner's role as being that of a spokesperson, delivering the message only."

The staff members interviewed did point out instances in which the communication staff played an important role in crisis situations—providing the same impetus for symmetrical communication that we have seen in other cases. Although these instances occurred in the days of the CEO with a symmetrical mind-set, the current staff members brought them up—suggesting that the organization still would practice two-way symmetrical communication in a crisis situation. On one occasion, the state lottery had accumulated a $25 million jackpot. The machine that selected the winner malfunctioned, creating a public relations crisis. Thirty minutes later, a second drawing was held and the original malfunction was explained to the public over a televised statewide feed. The prompt and candid explanation of the malfunction helped the state lottery maintain credibility, largely through the efforts of its former "outsourced" public relations agency and the lottery's communication staff. This, in turn, helped to stave off a drop in lottery ticket sales.

Several problems with contract disputes also had surfaced in the past, and all were resolved through public relations efforts. On one occasion, the phone lines failed with a large jackpot at stake. The lottery staff worked with radio stations to inform the public of the problem. Phone lines are important because they transport information regarding ticket purchases instantaneously, which affects the size of the jackpot. "If you get to them before they get to you, you will be much better off," the assistant director of public affairs reported. "We must learn from other crises, hypothetically discuss situations internally, and place a high value on crisis management."

Essentially the same situation existed in a second insurance company, which scored in the 6th percentile of the Excellence scale—an emphasis on marketing communication limited the public relations function to mostly a technical, one-way model of practice. The top communicator reported that the communication department was part of the marketing department and that the communication department exists as a service or support unit to marketing. Communication was not viewed as a managerial function, and it had no role in strategic management.

As a result, "We are pretty much one-way, unfortunately," the top communicator said. "But we do so little public relations in the first place. And because we do not focus on public relations, the result is one-way communication. Basically, we disseminate brochures, direct mail, and press releases when it comes to public relations." "Communication in this organization is basically one-way," the vice president of underwriting, who represented the dominant coalition, said. "There is some two-way interaction, but it tends to be asymmetrical. For example, bounce-back cards are included with the newsletters in order to gauge our customers' feelings."

A Knowledgeable Top Communicator as a Catalyst

A state hospital association, ranked in the 97th percentile for excellence, provided an example of an organization in which the impetus for a change to symmetrical communication from traditional one-way models came not so much from the CEO or the dominant coalition as from a new and knowledgeable top communicator. In the quantitative portion of the Excellence study, this practitioner estimated the departmental knowledge to practice the two-way symmetrical model in the 98th percentile and to practice the two-way asymmetrical model in the 97th percentile. Before hiring this new director of public affairs, 4 years before our case study, the organization's public relations function used traditional one-way models of communication.

The new PR head built the communication function from scratch. When she was hired, she approached communication more strategically, based on her experience with public affairs and government affairs in previous positions. "The most important thing I've done is to combine public affairs and government affairs," she said. "I think big and understand what drives public opinion, policy, and situations where you can exert leadership."

When we asked the CEO about two-way communication with publics, he said his organization maintained ongoing communication with the legislature and other publics. A core function of his organization, the CEO said, is to understand issues and to address those issues in ways that people will understand. When he hired the current top communicator, her strategic approach to communication as a two-way process amounted to an introduction to a "whole new science." "She brought in a whole new view and way of thinking with her knowledge of communication," he added. "Then we realized how much we had needed her."

In the blood bank with an Excellence score in the 94th percentile, we interviewed two top communicators (a director of community relations to whom a director of public affairs reported) and found that they have extensive boundary-spanning duties that allow them to look at the blood bank from a community perspective. This contrasted with the worldview of medical "insiders" who look at the organization largely from a medical practitioner's perspective. In the blood bank, the expertise to practice the two-way models of public relations consisted of a seamless web of scanning and evaluation skills that spanned both traditional and emerging research skills in public relations.

Two top communicators had made the excellent program possible, but further interviews suggested that other senior managers believed that two-way practice was unique to these two excellent communicators. According to the blood bank's CEO, the director of community relations was "in an uncommon position to be aware of what's going on in the community. I marvel at her effectiveness." However, we asked how widely the communication function was understood among senior managers in the organization. According to the public affairs officer, some senior managers could articulate a two-way model of communication but many could not. Most also attributed the two-way nature of the blood bank's program to the skills of the communicators in this organization and did not see it as a characteristic of the communication function generally.

A state arts organization, for which we conducted in-depth interviews because it had a very low Excellence score—the 9th percentile—ironically illustrated the difference that a knowledgeable practitioner can have in moving an organization toward two-way communication. At the time of the quantitative survey, the communication department engaged in traditional one-way practices of disseminating information. Three years later, a new top communicator had begun to transform both the techniques of communication and the philosophical approach of the organization toward its publics.

A strong two-way symmetrical philosophy was practiced in a series of town hall meetings. This symmetrical orientation was reflected in the director of public relations' phrase, "We can listen to people about what we can do better." He added, "One of my roles is to bridge the gap between the different mentalities held by people in the arts organization and the state and federal legislators who definitely have a different perspective on things. I help both organizations understand each other." At the same time, there were two-way asymmetrical elements to the program. Research was used to persuade legislators to fund arts projects and to find the "hot buttons" that would convince a legislator to act favorably on funding legislation.

Mixed-Motive, Strategic Symmetry

Although most of the cases we have discussed thus far have been relatively pure cases of symmetrical communication, the case of the state arts association provides an example of the strategic mixture of collaboration and advocacy in an organization's approach to public relations. We also heard about this combination, the "mixed-motive model," in other cases. One illustration came as a communicator discussed his values:

> If we hold to the principle of being honest, there is honest manipulation and false manipulation. Manipulation is usually associated with false manipulation. If we're honest in what we do and how we do it, then I look on the role of the communicator as being one who achieves desirable outcomes. . . . What do we want you to do? We don't want to just inform and educate somebody for the sake of saying we've done our good deed. We want to inform and educate with the intent of buying our stock, of being a safer employee, of coming to work more than being absent, and in seeing a better article in the press.

One example of incorporating both advocacy and collaboration within a symmetrical framework came from the medical association we studied. The head of public affairs described his communication programs as largely two-way and balanced, although he said he uses persuasive techniques situationally. He explained that because his is a membership association, he must strive to listen to members, incorporate their input into decision making, serve those members, and ultimately serve their patients. At the same time, the association uses what only could be characterized as asymmetrical tactics to "sell" the membership on some of its programs and policies.

Four participants from the oil company headquartered in the United States described a mixture of the two-way symmetrical and asymmetrical models that also was situational in a way that resembles Cancel et al.'s (1997) contingency approach to advocacy and accommodation. After the Middle East oil embargo of the late 1970s and the Exxon Valdez oil spill in Alaska's Prince William Sound a decade later, public disfavor forced the oil company to professionalize its public relations staff. The result was an emphasis on research, on two-way asymmetrical campaigns, and on symmetrical communication when necessary.

For employee communication in its four operating companies, the oil company's dominant coalition preferred symmetrical communication: "You have to understand what the other manager's sensitivity is about an issue or whatever they're trying to do . . . understand their goals, which is sometimes different from what your goals might be from a public relations standpoint," the coordinator of corporate communication said.

For external publics, the company often used asymmetrical communication—persuasive messages based on research—such as a corporate advertising campaign on the environment to put the organization in a favorable light. When forced, however, the company turned to symmetrical communication. Overall, costs and consequences appeared to determine whether the oil company used the two-way asymmetrical or the two-way communication model. If the cost of a two-way symmetrical strategy were high and risk to the company low, it probably would choose the two-way asymmetrical model. If the potential costs associated with failure to change operating methods were high and there was a strong possibility that negative action would be taken against the company, then it likely would choose the two-way symmetrical model.

"I think it would depend on what you could get away with, to be frank," the coordinator of corporate contributions said. "If we keep operating the way we were and we could portray it so that the community understood the good and valid reasons for operating in that way, then that's what we would do. If, on the other hand . . . the risk was too high and seemed likely, then we would have to change."

This limited acceptance of the two-way symmetrical model also can be seen in the quantitative results for this company. Although the company scored in the 97th percentile on overall excellence and the 85th percentile for knowledge to practice the two-way asymmetrical model, it scored only in the 76th percentile on knowledge for the two-way symmetrical model. The CEO scored in the 87th percentile in his preference for the two-way asymmetrical model but only the 79th percentile for the two-way symmetrical model.

A medical products subsidiary of a major corporation, which scored in the 97th percentile of the Excellence scale, also seemed to practice both symmetrical and asymmetrical, one-way and two-way communication, based on an analysis of the situation and publics involved. Most internal communication was two-way, with a "free flow" of information between management and employees. The company practiced two-way asymmetrical and one-way communication in crisis situations to restrict the flow of information that might have a negative impact on the company and its parent corporation. Product-based communication employed one-way models (press relations and product demonstrations) as well as two-way models (customer focus groups and surveys along with sales training).

The heart health association, which had an Excellence score in the 99th percentile, also demonstrated a mixture of the two-way symmetrical and asymmetrical models. An emphasis on two-way asymmetrical communication is common in health communication programs, which typically are based on principles of social marketing and use research to change the behaviors of publics to improve their health. Because the purpose of such asymmetrical programs is to enhance the health of target publics, there generally are fewer ethical problems with asymmetrical communication in comparison to many corporate programs that promote a special interest asymmetrically.

Although the top communicator estimated the department's knowledge to practice the two-way symmetrical model at the 90th percentile, she estimated two-way asymmetrical knowledge in the 97th percentile. Likewise, the CEO expressed a preference for the two-way asymmetrical model in the 94th percentile, compared with a score in the 69th percentile for the two-way symmetrical model.

Our interviews showed that the association's communication programs used both two-way models as well as the traditional publicity and public information models—reflecting the use of mediated communication within the context of two-way communication that we described when we analyzed the quantitative data. News media opportunities served as "stepping stones" to reach relevant publics (described as "markets"). The association also ran programs at the grassroots level in parallel with media promotions. Rather than simply providing information subsidies to the media, the heart health communicators also used the media as a platform to build their own agenda of issues.

In addition to this asymmetrical approach, the association used symmetrical techniques to build coalitions with organizations with similar interests. The top communicator also described negotiated symmetrical relationships with the media and outside groups as, "you scratch my back and I'll scratch yours." She pointed out the importance of standing in the shoes of members of a public and asking: "So what? Why is this important to me?"

In the interview, the CEO mirrored the quantitative results when he demonstrated more knowledge of the two-way asymmetrical model than of the symmetrical model. He described in detail the rationale behind the association's "market" targeting policy and its plan for communicating message points effectively. The top communicator provided a detailed analysis in a video presentation of how the organization developed its logo and how the organization builds awareness of its goals among volunteers. An ongoing image survey provided further evidence of using research to tailor messages—in a way that is typical of the two-way asymmetrical model.

Two-Way, Research-Based Communication

Each of the two-way communication models—symmetrical or asymmetrical—requires a degree of sophistication in research, and the quantitative results show that CEOs prefer research-based, two-way communication programs. In the qualitative study, we were curious about the kind and extent of research, if any, being conducted to support the two-way models.

The heart health association, which we just described, provides an example of an organization that used extensive research in support of its asymmetrical communication campaigns. When we asked the CEO of the blood bank about two-way communication with publics, he indicated that the more traditional media relations expertise of the community relations director provided him with important intelligence about the organization's environment. The use of media contacts—an informal technique for monitoring the organizational environment—was supplemented and enhanced by focus group studies, surveys of blood-drive chairs, and summative evaluations of each blood drive. Each type of research, whether formal or informal, was a source of information that contributed to management decision making.

The oil company affiliate, in contrast, was typical of an Excellent communication function that still does little research. Despite an overall excellence rating in the 92nd percentile, the oil company's practice of public affairs can best be characterized as press agentry. When we asked what sort of research the department conducts, its media relations manager answered, "None at all." However, this department involves itself with its trade association to such a degree that its media relations manager described it as an extension of public affairs—an indicator of how indirect research may undergird press agentry and public information activities in excellent public relations departments. The company relies on industry research on the image of the oil industry carried out by the association. So, as he explained, "Although we don't get feedback on, perhaps, how people view [the company], we do get feedback on how people view the oil industry and also people's concerns about the oil industry." In addition to this kind of *formal* research generated by the association, the interviewee used *informal* means to glean information from "the outside world": monitoring the media, talking to journalists, and participating in activities sponsored by his trade association.

The U.S. oil company was different, however. That company had institutionalized a research unit within the public affairs department. The research manager told us that communication research data were carefully analyzed and used as a base on which public affairs recommendations were designed. "Oh, definitely, we make recommendations," the research manager said. "We are charged in research to provide insight and foresight, not just data." Research results were transmitted to a public affairs committee through formal presentations, less formal presentations by the vice president of public affairs, and memos.

The assistant executive director of the medical association also emphasized the focus of his department on measurement and its ability to show measurable effects. He described research frequently—80% of members thought this, 60% of this public thought it was a good campaign, and the government changed its policy. He also described the association's communication as "not just reactive." He said it is important to use research to understand the members of the association and to shape the association's agenda to reflect members' needs.

The senior communication specialist in the electric utility that scored in the 99th percentile of the Excellence scale told us that his department within the parent company conducts a great deal of research on its customers and that he thinks the needs of an organization's publics are very important. "We do a lot of surveying, a lot of focus group analysis, to try to stay on top of where the customer is," he said. "Last year, I probably went to 50 focus groups in 20 cities across our system."

The disabled services agency, which scored in the 95th percentile of the Excellence scale, was headed by a top communicator who was a part-time public relations educator familiar with the literature of the field. She posted knowledge scores in the 85th and 84th percentiles for the two-way symmetrical and asymmetrical models. The agency did not conduct formal research with any regularity, and the quantitative research was conducted 10 years before our interview. However, the agency used qualitative research and planned a major focus group project for the year after our interview to gain information on how to provide better educational services to the disabled. The agency constantly used informal research methods. One example was gleaning information from telephone conversations with members of a public and adding the results to an information base. The agency also used quasi-formal methods such as tracking donations from gift envelopes.

The top communicator in the medical products subsidiary, who came into the position between the quantitative and qualitative phases of our research, reported that he had implemented a number of two-way communication activities. They had included employee focus groups, customer focus groups, sales and training focus groups, customer surveys, and sales training seminars.

One of the three insurance companies we studied, a major international company that scored in the 81st percentile of the Excellence scale, depended strongly on research for its campaign of reconstruction and renewal after a financial crisis. To build and maintain relationships with its members, regulators, financial analysts, the media, and similar groups, the company held seminars, conferences, meetings, press conferences, and interviews. The campaign depended on research, which the senior communication officer described as "intelligence gathering," to determine the extent to which the campaign strategy was working. Over 2 months, the corporate communications department commissioned a leading research firm to conduct tracking surveys among representative samples of the company's members. The studies tested members' opinions on the options being placed before them—some of which were alternatives to the company's own reconstruction and renewal program.

Three organizations that we interviewed because they scored at the bottom of the Excellence scale provided evidence that research-based, two-way communication is one of the primary changes that an organization makes when it revises its communication function to fit better with our profile of excellence. The metal manufacturing company mentioned previously, for example, scored in the 11th percentile of the Excellence scale and in the 9th and 14th percentiles of knowledge to practice the two-way symmetrical and asymmetrical models. When a new CEO created the position of vice president of public affairs at a higher level in the organization between the quantitative and qualitative stages of this project, the new CEO and the new vice president based the revamped communication function on a foundation of research.

In our case study, we found that the public affairs department used all four models of communication. The one-way models still were used in the public relations unit, which remained staffed by "journalists-in-residence" and specialized in media relations. For governmental, labor, and community relations, however, the company used a mix of the two-way models, typified by sophisticated research activities to understand publics. Sometimes, that understanding helped the organization negotiate and collaborate with key publics, as when the corporation formed strategic alliances with other companies in metal manufacturing and other heavy industries. At other times, that understanding was used to persuade, as with legislators and regulators.

We also interviewed a state economic development agency because it had scored near the bottom of the Excellence scale in the quantitative portion of the study. Since that time, however, the agency hired a new communication manager and the direction of its communication program made a dramatic change. "Originally, our public relations concept was to crank out a newsletter every quarter and an annual report once a year and we thought that's all they ought to do," according to the vice president of management services. "We've learned to involve the communication department in the process and that's the trick to all of it." An important part of the switch was evaluative research. As part of the communication manager's 2-year plan, the organization will collect hard data to measure the impact of the communication department in attracting and retaining clients.

The third organization—a hotel chain—that we interviewed because of its low Excellence score—the 18th percentile—provides an example of an organization that practices largely an asymmetrical model because of the fragmentation of the communication function and its subservience to marketing: "PR in the [hotel chain] culture has always been a strong part of the marketing environment and there's always been an appreciation of its value," according to one of the top communicators. However, the chain still uses a great deal of research to support its two-way asymmetrical approach. As we saw in chapter 7, the chain has several operating groups and each has its own public relations function. A separate employee communication group provides photographic services, audiovisual services, and management communication services such as brochures, pamphlets, and employee vehicles for the organization as a whole on a cost-recovery basis.

The communication units in the chain's lodging and contract management divisions do use communication research, although their level of expertise to practice the two-way models was low in the quantitative results—probably because a top communicator in another division completed the questionnaire. Communication research methods reported in the case study included focus groups, interviews, and other forms of qualitative study. "When we are out on the road, we will take an extra day or two in whatever city we're in to do focus groups and other kinds of things," one top communicator reported. "We're right in the middle of really developing a comprehensive communication strategy. And part of that is going out and talking to each of the presidents and then going into units and interviewing, not for quantitative data but really qualitative data."

Most of this research seems to support a two-way asymmetrical model of public relations: "Are we modifying . . . the way we're doing things to respond to feedback . . . or are we just modifying our message," the top communicator in contract management asked. "It's the latter to a certain extent." The top communicator in lodging added, "I think there's more functional time, if you will, spent on designing and issuing messages than there is on shaping messages." Because employee communication acted only as a service bureau for the technical communication needs of its internal clients, employee communication did not use two-way models of communication.

SUMMARY AND CONCLUSIONS

J. Grunig first introduced the concept of models of public relations in the 1970s as a way of understanding and explaining the behavior of public relations practitioners. At that time, public relations educators routinely advocated two-way communication but few made a distinction in the purpose of public relations in an organization. J. Grunig conceptualized the press agentry and public information models to improve on the simple concept of one-way communication. He also did not believe that all two-way communication was the same. Some was asymmetrical: Public relations people did research and listened to publics in an effort to determine how best to change their behavior to benefit the organization. But, he believed that public relations professionals had a calling beyond this asymmetrical approach: serving as the organizational function that attempts to balance the interests of organizations with those of their publics, an approach he called "symmetrical" communication.

Over the years, these public relations models have been researched and debated. Do they really describe actual public relations practice? Is the symmetrical model only an idealized, normative model? Are critical scholars correct: Is it unlikely that a large organization with more power than its publics would ever deliberately choose to practice symmetrical public relations? Is symmetrical public relations simply a deceptive term used by educators and practitioners to cover up the damage that public relations does to the interests of publics?

In the first section of this chapter, we summarized and responded to these questions. We concluded that the four models are both positive and normative and that the two-way symmetrical model still appears to be a normative ideal for public relations practice. We maintained that public relations professionals can use the power of their knowledge—if they have it and if society recognizes the value of public relations—to advocate a symmetrical approach to public relations. They should be able to advocate symmetry in public relations for the same reason that a physician tells an overweight person to exercise—because it is good for the organization just as exercise is good for one's health.

The quantitative and qualitative data reported in this chapter provide the most comprehensive information ever collected on the models of public relations. As a result, the data suggest a significant reconceptualization of the models. We did find that the four models still provide an accurate and useful tool to describe public relations practice and worldview. Practitioners and CEOs do think about public relations in these ways, and the four models do describe the way communication programs are conducted for different types of publics. However, the differences among the two one-way and the two two-way models typically blur in the minds of CEOs and in the practice of some, but not all, programs. CEOs, in particular, view an excellent public relations function as including the two-way asymmetrical model as often as the two-way symmetrical model.

We found the answer to that dilemma in the two-way component of the two-way asymmetrical model. CEOs like the two-way asymmetrical model because they appreciate the systematic use of research in that model. Most do not distinguish research conducted for symmetrical purposes from research conducted for asymmetrical purposes. Most CEOs do not want asymmetrical communication programs, although we did find exceptions in our survey of cases. Organizations that define public relations as a marketing function, in particular, tend to see public relations only in asymmetrical terms—or in one-way terms.

We successfully isolated three dimensions underlying the four models—one-way versus two-way, symmetry versus asymmetry, and mediated and interpersonal techniques. We also suggested further research on a fourth dimension, the ethics of communication. The overlapping concepts and practices of the models that we had found before—such as practicing the two-way symmetrical, two-way asymmetrical, and public information models concurrently—now seem to have occurred because an organization had a symmetrical public relations worldview, favored extensive research, and practiced mediated as well as interpersonal communication.

Excellent public relations, therefore, can be described better in terms of these underlying dimensions than in terms of the four discrete models themselves. Excellent public relations is research based (two-way), symmetrical (although organizations constantly struggle between symmetry and asymmetry when they make decisions), and based on either mediated or interpersonal communication (depending on the situation and public). We also believe it is more ethical, although we did not measure ethics as a component of the models in the Excellence study. Future research, we predict, will establish ethics as a crucial component of excellent public relations (see chap. 12).

We also learned from both our quantitative and qualitative data that organizations typically turn to a symmetrical approach when activist pressure or a crisis makes an asymmetrical approach too costly. Then, the CEO tends to upgrade the communication function and hire a knowledgeable top communicator—although sometimes the top communicator comes first and convinces the CEO of the need to enhance the communication function. By and large, organizations practice symmetrical public relations when the CEO understands its value and *demands* it and the senior communicator and his or her communication staff have the knowledge to *supply* it. Much of that knowledge comes from the ability to do research, to understand publics, and to collaborate and negotiate—skills that excellent communicators must have.

REFERENCES

Anderson, D. S. (1992). Identifying and responding to activist publics: A case study. *Journal of Public Relations Research, 4,* 151–165.

Bakhtin, M. M. (1981). *The dialogic imagination: Four essays by M. M. Bakhtin* (M. Holquist, Ed.; C. Emerson & M. Holquist, Trans.). Austin: University of Texas Press.

Baxter, L. A. (1994). A dialogic approach to relationship maintenance. In D. J. Canary & L. Stafford (Eds.), *Communication and relational maintenance* (pp. 233–254). San Diego: Academic Press.

Baxter, L. A., & Montgomery, B. M. (1996). *Relating: Dialogues & dialectics.* New York: Guilford.

Beam, R. A. (1990). Journalism professionalism as an organization-level concept. *Journalism Monographs, 121.*

Cameron, G. T. (1997, October). The contingency theory of conflict management in public relation. In *Proceedings of the conference on two-way communication* (pp. 27–48). Oslo: Norwegian Central Government Information Service.

Cancel, A. E., Cameron, G. T., Sallot, L. M., & Mitrook, M. A. (1997). It depends: A contingency theory of accommodation in public relations. *Journal of Public Relations Research, 9,* 31–63.

Cancel, A. E., Mitrook, M. A., & Cameron, G. T. (1999). Testing the contingency theory of accommodation in public relations. *Public Relations Review, 25,* 171–197.

Cawson, A. (1986). *Corporatism and political theory.* New York: Basil Blackwell.

Charlton, R. (1986). *Comparative government*. London: Longman.

Cheney, G., & Christensen, L. T. (2001). Public relations as contested terrain: A critical response. In R. L. Heath (Ed.), *Handbook of public relations* (pp. 167–182). Thousand Oaks, CA: Sage.

Clark, M. S., & Mills, J. (1993). The difference between communal and exchange relationships: What it is and is not. *Personality and Social Psychology Bulletin, 19*, 684–691.

Coombs, W. T. (1993). Philosophical underpinnings: Ramifications of a pluralist paradigm. *Public Relations Review, 19*, 111–120.

Culbertson, H. M., & Chen, N. (1997). Communitarianism: A foundation for communication symmetry. *Public Relations Quarterly, 42*(2), 36–41.

Cutlip, S. M., Center, A. H., & Broom, G. M. (1994). *Effective public relations* (7th ed.). Englewood Cliffs, NJ: Prentice-Hall.

Deetz, S. A. (1992). *Democracy in an age of corporate colonization*. Albany: State University of New York Press.

Dozier, D. M., with Grunig, L. A., & Grunig, J. E. (1995). *Manager's guide to excellence in public relations and communication management*. Hillsdale, NJ: Lawrence Erlbaum Associates.

Dozier, D. M., & Lauzen, M. M. (1998, August). *The liberation of public relations: Activism and the limits of symmetry in the global market*. Paper presented at the meeting of the Association for Education in Journalism and Mass Communication, Baltimore.

Dozier, D. M., & Lauzen, M. M. (2000). Liberating the intellectual domain from the practice: Public relations, activism, and the role of the scholar. *Journal of Public Relations Research, 12*, 3–22.

Gandy, O. H., Jr. (1982). *Beyond agenda setting: Information subsidies and public policy*. Norwood, NJ: Ablex.

Gray, B. (1989). *Collaborating: Finding common ground for multiparty problems*. San Francisco: Jossey-Bass.

Grunig, J. E. (1976). Organizations and publics relations: Testing a communication theory. *Journalism Monographs, 46*.

Grunig, J. E. (1984). Organizations, environments, and models of public relations. *Public Relations Research & Education, 1*(1), 6–29.

Grunig, J. E. (1989). Symmetrical presuppositions as a framework for public relations theory. In C. Botan & V. T. Hazelton (Eds.), *Public relations theory* (pp. 17–44). Hillsdale, NJ: Lawrence Erlbaum Associates.

Grunig, J. E. (Ed.). (1992a). *Excellence in public relations and communication management*. Hillsdale, NJ: Lawrence Erlbaum Associates.

Grunig, J. E. (1992b). Symmetrical systems of internal communication. In J. E. Grunig (Ed.), *Excellence in public relations and communication management* (pp. 531–576). Hillsdale, NJ: Lawrence Erlbaum Associates.

Grunig, J. E. (1994). Worldview, ethics, and the two-way symmetrical model of public relations. In W. Armbrecht & U. Zabel (Eds.), *Normative aspekte de public relations* (pp. 69–90). Opladen, Germany: Westdeutscher Verlag.

Grunig, J. E. (1997). A situational theory of publics: Conceptual history, recent challenges and new research. In D. Moss, T. MacManus, & D. Verčič (Eds.), *Public relations research: An international perspective* (pp. 3–46). London: International Thomson Business Press.

Grunig, J. E. (1998, May). *The contribution of research to professionalism in public relations*. Glassboro, NJ: Rowan University Public Relations/Advertising Department.

Grunig, J. E. (2000). Collectivism, collaboration, and societal corporatism as core professional values in public relations. *Journal of Public Relations Research, 12*, 23–48.

Grunig, J. E. (2001a). Bernays' *The Engineering of Consent. Journalism Studies, 2*, 302–305.

Grunig, J. E. (2001b). Two-way symmetrical public relations: Past, present, and future. In R. L. Heath (Ed.), *Handbook of public relations* (pp. 11–30). Thousand Oaks, CA: Sage.

Grunig, J. E. (in press). Constructing public relations theory and practice. In B. Dervin & S. Chaffee with L. Foreman-Wernet (Eds.), *Communication, a different kind of horse race: Essays honoring Richard F. Carter*. Peekskill, NJ: Hampton Press.

Grunig, J. E., & Grunig, L. A. (1989). Toward a theory of the public relations behavior of organizations: Review of a program of research. In J. E. Grunig & L. A. Grunig (Eds.), *Public relations research annual* (Vol. 1, pp. 27–66). Hillsdale, NJ: Lawrence Erlbaum Associates.

Grunig, J. E., & Grunig, L. A. (1992). Models of public relations and communication. In J. E. Grunig (Ed.), *Excellence in public relations and communication management* (pp. 285–326). Hillsdale, NJ: Lawrence Erlbaum Associates.

Grunig, J. E., & Grunig, L. A. (1996, May). *Implications of symmetry for a theory of ethics and social responsibility in public relations.* Paper presented at the meeting of the International Communication Association, Chicago.

Grunig, J. E., & Grunig, L. A. (1997, July). *Review of a program of research on activism: Incidence in four countries, activist publics, strategies of activist groups, and organizational responses to activism.* Paper presented at the Fourth Public Relations Research Symposium, Managing Environmental Issues, Lake Bled, Slovenia.

Grunig, J. E., Grunig, L. A., Sriramesh, K., Huang, Y. H., & Lyra, A. (1995). Models of public relations in an international setting. *Journal of Public Relations Research, 7,* 163–186.

Grunig, J. E., & Hunt, T. (1984). *Managing public relations.* New York: Holt, Rinehart & Winston.

Grunig, J. E., & Jaatinen, M. (1999). Strategic, symmetrical public relations in government: From pluralism to societal corporatism. *Journal of Communication Management, 3,* 218–234.

Grunig, J. E., & Repper, F. C. (1992). Strategic management, publics, and issues. In J. E. Grunig (Ed.), *Excellence in public relations and communication management* (pp. 117–158). Hillsdale, NJ: Lawrence Erlbaum Associates.

Grunig, J. E., & White, J. (1992). The effect of worldviews on public relations theory and practice. In J. E. Grunig (Ed.), *Excellence in public relations and communication management* (pp. 31–64). Hillsdale, NJ: Lawrence Erlbaum Associates.

Grunig, L. A. (1986, August). *Activism and organizational response: Contemporary cases of collective behavior.* Paper presented at the meeting of the Association for Education in Journalism and Mass Communication, Washington, DC.

Grunig, L. A., Grunig, J. E., & Verčič, D. (1998). Are the IABC's excellence principles generic? Comparing Slovenia and the United States, the United Kingdom and Canada. *Journal of Communication Management, 2,* 335–356.

Habermas, J. (1984). *The theory of communicative action* (Vol. 1; T. McCarthy, Trans.). Boston: Beacon Press.

Heath, R. L. (1992). The wrangle in the marketplace: A rhetorical perspective of public relations. In E. L. Toth & R. L. Heath (Eds.), *Rhetorical and critical approaches to public relations* (pp. 17–36). Hillsdale, NJ: Lawrence Erlbaum Associates.

Heath, R. L. (1998, November). *Rhetorical enactment theory: Another piece in the paradigm shift.* Paper presented at the meeting of the National Communication Association, New York.

Heath, R. L. (2001). A rhetorical enactment rationale for public relations: The good organization communicating well. In R. L. Heath (Ed.), *Handbook of public relations* (pp. 31–50). Thousand Oaks, CA: Sage.

Hofstede, G. (1980). *Culture's consequences.* Beverly Hills, CA: Sage.

Holtzhausen, D. R. (2000). Postmodern values in public relations. *Journal of Public Relations Research, 12,* 93–114.

Karlberg, M. (1996). Remembering the public in public relations research: From theoretical to operational symmetry. *Journal of Public Relations Research, 8,* 263–278.

Kersten, A. (1984). The ethics and ideology of public relations: A critical examination of American theory and practice. In W. Armbrecht & U. Zabel (Eds.), *Normative aspekte der public relations* (pp. 109–130). Opladen, Germany: Westdeutscher Verlag.

Kim, Y., & Hon, L. C. (1998). Craft and professional models of public relations and their relation to job satisfaction among Korean public relations practitioners. *Journal of Public Relations Research, 10,* 155–176.

Kovacs, R. S. (1998). *Pressure group strategies and accountability in British public service broadcasting*. Unpublished doctoral dissertation, University of Maryland, College Park.

Kruckeberg, D., & Starck, K. (1988). *Public relations and community: A reconstructed theory*. New York: Praeger.

Kunczik, M. (1994). Public relations: Angewandte Kommunikationswissenschaft oder ideologie? Ein Beitrag zur ethik der offentlichkeitsarbeit [Public relations: Applied communication science or ideology? A contribution to the ethics of public relations]. In W. Armbrecht & U. Zabel (Eds.), *Normative aspekte der public relations* (pp. 225–264). Opladen, Germany: Westdeutscher Verlag.

Leeper, R. (2001). In search of a metatheory for public relations: An argument for communitarianism. In R. L. Heath (Ed.), *Handbook of public relations* (pp. 93–104). Thousand Oaks, CA: Sage.

Leichty, G. (1997). The limits of collaboration. *Public Relations Review, 23*, 47–56.

Leichty, G., & Springston, J. (1993). Reconsidering public relations models. *Public Relations Review, 19*, 327–340.

Leitch, S., & Neilson, D. (2001). Bringing publics into public relations: New theoretical frameworks for practice. In R. L. Heath (Ed.), *Handbook of public relations* (pp. 127–138). Thousand Oaks, CA: Sage.

L'Etang, J. (1995, July). *Clio among the patriarchs: Historical and social scientific approaches to public relations: A methodological critique*. Paper presented at the Second International Public Relations Symposium, Bled, Slovenia.

L'Etang, J. (1996a). *Corporate responsibility and public relations ethics*. In J. L'Etang & M. Pieczka (Eds.), *Critical perspectives in public relations* (pp. 82–105). London: International Thomson Business Press.

L'Etang, J. (1996b). *Public relations and rhetoric*. In J. L'Etang & M. Pieczka (Eds.), *Critical perspectives in public relations* (pp. 106–123). London: International Thomson Business Press.

Miller, G. R. (1989). Persuasion and public relations: Two "Ps" in a pod. In C. H. Botan & V. Hazleton, Jr. (Eds.), *Public relations theory* (pp. 45–66). Hillsdale, NJ: Lawrence Erlbaum Associates.

Mintzberg, H. (1983). *Power in and around organizations*. Englewood Cliffs, NJ: Prentice-Hall.

Moloney, K. (1997). Teaching organizational communication as public relations in UK universities. *Corporate Communication: An International Journal, 2*, 138–142.

Murphy, P. (1991). The limits of symmetry: A game theory approach to symmetric and asymmetric public relations. In J. E. Grunig & L. A. Grunig (Eds.), *Public relations research annual* (Vol. 3, pp. 115–132). Hillsdale, NJ: Lawrence Erlbaum Associates.

Murphy, P., & Dee, J. (1996). Reconciling the preferences of environmental activists and corporate policymakers. *Journal of Public Relations Research, 8*, 1–34.

Pearson, R. (1989). Beyond ethical relativism in public relations: Coorientation, rules, and the idea of communication symmetry. In J. E. Grunig & L. A. Grunig (Eds.), *Public relations research annual* (Vol. 1, pp. 67–86). Hillsdale, NJ: Lawrence Erlbaum Associates.

Pieczka, M. (1995, July). *Symmetry in communication and public relations*. Paper presented at the Second International Public Relations Symposium, Bled, Slovenia.

Pieczka, M. (1996a). Paradigms, systems theory and public relations. In J. L'Etang & M. Pieczka (Eds.), *Critical perspectives in public relations* (pp. 124–156). London: International Thomson Business Press.

Pieczka, M. (1996b). Public opinion and public relations. In J. L'Etang & M. Pieczka (Eds.), *Critical perspectives in public relations* (pp. 54–64). London: International Thomson Business Press.

Pieczka, M., & L'Etang, J. (2001). Public relations and the question of professionalism. In R. L. Heath (Ed.), *Handbook of public relations* (pp. 223–236). Thousand Oaks, CA: Sage.

Raiffa, H. (1982). *The art and science of negotiation*. Cambridge, MA: Harvard University Press.

Rodino, V., & DeLuca, K. (1999, June). *Unruly relations: Not managing communication in the construction of the activist model of public relations*. Paper presented at the PRSA Educator Academy Second Annual Research Conference, College Park, MD.

Serini, S. A. (1993). Influences on the power of public relations professionals in organizations: A case study. *Journal of Public Relations Research, 5*, 1–25.

Shapere, D. (1977). Scientific theories and their domains. In F. Suppe (Ed.), *The structure of scientific theories* (2nd ed., pp. 518–565). Urbana: University of Illinois Press.

Spicer, C. (1997). *Organizational public relations: A political perspective.* Mahwah, NJ: Lawrence Erlbaum Associates.

Sriramesh, K., Grunig, J. E., & Dozier, D. M. (1996). Observation and measurement of two dimensions of organizational culture and their relationship to public relations. *Journal of Public Relations Research, 8*, 229–262.

Starck, K., & Kruckeberg, D. (2001). Public relations and community: A reconstructed theory revisited. In R. L. Heath (Ed.), *Handbook of public relations* (pp. 1–60). Thousand Oaks, CA: Sage.

Stauber, J., & Rampton, S. (1995). *Toxic sludge is good for you: Lies, damn lies, and the public relations industry.* Monroe, ME: Common Courage Press.

Suppe, F. (1977). *The structure of scientific theories* (2nd ed.). Urbana: University of Illinois Press.

Susskind, L., & Field, P. (1996). *Dealing with an angry public: The mutual gains approach to resolving disputes.* New York: The Free Press.

Thayer, L. (1968). *Communication and communication systems.* Homewood, IL: Irwin.

Van der Meiden, A. (1993). Public relations and "other" modalities of professional communication: Asymmetric presuppositions for a new theoretical discussion. *International Public Relations Review, 16*(3), 8–11.

Vasquez, G. M. (1996). Public relations as negotiation: An issue development perspective. *Journal of Public Relations Research, 8*, 57–77.

Verčič, D. (1997). Toward fourth wave public relations: A case study. In D. Moss, T. MacManus, & D. Verčič (Eds.), *Public relations research: An international perspective* (pp. 264–279). London: International Thomson Business Press.

Verčič, D., Grunig, L. A., & Grunig, J. E. (1996). Global and specific principles of public relations: Evidence from Slovenia. In H. M. Culbertson & N. Chen (Eds.), *International public relations: A comparative analysis* (pp. 31–65). Mahwah, NJ: Lawrence Erlbaum Associates.

Wakefield, R. I. (1997). *International public relations: A theoretical approach to excellence based on a worldwide delphi study.* Unpublished doctoral dissertation, University of Maryland, College Park.

Wallack, L., Dorfman, L., Jernigan, D., & Themba, M. (1993). *Media advocacy and public health: Power for prevention.* Newbury Park, CA: Sage.

Wetherell, B. J. (1989). *The effect of gender, masculinity, and femininity on the practice of and preference for the models of public relations.* Unpublished master's thesis, University of Maryland, College Park.

Wilson, L. J. (2001). Relationships within communities: Public relations for the new century. In R. L. Heath (Ed.), *Handbook of public relations* (pp. 521–526). Thousand Oaks, CA: Sage.

Yarbrough, C. R., Cameron, G. T., Sallot, L. M., & McWilliams, A. (1998). Tough calls to make: Contingency theory and the Centennial Olympic Games. *Journal of Communication Management, 3*, 39–56.

Ziegler, H. (1988). *Pluralism, corporatism, and Confucianism: Political association and conflict resolution in the United States, Europe, and Taiwan.* Philadelphia: Temple University Press.

CHAPTER NINE

The Origins, Management, and Outcomes of Programs for Key Publics

In these early days of the 21st century, two themes seem to dominate discussions in the professional public relations literature, at meetings of professional societies, and in discussions between public relations professionals and their employers or clients. The first is the need to make communication programs more strategic—to connect them to organizational goals. The second is the need to demonstrate that communication programs are effective—to develop evaluation research methods to demonstrate that the programs have measurable outcomes.

In chapter 5, we discussed the difference in meaning of the term "strategic" when it is attached to "public relations." Most commonly, "strategic" means that public relations managers align messages with organizational goals. We call this the *message-only* approach. Communicators using this strategic approach have little involvement in decision making. After the dominant coalition makes a decision, they are called in to develop messages to persuade publics to accept and support the decision.

In place of this common understanding of strategic public relations, we advocated a *full-participation* approach in which communicators are involved before strategic decisions are made. When they participate fully in strategic management, communicators scan the environment to identify stakeholder publics likely to be affected by a potential decision or who can affect the implementation of the decision, communicate with publics to involve them in the decision process, and develop ongoing communication programs to develop relationships with the publics affected by the consequences of decisions. At each step of the strategic process depicted in Fig. 5.1 (the stakeholder, publics, issue, and crisis stages), we pointed out, organizations need to communicate with publics who affect or are affected by an organization's decisions and behaviors.

To this point in the book, we have discussed the characteristics of excellent public relations at the organizational and departmental levels. In this chapter, we move down a level. This is the level of ongoing programs that excellent communication departments devise to develop and maintain relationships with their key publics—those identified by top communicators who participate fully in top-management decisions. (These programs are located in the center oval in Fig. 5.1.) It is at this level that we address the two concerns that pervade current discussions of public relations—strategic origination of programs and evaluation of their outcomes.

In this chapter, we analyze communication programs for seven specific publics: the media,[1] employees, investors, the community, customers, government, and members. (We did not include the donor public in the analysis as we did in chap. 8 because the small number made analysis impossible.) We look for support for our theoretical prediction that organizations and public relations departments that are excellent overall also will have specific communication programs that are excellent. We believe that communication programs in excellent departments will be more likely to have strategic origins and less likely to have historicist origins than those in less excellent departments. We also believe that excellent programs will be based on environmental scanning research and that they are more likely to use evaluation research to gather evidence that shows positive outcomes from the programs. Less excellent programs, in contrast, continue year after year with little or no research to identify new or changing publics, without setting measurable objectives, and without conducting evaluation research to determine whether these objectives have been met.

The questionnaire for the top communicator provided a list of 17 publics that serve as the focus of public relations programs in many organizations. Top communicators were asked to provide a detailed breakdown of the origins, management, and outcomes of communication programs for their top three publics, as defined by budget allocations. The questions we asked about these programs can be found in Part I of the PR head questionnaire in Appendix A.

We treat the participating department as the unit of analysis. Several organizations in the Excellence study provided data from multiple departments handling different aspects of the communication function. Thus, data in this chapter were reported by 407 communication departments, with program-level data reported by 316 primary departments (either the only department in the organization or the one with the biggest overall budget) and 91 secondary departments (those with smaller budgets in organizations with multiple communication departments). Of those, 361 departments reported data on at least one of

---

[1]The media cannot truly be said to be a public because they are important only as a means of communicating with publics that interact with an organization. If a key public does not use the media for information about an organization or its decisions, the media have little importance in a communication program. However, journalists behave like members of other publics (J. Grunig, 1983) when they seek information, so we refer to them loosely in this chapter as a public.

the top seven publics. Twenty-two additional departments implemented programs for less common publics not included in the top seven; they were excluded from subsequent analysis.

A total of 920 communication programs from the top seven were implemented by 361 departments. Some 72% of departments included media relations programs among their top three programs, followed by employee relations programs (55% of departments), community relations programs (41% of departments), customer relations programs (38% of departments), governmental relations programs (17% of departments), member relations programs (17% of departments), and investor relations programs (16% of departments).

As detailed in the meta-analysis at the end of this chapter, 546 relationships were tested, each of which provided an opportunity to confirm or disconfirm the propositions in the next section. For those tests, 468 (86%) yielded findings consistent with theoretical propositions of communication Excellence. Of those, 400 (73% of all relationships tested) were statistically significant. Only eight relationships (1.4% of all relationships tested) yielded findings disconfirming Excellence propositions; only four (0.7% of total) were statistically significant. That is, propositions derived from the Excellence theory were strongly confirmed by the data. Disconfirming findings were well within expected sampling error.

PROPOSITIONS ABOUT EXCELLENCE

In *Excellence in Public Relations and Communication Management* (J. Grunig, 1992), we put forth several propositions about relationships between communication Excellence, the strategic origins of communication programs, environmental turbulence, environmental scanning, program evaluation, and positive outcomes of specific communication programs targeted at key publics. The list of propositions expanded when data from the Excellence study were examined in the *Manager's Guide to Excellence in Public Relations and Communication Management* (Dozier with J. Grunig & L. Grunig, 1995).

Proposition 1 states that overall communication Excellence in organizations, as conceptualized in chapter 1 and as operationalized in chapter 3, leads to the strategic (rather than historicist) origination and implementation of specific communication programs for publics: *The greater the communication Excellence in organizations, the greater the levels of strategic planning in the origination, planning, and execution of programs for key publics.*

Of course, the underlying assumption of excellence as an attribute of departments and organizations is that it materially affects how communication programs originate and are implemented. Broom's (1986) conceptual work with open-system versus closed-system approaches to the practice of public relations provides a useful framework for understanding the historicist versus strategic origins of public relations programs:

Professional etiquette often demands going along with the conventional wisdom that public relations activities are rational, goal-directed management responses to an organization's environment. The more historically accurate portrayal, however, would show routine and institutionalized public relations responses that are unsystematically related to organizational survival and growth, or demise. Explanation of the relationship between public relations activities and organizational environment would draw more from Darwin's theory of evolution by natural and chance selection than from a model of scientific management and decision-making. (p. 1)

Broom later revised his pessimistic assessment and viewed organizations arrayed along a continuum from a relatively closed-system, historicist approach to the practice to a more strategic, open-systems approach (Broom & Dozier, 1990). In a closed-system or historicist approach to communication programs, the organizational boundary is relatively "impermeable to environmental inputs" and communication programs "increasingly reflect historical, routine, and institutionalized behaviors" reminiscent of "perpetual motion machines—infinite, self-replicating causal loops with the original causes or motivations lost in history" (Broom, 1986, p. 7).

Organizations using the open-systems approach, on the other hand, develop communication programs in direct response to perceived threats or turbulence in the environment and among key publics. Such an approach depends heavily on environmental inputs, provided by such mechanisms as environmental scanning. Goal states or desired outcomes are compared with the existing relationships with key publics. Such an open-systems approach relies on information provided by environmental scanning and evaluation research to identify problems and measure progress toward their solution (Dozier, 1990). In the Excellence study, indexes were constructed to measure both historicist and strategic origins of communication programs for key publics.

Proposition 2 states: *The more turbulent and uncertain the organizational environment, the greater the environmental scanning among key publics.* Embedded in this proposition is a broad theoretical area of concern to organizational theorists in general and public relations scholars in particular. Robbins (1990) provided a useful synthesis of the environmental imperative in organizational theory. Summarizing a large body of earlier research, he established that organizations face varying degrees of environmental uncertainty and turbulence. Environmental uncertainty and turbulence, Robbins concluded, is as much perceptual as it is rooted in objective indicators.

In public relations, several scholars have considered the impact of organizational environment on aspects of the communication function (Broom & Dozier, 1990; Dozier, 1987, 1990; Dozier & Broom, 1995; Dozier & Ehling, 1992; Dozier & L. Grunig, 1992; Dozier & White, 1992; Lauzen & Dozier, 1992, 1994). This issue has been central to the Excellence study. Organizations that perceive little environmental uncertainty and turbulence are likely to become comfortable with a closed-system, historicist approach to the management of communication programs. As Broom argued (1986), existing public relations programs have considerable sunk costs; maintaining existing programs as they have been historically executed costs less in terms of budgetary and intellectual resources than instituting new programs in response to new environmental conditions. He explained, "Past investments in human and physical resources are maintained because of the high cost of replacement or redesign" (p. 8). In addition, managers often bet that doing a communication program like the last one will encounter fewer objections from other managers jealous of scarce resources than would doing a new, innovative program.

Organizations that encounter and perceive environmental uncertainty and turbulence are likely to develop communication programs in response to those perceived changes and uncertainties. The power-control perspective to organizational theory suggests that communication programs change—and new ones are added—when the current, historically driven programs no longer satisfice. Dozier and White (1992) argued that managers enact organizational environments that generally are self-serving, socially constructed representations of the world outside the organization's loosely defined boundaries. As boundary spanners, public relations practitioners often interact with an outside world that is markedly different from the way managers inside the organization perceive it. By contrast, organizations and public relations practitioners originate communication programs strategically when they perceive that circumstances in the environment require a strategic response.

The strategic origin of communication programs has a number of important conceptual corollaries. First, strategic communication programs originate when dominant coalitions are generally strategically oriented and apply that orientation to specific communication programs. Strategic communication programs are thoughtful responses to perceived problems or threats to the organization posed by one or more publics. The communication program is carefully planned, taking advantage of the best available information about target publics involved. Environmental scanning research is important to designing strategic communication programs. Strategic programs have measurable goals and objectives; evaluation research helps determine if goals and objectives have been met. Strategic programs are dynamic, adapting on a regular basis as the organization–public relationship changes.

As Dozier and Ehling (1992) and Ehling and Dozier (1992) argued, operations research and evaluation are critical components to the strategic management of communication programs. A communication program driven by historicist logic does not require research; it operates independently of environmental conditions and independently of the effects (if any) of the program itself. Broom and Dozier (1990) constructed a typology of the uses of research in public relations and communication management. The *no-research* approach fits the closed-system, historicist approach best. The *informal* approach collects useful preliminary information; but then it uses such tentative information inappropriately to make strategic decisions that require more rigorous, scientific information. The *media-event* approach funds research projects for the sole purpose of generating publicity for the organization that sponsors the research; the information plays no role in management decision making. The *evaluation-only* approach occurs in organizations where dominant coalitions demand accountability from communication departments ill equipped by predilection or training to use research to plan and implement communication programs. Evaluation research becomes a feared weapon wielded by budget cutters rather than a powerful tool for communicators to plan, manage, and evaluate the programs they execute.

Only the *scientific management* approach uses environmental scanning and program evaluation research to manage communication programs strategically. As indicated in chapters 1, 3, and 6, excellence hinges on the knowledge base or expertise of personnel in the communication department to enact the manager role. Excellence also depends on frequent enactment of the manager role by top communicators. The strong linkage between managerial role playing and the use of program or operations research was well documented before the Excellence study (see Dozier, 1990, for a summary of this research). When communication managers enact a managerial role more frequently, they also increase their environmental scanning and program evaluation.

Propositions 3–6, therefore, spell out the expected relationships among manager role expertise, manager role enactment, environmental scanning, and program evaluation for key publics:

3. *The greater the managerial role expertise in the communication department, the greater the levels of environmental scanning of key publics.*
4. *The greater the managerial role enactment by the top communicator, the greater the levels of environmental scanning of key publics.*
5. *The greater the managerial role expertise in the communication department, the greater the efforts to evaluate programs for key publics.*
6. *The greater the enactment of the manager role among top communicators, the greater the efforts to evaluate programs for key publics.*

As noted in chapter 1, the original mandate to the Excellence research team from the IABC Foundation was to answer the effectiveness question: How, why, and to what extent does communication affect the achievement of organizational objectives? At the level of individual communication programs, the question can be recast as: What factors contribute to the positive outcomes of communication programs for key publics? Propositions 7–10 address the bottom-line concerns of practitioners as well as scholars:

7. *The greater the communication Excellence in organizations, the more successful such organizations are at reducing conflicts with key publics.*

8. *The greater the communication Excellence in organizations, the more successful such organizations are at achieving positive change in relationships with key publics.*

9. *The more strategic the origins and management of programs for key publics, the more positive are the outcomes achieved with publics.*

10. *The more scanning and evaluation research conducted on key publics, the more demonstrable are the outcomes achieved with publics.*

As outlined in chapter 1, a major goal of communication programs targeted at important publics is to reduce conflict—either actual or potential—and to seek positive change in relationships in order to build stable, open, and trusting ones. These bottom-line indicators of success at the programmatic level are a function of the overall Excellence of the communication function. This includes the knowledge core in the communication department to provide excellence, shared expectations with a dominant coalition that demands excellence, and a participative organizational culture that provides fertile soil where excellence can grow. These expectations are reflected in Propositions 7 and 8.

Proposition 9 ties the strategic origins and management of communication programs to desired outcomes with key publics. Proposition 10 argues that the use of scanning and evaluation provides communicators with the evidence they need to demonstrate success to dominant coalitions. That is, if the general theory of excellence is true in a positive sense, one would expect that overall Excellence of the organization and the communication department would result in communication programs that have demonstrably positive outcomes on relationships with strategic constituencies.

Note that the variables analyzed in this chapter are *not* components of the general measure of excellence, operationalized as the Excellence factor in chapter 3. Rather, these measures at the program level permit a test (in the hypothetical-deductive sense) of the general theory on essentially new data not employed previously in the construction of the Excellence factor.

CONSTRUCTING INDEXES FOR PROGRAMS AND PUBLICS

Nine indexes were constructed for each of the seven most popular communication programs listed by top communicators. These indexes permitted the Excellence research team to test the 10 propositions listed earlier. These included a 4-item index measuring the historical origins of public relations programs for key publics; a 15-item index measuring strategic origins; a 5-item index measuring formal environmental scanning; a 5-item index measuring informal environmental scanning; a 4-item index measuring scientific evaluation of programs for key publics; a 4-item index measuring clip-file evaluation of programs; and a 4-item index measuring informal, seat-of-the-pants evaluation of program. The two indexes of environmental scanning and the three indexes of program evaluation were then combined into a single, 5-item index measuring operations or program research, inclusive of both scanning and evaluation efforts at various levels of rigor. A 7-item index was constructed that measured the degree to which communication programs avoided or reduced conflict with each of the seven publics. A 6-item index was constructed that measured the degree to which communication programs resulted in positive changes in relationships with the seven publics.

In addition to conflict avoidance and positive changes in relationships, other measures of positive program outcomes were made for each of the seven publics. These single-item indicators included positive media coverage, accurate reception of program messages, increased sales of products or services, making money for the organization, saving money for the organization, and helping the organization achieve its goals.

All indexes used transformed versions of original variables from the fractionation scales in the questionnaire. These transformations are square roots of original responses to each item. Whereas 100 was a hypothetical average score for an item on the original fractionation scale, 10 was the average for a typical transformed item. Of course, the average for any item is based on actual frequency of the reported activity. The average of 10 simply provides a basis for the reader to orient to the transformed fractionation-scale scores. All indexes were computed as the mean of the items making up that index, so an average of 10 applies to indexes as well as individual items.

Historical and Strategic Origins of Communication Programs

Table 9.1 displays the four items used to measure the historical origins of communication programs for key publics. These measures operationalize the closed-systems, historicist approach to public relations programming, as Broom (1986; Broom & Dozier, 1990) originally conceptualized it. Means and standard deviations of the historicist origins index are provided for each of the seven key publics. Cronbach's alpha reliability coefficients are low, especially for customer relations programs, but analysis of the item set did not indicate that removal of any items would increase reliability for any of the seven publics. Reliability coefficients range from a low of .37 for customer relations programs to a high of .61 for member relations programs.

Table 9.2 displays the 15 items that make up the strategic origins index. The strategic origins index goes beyond simply measuring the origins of communication programs; this index also operationalizes the strategic manner in which

TABLE 9.1
Historical Origins for Public Relations Programs by Key Publics

Items
We continue the program because we have had it for many years.
For this program, public relations produces publications, news releases, video tapes, and the like but did not participate in the decision to begin the program.
Senior management made the decision with little input from the public relations head and instructed the public relations department to implement the program.
Although the public relations head was not part of senior management, senior management asked for input from public relations before making the decision to begin the program.

Characteristics by Key Publics	Mean	Stand. Dev.	Cronbach's alpha
Employees	4.23	3.36	.47
Media	3.99	3.60	.53
Investors	4.05	3.28	.55
Community	4.93	3.72	.53
Customers	4.49	3.82	.37
Government	4.27	3.49	.54
Members	4.91	3.70	.61

the program was planned, executed, and evaluated. As the items indicate, programs with strategic origins are developed in response to problems or issues involving the organization and each public; organizational responses are planned strategically; the impact of programs is evaluated; and the program changes dynamically in response to a changing organizational environment. This index provides reliable measures for all seven publics, with Cronbach's alphas ranging from .80 to .86.

Note that for each of the seven publics, the mean strategic origin scores are higher than the mean historical origin scores. These differences are statistically significant for employee relations programs ($T = 9.51$, $df = 147$, $p < .01$), media relations programs ($T = 11.21$, $df = 205$, $p < .01$), investor relations programs ($T = 4.78$, $df = 42$, $p < .01$), community relations programs ($T = 7.01$, $df = 110$, $p < .01$), customer relations programs ($T = 7.11$, $df = 78$, $p < .01$), governmental relations programs ($T = 4.04$, $df = 38$, $p < .01$), and member relations programs ($T = 3.47$, $df = 40$, $p < .01$). Across the board, the origin of communication programs tends to be more strategic than historicist.

Environmental Scanning for Communication Programs

Table 9.3 shows the items that make up both the formal and informal environmental scanning indexes for each of the seven publics. The formal evaluation index measured use of surveys, public opinion research firms, audits, demographic data, and formal research to scan the organizational environment with

TABLE 9.2
Strategic Origins and Management for Public
Relations Programs by Key Publics

Items
We started the program after strategic planning showed the public could hurt or help the organization.
The public relations head was part of senior management and participated fully in the decision to conduct the program.
The public relations department has reviewed management decisions to identify public relations problems with this public.
The public relations department has identified a public relations problem by reviewing the extent to which the organization has been socially responsible with this public.
The public relations department has used techniques such as VALS or Prizm to segment this public.
The public relations department has used focus groups to research this public.
A committee or other formal mechanism is used to track issues with this public.
The program for this public was developed because of a specific issue or set of related issues.
A crisis communication plan exists in the program for this public.
The actual communication program for this public is based on research on the issue and public.
The program for this public changes every year or two as issues and publics change.
The program for this public was developed and is reviewed through a formal planning process.
The program for this public has written objectives.
Management by objectives (MBO) is used in the program for this public.
At budget time, funding depends on the demonstrated effectiveness of the program for this public.

Characteristics by Key Publics	*Mean*	*Stand. Dev.*	*Cronbach's alpha*
Employees	7.88	3.28	.81
Media	7.64	3.07	.80
Investors	7.24	3.15	.86
Community	8.17	3.12	.84
Customers	8.09	3.51	.81
Government	7.45	3.46	.84
Members	7.94	2.88	.81

regard to each of the seven publics. The formal scanning index is reliable, ranging from .75 for member publics to .90 for employees and investors.

Informal environmental scanning depends more on informal information gathering, similar to the tools journalists use, than does a formal process. These tools include informal discussions and call-backs to representatives of key publics and field personnel, as well as reviewing complaints. The means and standard deviations for the informal scanning index are provided for each of the seven publics. The reliabilities of the informal scanning indexes are lower than those for the formal scanning indexes, but they are sufficiently reliable for testing propositions explicated earlier. Reliability coefficients for the informal scan-

TABLE 9.3
Formal and Informal Environmental Scanning by Key Publics

Formal Environmental Scanning Items

Formal research studies are used to track public reactions to the organization.
Surveys are conducted of this key public.
This program subscribes to or uses the services of public opinion research agencies.
Communication or public relations audits are conducted to find out about this public.
Demographic data are used to help make decisions concerning this public.

Characteristics by Key Publics	Mean	Stand. Dev.	Cronbach's alpha
Employees	6.46	5.63	.90
Media	5.27	4.97	.85
Investors	6.35	7.60	.90
Community	6.04	4.74	.87
Customers	7.48	6.41	.85
Government	5.00	4.47	.86
Members	6.20	4.25	.75

Informal Environmental Scanning Items

Phone calls are made to members of this public to keep in touch.
In-depth interviews are conducted with members of this public.
After the organization conducts special events, people are called back to get their reaction.
Program managers talk with field personnel to find out about this public.
Complaints are reviewed to find out how this public feels about the organization.

Characteristics by Key Publics	Mean	Stand. Dev.	Cronbach's alpha
Employees	8.39	4.26	.78
Media	7.35	3.70	.65
Investors	8.07	3.55	.61
Community	8.00	3.75	.75
Customers	9.43	4.90	.62
Government	6.89	3.41	.57
Members	9.31	3.87	.74

ning index range from a low of .57 for governmental relations programs to a high of .78 for employee relations programs.

Note that informal scanning techniques are generally employed more frequently than are formal scanning techniques. As scholar-turned-practitioner David Clavier noted, all decisions about research in public relations are constrained by time and budget, as well as the philosophy of the dominant coalition (Broom & Dozier, 1990, p. 90). Because the purpose of environmental scanning is early detection of public relations problems, the rigor of the information collected must be balanced against the time and budget constraints. Informal environmental scanning is used significantly more often than formal scanning for employee publics ($T = 6.37$, $df = 182$, $p < .01$), media publics ($T = 7.80$, $df = 250$,

$p < .01$), investor publics ($T = 2.17$, $df = 52$, $p = .03$), community publics ($T = 5.67$, $df = 134$, $p < .01$), customer publics ($T = 3.39$, $df = 93$, $p < .01$), government publics ($T = 3.44$, $df = 48$, $p < .01$), and member publics ($T = 4.77$, $df = 55$, $p < .01$). For all publics, then, informal scanning is used significantly more frequently than formal scanning.

Evaluating Communication Programs

Three separate indexes of program evaluation were used in the Excellence study, based on previous studies of how practitioners go about evaluating the impact of communication programs (Dozier, 1990). These included an index for each program that measured program impact through formal, scientific methods; a hybrid index that focused on both formal and informal evaluation of clip files; and an informal, seat-of-the-pants index that focused on largely subjective evaluations of low rigor.

Unlike environmental scanning, where early detection of problems or issues with publics permits a more egalitarian view of formal and informal methods, program evaluation is arguably much more hierarchical with regard to quality and rigor. Based on the theory of excellence, scientific evaluation is clearly superior to either clip-file or seat-of-the-pants evaluation. Only scientific evaluation provides the kind of rigorous, objective data that dominant coalitions are likely to regard as compelling. Evaluating clip files can be done formally and informally, but attention is focused on process variables (message dissemination), not outcomes of inherent value to organizations and dominant coalitions. Seat-of-the-pants evaluation, when used alone, is the last bastion of the one-way communicator, disseminating messages and relying on such devices as gastrointestinal feedback (see index) as indicators of success.

Table 9.4 displays the four items used to measure scientific evaluation for each of the seven communication programs. This method of evaluation uses cross-sectional surveys and before–after field experimental designs to measure program impact. The means and standard deviations for these indexes are provided for the seven communication programs. Cronbach's reliability coefficients range from a low of .54 for employee communication programs to a high of .79 for member communication programs.

Table 9.5 displays the four items used to measure program evaluation through analysis of clip files. These evaluations range from formal, scientific content analysis of clip files to more informal monitoring of message dissemination through media contacts. Cronbach's reliability coefficients range from a low of .54 for government relations programs to a high of .84 for media relations and investor relations programs.

When comparing the use of clip-file evaluation to more rigorous scientific evaluation across programs, the relative frequency depends on the degree to which public media are used to disseminate messages. When public media pro-

TABLE 9.4
Scientific Evaluation of Programs for Key Publics

Scientific Evaluation Items

The effectiveness of the program is checked through interviews with a scientifically selected cross-section of this public.

Communications are prepared in this program after first reviewing published surveys (Gallup, Harris) on attitudes of this public.

The communication effectiveness of this program is measured by comparing before-program and after-program measures of this public.

The communication program is designed as though it were a field experiment of communication effects.

Characteristics by Key Publics	*Mean*	*Stand. Dev.*	*Cronbach's alpha*
Employees	4.63	3.56	.54
Media	6.65	13.41	.69
Investors	4.34	3.75	.60
Community	5.02	4.07	.76
Customers	5.71	4.23	.54
Government	4.23	3.52	.56
Members	4.20	4.04	.79

TABLE 9.5
Clip-File Evaluation of Programs for Key Publics

Clip-File Evaluation Items

This program monitors the dissemination of messages (news stories, editorials, letters to editors) through a formal, ongoing content analysis of items in a clip file.

This program tracks news releases and other placements through a comprehensive clip file.

In this program, the number of inches placed, reach, and other vital statistics are logged for clip files.

Personnel in this program monitor dissemination of messages through close personal contacts among mass media professionals.

Characteristics by Key Publics	*Mean*	*Stand. Dev.*	*Cronbach's alpha*
Employees	3.06	3.62	.64
Media	5.32	6.42	.84
Investors	4.87	5.29	.84
Community	6.44	4.22	.80
Customers	6.11	5.25	.73
Government	5.53	3.38	.54
Members	4.86	4.33	.81

vide the primary vehicle for message dissemination, the frequency of clip-file evaluation is generally much higher than scientific evaluation. When controlled media are used primarily for message dissemination, scientific evaluation remains about the same as for other publics; but the use of clip-file evaluation drops dramatically.

For employee relations programs, scientific evaluation is used significantly more frequently than clip-file evaluation ($T = 5.42$, $df = 176$, $p < .01$), probably because employee communication programs depend heavily on internal or controlled media, rather than public media, for the dissemination of program messages. The same is true for member relations programs, with the use of scientific evaluation significantly higher than clip-file evaluation ($T = 5.42$, $df = 176$, $p < .01$). As with employee relations programs, clip-file evaluation is less relevant, because controlled rather than public media are primary vehicles for message dissemination.

On the other hand, clip-file evaluation is used much more frequently than scientific evaluation when the media are the target public ($T = 9.75$, $df = 252$, $p < .01$). This also makes sense conceptually, because media relations programs typically focus on message dissemination as a key indicator of success. Clip-file evaluation is used significantly more often than scientific evaluation for community relations programs ($T = 4.32$, $df = 136$, $p < .01$) and government relations programs ($T = 2.22$, $df = 49$, $p = .03$).

Clip-file evaluation is used somewhat more frequently to evaluate investor relations programs than is scientific evaluation, but the difference is not statistically significant ($T = 1.03$, $df = 48$, $p > .05$). Customer relations programs also use clip-file evaluation somewhat more frequently than scientific evaluation, but again the differences are not statistically significant ($T = .79$, $df = 90$, $p > .05$).

Table 9.6 displays the four items used in indexes to measure informal, seat-of-the-pants evaluation of the seven communication programs. These items involve informal, subjective impressions of program impact—collected by the communicator—using eyes, ears, and intestines as data-collection instruments. Cronbach's reliability coefficients vary considerably, from a low of .65 for investor and government relations programs to a high of .93 for media relations programs.

Across the board, informal, seat-of-the-pants evaluation is used much more frequently than either scientific or clip-file evaluation. Although informal evaluation is least consistent with the theory of excellence, the use of such informal techniques reflects the time and budget constraints identified by Clavier (Broom & Dozier, 1990). Such evaluation techniques are also consistent with Broom and Dozier's argument (1990) that communication programs be designed and evaluated using the *best available evidence*. The ideal of treating every communication program as a field experiment in communication effects, using probability sampling of target publics to ensure that measures of impact can be generalized from those surveyed to the entire population, simply does not re-

TABLE 9.6
Informal Seat-of-the-Pants Evaluation of Programs for Key Publics

Informal Evaluation Items

Personnel in this program check its impact by keeping their eyes and ears open to the reactions of their personal and public contacts.

Personnel working on this program prepare communications by drawing on their own professional experience.

The impact of this communication program is checked by having personnel attend meetings and hearings of groups representative of this public.

Personnel working on this program can tell how effective it is by their own gut-level reactions and those of other communicators.

Characteristics by Key Publics	*Mean*	*Stand. Dev.*	*Cronbach's alpha*
Employees	9.82	3.86	.77
Media	10.92	3.68	.93
Investors	10.92	3.68	.65
Community	10.49	3.19	.66
Customers	9.88	4.24	.73
Government	10.90	3.25	.65
Members	10.12	3.16	.67

flect the real-world constraints of running communication programs. Rather, the imperative to gather and use the best available evidence suggests that various scanning and evaluation methods be treated as tools in a common tool box, with each tool used as constraints of the situation permit.

Toward that end, the two indexes of environmental scanning and the three indexes of program evaluation were combined into a single index of operations or program research. The structure of the index is displayed in Table 9.7. The index consists of five separate indexes and 22 separate items. Table 9.7 displays the means and standard deviations for the seven programs, as well as Cronbach's reliability coefficients for each program. These indexes are generally reliable across all seven programs, ranging from a low of .75 for government relations to a high of .89 for investor relations.

Outcomes of Communication Programs

In all, we measured eight positive outcomes of communication programs for each of the seven publics. For two outcomes most directly related to successful communication programs, we constructed indexes to provide multiple indicators and measures of reliability. For the remaining six, which either focus on process variables or are less directly linked to communication program activities, we used single indicators.

TABLE 9.7
The Operations Research Index
(Combined Scanning and Evaluation Indexes)

Research Indexes

Formal Environmental Scanning Index (5 items)
Informal Environmental Scanning Index (5 items)
Scientific Program Evaluation Index (4 items)
Clip File Program Evaluation Index (4 items)
Informal Seat-of-the-Pants Program Evaluation Index (4 items)

Characteristics by Key Publics	Mean	Stand. Dev.	Cronbach's alpha
Employees	6.47	3.30	.83
Media	9.19	9.52	.78
Investors	6.98	4.23	.89
Community	7.19	3.11	.83
Customers	7.83	4.10	.84
Government	6.34	2.60	.75
Members	6.92	2.80	.76

Table 9.8 displays the seven items measuring the success of communication programs to avoid conflicts with each of the seven publics. These items address the proactive side of public relations, wherein strikes, boycotts, complaints, disagreements, and governmental or legislative interference were avoided and negotiations with activists were undertaken. The Cronbach's reliability coefficients generally are reliable and remarkably stable across all seven publics, ranging from .78 (community relations) to .85 (media relations).

Table 9.9 displays the six items that measure positive change in relationships with the seven publics. Some of these involve pushing publics toward the win–win zone and closer to the position of the dominant coalition. Others involve the larger symmetrical concerns of building stable, long-term relationships based on improved understanding and cooperation between organizations and publics. Cronbach's reliability coefficients indicate the indexes are reliable. With the exception of customer relations programs (alpha = .75), Cronbach's reliability coefficients range from .82 to .90.

Table 9.10 displays the six single-item indicators of positive program outcomes. These include process measures, such as accurate message reception by the target public or positive media coverage with regard to the target public. This set also includes other items that may be indirect consequences of excellent communication programs, but dependent on other departments in the organization performing successfully as well. These include increased sales of products or services, helping the organization make money, helping the organization save money, and helping the organization achieve its objectives.

TABLE 9.8

Conflict Avoidance Outcomes for Key Publics

Conflict Avoidance Items

Litigation was avoided.
A strike or boycott was avoided.
Complaints from this public were reduced.
There were fewer disagreements and disputes with this public.
There was less interference by government in the management of the organization.
Activist groups were willing to negotiate with the organization.
Desirable legislation was passed or undesirable legislation was defeated.

Characteristics by Key Publics	Mean	Stand. Dev.	Cronbach's alpha
Employees	3.74	3.30	.80
Media	3.83	3.60	.85
Investors	3.78	3.34	.82
Community	3.89	3.40	.78
Customers	4.38	3.63	.82
Government	4.11	3.42	.80
Members	3.95	3.36	.80

TABLE 9.9

Change of Relationship Outcomes of Programs for Key Publics

Change of Relationship Items

Attitudes of this public changed in support of our position.
The quality of communication with this public improved.
There was greater cooperation between my organization and this public.
This public changed its behavior in the way my organization wanted.
Understanding improved between the organization and this public.
A stable long-term relationship was developed with this public.

Characteristics by Key Publics	Mean	Stand. Dev.	Cronbach's alpha
Employees	10.16	2.82	.82
Media	10.21	3.56	.86
Investors	10.58	3.03	.82
Community	10.71	3.20	.85
Customers	10.54	3.81	.74
Government	10.68	3.73	.90
Members	10.09	3.60	.86

TABLE 9.10
Outcomes With Single-Item Measures for Key Publics

Single-Item Outcome Measures
Positive media coverage resulted [from this program].
Our message was received accurately [from this program].
Product sales or use of the organization's services increased [from this program].
The program [for this public] helped the organization make money.
The program [for this public] saved money for the organization.
The program [for this public] helped the organization meet its goals.

TESTING PROPOSITIONS ABOUT ORIGINS AND OUTCOMES

The propositions listed earlier specify how the overall Excellence of communication in organizations affects the ways in which specific communication programs are originated, how they are managed, how they are evaluated, and how they bring about desired outcomes for organizations and publics. The nine indexes and six single-item measures detailed in the previous section, "Constructing Indexes for Programs and Publics," permit testing of those propositions. As noted in chapter 2, tests of statistical significance are provided as indicators of the strength of relationships in the sample. Strictly speaking, the multistage sampling strategy used in the Excellence study (see chap. 2) does not allow for the use of such inferential statistics without a note of caution. Furthermore, the sample size varies considerably from one public to another. Among the 361 communication departments that run communication programs for at least one of the seven publics, 258 departments have media relations programs, 198 have employee relations programs, 148 have community relations programs, 137 have customer relations programs, 62 have government relations programs, 61 have member relations programs, and 56 have investor relations programs. Thus, for government, member, and investor relations programs, the effect size must be quite large in the population for any relationship to be detected as statistically significant in the sample. The probability of Type 2 error is large.

A useful way to interpret the Pearson product–moment correlation coefficients in the analysis that follows is to generate estimates of explained variance by squaring the correlation coefficient. For example, if the correlation between manager role expertise in the department is correlated with the strategic origins of the employee relations program at $r = .49$, then the variance in the strategic origins of the employee relations program explained by manager role expertise is .24 ($.49 \times .49 = .24$) or 24%. That is, expertise in the communication department to enact the manager role accounts for 24% of the variance in the strategic origins of employee relations programs. Note that this variance is not uniquely accounted for by the independent variable, because the independent variable may be correlated with a host of other antecedent variables. However, explained variance does provide a useful tool for understanding the strength of relationships between variables, especially when some publics have substantially smaller sample sizes than others.

Historicist Origins of Communication Programs

Table 9.11 displays the relationship between the historical origins of communication programs for the seven publics with key measures of communication Excellence, as spelled out in the propositions. Regarding overall Excellence as indicated by the organization's Excellence score (see chap. 3), excellence is negatively related to the historicist, closed-system approach to running public relations programs. Three of these negative relationships are statistically significant, accounting for 3% to 17% of the variance. The greater the excellence in a communication department, the less the use of historicist, closed-system thinking in the design and continuance of communication programs for specific publics.

Although no measure of environmental turbulence was collected for individual publics, a global measure asked top communicators to indicate "the extent to which your organization has experienced pressure from activist groups." This measure was correlated with historicist origins for each of the seven publics. As expected, environmental turbulence—operationalized as general pressure from activist groups—usually was unrelated to historicist, closed-system approaches to originating communication programs. For investor relations, the relationship was significant and negative, accounting for 12% of the variance. The greater the pressure from activists, the less likely was the use of closed-system thinking in originating investor relations programs.

Top communicators were also asked to estimate how successful they (and their organizations) were in achieving their goals with regard to activist pressure groups. As expected, success with activist groups was generally unrelated to the historicist, closed-system origins of communication programs for most programs. For member relations programs, the relationship was significant and negative, accounting for 14% of the variance. The more successful the organization in dealing with activist pressure, the less its member relations program depended on historicist origination.

As explained in chapter 6, one of the prerequisites to the effective management of communication programs is core knowledge in the communication department to design and implement excellent communication programs. Along with the expertise to use the two-way symmetrical and asymmetrical model as originally conceptualized (see chap. 8 for our refinement of the two-way model), excellent communication departments require the expertise to enact the manager role. As shown in Table 9.11, manager role expertise in the com-

TABLE 9.11

Correlations of Excellence, Environmental Turbulence, Turbulence Management, and Manager Role Characteristics With Historical Origins of Public Relations Programs for Key Publics

Historical Origins of Programs for:	Employees	Media	Investors	Community	Customers	Government	Members
Overall Excellence Score	-.17*	-.09	-.27*	-.03	-.05	-.06	-.41**
Environmental Turbulence (Activists)	-.06	-.05	-.34**	.04	.05	.06	.01
Success With Activist Publics	-.01	-.03	-.12	-.01	.03	-.20	-.37**
Manager Role Expertise in Department	-.05	-.08	-.14	-.10	-.12	.09	-.34**
Technician Role Expertise in Dept. (partial corr.)	.03	.06	-.18	.16*	.18*	.03	-.08
Top Communicator Manager Role Playing	-.22**	-.21**	-.17	-.29**	-.14	-.07	-.38**

Note. Average sample sizes for this analysis: employees = 159; media = 217; investors = 46; community = 121; customers = 85; government = 44; and members = 48. Sample size may vary for each coefficient, depending on number of missing cases.

$*p < .05$. $**p < .01$.

munication department is negatively correlated with use of the historicist model to originate communication programs. For member relations, this negative relationship is statistically significant, accounting for 12% of the variance. The greater the manager role expertise in the department, the less the use of the historicist model to originate communication programs for specific publics.

Expertise to enact the technician role was also correlated negatively in some cases with the historicist model. This may seem surprising, because technician expertise would be logically associated with historicist rather than strategic origination of communication programs. However, as detailed in chapter 6, the best single predicator of technician role expertise in the communication department is manager role expertise. Excellent communication departments have strong expertise in both the managerial and technical roles. The best indicator of relations between technician role expertise and other measures of excellence is the partial correlation coefficient, wherein the relationship between technician expertise and other variables is tested *after* the influence of manager role expertise is removed.

In Table 9.11, the partial correlation is displayed between historicist origins of the seven programs and technician role expertise in the department. Five of the seven relationships are insignificant. Historicist origins of community and customer relations programs are positively related to technician role expertise in the department, accounting for 3% of the variance in both cases. For those two programs, the greater the technician role expertise in the department, the more likely that community and customer relations programs will have higher historicist origin scores. For the rest of the programs, technician role expertise is not related to historicist origins.

As we showed in chapter 6, top communicators were asked to describe their own organizational behavior with regard to communicator roles. The manager role index used in this chapter is the index detailed in Table 6.8, which combines attributes of both the manager and senior adviser role as originally conceptualized. Table 9.11 shows the relationship between manager role enactment by the top communicator and historicist origins of the seven communication programs. All the relationships are negative. Four of the seven are statistically significant, accounting for 4% to 14% of the variance. The more the top communicator enacts the manager role, the lower the historicist origin scores for communication programs that he or she manages.

Strategic Origins of Communication Programs. Table 9.12 displays the same set of Excellence indicators, broken down by the strategic origins and management scores for each of the seven programs. As expected, the organization's overall Excellence score is significantly and positively correlated with the strategic origins and management of all seven communication programs. Overall Excellence accounts for 8% (governmental relations) to 40% (community relations) of the variance in the strategic origins and management of communi-

TABLE 9.12

Correlations of Excellence, Environmental Turbulence, Turbulence Management, and Manager Role Characteristics With Strategic Origins of Public Relations Programs for Key Publics

Strategic Origins of Programs for:	Employees	Media	Investors	Community	Customers	Government	Members
Overall Excellence Score	.57**	.56**	.43**	.63**	.57**	.29**	.78**
Environmental Turbulence (Activists)	.23**	.16**	.14	.25**	.23*	-.06	.19
Success With Activist Publics	.11	.25**	.18	-.02	.14	.18	.41**
Manager Role Expertise in Department	.49**	.47**	.62**	.48**	.54**	.37**	.66**
Technician Role Expertise in Department (partial corr.)	.16*	.01	.20	-.07	.09	-.30*	.07
Top Communicator Manager Role Playing	.37**	.39**	.23	.38**	.53**	.47**	.79**

Note. Average sample sizes for this analysis: employees = 159; media = 217; investors = 46; community = 121; customers = 85; government = 44; and members = 48. Sample size may vary for each coefficient, depending on number of missing cases.

*p < .05. **p < .01.

cation programs for specific publics. The greater the overall Excellence of the organization, the greater the strategic origins of all its major communication programs.

With the exception of governmental relations programs, pressure from activist groups on the organization is significantly correlated with the strategic origins of communication programs. Four of these relationships are statistically significant, with explained variance ranging from 3% to 6%. The greater the pressure from activist groups, the greater the strategic origin of communication programs. The only exception is strategic origins of governmental relations programs, which are negatively related (but not significantly so) to activist pressure.

The strategic origins and management of communication programs are generally related to increased success with activist publics, although the relationships are weak. Two such relations are statistically significant. Strategic origins of media relations programs account for 6% of success with activist publics; strategic origins of member relations programs account for 17% of success with activists.

Manager role expertise is significantly and positively related to the strategic origins and management of communication programs for all publics. Manager role expertise accounts for 14% (governmental relations) to 44% (member relations) of the variance in the strategic origin of communication programs for the seven publics.

Technician role expertise, on the other hand, is generally unrelated to the strategic origins of communication programs, once the influence of manager role expertise is removed. The only exceptions are the positive relationship with the strategic origins of employee relations programs (3% of the variance) and the negative relationship with governmental relations programs (9% of the variance).

Enactment of the manager role by the top communicator is positively related to the strategic origin of communication programs for all publics. Six of the seven relationships are statistically significant. Enactment of the manager role by the top communicator accounts for 14% (employee relations) to 62% (member relations) of the variance in the strategic origin of programs. Even for the relationship that is not significant (investor relations), manager role enactment still accounts for 6% of the variance in the sample; small sample size ($N = 42$ for this test) helps explain the nonsignificance of the relationship.

In summary, strategic origins of communication programs are consistently linked to indicators of communication Excellence, as posited in the propositions. Strategic origins of communication programs are linked to the overall Excellence of communication in the organization. The origins of communication programs are more likely to be strategic when the organization experiences pressure from activist groups. Programs with strategic origins tend to achieve greater success with activists, although these relationships are generally weak. The strategic origins of programs are consistently and positively associated with manager role expertise in the communication department and manager role enactment by the top communicator. Technician role expertise, on the other hand, is generally unrelated to the strategic origins of programs, once the influence of manager role expertise is controlled.

Environmental Scanning for Strategic Constituencies.   Table 9.13 displays the relationships between formal environmental scanning and key indicators of excellence for each of the seven publics analyzed. The overall communication Excellence of the organization is positively and significantly correlated with formal environmental scanning for each of the seven publics. Overall communication Excellence accounts for 6% (governmental relations) to 35% (customer relations) of the variance in formal evaluation activities.

When organizations are confronted with pressure from activist groups, they are more likely to engage in formal environmental scanning for six of seven publics. Activist pressure accounts for 4% (community relations) to 25% (investor relations) of the use of formal environmental scanning. The only anomaly is the significant, negative correlation between activist pressure and formal scanning of member publics.

When organizations engage in formal scanning of strategic constituencies, they are generally more successful in dealing with activists. Four of the seven relationships are significant and positive, with formal scanning accounting for 8% (media relations) to 29% (investor relations) of success with activists. Two other relationships are positive but not significant. One relationship (government relations) is negative but near zero and not significant.

As expected, programs with strategic origins are positively and significantly correlated with the use of formal evaluation methods for all seven publics. Strategic origins of programs account for 22% (member relations) to 67% (investor relations) of the variance in the use of formal environmental scanning methods.

Manager role expertise in the department is significantly and positively related to the use of formal scanning methods for six of seven publics. Manager role expertise in the department accounts for 18% (member relations) to 48% (investor relations) of the variance in the use of formal environmental scanning methods. The only nonsignificant relationship (government relations) is nevertheless positive.

Technician role expertise in the department is generally unrelated to the use of formal scanning techniques, once the influence of manager role expertise is controlled. Of the seven relationships, only two are significant. One (investor relations) is positive; the other (community relations) is negative. Five of the six nonsignificant relationships are weak and negative.

Manager role enactment of the top communicator is significantly and positively related to formal environmental scanning for six of seven publics. Manager role enactment accounts for 5% (media relations) to 12% (customer relations) of the variance in the use of formal scanning techniques. The greater the

TABLE 9.13

Correlations of Excellence, Environmental Turbulence, Turbulence Management, Strategic Origins, and Manager Role Characteristics With Formal Environmental Scanning for Key Publics

Formal Environmental Scanning for:	Employees	Media	Investors	Community	Customers	Government	Members
Overall Excellence Score	.53**	.50**	.58**	.58**	.59**	.25**	.32**
Environmental Turbulence From Activists	.28**	.21**	.50**	.20**	.33**	.26**	-.23**
Success With Activist Publics	.33**	.28**	.54**	.08	.43**	-.04	.16
Strategic Origins of Program	.56**	.57**	.82**	.64**	.63**	.57**	.47**
Manager Role Expertise in Department	.51**	.47**	.69**	.65**	.65**	.07	.43**
Technician Role Expertise in Department (partial corr.)	-.01	-.07	.28*	-.15*	.07	-.11	-.05
Top Communicator Manager Role Playing	.27**	.23**	.28**	.30**	.35**	.03	.28*

Note. Average sample sizes for this analysis: employees = 159; media = 217; investors = 46; community = 121; customers = 85; government = 44; and members = 48. Sample size may vary for each coefficient, depending on number of missing cases.

*p < .05. **p < .01.

manager role enactment by the top communicator, the greater the use of formal scanning techniques. The only nonsignificant relationship (government relations) is positive but near zero.

In summary, the use of formal environmental scanning techniques is related to a number of indicators of communication Excellence. The overall communication Excellence of the organization is a strong, positive predictor of the use of formal evaluation techniques for all seven publics. Environmental turbulence from activist groups tends to increase the use of formal scanning for most publics. Use of formal scanning with most publics also increases organizational success in dealing with activists. The use of formal scanning techniques is driven by the strategic origins of communication programs for all seven publics. Generally, formal scanning techniques are used more frequently as a function of manager role expertise in the department and enactment of the manager role by the top communicator. Technician role expertise in the communication department is generally unrelated to the use of formal scanning methods.

Table 9.14 displays the correlations between the use of informal scanning techniques and key indicators of communication Excellence. The overall communication Excellence of the organization is significantly and positively correlated with the use of informal scanning for all seven publics. Overall Excellence accounts for 8% (government relations) to 28% (member relations) of the use of informal scanning techniques.

Informal scanning increases when organizations experience pressure from activist publics, although only three relationships are statistically significant. Activist pressure accounts for 2% to 9% of the variance in the use of informal scanning. Three of the four nonsignificant relationships are positive; one is negative (member relations) but near zero. When organizations do use informal scanning techniques, they are generally more successful in dealing with activists. All seven relationships are positive; five are statistically significant. Use of informal scanning techniques accounts for 5% (media relations) to 18% (investor relations) of the variance in successfully dealing with activists.

When the origins of communication programs are strategic, we see more use of informal scanning techniques. The relationships are positive and significant for all seven publics. Strategic origins of programs account for 19% (government relations) to 48% (community relations) of the variance in the use of informal scanning techniques.

Manager role expertise in the communication department is also significantly and positively related to the use of informal scanning techniques for all seven publics. Manager role expertise accounts for 8% (member relations) to 21% (investor, community, and customer relations) of the variance in the use of informal scanning techniques. Technician role expertise, on the other hand, is generally unrelated to informal scanning, once manager role expertise is con-

TABLE 9.14

Correlations of Excellence, Environmental Turbulence, Turbulence Management, Strategic Origins, and Manager Role Characteristics With Informal Environmental Scanning for Key Publics

Informal Environmental Scanning for:	Employees	Media	Investors	Community	Customers	Government	Members
Overall Excellence Score	.45**	.43**	.39**	.53**	.39**	.28**	.46**
Environmental Turbulence (Activists)	.15**	.04	.30*	.13	.20*	.08	-.01
Success With Activist Publics	.26**	.22**	.42**	.02	.36**	.05	.38**
Strategic Origins of Program	.54**	.59**	.66**	.69**	.65**	.44**	.60**
Manager Role Expertise in Department	.45**	.39**	.46**	.46**	.46**	.30**	.28**
Technician Role Expertise in Department (partial corr.)	.05	.05	.20	.01	.17*	-.06	.21
Top Communicator Manager Role Playing	.35**	.30**	.11	.32**	.35**	.22	.41**

Note. Average sample sizes for this analysis: employees = 159; media = 217; investors = 46; community = 121; customers = 85; government = 44; and members = 48. Sample size may vary for each coefficient, depending on number of missing cases.

$*p < .05.$ $**p < .01.$

trolled. Only one positive relationship (customer relations) is statistically significant, accounting for 3% of the variance in the use of informal scanning.

Manager role enactment by the head of public relations is positively correlated with informal scanning activities for all seven publics; five of these relationships are statistically significant. Manager role enactment accounts for 9% (media relations) to 17% (member relations) of the variance in the use of informal scanning activities. Both nonsignificant relationships are positive and involve publics with small sample sizes.

In summary, the use of informal scanning techniques parallels the use of formal scanning techniques. Overall communication Excellence of the organization is a powerful predictor of informal scanning for all seven publics. Informal scanning increases with pressure from activist groups; informal scanning is correlated with organizational success in dealing with activists. For all seven publics, programs with strategic origins frequently use informal scanning techniques. Manager role expertise in the public relations department and manager role enactment by the top communicator increase the use of informal scanning techniques.

Evaluation for Key Programs.   Although scientific program evaluation is used less frequently than less rigorous methods of evaluation, such evaluation is significantly and positively associated with overall communication Excellence. As shown in Table 9.15, overall Excellence accounts for 6% (media relations) to 37% (community relations) of the variance in the use of scientific evaluation of communication programs.

For five of the seven programs, scientific evaluations are more likely to increase as a result of pressure from activists. Activist pressure on the organization accounts for 3% (media relations) to 21% (investor relations) of the variance in the use of scientific program evaluation. Both of the two programs with nonsignificant relationships (government and member relations) are negative but account for less than 1% of the variance in the use of scientific evaluation.

For four of the seven programs, use of scientific evaluation significantly increases organizational success in dealing with activists. Scientific program evaluation accounts for 3% (employee relations) to 19% (investor relations) of the variance in success with activists. The three nonsignificant relationships account for less than 1% of the variance in success with activists.

For all seven programs, strategic origins of programs are positively and significantly correlated with scientific evaluation of those programs. Strategic origins account for 28% (media relations) to 66% (customer relations) of the variance in the scientific evaluation of those programs.

For six of the seven programs, manager role expertise in the department is significantly and positively correlated with scientific evaluation of those programs. Manager role expertise accounts for 8% (media relations) to 41% (member relations) of the variance in the use of scientific evaluation of programs. The one nonsignificant relationship (government relations) is nevertheless positive

TABLE 9.15

Correlations of Excellence, Environmental Turbulence, Turbulence Management, Strategic Origins, and Manager Role Characteristics With Scientific Evaluation of Public Relations Programs for Key Publics

Scientific Evaluation of Programs for:	Employees	Media	Investors	Community	Customers	Government	Members
Overall Excellence Score	.51**	.25**	.50**	.61**	.57**	.30**	.57**
Environmental Turbulence (Activists)	.21**	.18**	.46**	.20**	.35*	-.02	-.06
Success With Activist Publics	.17**	.32**	.44**	.03	.36**	-.05	.05
Strategic Origins of Program	.65**	.53**	.60**	.63**	.81**	.62**	.68**
Manager Role Expertise in Department	.40**	.29**	.48**	.54**	.58**	.17	.64**
Technician Role Expertise in Department (partial corr.)	-.05	-.07	.22	-.15**	.14	-.13*	-.09
Top Communicator Manager Role Playing	.22**	.14*	.16	.36**	.39**	.30**	.42**

Note. Average sample sizes for this analysis: employees = 159; media = 217; investors = 46; community = 121; customers = 85; government = 44; and members = 48. Sample size may vary for each coefficient, depending on number of missing cases.

*p < .05. **p < .01.

and manager role expertise accounts for 3% of the variance in the scientific evaluation of government relations programs. Small sample size ($N = 47$ for this
test) reduces the chances of detecting a relationship in the population as significant; thus there is a high probability of Type 2 error.

Technician role expertise in the department, on the other hand, is generally
unrelated to scientific program evaluation, once manager role expertise is controlled. Six of the seven relationships are nonsignificant. The only significant relationship (community relations) is negative, meaning that greater technician
role expertise is associated with lower levels of scientific evaluation of community relations programs, once manager role expertise is controlled.

Manager role enactment by the top communicator is significantly and positively related to scientific program evaluation for six of the seven programs.
Manager role enactment accounts for 2% (media relations) to 18% (member relations) of the variance in the use of scientific program evaluation. The only
nonsignificant relationship (investor relations) involved a small sample ($N = 48$)
and was nevertheless positive, accounting for 3% of the variance in the scientific
evaluation of investor relations programs.

Table 9.16 shows the relationships between clip-file evaluation and key indicators of communication Excellence. Overall communication Excellence for
the organization is positively and significantly correlated with clip-file evaluation for five of the seven programs. Overall Excellence accounts for 5% (media
relations) to 20% (investor relations) of the variance in the use of clip-file evaluation. Overall Excellence is positively correlated with clip-file evaluation of
member relations programs, although the relationship is not statistically significant. A major anomaly is the significant, negative relationship between overall
Excellence and clip-file evaluation of government relations programs.

Clip-file evaluation increases as a function of activist pressure on organizations. For five of the seven programs, the relationship is statistically significant.
Activist pressure accounts for 3% (community relations) to 26% (investor relations) of the variance in the use of clip-file evaluation. Both of the nonsignificant
relationships (government and member relations) are positive and involve
small samples ($N = 51$ and $N = 57$, respectively, for these tests). For these programs, activist pressure accounts for about 2% of the use of clip-file evaluation.

For four of the seven programs, use of clip-file evaluation increases success in
dealing with activists. Use of clip-file evaluation accounts for 2% (employee relations) to 17% (investor relations) of variation in success with activists. One
nonsignificant relationship (community relations) is positive. Two other nonsignificant relationships (governmental and member relations) are negative.
However, sample sizes are small ($N = 40$ and $N = 43$, respectively); clip-file evaluation for these programs accounts for less than 1% of the variance in success
with activists.

Strategic origins of communication programs are positively correlated with
the use of clip-file evaluation for all seven programs. For six, the relationship is

TABLE 9.16

Correlations of Excellence, Environmental Turbulence, Turbulence Management, Strategic Origins, and Manager Role Characteristics With Clip-File Evaluation of Public Relations Programs for Key Publics

Clip-File Evaluation of Programs for:	Employees	Media	Investors	Community	Customers	Government	Members
Overall Excellence Score	.32**	.23**	.53**	.45**	.33**	-.28**	.17
Environmental Turbulence (Activists)	.17**	.18**	.51**	.16**	.29**	.15	.13
Success With Activist Publics	.15*	.35**	.51**	.06	.41**	-.08	-.05
Strategic Origins of Program	.40**	.33**	.64**	.49**	.50**	.25	.31**
Manager Role Expertise in Department	.36**	.31**	.62**	.37**	.36**	.14	.28*
Technician Role Expertise in Department (partial corr.)	.17*	.01	.26*	.06	.20*	.01	-.14
Top Communicator Manager Role Playing	.17*	.20**	.25*	.24**	.25**	-.09	.13

Note. Average sample sizes for this analysis: employees = 159; media = 217; investors = 46; community = 121; customers = 85; government = 44; and members = 48. Sample size may vary for each coefficient, depending on number of missing cases.

$*p < .05$. $**p < .01$.

statistically significant. Strategic origins of programs account for 10% (member relations) to 38% (investor relations) of the variance in the use of clip-file evaluation for these programs. The one nonsignificant relationship (government relations) is positive and involves a small sample ($N = 41$). Yet strategic origins still account for 6% of the variance in the use of clip-file evaluation for government relations programs.

Manager role expertise in the communication department is positively related to the use of clip-file evaluation. For six of the seven programs, the relationship is statistically significant. Manager role expertise accounts for 8% (member relations) to 38% (investor relations) of the variance in the use of clip-file evaluation. For the single nonsignificant relationship (government relations), the relationship is positive, the sample size is small ($N = 49$), and manager role expertise nevertheless accounts for 2% of the variance in the use of clip-file evaluations of government relations programs.

Technician role expertise in the department also shows significant, positive correlations for three of the seven programs, even after controlling for manager role expertise. Technician role expertise accounts for 3% (employee relations) to 7% (investor relations) of the variance in clip-file evaluation of these programs. Three of the nonsignificant relationships are near zero. A negative relationship exists between technician role expertise and clip-file evaluation of member relations programs, accounting for about 2% of the variance.

For five of the seven programs, manager role enactment by the top communicator is positively and significantly correlated with the use of clip-file evaluation for these programs. Manager role enactment accounts for 3% (employee relations) to 6% (investor and customer relations) of the variance in use of clip-file evaluations for these publics. Manager role enactment is positively related to clip-file evaluation of member relations programs, but the relationship is not significant. Manager role enactment is negatively related to clip-file evaluation of government relations programs; however, manager role enactment accounts for less than 1% of the variance.

In summary, clip-file evaluation is linked to various aspects of communication Excellence in a manner similar to scientific evaluation. However, several differences are worth noting. First, technician role expertise remains significantly correlated with clip-file evaluation for three programs, even after controlling for manager role expertise. None of these relationships is significant when scientific evaluation is the dependent variable. A strong link exists between technician role expertise and clip-file evaluation that is independent of manager role expertise in the department. Second, clip-file evaluation of governmental relations programs does not seem to be linked to characteristics of excellence, linkages that are manifest for other programs. The many anomalies associated with government relations programs cannot be fully dismissed as a function of small sample size. Several other programs (e.g., investor, customer, and member relations) have similarly small samples, yet linkages to characteristics of excellence are sufficiently robust to manifest themselves in small samples (i.e., large effect size).

Table 9.17 shows the relationships between informal, seat-of-the-pants evaluation of programs and key indicators of excellence. Informal evaluation is tied to the overall communication Excellence of organizations in six of seven programs. Overall communication Excellence accounts for 4% (media relations) to 24% (community relations) of the variance in the use of informal evaluation. For governmental relations programs, the relationship is positive but not significant, with overall Excellence accounting for less than 2% of the variance in the use of informal evaluations of governmental relations programs.

Informal evaluation increases when organizations experience activist pressure, as indicated by the correlations for four of the seven programs. Environmental turbulence in the form of activist pressure accounts for 2% (media relations) to 12% (investor relations) of the variance in the use of informal evaluation. For the nonsignificant relationships, all are near zero, with activist pressure accounting for less than 1% of the variance in the use of informal evaluation for those programs.

When programs are evaluated using informal techniques, success with activist groups increases for five of the seven programs. Informal evaluation accounts for 3% (community relations) to 28% (customer relations) of the variance in success with activists. For member relations, the correlation is positive but not significant. For governmental relations, however, the relationship is not significant but negative; informal evaluation of governmental relations programs is negatively related to success with activist pressure.

The more strategic the origins of communication programs, the greater the use of informal evaluation techniques. This relationship is significant and positive for all seven programs. The strategic origins of programs account for 13% (employee relations) to 37% (investor relations) of the variance in the use of informal evaluation techniques.

Manager role expertise in the communication department is significantly and positively related to the use of informal evaluation techniques for six of the seven programs. Manager role expertise accounts for 7% (media relations) to 37% (investor relations) of the variance in the use of informal evaluation techniques. The relationship between manager role expertise and the informal evaluation of governmental relations programs is positive but not significant; small sample size ($N = 46$) helps explain the nonsignificance of the correlation. Manager role expertise does account for about 5% of the variance in the informal evaluation of governmental relations programs.

Technician role expertise is unrelated to informal evaluation for six of the seven programs, once manager role expertise is controlled. However, technician role expertise is significantly and positively correlated with the informal evaluation of investor relations programs, accounting for about 6% of the variance.

TABLE 9.17

Correlations of Excellence, Environmental Turbulence, Turbulence Management, Strategic Origins, and Manager Role Characteristics With Informal, Seat-of-the-Pants Evaluation of Public Relations Programs for Key Publics

Informal Evaluation of Programs for:	Employees	Media	Investors	Community	Customers	Government	Members
Overall Excellence Score	.40**	.21**	.45**	.49**	.46**	.14	.31*
Environmental Turbulence (Activists)	.18**	.15**	.35**	.07	.29**	-.08	-.01
Success With Activist Publics	.28**	.29**	.52**	.16*	.53**	-.11	.08
Strategic Origins of Program	.36**	.57**	.51**	.55**	.45**	.37**	.39**
Manager Role Expertise in Department	.42**	.27**	.61**	.42**	.43**	.22	.28**
Technician Role Expertise in Department (partial corr.)	.02	.01	.25*	-.02	.02	.03	.12
Top Communicator Manager Role Playing	.21**	.14*	.23*	.30**	.43**	.30*	.29*

Note. Average sample sizes for this analysis: employees = 159; media = 217; investors = 46; community = 121; customers = 85; government = 44; and members = 48. Sample size may vary for each coefficient, depending on number of missing cases.
$*p < .05.$ $**p < .01.$

Enactment of the manager role by the top communicator in the department is positively and significantly correlated with informal evaluation of all seven programs. Manager role enactment accounts for 2% (media relations) to 18% (customer relations) of the variance in the use of informal evaluation techniques.

In summary, the use of informal evaluation techniques is linked to excellence in ways similar to scientific and clip-file evaluation techniques. For employees, media, investors, and customers, informal evaluation techniques are significantly and positively correlated with overall communication Excellence in the organization, activist pressure, success in dealing with activists, strategic origins of programs, manager role expertise in public relations departments, and manager role enactment by top communicators. The relationships are also significant for community and member publics, with the exception of near-zero correlations between activist pressure and informal evaluation of those programs. Governmental relations programs remain somewhat anomalous, showing weaker but positive relationships with most indicators of excellence. Also, informal evaluation of governmental relations programs is negatively correlated with activist pressure and success in dealing with activist pressure, although these relationships are not significant and account for little variance.

Operations Research

As noted previously, formal versus informal scanning is not an either/or proposition. Although evaluation research varies substantially from rigorous scientific evaluation to less rigorous, informal, seat-of-the-pants techniques, excellent communication programs rely on the full range of evaluation techniques to measure program success or failure. For these reasons, the two scanning indexes and three evaluation indexes were combined into a common operations research index; this index proved reliable across all seven programs (see Table 9.7).

Table 9.18 displays the relationships between the operations research index and key indicators of excellence. For six of the seven programs, the operations research index is positively correlated with overall communication Excellence. Communication Excellence accounts for 10% (media relations) to 48% (community relations) of the variance in the use of operations research techniques to scan organizational environments and evaluate programs for these publics. The correlation between overall Excellence and the use of research with governmental relations programs is positive but not significant. This is due in part to small sample size (N = 39); overall Excellence accounts for about 4% of the variance in the use of research with governmental relations programs.

The use of operations research increases with greater perceived environmental turbulence in the form of pressure from activist groups. The relation-

TABLE 9.18

Correlations of Excellence, Environmental Turbulence, Turbulence Management, Strategic Origins, and Manager Role Characteristics With Scanning and Evaluation Research Index for Key Publics

Operations Research Index for:	Employees	Media	Investors	Community	Customers	Government	Members
Overall Excellence Score	.58**	.32**	.59**	.69**	.61**	.20	.53**
Environmental Turbulence (Activists)	.27**	.18**	.53**	.22**	.37**	.12	-.03
Success With Activist Publics	.32**	.34**	.58**	.09	.52**	-.06	.12
Strategic Origins of Program	.71**	.74**	.82**	.78**	.85**	.65**	.69**
Manager Role Expertise in Department	.56**	.34**	.69**	.64**	.63**	.27*	.57**
Technician Role Expertise in Department (partial corr.)	.02	-.02	.31*	-.09	.17	-.06	.01
Top Communicator Manager Role Playing	.31**	.18**	.25*	.37**	.45**	.28*	.47**

Note. Average sample sizes for this analysis: employees = 159; media = 217; investors = 46; community = 121; customers = 85; government = 44; and members = 48. Sample size may vary for each coefficient, depending on number of missing cases.

*$p < .05$. **$p < .01$.

ship is positive and significant for five of the seven publics. For these significant relationships, activist pressure accounts for 3% (media relations) to 28% (investor relations) of the variance in the use of program research. For investor relations, the relationship is positive but not significant, accounting for about 1% of the variance. For member relations programs, the relationship is negative but near zero.

Success with activists is significantly and positively correlated with use of program research for four of the seven publics. For these significant relationships, use of program research accounts for 10% (employee relations) to 34% (investor relations) of the variance in success with activists. The relationship is positive but not significant for member relations and community relations programs, accounting for about 1% of the variance in the sample for both cases. The relationship is negative but near zero for government relations programs.

The strategic origins of programs is positively and significantly correlated with the use of operations research for all seven programs. Strategic origins account for 42% (government relations) to 72% (customer relations) of the variance in the use of operations research.

Manager role expertise in the communication department is positively and significantly correlated with the use of operations research for all seven programs. Manager role expertise accounts for 7% (governmental relations) to 48% (investor relations) of the variance in the use of operations research. Technician role expertise, on the other hand, is generally unrelated to operations research, once manager role expertise is controlled. The sole exception is investor relations programs, where the partial correlation is positive and significant, accounting for about 10% of the variance in the use of operations research.

Manager role enactment by the top communicator is significantly and positively correlated with use of operations research for all seven programs. Manager role enactment accounts for 3% (media relations) to 22% (member relations) of the variance in the use of operations research.

In summary, overall Excellence is positively tied to the use of operations research for all but government relations programs. Operations research increases when organizations experience activist pressure; organizations are more successful with activists when they employ operations research. This generalization holds true for employee, media, investor, and customer relations programs. For community relations programs, operations research increases with activist pressure, but such research is not so highly correlated with success with activists. For government and member relations programs, operations research is not significantly related to activist pressure or success in dealing with such pressure. Use of operations research increases significantly as a function of manager role expertise in the department and manager role enactment by the top communicator. Technician role expertise, on the other hand, is generally unrelated to the use of operations research.

Conflict Avoidance Outcomes for Key Publics

One major goal of proactive public relations programs is to avoid conflict with key constituents. As shown in Table 9.8, seven items were used to study conflict avoidance outcomes for the seven publics. These items measured positive program outcomes in terms of avoiding strikes, boycotts, litigation, disagreements, disputes, and governmental interference for each of the seven key publics. Table 9.19 displays the relationships between the index of conflict avoidance outcomes and key indicators of excellence.

Avoidance of conflicts is positively and significantly correlated with overall Excellence for six of the seven programs. For these significant relationships, overall Excellence accounts for 6% (member relations) to 31% (investor relations) of the variance in the avoidance of conflict as a positive program outcome. For government relations, the correlation is negative but near zero.

Positive program outcomes increase as a function of activist pressure for five of the seven programs. For these significant relationships, activist pressure accounts for 3% (community relations) to 22% (investor relations) of the variance in conflict avoidance outcomes. For member relations, the relationship is positive but not significant, accounting for 3% of the variance. Again note that the sample size is small ($N = 48$), reducing the probability of finding statistically significant relationships and increasing the probability of making a Type 2 error. For government relations programs, the relationship is also positive but not statistically significant. Activist pressure accounts for 2% of the variance in conflict avoidance outcomes for government relations programs. Small sample size ($N = 45$) reduces the probability of detecting statistically significant relationships.

Success with activists is positively correlated with conflict avoidance outcomes for six of the seven programs; four are statistically significant. For those significant relationships, success with activists accounts for 4% (employee relations) to 17% (customer relations) of the variance in conflict avoidance outcomes for those programs. For investor relations and government relations, the relationships are not significant, but they account for about 6% of the variance in the sample. For community relations, however, the explained variance is near zero.

Manager role expertise in the communication department significantly increases the level of conflict avoidance outcomes for six of the seven programs. For these significant relationships, manager role expertise explains 2% (media relations) to 24% (investor relations) of the variance. For governmental relations programs, however, the relationship is negative but not statistically significant. Manager role expertise accounts for about 2% of the variance in the sample. Technician role expertise in the department, on the other hand, is generally unrelated to conflict avoidance outcomes, once manager role expertise is controlled. For government relations, however, the relationship is significant but negative. For investor relations, the relationship is significant and positive.

TABLE 9.19

Correlations of Excellence, Environmental Turbulence, Turbulence Management, and Manager Role Characteristics With Conflict Avoidance Outcomes of Public Relations Programs for Key Publics

Conflict Avoidance Outcomes of Programs for:	Employees	Media	Investors	Community	Customers	Government	Members
Overall Excellence Score	.32**	.29**	.56**	.34**	.45**	−.03	.25*
Environmental Turbulence (Activists)	.21**	.24**	.47**	.18*	.19*	.14	.18
Success With Activist Publics	.19**	.26**	.24	.07	.41	.25	.28*
Manager Role Expertise in Department	.22**	.14*	.49**	.29**	.33**	−.17	.35**
Technician Role Expertise in Department (partial corr.)	.11	.09	.31*	−.05	.10	−.27*	.08
Top Communicator Manager Role Playing	.07	.13*	.27*	.24**	.24*	−.10	.31*

Note. Average sample sizes for this analysis: employees = 159; media = 217; investors = 46; community = 121; customers = 85; government = 44; and members = 48. Sample size may vary for each coefficient, depending on number of missing cases.

*p < .05. **p < .01.

Manager role enactment by the top communicator is positively and significantly related to conflict avoidance outcomes for five of the seven programs. For these significant relationships, manager role enactment explains 2% (media relations) to 10% (member relations) of the variance in conflict avoidance outcomes. For employee relations, manager role enactment posts a weak positive correlation with conflict avoidance outcomes, accounting for less than 1% of the variance in the sample. For government relations programs, the relationship is negative, accounting for 1% of the variance in the sample.

In summary, conflict avoidance outcomes are correlated with key indicators of excellence for most publics. Conflict avoidance generally increases as a function of overall Excellence, environmental pressure, manager role expertise in the department, and manager role enactment. When these relationships are not significant, they are nevertheless positive correlations in the sample. Government relations programs, however, remain anomalous, posting insignificant and sometimes negative correlations with Excellence indicators, counter to theory.

Change in Relationship Outcomes for Key Publics

A second major goal of public relations programs is to bring about positive changes in relationships with key publics. Table 9.9 displays the six items used to measure positive relationship changes for each public. As noted, these items involve efforts to move publics to positions more compatible with the views of dominant coalitions in organizations as well as items measuring the building of stable, long-term relations of cooperation and understanding. Table 9.20 shows correlations between positive changes in relationships as program outcomes with key indicators of excellence.

Overall communication Excellence in the organization is positively and significantly correlated with positive change in relationships with six of the seven publics. For these significant correlations, overall Excellence accounts for 10% (media relations) to 24% (investor relations) of the variance in positive relationship changes as program outcomes. For government relations programs, the overall Excellence accounts for almost no variance in positive relationship changes.

Contrary to expectations, positive changes in relationships generally are not correlated with pressure from activist groups. The only significant relationship is the positive one for investor relations programs. For investor programs, activist pressure accounts for about 12% of the variance in positive change in relationships. The relationship is positive but weak for employee, media, customer, and member relations programs. The relationship is negative for government and community relations programs; however, explained variance is near zero.

Success in dealing with activists shows positive and significant correlations with positive relationship changes for five of the seven programs. For these significant relationships, success with activists accounts for 35% (employee rela-

TABLE 9.20

Correlations of Excellence, Environmental Turbulence, Turbulence Management, and Manager Role Characteristics With Positive Change of Relationship Outcomes of Public Relations Programs for Key Publics

Positive Change in Relationship Outcomes of Programs for:	Employees	Media	Investors	Community	Customers	Government	Members
Overall Excellence Score	.36**	.31**	.49**	.36**	.41**	.02	.47**
Environmental Turbulence (Activists)	.10	.06	.34**	-.04	.12	-.03	.05
Success With Activist Publics	.17**	.29**	.48**	.12	.32**	.16	.44**
Manager Role Expertise in Department	.18**	.20**	.50**	.35**	.44**	-.25*	.38**
Technician Role Expertise in Dept. (partial corr.)	.08	.13*	.23	-.08	.12	-.12	.10
Top Communicator Manager Role Playing	.14*	.24**	.17	.29**	.47**	-.02	.49**

Note. Average sample sizes for this analysis: employees = 159; media = 217; investors = 46; community = 121; customers = 85; government = 44; and members = 48. Sample size may vary for each coefficient, depending on number of missing cases.

$*p < .05.$ $**p < .01.$

tions) to 48% (investor relations) of the variance in positive relationship changes with these publics. The relationship is positive but not significant for government and community relations programs. Nevertheless, success with activists accounts for 3% and 1% of the variance, respectively, in the sample.

Manager role expertise in the department is significantly and positively related to positive change in relationships with six of the seven publics. For these significant relationships, manager role expertise accounts for 3% (employee relations) to 25% (investor relations) of the variance in positive change in relationships with these publics. For government relations programs, however, the relationship is negative and significant. Manager role expertise accounts for 6% of the variance in positive changes in relationships with government publics; the greater the manager role expertise, the less positive are changes in relations with government publics.

Technician role expertise, on the other hand, is generally unrelated to positive changes in relationships with the seven publics analyzed, once manager role expertise is controlled. The only significant partial correlation is the positive relationship between technician role expertise and positive change in relationships with the media.

Manager role enactment by the top communicator is positively and significantly correlated with positive relationship changes for five of the seven publics. For these significant relationships, manager role enactment accounts for 2% (employee relations) to 24% (member relations) of the variance in positive change in relationships with these publics. The relationship is positive for investor relations as well, although not significantly so. Nevertheless, in the sample, manager role enactment accounts for about 3% of the variance in positive relationship changes with investors. Government relations programs, on the other hand, show a negative correlation with manager role enactment. The correlation is small; explained variance is near zero.

In summary, positive changes in relationships with key publics are related to several indicators of excellence for most publics analyzed. Positive change in relationships occurs as a function of overall Excellence, manager role expertise in the department, and manager role enactment by the top communicator. This generalization is the case for employees, media, community, customer, and member relations programs. The generalization also applies to investor relations programs; however, the correlation with manager role enactment is slightly less than significant, probably due to small sample size ($N = 42$). General activist pressure on organizations, however, does not stimulate positive changes in relationships with key publics. Once again, government relations programs are anomalous; these programs are not significantly correlated in a positive manner with any indicator of excellence. The only significant relationship is negative; greater manager role expertise in the communication department is correlated with less success in the positive change of relationships with government publics.

The Impact of Overall Excellence on Eight
Program Outcomes

In addition to conflict avoidance and positive change in relationships, communication programs seek other outcomes as well. Six of these other outcomes are displayed in Table 9.10. In Table 9.21, all eight measures of positive program outcomes are correlated with each of the seven publics. That is, each column in Table 9.21 displays the correlation coefficient between the organization's overall Excellence score and eight program outcomes for that public.

The influence of overall Excellence on conflict avoidance and change in relationship outcomes is reported in the previous sections. As noted and as theoretically expected, these relationships are significant and positive for six of the seven publics. Government relations programs are anomalous, with overall Excellence posting low correlations that account for near-zero variance in these two outcomes for government publics.

Many public relations programs use communication to help organizations achieve larger organizational objectives. The third row of Table 9.21 displays correlations between overall Excellence and success in achieving organizational goals for the seven publics analyzed. The relationship is positive and significant for six of the seven publics. For these significant relationships, overall Excellence accounts for 5% (employee relations) to 35% (member relations) of the variance in helping organizations achieve their objectives. The relationship between excellence and helping organizations achieve objectives through government relations programs is positive but not significant. Nevertheless, overall Excellence accounts for 5% of the variance in success at achieving organizational objectives with government publics. Small sample size ($N = 45$) reduces the probability of detecting significant relationships.

A process objective of any communication program is to ensure that programmatic messages are accurately received. The fourth row of Table 9.21 displays correlations between overall Excellence scores and accurate message reception for the publics analyzed. The relationships are positive and significant for five of seven programs. For those significant relationships, overall Excellence accounts for 3% (employee relations) to 10% (customer relations) of the variance. The relationship is positive but not significant for member and government relations programs; explained variance is near zero for both.

Many communication programs try to help organizations save money. The fifth row of Table 9.21 displays the correlations between overall Excellence and saving organizations money as a function of the seven programs analyzed. Three of the correlations are positive and significant. Among those, excellence accounts for 6% (employee relations) to 11% (investor relations) in variance in saving money for organizations. The remaining relationships are all positive but weak, ranging from about 3% variance in the sample for member relations programs to near-zero explained variance for government and customer relations programs.

TABLE 9.21

Correlations of Overall Communication Excellence With Positive Program Outcomes for Key Publics

Outcomes of Programs for:	Employees	Media	Investors	Community	Customers	Government	Members
Conflict avoidance index	.32**	.29**	.56**	.34**	.45**	-.03	.25*
Positive change in relationship index	.36**	.31**	.49**	.36**	.41**	.02	.47**
Program helped organization achieve goals	.22**	.37**	.47**	.39**	.34**	.22	.59**
Program message accurately received	.17**	.21**	.28*	.30**	.31**	.01	.05
Program helped organization save money	.25**	.10	.33*	.30**	.03	.05	.17
Positive media coverage resulted	.04	.21**	.11	.24**	.13	-.09	.14
Program helped organization make money	.11	.07	.24	.16*	.06	-.17	-.07
Program helped sales/services increase	.13	.05	.16	.13	-.01	-.26*	.37**

Note. Average sample sizes for this analysis: employees = 159; media = 217; investors = 46; community = 121; customers = 85; government = 44; and members = 48. Sample size may vary for each coefficient, depending on number of missing cases.

*p < .05. **p < .01.

Public relations programs that depend on the public media for message dissemination seek to generate positive coverage. The sixth row of Table 9.21 displays the correlations between overall Excellence and positive media coverage for the seven publics analyzed. Only two correlations are positive and statistically significant. Overall Excellence accounts for 4% of the variance in media relations programs and 6% of the variance in community relations programs. The correlations are positive but weak for employee, investor, customer, and member relations programs. The relationship is negative but weak for government relations programs, accounting for less than 1% of the variance in the sample. These correlations do not match the stronger relationships noted for accurate message reception because public media are not the critical channels of dissemination for publics such as employees, investors, and members. Controlled media, it seems, are used to disseminate messages accurately to these publics as a function of overall Excellence, whereas overall Excellence is only weakly linked to positive media coverage for these publics.

Many public relations programs also help organizations make money. The seventh row of Table 9.21 shows correlations between overall Excellence and helping make money. Overall Excellence is significantly and positively correlated with helping organizations make money for community relations programs. It accounts for about 3% of the variance in helping organizations make money through community relations programs. Overall Excellence also accounts for 6% of the variance in helping organizations make money through investor relations programs. This positive correlation is not significant, however, probably because of the small sample size ($N = 43$). The correlations are positive but very weak for employee, media, and customer relations programs, accounting for 1% or less of the variance in the sample. For government relations programs, the correlation between overall Excellence and helping organizations make money is negative but not significant, accounting for less than 3% of the variance.

Many communication programs help increase the sales of goods or services provided by organizations. The eighth row of Table 9.21 shows correlations between overall Excellence and increasing sales for the seven programs analyzed. Five of the seven relationships are positive, but only one is statistically significant. For member relations programs, excellence accounts for 14% of the variance in helping organizations increase sales. For investor relations, excellence accounts for about 3% of the variance; but this positive correlation is not statistically significant. The correlations for employee, media, and community relations programs are positive but weak, with each accounting for less than 2% of the variance in the sample. Interestingly, the correlation for customer relations programs is near zero. For government relations programs, the correlation is significant but negative. Greater overall communication Excellence in organizations is correlated with decreases in sales as a result of government relations programs.

In summary, overall Excellence is positively related to reduced conflict and positive change in relationships for most publics. Excellence helps organizations achieve their goals and ensure that program messages are received accurately. In addition, overall Excellence leads to positive media coverage for those programs where public media are germane. It also helps organizations save money through employee, investor, and community relations programs. On the other hand, overall Excellence is generally unrelated to helping organizations make money or increase sales.

None of these generalizations about program outcomes applies to government relations programs. Overall communication Excellence in the organization seems to exert little influence over the outcomes of government relations programs. For government relations, four of the eight program outcomes are negatively correlated with overall Excellence.

The Impact of Strategic Program Origins on Eight Outcomes

Table 9.22 displays the correlations between the strategic origins and management of communication programs and eight program outcomes for the seven publics analyzed. The greater the strategic origins and management of a program, the greater the success in avoiding conflict with all seven publics. Six of the relationships are statistically significant. Of these significant relationships, strategic origins of a program account for 4% (employee relations) to 32% (customer relations) of success in avoiding conflicts with those publics. The correlation is also positive for government relations programs, but the relationship is not significant. However, strategic origins account for 14% of the variance in conflict avoidance for government relations programs.

The second row of Table 9.22 displays correlations between strategic origins and management of programs and positive changes in relationships with each public analyzed. Strategic origins of programs correlate significantly with positive change in relationships with six of the seven publics. For these significant relationships, strategic origins of programs account for 8% (employee relations) to 46% (investor relations) of the variance in positive relationship changes for these publics. For government relations, the correlation is positive but not significant, accounting for less than 1% of the variance in the sample.

The third row of Table 9.22 shows the correlations between strategic origins of programs and success in helping organizations achieve their goals for each of the seven programs analyzed. Strategic origins of programs are positively and significantly correlated with helping organizations achieve their objectives for six of the seven publics. Strategic origins account for 7% (customer relations) to 28% (member relations) of the variance. For government relations programs, the correlation is positive but not significant. Nevertheless, in the sample, stra-

TABLE 9.22

Correlations of Strategic Origins and Management With Program Outcomes for Key Publics

Outcomes of Programs for:	Employees	Media	Investors	Community	Customers	Government	Members
Conflict avoidance index	.20*	.40**	.51**	.48**	.57**	.38	.36*
Positive change in relationship index	.29**	.36**	.68**	.57**	.55**	.08	.59**
Program helped organization achieve goals	.52**	.28**	.47**	.44**	.27**	.16	.53**
Positive media coverage resulted	.07	.28**	.43**	.43**	.53**	.43**	.37**
Program message accurately received	.10	.31**	.31*	.41**	.29**	.37*	.20
Program helped organization save money	.12	.40**	.45**	.30**	.41**	.32*	.25
Program helped sales/services increased	.21**	.26**	.38**	.36**	.44**	.15	.15
Program helped organization make money	.16*	.25**	.20	.20*	.22*	.21	-.06

Note. Average sample sizes for this analysis: employees = 159; media = 217; investors = 46; community = 121; customers = 85; government = 44; and members = 48. Sample size may vary for each coefficient, depending on number of missing cases.

*p < .05. **p < .01.

tegic origins of government relations programs account for about 3% of the variance in achieving organizational goals.

The fourth row of Table 9.22 displays correlations between strategic origins and management of programs and positive media coverage for the seven publics analyzed. For six of seven publics, these correlations are positive and significant. Strategic origins of programs account for 8% (media relations) to 28% (customer relations) of the variance in positive coverage. The relationship is positive but not statistically significant for employee relations programs, perhaps because public media play a minor role in message dissemination to this public.

The fifth row of Table 9.22 shows correlations between strategic origins of programs and whether publics accurately receive messages. The correlations are positive and significant for five of seven programs. For those significant relationships, strategic origins of programs account for 8% (customer relations) to 17% (community relations) of the variance in accurate reception of program messages. For employee relations and member relations programs, the correlations are positive but not statistically significant.

The sixth row of Table 9.22 displays the correlations between the strategic origins of programs and the degree to which the program help the organization save money. These correlations are significant for five of the seven programs. For these significant relationships, strategic origins account for 9% (community relations) to 20% (investor relations) of the variance in helping organizations save money. The relationships for employee and member relations are positive but not significant.

The seventh row shows correlations between strategic origins of programs and each program's contribution to increased sales of goods and services or both. These correlations are positive and significant for five of the seven programs. For these significant relationships, strategic origins account for 4% (employee relations) to 19% (customer relations) of the variance in increased sales. For government and member relations programs, the correlations are positive but not significant.

The eighth row of Table 9.22 displays correlations between strategic origins of programs and each program's contribution to helping organizations make money. The correlations are positive and significant for four of seven programs. For these significant relationships, strategic origins account for 3% (employee relations) to 6% (media relations) of the variance in helping organizations make money. For investor and government relations programs, the correlations are positive but not significant. For member relations, the correlation is negative but the explained variance is near zero.

In summary, the strategic origins and management of communication programs for key publics generally result in positive outcomes for organizations and publics. For media, community, and customer relations programs, the correlations are both positive and statistically significant for all eight program outcomes (see Table 9.22). For investor relations programs, correlations are all positive; seven of eight are statistically significant. For employee relations programs, all correlations are positive; five are statistically significant, two are positive but not significant, and one is near zero (<1% explained variance). For government relations programs, all relationships are positive; three are statistically significant, four are positive but not significant, and one is near zero (<1% explained variance). For member relations programs, seven of eight are positive; of those, four are statistically significant. The one negative relationship is weak, accounting for less than 1% of the explained variance.

Demonstrating Outcomes Through Operations Research

In the Excellence questionnaire, we asked top communicators to quantify program outcomes using the fractionation scale. Specifically, we asked them to "please estimate the extent to which you believe *observable evidence shows* that the program has had one of the effects listed." The question was structured this way because we wanted to move beyond subjective impressions of "success" in the minds of top communicators and measure outcomes in ways that could be demonstrated to dominant coalitions. We posited that higher levels of scanning and evaluation research would be positively correlated with higher levels of demonstrable, successful program outcomes. Not only would operations research improve the quality of programs executed, research would also provide the needed feedback to demonstrate outcomes objectively to communicators and dominant coalitions.

Table 9.23 displays correlations between the operations research index and the eight program outcomes for each of the seven publics analyzed. As we expected, the correlations are positive and significant for avoiding conflict, generating positive media coverage, helping organizations save money, and helping increase sales. Operations research accounts for 16% (media and government relations) to 34% (customer relations) of the variance in demonstrating conflict avoidance with target publics. Operations research accounts for 3% (employee relations) to 18% (community relations) of the variance in demonstrating generation of positive media coverage. Operations research accounts for 7% (member relations) to 21% (employee relations) of the variance in documenting how programs save organizations money. Operations research accounts for 5% (media relations) to 19% (investor relations) of the variance in demonstrating increased sales as a result of communication programs.

With the exception of government relations programs, correlations are positive and significant between operations research and documenting how programs help organizations achieve their objectives. For these significant relationships, operations research accounts for 8% (media relations) to 27% (member relations) of the variance. For government relations, the relationship is positive but not significant.

TABLE 9.23

Correlations of Scanning and Evaluation Research Index With Program Outcomes for Key Publics

Scanning and Evaluation for:	Employees	Media	Investors	Community	Customers	Government	Members
Conflict avoidance index	.40**	.44**	.57**	.54**	.58**	.40**	.41**
Positive media coverage resulted	.17*	.28**	.37**	.42**	.37**	.33*	.33**
Program helped organization save money	.46**	.27**	.42**	.40**	.28**	.33*	.26*
Program helped sales/services increased	.35**	.23**	.44**	.29**	.32**	.30*	.38**
Program helped organization achieve goals	.34**	.29**	.48**	.47**	.46**	.08	.52**
Positive change in relationship Index	.45**	.41**	.57**	.56**	.52**	-.01	.48**
Program message accurately received	.24**	.26**	.23	.43**	.34**	.09	.20
Program helped organization make money	.36**	.24**	.19	.30**	.15	.37**	.13

Note. Average sample sizes for this analysis: employees = 159; media = 217; investors = 46; community = 121; customers = 85; government = 44; and members = 48. Sample size may vary for each coefficient, depending on number of missing cases.

$*p < .05.$ $**p < .01.$

Excepting government relations, correlations also are positive and significant between operations research and demonstrating positive changes in relationships with target publics. Operations research accounts for 17% (media relations) to 31% (community relations) of the variance in demonstrating positive relationship change. For government relations, the correlation is negative but not significant; explained variance is near zero.

Operations research is positively and significantly correlated with documenting accurate message reception for four of seven programs. For these significant relationships, operations research accounts for 6% (employee relations) to 18% (community relations) of the variance in demonstrating accurate message reception. For investor, member, and government relations, correlations are positive but not significant.

For four of the seven publics, operations research is positively and significantly correlated with showing how programs help organizations make money. For these significant relationships, scanning and evaluation research accounts for 6% (media relations) to 14% (government relations) of the variance. For investor, customer, and member relations, the correlations are positive but not significant.

In summary, operations research is positively and significantly correlated with all eight positive program outcomes for employee, media, and community relations programs. For customer relations programs, scanning and evaluation research is positively and significantly related to seven of eight positive program outcomes. The one nonsignificant correlation (helping organizations make money) is nevertheless positive and accounts for about 2% of the variance in the sample. For investor and member relations, scanning and evaluation research is positively and significantly associated with six of eight positive outcomes. The remaining nonsignificant relationships are positive, accounting for 2% to 5% of the variance in the sample. For government relations, scanning and evaluation research is positively and significantly correlated with five of the eight positive program outcomes. Of the three remaining nonsignificant relationships, two are positive but account for less than 1% of the variance in the sample. One nonsignificant relationship is negative but the explained variance is near zero.

QUALITATIVE EVIDENCE ON STRATEGIC ORIGINS

As noted elsewhere in this book, the quantitative survey provides a detailed snapshot of many organizations at a single point in time. This freeze frame, however, does not directly answer the core question that drove the statistical analysis in this chapter: Where does strategic management of communication programs come from? What are the antecedents—the origins—of the strategic communication programs? The relationships between activist pressure and the many indicators of excellence provide a clue. To answer more fully, we turn to the follow-up case studies and examine biographies of organizations with excellent and less-than-excellent public relations programs.

The biographies of organizations in the Excellence study demonstrate over and over the critical role of environmental turbulence as the catalyst for pushing public relations and communication management to center stage. At the same time, communicators needed the expertise to help dominant coalitions manage the environmental challenge.

Consider the blood bank on the West Coast of the United States. In the early 1980s, when the AIDS epidemic was high on the public agenda but poorly understood, people refused to donate blood to blood banks, based on the irrational fear that one could contract the deadly virus through the act of donating blood. In San Francisco, donations dropped 25%. In Los Angeles, donations dropped 15%. The blood bank that participated in our case study experienced only a 3% drop in donations. Faced with the same potential crisis of public perception, this blood bank used old-fashioned media relations expertise to provide a clear, rational voice to the public that won the perceptual battle. At the same time, the communication department brought scanning and evaluation skills to the table. Together, these two practitioners—one specializing in media and the other in research—ssuccessfully transformed what the dominant coalition expected from its public relations department. This is a specific exemplar of the demand–delivery loop (Dozier with L.Grunig & J. Grunig, 1995), wherein management expectations of communicators are transformed in times of crisis and locked into higher expectations from that point forward.

Now consider the chemical manufacturer with high overall Excellence scores. The dominant coalition includes the top communicator in strategic planning because, according to the top communicator's supervisor, "everything you do strategically in a company has to do with relations with the outside world." A key event in the chemical industry that played a role in pushing communicators to center stage was the Bhopal chemical gas leak in 1984. The gas leak resulted in 16,000 deaths and a $470 million settlement in 1989 from the company. This thrust many communicators with chemical firms into new roles with higher expectations from dominant coalitions.

Consider also the heavy-metal manufacturer that we studied because its overall Excellence score was among the lowest reported in the 1990–1991 survey. In 1994, when the long interviews were conducted, this manufacturer had gone through significant internal changes. The former top communicator, who enacted the technician role frequently, had retired. A new CEO and chairman of the board ran the corporation. In his climb up the corporate ladder, the new CEO had once managed corporate communication as one of his responsibilities. He had different ideas about what communication could do for the company. His first move was to put the communication department into a common unit with strategic planning. In this example, the turbulence was internal rather than environmental. The effect was the same, however. Communication became part of the strategic management team.

Consider the oil products manufacturer with high overall Excellence scores. Of the organizations surveyed, this company had perhaps the most sophisticated operations research expertise in house. When asked how the public relations department became such an important conduit for information used by the dominant coalition in decision making, the top communicator told the Excellence team that the 232,000-gallon spill from the Exxon Valdez oil tanker in 1989 had consequences for the entire oil industry. Even though his company was not involved in the oil spill, the dominant coalition of that oil company decided to treat its constituent relations with greater managerial expertise.

Finally, consider a gas and electric utility in the Midwest of the United States with a high overall Excellence score. In the follow-up case study, the Excellence team asked key informants how the utility had achieved such excellence. Our long interviews indicated that the CEO played a crucial role in making public relations proactive and communication two-way. However, a crucial historical event was the "rude" and expensive awakening when the utility encountered difficulties constructing a nuclear power plant. Before this event, the dominant coalition had a strong engineering or technology orientation and little sensitivity to public perceptions. The expensive consequences of the organization's failure to attend to public opinion again thrust the communication department to center stage.

In summary, events internal or external (or both) to organizations cause dominant coalitions to reconsider the communication function. Paradoxically, activist pressure resulting from oil spills, chemical gas leaks, nuclear power plant construction, the AIDS epidemic, and the like all serve to place the communication function in center stage. Often, dominant coalitions redefine their expectations of public relations based on how communicators perform. Proactive or reactive, strategic or historicist, managerial or technical, the performance of communicators is determined by what they know how to do.

A META-ANALYSIS OF FINDINGS

The findings reported in Tables 9.11 to 9.23 provide a detailed test of the theory of excellence as applied to specific communication programs. In all, the Excellence team tested 546 unique relationships where we expected significant correlations, based on theoretical propositions of communication Excellence. We expected many of these relationships would be disconfirmed because of small sample size and Type 2 error. For example, fewer than 100 communication departments in the Excellence study ran investor, government, and member relations programs. In this context, Type 2 error means that expected relationships among excellence, origins, activist pressure, operations research, and outcomes exist in the population; however, the correlations for those relationships were not statistically significant in the sample. For this reason, counting only statistically significant relationships in the meta-analysis would not adequately reflect the findings of the data analysis.

For purposes of this analysis, therefore, the outcomes of the correlation tests were divided into five possible outcomes. The relationships, as suggested in the propositions, may be both consistent with theory and statistically significant (confirmed and statistically significant).[2] On the other hand, relationships may be consistent with theory but not statistically significant (confirmed but not statistically significant).

Further, relationships may be positive or negative but essentially near zero, meaning that there is no relationship of any magnitude in the sample and probably none of any magnitude in the population. For this category of outcomes, a relationship was classified as null or near zero if the independent variable accounted for (or explained) less than 1% of the variance in the dependent variable. Thus, a correlation (which is the square root of explained variance) ranging from −.09 to +.09 was treated as near zero.

In addition, correlations may be inconsistent with theory and greater than zero (>1% explained variance) but not statistically significant (disconfirmed but not statistically significant). True anomalies are those correlations that are both inconsistent with theory and statistically significant (disconfirmed and statistically significant). The five possible outcomes for all the unique tests of excellence in Tables 9.11–9.23 are summarized in Table 9.24.

Of the 546 relationships tested, 468 correlation coefficients were positive and 400 were statistically significant. That is, 86% of the hypothesized relationships were positive as posited with 85% of the positive relationships (73% of all relationships) statistically significant, according to the 95% decision rule. The statistical analysis generated only four genuine anomalies—where correlations were both negative and statistically significant. This is less than 1% of the relationships tested, well below the 5% one would expect by chance alone, given the use of the 95% decision rule. In addition, the analysis indicated four additional negative relationships with the independent variable accounting for more than 1% of the variance in the dependent variable, but not statistically significant. In all, negative relationships, both significant and not significant, involving 1% or more of explained variance accounted for only 1.4% of all relationships tested. Some 70 relationships (nearly 13% of those tested) involved correlation coefficients near zero (<1% explained variance).

Regarding historical origins of communication programs (Table 9.11), we expected weak or negative correlations with excellence. Of 35 relationships tested, 49% were negative and 59% of those were statistically significant. The

---

[2]The only exceptions are theoretical expectations regarding historicist origins of programs and excellence. Regarding historicist origins, propositions derived from excellence suggest that programs with high historicist origin scores would be either unrelated or negatively related to indicators of excellence. In Table 9.24, the outcomes for Table 9.11 that confirm the propositions are negative relationships.

TABLE 9.24
A Meta-Analysis of the Tests of Excellence for Seven Key Publics/Programs

Table	Description	Confirm (SIG.) % (N)	Confirm (N.S.) % (N)	Null (<1% E.V.) % (N)	Disconfirm (N.S.) % (N)	Disconfirm (SIG.) % (N)	TOTAL % (N)
9.11	Historical Origins	29% (10)	20% (7)	51% (18)	0% (0)	0% (0)	100% (35)
9.12	Strategic Origins	74% (26)	20% (7)	6% (2)	0% (0)	0% (0)	100% (35)
9.13	Formal Scanning	86% (36)	5% (2)	7% (3)	0% (0)	2% (1)	100% (42)
9.14	Informal Scanning	81% (34)	7% (3)	12% (5)	0% (0)	0% (0)	100% (42)
9.15	Scientific Evaluation	83% (35)	5% (2)	12% (5)	0% (0)	0% (0)	100% (42)
9.16	Clip-File Evaluation	74% (31)	14% (6)	10% (4)	0% (0)	2% (1)	100% (42)
9.17	Informal Evaluation	83% (35)	5% (2)	10% (4)	2% (1)	0% (0)	100% (42)
9.18	Operations Research	86% (36)	7% (3)	7% (3)	0% (0)	0% (0)	100% (42)
9.19	Conflict Avoidance	71% (25)	14% (5)	9% (3)	6% (2)	0% (0)	100% (35)
9.20	Relationship Change	66% (23)	14% (5)	17% (6)	0% (0)	3% (1)	100% (35)
9.21	Excellence & Outcomes	43% (18)	26% (11)	26% (11)	2% (1)	2% (1)	100% (42)
9.22	Strategic Origins & Outcomes	77% (43)	18% (10)	5% (3)	0% (0)	0% (0)	100% (56)
9.23	Operations Research & Outcomes	86% (48)	9% (5)	5% (3)	0% (0)	0% (0)	100% (56)
TOTAL %		73.3%	12.5%	12.8%	0.7%	0.7%	100%
(N)		(400)	(68)	(70)	(4)	(4)	(546)

remaining correlation coefficients (51% of those tested) were near zero.[3] Regarding strategic origins of programs (Table 9.12), 94% of the relationships were positive as posited; of those, 79% were statistically significant. Statistical analysis revealed no anomalies (i.e., statistically significant negative relationships). The remaining correlations were near zero.

Regarding environmental scanning and program evaluation (Tables 9.13 to 9.18), statistical analysis revealed consistently strong, positive relationships with other indicators of excellence. Regarding formal scanning, 91% of the 42 correlations tested were positive. Of those, 95% were statistically significant. Regarding informal scanning, 88% of the 42 relationships were positive as posited; of those, 92% were statistically significant. Regarding scientific evaluation, 88% of the 42 relationships were positive as posited; of those, 95% were statistically significant. Regarding clip-file evaluation, 88% of the 42 relationships tested were positive as posited; of those, 84% were statistically significant. Regarding informal, seat-of-the-pants evaluation, 88% of the 42 relationships tested were positive; of those 95% were statistically significant. Using the operations research index that combined the two types of scanning and three types of evaluation, 93% of the 42 relationships tested were positive as posited. Of those, 93% were statistically significant.

Regarding program outcomes, conflict avoidance and changes in relationships (Tables 9.19 and 9.20) were tested with measures of overall Excellence, environmental turbulence, and manager role expertise and enactment. Of the 35 relationships tested for conflict avoidance outcomes, 85% of the correlations were positive as posited; of those, 83% were statistically significant. Of the 35 relationships tested for positive changes in relationships, 80% of the correlations were positive as posited; of those, 82% were statistically significant.

Other indicators of desired program outcomes used single measures (Table 9.21). These variables were correlated with overall Excellence, strategic origins of communication programs, and the operations research index (scanning and evaluation combined). For the 42 unique relationships in Table 9.21 (excluding conflict avoidance and relationship change previously included for Tables 9.19 and 9.20), overall Excellence scores correlated positively with 69% of six additional positive program outcomes (positive media coverage, accurate message reception, helping organizations achieve goals, helping organizations save money, helping organizations make money, and increasing sales). However, only 62% of those correlations were statistically significant. Over 26% of these tests were classified as null (<1% explained variance). Several factors contribute to weaker relationships between overall Excellence and these six additional pro-

---

[3]The partial correlations for technician role expertise in Tables 9.11 to 9.20 are not considered in this meta-analysis, because theory would suggest orthogonal or even negative relationships between attributes of excellence and technician role expertise, once manager role expertise is controlled.

gram outcomes. First, some process outcomes (e.g., positive media coverage) are not germane to all publics (e.g., employees, investors, and members). Second, overall communication Excellence is only weakly linked to some outcomes (e.g., making money and increasing sales) that are primary responsibilities of other departments in the organization (e.g., marketing).

The eight positive program outcomes were correlated also with the strategic origins and management of communication programs. Of the 56 relationships tested, 95% were positive; of those, 81% were statistically significant. The eight program outcomes were correlated with the use of operations research (scanning and evaluation index) for each public. Of the 56 relationships tested, 95% were positive; of those, 91% were statistically significant.

SUMMARY AND CONCLUSIONS

The meta-analysis of findings provides remarkably robust support for the propositions laid out at the beginning of this chapter. Our data show in detail how excellent communication programs can be made strategic and how they can be evaluated. These are two questions discussed by public relations people almost every day, although most do not have the answer. Our excellent programs have the answer.

When the organization and the communication department are excellent overall, communication programs for specific publics are more likely to have strategic origins and less likely to have historicist origins. Excellent departments are more than the routine publicity mills of traditional departments. Excellent programs arise from environmental scanning research, and they are evaluated through all forms of evaluation (scientific, clip-file, and informal). Managers of excellent departments also report that evidence is available that their programs have positive outcomes, such as meeting their objectives, changing relationships, and avoiding conflict.

Strategic origins for communication programs occur in organizations experiencing pressure from activist groups. When program origins are strategic, top communicators report greater success in dealing with activist pressure on the organization. Programs are more likely to have strategic origins if the communication department has the expertise to enact the manager role and the top communicator enacts that role frequently. When organizations experience activist pressure, they are more likely to use both formal and informal environmental scanning research. Communication programs are more likely to be evaluated through scientific, clip-file, and informal evaluation when activist pressure is high. Generally, organizations are more successful in dealing with activists when they evaluate their communication programs. Formal and informal scanning and the three forms of program evaluation all increase when the communication department has higher levels of managerial expertise and the head of public relations enacts that role frequently. Positive program outcomes increase as a function of overall Excellence, manager role expertise, and manager role enactment.

Government relations programs generated three of the four anomalies (significant negative correlations when we expected significant positive relationships) in the 546 relationships tested. Indeed, government relations programs show generally weaker correlations than those posited at the beginning of this chapter (see Tables 9.12 to 9.23), when compared to the six other publics. Excellence team member Fred C. Repper, retired vice president of public relations for Gulf States Utilities, provided an explanation. Having worked several years for Gulf States Utilities in Washington, DC, Repper and other members of the Excellence team generated two post hoc explanations for the anomalies of government relations programs. First, in many organizations, government relations programs and especially lobbying are functions often dominated by lawyers and CEOs directly. Communication departments typically exert little control over these programs, even if government relations is situated in the communication department on the organizational chart.

For this reason, government relations programs often operate somewhat orthogonally to communication departments, independent of both strengths and weaknesses in those departments, as indicated by various measures of communication Excellence. Second, lobbyists lean heavily on personal experience and interpersonal relations with legislators or regulators as the basis for their actions. More so than others under the public relations umbrella in organizations, these practitioners are less likely to have formal training in communication management. Because expertise (e.g., manager role and two-way symmetrical communication) in the communication function is at the core of overall Excellence, quasi-autonomous government relations programs appear to operate less directly as a function of communication Excellence.

REFERENCES

Broom, G. M. (1986, August). *Public relations roles and systems theory: Functional and historicist causal models*. Paper presented at the meeting of the Public Relations Interest Group, International Communication Association, Chicago.

Broom, G. M., & Dozier, D. M. (1990). *Using research in public relations: Applications to program management*. Englewood Cliffs, NJ: Prentice-Hall.

Dozier, D. M. (1987, May). *Gender, environmental scanning, and participation in management decision-making*. Paper presented at the meeting of the Public Relations Interest Group, International Communication Association, Montreal.

Dozier, D. M. (1990). The innovation of research in public relations practice: Review of a program of study. In L. A. Grunig & J. E. Grunig (Eds.), *Public relations research annual* (Vol. 2, pp. 3–28). Hillsdale, NJ: Lawrence Erlbaum Associates.

Dozier, D. M., & Broom, G. M. (1995). Evolution of the manager role in public relations practices. *Journal of Public Relations Research, 7*(1), 3–26.

Dozier, D. M., & Ehling, W. P. (1992). Evaluation of public relations programs: What the literature tells us about their effects. In J. E. Grunig (Ed.), *Excellence in public relations and communication management* (pp. 159–184). Hillsdale, NJ: Lawrence Erlbaum Associates.

Dozier, D. M., & Grunig, L. A. (1992). The organization of the public relations function. In J. E. Grunig (Ed.), *Excellence in public relations and communication management* (pp. 395–418). Hillsdale, NJ: Lawrence Erlbaum Associates.

Dozier, D. M., with Grunig, L. A., & Grunig, J. E. (1995). *Manager's guide to excellence in public relations and communication management.* Hillsdale, NJ: Lawrence Erlbaum Associates.

Dozier, D. M., & White, J. (1992). Public relations and management decision making. In J. E. Grunig (Ed.), *Excellence in public relations and communication management* (pp. 91–108). Hillsdale, NJ: Lawrence Erlbaum Associates.

Ehling, W. P., & Dozier, D. M. (1992). Public relations management and operations research. In J. E. Grunig (Ed.), *Excellence in public relations and communication management* (pp. 251–284). Hillsdale, NJ: Lawrence Erlbaum Associates.

Grunig, J. E. (1983). Washington reporter publics of corporate public affairs programs. *Journalism Quarterly, 60,* 603–615.

Grunig, J. E. (Ed.). (1992). *Excellence in public relations and communication management.* Hillsdale, NJ: Lawrence Erlbaum Associates.

Lauzen, M. M., & Dozier, D. M. (1992). The missing link: The public relations manager role as mediator of organizational environments and power consequences for the function. *Journal of Public Relations Research, 4,* 205–220.

Lauzen, M. M., & Dozier, D. M. (1994). Issues management mediation of linkages between environmental complexity and management of the public relations function. *Journal of Public Relations Research, 6,* 163–184.

Robbins, S. P. (1990). *Organizational theory: Structure, design, and applications* (3rd ed.). Englewood Cliffs, NJ: Prentice-Hall.

CHAPTER TEN

Activism and the Environment

Activism pushes organizations toward excellence. Counterintuitive though this may sound, both the survey results and insights from the case studies firmly establish this relationship. The explanation is multifaceted, but it begins with an understanding of the importance of support from the dominant coalition for the public relations function. In the case studies, activism emerged as the second greatest determinant of the value top management holds for public relations. Only providing a broad perspective both inside and outside of the organization was mentioned more frequently and with more conviction by the CEOs we talked with. They and their top communicators both described what some called the "infinite value" of public relations during times of crisis or activist pressure.

Coping with a turbulent, complex environment requires sophisticated, strategic, two-way communication. Activist groups put pressure on organizations. Excellent public relations programs are most successful in contending with that pressure.

More specifically, the theoretical framework for the Excellence study suggested a series of propositions about activism and managed communication. The findings reported in this chapter are organized around each of the seven propositions. The chapter begins by reviewing briefly the literature that led to those expectations.

THE ENVIRONMENT

More than three decades ago, the relationship between organizations and their environments became critically important to organizational sociologists (Aldrich, 1979; Aldrich & Pfeffer, 1976). They reasoned that organizational survival hinges on adaptation to the external context. Adaptation, in turn, requires the development of a monitoring and feedback mechanism for systematic assessment of the environment.

Andrews introduced the concept of an uncertain environment to strategic management in the Harvard textbook, *Business Policy: Text and Cases* (Learned, Christensen, Andrews, & Guth, 1965). Since then, the literature on strategic management has been permeated by two words, *mission* and *environment* (J. Grunig & Repper, 1992). Together, these concepts suggest that organizations must make long-term, strategic choices that are feasible in their environments. Chapter 5 showed the critical role of excellent public relations departments in strategic decision making. Public relations professionals, in their boundary-spanning role as the eyes and ears of the organization, are a key part of the environmental-scanning process. They serve as a kind of early-warning system. They have the knowledge and skill needed to bring the voices of publics into strategic decision making.

Although the concept of environment has pervaded the literature on strategic management, until recently it has been conceptualized in "general, even rather vague" terms (Rumelt, Schendel, & Teece, 1994, p. 22). Pearce and Robinson (1982), for example, defined environment as "the sum total of all conditions and forces that affect the strategic options of a business but that are typically beyond its ability to control" (p. 62). The commonality among scholars' many definitions of the environment, as Robbins (1990) expressed it, is "consideration of factors outside the organization itself" (p. 149).

In general, these *external* forces encompass the political arena, the economy, legal and social systems, and culture. Specific manifestations of the external context include customers or clients, suppliers, competitors, legislators, neighbors, the mass media, the trade press, and—of course—activist or special-interest groups. Mintzberg (1983) categorized these powerful influencers into three types of external publics that have special relevance for public relations practitioners: the mass media, government, and special-interest groups.

Media coverage conveys legitimacy. When activist groups find their target organizations unresponsive, they typically contact journalists. Of course, media coverage of activism is not unilaterally favorable to the activist group and unfavorable to the offending organization. However, activists do enjoy certain advantages. Harris (1982), for example, found that interest groups use the media to influence public opinion that serves as a court of appeal. Mazur (as cited in "Too Much Media," 1986) explained that the more the media report on an issue, the more negative the public's opinion of the organization being covered. Olien, Donohue, and Tichenor (1984) concluded that press coverage defines the importance of events that activist groups stage.

Whereas controversies escalate when the media get involved, consequences become more serious when the *government* becomes involved. Activists often work with government as well as with the press in their protests against organizations. At that point, the organization faces opposition from more than a single source. More significantly, governmental intervention reduces organizational autonomy. As Mintzberg (1983) emphasized, government represents the ultimate legitimate authority of a society. Governmental regulation results in what Jones (1978) called the "institutionalization of activism" (p. 19).

Although scholars of strategic management originally conceptualized the environment as a constraint on an organization's mission and choices, Porter (1980, 1985, 1990, 1994) turned the relationship around and conceptualized the environment as a source of competitive advantage. For example, he found that multinational corporations with strong competitors in their home country were better able to compete in other countries because of the pressure to excel at home (Porter, 1994). Likewise, he found that government regulation, traditionally seen by corporate managers as an intrusion on their decision making, can stimulate changes in organizational behavior that provide a competitive advantage.

Verčič and J. Grunig (2000) extended Porter's idea that an organization can gain competitive advantage from successful relationships with competitors and governments in the environment to relationships with other stakeholder publics. For example, a corporation that successfully solves its environmental problems, usually when pressured by environmental activists, will gain an advantage from relationships with stockholders, consumers, employees, government, and communities that can support or constrain that corporation.[1] Likewise, a government agency that responds well to pressures from its constituents will be more likely to gain support from those publics as it competes for limited public funding.

Most studies of *activism* and public relations date from the mid-1980s (e.g., L. Grunig, 1986). This body of knowledge leads to insights explored more fully in the next section. In short, the failure of most organizations to deal effectively with activist pressure suggests that they adopt a two-way symmetrical approach—rather than relying on more traditional asymmetrical models to try to quell antagonistic groups that exist in their environment.

To some scholars, factors *inside* the organization are part of its landscape as well. However, in this chapter we (following Robbins, 1990) restrict our consideration of environment and any activism that emerges from that environment to its external dimensions. We explore in considerable detail what goes on internally in the next chapter.

---

[1]An article in the trade press made much the same point—helping practitioners understand why advocacy groups can be a boon to organizations. Clark (1997) explained that by coming to understand activists' concerns, a company equips itself to deal effectively with similar advocates in future. The organization also may form and maintain a strong alliance with the activist group, helping ensure cooperation rather than confrontation in the future because of that alignment. Thus Clark promoted the development of an Advocacy Alliance Plan, through which the corporation establishes a relationship with activists designed to connect social responsibility with profitability.

For now, consider how managers—rather than scholars—look at their environments. An understanding of the concept of "enactment" adds more weight to the importance of the scanning function of public relations practitioners. Research has shown that the correspondence between actual environment and managers' perceptions of that context can be minimal (Downey, Hellriegel, & Slocum, 1975). Interestingly, managers tend to base their decisions more on their perceptions than any actuality. That is, they enact their environment and act accordingly.

Enacting the environment may be a more vital role now than when we conceptualized the Excellence project. A survey (Davis, 1995) conducted by the International Consortium for Executive Development Research and sponsored by Gemini Consulting found, in the words of Gemini's senior vice president: "With the arrival of the global village, you have to redefine yourself in relation to your environment much faster now. The evolution of the species has become more complex" (p. 15).

Because of the research they do or the interactions they have with external publics, public relations professionals can help to enact that global and rapidly changing environment. This is especially likely to happen when they are involved in the strategic management of their organization. Scanning is essential because it reduces uncertainty in the environment (Lauzen, 1995; Stoffels, 1994). Aspects of environmental uncertainty include dynamism (Robbins, 1990), heterogeneity, instability, dispersion, and turbulence (J. Grunig, 1984). High uncertainty, according to the literature, forces organizations to seek information from their environments as well as disseminating information to their external publics.

These concepts that organizational theorists use to describe the environment define it in general terms, but they are too general to be of practical use to professional environmental scanners, such as public relations professionals. In contrast, the theories that we and other public relations scholars have developed to identify stakeholders, publics, and activists and to explain their role in creating issues add substance to the vague concept of the environment found in organizational literature. These groups constitute the social and political environment that organizations need the assistance of public relations professionals to enact. They are the strategic groups that excellent public relations practitioners identify and monitor when they scan the environment. They are the groups with which organizations must communicate and build relationships.

The typical environment is dynamic and turbulent, rather than static and placid—that is, it is filled with active publics and activist groups. Therefore, we theorized that two-way symmetrical communication would be more valuable than one-way communication for most organizations. The interdependence between the organization and the specific or strategic constituencies in its environment also suggests the importance of the two-way symmetrical model.

ACTIVISM

But why, you may ask, would a large, powerful organization consider itself mutually dependent on smaller, less powerful elements even if they exist in its strategic environment? We believe that the leaders of some multinational conglomerates undoubtedly fail to enact their environment in a way that acknowledges (much less legitimizes) their interdependence with, say, small activist groups. We have called this the "snail darter fallacy."

Olson's (1971) theory of collective action explains the power of even very small groups to affect organizational power and autonomy. Olson believed that small interest groups can be more effective than larger, more established groups. Members of small groups tend to be more personally committed. Members of large groups—at least those who are rational—realize that their individual efforts rarely affect the outcome. They believe that the situation will turn out the same regardless of their personal contribution.

By contrast, people who join small activist groups are characterized by their motivation, even fervor. They persevere until they achieve their goal: exerting pressure on the organization on behalf of a cause. They often seem to have wider support than they actually enjoy, in part because they display more "action-taking" behavior than do larger groups. As a result, Olson (1971) concluded that special-interest groups with relatively few members have disproportionate power.

Our working definition of activism encompasses all such groups, regardless of their size: An activist public is a group of two or more individuals who organize in order to influence another public or publics through action that may include education, compromise, persuasion, pressure tactics, or force.

Without a thorough understanding of adversarial groups and their issues, the organization may be at their mercy. Activism is a problem for the majority of organizations (Mintzberg, 1983). Most issues are discrete, rather than escalations of what began as limited concerns. However, the typical dispute endures until there is some satisfactory resolution for the activist group. For example, Anderson (1992) conducted an extensive case study of a multinational food company that wanted to cut down part of the rain forest to plant orange groves in the Central American country of Belize. The company met no opposition in Belize; but Friends of the Earth, based in London, opposed the project. The company eventually canceled it.

Anderson (1992) found that when activists are dissatisfied with the information they receive from the organization, they go elsewhere to find information. Thus she suggested that if the organization had identified the relevant issue early in its decision process, it could have been proactive in, first, identifying the contentious public and, second, communicating with it. Representatives of the company and the activist groups accidentally engaged in symmetrical communication after a broadcast debate. When they finally engaged in dialogue, they

were able to resolve the issue. Anderson's case study, like many others conducted in the last decade, supports the two-way symmetrical model of public relations as the most effective strategy for dealing with activism.

Both activists and the organizations they pressure rely on public relations
practitioners to help communicate with each other. Many organizations, however, try to ignore activist groups. When they are willing to communicate, they
practice either one-way or two-way asymmetrical public relations. This approach rarely works. Only a few instances even of compromise could be found
in an extensive study of almost three dozen cases of activism in the 1980s (L.
Grunig, 1986).

Failure to establish good relationships with these often-belligerent groups
may result in crisis situations for the organization. Thus this chapter concludes
with findings of the qualitative research related to crises. We do not label this
section "crisis management," because we are convinced that no organization (at
least none we have studied) can manage a crisis. The best that can be expected is
that the organization manages its *response* to the crisis in an effective and responsible way. Fortunately, we have a number of these "best practices" in times of
crisis to report. Not surprisingly, they tend to come from organizations ranked
at or near the top of the Excellence scale.

RESULTS

Extent and Success of Activism

We begin our presentation of findings about activism and the way organizations respond by considering the problem (or opportunity) activism typically
represents. The questionnaires for the head of the public relations department
and the CEO in the quantitative portion of the Excellence study contained three
questions about the perceived incidence of activism and the success of the organization and activists in achieving their goals vis-à-vis the other. Table 10.1
shows the mean scores for these variables: an estimate of the extent of activist
pressure faced by the organization, an estimate of the success of the organization in achieving its goals that were affected by a recent case of activist pressure,
and an estimate of the success of the activists in the same case.

The respondents estimated these three variables on the open-ended fractionation scale described in chapter 2, from which they could give a number from
zero to as high as desired. For most responses to this scale, we transformed the
variables by taking their square root to minimize the impact of extreme responses on measures of central tendency and correlational statistics. As can be
seen in Table 10.1, a few extreme responses especially affected the means for activism, so that the raw means were well above the hypothetical mean of 100.

For the CEOs, the mean score on the untransformed scale was 149, which
suggests that the average CEO believed his or her organization experienced

TABLE 10.1
Activist Pressure on Organizations

Variable	CEOs	PR Heads
Extent of Activist Pressure		
Mean	149	117
Median	100	100
Transformed Mean	10.1	8.6
Pearson Correlation With Excellence Index	.24**	.38**
Success of Organization With Activists		
Mean	154	115
Median	100	100
Transformed Mean	11.4	10.2
Pearson Correlation With Excellence Index	.17*	.29**
Success of Activists With Organization		
Mean	74	83
Median	50	75
Transformed Mean	7.6	8.0
Pearson Correlation With Excellence Index	.08	.10
Number	286	375

Note. The means and medians reported in this table are based on an open-end fractionation scale for which respondents were told that 100 is a typical response on all of the items in the questionnaire. The transformed mean is based on a square-root transformation to reduce the skew of the data. A score of 10 on the transformed scale is equivalent to the typical response of 100 on the original scale.

$*p < .05.$ $**p < .01.$

50% more activism than the typical organization. A frequency count of individual scores showed, likewise, that 60% of the CEOs said that their organizations experienced as much or more activism than the typical organization (a score of 100 or more).

The median score, by contrast with this mean, was 100. Likewise, the transformed mean was just above the hypothetical average of 10. These differences resulted from a few high scores (e.g., two of 1,000 and one of 5,000), which skewed the untransformed mean. The overall picture from these data is that a few organizations faced extreme activist pressure but that the typical CEO thought that his or her organization coped with at least an average amount of activism.

Heads of public relations rated activist pressure somewhat lower than did their CEOs. The untransformed mean score for communicators was 117. However, their median score also was 100, and their transformed mean was 8.6. Fifty-two percent said their organizations faced as much or more activism as typical organizations. It is not clear why CEOs perceived more activism, although it is possible that heads of public relations were more aware of activism and therefore believed that the pressure experienced by their organization was normal whereas CEOs thought activists targeted them more than other organizations. Important to note, however, we can conclude that most organizations in our study are affected by activism.

When asked how successful the organization had been in dealing with activist groups and how successful the activist groups had been in dealing with the organization, both CEOs and heads of public relations rated their organization as more successful. However, CEOs rated the organization as more effective and the activists as less successful than did their top communicators. Again, the reason for the difference is not clear; although it is possible that the heads of public relations had a more accurate assessment of the relative success of the organization and activists because they are closer to the interaction with activists.

Table 10.1 also reports the correlations of these same three variables with the overall index of excellence in public relations. In our original theorizing, we had hypothesized that activism would push organizations toward excellence. Organizations that face activist pressure would be more likely to assign public relations a managerial role, include public relations in strategic management, communicate more symmetrically with a powerful adversary or partner, and develop more participative cultures and organic structures that would open the organization to its environment—the key variables in our index of excellence.

Table 10.1 provides at least moderate support for this hypothesis. The perceived incidence of activism correlated moderately and significantly with excellence in public relations, especially when estimated by the head of public relations. For the estimates of both CEOs and senior communicators, organizations with excellent public relations were more likely to report success in dealing with activists than were organizations with less excellent departments. The success of activists, however, did not correlate significantly with excellence. Important to note, these correlations were not negative: Communication Excellence seems to mean that activists do not fail to achieve their goals when organizations achieve their goals.

In summary, then, Table 10.1 suggests that activism stimulates excellence. The correlations probably were moderate, however, because most of the organizations studied reported facing activism. Many, but not all, seem to have responded by developing excellent public relations departments, which make them more successful in dealing with activists. Activists probably achieve some level of success regardless of how the organization responds; the difference provided by excellence is that the organization can achieve success as well as the activists—a symmetrical outcome for the organization and the activists.

Before turning to an analysis of additional quantitative results and of the qualitative research in an effort to explain and understand these findings, think back to the factor analyses of excellence or mediocrity in public relations as seen by CEOs and professional communicators. These results are presented in Table 3.3 in chapter 3, which represented the first step in isolating the Excellence factor. There, we saw that CEOs in effective organizations valued the contribution public relations makes when responding to major social issues much more highly than did their counterparts in mediocre operations (loadings of .67 vs. −.15, respectively). Similarly, heads of public relations in excellent departments valued their own contribution in responding to major social issues far more than did their counterparts in mediocre departments (loadings of .47 vs. −.20, respectively).

Taken together, these findings about the extent of activism perceived by CEOs and their top communicators and the value placed on responding to issues in that turbulent, dynamic, often hostile environment demonstrate the critical nature of this chapter. Activism represents an enormous problem in the typical organization. Effective organizations may overshadow the ineffective ones in part because they rely on the expertise of their public relations staffs to help contend with that pressure from outside forces.

As chapter 8 showed, we equate expert public relations with practice that is both ethical and effective. And that, we found, is two-way, balanced communication. The propositions that follow explore the role of two-way symmetrical public relations in enacting the environment, in establishing programs to communicate with elements of that external context deemed strategic to the organization (regardless of their size or perceived legitimacy and power), and in evaluating the long-term outcome of strategic communication with activists. One final proposition argues that to realize the potential of this kind of public relations, the top communicator must be in a position to interact with the dominant coalition. Evidence to support or refute these expectations, based on the theoretical literature reviewed briefly at the beginning of this chapter, comes both from our lengthy personal interviews and from additional questions in the survey instruments.

Proposition 1: Listening to All Strategic Constituencies

Excellent organizations use two-way communication to learn the consequences of what they are doing on all of their relevant publics—not just their owners, their employees, and their associates.

Listening is the aspect of communication that often gets short shrift in the professional public relations literature, although it is a critical element of symmetrical public relations. Textbooks typically concentrate on teaching students how to write, how to edit, how to take pictures, how to deliver speeches, how to host plant tours or other special events, how to lay out publications, and how to plan press conferences. Only rarely does the undergraduate in public relations concentrate on the other half of the process of two-way communication: gathering intelligence through research, through systematic observation, and—perhaps primarily—through listening. Because we on the Excellence team learned from our preliminary literature review about the critical nature of scanning the environment in order to enact it with any degree of accuracy, we chose to emphasize this aspect of two-way public relations as our first proposition related to activism. *Listen* is the first word of Benedict's *Rule*. Soundings, paying attention, remain a serious matter for the Benedictines. So, too, with some of the most effective executives we interviewed.

Results relevant to this first proposition came from both the qualitative and quantitative portions of our study. We examine the qualitative results first to understand the specifics of listening in excellent organizations and then analyze portions of the survey data to show their relationship to our index of communication Excellence.

Qualitative Results

The CEO of one of the organizations ranked at the top of the Excellence scale explained what he considered to be the value of listening, even when hearing from the activists that frequently constrained his industry. The chemical industry has numerous consequences on its strategic publics. After the 1984 tragedy in Bhopal, India, it became obvious that not all consequences were positive. Nevertheless, this CEO reminisced about his lengthy career in the industry at the time of his retirement: "I've found that if you listen, more often than not you'll hear as much stuff that you like, and that encourages you, as you will hear that discourages you and p-----s you off. And if you can't deal with that, then you're in trouble today because the scheme of things demands that you have this kind of symmetrical relationship." That "scheme of things" to which he referred, of course, is activism.

The industry association CEO emphasized the progress that often results from dialogue with strategic publics. However, he was careful to qualify "progress" as perhaps "only that they respect your willingness to engage in the dialogue." Respect, of course, may lead to the neutral stance he further described as, "If you won't help us, don't hurt us."

The heart-health organization was successful in parlaying symmetrical relationships with other health organizations and groups concerned with the same publics into coalitions. According to the top communicator there, the process began by standing in the shoes of the target audience and asking: "So what? Why is this important to me?" To him, this was the essence of the boundary-spanning function. He characterized the relationships that resulted as, "You scratch my back and I'll scratch yours." He added that research provides much of the raw data needed to answer the "so what?" question.

The major purpose of public relations at the midwestern gas and electric company seemed to be building a socially responsible profile in the community. To do so, the senior vice president described his department's systematic effort to accomplish "a lot of partnering with people . . . in raising money for whatever needs to be done in the community." His program consisted of "ongoing involvement, support, cheerleading, boosting." Both employees and the CEO belonged to organizational boards that also included the editors of the city's newspapers and the manager of the largest television station. The long-range goal, the top communicator explained, was to maximize the quality of life in the area. Altruistic? No, not entirely. The larger goal was to attract good people to the company.

Before new management at this utility embraced a philosophy of openness with the community it served, it focused solely on technology and the engineering aspects of its operation. Public relations problems, according to a senior vice president there, forced it to listen to the concerns of area residents in an effort to make sure their perceptions of the business were aligned with the reality.

At least one organization described its process of listening to publics as keeping an "ear to the ground." The goal of this medical products division of a Fortune 500 company was to correct for problems before they escalate. The company relied on ongoing assessment to help avoid crises, especially in its international operations. Its top communicator explained: "That's where things can really hurt you. When a crisis happens overseas, we try not to let it get in the press in the United States, because that is basically like throwing gas on a fire. No matter who is at fault, it doesn't do any good to have half-truths from either side come back and reflect on our company."

This communication manager went on to cite two instances in countries outside of the United States where he credited proactive assessment and fast thinking with helping avoid lawsuits that could have cost the company, in his words, "hundreds of millions of dollars, if not more."

Another organization, the blood bank, closely tracked telephone complaints to listen to the dissatisfactions of its publics. The public affairs officer there explained that this provides an early-warning system for senior management about emerging issues and problems.

The blood bank also listened systematically, primarily through focus group studies of donors, surveys of chairs of blood drives, and summative evaluations of each blood drive. It used its extensive media contacts as an informal technique for monitoring the organizational environment. As a result of this extensive research, the blood bank equated the role of communication with a conduit of information—a relatively new role, according to its chief financial officer. The CFO explained that media relations had served as the "foot in the door" for public relations. As a result of communicators' expertise, they performed "exceptionally well" during crises, in her opinion.

A third organization, the U.S.-based oil company, accomplished its listening in a similarly formal, systematic way—and with equally impressive results. For example, it relied on survey research to gauge public perceptions of the industry. During and after the Middle East oil embargo of the 1970s, it found increased public disfavor—as well as state and federal legislative proposals it considered negative. Its emphasis had been on forecasting. After this crisis period, it developed a strong research capability in its public affairs department.

By institutionalizing communication research, the oil company was able to establish an extensive program of two-way public relations. Two-way communication, both symmetrical and asymmetrical, characterized its interaction with environmentalists and its operating companies as well. As the coordinator of corporate contributions told us: "You have to understand what the other manager's sensitivity is about an issue or whatever they're trying to do . . . understand their goals, which is sometimes different from what your goals might be. . . ."

From all of these relevant cases, we found considerable support for this first proposition about the need to listen even to what the organization undoubtedly would prefer not to hear: the concerns of constituencies hostile to it. We can elaborate on the proposition in the following ways. We know, now, about the variety of approaches both effective and ineffective operations rely on to hear their publics. They include formal and informal means to bring information about emerging or existing issues in. Some, such as the oil company affiliate based in England, took advantage of research conducted by their industry associations. Others, such as the blood bank, do their own scanning. They use strategic alliances, focus groups, media contacts, survey research, programs of public participation, and hot lines for complaints.

We also gained a good grasp of the utility of this process of opening up the organization to its environment and thus reducing the uncertainty inherent in that external context. Advantages seem most apparent in the environment that is antagonistic or at least tumultuous. They are also obvious on the global scale. The benefits of listening made manifest from these cases include gathering intelligence about what is on the horizon, having the opportunity to learn about and thus form alliances with other entities similarly affected, and correcting any misperceptions.

These advantages take the organization beyond lip service paid to involvement with its strategic constituencies. They offer concrete values that accrue from helping and, in turn, being helped. Earning the respect of formerly hostile publics, in particular, may neutralize their overt opposition. Thus, by acknowledging its interdependence with strategic aspects of its environment, the organization actually gains autonomy in the long run. Along the way, it also may attract good employees.

Quantitative Results

Methods and Programs for Communicating With Activists. In the two quantitative Excellence questionnaires, we asked CEOs and the heads of public relations questions about how they heard about activists, who was responsible for dealing with activists, and how the organization communicated with activists. For each of these questions, the respondents had several fixed choices as well as the chance to add additional responses. The first column of Table 10.2 shows the frequency of the fixed responses. We also tabulated the frequency of the most common open-end responses but did not include them in the table because of the large number of categories and infrequency of particular responses. We do

TABLE 10.2
Comparison of Means on Excellence Index
With Methods of Communicating With Activists

Variable	Percentage (Multiple Responses)	Mean Yes (Z Scores)[a]	Mean No (Z Score)[a]	T
How Hear About Activist Pressure				
CEO Response				
Pressure Group Itself	69	.10	−.19	2.52**
Media Coverage	66	.12	−.19	2.86**
Public Relations Dept.	58	.17	−.20	3.51**
PR Head Response				
Pressure Group Itself	66	.16	−.24	3.70**
Media Coverage	60	.19	−.23	4.11**
Others in Organization	53	.07	−.04	1.04
Who in Organization Is Responsible for Dealing With Activists (PR Head)				
CEO	52	.12	−.08	1.97*
Head of PR	58	.28	−.33	6.16**
Attorneys	33	.11	−.02	1.23
Special Department	16	.35	−.04	2.79**
Standing Committee to Deal With Activist Issues	25	.32	.05	2.09*
Developed Special Program	51	.31	−.02	2.95**
How Organization Involves Activist Groups				
Informal Conversation	50	.24	−.20	4.22**
Special Committee	26	.41	−.11	4.47**
Include on Board of Directors	9	.15	.02	0.57

*p < .05. **p < .01.
[a]Because of the regression procedure used to calculate missing data, the Excellence index was recomputed as standardized z scores. Z scores have a mean of zero and a standard deviation of 1.0.

discuss the most frequent responses, however; and later we examine the cross-tabulation of these responses with three levels of our index of excellence.

First, we gave the CEOs and heads of public relations three choices about where they tend to find out about activist pressure on their organization. Both had the choice of the pressure group itself and media coverage. The third choice for CEOs was the public relations department, where theoretically we would hope they would get the news because of the environmental scanning role of public relations. The third choice for PR heads was "others in the organization." Table 10.2 shows that CEOs reported the pressure group itself and media coverage as sources somewhat more often than did the public relations department.

Forty-two CEOs volunteered one or more other sources of information about activists. In order of frequency, these sources were federal agencies or government (18), clients or customers (11), trade associations (9), lawsuits or legal challenges (5), employees (4), the department affected (3), competitors (1), and consultants (1).

Table 10.2 shows that heads of public relations said they got information more from the pressure group itself and media coverage than from others in the organization, suggesting that they—rather than others in the organization—are indeed scanning the environment as public relations theory suggests they should. Seventy-six heads of public relations volunteered one or more additional sources. The most common response was "other" (25), a category consisting of unique sources (mentioned by only one top communicator in each instance), which suggests many have personal sources of information. The remaining 51 responses were the same as CEOs': trade associations (16), federal agencies or government (15), employees or members (13), customers and investors (9), and lawsuits or legal challenges (3). In addition, PR heads mentioned networks, contacts, or "moles" (11); specific interest groups (6); analysts (2); and research (2).

Both CEOs and PR heads, therefore, seem to get information from formal sources with which they are in contact regularly. In addition, however, PR heads develop informal contacts and do more research to keep in touch with activists—again, the environmental scanning role they are supposed to enact.

We then asked the heads of public relations who in their organization was responsible for dealing with activist groups: the CEO, the head of public relations, attorneys, or a special department. In a separate question, we also asked if their organization had a standing committee to deal with activist pressure. Table 10.2 shows that the CEO and the PR head were about equally likely to be responsible. Attorneys were well down the list (33%). Seventeen percent of the organizations reported that a special department was responsible for dealing with activists, and 25% said they had a standing committee to deal with activists. These results suggest that about a quarter of the organizations we studied have created special committees or departments, such as issues-management departments, to do work that, theoretically, should be done by the public relations department.

In addition to the fixed responses to the question about who in the organization was responsible for dealing with activists, 112 heads of public relations suggested others in their organization who were responsible. Nearly half (53) were too diverse to code. Others, in order, were the affected department (29), consumer or community affairs (16), an ad hoc manager with relevant expertise (14), a senior vice president or assistant to the CEO (10), divisional public relations staff (9), a program director (7), board of supervisors (4), media relations (4), the communication director (2), and the president (1). These responses indicate that noncommunication managers directly affected by activists have primary responsibility either alone or together with top communicators (these were multiple responses) or that specialized public relations professionals take responsibility.

Table 10.2 also shows, however, that about half of the organizations developed special programs to respond to activist pressure. When the PR heads were asked what this special program was, 148 gave one or more of 22 responses. The most frequently mentioned program fit clearly into the category of a two-way symmetrical program: 55 of the PR heads said the program was "dialogue or dispute resolution." The next two responses were more one-way in nature, but they support the importance of the next proposition to be discussed (talking with all strategic constituencies). They were "preparing a position paper or preparing and writing a communication strategy," mentioned by 25 top communicators, and "media relations," mentioned by 19.

Other programs listed by one to five top communicators mostly fit the category of symmetrical communication, although they also included communication campaigns, seeking of inside or outside counsel, and ignoring or confronting the activists. Specifically, these responses were reliance on industrial relations staff, reliance on public affairs or government relations experts, assistance from outside public relations firms, assistance from outside legal counsel, social responsibility committees, establishment of an ongoing relationship, tour of facilities, consumer advisory panel, ignoring, confrontation, adding conference sessions, public information or grassroots campaign, change of policy, and communication to the sales force in support of a policy or to avoid confrontation.

The last set of variables in Table 10.2 came from the question to top communicators of how the organization typically involves the activist group in planning a response to the group's initiative. Informal conversation was used to involve activist groups by half of the organizations. A quarter said they set up special committees. However, few organizations placed representatives of activist groups on the board of directors.

Fifty-five top communicators alluded to other ways of involving the activist group. By far the most frequent response was meeting with the group, mentioned by 33 of the 55. Five said they sent a response, letter, or news release to the activist group. Five placed a representative in the activist organization, and one organized a tour. Two said they monitored the organization's publications and the news media. Only one top communicator said the program was a lawsuit and one a "media battle." Seventeen responses did not fit a particular category. These programs again were mostly symmetrical in nature, or they involved disclosure of information. Few were confrontational.

Relationships of Methods of Communicating With Excellence in Public Relations. After calculating the frequency with which organizations used these different means to communicate with activists, we wanted to determine if excellent departments responded differently than less excellent departments. The responses to each of the methods were dichotomous, meaning that the CEOs and PR heads checked either using or not using that method. Thus, we could explore the relationship of the method to overall excellence in public relations by comparing the means on the index of excellence for those who checked and those who did not check the possible method. We used t tests to determine the significance of the differences.

The last three columns of Table 10.2 show that excellent public relations departments were more likely to use nearly all methods of communicating with activists than were less excellent departments. The only nonsignificant differences occurred for public relations heads relying on others in the organization for information on activists, for making attorneys responsible for dealing with activists, and for including activists on the board of directors. The greatest differences in excellence were associated with the head of public relations being responsible for dealing with activists, for using informal conversation and special committees to involve activists, and for PR heads using media coverage and the pressure group itself to learn about activist pressure. For the CEOs, excellence was associated most with learning about activism from the public relations department. In short, these data provide strong evidence that excellent public relations departments do environmental scanning of activist groups, that they communicate symmetrically with those groups, and that the dominant coalition relies on public relations to deal with activists.

We also cross-tabulated high, average, and low levels of communication Excellence[2] with the open-end responses that CEOs and top communicators volunteered as "other" responses to the fixed responses to the questions included in Table 10.2. Generally, the responses were too specific and too few in any category to be meaningful; but we gained the following impressions from these cross-tabulations. The PR heads in excellent organizations reported a few more instances of learning about activists from informal sources (employees or members, networking, and the interest groups directly) than did PR heads in organizations with average or low levels of public relations Excellence. No similar difference could be found among the CEOs, however. Likewise, top communicators in excellent departments were somewhat more likely to say that "the department affected" was responsible for dealing with activists—most likely along with the public relations department.

Next, the top communicators in the most excellent and the average organizations were far more likely to mention some specific special program that had been developed to involve activists than were PR heads in the least excellent organizations. There were no discernible differences in the methods used by excellent and average organizations, however. Dialogue and dispute resolution, position papers and communication strategies, and media relations were used most often by both kinds of organizations. Likewise, excellent and average organizations mentioned more ways of involving the activist group than did the

---

[2]Organizations with a high level of excellence had a z score greater than 1.0 on the overall index of excellence, those with an average level had z scores between −1.0 and 1.0, and those with a low level had a z score below −1.0.

less excellent organizations. Meetings were most popular with the average and excellent organizations, but none of the least excellent organizations mentioned them.

In summary, both the results of the qualitative and quantitative portions of the Excellence study provide strong evidence in support of our first proposition. Organizations with excellent public relations departments listen to their strategic constituencies. The public relations department in excellent organizations is most likely to be responsible for listening to and communicating with activists. Likewise, excellent public relations departments set up many and varied methods to communicate with activists and work with others in the organization affected by the activists. Finally, they are more likely than CEOs to do informal environmental scanning. Excellent public relations heads reported having many sources of information about their environment.

Proposition 2: Talking With All Strategic Constituencies

Excellent organizations use two-way communication to tell the publics what they are doing about negative consequences.

When asked how often his association would respond positively to an invitation to tell its story to the activist groups that oppose it, one vice president for communication responded that he "almost never" turned down such an opportunity. We think this helps explain why the chemical association scored at the very top of the Excellence scale. It communicated frequently and openly with activists and demonstrated a willingness to change the organization rather than trying only to dominate these groups. That, in turn, resulted in an all-important credibility. The CEO called this "perception and reputation," and he credited his association's reputation for trustworthiness and technical expertise with helping it deal effectively with pressure groups over the long haul. Even though few of our participants were able to attach a dollar amount to what credibility or reputation is worth, readers familiar with chapter 4 on the value of public relations understand that this can be vitally important—especially in times of crisis.

But how do organizations use communication to explain their position on controversial issues? In the open-end responses reported under Proposition 1, we heard that organizations often use position papers, strategy papers, publications, media relations, and public-information or grassroots campaigns to communicate with activists. In the qualitative study, likewise, we learned that one organization included in our survey of cases relied on a corporate advertising campaign to respond to a number of environmental crises. The manager of research in the oil company described the positive effect of this 10-year effort: "Where we do run that campaign, we have public favorability and are getting our message out in a favorable light."

Another organization, the metal manufacturer, tried a number of approaches to reassure its community public and environmental activists that its planned surface mining would be environmentally sound. It communicated this message of responsibility and responsiveness via traditional, aggressive media relations. However, it also hosted site visits that included demonstrations of damage control and landscaping. As a result, it was able to forestall the restrictive legislation activists had threatened. The process, however, took time. Only eventually did the press back off in its investigation and coverage of the proposed above-ground operation. The outcome was worth the wait: Representatives of this organization said the legislation would have cost millions.

A second instance involving media relations is relevant here as well. The real estate and development company spared no expense to respond to a shooting on one of its properties. There were a number of injuries in this crisis situation. The company immediately sent an emergency response team, including its top communicator, to the site. This vice president and director for corporate public affairs explained what happened next: "We brought in doctors; we brought in counselors; anybody whom anybody wanted, we got—no questions asked. Nobody was billed for anything, and we just stayed with it." She credited this approach with alleviating what might have developed into extremely negative publicity for her company. It was ranked in the 99th percentile on the Excellence scale—a stronger showing than all but three of the 283 organizations included in the survey. It relies on two-way models of communication to relate to both external and internal publics in similar ways.

The critical event of facing hostility in the environment when trying to build the nuclear power plant served as catalyst for more straightforward and effective communication in the midwestern utility. Other organizations have yet to make the transition from closed to open communication, despite the problems they face with external publics. One top communicator in an insurance company held out the hope, though, that the threat of increased government regulation may spur her company toward a stronger public relations program if it does not respond appropriately to the issue of redlining, in particular.

One CEO from the East Coast explained how a *series* of crises changed the way his industry responds to such predicaments. It has moved from a closed to a far more open posture with its publics:

> Fifteen years ago we used to have seminars on confrontational television . . . where somebody'd come up and shove a microphone in your face. Today, you've got to be beyond that. You have to prevent that from ever being considered. You have to open your doors and open your minds and open your ears because that's what the practice of communication is about today.

Openness seems to be the key to both short-term and long-term gains. Candor helps the organization survive the crisis. It also may lead to a transformation in the way public relations is practiced across the board. In analyzing the highly publicized crises two other companies were experiencing at the time of the interview, one visionary public relations director characterized openness as the most important aspect of crisis communication: "Let the public see inside of your deliberations, that you take all of this very seriously. If you have the answers, let them know it; and if you don't, you let them know that too and how you're working to resolve the problem. We've learned these lessons in recent years."

His CEO agreed. He believed the public is more impressed with an organization's willingness to respond than with any details of what it intends to do about the crisis.

Thus Proposition 2 is supported, primarily in the sense that their publics perceive effective organizations as open to them. Willingness to engage with activists on their terms goes a long way toward establishing a quality relationship with those pressure groups. Relationships based on trust or credibility, as found for example in the chemical association, help organizations weather crises in the short term and survive—even prosper—in the long term. Some organizations relied on traditional media relations or advertising programs to tell their story to strategic constituencies. Others, including the most excellent in our survey, worked continuously through interpersonal and small-group means. They recognized that high-quality relationships, especially with activists initially bent on curtailing their power, take time to develop.

Proposition 3: Continuous Communication With Activists

Continuous efforts at communicating with activists are necessary to contend with their shifting stances.

Qualitative Support for the Proposition

Even the best-intentioned, most sophisticated approaches to public relations cannot guarantee a successful relationship with strategic constituencies, especially those whose raison d'etre hinges on opposition to the organization. However, we learned in the qualitative portion of the Excellence study that savvy practitioners never give up entirely in their efforts to communicate with activists. The top communicator with the chemical association explained his organization's constant bias "toward openness and toward dialogue." As this vice president put it: "I'm not going to waste a lot of my good time, or limited time, on groups that have proven to me over the years that their interests are diametrically opposed to mine and I'm never going to change them no matter what I do. But, by the same token, if I get invited to come and talk about what we're doing, I almost never turn down an invitation."

The medical products company, as we have seen throughout this book, relied on a mix of one-way and two-way public relations to communicate with its strategic constituencies. However, certain of its initiatives required the more interactive approach inherent in the two-way models. As its director of human resources explained: "Producing equipment used in hospitals that maintains and saves people's lives—working with hospitals in general—is a sensitive area that requires constant communication with your clients and affiliated sales staffs, both in the United States and in foreign countries."

The head of human resources, himself a member of the dominant coalition, credited the constancy of two-way public relations with helping his organization achieve several major goals. He described its ongoing communicative efforts in building and maintaining a high level of integrity with its publics, limiting the amount of negative publicity associated with an issue facing the company, and generating favorable publicity about a new product or service.

We also encountered an instance where *lack* of ongoing communication with at least one public, customers, resulted in perhaps needless difficulties. We believe this negative example also helps support the proposition that start-to-finish, two-way communication may be the only way of dealing effectively with contentious issues.

The scenario unfolds in the United Kingdom in the 1960s and 1970s, when consumers relied on petroleum for central heating of their houses. Central tanks supplied fuel through lines reaching out to each home. The media relations director at this oil company affiliate explained what developed as the tanks aged: They became "pitted, busted, starting to leak, hellish problems." By that time, people preferred gas heat. The energy company, then, wanted to get out of the old system. But how to communicate the decision to long-term customers? As one of the top communicators there said, "Are you just going to tell them, 'Sorry, we're not going to supply you anymore'?"

Recognizing the disruption (and the added cost of conversion) this corporate decision undoubtedly would cause, the public affairs staff considered such issues as how much notice to give and whether to offer an incentive to have the existing boiler converted to gas or a new boiler installed. It then approached the marketing department about the need to "perhaps be a little more gentle in the way you're approaching customers and give them more time to make other arrangements."

However, the public affairs staff was not consulted early on in the process and—predictably—problems developed. One top communicator told us that "as typical, [the marketing department] called us in once they got into difficulties." Ultimately, public affairs was responsible for amending the policy and consumers received about £500 each as a sort of loyalty bonus. The director of media relations we interviewed at this oil company concluded, "[W]e do have an influence on the way marketers behave and the way the company behaves."

Proposition 3, then, was supported at least in part in our survey of cases. We heard little about activists shifting their stances toward the organizations they pressure. On the other hand, we heard a great deal about the importance of constant communication with those hostile elements of the organizational environ-

ment. We also became convinced of the value of being in on the communicative efforts from the beginning rather than relying, say, on the marketing
department to launch an information campaign. In such instances, where public
relations is brought in to the interaction with disgruntled publics belatedly, it
amounts to little more than "mopping up."

Strong evidence in favor of continuing symmetrical dialogue and involvement of activists also came from our quantitative data. We report the rest of
those results related to activism, therefore, as support for this third proposition.

Quantitative Results on Models of Public Relations Related to Activism

Among the 20 variables that make up the index of excellence, 6 measure the
two-way symmetrical and two-way asymmetrical models of public relations
practice. As we discussed in chapter 3, both of these models correlated strongly
with the other variables of the Excellence factor. Chapter 8 presented extensive
data on the measurement and scaling of these models. In that chapter, we
pointed out that the two-way asymmetrical model correlated with excellence
not so much because of its asymmetrical nature but because three of the four
items measuring the model asked about the extent to which research is or
should be used in public relations. The only item measuring asymmetrical purpose did not scale so well as the three research items; as a result, the index of
two-way asymmetrical public relations actually seems to represent a *two-way*
model more than a two-way *asymmetrical* model. Thus, in chapter 8, we combined the two two-way models into a two-way contingency model of symmetrical public relations.

In this chapter, however, we use the original indexes of the models that were
included in the overall index of excellence. Our research on activism before and
during the Excellence study has shown that the two-way symmetrical model is
an especially important and generally effective way for organizations to communicate with activists. Likewise, the data reported in this chapter in support of
Proposition 1 strongly support the importance of the symmetrical model.
Therefore, to relate the excellent models of public relations to this proposition
on the importance of continuous communication with activists, we correlated
the measures of the excellent models with several activist variables to test the
importance of the two-way and symmetrical models for responding to activist
pressure.

Table 10.3 shows the correlations of three different measures of the two excellent models of public relations with incidence of activism and the success of
activists and organizations in dealing with each other. The first measure of the
models came from the PR head's questionnaire: the top communicator's prediction for the models preferred by the dominant coalition. The second measure

TABLE 10.3
Pearson Correlations of Models of Public Relations With Activist Pressure

	Activist Pressure		Success of Activists		Success of Organization	
	CEOs	PR Heads	CEOs	PR Heads	CEOs	PR Heads
Two-Way Symmetrical:						
PR Prediction for Dominant Coalition	.17**	.24**	.11	.08	.07	.19**
Dominant Coalition	.23**	.23**	.08	.10	.12	.11
Knowledge	.16**	.41**	.05	.10	.12	.22**
Two-Way Asymmetrical:						
PR Prediction for Dominant Coalition	.12*	.17**	.10	.07	.04	.12*
Dominant Coalition	.21**	.24**	.05	.06	.10	.09
Knowledge	.18**	.33**	.08	.13*	.12	.15*
Press Agentry:						
PR Prediction for Dominant Coalition	−.10	−.06	.05	.12*	−.06	−.05
Dominant Coalition	−.10	−.02	.03	−.09	.00	.02
Knowledge	.13*	.20**	.00	−.05	.07	.15**
Public Information:						
PR Prediction for Dominant Coalition	−.04	−.03	.12	.16**	−.10	−.10
Dominant Coalition	−.19**	−.08	−.06	−.15*	.01	.09
Knowledge	.05	.29**	−.03	−.03	.07	.18**

*$p < .05$. **$p < .01$.

was the CEO's choice of models. The third measure came from the index measuring the extent to which the public relations department possessed the knowledge needed to practice the four models.

Like Table 10.1, which reported the correlations of these activist variables with the overall index of excellence, Table 10.3 shows that activist pressure increases the likelihood that an organization will practice excellent, including two-way and symmetrical, public relations—although the correlations were only moderately high. The indexes of knowledge were the best predictors, which indicates that activist pressure stimulates organizations to build communication departments with the knowledge needed to practice excellent public relations. The success variables for activists and organizations did not correlate so well with the models, although the PR heads' estimates of these success variables and their prediction of the extent to which the dominant coalition would prefer the excellent models generally had low, but significant, correlations with the success of the organization in dealing with activists.

For comparison, Table 10.3 also presents a similar set of correlations for the two nonexcellent models (press agentry and public information). As we had theorized, these models did not correlate with activist pressure or success of the organization in dealing with activists. The exceptions were a few significant correlations of the knowledge indicators with activist pressure and success of the organization. As we discussed in chapter 8, excellent public relations departments generally had the knowledge to practice the traditional one-way models as well as the two-way models, which would explain these correlations.

The intriguing correlations in Table 10.3, however, were the small but significant positive correlations between the top communicators' prediction that the dominant coalition preferred the one-way models and the success of activists. The dominant coalition's own preference for these models did not correlate significantly. Apparently, when the public relations head believes the dominant coalition prefers press agentry, he or she also believes that activists succeed. The evidence is far from strong, but Table 10.3 does suggest that activists succeed more often than the organization when the organization uses a one-way and asymmetrical model.

The questionnaire completed by the senior communicator also contained four questions about organizational responses to activism that are directly related to two-way and symmetrical means of communication. The PR head estimated the "extent to which the entire organization, both senior management and other employees, was involved with the response to the activist group," "the extent to which activist groups have a direct involvement in planning your organization's response to them," "the extent to which your organization researched the activist group," and "the extent to which the organization evaluates its response to activist groups." The first two questions are indicators of symmetrical communication, the second two of two-way communication.

Table 10.4 shows the correlations of these variables with the overall index of excellence and the indicators of the models of public relations. The pattern of responses is generally strong and clear. Active involvement of the organization with activists and research on activists correlated positively with both overall Excellence and the two-way and symmetrical models. The correlations were weaker for the CEOs' preferences for these models, however. In part, these lower correlations could have resulted because the independent variable came from a different person than did the dependent variable. In part, also, the PR heads may be in a better position to know what model actually is practiced. Important to note, though, the knowledge potential to practice two-way and symmetrical communication was the best predictor of the extent to which involvement and research occurred.

In contrast, Table 10.4 also shows that press agentry and public information generally had no correlation or lower correlations with involvement of activists in organizational decisions and research on activists. As before, knowledge to practice these models did correlate positively because excellent departments have knowledge to practice all four models.

Overall, then, these quantitative data generally support the conclusion that activist pressure stimulates organizations to develop two-way and symmetrical public relations departments. Excellent public relations departments then respond to activists with two-way communication, symmetrical communication,

TABLE 10.4
Pearson Correlations of Involvement With Activists and Research
of Activists With Excellence Index and Models of Public Relations

	Entire Organization Involved	Activists Had Direct Involvement	Researched Activist Group	Evaluated Response
Overall Excellence Index	.36**	.24**	.43**	.42**
Two-Way Symmetrical:				
PR Prediction for Dominant Coalition	.24**	.16**	.27**	.32**
Dominant Coalition	.13**	.07	.15*	.20**
Knowledge	.27**	.19**	.35**	.31**
Two-Way Asymmetrical:				
PR Prediction for Dominant Coalition	.21**	.19**	.29**	.25**
Dominant Coalition	.21**	.16**	.23**	.25**
Knowledge	.26**	.12	.30**	.22**
Press Agentry:				
PR Prediction for Dominant Coalition	−.09	.15*	−.09	.03
Dominant Coalition	−.13	.17**	−.11	−.06
Knowledge	.16**	.10	.24**	.19**
Public Information:				
PR Prediction for Dominant Coalition	−.10	.14*	− .12	−.09
Dominant Coalition	−.12	.02	−.07	−.02
Knowledge	.17**	.17**	.27**	.18**

*$p < .05.$ **$p < .01.$

involvement of activists in organizational decisions, and both formative and evaluative research on the activists. That pattern of results fits the Excellence theory: Excellent public relations departments scan the environment and continuously bring the voices of publics, especially activist publics, into decision making. Then, they develop programs to communicate symmetrically with activists and involve them with managers throughout the organization. Finally, they use both formative and evaluative research to manage their communication programs strategically.

Proposition 4: Acknowledging the Legitimacy of All Constituencies

An ongoing, balanced, and proactive program of constituency relations must acknowledge the legitimacy of all constituent groups—regardless of size.

We may have heard more evidence in our qualitative analysis to support this fourth proposition than any other related to activism and the environment. Perhaps the most cogent discussion came from the CEO of the chemical association. He explained that all business operates under a public franchise. Without appreciation for the legitimacy of even the smallest publics:

You can be closed down or closed out by a handful of people with some placards who go down on the steps of your company and the camera comes in and they zoom that thing down as tight as they can and there are only 14 but it looks like 1,400. There are only four yelling but it sounds like 4,000 and they only got one minute on the 6 o'clock news but it is just devastating to you and your product and your company.

By contrast, interview participants in the blood bank emphasized the value to be gained from communicating with virtually everyone rather than the downside of failing to acknowledge those who are potentially strategic. It had successfully dealt with a number of crises. Its public affairs officer credited proactivity and the willingness to work bilaterally with everyone: "We often are able to catch stuff at the spark stage. We try to avoid crises by trying to work through issues with anybody with an idea."

Effective organizations, then, credit all of their strategic constituencies with the potential for affecting them both positively and negatively. On the minus side, a few dissidents can create the perception of impressive numbers—at least in the minds of the larger audience. Ignoring the concerns of even small activist groups thus can lead to problems, sometimes crises.

More important, the plus side suggests that organizations play a win–win game when they acknowledge the legitimacy of the groups within the larger society that allows them to exist in the first place. Two-way communication with all organized activist interests helps avoid the public perception of an insensitive, unresponsive organization. It also offers the potential for satisfying activists' concerns when factoring their ideas or insights into the decisional equation. The outcome may be favorable to both the organization and the environment in which it does business.

Proposition 5: Expertise of the Communicators

Conducting a two-way symmetrical communication program hinges on employing people with the necessary background and education.

In chapter 4 and again earlier in this chapter, we described the blood bank that had successfully managed its response to a crisis of confidence in its procedures during the early years of AIDS consciousness. It minimized the drop in blood donations largely through strategic media relations and thus continued to achieve its goal of meeting the demand for blood. It even managed to develop awareness and understanding in the city's growing Latino community to increase blood donations from this traditionally reluctant donor population.

We asked participants at the blood bank how all this was possible. The public affairs director simply said, "We are pretty good at catching things before they escalate into fire." Through our long interviews, we learned more. At least two communicators in this organization have extensive boundary-spanning duties that allow them to look at the blood bank from the community's perspective.

This contrasts with the worldview of medical "insiders" who view the organization largely from a medical practitioner's perspective. The expertise to practice the two-way models of public relations consists of a seamless web of scanning and evaluation skills that encompass both traditional and emerging skills in public relations. The CEO of the blood bank told us that the more traditional expertise in media relations of the community relations director provided him with important intelligence about the organization's environment.

The uncertain, often hostile environment of the typical oil company may require equally sophisticated and extensive intelligence. As a result of crises it had experienced, the U.S.-based company we studied in depth sought out professionals who would have the requisite competencies. Its new hires included researchers, legislative analysts, and communicators with the ability to scan their environment and help the dominant coalition prepare for contingencies in a proactive way.

In the fifth and sixth chapters, we discussed how expertise can empower the communication professional to serve at the highest levels of the organization. Likewise, in the quantitative data presented in this chapter to support Proposition 3, we saw that knowledge to practice the two-way models correlated with several activist variables. The cases described in this chapter further the understanding that communicating with activists, in particular, challenges the capability of even the most experienced, well-educated practitioner. Support for this proposition also comes with an awareness of what that expertise includes: boundary spanning and other kinds of formative research, proactivity, appreciation for cultures different from one's own, the ability to communicate with diverse groups, skill in interpersonal communication, and crisis management.

Proposition 6: Evaluating Effectiveness in the Long Run

Excellent organizations learn to measure their effectiveness in terms of more than simplistic, short-term gains or losses.

In Table 10.4, we presented quantitative data showing that excellent public relations departments, in general, and those that practiced two-way models of public relations, in particular, involve the entire organization in the response to activists, directly involve activists in decisions that affect them, research the activist group, and evaluate the organization's response to the activists.

We found similar results in our qualitative research. Over and over, throughout our interviews with organizational elites, we heard that the value of ongoing dialogue with activist groups may not be obvious in the short run. Even so, top communicators and their CEOs tended to agree that two-way programs of communication could result in long-term gains that were critically important to the organization. Thus we consider the essence of this proposition supported, despite the lack of evaluative research conducted over time that would have supported it definitively and in its entirely.

For example, the CEO of the chemical industry association offered two examples of activism and concluded that in both cases, environmental organizations could have "*trashed* these activities publicly." Instead, the groups gave the programs a chance because they understood what the association's principles were as a result of its discussions with them. The CEO explained his position with the activists as, "If you don't like it, if you don't believe this, if you don't trust us, why don't you just wait and see what happens—but don't destroy it [an initiative to clean up toxic waste sites] before it gets a chance." His association got that chance, which was worth—in his words—"a lot."

Quantifying that return on investment in two-way communication—whether it is symmetrical, asymmetrical, or mixed-motive—requires a degree of sophistication in evaluative research. We found little evidence of expertise in any kind of research among the people with whom we talked. We also were curious about the kind and extent of research, if any, being conducted to support the one-way models.

Perhaps the oil company affiliate in the United Kingdom was typical. Like the chemical industry, the oil industry has experienced a great deal of turbulence in its environment. Despite an overall Excellence rating in the 92nd percentile, its practice of public affairs can best be characterized as press agentry. When we asked what sort of research the department conducts, its media relations manager answered, "None at all."

However, this department involves itself with its trade association to such a degree that its media relations manager described the association as an extension of public affairs. His company relies on research on the image of the oil industry carried out by the association. So, he explained, "Although we don't get feedback on, perhaps, how people view [the company], we do get feedback on how people view the oil industry and also people's concerns about the oil industry." In addition to this kind of *formal* research generated by the association, this communicator used *informal* means to glean information from "the outside world": monitoring the media, talking to journalists, and participating in activities sponsored by his trade association.

Finally, we heard about the glacial rate at which most positive change occurs—even when it happens as a result of something as instantaneous as the Bhopal calamity. This crisis led to what approaches a transformation of public affairs in the chemical industry and the chemical corporation, in particular. The communication director there explained that crisis was one within a convergence of factors that helped alter the thinking of senior management about public relations. Although he described "tremendous strides" within the dominant coalition, he acknowledged that "senior managers still have a fundamentally conservative mind-set." He called the shift in their worldview from more closed to more open with publics as "a slow process."

Proposition 7: Public Relations in the Dominant Coalition

Excellent departments practice public relations appropriately for their environment in part because the structure of their organization places the head of public relations in a position both to monitor that environment and to interact with the dominant coalition internally.

Earlier chapters described the importance of including public relations in top management from many perspectives. Basically, participating in the decisions made by the dominant coalition allows the issues of the organization's strategic publics to be factored into those decisions before they are set in concrete. Thus the public relations practitioner serves more as a counselor and top-level manager him- or herself than as a lower level technician who communicates decisions to the publics affected by them. This enhances the professionalism of the field and also its centrality as an organizational function.

Without this kind of autonomy and participation in decision making, public relations becomes more functionary than functional. More directly relevant to this proposition, without the representation of public relations in the dominant coalition, policymakers may dictate a program of communication inappropriate for the organization's environment. Public relations professionals, in their boundary-spanning role and as part of the power elite, help to enact the environment externally and communicate that intelligence internally. This kind of information is especially important during crises.

When the organization employs communicators with a track record of success in handling crises or other activist issues, it not only benefits but so do those expert practitioners. The vice president of corporate communications at the financial services company explained how the process worked in her organization. The top communicator there had made the transition from technician to strategist by gaining recognition from the dominant coalition during times of crisis. She said: "You have to earn it—show them you're worth it. If you can bring value to the equation, you will be recognized and [top management] will seek your input."

Now, this vice president said, senior managers involve the communication department early on, rather than waiting until a crisis develops. We agreed that the company's approach to crisis management had developed from reactive to proactive. We saw a similar shift in the blood bank, where the successful management of its response to crises also garnered the respect of the CEO and his senior leadership team. This relationship gave communicators access to the daily decision making of the dominant coalition.

These two qualitative cases illustrate how this proposition works in two of our excellent organizations. In addition, three of the quantitative variables related to the relationship of public relations to top management allowed us to test the proposition. Data already reported provide general support for the idea that public relations can do a better job of monitoring the environment if it is close to the dominant coalition. The overall index of public relations Excellence contained several variables indicating that the senior public relations person is involved in strategic management and that he or she enacts a managerial role. In chapter 3, we also saw that the Excellence index correlates with the top communicator being named a member of the dominant coalition. In this chapter, we saw that this Excellence index correlates with activist pressure, success of the organization in responding to activists, and several methods of involving and communicating with activists.

Table 10.5 presents data to test this proposition more directly. However, these data provide only modest support for the importance of public relations being in a position in the organizational structure where it can monitor the environment and alert management to changes in it. The first indicator of the management role of public relations is the contribution it makes to strategic management. The first column of Table 10.5 shows low but significant correla-

TABLE 10.5
Comparison of Activist Pressure and Success
With Public Relations Role in Management

	Activist Pressure		Success of Activists		Success of Organization	
	CEOs	PR Heads	CEOs	PR Heads	CEOs	PR Heads
Pearson Correlations With PR Contribution to Strategic Management	.12	.16**	.08	.09	.11	.23**
Public Relations in Dominant Coalition						
Means if Yes (N)[a]	11.52	8.38	7.73	8.23	11.94	10.28
	(118)	(172)	(106)	(124)	(106)	(125)
Means if No (N)	9.04	8.87	7.48	8.04	11.03	10.20
	(161)	(201)	(133)	(160)	(131)	(159)
T	2.92**	0.72	0.49	0.39	1.34	0.23
Management Level of Public Relations						
Means If Reports Directly to CEO	9.82	8.66	8.06	8.41	11.10	10.50
(N)	(159)	(207)	(129)	(151)	(129)	(152)
Means If Reports Indirectly to CEO	10.76	7.36	6.79	6.94	12.17	9.90
(N)	(75)	(100)	(69)	(76)	(67)	(76)
Means If Reports to Manager Who Reports to CEO (N)	9.48	9.82	7.18	8.32	11.24	9.95
	(42)	(61)	(38)	(52)	(37)	(52)
Means If Reports to Junior Management (N)	13.54	15.41[b]	11.88[b]	11.64[b]	10.56	10.15
	(6)	(6)	(5)	(6)	(5)	(6)
F	0.93	4.26**	3.61**	3.76**	0.80	0.72

Note.   The means reported in this table are the square-root transformation of the open-end fractionation scale. A score of 10 on the transformed scale is equivalent to the typical reponse of 100 on the original scale.

[a]The number in similar categories may differ because of missing values.

[b]The category "reports to junior management" is significantly different from the category "reports indirectly to CEO," based on the Tukey procedure.

$*p < .05$. $**p < .01$.

tions between activist pressure and the likelihood of the public relations head saying that she or he contributes to strategic management. Likewise, the PR head's reported contribution correlated moderately with his or her reported success in dealing with activists. The correlations for CEOs were similar but not significant. There were no significant correlations with the reported success of activists.

Table 10.5 next compares the means on these three activist variables for top communicators and CEOs who said public relations is part of the dominant coalition with those who said public relations is not a member. Only one difference was significant: The CEOs' report that public relations is in the elite coalition and the amount of activist pressure. This difference indicates that CEOs who experience activism are more likely to include public relations in the dominant coalition. Being in the dominant coalition seems to make no difference, however, in success in dealing with activists.

The third comparison in Table 10.5 is among the four levels at which the CEO and heads of public relations said that public relations reports to the CEO—directly, indirectly, through a second-level manager, or through junior management. As we saw in chapter 4 on the empowerment of public relations, most of the CEOs and PR heads said that public relations reports directly or indirectly to the CEO. For these two reporting relationships, as well as reporting through a second-level manager, there were no significant differences in incidence of activism or success of either the organization or the activists.

The only significant differences occurred for the public relations departments that reported to junior management. In this situation, the success of activists was higher. Interestingly, the incidence of activism also was reported as higher for both the CEOs and PR heads who reported this relationship for public relations. However, only five or six public relations departments (depending on missing data) reported to junior management, as indicated by both CEOs and top communicators. Apparently, these half-dozen organizations believed they faced a lot of activist pressure and that the activists were successful. These means hint that placing public relations low in the organization's management leads to failure in dealing with activists. All three higher levels of reporting relationships are more effective.

If we compare these data with those reported earlier in this chapter, we come to the conclusion that the structural position of public relations is less important than the knowledge needed to scan the environment and deal with activists and the symmetry of the programs set up to communicate with activists. About half of the PR heads are in the dominant coalition and most have direct or indirect contact with the CEO. What seems to matter most is whether the department has the knowledge needed to take advantage of this access and the support from top management to set up programs to communicate symmetrically with activists.

Revisiting Our New Perspective on Two-Way Public Relations: Using the Two-Way Contingency Model to Communicate With and About Activists

All seven propositions about the role of excellent public relations in dealing with hostile elements of the environment are based on the assumption that two-way communication would be most effective. Upon completion of our data analysis, we do not back away from this perspective. However, if we were to revise those expectations based on the insights gleaned from our qualitative research, in particular, we find evidence of what Murphy (1991) called a mixed-motive model and Spicer (1997) called collaborative advocacy. In chapter 8, we combined the former two-way symmetrical and two-way asymmetrical models of public relations into a two-way contingency model. This new model resembles Murphy's mixed-motive model, although we said in chapter 8 that we now see little conceptual difference between a symmetrical model and a mixed-motive model of public relations.

In both our qualitative and quantitative analyses in this chapter, we found no organization and no communication program to be exclusively symmetrical or asymmetrical. Using concepts from game theory, we would say that public relations is neither a pure "positive sum" (symmetrical) nor a pure "zero sum" (asymmetrical) game. Rather, managed communication is perhaps most usefully conceptualized as a process in which organizations and publics both seek their own advantage in a context of enlightened self-interest. Murphy (1991) emphasized that in this mixed-motive model, the needs and wants of the other party also are respected. What is contingent about the new model is the need for public relations professionals to make decisions about whom most needs to be persuaded in particular situations—the dominant coalition, the public, or both. These contingent decisions must be made, however, with the interests of both the organization and the public in mind.

From our participants in the 24 case studies, we heard about approaches to public relations that suggest a deliberate fusion of advocacy and collaboration—collaborative advocacy—when coping with activist pressure or when attempting to survive a crisis. This juncture is illustrated in one communicator's depiction of his values of communicating openly with activists and trying to persuade those groups at the same time:

> If we hold to the principle of being honest, there is honest manipulation and false manipulation. Manipulation is usually associated with false manipulation. If we're honest in what we do and how we do it, then I look on the role of the communicator as being one who achieves desirable outcomes. . . . What do we want you to do? We don't want to just inform and educate somebody for the sake of saying we've done our good deed. We want to inform and educate with the intent of buying our stock, of being a safer employee, of coming to work more than being absent, and in seeing a better article in the press.

In this comment, we have an obvious instance of the win–win zone graphically depicted in chapter 8. This quote also illustrates the asymmetrical extremes of the continuum describing professional, contemporary public relations. In advocating for the organization's position, the communicator tried to establish his employer as a credible company for which to work or in which to invest. At opposite end of the continuum, in advocating for the public, the communicator established his responsibility for informing and educating the strategic constituencies.

Communication When Crises Develop

Regardless of the model of public relations practiced or the expertise of the communicator, crises inevitably befall organizations. Of course, some fields, such as energy, seem to experience more than their share. As one top communicator said of her industry, "The insurance industry is a crisis by definition."

Crises in any organization may result from poor relationships with activists, as we saw in the case of consumers at the oil company affiliate in the United Kingdom. Or, they may be beyond the control of anyone in the organization, as we saw in the case of the natural disasters that affected the utility company, the insurer, and the metal manufacturer. These crises are what Perrow (1984) called "normal accidents." The analogy to consider is with the human body. Crises in organizations are like death in people: They may not happen often, but they are inevitable. In such cases, we learned, effective public relations at least can mitigate the damage to the organization (if not resuscitate it).

Communication played this vital role in several crises at the state lottery. On one occasion, the pool had accumulated ticket purchases to support a U.S. $25 million jackpot. The machine that selected the winner malfunctioned at this most inopportune time, creating a major crisis. Just a half-hour later, a second drawing was held and the original malfunction was explained to the public over a televised statewide feed. The prompt, candid explanation of the mechanical failure helped the lottery maintain its credibility. Salvaging its reputation for trustworthiness took the best efforts of both the lottery's own communication staff and a public relations firm it hired. This investment, in turn, was credited with helping stave off a drop in sales of lottery tickets.

On a second occasion, a crisis arose when the telephone lines failed with another large jackpot at stake. The lottery's communication staff worked with radio stations to inform the public of the problem. Phone lines are critical because they transport information about ticket purchases instantaneously, which affects the size of the jackpot. In explaining the philosophy behind his agency's speedy and open response to this kind of predicament, the assistant director of public affairs said, "If you get to them before they get to you, you will be much better off."

The lottery we explored in depth during our survey of cases faced several additional problems, deemed at least minor imbroglios by the people we interviewed. These small-scale crises involved contract disputes and the organization's image. All were resolved through the efforts of what our participants considered "proactive" public relations. As the assistant director of public affairs explained, he and his colleagues exploited these situations as potential opportunities to develop professionally: "We must learn from other crises, hypothetically discuss situations internally, and place a high value on crisis management."

Interestingly, this organization already had scored in the top 1% of all organizations included in our survey research; yet one of its top communicators saw the need for continuous improvement (and the inevitability of crises, even in top-performing operations). Of course, much is at stake. We understood from our conversation with several members of the dominant coalition in this agency that crises can undermine the public's support for state lotteries across the nation.

Few industries have experienced as many far-reaching crises as has energy. During the late 1970s and again in the late 1980s, the oil industry in particular suffered from the turbulence of an environment rife with activists and the crises that precipitated that pressure in the first place. The oil company we studied increasingly relied on the expertise of its public affairs department to help it weather the storm of public outrage in the wake of the Middle East oil embargo and, a decade later, the Exxon Valdez oil spill in Alaska's Prince William Sound. Top management there deliberately sought out sophisticated practitioners with the skill to manage relationships with key constituencies in that hostile environment.

The embargo forced senior management to approach communication from a broader, more strategic perspective than ever before. The director of research at the oil company explained that the industry was hit by surprise with the idea of blame for what Middle Eastern countries had caused. This member of the dominant coalition went on to point out the value of having had to learn to cope with such crises—and allocating the necessary financial resources to prepare for and contend with similar eventualities: "I think what we've done has inoculated us a bit and it's more than just communications. There's a whole structure in the company to respond to environmental issues in a responsible manner."

We concluded that this organization, ranked in the 97th percentile in terms of excellence at the time of the survey, had become even more effective. Increasingly, it relied on its top communicator to play the communication manager or senior advisor role. Its communication department was increasingly involved in strategic planning and it received increased support from the dominant coalition overall. Emphasis shifted from crisis containment and control to crisis prevention. Even if this ambitious goal were unobtainable, it bespeaks the proactivity that has become the hallmark of the company's public relations program. Its manager of quality and support services said of the company's new strategic thrust: ". . . preventing fires. That's certainly where we're trying to go. That's part of the reason for this concern about our previous planning process. We're trying to be more strategic and less reactive."

However, we learned from the blood bank that some aspects of media relations, in particular, are inherently reactive. Inquiries from the press in times of crisis require immediate response, the public affairs officer emphasized.

Analysis of the real estate development case reinforced the understanding that underlies chapter 4 on the value of public relations: Even successful resolution of a crisis may not have an immediately positive effect on the bottom line. The top communicator there—a woman of uncommon education, experience, skills, and access to the CEO—explained that turning around a crisis does not necessarily generate sales but that it does build what she called "a tremendous amount of goodwill."

Using communication to help cope with a crisis also can help the communicator. Throughout this book, we have explored avenues through which expert public relations professionals can gain the credibility necessary for access to their organization's top decision makers. Research to help avoid crises certainly is one such means. Another, though, is to be responsive when the inevitable eventually happens. At the cosmetics company, for example, the director of sales force communication began to establish rapport with the president in the process of helping him write a eulogy for a deceased vice president. She considered her contribution at a time of upheaval the beginning of a long-term relationship of trust with the head of the company.

As a result of crises in his industry, one top communicator we interviewed said that management had become more outreach- and communication-minded than ever before. Unfortunately, he added, this appreciation did not automatically translate to higher marks for public relations professionals. He concluded that even if communicators saw the demand for their services increasing dramatically during crises, they could not count on seeing bigger budgets or higher salaries as a result.

Inclusion in the strategic management of the organization is likely, however. Recall from chapter 5, which dealt with empowerment of the communication function, that the number-one reason cited by CEOs for valuing public relations is that it helps them deal with the many problems they face. More specifically, public relations helps the organization deal with crises or the activist groups that often prompt those predicaments. The crises facing the chemical company we studied led in large part to the development of an excellent communication department there—a department valued for its ability to anticipate problems and deal with them ethically and effectively should they develop into crises. Once again, then, we see that surviving the pressure of activist groups calls for a sophisticated, interactive, negotiational approach to public relations.

SUMMARY AND CONCLUSIONS

Excellence in public relations is characterized by two-way, balanced relationships with strategic publics, especially activist groups. Open communication—explaining one's position, listening to others, and making adjustments in response to what one is hearing—helps improve the functioning of the organization overall. Practitioners of public relations and their top management agreed that this kind of interactive communication (including a mix of symmetrical and asymmetrical approaches) is essential for survival in an uncertain, often hostile, environment.

Two-way symmetrical communication, touted in the scholarly literature as the normative approach to excellence, seems to be emerging in the actual practice of the field as well. This research firmly establishes the two-way symmetrical approach to public relations as a positive or descriptive model as well as the ideal. We can make this assertion because we heard a great deal about symmetry in response to our questions about activism in the environment. Recall the industry association and its head of public relations who described a community program he had developed that has won national prominence and acclaim. The program's first principle is listening and responding to the community's concerns. He emphasized that responsiveness may include change on the organization's part when pressure groups do not agree with it.

In organizations with the most excellent communication programs, such as this chemical industry association and the chemical corporation, members of the dominant coalition value the contribution of public relations in several senses. They not only consider their communicators to be the mouthpiece of the organization, but to be its eyes and ears as well. Capable public relations professionals use a variety of means to enact their environment, thus reducing the uncertainty that plagues most organizations. That intelligence, gathered through the formal process of environmental monitoring but also through ongoing dialogue with the media and the organization's strategic constituencies, is brought to bear at the decision-making table.

In the most effective organizations, the input of professional communicators is sought before the decision is made—a process inevitably called "proactive" by our participants in the case study phase of the Excellence project. In organizations such as the UK-based oil company affiliate, the chemical association, the chemical corporation, and the medical products company, the public relations department truly functioned as an early-warning system. It was alert to the concerns of activist groups in its dynamic environment, even at the international level. Then, when a decision had been made, the public relations department engaged in the other part of the two-way process of communicating: crafting and disseminating the message.

Only rarely did organizations—even the most excellent ones we studied—have sophisticated, ongoing, systematic ways of evaluating the effectiveness of those programs. In fact, even informal, seat-of-the-pants research on efforts to communicate with activist groups was unusual.

We conclude this chapter, then, by referring back to chapter 6. There we described the importance of environmental research to both the careers of public relations practitioners and to the efficacy of their organizations. When top communicators have the expertise necessary to scan the environment, they can anticipate much of the activism that inevitably besets today's organization. Also in chapter 6 and in chapter 8 as well, we emphasized the necessity of having the expertise to practice all aspects of two-way public relations. These skills go beyond formative research to include evaluative research, small-group communication, negotiation, conflict resolution, and means of public participation. If the top communicator possesses these skills, as we saw in the quantitative data and in several of the cases reviewed here, the organization is able to capitalize on the opportunities presented in crises that would knock a more mediocre operation to its knees.

Thus we end where we began this chapter: with the potential that activism provides. Perhaps in no case was this more obvious than the chemical corporation. Crises and improving company performance both played a part in its overcoming what might have been crippling pressure from outside groups. As its vice president explained, since the catastrophe in Bhopal, his entire industry has become more willing to be open to the public.

Crises also have the potential to enhance the career opportunities of public relations practitioners. Recall that the U.S.-based oil company sought sophisticated communicators to help it contend with a series of industry crises. Only 3% of the organizations we surveyed were ranked equal to or greater than this corporation on the Excellence scale. Environmental turbulence dating from the late 1970s caused top management to place great value on communication and thus demand skilled professionals to head its public relations function.

Participants in only a handful of our two dozen cases failed to discuss at least one crisis situation that had resulted in a real shift both in their organization's culture and in its practice of public relations. More often, they spoke of increased appreciation for their function on the part of others in the organization; greater access to the dominant coalition as a result; more openness in communication; a new willingness to cooperate with pressure groups and the community at large; the concomitant likelihood of learning from these strategic constituencies; and greater support for or at least understanding of the organization from the community, the clients or customers, the media, and even government regulators.

The effective organization exists in an environment more characterized by dynamism and even hostility than by stability. We learned that this activism pushes organizations toward excellence as they try to cope with the expectations of all their strategic constituencies. Such demands require greater sophistication in public relations than the simple one-way communication found in press agentry or public information. Thus public relations adds value because it helps the organization deal with pressing social issues—but only if the top communicator is empowered to play a role in strategic decision making. To some of our participants, effective communication adds "infinite" value during the times of crisis described throughout this chapter.

REFERENCES

Aldrich, H. E. (1979). *Organizations and environments.* Englewood Cliffs, NJ: Prentice-Hall.
Aldrich, H. E., & Pfeffer, J. (1976). Environments of organizations. *Annual Review of Sociology, 2,* 79–105.
Anderson, D. S. (1992). Identifying and responding to activist publics: A case study. *Journal of Public Relations Research, 4,* 151–165.
Clark, C. E. (1997, Spring). If you can't beat 'em . . . A new strategy for advocacy groups. *The Public Relations Strategist,* pp. 36–40.
Davis, E. (1995, April). What's on American managers' minds? *Management Review,* pp. 14–20.
Downey, H. K., Hellriegel, D., & Slocum, J. W., Jr. (1975). Environmental uncertainty: The construct and its applications. *Administrative Science Quarterly, 20,* 613–629.
Grunig, J. E. (1984). Organizations, environments, and models of public relations. *Public Relations Research and Education, 1*(1), 6–29.
Grunig, J. E., & Repper, F. C. (1992). Strategic management, publics, and issues. In J. E. Grunig (Ed.), *Excellence in public relations and communication management* (pp. 117–158). Hillsdale, NJ: Lawrence Erlbaum Associates.
Grunig, L. A. (1986, August). *Activism and organizational response: Contemporary cases of collective behavior.* Paper presented at the meeting of the Association for Education in Journalism and Mass Communication, Norman, OK.
Harris, P. (1982). Pressure groups and protest. *Politics, 17,* 111–120.
Jones, B. L. (1978). Issue management by objective: The new frontier for business. *Enterprise, 23,* 19–21.
Lauzen, M. M. (1995). Toward a model of environmental scanning. *Journal of Public Relations Research, 7,* 187–203.
Learned, E. A., Christensen, C. R., Andrews, K. R., & Guth, W. D. (1965). *Business policy: Text and cases.* Homewood, IL: Irwin.
Mintzberg, H. (1983). *Power in and around organizations.* Englewood Cliffs, NJ: Prentice-Hall.
Murphy, P. (1991). The limits of symmetry: A game theory approach to symmetric and asymmetric public relations. *Public Relations Research Annual, 3,* 115–131.
Olien, C. N., Donohue, G. A., & Tichenor, P. T. (1984). Media and stages of social conflict. *Journalism Monographs, 90.*
Olson, M. (1971). *The logic of collective action: Public goods and the theory of groups.* Cambridge, MA: Harvard University Press.
Pearce, J. A., II, & Robinson, R. B., Jr. (1982). *Strategic management: Strategy formulation and implementation.* Homewood, IL: Irwin.
Perrow, C. (1984). *Normal accidents: Living with high-risk technologies.* New York: Basic Books.
Porter, M. E. (1980). *Competitive strategy: Techniques for analyzing industries and competitors.* New York: The Free Press.
Porter, M. E. (1985). *Competitive advantage: Creating and sustaining superior performance.* New York: The Free Press.
Porter, M. E. (1990). *The competitive advantage of nations.* New York: The Free Press.

Porter, M. E. (1994). Toward a dynamic theory of strategy. In R. P. Rumelt, D. E. Schendel, & D. J. Teece (Eds.), *Fundamental issues in strategy* (pp. 423–461). Boston: Harvard Business School Press.

Robbins, S. P. (1990). *Organization theory: Structure, design, and applications* (3rd ed.). Englewood Cliffs, NJ: Prentice-Hall.

Rumelt, R. P., Schendel, D. E., & Teece, D. J. (1994). Fundamental issues in strategy. In R. P. Rumelt, D. E. Schendel, & D. J. Teece (Eds.), *Fundamental issues in strategy* (pp. 9–47). Boston: Harvard Business School Press.

Spicer, C. (1997). *Organizational public relations: A political perspective.* Mahwah, NJ: Lawrence Erlbaum Associates.

Stoffels, J. D. (1994). *Strategic issues management: A comprehensive guide to environmental scanning.* Oxford, England: Pergamon.

Too much media coverage backfires. (1986, January 6). *pr reporter,* p. 4.

Verčič, D., & Grunig, J. E. (2000). The origins of public relations theory in economics and strategic management. In D. Moss, D. Verčič, & G. Warnaby (Eds.), *Perspectives on public relations research* (pp. 7–58). London: Routledge.

CHAPTER ELEVEN

Inside the Organization: Culture, Structure, Systems of Internal Communication, Gender, and Diversity

Public relations practitioners working in or for organizations are professionals whose role is to establish and maintain a system of communication within that organization and between that organization and stakeholders in the environment. An organization and its environment constitute a system, however; and systems theory tells us that all parts of a system and its environment interact and influence one another. Being part of a system makes professionalism difficult because the interactions that characterize systems produce constraints on professional behavior. The systemic nature of organizations is especially important for communication managers because they must work for and with most other subsystems in and around the organization.

Professionals are most free to carry out their professional roles when they face little interference from clients or employers who want to impose what often are nonprofessional behaviors on them. The excellence of a public relations function, therefore, does not depend on the knowledge and behavior of public relations professionals alone. How communicators behave depends greatly on their interaction with other people in the organization and with strategic constituencies in the environment. In chapter 10, we examined the effect of the environment—of activists in particular—on public relations. In this chapter, we examine the interactions of public relations with internal groups and processes.

As we explore the organizational context in which public relations must function in this chapter, we also devote particular attention to the system of internal communication in the organization and to the context for women. On the one hand, internal communication is one of the most important specialties of public relations. Without internal communication, organizations would not develop structures and cultures. Internal communication, therefore, is the force that produces the context in which a public relations department must function.

At the same time, though, structure and culture have a strong influence on the nature of the communication system. As a result, the system of internal communication is both a public relations program and an important component of the organizational context that shapes public relations.

In chapter 5, we also saw that the conditions under which women work in an organization have a great effect on the excellence of the public relations function because a large proportion of the most knowledgeable public relations practitioners are women. In this chapter, we examine how the context for all women in an organization relates to the other features of the organizational context. That information should help us to understand why excellent female communicators may be restricted or supported when they attempt to implement an excellent public relations program.

We conceptualized the organizational context for public relations in five main ways: culture, structure, internal communication, employee satisfaction with the organization, and status and treatment of women. Analysis of several questions in the survey of employees resulted in reliable indexes of each of these concepts. The interrelationships among them provide strong support for the general theory of excellence. In brief, we theorized that the culture of the excellent organization is participative, rather than authoritarian. Participative culture usually is found in an organization that has a decentralized, deformalized, destratified, and complex structure. Such a structure, which organization theorists call "organic," promotes extensive and open communication. The system of internal communication is two-way and symmetrical.

Symmetrical systems of internal communication typically increase the likelihood that employees will be satisfied with their individual jobs and with the organization as a whole. In addition, satisfied employees are more likely to be loyal to the organization and to identify with it. Symmetrical communication also has a reciprocal relationship with participative culture: The more symmetrical the communication the more participative the culture; and the more participative the culture the more symmetrical the system of communication.

These factors often work in tandem with contemporary initiatives such as Total Quality Management to facilitate shared decision making. Finally, the workforce of the effective organization is diverse in both race and gender, allowing the organization to understand adequately the heterogeneity of its environment and to maximize the value of all employees.

More specifically, the qualities of an effective organization identified in the literature on excellence, reviewed briefly throughout this book and exhaustively in the theory book that preceded it, include the following: organic structure, intrapreneurship, symmetrical communication systems, human resources, leadership, participative culture, strategic planning, social responsibility, support for women and minorities, quality as a priority, effective operational systems, and a collaborative societal culture. The propositions framing this chapter touch on each of these concepts, linking them both to excellent public relations and to effectiveness in organizations. As we established in the third chapter, in which the Excellence factor was isolated, excellent public relations helps the organization become effective. The relationship, however, is reciprocal: Organizational excellence provides a hospitable climate for excellent public relations. In this chapter, we offer further evidence to support this guiding premise about the organizational setting.

THEORETICAL OVERVIEW

Organizational Culture

In the theory book that conceptualized this study, we called culture "the glue that holds excellent organizations together and keeps mediocre organizations mediocre" (Sriramesh, J. Grunig, & Buffington, 1992, p. 577). We traced the development of the concept of organizational culture and arrived at the understanding that public relations departments can become countercultures that change the larger culture of the organization—thus making it more effective. We generated theoretical propositions about two distinct types of culture, which we contrasted as *authoritarian* and *participative*.

Before describing each type of culture, a definition of the larger concept is in order. Although no unanimously accepted definition has emerged from anthropology, the field in which it originated, we reviewed the many extant definitions and descriptions in the literature. To Kluckhohn (1951), culture meant patterned ways of thinking, feeling, and reacting. Hofstede (1980) considered culture a system of values and defined it as the collective programming of the mind. Similarly, to Deal and Kennedy (1982) culture was the set of dominant or core values espoused by an organization and to Peters and Waterman (1982), the set of values that helps unify the social dimensions of the organization. Mitroff (1983) defined culture as shared meanings or symbols. Schein (1984, 1985) defined culture as the synthesis of basic assumptions that members of an organization share. To Wallach (1983), culture was simply "how we do things around here" (p. 29).

We worked from what we found to be the points of consensus among those and many additional, similar definitions: *Culture is the sum total of shared values, symbols, meanings, beliefs, assumptions, and expectations that organize and integrate a group of people who work together.* In essence, we determined that corporate or organizational culture consists of the set of presuppositions that make up a worldview and also the products of that worldview. (Products might consist of values, stories, myths, artifacts, and rituals.)

In organizations with authoritarian cultures, decision making is centralized with the CEO and a few trusted high-level managers. Different departments pursue their separate agendas that may conflict with each other. Employees believe they are given little flexibility to try innovative approaches to their work. They also believe that senior managers are interested in them only as workers, not as whole people. Employees in such authoritarian organizations may express fear of their supervisors and other top managers. Authoritarian cultures are generally closed and resistant to ideas from outside the organization.

In organizations with participative cultures, employees describe a common value: teamwork. All departments in such organizations work together like a well-oiled machine. Departmental agendas match the overall goals and objectives of the organization. Employees say they would run the organization in much the same way as does the current dominant coalition. These workers believe management values them as whole people, not just employees. Participative organizations are open to ideas from the external as well as the internal environment.

These notions of two distinct organizational cultures came largely from the work of Ouchi (1981) on managerial styles. He (like Pascale & Athos, 1981) considered organizational culture to be the philosophy that guides an organization's policy toward employees and customers. Over time, that philosophy is reflected in the organization's preferred style of management. Ouchi contrasted Theory J, Japanese style, with Theory A, U.S. style. Key characteristics of each are:

- Collective versus individual responsibility.
- Collective versus individual decision making.
- Collective versus individual values.
- Holistic concern versus lack of such concern for employees.
- Long-term versus short-term employment.
- Slow versus fast evaluation and promotion.
- Nonspecialized versus specialized career paths.

We took several additional characteristics from our own previous research on the relationship between organizational ideology and presuppositions and models of public relations. These variables are:

- Authoritarian versus participative management style.
- Liberal versus conservative values.
- Cooperation versus domination in relationships with publics.
- System open versus closed to its environment.
- Innovation versus tradition and efficiency as organizational values.

We expected that characteristics on the left would characterize participative cultures and those on the right authoritarian cultures. However, we kept our minds open to the possibility that more than two dimensions might emerge from our analysis of responses to questionnaires measuring these concepts.

Finally, we considered the following aspects gleaned from the broad literature of organizational culture: shared mission, rewards for performance rather than personal connections, social atmosphere among employees and managers off the job, integration versus individualism, emphasis on time, style of decision making (by tradition, rational process, open debate, trial-and-error, scientific research, or authority), and consensual process.

Organizations with excellent communication programs, we reasoned, would tend to have participative organizational cultures. Of course, even before we collected the data we acknowledged that no organization is totally participative or totally authoritarian.

Organizational Structure

The previous chapter showed how organizations become excellent because they must cope with turbulent, complex environments. Such environments produce activist publics that pressure the organization. This, in turn, requires expert communication management to develop and maintain high-quality relationships with interest groups. However, effective public relations departments usually cannot exist unless they are in organizations that also are excellent. Such organizations tend to have a strong—often participative—culture. Excellent organizations also have certain management structures that empower employees and allow them to participate in decision making.

Organizational structure addresses the questions of what is the best form of organization and why. Horizontal structure speaks to the way in which tasks are allocated in a single department or plane of the organization. We addressed the horizontal structure of public relations departments in chapter 7. Even more important, vertical structure speaks to reporting relationships, coordinating mechanisms, and patterns of interaction throughout the organization (Robbins, 1990). We determined that vertical structure was a critical aspect of excellence to be explored in our study because, as J. Grunig (1976) pointed out a quarter century ago, the role and behavior of the public relations practitioner are influenced by organizational structure. J. Grunig and Hunt (1984) also held that structural variables help predict the model of public relations practiced. More specifically, we used Hage's (1980) set of four structural variables to allow for comparisons among organizational types.

Centralization represents the hierarchy of authority that determines the extent to which decision making is concentrated at the top of the organization. Hage (1980) believed that centralization inhibits communication in organizations, whereas decentralization encourages the dispersion of information and decision making throughout the organization. *Stratification*, the second of Hage's structural considerations, represents the way in which rewards are distributed within the organization. The extent to which there are obvious differences between status levels indicates the level of stratification or destratification. Low levels of communication are associated with stratification. *Formalization* represents the importance of rules and the degree to which they are enforced in the organization (Hage & Aiken, 1970). A preponderance of rules and regulations discourages both innovation and communication. Communication helps an organization coordinate its members, whereas formalization controls them.

Finally, Hage (1965) defined *complexity* as the number of occupational specialties in the organization and the level of training required for each specialty. Later, he and Aiken (1967a, 1967b) added the concept of professionalism to this definition. Upward communication, rather than a downward flow of communication, correlates with complexity far more than with the other three structural variables.

Hage (1980) found that the size of the organization or its scale and measures of nonvariability (task complexity) both affect organizational structure. He and his colleague Hull (Hull & Hage, 1982) used these two dimensions to construct a four-cell typology of organizations. *Traditional* or *craft* organizations are small in scale and low in complexity. *Mechanical* organizations are large-scale, low-complexity operations. *Organic* organizations are small in scale but high in complexity. *Mixed mechanical/organic* organizations are both large in scale and high in complexity.

A 3-year program of research in public relations (Schneider, aka L. Grunig, 1985a, 1985b) concluded that the Hull–Hage (1982) typology provides only a minimal explanation for the effect of vertical structure on the public relations department. Instead, and once again, the power-control theory perspective provides a more positive than normative theory to help explain organizational structure. That is, as Child (1972) and Robbins (1990) argued, the dominant coalition chooses a course of action that becomes the organization's goals because it has the power. That course remains the structure until a new dominant coalition restructures to correct what it considers to have been the mistakes of the previous group. However, the mixed mechanical/organic organizational type did predict the model of public relations practiced. In fact, practitioners there adopt two-way models, both the symmetrical and asymmetrical, to contend with their heterogeneous, dynamic, large-scale environment (J. Grunig & L. Grunig, 1989).

In his chapter on internal communication in the first *Excellence* book, J. Grunig (1992) used Hage's (1980) four dimensions of organizational structure—centralization, stratification, formalization, and complexity—to conceptualize organizational structure and its effect on organizational communication and employee satisfaction with the organization. He added a fifth structural variable, *participation in decision making*, which often has appeared in audits of employee communication (e.g., Monge & Miller, 1988) and in psychological theories of leadership (e.g., Lawler, 1986; Vroom & Jago, 1988).

J. Grunig (1992) said that scholars of organizational communication have considered participation in decision making to be a communication variable, but he explained that it fits more logically with related structural variables that affect communication rather than as a communication variable itself:

> It is a structural variable because participation strategies—such as participative management, quality circles, teams, or delegations of responsibility—increase the autonomy of individuals and reduce their constraints. Participation is particularly relevant to communication because it increases the amount and symmetry of communication and increases the likelihood of organizational outcomes associated with communication—involvement, innovation, and job satisfaction.
>
> Participation has strong positive effects on job satisfaction in particular (Lawler, 1986; Monge & Miller, 1988), as do other structural variables that increase autonomy. Thus, it is likely that some of the effects of communication on job satisfaction occur not because of communication but because participation— a structural variable that affects communication—was included in the audit instrument as a characteristic of communication. (p. 561)

J. Grunig (1992) then followed the literature in organizational sociology (e.g., Burns & Stalker, 1961; Hage, 1980; Hage & Aiken, 1970) and combined these five variables into two general types of organizational structure. Organizations with *mechanical* structures are centralized, formalized, stratified, and less complex and do not allow employees to participate in decision making. Organizations with *organic* structures are decentralized, less formalized, less stratified, and more complex and facilitate participation in decision making. He developed propositions associating organic structure with symmetrical communication systems and greater employee satisfaction with the organization and mechanical structure with asymmetrical communication system and lower employee satisfaction.

Internal Communication

In *Excellence in Public Relations and Communication Management*, J. Grunig (1992) also reviewed the literature of organizational communication, a specialized subdiscipline of communication that examines how people communicate in organizations and the nature of effective communication systems in organizations. He identified eight research traditions in this literature and concluded that the concept of symmetrical communication can be found throughout these eight traditions. He also proposed that symmetry of communication could be used to integrate the research that has been produced by these traditions.

J. Grunig (1992) concluded that, "Symmetrical concepts such as trust, credibility, openness, relationships, reciprocity, network symmetry, horizontal communication, feedback, adequacy of information, employee-centered style, tolerance for disagreement, and negotiation pervade the literature" (p. 558). He reviewed a number of studies designed to develop and use instruments to audit the effectiveness of organizational communication. He concluded that these audits also suggest the presence of symmetrical communication. He said that audit studies have shown that employees are most satisfied with information that helps them make sense of their situation by explaining how their jobs fit into "the organizational mission, about organizational policies and plans, and about relationships with key constituencies in the organization's environment" (p. 558).

The research reviewed also shows that employees, especially in managerial ranks, express a preference for open communication with top management, which J. Grunig (1992) interpreted as a desire for symmetrical communication. Finally, research shows that interpersonal communication is strongly related to employee satisfaction. According to J. Grunig, "Face-to-face communication makes symmetrical communication easier, although mediated communication also can be symmetrical if its content meets the employee's need to know rather than management's need to tell" (p. 559).

Asymmetrical communication in organizations, in contrast, is generally one-way, top-down, and designed to control the behavior of employees in ways that management desires. Such a system is typical in mechanical organizations with authoritarian cultures. Asymmetrical communication remains popular among dominant coalitions that strive to increase their power and to control others, rather than to empower employees throughout the organization.

Employee Satisfaction

The level of satisfaction that employees express with their jobs and with the organization as a whole has been the outcome of employee communication studied most frequently by communication scholars. Organizational psychologists also have studied employee satisfaction extensively (Locke, 1976). Scholars of organizational communication have explored the effect of communication on other outcomes, such as employee identification with the organization (Van Riel, 1995); absenteeism, turnover, safety records, and indexes of health (Downs, Clampitt, & Pfeiffer, 1988); and role stress, organizational commitment, and socialization (B. Schneider, 1985).

Although these other possible outcomes of internal communication are not subsumed by the concept of organizational satisfaction, organizational satisfaction generally is an indicator of their presence. In the first *Excellence* book, J. Grunig (1992) pointed out the communication may not directly affect employee behaviors such as job performance or absenteeism. However, he cited Hall (1987), who said that internal participants in organizations are strategic constituencies that can constrain the ability of an organization to meet its goals. J. Grunig added, "Measures of job satisfaction and the other individual outcomes of organizational behavior and communication, therefore, provide valuable indicators of the extent to which employees are likely to support or constrain the mission of the organization" (p. 549). In the Excellence study, therefore, we included measures of satisfaction as surrogate variables for a number of indicators of the extent to which employees are likely to support rather than constrain organizational goals.

J. Grunig found two types of satisfaction in the literature (such as Hage, 1980), which he also had used in previous audits of employee communication (J. Grunig, 1985, 1987): satisfaction with an individual's job and satisfaction with the organization overall. He concluded that satisfaction with the organization is the best indicator of the effect of the organization's system of communication.[1] Individual job satisfaction tends to be correlated with variables such as complexity of a job rather than with characteristics of the organization.

Employee satisfaction also is affected strongly by the structure and culture of the organization as well as by its communication system. J. Grunig (1992) theorized that organizational structure and the communication system interact closely with each other to produce employee satisfaction—especially satisfaction with the organization. He added that the dominant coalition chooses a structure and communication system, as power-control theory suggests. As a result, the organizational context for excellent communication ultimately results from the choices made by those who are most empowered in the organization.

When the organization's culture is participative, though, more people are empowered in the organization, public relations professionals are more likely to be in the dominant coalition, the structure more often will be organic than mechanical, communication will be more symmetrical, *and* employees will be more satisfied with the organization. J. Grunig (1992) summarized these interactions in a figure in the theory book, which is reproduced here as Fig. 11.1.

Diversity

The value of diversity in an organization can be explained by Weick's (1979) principle of requisite variety—the idea that organizations are most effective when they have as much variety in the organization as there is in the environment. L. Grunig, J. Grunig, and Ehling (1992) included this principle of diversity in their discussion of organizational effectiveness in the theory book underlying this study.

Weick (1979) explained the principle by pointing out that the environments of organizations are enacted rather than objective. Enacted means that different people in an organization will perceive the organization's environment differently. In addition, people outside the organization will perceive the environment even more differently. Therefore, the more diverse the employees in an organization, the more diversely they will perceive the environment.

---

[1]D'Aprix (1996) also suggested that employees can be loyal to their jobs but not to their employers.

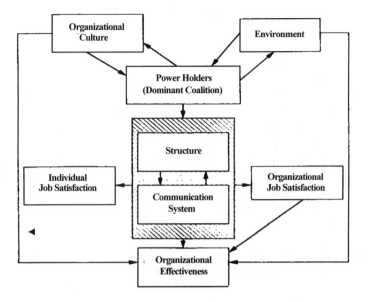

Source: J. Grunig (1992), p. 566

FIG. 11.1.   Power-control model of organizational communication and structure.

Diversity is especially important in public relations because of its key role in environmental scanning. A public relations staff that is mostly male and White would be less likely to perceive the environment of women and racioethnic minorities than would be the case if some members of these groups are in the public relations department, interacting with White men and with each other. This does not mean that there must be a representative of every group in an organization's public relations department. Rather it means that some diversity will force everyone in the department to interact and to think more diversely.

We examined diversity in the Excellence study in two ways. In the quantitative survey, we asked the top communicator, the CEO, and the employees to respond to the same battery of questions about the treatment of women in the organization. In the qualitative interviews, we asked more questions about the treatment of women in public relations and throughout the organization. The results for women in public relations were discussed in chapter 5. In this chapter, we discuss the overall organizational context for women throughout the organization and relate it to culture, structure, internal communication, and job satisfaction. In the qualitative interviews, also, we asked in-depth questions about the status of racioethnic minorities in the organization to extend the concept of diversity beyond gender.

RESULTS RELATED TO ORGANIZATIONAL CULTURE AND PUBLIC RELATIONS

Quantitative Results Related to Culture

The literature reviewed showed organizational culture to be a key determinant of organizational effectiveness. Culture also helps explain why some organizations practice excellent public relations. In fact, four major propositions about culture and public relations grew out of the theoretical conceptualization of the Excellence study. In our survey, we measured the nature of an organization's culture through 45 questions administered to 4,631 employees. We also discussed culture during our long interviews with participants in organizations selected from the top and bottom of the Excellence scale.

In our preliminary analyses of these cultural data, we first developed indexes for the concepts of authoritarian and participative cultures. We then correlated the indexes with the communication structures and activities of the organizations. We developed these indexes by isolating interrelated variables that describe the cultures of organizations and then by determining items for questionnaires to be completed by members of organizations. With this procedure, each employee provided a "window" into the culture of her or his organization. The aggregated responses of employees provided a "picture" of that culture.

To calculate the indexes, we used exploratory factor analysis to develop factors or underlying dimensions of culture. The loadings of the cultural variables on these factors indicate the extent to which each variable describes the culture identified by the factor. Our review of theories of organizational culture suggested that there are two major types of culture in organizations that affect the excellence of its management and of its communication efforts.

The factor analysis, shown in Table 11.1, did indeed produce two factors that reflect these two types of culture almost perfectly. One factor can be described as a *participative* factor and the other as an *authoritarian* factor.

An exploratory factor analysis (principal axis method, varimax rotation) of the 48 items describing organizational culture initially produced 10 factors with an eigenvalue greater than 1.0. An eigenvalue measures the strength of a factor, and a value of 1.0 or higher is used conventionally to indicate whether an additional factor should be added to explain the correlations among the variables being analyzed. In this factor analysis, however, the eigenvalues of the first two factors were much greater than those of the other eight. The eigenvalue of the first factor was 9.87 and of the second, 6.65. The eigenvalues of subsequent factors were 1.99, 1.57, 1.52, 1.38, 1.30, 1.22, 1.10, and 1.07. The first factor accounted for 21% of the variance and the second for 14%. The third factor accounted for 4% of the variance, the next five for 3% of the variance each, and the last two for 2% each.

Based on the small eigenvalues and low percentage of variance explained by factors extracted after the first two, we concluded that the variance produced in

TABLE 11.1
Factor Analysis of 45 Indicators of Organizational Culture

Concept and Question	Communality	Participative Factor	Authoritarian Factor
Collective vs. individual responsibility			
Each project in this organization, even if it is a complicated one requiring a team effort, usually is divided into tasks and subtasks. Each employee is assigned subtasks and is solely responsible for the results of his or her work.	.34	.42	.18
Most projects are done here through teamwork. Each individual is expected to contribute to the team effort, but the team as a whole is ultimately held accountable and rewarded or punished for its efforts.	.43	.58	−.07
Collective vs. individual decision making			
Most decisions in this organization are made by individuals largely working alone.	.48	−.13	.57
Most decisions in this organization are made after thorough discussion between all people who will be affected in a major way.	.48	.64	−.23
Collective vs. individual values			
Most employees in this organizations share a common sense of mission that most think is worth striving to achieve.	.49	.54	−.20
Most departments in this organization do not share a common mission; each has different priorities that conflict with the priorities of other departments.	.49	−.11	.64
Holistic concern vs. lack of such concern for people			
This organization is a place where people tend to separate their work life from their home and social life. Most superiors feel that it is not their responsibility nor their right to know very much about the personal problems of their subordinates.	.33	.04	.42
People take interest in each other in this organization. It is common to find supervisors who feel that it is part of their job to know about personal problems that may be bothering their subordinates.	.54	.60	−.00
Long-term vs. short-term employment			
People in this organization move frequently to other employers, including those who are successful as well as those who are not.	.30	.07	.40
The typical career in this organization is long term; the organization rarely has layoffs and terminations.	.38	.40	−.02
Slow vs. fast evaluation and promotion			
Performance is important in this organization, but promotions are made only after careful evaluation of an individual over a long period of time.	.25	.32	.17
People are evaluated often in this organization through hard measures such as sales, profitability, or production. For those who receive favorable evaluations, promotion can be rapid.	.31	.41	.20

TABLE 11.1
(Continued)

Concept and Question	Communality	Participative Factor	Authoritarian Factor
Nonspecialized vs. specialized career paths			
Most people in this organization are specialists who are known outside the organization as experts in engineering, marketing, accounting, or a similar field.	.35	.39	.20
Most people do not specialize in this organization. They rotate among areas such as marketing, operations, sales, engineering, personnel, or similar functions.	.36	.28	.31
Shared mission			
This organization has clearly defined goals.	.47	.51	−.18
If I were one of the four or five most powerful executives of this organization, I would manage the organization in the same way as the executives now in power are managing it.	.47	.55	−.27
The goals of this organization are different from my personal goals.	.41	−.08	.51
Rewards for performance rather than personal connections			
Advancement in this organization is based more on who you know than on how well you perform.	.48	−.12	.58
Social atmosphere among employees and managers off the job			
People who work here meet frequently off the job.	.50	.41	.05
Senior managers of this organization frequently socialize with other employees off the job.	.50	.46	.05
Integration vs. individualism			
The departments in this organization seem to work together like a well-oiled machine.	.66	.66	−.16
Nearly everyone feels like he or she is part of a team in this organization.	.66	.71	−.17
Senior managers in this organization care deeply about other employees.	.61	.66	−.17
Emphasis on time			
Being on time is extremely important in this organization.	.38	.31	.24
Decision making by tradition, rational process, open debate, trial-and-error, scientific research, or authority			
Decisions usually are based on tradition here—the way things always have been done.	.45	−.00	.55
Before decisions can be made here, committees usually are set up to study the issue.	.30	.32	.20
Major decisions usually are based on open debate in this organization.	.44	.50	.01
Usually, we make decisions by trial-and-error. We try things and see if they work.	.39	.29	.31
Decisions here usually are based on scientific research.	.35	.50	.18
Decisions usually are based on authority here—the way the CEO and the people close to him or her want things done.	.48	−.01	.63

TABLE 11.1

(Continued)

Concept and Question	Communality	Participative Factor	Authoritarian Factor
Consensual processes			
Everyone is treated as an equal in this organization.	.60	.64	−.12
Everyone works together here to make the organization effective.	.64	.69	−.18
Importance of innovation, tradition, and efficiency as organizational values			
This organization is open to new ideas from outside.	.58	.60	−.23
This organization looks to the future rather than to the past.	.48	.57	−.06
Innovation probably is the most important goal of this organization.	.48	.59	−.06
Efficiency probably is the most important goal in this organization.	.38	.48	.17
Authoritarian vs. participative management style			
Senior management in this organization believes that it must have nearly total control over the behavior of subordinates.	.54	−.03	.69
Rigid control by management often makes it difficult for me to be innovative in this organization.	.60	−.14	.73
Managers in this organization seem to believe that employees lack initiative and must constantly be given instructions.	.60	−.05	.67
Senior administrators in this organization believe that they know best because they have more knowledge than lower-level employees.	.54	−.11	.65
Senior managers here believe in the sharing of power and responsibility with lower-level employees.	.60	.63	−.17
Most people who work here seem to be afraid of senior managers.	.49	−.01	.65
Liberal vs. conservative values			
This organization can be classified as conservative.	.37	−.02	.39
This organization can be classified as liberal.	.45	.44	−.06
Cooperation vs. domination in relationships with publics			
This organization usually is willing to negotiate with groups outside that disagree with it.	.50	.49	.07
This organization tries to dominate people outside who disagree with it.	.42	.06	.54
System open vs. closed to its environment			
This organization usually is closed to new ideas from outside.	.51	−.09	.64
This organization is open to ideas from outside.	.58	.58	−.18
Percentage of variance explained		21%	14%
Eigenvalue		9.87	6.65

Note. Factor analysis was based on the principal axis method with varimax rotation.

the correlational matrix of 48 cultural items could be explained well by the two dominant factors. Therefore, we conducted a final factor analysis specifying two factors, as shown in Table 11.1. The first factor can be described as a participative factor and the second as an authoritarian factor. All but 5 of the 48 variables included in the analysis loaded clearly on one of the factors. If more than two factors are rotated, these items could become additional factors; but we did not judge them to be strong enough factors to merit calling them additional dimensions of culture. Although we cannot say that the two dimensions we identified through factor analysis are the only two dimensions of organizational culture, we can conclude that they are two dominant dimensions—at least when the items we generated to measure organizational culture are used as indicators.

Further, the variables on the two factors in Table 11.1 loaded logically. Organizations with participative cultures emphasize collective responsibility, decision making, and values. By contrast, organizations with authoritarian cultures emphasize individual responsibility and values. Managers in participative cultures have a holistic concern for people. Managers in authoritarian cultures have little concern for the lives of their employees outside of the organization. Employees in participative cultures socialize off the job; in authoritarian cultures, they separate their work life from their home life.

Workers in participative cultures typically are employed for long terms. In authoritarian cultures, they move from organization to organization more frequently. Employees in participative cultures also share a mission, whereas those in authoritarian cultures separate their personal goals from those of the organization. Advancement depends on whom they know. Participative cultures tend to integrate all members of the organization, whereas authoritarian cultures value individualism.

Both cultures stress being on time, although, somewhat surprisingly, participative cultures emphasize time somewhat more. Both types also use rational processes and scientific research to make decisions. However, participative organizations strive more for equity and consensus than do authoritarian organizations. When authoritarian cultures make decisions, they often use tradition, trial-and-error, and authority as the basis for those decisions.

As expected, participative organizations emphasize innovation as a value and authoritarian organizations tradition. Both types of culture value efficiency, which we believe is explained by the broader societal cultures of the three countries studied. Surprisingly, however, participative organizations strive for efficiency more than do the authoritarian. Perhaps the explanation for this unanticipated finding lies in Total Quality Management. TQM empowers workers to look for new and more efficient operating methods. Organizations embracing TQM also encourage participative culture.

Participative culture is characterized by liberal values and authoritarian culture by conservative values. Finally, in relation to their environments, participative organizations work toward negotiation and compromise. They are open systems. Authoritarian organizations try to dominate their environment. They are closed systems.

Some of the characteristics of Japanese organizations did not distinguish between the two kinds of culture in these three English-speaking countries. In particular, both kinds of cultures have specialists and do not have nonspecialized career paths. Promotion can be rapid in both kinds of cultures, although it is more likely to be slow in participative than in authoritarian cultures.

In chapter 3, Table 3.8, we compared cultures across organizational types. We juxtaposed the indexes of participative and authoritarian culture with corporations, not-for-profits, governmental agencies, and professional or trade associations. Table 3.8 showed no significant differences across these types for participative culture, although government agencies and associations had lower average scores than did corporations and not-for-profits. Significant differences did occur in authoritarian culture, however. Associations and not-for-profits were less likely to have authoritarian cultures than were corporations, especially, and government agencies, to a lesser extent. In short, the larger organizations tended to be more authoritarian in their cultures, although their cultures are just as likely to be participative as in the smaller organizations.

In Table 3.7 of chapter 3, we also compared cultures across nations. Only slight differences emerged. Organizations in the United Kingdom had significantly lower scores for participative culture than did American and Canadian organizations. Differences were negligible for authoritarian culture: Organizations in the United Kingdom also were slightly lower than the North American countries on authoritarian culture, but the differences were not significant.

Taken together, these data establish that we have developed valid measures of the two types of organizational culture. They seem to transcend international, societal boundaries. The next step, then, was to correlate the two indexes of culture with other characteristics of organizational Excellence. In this analysis, we looked for confirmation that participatory culture produces excellent public relations and that authoritarian cultures result in mediocre public relations.

Individual correlations of the indexes of culture with the other variables that made up the Excellence factor generally were low or nonsignificant. Significant correlations ($p < .05$ or less) were found between participatory culture and knowledge needed for the two-way symmetrical model (.18), playing the manager (.09) and senior advisor roles (.14), and knowledge needed for the manager role (.10).

The impact of the two types of culture on public relations can be seen most clearly from their loadings on (correlations with) the Excellence factor. Participatory culture had a significant correlation of .22 with the Excellence factor; authoritarian culture a nonsignificant correlation of .05. Participatory culture had the lowest loading of any of the variables loading on the Excellence factor, however. The other loadings ranged from .29 to .76.

These results can be interpreted as suggesting that participatory culture is neither a necessary nor a sufficient condition for excellent public relations. An authoritarian culture does not make excellent public relations impossible because it does not correlate negatively with the Excellence factor. At the same time, a participative culture provides a more supportive, nurturing environment for excellent public relations than does an authoritarian culture. Nevertheless, a participative culture does not produce an excellent public relations department unless that department possesses the knowledge and skills to practice public relations symmetrically, in a two-way manner, strategically, and as a managerial function. Likewise, a department that possesses such knowledge can practice excellent public relations even in an authoritarian culture. All in all, however, public relations departments will find it easier to apply their knowledge in a participatory than authoritarian culture.

The nurturing role of culture can be seen most clearly when the two indexes are correlated with the other internal characteristics of organizations. We examine those relationships after we explore the qualitative results for culture and develop indexes to measure the other internal characteristics.

Qualitative Results Related to Culture

The qualitative interviews helped paint a more detailed picture of the nature of organizational cultures. In particular, however, these long interviews provided results that shed light on each of four propositions:

1. *The presuppositions about public relations in an organization will reflect that organization's internal and external culture.*

2. *Public relations managers will be most likely to change the model of public relations practiced in an organization when organizational culture is changing.*

3. *A public relations department that is high in potential (because of managerial roles, education in public relations, and professionalism) will develop a counterculture when the organization's culture and worldview for public relations do not reflect the presuppositions and worldview for public relations of the department.*

In our interviews in the chemical corporation, public relations was credited with helping top management shift the culture of the chemical corporation from a relatively authoritarian culture to a more participative one. By contrast, the conservative, authoritarian culture of an insurance company whose employee scores ranked it in the 8th percentile in terms of their participation is likely to limit the potential of public relations there. No one on the communication staff was a member of the dominant coalition. Even the director of communication did not play a part in the strategic decision making of the company (although the public relations department's yearly plan is presented to the officers of the company for discussion at their annual strategic planning session).

The culture of some of our organizations was so financially driven that questions of social responsibility and value of public relations were considered irrelevant. The relevant question was, "How's the company doing for our stockholders?" In others, such as the medical association, the opposite was the case. There, the ultimate focus was on treating patients. Its head of public affairs described this "visceral" concern for patient well being as permeating the leadership of the organization. Its medical ethos created a climate where symmetrical communication came naturally.

4. *Participative cultures foster organic structures, symmetrical communication systems, and organizational Excellence and effectiveness. Authoritarian cultures, in contrast, foster mechanical structures, asymmetrical systems of communication, and mediocrity and ineffectiveness.*

We return to this proposition after we calculate indexes for structure and symmetrical and asymmetrical systems of internal communication. At this point, however, we can examine the relationship between culture and organizational Excellence and effectiveness. We did not include direct indicators of organizational Excellence or effectiveness in any of the three questionnaires. However, we did ask the CEO to estimate the rate of return on public relations and the value of public relations in comparison with other organizational functions—indicators that public relations increases organizational effectiveness in the mind of the CEO. As we saw in chapter 3, the measures of public relations Excellence correlated strongly with these measures of value. As a result, it is reasonable to look at the correlations of culture with the overall index of excellence as a surrogate indicator of the relationship between organizational culture and effectiveness.

As we have already seen, participatory culture did not necessarily result in communication Excellence, nor did authoritarian culture doom the public relations unit to mediocrity. The qualitative data provide at least a partial explanation for the unanticipated lack of correspondence between type of culture and degree of excellence. Of all the organizational attributes that we hypothesized would contribute to excellence in communication, participative culture turned out to be least important.

The case of the U.S. insurance company helps explain why. It made a strong showing in the survey phase of our research regarding participative culture, ranked in the 97th percentile on this dimension. The top communicator said that the company placed even greater emphasis on participative values in 1994 than it did in 1991. She described its management style as becoming more participatory and less top-down (although she acknowledged that the improvement is coming slowly).

However, the core elements of communication Excellence are absent. In this organization, ranked toward the bottom (in the 6th percentile) of the Excellence scale, the communication department did not have the knowledge base to enact the managerial role nor the expertise to practice the sophisticated two-way models of public relations. Further, the dominant coalition regarded communication largely as a technical support function for marketing, with little to contribute to strategic planning or managerial decision making. The head of the communication department was excluded from the dominant coalition.

Given these constraints, a participative organizational culture contributes little to excellence because the more fundamental aspects of strategic management and symmetrical communication are missing. We concluded that without the knowledge base to practice communication Excellence and shared expectations with the power elite to provide such excellence, organizational culture is largely irrelevant. Participative culture can provide only a conducive, supportive environment for communication Excellence.

Similarly, the hotel chain that encouraged participative culture (largely through its TQM initiative) ranked only in the 18th percentile in overall Excellence. This case study supported the finding of the survey research that participative organizational culture does not lead necessarily to the development of an excellent communication department within the organization. Why? Its communication function was fragmented among several subunits within the larger structure and the head of public relations did not participate in strategic planning, nor did he act as a senior adviser to the dominant coalition.

On the other hand, the participative organizational culture and a structure that fostered teamwork, shared decision making, and openness to ideas from outside undoubtedly contributed to the 91st-percentile score in overall Excellence for the financial services corporation included in our study of cases. The company had a higher-than-average score, 68%, in terms of participative culture as reported by its employees in the survey research.

In the qualitative research, we also explored briefly the CEO's critical role in developing or changing organizational culture. Although no proposition guided data collection in this area, the power-control perspective that pervades the Excellence research suggests that members of the dominant coalition must play a significant part in developing, changing, or strengthening the culture of their organization. One of our participants went so far as to call the CEO "the keeper of the corporate culture." In his opinion, it is also the CEO who decides when the culture will shift: "If the CEO is out of whack with the corporate culture or the corporate culture is out of whack with the CEO, then the situation is not going to work."

One CEO, in particular, emphasized the importance of his part in establishing organizational culture. He put this concept in terms of creating an environment in which the best minds can do their work—and he included the physical environment as well as the climate of the company. He made much of the fact that his association hosts five parties a year for its 300 employees, "to make sure everyone knows, likes, understands everyone else."

Another top manager, this one a senior vice president in the midwestern utility company, talked about culture more in relation to the external than internal public. To him, culture was the "persona" of the company. In his company, that meant boosterism. Public relations reinforces this persona by "a lot of partnering with people . . . in raising more money for whatever needs to be done in the community."

Finally, we learned that the gender of the CEO may affect the culture of the organization. In the medical association whose top communicator ranked it only in the 12th percentile in support for women employees 3 years before our analysis of the qualitative data, the new president—a woman—was credited with pushing for more participative management. Another senior woman in the organization, the manager of communication, worked toward more symmetrical public relations. She stressed listening and trying to improve her department's service to members. The assistant executive director of corporate affairs there linked positive changes in the association with these new roles for women. Women's emergence at the highest levels, then, may be playing a part in some underlying transformations occurring in organizational culture.

RESULTS RELATED TO ORGANIZATIONAL STRUCTURE, INTERNAL COMMUNICATION, AND EMPLOYEE SATISFACTION

Now we turn to our basic theoretical premise that organic structures and symmetrical systems of communication make the organization more effective because they empower people. Under these conditions, politics in the organization becomes constructive because it embodies negotiation and compromise. In organizations with mechanical structures, in contrast, power holders use asymmetrical communication in a continual battle between independence and dependence.

We proposed that organizations are effective—the organizational effectiveness variable increases—when their structure, culture, and environment are in harmony. The environment is important because the strategic constituencies in it constrain or enhance the mission of the organization. Employees, a key constituency in the internal environment of an organization, can have a similar impact. That is why satisfaction with the organization is a critical outcome of the structure-communication system of the organization and a critical link to organizational effectiveness (J. Grunig, 1992).

We tested this line of reasoning in three specific propositions:

1. *Excellent systems of internal communication reflect the principles of symmetrical communication.*

2. *Organizations with organic structures have symmetrical communication systems and organizations with mechanical structures have asymmetrical communication systems.*

3. *Symmetrical communication can help to create organic structures in organizations.*

We further proposed that high levels of employee satisfaction, especially satisfaction with the organization, indicate good relationships with employee constituencies. We proposed that:

4. *Job satisfaction, especially satisfaction with the organization, is higher in organizations with organic structures than in organizations with mechanical structures.*

Finally, as stated in a proposition introduced in our discussion of culture, we proposed that organizational culture would covary with the system of communication, organizational structure, and employee satisfaction. In particular, we proposed that a participative culture would be associated with symmetrical communication, organic structure, and high levels of satisfaction. Authoritarian culture, in contrast, would be associated with asymmetrical communication, mechanical structure, and low levels of satisfaction.

Quantitative Results Related to Internal Communication, Structure, and Satisfaction

Means and Reliability.   We began the analysis of the hypothesized relationships between these three sets of variables by analyzing the reliability of the questionnaire items used to construct an index to measure each concept. Tables 11.2, 11.3, and 11.4 report these results. Again, a total of 4,631 employees from 320 organizations participated in the employee survey. For these three sets of variables, individual responses were aggregated for each organization by averaging the responses of all employees completing the questionnaire for each organization. The analyses of reliability were based on the aggregated responses. Therefore, the sample size was 320 for each of these three tables.

Each table reports the mean of the transformed fractionation scale used in the Excellence study. A mean of 10 (the square root of 100 in the original scale) was defined as an "average" answer to all of the questions in the questionnaire in the instructions to the employees participating in the survey. Each table reports the Cronbach's alpha for each index. An alpha of over .70 is good, whereas an alpha approaching .90 is excellent. However, alphas generally are higher when there are more items in a scale so that a lower alpha can be expected for indexes with fewer items. Tables 11.2, 11.3, and 11.4 also contain two columns

TABLE 11.2

Means and Reliability of Internal Communication Variables

Concept and Question	Mean (Transformed Scale)	Item–Total Correlation	Alpha If Item Deleted
Asymmetrical Communication			
The purpose of communication in this organization is to get employees to behave in the way administrators want them to behave.	7.35	.56	.76
Most communication in this organization is one-way: from administrators to other employees.	8.47	.71	.58
I seldom get feedback when I communicate to administrators.	7.14	.58	.74
Symmetrical Communication			
I am comfortable in talking with administrators about my performance.	11.64	.63	.85
Most communication between administrators and other employees in this organization can be said to be two-way communication.	9.78	.68	.85
This organization encourages differences of opinion.	9.03	.73	.84
The purpose of communication in this organization is to help administrators to be responsive to the problems of other employees.	8.97	.65	.85
My supervisor encourages differences of opinion.	10.22	.62	.86
I am usually informed about major changes in policy that affect my job before they take place.	9.97	.64	.86
I am comfortable in talking with my immediate supervisor when things are going wrong.	12.77	.58	.86

Note. Cronbach's alpha for the asymmetrical communication scale = .78. Cronbach's alpha for the symmetrical communication scale = .87.

that indicate the strength of each item in defining the index of a concept. The most important of these is the "alpha if item deleted." If alpha goes up substantially when an item is deleted, that item is not a good indicator of the concept because the alpha would be stronger without it. The "item–total correlation" simply tells how strongly each item correlates with all of the other items added together.

Table 11.2 shows the reliability results for the indexes used to measure asymmetrical and symmetrical internal communication. Three items were used to measure asymmetrical communication, and seven items were used to measure symmetrical communication. Cronbach's alpha was high for both indexes and approached the ideal level of .90. It was higher for the symmetrical index than for the asymmetrical index, but this could be expected because of the larger number of items used to measure symmetrical communication. It was not necessary to delete any of the items because eliminating any of them would not

TABLE 11.3
Means and Reliability of Structural Variables

Concept and Question	Mean (Transformed Scale)	Pearson's Correlation of Related Items	Item–Total Correlation	Alpha If Item Deleted
Centralization				
In this organization, important decisions generally are made by a few administrators alone rather than by people throughout the organization.	7.35		.36	.69
I have a great deal of freedom in making decisions about my work without clearing those decisions with people at higher levels of the organization. (reversed)	10.62	−.18**	.52	.66
Participation in Decision Making				
I have a personal influence on decisions and policies of this organization.	7.50		.64	.63
I have a say in decisions that affect my job.	10.47	.64**	.63	.63
Stratification				
It is difficult for a person who begins in the lower ranks of this organization to move up to an important administrative or supervisory position within about 10 years.	8.68		.29	.70
In this organization, there are clear and recognized differences between superiors and subordinates. These differences can be seen in larger offices, quality of office furniture, close-in parking spaces, or frequency of superiors and subordinates having lunch together.	10.77	.30**	.18	.72
Formalization				
My organization has a printed organization chart, which nearly everyone follows closely.	7.86		−.10	Deleted
My actual work seldom deviates from a written job description for my position.	7.25	.13*	.21	.71
Complexity				
I must keep reading, learning, and studying almost every day to do my job adequately.	9.98		.33	.69
Employee education (1–5 scale).	2.34	.38**	.34	.69

Cronbach's alpha = .71.

$*p < .05.$ $**p < .01.$

TABLE 11.4
Means and Reliability of Employee Satisfaction Variables

Concept and Question	Mean (Transformed Scale)	Item–Total Correlation	Alpha If Item Deleted
Individual Job Satisfaction			
On the whole, my job is interesting and challenging.	13.06	.73	.77
I look forward to coming to work almost every day.	12.03	.73	.77
My work gives me a sense of accomplishment.	12.58	.70	.78
My work is a dead-end job. (reversed)	5.63	.49	.84
My work is boring. (reversed)	3.85	.52	.83
Satisfaction With the Organization			
In general, this organization has treated me well.	13.12	.77	.91
I feel as though I have a real chance to get ahead in this organization.	9.91	.75	.91
The best-qualified people usually are chosen for promotion in this organization.	9.73	.72	.91
I am satisfied with my pay and benefits.	10.81	.63	.92
This organization has a genuine concern for the welfare of its employees.	10.68	.68	.91
I am satisfied with my day-to-day working conditions.	11.16	.65	.92
I am satisfied with the recognition I receive for good performance in my job.	10.68	.78	.91
I have found this organization to be a good place to work.	12.45	.86	.91
Both men and women are treated well in this organization.	11.29	.76	.91
It is easy to work with my coworkers.	12.24	.45	.92
There is good opportunity for advancement in my job.	8.76	.72	.92
Minorities are treated well in this organization.	11.26	.48	.92

Note.   Cronbach's alpha for the individual job satisfaction scale = .83. Cronbach's alpha for the satisfaction with the organization scale = .92.

increase alpha. The means for the individual items show that symmetrical communication was more common in these 320 organizations than was asymmetrical communication.

Table 11.3 reports the analysis of reliability for 10 items used to measure five structural variables—centralization, participation in decision making, stratification, formalization, and complexity. Two items measured each of the five concepts. All of the items were Likert-type agree or disagree statements except for one of the indicators of complexity. The second indicator of complexity was the amount of education employees had completed.

The structural characteristics were combined first for each of the five concepts and then as a single scale in which a high score indicated an organic structure and a low score a mechanical structure. In that way, we could look at the overall impact of structure on the other internal variables as well as the impact of each structural characteristic. To compute that scale, the first item listed in Table 11.3 measuring centralization and both of the items measuring stratification and formalization were reversed because low centralization, stratification, and formalization characterize organic organizations. Combining all of the structural items into a single scale rather than putting them into separate organic and mechanical scales, as we did to calculate the Excellence factor in chapter 3, improved the reliability of the final scale and simplified data analysis because organic and mechanical structures are polar opposites and because of the larger number of items used to calculate the index.

The second column of Table 11.3 shows the correlation between each of the two concepts used to measure each structural characteristic, because it is not meaningful to compute Cronbach's alpha for only two items. These correlations ranged from low for centralization and formalization to moderate for stratification and complexity and high for participation in decision making. The overall Cronbach's alpha for structure was .71, which is good although not high. The two items measuring participation in decision making and the positive item measuring low centralization were the best indicators of the organic–mechanical continuum.

The first item measuring formalization, which asked the extent to which employees in each organization follow a formal organization chart, correlated negatively with the other structural items and only $r = .13$ with the second formalization item, the extent to which an employee's work deviates from a written job description. As a result, we deleted the first item from the overall index of structure and used only the second item as a measure of formalization in later analyses.

Just as the means for the communication items showed that the organizations in our sample were more likely to have symmetrical than asymmetrical systems of communication, the means of the structure items showed that organic structure was more common in the sample than mechanical structure.

Table 11.4, finally, shows the reliability of 5 items that we used to measure individual job satisfaction and 12 items used to measure satisfaction with the organization. Both indexes were highly reliable (alpha = .83 and .92 respectively), and all items contributed equally well to the final index as indicated by the alphas if item deleted and item–total correlations. The mean scores again showed that employees were more satisfied than dissatisfied in our sample, although individual satisfaction is slightly higher than satisfaction with the organization. The greatest expression of dissatisfaction with the organization came on three items asking about opportunities for promotion and advancement, which were the only items with means below the nominal "average" score.

Correlations of Internal Variables.   With these indexes of our key variables in place, we now can test the propositions for systems of employee communication. We hypothesized that organizations with excellent public relations would be characterized by symmetrical systems of internal communication and that symmetrical communication would correlate positively with organic structure, individual and organizational job satisfaction, and participative culture. All of these internal contextual variables should correlate with the overall index of excellence in public relations.

These correlations are reported in Tables 11.5 and Table 11.6. In both tables, the correlations are based on the aggregated data—that is, the correlations were based on average data for 320 organizations. Before deciding to use the aggregated data, we also calculated the same correlations based on the individual scores of the 4,631 employees. The correlations were similar for the aggregated organizational data and the individual data, but they were consistently higher for the aggregated data. The higher organizational correlations confirmed that these variables are characteristics of the organization rather than characteristics of individual employees regardless of the organization in which they work. As a result, the two tables contain only the correlations from the aggregated data.

Table 11.5 examines the relationship between structure and the other internal variables. The correlations with the overall index of structure in column 1 strongly confirm our theoretical expectations. Organizations with organic structures also have symmetrical systems of internal communication, participative cultures, and high levels of individual job satisfaction and satisfaction with the organization. Organizations with mechanical structures have asymmetrical systems of internal communication, authoritarian cultures, and low levels of individual and organizational job satisfaction. We had expected that the correlation between structure and organizational satisfaction would be higher than with individual satisfaction; but both were equally high, suggesting that structure, especially complexity, affects the nature of a job itself as well as the organizational context.

The same pattern of correlations resulted for three of the individual structural variables—participation in decision making, centralization, and stratification—as well as for the overall index. The correlations with formalization and complexity deviated from the pattern, however, and were not so high. Formalized organizations had a tendency to have asymmetrical communication, authoritarian cultures, and low individual satisfaction; but they also had participative cultures. Formalization did not correlate significantly with symmetrical communication or satisfaction with the organization. We suspect that formalization probably varies with size of the organization and, as we saw in chapter 3, size did not affect excellence in communication.

Complexity did tend to be associated with symmetrical communication, participative culture, and satisfaction; but it also was associated with authoritarian culture. The two highest correlations, however, support our prediction that employees with more complex jobs like their jobs more than those with less complex jobs. It also is interesting that employees with complex jobs engage more in symmetrical communication. Job complexity, however, was not highly associated with the other structural variables.

TABLE 11.5

Pearson's Correlations of Structural Variables With Internal Communication, Culture, and Satisfaction Variables and With Overall Communication Excellence

Other Internal Variables	Overall Structure (High = Organic, Low = Mechanical)	Participation in Decision Making	Centralization	Stratification	Formalization	Complexity
Symmetrical Communication	.61**	.59**	-.62**	-.28**	-.00	.29**
Asymmetrical Communication	-.40**	-.24**	.45**	.50**	.16**	.07
Participative Culture	.40**	.41**	-.50**	-.23**	.13*	.13*
Authoritarian Culture	-.38**	-.21**	.45**	.59**	.12*	.13*
Individual Job Satisfaction	.50**	.48**	-.44**	-.23**	-.13*	.23**
Satisfaction with the Organization	.42**	.43**	-.44**	-.28**	.07	.12*
Overall Excellence Score	.12	.12	-.09	-.06	.14*	.14*

$*p < .05. **p < .01.$

TABLE 11.6

Pearson's Correlation Among Internal Communication, Culture,
Satisfaction, and Overall Excellence Variables

	Symmet. Comm.	Asymm. Comm.	Partic. Culture	Author. Culture	Ind. Job Satisfaction	Satisfaction With Org.	Overall Excellence
Symmet. Comm.	—	−.33**	.68**	−.30**	.54**	.63**	.20**(.09)[a]
Asymmet. Comm.		—	−.15**	.71**	−.22**	−.20**	−.03 (−.02)
Partic. Culture			—	−.16**	.35**	.61**	.26**(.14*)
Author. Culture				—	−.24**	−.16**	.02 (.01)
Ind. Job Satisfaction					—	.66**	.16**(.09)
Satisfaction with Org.						—	.17**(.05)
Overall Excellence							—

[a]Correlations in parentheses are with the Excellence scale with participative culture removed.
*$p < .05$. **$p < .01$.

As we saw in chapter 3, none of these structural characteristics correlated highly with overall Excellence in public relations. As we see later, the variables affected by structure (communication, culture, and satisfaction) are correlated more with excellence in public relations than is structure itself—probably because these variables can be affected by excellent public relations and structure cannot. The only significant correlations with overall Excellence were with formalization and complexity, but these still were small. These correlations suggest, though, that an organization with excellent public relations is more formalized and complex than one whose public relations is less excellent.

Table 11.6 shows the correlations among the system of communication, culture, and satisfaction and the correlations of these variables with the overall index of excellence in public relations. Our same predicted pattern emerged again in this table. Symmetrical communication, participative culture, and both individual job satisfaction and satisfaction with the organization correlated highly with each other. As we predicted, however, symmetrical communication and participative culture correlated higher with organizational satisfaction than with individual satisfaction. Employees were more satisfied with organizations that have participative cultures—organizations in which communication and culture interact to produce a harmonious environment in which employees can work.

Although the correlations were moderate to low, a symmetrical system of internal communication, participative culture, and both individual and organizational satisfaction correlated positively and significantly with overall Excellence in public relations. However, because participative culture was one of the 20 variables in the Excellence scale, we removed that variable from the scale to eliminate the possibility of autocorrelation—of the variable correlating at least in part with itself. With participative culture removed from the Excellence scale, the correlation of participative culture dropped to a low level. However, it still was significant. None of the other internal variables correlated significantly with the truncated Excellence scale—reflecting the reason we included only participative culture in the scale. These other variables correlated with overall Excellence only because of their correlations with participative culture.

As we explained in chapter 3, these correlations probably were not higher because the data used to calculate the internal variables came from the employee sample whereas most of the other variables in the index of excellence came from the samples of PR heads and CEOs. At the same time, the absence of significant correlations shows that the organizational context alone cannot produce excellent public relations. However, these contextual variables do make a more hospitable home for excellent public relations, largely by producing a culture conducive to excellence.

From Correlations to a Causal Model.   The correlations reported in the previous section revealed a strong pattern of relationships among structure, communication, culture, and employee satisfaction. However, the communication professional needs to know more if she or he would like to change the pattern for his or her organization from one that leads to an ineffective organization to one that leads to an effective organization. He or she needs to know which variables come first in order to intervene and change the pattern. Can communication help to create organic structures, as we proposed in Proposition 3, or does structure determine the nature of the communication system? Can communication affect individual job satisfaction and satisfaction with the organization, or does structure largely determine how satisfied employees will be regardless of what the communicator does? And, how does culture fit into the picture? Does communication create culture or does culture create a system of communication? Likewise, we can ask which comes first, culture or structure? Can we manage variables that affect culture, such as communication, or does culture exist independently of the variables a communicator can manage—predetermining the outcomes of communication programs?

Recall that Fig. 11.1, reproduced from the chapter on internal communication in our theory book, suggests that structure and the system of communication are closely intertwined and that both affect the other. In the model, however, the dominant coalition chooses a closely related structure and system of communication, which jointly affect employee satisfaction. Figure 11.1, also proposed that organizational culture and the organization's environment each affect who gains power in the organization. Figure 11.1 further proposed that organizational effectiveness is a product of the combination of culture, environment, structure, communication, and satisfaction with the organization. However, Fig. 11.1 also indicated that decisions made by the dominant coalition largely determine what structure an organization will have, the nature of its system of internal communication, and how satisfied employees will be. As a result, as we showed in chapter 5, the top communicator must be a part of the dominant coalition if she or he hopes to help choose an organizational structure and system of communication that, in turn, affect employee satisfaction and ultimately organizational effectiveness.

We tested the model in Fig. 11.1 by constructing a structural equation model from the correlational data we have reported thus far. A structural equation model reveals apparent causal relationships among theoretical constructs. Rather than showing that several concepts merely are related, as correlations do, the structural equation model shows *how* they are related—which variables precede others in a causal pattern of relationships. The structural equation model that we developed is shown in Fig. 11.2.[2]

Figure 11.2 can be interpreted most easily by concentrating on the five theoretical constructs depicted by circles in the middle of the diagram: organic structure, mechanical structure, symmetrical communication, participative culture, and job satisfaction. For each of these constructs, arrows pointing to the outside show connections to the questionnaire items that were combined to measure the construct. A box represents each questionnaire item, with a variable number inside.

Each variable, in turn, has an arrow pointing farther outside connecting it to the error variance of the item, labeled with E and a number, such as E25 for Variable 25 (V25). The error variance is the variation in an item that is not explained by its association with the theoretical construct measured. To improve the overall fit of the model to the data, some of these variances were allowed to covary, which is indicated by the double-headed arrows at the outside of the diagram. For example, the errors for two of the items used to measure organic structure covaried with two of the items that measured mechanical structure. Most likely, they covaried because of response effects—that is, a tendency of participants in the survey to respond to the items in the opposite direction because the items measured similar but opposite concepts.

Because we used a large number of variables to measure each theoretical concept in the Excellence study, we chose a smaller number of the best indicators of each concept to reduce the complexity of the model. Some of the indicators also were chosen for their face validity—that is, they were logical indicators of the concepts.

The three indicators of organic structure consisted of the two items used to measure participation in decision making (V25: I have a personal influence on decisions and policies of this organization; and V31: I have a say in decisions that affect my job) and one that was used to measure low centralization (V27: I have

---

[2]The structural equation model shown in Fig. 11.2 was developed by Collin Elliot, a graduate student in public relations at the University of Maryland, working in collaboration with James Grunig. To maximize the sample size and improve the fit of the model, the analysis was based on the individual data of the sample of 4,631 employees rather than on the aggregated sample used in previous analyses.

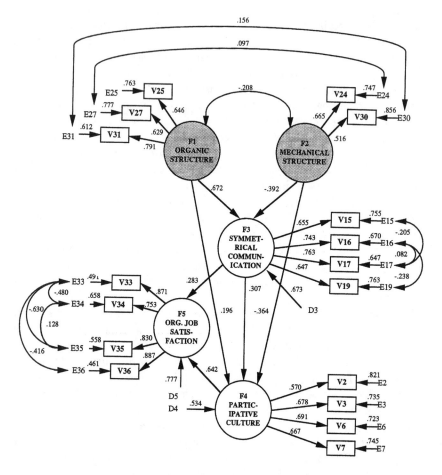

FIG. 11.2.   Structural equation model of internal variables.

a great deal of freedom in making decisions about my work without clearing those decisions with people at higher levels of the organization). Of the indicators of mechanical structure, one was a measure of centralization (V24: In this organization, important decisions generally are made by a few administrators alone rather than by people throughout the organization) and the other a measure of stratification (V30: In this organization, there are clear and recognized differences between superiors and subordinates. These differences can be seen in larger offices, quality of office furniture, close-in parking spaces, or frequency of superiors and subordinates having lunch together).

Symmetrical communication was measured by four indicators (V15: I am comfortable talking with administrators about my performance; V16: Most communication between administrators and other employees in this organization can be said to be two-way communication; V17: This organization encourages differences of opinion; and V19: My supervisor encourages differences of opinion).

The four items used for participative culture were indicators of collective values (V2: Most employees in this organization share a common sense of mission that most think is worth striving to achieve), collective decision making (V3: Most decisions in this organization are made after thorough discussion between all people who will be affected in a major way), integration of the organization (V6: Senior managers in this organization care deeply about other employees), and participative management style (V7: Senior managers here believe in the sharing of power and responsibility with lower-level employees).

Finally, the four items used to measure job satisfaction in Fig. 11.2 all were measures of satisfaction with the overall organization, which we believed would be affected more by the other variables than individual job satisfaction (V33: In general, this organization has treated me well; V34: I am satisfied with my day-to-day working conditions; V35: I am satisfied with the recognition I receive for good performance in my job; and V36: I have found this organization to be a good place to work).

The final structural model depicted in Fig. 11.2 was constructed using the EQS computer program. The model fit the data well. It had a Comparative Fit Index (CFI) of .949,[3] when a CFI of .90 is considered a minimum for an adequate fit. The numbers on the arrows connecting concepts are standardized path coefficients, which can be interpreted much like correlation coefficients, although the direction of the arrows indicate the most likely direction of cause and effect.

To understand the model, begin by looking at the boxes representing organic and mechanical structure. These concepts are not affected by other concepts in the model, suggesting that the types of structure are the initial conditions that affect communication, culture, and employee satisfaction. Although the choices made by the domination coalition were not measured in the Excellence study, the best explanation of how the model begins is that the dominant coalition chooses a structure for the organization, which then has a snowball effect on communication, culture, and satisfaction.

Figure 11.1 shows that organizational structure has a strong direct effect on symmetrical communication (a coefficient of .672), which confirms the importance of having an organic structure in place before a symmetrical system of communication can be developed. Mechanical structure has an opposite but smaller effect on symmetrical communication ($-.392$), showing that symmetrical communication will be difficult in a mechanical structure. Symmetrical communication then has a moderate direct effect on participative culture (.307). Organic structure also has a positive direct effect on participative culture (.196), and mechanical structure has a negative direct effect ($-.364$).

In other words, the path coefficients show that structure affects the nature of an organization's culture through the kind of communication system that is

---

[3]Chi-square of the final structural model was 1476.003, with 102 df.

most common in each structure and directly regardless of the nature of communication. Multiplying the path coefficients shows that organic structure has a stronger effect on participative culture through symmetrical communication $(.672 \times .307 = .206)$ than a direct effect $(.196)$. This supports the assertion in Fig. 11.1 that structure and communication are intertwined and have a stronger influence when they act together. Figure 11.2, finally, shows that participative culture has a strong direct effect on satisfaction with the organization $(.642)$. Symmetrical communication has a smaller but still moderate direct effect on satisfaction independent of its effect on culture.

Altogether, Fig. 11.1 supports our theoretical reasoning that communication alone cannot produce satisfied employees. Rather, the system of communication must function within a context of structure and culture. Organic structure and symmetrical communication working together can produce participative culture, and participative culture is the biggest contributor to employee satisfaction with the organization. A communicator cannot step into any organization and implement a system of symmetrical communication. If organic structure does not exist, the communicator must work simultaneously with the dominant coalition to develop an organic structure for the organization while he or she is developing a system of symmetrical communication—especially a structure characterized by employee participation in decision making throughout the organization, low centralization, and low stratification. These findings, therefore, support not only the need for symmetrical communication in an effective organization but the need for representation of the public relations function in the dominant coalition to help create the organic structural context that is necessary for a participative culture and subsequent employee satisfaction.

Our quantitative analysis of the key concepts of the internal context of organizations, culminating in the causal model shown in Fig. 11.2, has provided strong evidence that power holders in an organization—the dominant coalition—make decisions about organizational structure that have subsequent effects on communication, culture, employee satisfaction, and organizational effectiveness. Professional communicators must manage communication in an organization, but they must also communicate to the power holders the importance of sharing power with other employees before communication can help the organization. We turn, then, to our qualitative data for examples of how these processes work themselves out in real organizations.

Qualitative Results Related to Internal Communication, Structure, and Satisfaction

Although we did not ask our case study respondents to address each of these internal variables specifically, they did talk about them extensively as they discussed the importance of internal communication and the value of empowering employees to participate in organizational decision making. The case studies provided strong support for the proposition that excellent internal communication would follow the principles of symmetrical communication. They also supported the importance of the CEO and the dominant coalition in choosing a structure and system of internal communication for the organization. In particular, the interviewees described the important interactions among structure, communication, and culture that we found in the quantitative results. We also learned that organic structure, symmetrical communication, and participative culture can be created and nurtured through change programs such as Total Quality Management and flexible reporting relationships such as those found in a matrix structure.

Symmetrical Internal Communication. Our first proposition related to internal communication was that excellent systems of internal communication reflect the principles of symmetrical communication. Those principles hinge on two-way public relations. To the top communicator in the heart health organization, this translates into talking and listening. She contended that "talking to people," both inside and outside the organization, is one of her organization's highest priorities. As a result, she spent much of her time in the field with grassroots staff, "doing what they do." She emphasized "keeping in touch with the real world" and working "in the trenches." Such listening and interacting constitute the informal research that constantly informs the public relations program and overall strategic thinking in the organization. Its Excellence score equaled or bettered 99% of all organizations taking part in the study.

Effective internal communication, considered vital, ranged from weekly liaison meetings among department heads who share information to universally available voice mail. The CEO described the organization as tightly integrated; "no one is left out" in terms of consultation. The CEO indicated that every employee has a voice and everyone is involved in total quality. The top communicator merely said: "It's simple. We talk to each other." Although this exemplary operation combines traditional, one-way publicity and public information models with the more sophisticated two-way practice, it achieves excellence in communication. The goal of communication, whether internal or external, is to be proactive rather than reactive and submerged in the process of communication as an end in itself.

Symmetrical systems of communication make organizations more effective by building open, trusting, and credible relationships with strategic employee constituencies. Support for this proposition came largely from our long interviews with selected participants, primarily in organizations rated toward the top of the Excellence scale. Only 9% of the 281 organizations that provided employee questionnaires in the survey research ranked higher than the financial services company. Its top communicator said that her department enjoys an excellent relationship with the other corporate units. She attributed this to the caliber of the department's staff, which was expected to practice two-way public relations. She credited the excellence of her staff with instilling a high level of trust in the communication function throughout the organization.

This woman, who heads a staff of 40 full-time employees, explained that her CEO fostered an emphasis on internal communication. She cited these two reasons: the CEO's conviction that good internal communication is a part of a larger trend in management and, second, the CEO's personality and personal objectives.

The company implemented a Total Quality Management training program in hopes of improving both internal and external communication. The top communicator stressed that the TQM process was designed so all staff members would understand "the flow of what's needed in accomplishing a specific goal." She saw a strong connection between the principles of TQM and excellence in communication. She explained that the actions of every employee contribute to the overall success of the company, and that empowering every employee through communication is an important motivational factor.

The highly rated disabled services organization based its philosophy of internal communication on the belief that customer relations mirrors employee relations. The top communicator used her newsletter to help develop pride in the organization and to infuse the idea of responsibility among employees. Every employee in this not-for-profit is responsible for fund-raising, in particular. All employees—not just those in development—are expected to spread the word about the agency and look for new donation opportunities. The CEO concurred: "The custodian is just as important to the overall operations of this organization as I am."

Even in a less highly ranked operation, the philosophies of total quality and employee communication were apparent. Consider the aerospace corporation. Its Excellence score was in the 12th percentile. Because it depends on manufacturing, internal communication is critical. The head of public relations explained that product quality and meeting production deadlines are key values stressed through internal communication:

> Because we are in a manufacturing industry, total quality is rooted in the production departments. Management made it a point not to make total quality a department but rather a philosophy. Management wants [total quality] instilled in the company and not relegated to a specific area within the corporation. I do not see a direct relationship between excellence in public relations and total quality except that you should be practicing public relations with the total quality philosophy.

Why Some CEOs Emphasize Internal Communication.   One of the themes that repeated itself several times in our in-depth interviews was the important role of the CEO in determining the culture, structure, and system of internal communication in the organization—a theme that mirrored the influence of the dominant coalition in Fig. 11.1 and that we alluded to in explaining Fig. 11.2.

Some chief executive officers valued public relations for its role in internal *advocacy*. As the CEO in an excellent association explained, his vice president for communication supports him in where he wants to take the association: "He's helping me propagate those ideas both within and without the organization. Once that happens, you get a kind of synergism. . . ."

Other senior managers we spoke with, such as a vice president in the chemical corporation, alluded to the role public relations can play in *changing the organization's culture*. As in the chemical company, top management at one gas and electric company wants to transform its old-line, bureaucratic, and authoritarian ways into a more participative style: "An organization that is nimble and flexible and is positioned to be able to be successful in a competitive environment." The dominant coalition there also believed that although the process of transfiguring culture starts and stops at the top, employee participation is vital. Thus the company uses internal communication vehicles, print and video, to share this initiative with employees.

Still other executives see an obvious link between two-way communication with employees and their *productivity*. Total quality management programs may reinforce the role that public relations plays not only in informing workers but also in listening to their ideas. So, too, does the popular notion of *reengineering* the company. One vice president we interviewed described his chemical company's efforts at restructuring. In the process, employees became the strategic public and communication the strategic tool. The only way to gain productivity, he added, was by downsizing: "a nice simple strategy that must be explained to employees and stockholders." Communication also will enjoy an expanded role in relations between the company and its international subsidiaries. As an employee communication manager there explained it, "Part of the vision the human resources team has is to have communication strategies and plans in place within five years for all of the major locations." In surviving a hostile takeover, this company had to cut its workforce by 85%. This fact alone suggests that the remaining workers have become a strategic public. Management of the corporation interacts with its internal audience using a combination of one- and two-way communication.

Multinational organizations seemed to place high value on the role of communication for coordinating their operations. A communication manager in the oil company affiliate, which does business in a country apart from the parent company, described the decentralized structure that allowed for each affiliate's autonomy. For example, each company had a distinctly local system of internal communication—yet all needed to be linked strategically to headquarters.

Finally, we heard about the importance of the CEO's *basic orientation*: people or the bottom line. Some executives simply seem more attuned to their internal and external publics. We do not consider this dichotomy a necessary one, as indicated by the literature that supports a positive correlation between good relationships and profitability. However, at least one participant in this study alluded to presidents who, in her experience, give lip service to communication but provide little actual support: "I think they just aren't as people oriented or don't always see the importance of good relations with your employees in order to help that bottom line."

In other organizations, the split was between an internal and external focus on the part of the CEO. At the cosmetics company, for example, communicating with the sales force had been the key concern of top management. The independent contractors who make up the force outnumber employees by more than 10 to 1. The company's slogan holds that sales consultants are in business for themselves but not by themselves. However, senior management is increasingly concerned with communication inside the company, with employees, according to the agency head responsible for public relations there.

Quality Programs and Public Relations.   Between the quantitative research and our follow-up case studies, we observed an important change. More than half the organizations included in our survey of cases had instituted a program of total quality management, or TQM. The process went by different labels, such as "quality improvement" and "corrective action." Regardless of its name, its most pronounced effect seemed to be the empowerment of employees. As one of our own association CEOs put it, "TQM goes hand in glove with empowerment."

At this point, some readers may be experiencing the same cynicism we heard expressed by a handful of our interviewees. The independent public relations counsel retained by the cosmetics company, for example, said he believed the action teams suggested by TQM accomplish little. However, he acknowledged that the program does provide these groups of employees with a sense of ownership in various initiatives. And that, he reminded us, "leads to programs coming down the pike as partially presold."

Despite this kind of skepticism, TQM overlaps with many of the other concepts central to this study. A treatise by Shafer (1994)[4] on using quality to improve the public affairs function pointed out that as staffs are cut, TQM provides the instrument to eliminate unnecessary programs and to enhance the effectiveness of the vital initiatives that remain. In this sense, the book reinforces the *strategic* nature of public affairs—relating all activities to the organization's mission. It defines the stakeholders who can support or interfere with those goals in a broader sense than many previous discussions of publics. For example, it flags the CEO as a critical user of the output of the public affairs de-

---

[4]In particular, we recommend the chapter by Walter K. Lindenmann, "Believe It or Not, Measuring Public Relations Is Possible," to our readers. Before retiring, Lindenmann was senior vice president and director of research at Ketchum Public Relations.

partment. Employees, too, are considered vital. Perhaps most important, this book for the Public Affairs Council emphasizes the value of research. Benchmarking emerges as a key factor. Shafer cited the definition attributed to Xerox CEO David Kearns: continuously measuring products, services, or processes against the competitors' or industry's leaders. To engage in this kind of management requires criteria and measurement instruments that help determine what value public relations adds to achieving overall organizational goals.

We found that this expertise both in management and in research was lacking in many of our interview participants. The need to do more research to improve communication with its *international* sites was a particular concern of the top communicator in the chemical company we studied. Despite the growing sophistication of public relations in this above-average organization, he conceded that "we're still not big on research."

Feedback was a scarce commodity in the lowest ranked organizations. In a typical comment about the inability of many top communicators to assess their effectiveness, the director of public relations at an insurance company said: "I think we do a good job of telling associates what management wants. I'm not sure we do a good job of getting feedback." She predicted this would change with the recent initiation of a quality improvement program. Already the effort had succeeded in encouraging employees to become more involved—to offer ideas and to work in small groups to resolve problems on the job. She considered this initiative "a step toward improving openness and recognizing the ability of associates to give input."

In at least one organization, the engineering research agency, IABC had played an important part in the incorporation of the TQM principle of teamwork. The local IABC chapter had sponsored a series of TQM talks with a sister organization. The manager of communication became so enthusiastic that she paid for two half-day workshops just for her own staff. Although her division already operated in teams, she believed they could improve: "There are old behaviors we were still hanging onto." She herself continued to make too many unilateral decisions. TQM, on the other hand, "is about shared responsibility and shared decision making. I had to learn new ways of doing things. And it is absolutely one of the most exciting things that ever happened to me." As one concrete instance of what the TQM approach has meant to her department as well, this manager described several long-standing problems. The foremost was too much work. "Now," she said, "we work better and more efficiently in the production shop and in advising clients."

TQM also may help motivate communicators—especially those involved with promotion or sales, as we saw in the direct-marketing cosmetics concern we studied. The company has become heavily involved in what it calls not "TQM" or even "corrective action" but "creative action." We spotted a copy of Stephen Covey's popular *Seven Habits of Highly Effective People* on the desk of the director of sales force communications we interviewed there.

The question becomes, then, what relationship (if any) do public relations practitioners see between the practice of excellent public relations and "total quality"?

One vice president of communication called TQM a "fabulous opportunity" for practitioners to learn new things, including management skills, that add value to their practice. He acknowledged that TQM has "taken some pretty heavy hits in the media lately," but he explained the criticism more as a function of the trappings of the process than its philosophy. That ideology, he said, hinges on empowerment: mentoring and the opportunity for employees at all levels to make decisions about their everyday work. He summed up TQM in his association as "responsibility yet accountability."

Quality improvement also offers the promise of better feedback for ambitious public relations practitioners—especially those who work in organizations that traditionally have not appreciated their contribution beyond day-to-day problem solving. The top communicator in the contract management group of the hotel chain we studied in depth was responsible for the development of TQM communication strategies for his group. He explained how the concepts of TQM apply in the context of communication: "We established what the goals of the communication group would be, what we were trying to accomplish, who we were trying to move, and what messages were needed to move that. Based on those things, what were the vehicles that made sense and how do we execute those vehicles?"

However, this top communicator was not directly involved in TQM. Instead, members of the hotel chain's dominant coalition make up its TQM steering committee. A working committee, composed of outside consultants and representatives from several other corporate units, operates in conjunction with the steering committee to develop TQM policy. A working group representing staff and operations provides feedback on policies developed by the steering and working committees. Still, the head of public relations told us that "long before TQM was a popular buzzword, quality was always in at [the company] and hopefully long after TQM has passed as a buzzword or process, quality will still be in."

TQM principles encourage quality customer service. TQM has the potential to instill confidence in consumers and stockholders, two primary publics that many communication departments attend to. According to the head of public relations at the financial services corporation, TQM also helps empower employees. Together with diversity in hiring and a participative organizational culture, TQM has led to an outstanding internal communication effort in this top-ranked company. So, too, in the hospital association. There the top communicator explained that TQM is critical to the public relations function: "Communicators have to be an integral part of the TQM team and should be prepared to teach some communication skills down through the organization. People working on employee communications really need to do this and learn not to be possessive of their communication skills." The CEO of this state association also saw a central role for public relations in the TQM process. Because TQM hinges on tighter communication linkages to connect the "top" and "bottom" of the organizational hierarchy, the CEO believed a participative organizational culture makes the communication function inherently important.

Matrix Structure. In addition to the openness, participation, and organic structure fostered by quality programs, we also found evidence of the value of organic structure in the matrix structure employed by several of our case study organizations. The matrix structure, in particular, leads to open communication. We found such a structure in both the real estate development company and an industry association. The association CEO described his organization's design not in terms of "lines and boxes" or what most of us know as turf. Instead, he spoke of "grazing rights." This, he explained, allows employees to share information—both problems and solutions.

Although levels do exist within matrix structure, the matrix is less hierarchical than most organizational configurations. Responsibilities, as well as knowledge, are shared. Matrix structure goes hand in hand with openness. The top communicator in the real estate company described her organization as "very open. It's a very supportive environment which will allow people to take on jobs which aren't in their job descriptions." As with most participative *cultures* as well, people are allowed to make mistakes—"even big ones once in a while"—and still feel supported.

RESULTS RELATED TO GENDER AND DIVERSITY IN THE WORKFORCE

The effective organization provides an hospitable environment for its increasingly multicultural and female workforce in all departments, not just public relations. We expected that there would be a close correlation between the extent to which organizations embraced women and diversity and their culture, structure, and communication system. We also expected to find a correlation between employee satisfaction with the organization and the way organizations treated women and minorities. In our quantitative analysis, we examined only how the organization treats women, but in the qualitative analysis we also examined how organizations respond to cultural, racial, and ethnic diversity.

Quantitative Results Related to Gender

To determine how women were treated throughout the organizations we studied, we developed 22 items asking the extent to which our survey participants thought that each organization had enacted policies and established programs to support women and further their careers. The same questions were included in the questionnaires for employees, CEOs, and heads of public relations. Including the questions in all three questionnaires allowed us to compare differences in perceptions of employees and the CEO, in particular, but also to determine if the top communicator perceived the situation for women more from the perspective of the dominant coalition or from the perspective of employees.

Our guiding hypothesis here was that organizations that eliminated discriminatory practices against women and took positive steps to enhance their careers would provide an organizational context conducive to excellent public relations. The context would lead to excellent public relations because it would enhance the practice of public relations for the female majority in the field and also because organizations that provide a conducive environment for all employees also would be more likely to provide a conducive environment for women and minorities.

Constructing Indexes From the Variables on the Status of Women. We conducted an exploratory factor analysis of these variables, first, to determine if any of the policies and programs fit into categories that could be used to reduce the data to more manageable scales. For the employee data, we used the aggregated sample because it consistently produced the higher correlations among the employee variables than did the individual data. For each of the three samples (employees, CEOs, and PR heads), the factor analysis produced one dominant factor. The factor loadings for that dominant factor are shown in Table 11.7. The fact that all 22 items correlated strongly with one another when seen by employees, CEOs, and PR heads suggests that the climate for women is perceived consistently throughout an organization and extends both to policies and proactive programs.

Although Table 11.7 shows that most of the variables loaded highly on the single factor, some variables loaded higher than others. For each set of data, therefore, we examined the results of the factor analysis to determine if more than one factor might explain the data better than a single factor. Each of the three factor analyses produced at least three factors with an eigenvalue greater than 1.0 (the standard criterion for extracting additional factors), although the eigenvalue of the first factor was always much higher that the second and subsequent factors (e.g., 9.4 vs. 2.0 for the employee sample). We were able to interpret only three factors meaningfully, however. Nevertheless, all variables loaded highly on all three of these factors, even though patterns could be discerned that separated the variables into three groups.

These three sets of items consisted of (a) nondiscriminatory policies enacted to protect female employees (such as equal pay for comparable work, policies against sexual discrimination, and eliminating "perks" for men such as all-male clubs or executive dining rooms), (b) steps taken to provide a supportive work environment for women (such as providing opportunities for women to take risks, fostering women's leadership abilities, and encouraging women who

TABLE 11.7
Factor Analysis of Variables Measuring the Treatment
of Women Throughout the Organization

Question	Employees	PR Heads	CEOs
This organization has:			
Enacted specific policies, procedures, or programs designed to promote an understanding of the concerns of female employees.	.78	.61	.70
Provided a supportive climate for women at work.	.70	.70	.72
Monitored the use of sexist language in all realms of the organization's communication.	.73	.62	.56
Reviewed organizational policies for their effect on women.	.82	.71	.72
Provided opportunities for women who must relocate or who have relocated.	.68	.54	.60
Allowed flex time for employees.	.42	.51	.44
Avoided "perks" that divide employees on the basis of their gender and tenure, such as all-male clubs or executive dining rooms.	.53	.49	.49
Established effective policies to deal with sexual discrimination.	.71	.72	.72
Developed specific guidelines for handling problems of sexual harassment.	.70	.68	.63
Set up a system of maternity and paternity leave.	.69	.55	.46
Provided child-care services.	.44	.33	.28
Built a system of multiple employment centers that allows mobility for employees.	.60	.37	.39
Furthered the talents of women through mentoring programs.	.73	.53	.49
Fostered women's leadership abilities.	.75	.71	.63
Funded or reimbursed employees for work-related travel.	.44	.52	.47
Included membership in professional associations as an employee benefit.	.18	.32	.41
Provided opportunities for women to take risks.	.71	.70	.59
Encouraged women who may seem less "serious-minded" about their careers than men.	.75	.63	.51
Groomed women for management by selecting them as "informal assistants" to those in the next-higher position.	.65	.52	.47
Included women in the informal informational network.	.59	.61	.53
Made available comparable data to help women in salary negotiations.	.61	.45	.42
Paid men and women equally for equal or comparable work.	.48	.50	.59
Percentage of variance explained	42.8	35.2	33.2
Eigenvalue	9.42	7.74	7.30

Note. When a factor analysis produces only one factor, the communality is the loading of each variable on that factor squared. Therefore, communalities were not included in this table. This factor analysis was based on the principal axis method.

might seem less "serious-minded" than men), and (c) establishing formal mentoring and advancement programs for women (such as furthering the talents of women through mentoring programs; reviewing organizational policies for their effect on women; and enacting policies, procedures, or programs to promote an understanding of the concerns of female employees).

The differences between these three sets of variables were interesting enough that we decided to construct three indexes for further analysis. The differences were interesting because they seemed to distinguish among policies required by law, improvement of background conditions for women, and formal proactive programs to enhance the careers of women. Excellent organizations would seem likely to enact all three sets of policies. The least excellent organizations would not be likely to enact any of them. As organizations become more excellent, they would seem likely to begin with legally required policies, move to improvement of background conditions for women, and end with proactive policies.

We decided not to use the factor scores to measure these three types of policies and programs, however, because of the high cross-loading of all variables on all of the factors. Had we used factor scores, most of the variables would have contributed to defining all three indexes; and it would have been difficult to measure the three types of policies and programs separately. Therefore, we placed the variables into one of the three indexes for which they most consistently loaded the highest on the three separate factors. Indexes were constructed using the same variables for the employee, CEO, and top-communicator samples.

We then analyzed the reliability of these three indexes, the results of which can be found in Tables 11.8, 11.9, and 11.10. All three indexes for each sample had high reliabilities, with Cronbach's alpha ranging from .72 to .87. Most of the individual items correlated with the overall indexes at about the same levels, although there were some interesting differences. For example, on the Index of Nondiscrimination Policies setting up a system of parental leave and paying men and women equally for comparable work correlated highly, but not so highly, with the index as other items (Table 11.8). The means of these two items (9.84 and 10.30, where 10 is an "average" answer) were roughly equivalent to the means of the other variables on this index (which ranged from 9.97 to 10.33), so these nondiscriminatory policies appeared to be offered as frequently as the others. The best explanation for the lower correlation seems to be that parental leave and equal pay for men and women are more often offered independently of avoiding "perks" for men, establishing policies to deal with sexual discrimination, and developing guidelines for handling sexual harassment.

Similarly, allowing flex time for employees and paying for membership in professional associations correlated lowest with the Index of Steps Taken to Provide a Supportive Work Environment for Women. The correlations were only moderate. Again, the means for these items were similar to those of others in this index (8.77 and 8.39), suggesting that they more often are offered inde-

TABLE 11.8
Reliability Analysis of Index of Nondiscrimination
Policies Enacted to Protect Female Employees

Question	Employees		PR Heads		CEOs	
	Item–Total Correlation	Alpha If Item Deleted	Item–Total Correlation	Alpha If Item Deleted	Item–Total Correlation	Alpha If Item Deleted
This organization has:						
Avoided "perks" that divide employees on the basis of their gender and tenure, such as all-male clubs or executive dining rooms.	.59	.77	.44	.76	.53	.66
Established effective policies to deal with sexual discrimination.	.75	.72	.75	.65	.66	.63
Developed specific guidelines for handling problems of sexual harassment.	.67	.75	.69	.66	.58	.64
Set up a system of maternity and paternity leave.	.52	.79	.38	.77	.42	.70
Paid men and women equally for equal or comparable work.	.45	.81	.47	.74	.36	.75
Cronbach's alpha		.81		.76		.72

pendently of the other steps to provide a supportive work environment. Finally, providing child-care services correlated the lowest with the Index of Mentoring and Advancement Programs. This correlation still was relatively high, but the mean for the item (3.00) was by far the lowest of any of the questions asked about the treatment of women—suggesting that the lower correlation occurred because of the relative rarity of child-care programs in the organizations we studied as well as the greater independence of such programs from the other proactive programs.

Table 11.11 then compares the mean scores of these three sets of policies and programs to enhance the careers of women. In this table, an average of 10.0 would reflect the hypothetical average on the fractionation scale used in the Excellence study. Table 11.11 shows that the organizations we studied—in the eyes of employees, PR heads, and CEOs—more often provide nondiscrimination policies than they take steps to provide a supportive work environment and, especially, to develop proactive mentoring and advancement programs for women. CEOs, in particular, were more likely to believe their organizations have established such programs than are employees. PR heads fell between CEOs and employees on these indexes, suggesting that they do bridge the gap between employees and management.

TABLE 11.9
Reliability Analysis of Index of Steps Taken to Provide
a Supportive Work Environment for Women

Question	Employees		PR Heads		CEOs	
	Item–Total Correlation	Alpha If Item Deleted	Item–Total Correlation	Alpha If Item Deleted	Item–Total Correlation	Alpha If Item Deleted
This organization has:						
Provided a supportive climate for women at work.	.67	.81	.66	.81	.70	.78
Monitored the use of sexist language in all realms of the organization's communication.	.54	.82	.52	.82	.47	.80
Allowed flex time for employees.	.36	.85	.37	.84	.41	.81
Fostered women's leadership abilities.	.75	.79	.68	.80	.64	.78
Funded or reimbursed employees for work-related travel.	.52	.82	.52	.82	.52	.80
Included membership in professional associations as an employee benefit.	.26	.86	.32	.84	.50	.80
Provided opportunities for women to take risks.	.78	.79	.73	.79	.66	.78
Encouraged women who may seem less "serious-minded" about their careers than men.	.72	.80	.53	.82	.35	.82
Included women in the informal informational network.	.61	.81	.61	.81	.47	.80
Cronbach's alpha		.84		.83		.81

Correlations With Internal Variables and the Excellence Factor.   Now that we have constructed an overall index (represented by a single-factor score) measuring the conditions for women in the organizations we studied and three specific indexes that represent components of this index, we can test our guiding hypothesis that the conditions for women are related to other contextual conditions favorable for excellent public relations. We tested this hypothesis by correlating these indexes with the indexes we constructed to measure the other internal contextual conditions and with the overall index of excellence in public relations (with the PR head's estimate of the climate for women removed to avoid autocorrelation). Table 11.12 shows a pattern of positive relationships among favorable conditions for women, excellence in public relations, a participative culture, organic structure, symmetrical internal communication, and satisfaction with the organization. The conditions for women also correlated significantly with individual job satisfaction for the employee sample, but at a low level— showing that women can be satisfied to some extent with their jobs when an or-

TABLE 11.10
Reliability Analysis of Index of Mentoring
and Advancement Programs Established for Women

	Employees		PR Heads		CEOs	
Question	Item–Total Correlation	Alpha If Item Deleted	Item–Total Correlation	Alpha If Item Deleted	Item–Total Correlation	Alpha If Item Deleted
This organization has:						
Enacted specific policies, procedures, or programs designed to promote an understanding of the concerns of female employees.	.73	.85	.52	.75	.55	.74
Reviewed organizational policies for their effect on women.	.75	.85	.58	.74	.54	.75
Provided opportunities for women who must relocate or who have relocated.	.71	.85	.51	.75	.53	.74
Provided child care services.	.46	.88	.35	.78	.40	.77
Built a system of multiple employment centers that allows mobility for employees.	.66	.85	.43	.76	.45	.76
Furthered the talents of women through mentoring programs.	.77	.84	.59	.73	.60	.73
Groomed women for management by selecting them as "informal assistants" to those in the next-higher position.	.51	.87	.49	.75	.42	.76
Made available comparable data to help women in salary negotiations.	.53	.87	.39	.77	.42	.76
Cronbach's alpha		.87		.78		.78

TABLE 11.11
Mean Scores on the Transformed Scale for Indexes
of Three Types of Programs to Support Women Employees

Type of Program	Employees	PR Heads	CEOs
Nondiscrimination policies enacted to protect female employees	10.11	10.24	11.50
Steps taken to provide a supportive work environment for women	8.93	9.59	10.71
Mentoring and advancement programs established for women	6.13	6.15	7.59

TABLE 11.12

Pearson's Correlations of Indexes Measuring the Treatment of Women Throughout the Organization With Culture, Structure, Communication, Satisfaction, and Overall Excellence Scale

Treatment of Women Index	Participative Culture	Authoritarian Culture	Overall Structure (High = Organic, Low = Mechanical)	Symmetrical Communication	Asymmetrical Communication	Individual Job Satisfaction	Satisfaction With the Organization	Overall Excellence Score[a]
Overall Factor								
PR Head	.11	.04	.05	.11	.06	-.04	.09	.33**
CEO	.10	.06	.07	.21**	.16*	.01	.09	.34**
Employees	.47**	.01	.29**	.46**	.01	.19**	.43**	.15**
Nondiscrimination Policies								
PR Head	.09	.09	.06	.08	.06	-.04	.07	.27**
CEO	.10	-.05	.13*	.18	.04	.05	.09	.28**
Employees	.36**	.04	.21**	.35**	.02	.14*	.33**	.11
Supportive Work Environment								
PR Head	.16**	-.08	.10	.15**	-.01	-.02	.07	.38**
CEO	.06	-.11	.08	.14*	.02	.08	.10	.36**
Employees	.53**	-.10	.39**	.50**	-.08	.22**	.47**	.16**
Mentoring and Advancement Programs								
PR Head	.14*	.04	.09	.18**	.07	.09	.19**	.24**
CEO	.12	.11	.07	.22**	.15*	.01	.11	.27**
Employees	.37**	.12	.21**	.38**	.10	.16**	.34**	.11

[a]Excellence scale with the PR head's estimate of the environment for women removed to avoid autocorrelation.

$*p < .05$. $**p < .01$.

ganization does not take steps to eliminate discrimination and enhance the careers of women but not satisfied with the organization that employs them. Favorable conditions for women were not related to authoritarian culture, mechanical structure, and an asymmetrical system of internal communication.

Table 11.12 reports correlations between the variables measuring conditions for women and the other contextual variables based on data from the employee, top-communicator, and CEO samples. The correlations were invariably higher for the employee sample, although a similar pattern of smaller correlations resulted from the PR head and CEO samples. There are two likely explanations for these differences. First, the employees probably provided a more accurate estimation of the conditions for women than the CEOs and PR heads because they are more likely to experience these conditions firsthand. Second, however, most of the other contextual variables were measured only in the employee sample; and, as we have found throughout our analysis of the Excellence data, correlations have been consistently higher among variables measured in the same samples. As a result, we pay the closest attention to the employee sample in Table 11.12 in interpreting the relationship of the women's variables with the other contextual variables.

The story is slightly different, however, for the correlations with the Excellence factor. The overall factor representing all of the variables related to conditions for women and each of the three indexes representing specific types of policies and programs correlated significantly with the overall Excellence score for the PR heads and CEOs. However, the correlations from the employee sample were lower and significant only for the overall factor and for the index of a supportive work environment. We saw this same pattern when we derived the Excellence factor in chapter 3, and for this reason we included only the overall women's factor from the sample of top communicators in the Excellence factor. Again, the correlations from both the PR head sample and the CEO sample most likely were higher than those from the employee sample because most of the variables in the Excellence factor came from those two samples. Because of this tendency for the variables from the same sample to correlate more highly with variables from the same sample than from another sample, the truest test of the relationship between the women's variables and the other internal variables can be found in the employee correlations in Table 11.12 and the truest test of the relationship of the women's variables with the Excellence factor can be found in the PR head and CEO correlations.

With this conclusion in mind, we can see in Table 11.12 that the overall treatment-of-women index correlated highly with excellence in public relations, participative culture, symmetrical communication, and employee satisfaction with the organization. It also correlated moderately with organic structure. The same pattern of high correlations can be found with the index of a supportive work environment for women—the specific index that seems to capture best the overall context in which women work. This overall supportive environment correlated higher with the other contextual variables than did the index of nondiscrimination policies, which most organizations are required to provide, and specific mentoring and advancement programs, which are less common in all organizations.

Overall, however, these quantitative data on the treatment of women provide strong evidence that a supportive environment for women interacts with organizational culture, organizational structure, and symmetrical communication to provide a context that produces employees who are satisfied with the organization and, as a result, also likely to identify with the organization, to support its goals, and to be loyal and committed to it. This overall supportive internal environment, in turn, provides a context in which excellent public relations is most likely to be found and to thrive.

Qualitative Results Related to Gender and Diversity

Our quantitative data suggest one overarching question about diversity that could be answered through our qualitative interviews: *How do excellent organizations manage to empower women and minorities?* More specifically, how does the organization intent on diversifying its workforce do so? During our long conversations with interview participants, we heard how the organization determined to diversify its employee base does so. These conversations provided a great deal of support for our quantitative results and insight into how the process of creating conducive conditions for both the public relations function and for women occur in excellent organizations.

Our intent was to move beyond the somewhat simplistic and oft-repeated suggestions summed up in one participant's comment: "It takes talent, hard work, personality, being in the right place at the right time." She acknowledged that "this is true for everybody, but it is harder for women." At the same time, however, her stance sounded much like "blaming the victim." It also bespeaks the contradiction inherent in what we heard from two other participants, including the top communicator at the heart health organization. She said, first, that gender discrimination is not an issue in her agency. However, she added that women generally do have to work harder and perform better than men to succeed there.

The top communicator at the disabled services agency was even more emphatic on this point. She said she was "sick and tired of the rhetoric surrounding the issue." She deplored women's "whining" about their status. Rather than weighing the relative merits of, say, women working harder or relying on affirmative action or equal employment opportunity laws, she proposed that women start behaving the way top executives do. She suggested reading the *Harvard Business Review*, in particular. Without taking such action, she contended, it is women's own failure when they fail to become part of the management team.

Similarly, the top communicator at a statewide public utility suggested that women should crash the glass ceiling through their own efforts—specifically by paying attention and doing a good job. She also urged women not to draw attention to the fact that they are female. When asked how women might do that, she replied: "It's just kind of doing business work and not paying attention to the fact that you're a female and everyone around you is male."

However, we speculate about the ramifications of these women's arguments. If women do come to emulate the male model, can they increase the diversity of their department? If they downplay or renounce the characteristics considered "feminine" in the cultures we studied, then will they bring a woman's perspective or traits or management style to their work? Can they serve as role models or mentors for their female colleagues? Mary Kay Ash (1995), who built a billion-dollar business as founder and chair of the cosmetics company that bears her name, asked much these same questions in her best-seller. Her goal in writing the book was to teach women how to balance career and family while not forgetting about themselves. She described women so zealous to climb the corporate ladder that they stopped "being ladies," losing their femininity in exchange for a chance to play with the "big boys." She concluded that in their effort to imitate men, these aggressive women compromise their major asset—their womanliness—and thus cannot be good role models for their own daughters.

We also questioned whether women who adopt the male model would realize their potential for the two-way symmetrical practice of public relations that many of our participants associated with women in the field. So, rather than exploring ways in which women might conduct themselves as mirror images of the men they see at the top of the hierarchy, we prefer to describe in some detail a number of *promising* suggestions we heard:

1. The two participants from an industry association agreed that *TQM programs,* which typically empower employees, also could be influential in accomplishing the organization's diversity goals. As the CEO put it:

> TQM . . . is done just to try to create . . . a culture . . . which says that you want to get as much as you can out of everybody in your organization—no matter what they look like, no matter what they talk like, no matter what their sex or religion or anything else is. Because nobody has a corner on all the brains. They come in different packages and we are consistently amazed at what we get out of everyone on our staff.

The director of human resources at the medical products company went so far as to declare, "diversity is really a quality issue. If you are too homogeneous, or don't have diversity, or the best people at all levels, the company isn't going to be as effective as it could be. If you do have diversity, everybody becomes more valuable."

2. *Promoting from within* was a second strategy for making the most of diverse human resources. That same CEO described the risks and benefits inherent in this process: "Take a chance. I don't care if you fail. I cannot tell you how many times we have found gold by giving a job to somebody where she's a little young, or she's never done a feature film, or she never really worked on the hill."

Many organizations included in our series of case studies were proactive regarding the advancement opportunities of their female employees. The heart health agency, for example, set up a Women and Minorities Leadership Committee with the object of developing professional growth internally. The CEO acknowledged that although the organization seeks better conditions for advancing women and minorities, this nonprofit is "far from where we need to be." To wit: Female employees make up 60% of the staff, but the dominant coalition includes only 4 female vice presidents among the 16 VPs in the organization. Minorities represent about 19% of the staff; only one vice president is a member of an ethnic minority.

3. Beyond a culture open to risk taking, providing opportunities for women and minorities often depends on the *mind-set of the people who hire*. We learned that these key people extend beyond the CEO and the head of public relations. As one CEO explained, "It's got to be on the treasurer's mind, because the treasurer is always going to try to find a way to do it easier or cheaper. . . ."

If those top managers who hire happen to be women themselves, as we found in the case of a medical association, then sexism may disappear gradually. This is even possible, we heard from a corporate affairs specialist, in an industry culture such as chemistry or medicine that remains male dominated. She told us that her association is one of the best she has worked for in terms of lack of gender bias. The manager of quality and support services in the U.S. oil company described top management's deliberate effort to recruit women and minorities to make sure that "it's not just a slam dunk for the White male to get the job."

By contrast, consider the problem described by the CEO at the hospital association:

> In communication, women seem to do really well but moving ahead is tough. I see things starting to change and now there is a natural progression from public relations to top management to becoming CEO. The problem is that 95% of the hospital administration committee is made up of men. These are the people who select [the CEO] so I can see how that would make it harder for women.

4. *Awareness* of the special problems people of color and women may face simply because of their race or gender also might help solve those problems. More than any specific action, the director of communication at the chemical

company believed that eliminating obstacles to promotion for women or minorities depends on "being more conscious of the need to work with them, to overcome the barriers that have grown up." The director of public relations in an insurance company explained that her operation is becoming similarly cognizant. It is taking its important first step toward filling more management positions with women. However, the top communicator in this company pointed out that his industry has not attracted minorities, in particular.

5. A fifth strategy—one only rarely mentioned—is the development of a *diversity training program*, or training per se. We heard about such an initiative in a chemical company: "In the past [women and minorities] might not have been involved in certain training groups. Now [the company] makes different types of training available to them . . . to give them a better chance to level the playing field against those who have had the edge or the perceived edge all these years."

6. Equally rare but promising was *hiring a diversity recruiter or a diversity manager*, as one midwestern utility in our study did. The manager's task is to help increase the number of women and minorities in top ranks and to use more women- and minority-owned suppliers. The company also sponsors activities in the community that benefit women and minorities. For example, it is launching, in conjunction with area universities, a high school cooperative program designed to mentor disadvantaged youths.

The chemical corporation we studied recruits nontraditional employees through its summer internship program. It commits to hiring these interns permanently when their performance is satisfactory. (The communication specialist we interviewed was recruited this way.) The human resources department of the heart health organization, like several others included in our case study research, boasts a minority recruiter. This deliberate approach is helpful because, according to the top communicator at the financial services corporation, "otherwise people have a tendency to hire people who are just like them." Her company seeks out diversity by specifically asking headhunters to help find employees of varied ethnic groups and genders.

7. All of this helps, but the director of public relations at the chemical corporation said she believes that progress there has been slow. As a result, women in her company have formed a women's group to "make a little noise." Thus we add *women making an issue out of women's concerns* as another strategy that may help top management understand the seriousness of diversity issues.

The top communicator at the hospital association was relatively pessimistic about the status of women across organizations. The only hope, as she saw it, was women themselves. She said that, in general, organizations do little to provide opportunities for their female employees: "Nobody does a particularly good job of empowering women. There is no question about it: There is a glass ceiling and women are going to have to empower themselves."

Interestingly, despite the apparent glass ceiling this woman described and her CEO's acknowledgment that women do experience special barriers to advancement, she plays a highly visible role in managerial decision making. We asked how this was possible and what advice she could offer to other communicators, female or male, who were equally ambitious. She answered that to empower themselves: "Communications people should not stay in one place forever. You're not stuck unless you 'stick' yourself. You can enhance your value by being in different situations and learning to see things from different perspectives. Show you can apply your skills in solving internal problems."

8. In a related point, we learned that *women through their own sustained efforts* may make changes in organizational culture. The female head of corporate affairs for the medical association exemplified this kind of incrementalism. Although the company had no formal programs for empowering women, she established work teams within her department and empowered them to make decisions.

Similarly, one insurance company seems to have made significant inroads in the representation and advancement of women. The track record is less clear with ethnic minorities. However, the top communicator there explained that 80% of the workforce and half of all managers are women. This has been possible, she said, because the company was founded in 1982 and so "there is not a lot of old tradition." The vice president of underwriting agreed that "the dynamic organizational culture encourages females, providing them with challenges to demonstrate their ability beyond entry-level positions." She believed that "it is relatively easy to advance." She added, however, that hard workers were valued in the company regardless of their gender.

Of course, not having a long history of authoritarian organizational culture to overcome does not guarantee equal opportunity for women. The economic development agency we studied was founded in 1983, making it a year younger than the insurance company described previously. However, women working in public relations in this state agency (ranked in the 4th percentile on the Excellence scale) labor under the heavy burden of trying to overcome centuries of male domination pervading the larger social culture of the U.S. South.

9. *Mentoring* was mentioned surprisingly few times. However, at least one woman we spoke with touted its value—even when handled informally. She said that her communication department in the chemical company is trying to formalize the mentoring process rather than relying on luck or just happening "to click with others." The publication editor of the experiment station added the understanding that the mentor does not have to be a woman—just "someone who is supportive of a woman." She considered a mentor vital to helping women break into top management, in particular. Finally, although the top communicator at the heart health organization described the mentor as "critical to success," she cited other, individual factors as more important avenues to women's career advancement: being proactive, taking the initiative, developing

leadership skills, broadening one's perspective related to communication, and interacting with others in the organization.

In a related point, the president of a public utility suggested that women must know and relate to the people with whom they deal to move into management positions. He also mentioned mentorship as very important in this process, along with the requisite communication skills and education.

Overall, we sensed a trend toward more inclusivity, more diversity, and more openness to communication—in large part because of the TQM programs that characterize so many of the organizations we studied in depth. In fact, the quality program was equated with a culture change in at least one organization. In a culture described as conservative and dominated by White males, we heard about progress toward more participation because of changing senior management. In the words of the Hispanic woman who serves as a communication specialist there, "The majority who came up in the old culture have taken a buy-out package or retired." Having more women at the highest levels, as we saw in this chemical corporation and in the medical association, may make a positive difference as well.

SUMMARY AND CONCLUSIONS

In this chapter, we have analyzed the organizational context in which excellent public relations is found. In chapter 3, we found that organizational culture and the conditions for women in an organization are the two contextual conditions most highly correlated with an excellent public relations function. However, these two conditions had the lowest correlations of any variables included in the Excellence factor. We interpreted those positive, yet low correlations, to mean that having an excellent *context* for public relations does not guarantee that an organization will have an excellent public relations function. The organization also must have a public relations department with the knowledge to practice strategic, symmetrical public relations and a dominant coalition that understands, values, and supports excellent public relations. Without one or both of these other necessary conditions for excellence, a favorable organizational context means little.

Nevertheless, this chapter demonstrates conclusively that excellent public relations will thrive in an organization with an organic structure, participative culture, and symmetrical system of communication and in which opportunities exist for women and racial-cultural minorities. Although these conditions alone cannot produce excellent public relations, they do establish a hospitable environment for excellent public relations. Most important, these conditions provide a favorable context in which all employees work most effectively—but especially women and minorities. Within such an organization employees are empowered to participate in decision making, As a result, they are more satisfied with the organization and are more likely to support than to oppose the goals of the organization. In addition, employees who are empowered to participate in decision making and to engage in symmetrical internal communication are likely also to be effective symmetrical communicators with members of external publics as well as internal. And, as we saw in chapter 5, the senior public relations person is more likely to be a member of the dominant coalition in organizations that empower more employees to be part of that coalition. Thus, the more empowering the total organization is, the more empowered public relations people will be.

In our long interviews with members of the most and least excellent organizations, we were able to explain our quantitative results further when we found that the structure that leads to the most open communication is the matrix. Although levels exist within a matrix structure, it is less hierarchical than most organizational configurations. Its decentralized, organic management structures offer autonomy to employees. As a result, job satisfaction—both with one's own job and with the organization—is higher than in centralized, stratified, and formalized structures.

We also found that the effective organization provides a hospitable environment for its increasingly diverse workforce. The CEOs and employees we surveyed seemed to agree on all 22 aspects we measured about how women, in particular, are treated in their organizations. Although top management's perceptions were at least somewhat more optimistic, we were encouraged by the general correspondence among the responses from the CEOs, top communicators, and other employees. All three groups of respondents clearly differentiated between areas in which women are most and least supported. The survey data suggested that equitable treatment of women, as evidenced primarily by economic equity, and programs to foster their careers (such as policies against sexual harassment and efforts to encourage women's leadership abilities) are an integral component of excellent organizations. Programs that provide a supportive work environment correlate especially highly with the other conditions found in excellent organizations. Likewise, excellent organizations are beginning to branch out and offer some deliberate mentoring and advancement programs for women. In the final phase of data collection, the case studies, we also found that quality programs offer the real possibility of supporting women and racioethnic minorities—largely through cultural transformation.

Our interviews also revealed that decentralization of operations within the multinational companies we studied and contention with competitors and suppliers from other countries both have presaged a need for two-way public relations. The globalization of business and an increasingly multicultural workforce are just two of the factors we found to be complicating the lives of the top managers we interviewed. Internal communication, in particular, must be open, extensive, symmetrical, and multidirectional rather than closed, secretive, asymmetrical, and top-down. The key is that excellent organizations distribute power and communication throughout. Public relations in the excellent organizations we studied was vested with enough power to implement effective two-way symmetrical programs.

Our data show that when the public relations function is given the power to implement symmetrical programs of communication, the result is a more participative culture and greater employee satisfaction with the organization. However, we also found that symmetrical communication is not likely in an organization with a mechanical structure and authoritarian culture. Organic structure and symmetrical communication interact to produce a participative culture, and participative culture contributes strongly to employee satisfaction with the organization.

An organic structure seems to be critical for developing an effective organization—triggering changes in culture, communication, and satisfaction. Symmetrical communication has a pervasive role in creating and implementing organic structure, but a communicator cannot step into any organization alone and establish an organic structure or symmetrical system of communication. The top communicator must work with the dominant coalition to develop an organic structure for the organization while he or she is developing a system of symmetrical communication. This chapter, therefore, supports not only the need for symmetrical communication in an effective organization but also the need for the public relations function to be represented in the dominant coalition to create the organic structural context that is necessary to create a participative culture and subsequent employee satisfaction.

REFERENCES

Ash, M. K. (1995). *Mary Kay you can have it all: Lifetime wisdom from America's foremost woman entrepreneur.* Rosevale, CA: Prima.

Burns, T., & Stalker, G. M. (1961). *The management of innovation.* London: Tavistock.

Child, J. (1972). Organizational structure, environment, and performance: The role of strategic choice. *Sociology, 6*(1), 2–22.

D'Aprix, R. M. (1996). *Communicating for change: Connecting the workplace with the marketplace.* San Francisco: Jossey-Bass.

Deal, T. E., & Kennedy, A. E. (1982). *Corporate culture: The rites and rituals of corporate life.* Reading, MA: Addison-Wesley.

Downs, C. W., Clampitt, G. G., & Pfeifer, A. L. (1988). Communication and organizational outcomes. In G. M. Goldhaber & G. A. Barnett (Eds.), *Handbook of organizational communication* (pp. 171–211). Norwood, NJ: Ablex.

Grunig, J. E. (1976). Organizations and public relations: Testing a communication theory. *Journalism Monographs, 46.*

Grunig, J. E. (1985, May). *A structural reconceptualization of the organizational communication audit, with application to a state department of education.* Paper presented at the meeting of the International Communication Association, Honolulu.

Grunig, J. E. (1987, July). An audit of organizational structure, job satisfaction, and the communication system in the Allegany County School System. Cumberland, MD: Allegany County Board of Education.

Grunig, J. E. (1992). Symmetrical systems of internal communication. In J. E. Grunig (Ed.), *Excellence in public relations and communication management* (pp. 531–576). Hillsdale, NJ: Lawrence Erlbaum Associates.

Grunig, J. E., & Grunig, L. A. (1989). Toward a theory of the public relations behavior of organizations: Review of a program of research. In J. E. Grunig & L. A. Grunig (Eds.), *Public relations research annual* (Vol. 1, pp. 27–63). Hillsdale, NJ: Lawrence Erlbaum Associates.

Grunig, J. E., & Hunt, T. (1984). *Managing public relations*. New York: Holt, Rinehart & Winston.

Grunig, L. A., Grunig, J. E., & Ehling, W. P. (1992). What is an effective organization? In J. E. Grunig (Ed.), *Excellence in public relations and communication management* (pp. 65–90). Hillsdale, NJ: Lawrence Erlbaum Associates.

Hage, J. (1965). An axiomatic theory of organizations. *Administrative Science Quarterly, 10*, 289–320.

Hage, J. (1980). *Theories of organizations; Form, process, and transformation*. New York: Wiley.

Hage, J., & Aiken, M. (1967a). Program change and organizational properties: A comparative analysis. *American Journal of Sociology, 72*, 503–519.

Hage, J., & Aiken, M. (1967b). Relationship of centralization to other structural properties. *Administrative Science Quarterly, 12*, 72–91.

Hage, J., & Aiken, M. (1970). *Social change in complex organizations*. New York: Random House.

Hall, R. H. (1987). *Organizations: Structures, processes, and outcomes* (3rd ed.). Englewood Cliffs, NJ: Prentice-Hall.

Hofstede, G. (1980). *Culture's consequences*. Beverly Hills, CA: Sage.

Hull, F., & Hage, J. (1982). Organizing for innovation: Beyond Burns and Stalker's organic type. *Sociology, 16*, 564–577.

Kluckhohn, C. (1951). The study of culture. In D. Lerner & H. Lasswell (Eds.), *The policy sciences: Recent developments in scope and method* (pp. 86–101). Stanford, CA: Stanford University Press.

Lawler, E. E., III (1986). *High-involvement management*. San Francisco: Jossey-Bass.

Locke, E. A. (1976). The nature and causes of job satisfaction. In M. D. Dunnettee (Ed.), *Handbook of industrial and organizational psychology* (pp. 1297–1349). Chicago: Rand McNally.

Mitroff, I. I. (1983). *Stakeholders of the organizational mind*. San Francisco: Jossey-Bass.

Monge, P. R., & Miller, K. I. (1988). Participative processes in organizations. In G. M. Goldhaber & G. A. Barnett (Eds.), *Handbook of organizational communication* (pp. 213–229). Norwood, NJ: Ablex.

Ouchi, W. G. (1981). *Theory Z: How American business can meet the Japanese challenge*. Reading, MA: Addison-Wesley.

Pascale, R. T., & Athos, A. G. (1981). *The art of Japanese management*. New York: Simon & Schuster.

Peters, T. J., & Waterman, R. H., Jr. (1982). *In search of excellence*. New York: Harper & Row.

Robbins, S. P. (1990). *Organization theory: Structure, design, and applications* (3rd ed.). Englewood Cliffs, NJ: Prentice-Hall.

Schein, E. H. (1984). Coming to a new awareness of organizational culture. *Sloan Management Review, 25*, 3–16.

Schein, E. H. (1985). *Organizational culture and leadership*. San Francisco: Jossey-Bass.

Schneider, B. (1985). Organizational behavior. *Annual Review of Psychology, 36*, 573–611.

Schneider (aka L. Grunig), L. A. (1985a). *Organizational structure, environmental niches, and public relations: The Hage-Hull typology of organizations as predictor of communication behavior*. Unpublished doctoral dissertation, University of Maryland, College Park.

Schneider (aka L. Grunig), L. A. (1985b). The role of public relations in four organizational types. *Journalism Quarterly, 62*, 567–576, 594.

Shafer, P. (1994). *Adding value to the public affairs function: Using quality to improve performance*. Washington, DC: Public Affairs Council.

Sriramesh, K., Grunig, J. E., & Buffington, J. (1992). Corporate culture and public relations. In J. E. Grunig (Ed.), *Excellence in public relations and communication management* (pp. 577–595). Hillsdale, NJ: Lawrence Erlbaum Associates.

Van Riel, C. B. M. (1995). *Principles of corporate communication.* London: Prentice-Hall.

Vroom, V. H., & Jago, A. G. (1988). *The new leadership: Managing participation in organizations.* Englewood Cliffs, NJ: Prentice-Hall.

Wallach, E. J. (1983). Individuals and organizations: The cultural match. *Training and Development Journal, 37*(2), 29–36.

Weick, K. E. (1979). *The social psychology of organizing* (2nd ed.). Reading, MA: Addison-Wesley.

CHAPTER TWELVE

New Directions for Research
Suggested by the Excellence Study

We began this book by posing the central research question of the Excellence study: What specific expertise can a public relations function offer, which other management functions cannot offer, that makes an organization more effective both in achieving its own goals and those of society? We provided a tentative answer to that question in the first chapter and then supported our answer with evidence, presented in considerable detail, as we moved through each chapter.

We begin this last chapter with a summary of the research that answered the question with which we opened the book. We believe the research-based portrait of an excellent public relations department that we have painted represents a critical milestone in the history of public relations research. However, it does not mean that research has answered every important research question in public relations. Therefore, we end this book with a look to the future. We identify four important gaps in our knowledge of public relations and recommend research needed to close those gaps.

AN OVERVIEW OF EXCELLENT PUBLIC RELATIONS PRACTICE

The Excellence study has shown that public relations is an unique management function that helps an organization interact with the social and political components of its environment. These components make up the institutional environment of an organization, which consists of publics that affect the ability of the organization to accomplish its goals and that expect organizations to help them accomplish their own goals. Organizations solve problems for society, but they also create problems for society. As a result, organizations are not autonomous units free to make money or to accomplish other goals they set for themselves.

They have relationships with individuals and groups that help set the goals they choose, define what the organization is and does, and affect the success of its strategic decisions and behaviors.

The value of public relations, therefore, can be determined by measuring the quality of the relationships it establishes with the strategic components of its institutional environment. However, not all public relations units are created equal. As we have seen in this book, excellent public relations units—those with a specific set of characteristics—are more likely to contribute to organizational and societal effectiveness than are less excellent units.

Excellent public relations departments serve a *managerial* role as well as a technical role in their organizations. The managerial role of excellent public relations departments goes beyond the administration of public relations programs, however. Excellent public relations units play an important role in the *strategic management* of their organizations. They identify critical publics that affect or are affected by management decisions and that can create issues and crises for the organization. Excellent public relations departments then *strategically plan, administer, and evaluate public relations programs* to communicate with their publics so that the organization can build and maintain good, long-term relationships with them. These strategic programs are developed as a result of environment scanning, they are guided by relationship and conflict management objectives, and they are evaluated both informally and scientifically.

Public relations professionals are one of many interacting subsystems in an organization, so their ability to help shape the strategic direction of the organization depends on the nature of the organization. Excellent public relations professionals, however, do not just adapt themselves to the organizational conditions that affect public relations: culture, structure, the system of internal communication, and conditions for women and employees with diverse backgrounds. Rather they help to shape these *underlying conditions of organizational Excellence.* Excellent public relations departments do not flourish in authoritarian cultures, mechanical structures, asymmetrical communication systems, and organizational conditions that devalue women and minorities. Fortunately, though, an excellent public relations function is not shackled by these conditions. Through participation in strategic decision making and by creating a symmetrical system of internal communication, public relations can help to create the conditions that enhance excellent public relations: participative culture, organic structure, symmetrical internal communication, and empowerment of women and minorities.

To do so, excellent public relations professionals must be *empowered* by the dominant coalitions of their organizations. Senior public relations officers either are part of this power elite themselves or they have ready access to other managers with the most power in the organization. The members of the dominant coalition and their public relations staffers share expectations for what public relations is and what it should help the organization accomplish.

In organizations with excellent public relations functions, communication activities are *integrated* into a central public relations department or coordinated through a senior corporate communication executive. Excellent public relations departments seldom report to another management function such as marketing, human resources, or finance. Public relations activities also are *not subordinated* to the role of providing only technical communication support for marketing or other management functions—although they do help other management functions manage communication.

Excellent public relations departments interact with publics in a way that is both *two-way* and *symmetrical*. They disclose relevant information to publics; but, most important, they also listen to publics both informally and formally through qualitative and quantitative research. Excellent public relations departments communicate symmetrically with publics in an attempt to balance their organization's self-interests with the interests of publics. They understand that public relations is dialogue and that its purpose is to manage conflict and build, maintain, and enhance relationships. Through two-way and symmetrical communication, excellent public relations departments become *ethics counselors* to management and *internal advocates of social responsibility*. The Excellence study also showed that public relations can enhance the financial success of an organization without reducing its social responsibility.

At the core of the excellent public relations practice we have just described is the knowledge and professionalism of communicators. More than anything else, excellent public relations departments are characterized by a *professional base of knowledge*—especially the knowledge needed to play a managerial, strategic, symmetrical, and ethics role in an organization. Increasingly, excellent public relations practitioners have studied public relations formally in a university, continuing education program, or lectures and seminars of a professional organization. Even more commonly, excellent practitioners continually read, study, and learn—through books, scholarly journals, and professional publications. They think about and approach their work like a scholar: thinking, searching the literature, planning, and evaluating what they do.

This brief description of excellent public relations programs may at first seem obvious and simple. Why, one might ask, would the Excellence research team need 15 years and three books to paint this clear and simple portrait of excellence? When we look below the surface of this summary, we are confronted by a much more perplexing question: Why do relatively few public relations people practice public relations in this excellent, effective way? Part of the answer lies in the last characteristic of excellence we mentioned: the lack of knowledge by most public relations practitioners needed to practice public relations as a managerial, strategic, two-way, symmetrical, and ethical function.

The rest of the answer lies in the body of knowledge available to public relations professionals. Even excellent public relations staffers are practicing with a body of knowledge that is limited in some critical areas. The foundations for the body of knowledge to practice excellent public relations have been developed both through research by academic scholars and the experience of enlightened practitioners. Nevertheless, when we reflect on what we heard and observed in the Excellence study, we can identify critical areas of research needed to help excellent public relations professionals fulfill the role we identified. The Excellence study has provided a framework for the professional practice of public relations. In some areas, we believe the framework has been filled with well-developed theories—such as in public relations roles, two-way communication, symmetrical communication, gender and communication, integration of communication activities, and internal communication.

In this last chapter, however, we describe four areas in which we believe additional research is needed to develop better theories and practical methods. These areas are the globalization of public relations, strategic management and the nature of relationships, ethics, and the role of public relations in change. In all of these areas, research has begun; so we describe each area and summarize the research underway.

GLOBALIZATION OF PUBLIC RELATIONS

Although the Excellence study was conducted in only three English-speaking countries, it has generated a great deal of interest among public relations scholars and practitioners worldwide. We have lectured about the study in more than 35 countries, ranging from Chile and Brazil in South America; China, Taiwan, and Korea in Asia; Australia and New Zealand in the South Pacific; South Africa in Africa; the United Arab Emirates and Egypt in the Middle East; and in many of the European countries. With so much global interest in the study, however, researchers must pause to ask if the principles of public relations are the same around the world.

Most organizations are affected by publics throughout the world or by competition or collaboration with organizations in other countries. As a result, all public relations is global or international. Thus, it becomes imperative for public relations professionals to have a broad perspective that will allow them to work in many countries—or to work collaboratively with public relations professionals, employees, or customers from many countries.

In public relations as well as in related fields such as management and marketing, scholars and practitioners have asked whether the principles and practices of their profession are the same regardless of the country in which they are practiced or whether the profession must be enacted differently in each country. On the one hand, public relations would not be a global profession if it had to be practiced differently in each country; and professionals in international associations such as the IABC or the International Public Relations Association (IPRA) would have little in common and little to share. On the other hand, there is great danger of ethnocentrism if scholars and practitioners from one country, region, or cultural grouping decide that their way of practicing public relations is most appropriate for all other parts of the world. Ethnocentrism is particularly dangerous for public relations because that profession often has been said to have developed in the United States and to be a U.S. profession and because North Americans are notoriously ethnocentric.

The great interest in the Excellence study worldwide suggests that the theoretical principles we have identified here are not limited to the United States and that they are applicable to public relations practice outside the three Anglo countries where the study was conducted. Although the United States, Canada, and the United Kingdom are similar in many ways, they also exhibit cultural, political, and social differences. Thus, the fact that we found no difference in excellent public relations among the three countries provides some evidence that the principles are not limited strictly to the United States.

Nevertheless, we believe that the first important research problem that should be addressed after the Excellence study is the need for a global theory of public relations. There is a substantial literature already on international public relations, but it consists mostly of descriptive research on and case studies of public relations practice in many countries of the world (as found, e.g., in Culbertson & Chen, 1996). Many of these studies suggest that public relations is practiced in substantially different ways in different countries—often reflecting cultural differences. At the same time, research has shown that the same four models of public relations we have used to describe U.S. practice (press agentry, public information, two-way asymmetrical, and two-way symmetrical) also describe practice in other countries (J. Grunig, L. Grunig, Sriramesh, Huang, & Lyra, 1995).

Research shows that the relative proportion of public relations practice that falls into these four models differs among countries, however. The one true universal of public relations practice around the world seems to be the press agentry/publicity model—the most antiquated and ineffective approach to our profession (see, e.g., Ali, 1995; Kaur, 1997; Scholz, 1998; see also J. Grunig et al., 1995).

The literature describing public relations practice in several countries suggests that public relations suffers from limited and confused concepts—limited to media relations and confused with advertising and marketing—often brought about by a lack of qualified professionals.[1] The United States was no exception. The press agentry model characterized much of the early practice of public relations in the United States; and, as the Excellence study has shown, it

---

[1]That generalization has been reported for China (Black, 1990–1991; Pintak, 1992), Spain (Noguero i Grau, 1992), Brazil (Giagrande, 1991), Israel (Eshkol, 1992), the Philippines (Nieva, 1993), Mexico (Noriega de Aragon, 1990), Japan (Japan PR Directory, 1991), India (Sriramesh, 1992), France (Tixier, 1993), Malaysia, and Singapore (VanLeuven, 1994).

continues to be practiced in all three countries we studied. Thus, U.S. ethnocentrism may indeed have negatively influenced the practice of public relations worldwide by disseminating this outdated and superficial model of media relations, publicity, and "image making" to practitioners in other countries.

A Normative Theory of Generic Principles and Specific Applications

Rather than continuing to conduct purely positive (i.e., descriptive) research on public relations, we propose that scholars construct a normative theory of excellent global public relations. A normative theory would specify how public relations *should be practiced*. A good normative theory is based on sound theory, but it also is built from research to identify the most effective existing, or positive, practices of public relations. This is exactly what we have done in the Excellence study, and the summary of our research at the beginning of this chapter qualifies as a potential normative theory for global public relations practice.

Before we can adopt the Excellence principles as a normative theory for global practice, we must do research to ensure that they are not an ethnocentric theory. At the same time, we do not believe that different polycentric theories are necessary for each country, region, or culture of the world. Verčič, L. Grunig, and J. Grunig (1996), L. Grunig, J. Grunig, and Verčič (1998), and Wakefield (1996) have collaborated to propose a global public relations theory of generic principles and specific applications—a middle-ground theory between an ethnocentric theory and polycentric theories.

"Generic principles" means that in an abstract sense, the principles of public relations are the same worldwide. "Specific applications" means that these abstract principles must be applied differently in different settings. For example, the concept of employee participation in decision making is the same concept throughout the world. However, when Stohl (1993) asked managers in Denmark, Germany, France, England, and the Netherlands how they implemented that principle, she found that they did so differently in each country—in ways that reflected the culture of their country.

As a starting point for research, we have proposed that our principles of excellence are generic principles. We also have proposed that public relations professionals must take six contextual conditions into account when they apply the principles:

- Culture, including language.
- The political system.
- The economic system.
- The media system.
- The level of economic development.

• The extent and nature of activism.

Our research to date has provided evidence supporting this theory of generic principles and specific applications. The most extensive test of the theory came in Slovenia. L. Grunig et al. (1998) replicated the quantitative portion of the Excellence study with 30 Slovenian firms with public relations departments. They found that the principles of excellence clustered into the same Excellence factor in Slovenia as they did in the United States, Canada, and the United Kingdom in spite of a different cultural, political, and economic context.

At the same time, the research showed that Slovenian practitioners were less involved in strategic management and were less valued by senior management than were practitioners in the English-speaking countries. We also found that privatization and political change in Slovenia had encouraged activism to the extent that it is now similar to that of the other countries. However, the old Yugoslavian cultural, political, and economic context in Slovenia had left its remnants inside Slovenian organizations, which still had more authoritarian cultures, asymmetrical communication systems, and low levels of job satisfaction than organizations in the Anglo countries.

To deal with these differences, public relations practitioners in Slovenia found it necessary to apply the generic principles differently than in the Anglo countries. For example, they learned that they needed to counsel CEOs to support and empower public relations managers. They also developed continuing education in public relations to deal with the lack of public relations knowledge, and they had to emphasize employee relations because of the negative context inside Slovenian organizations.

Wakefield (1997) asked a Delphi panel of 23 public relations experts in 18 countries to evaluate the extent to which they believed that the Excellence principles were generic principles that applied to their countries and whether additional principles were needed. He also asked them whether all of the six specific conditions were important for applying the generic principles. With the exception of the need for diversity in public relations departments, he found consensus that these principles are generic and that the list of specific conditions is complete. Wakefield (2000) also conducted a second Delphi study, which extended the database to 54 experts in 29 countries, and again found support for the principles of excellence and the contextual variables

Wakefield (2000, 2001) has begun research on the implications of this theory of generic principles and specific applications for the organization of a public relations function in a multinational organization and of the implications for using public relations firms in different countries. He found that in organizations with what he called a "world class" public relations function the generic principles provided a framework for public relations practice in all countries. However, he found that these world-class companies did not centralize the function or control it through the headquarters office. Rather:

- International public relations officers functioned as a global team with frequent interaction among headquarters and local officers and among local officers.

- The senior public relations officer at headquarters served as a team leader for achieving mutual goals and not as the only decision maker in a hierarchical structure.

- Ideas and solutions came from any source in the global team.

- The global team cooperatively set public relations values and guidelines, but every unit created and carried out local strategies based on these guidelines. (p. 69)

Another test of the theory came in Korea. Rhee (1999) replicated major portions of the Excellence study and also produced an index of excellence almost identical to the Excellence factor developed in chapter 3. As was true in Slovenia, however, she found that fewer Korean professionals were involved in strategic management than in the Anglo countries; and she learned that they had less knowledge of the two-way models and managerial role. She also found that symmetrical public relations in Korea had been adapted to fit Confucian culture, with its emphasis on hierarchical relationships combined with collective responsibility.

As we search for and test generic principles of public relations, we have found it beneficial to begin with the Excellence principles. However, it is important to remain open to revision of these principles and to the addition of new ones so that the generic principles are truly global and not ethnocentric. In that regard, Verčič et al. (1996) interviewed three principals of the public relations firm Pristop in Slovenia to determine if they agreed that the Excellence principles are generic, to ask them how they adapted the principles in their country, and to suggest additional principles.

The interviews confirmed the importance of the existing principles and provided examples of context-specific applications of the principles. In addition, the Slovenian professionals suggested a new generic principle: Ethics is a necessary component of excellent public relations. They pointed out that in the post-socialist context of Slovenia, corruption was common and the suspicion of corruption even more common. Therefore, they suggested that ethical practice was a crucial element of excellent public relations in order to avoid damage both to their individual reputations as well as to the reputation of the public relations profession.

Although we referred to integrity tangentially throughout the three books on the Excellence project, we did not include it as a principle of excellence or ask questions about it directly in our research. At this point, however, we have added ethical practice to our list of generic principles and consider ethics as an important area that needs additional study.

Research, therefore, is well underway on a normative theory of global public relations; but much more research is needed in many countries of the world to confirm the importance of the generic principles, to refine existing principles, to identify new principles, and to provide positive examples of how to apply the principles in the different local contexts in which global public relations professionals work.

Research on International Activism

Of the six specific conditions that we believe affect the local application of generic principles of public relations, the level of activism probably has received the least attention from practitioners and is least likely to come to mind when public relations people think of the contextual conditions that affect public relations practice. Yet, activism might be the most important of the six conditions. As we saw in chapter 10, activism provides an important incentive for organizations to practice excellent public relations. We found that all organizations in our English-speaking sample experienced activism but that excellent public relations departments responded to it more effectively than did less excellent ones.

In the replication of the Excellence study in Slovenia, J. Grunig and L. Grunig (1997) reported that Slovenian organizations experienced about the same level of activist pressure as organizations in Canada, the United States, and the United Kingdom. Slovenian organizations, however, had not developed the same effective means of dealing with activism as had organizations in the Anglo countries. Activism was relatively new in Slovenia in the postsocialist period, so even excellent public relations departments had not learned how to cope with it.

Although every country experiences some form of activism, it generally is less prevalent in countries with collective cultures and authoritarian political systems. Under those conditions, organizations feel less pressure for excellent public relations. As a result, public relations practitioners must develop rationales for excellent practice other than the threat of consequences of activism on organizational autonomy. Researchers can help professionals in different cultures and political systems discover and develop such rationales. Examples are the values of responsibility and collectivism found in Confucian cultures.

Activist groups occupy a central role in public relations. They constrain organizations when they oppose organizational behaviors, but collaboration with activist groups also can provide organizations with a strategic advantage (Verčič & J. Grunig, 2000). Therefore, we need research to understand how activist groups develop and how they behave once they have developed.

Most public relations research on activist groups has emphasized the individual level of analysis—that is, researchers have looked for variables that explain why individuals are motivated to join activist groups. The most common of these variables have come from J. Grunig's situational theory of publics: problem recognition, level of involvement, and constraint recognition (J. Grunig, 1989, 2000; J. Grunig, 1997). Sociologists and political scientists, however, have developed an extensive body of knowledge on social movements that includes the effect of macrolevel conditions such as culture and political systems on the origins of activist groups (e.g., Buechler, 2000; McAdam, McCarthy, & Zald, 1988). To develop a global theory of public relations, scholars should build on that literature to explore how and why activism develops differently under different contexts.[2]

McAdam et al. (1988) pointed out that little research has been done at a level between the "macro and micro factors that make movements and individual activism more likely" (p. 729):

> How do macro and micro propensities get translated into specific mobilization attempts? What are the actual dynamics by which movement activists reach decisions regarding goals and tactics? How concretely do SMOs [social movement organizations] seek to recruit new members? To answer these questions, what is needed is more systematic qualitative fieldwork in the dynamics of collective action at the intermediate meso level. We remain convinced that it is *the* level at which most movement action occurs and of which we know the least. (p. 779)

McAdam et al.'s call for more meso-level research on activism mirrors the call by Karlberg (1996) and Dozier and Lauzen (2000) for more research on how activist groups conduct, and should conduct, public relations. They pointed out that activist groups play a major role in representing the interests of publics and that scholars should devote as much attention to helping them develop a normative theory of public relations as they do to the other clients or employers of public relations professionals: powerful corporations and government agencies.

J. Grunig (2000) suggested that a normative theory of activist public relations should be based on the same generic principles as a normative theory for more powerful organizations—principles such as symmetrical communication, relationship building, and ethical behavior. In a study of activists pressuring the British Broadcasting Corporation, Kovacs (1998) found evidence that the most successful activists do indeed follow such principles.

Additional research on activism, therefore, would make public relations theory more global in at least two ways. It would help us to understand how this important incentive for excellent public relations develops in different countries. And, it would help to make the theory of excellent public relations more applicable in all kinds of organizations—those that apply activist pressure as well as those that experience the pressure in a democratic society.

---

[2]We acknowledge the contribution of Jeong-Nam Kim, a doctoral student at the University of Maryland, who identified much of this literature and developed a theory of activism with three levels of analysis.

RELATIONSHIP BUILDING IN STRATEGIC MANAGEMENT

The results of the Excellence study presented throughout this book have highlighted the central importance of participation in the strategic decision processes of an organization if a public relations department is to contribute to organizational effectiveness. Public relations makes an organization more effective, the data have shown:

- First, when it identifies the strategic publics that develop because of the consequences that organizations and publics have on each other.
- Second, when it uses symmetrical communication programs to develop and maintain quality long-term relationships with these strategic publics.

Although the excellent public relations practitioners we studied had developed procedures for scanning the environment to identify strategic publics and for assessing the quality of their organizations' relationships with these publics, most of these procedures remain rudimentary. As a result, we believe much additional research is needed to develop ways for public relations managers to participate in strategic management, to cultivate relationships with publics, and to assess the quality of these relationships.

As we discussed in chapter 5, public relations managers often follow a *marketing/message approach* to strategic management rather than the *full-participation approach* we described in that chapter. When they take a marketing/message approach, public relations managers cling to their typical behavior of waiting outside the door when strategic decisions are made. When they are called to the decision-making table, the important decisions have been made; and the public relations role is limited to choosing message strategies to promote and advocate those decisions. Typically, this is called "aligning messages with organizational goals." Too often, however, public relations people are forced to align messages with bad decisions—decisions whose consequences on publics have not been taken into account. As a result, they can contribute little to organizational effectiveness. Also, "strategic public relations" differs little from the traditional press agentry/publicity model of public relations. The only difference is that public relations practitioners align messages with organizational decisions and goals rather than publicize messages indiscriminately.

In 1997, Broom, Casey, and Ritchey wrote an article that renewed the interest of public relations scholars in Ferguson's (1984) suggestion that the central concept of public relations should be the relationship between an organization and its publics—a concept that also played a major role in our conceptualization of the Excellence theory. Broom and his colleagues developed a three-stage model of relationship management, which included antecedents of relationships, concepts of relationships, and outcomes of relationships.

J. Grunig and Huang (2000) used that model as a springboard to develop a similar three-stage model of the public relations process that incorporated strategic management of public relations, the models of public relations, and relationship outcomes into a single theory. The first stage consisted of environmental scanning to identify the strategic publics with which an organization needs relationships. The second stage incorporated the models of public relations into a set of communication strategies for developing and maintaining relationships with these publics. The third stage consisted of a set of relationship outcomes that could be used to assess the quality of organization–public relationships and, as a result, the contribution that public relations makes to organizational effectiveness. We believe these three stages provide an important framework for future research in public relations.

Environmental Scanning and Strategic Management

Chang (2000) conducted a Delphi study of senior public relations managers in major U.S. corporations and found that only a few of them reported using a sophisticated system of environmental scanning in their department. Most were skeptical that public relations professionals had the skills to do environmental scanning. Most also said they believed senior management did not have confidence in the ability of public relations professionals to be environmental scanners. Some did not even understand the term "environmental scanning," believing that it had something to do with reacting to pollution and other natural environmental issues.

In chapter 5, we saw that public relations managers reported contributing to strategic management more often using "judgment based on experience," "informal methods," and "contacts outside the organization" than formal research methods. In our qualitative research, we found that participation in strategic management meant different things to public relations professionals—even the excellent ones. In one case, strategic planning was done strictly on a financial basis and was no more than numbers crunching. In another case, strategic management in public relations referred almost exclusively to media relations. In other organizations, however, participation in strategic management involved environmental scanning and was an integral part of the public relations function.

As a result of this confusion and limited knowledge about strategic management and environmental scanning, we believe that much more research is needed to identify and develop methods of environmental scanning that public relations professionals can use when they participate in strategic decision processes. Books by Stoffels (1994) and Heath (1997) provide some ideas for these methods, but research is needed to explicate unique public relations methods of environmental scanning. In particular, we believe research is needed to learn how to use the Internet for identifying publics, activist groups, and issues—a process we call "cyber scanning." We also need methods for predicting scenarios that might result from the consequences of potential organizational decisions on publics. Insights might be found in chaos theory—as described by the familiar question of whether a butterfly flapping its wings in Brazil might have the consequence of causing a tornado in Texas (Aula, 1996). Many management decisions have such spreading effects, and public relations professionals need methods to detect which decisions might cause a tornado a continent away. Further research into the behavior of activist groups will help us construct such scenarios.

Strategies for Developing and Maintaining Relationships

After a strategic public relations manager has used formative research to identify the publics with which an organization needs relationships and the problems and issues that exist or might exist, a public relations staff should formulate objectives for programs to communicate with these strategic publics. Because the value of public relations to an organization and society exists in the relationships developed with strategic publics, objectives should consist of *strategies to develop, maintain, and enhance relationships* and the *relationship outcomes* that the organization strives to achieve with these strategies. Strategies to develop and maintain relationships can be specified as *process objectives* for public relations programs. Relationship outcomes can be specified as *outcome objectives*

Most of the knowledge that public relations professionals possess has something to do with how to communicate with publics to develop and maintain a relationship with those publics. Not all strategies for developing and maintaining relationships are equally effective, however. We must recognize that not all public relations strategies, techniques, and programs are equally likely to produce quality relationship outcomes. The Excellence study has shown that maintenance strategies that are symmetrical in nature generally are more effective than asymmetrical strategies.

In future research and theory building, therefore, we believe that the models of public relations should be integrated into a larger set of strategies for developing and maintaining relationships between organizations and publics. We developed our initial knowledge of these strategies by studying the models of public relations. We believe this knowledge can be expanded, however, by incorporating theories of conflict resolution and interpersonal communication into our maintenance strategies for organization–public relationships. Plowman (1996) and Huang (1997) conducted the first research using these literatures to expand our knowledge of public relations strategies.

Particularly promising, we believe, is the dialectical/dialogical approach to relationships developed by Baxter and Montgomery (1996). This approach recognizes the essential tension in all relationships—of wanting to be together and, at the same time, desiring autonomy. As we pointed out in chapter 8, Baxter and Montgomery's approach captures well the idea underlying the two-way symmetrical model that critics often have failed to understand. Symmetrical communication does not move relationships inexorably to consensus, equilibrium, or harmony. Rather, it is the give-and-take of persuasion and collaboration that organizations and publics use when they must interact with each other. Although both might prefer autonomy, they cannot have it because their actions have consequences on the other. Thus, they struggle to pursue their self-interest while simultaneously taking the interests of the other into account.

To fully understand how to improve relationships, we must develop theoretical strategies that manage their inherent dialectical tensions. Hon and J. Grunig (1999) developed a preliminary list of such maintenance strategies derived from Plowman's and Huang's research and from other academic studies of relationships and conflict resolution. We provide this list here as a starting point for additional research on maintenance strategies:

- **Access.** Members of publics or community or activist leaders provide access to public relations people. Public relations representatives or senior managers provide representatives of publics similar access to organizational decision-making processes.
- **Disclosure or openness.** Both organizations and members of publics are open and frank with each other. They are willing to disclose their thoughts, concerns, and problems as well as their satisfaction or dissatisfaction with each other.
- **Assurances of legitimacy.** Each party in the relationship attempts to assure the other that it and its concerns are legitimate and to demonstrate that it is committed to maintaining the relationship.
- **Networking.** Organizations build networks or coalitions with the same groups that their publics do, such as environmentalists, unions, or community groups.
- **Sharing of tasks.** Organizations and publics share in solving joint or separate problems. Examples of such tasks are managing community issues, providing employment, conducting high-quality research, and maintaining funding. These are in the interest of the organization, the public, or both.
- **Integrative strategies of conflict resolution.** These approaches are symmetrical because all parties in a relationship benefit by searching out common or complementary interests and solving problems together through open discussion and joint decision making. The goal is a *win–win* solution that values the integrity of a long-term relationship between an organization and its publics. **Integrative** strategies are more effective than **distributive** strategies, which are asymmetrical because one party benefits at the expense of another by seeking to maximize gains and minimize losses

within a *win–lose* or self-gain perspective. Distributive tactics include trying to control through domination, argument, insistence on a position, or
showing anger. Other forcing strategies are faulting the other party, hostile questioning, presumptive attribution, demands, or threats. Distributive strategies impose one's position onto that of an adversary without
concern for the adversary's position.

Relationship Outcomes

We and other public relations researchers who have studied the literature on relationships in related disciplines have identified key characteristics of relationships and have developed measures of the quality of long-term organization–public relationships. Hon and J. Grunig (1999) identified two types of
relationships and Huang (1997, 2001) and J. Grunig and Huang (2000) identified
four relationship outcomes that we believe define the quality of long-term relationships. These indicators can be measured periodically to monitor the overall
effect of public relations programs on each strategic public and, therefore, the
value that the public relations function has to an organization.

Types of Relationships.[3]   The psychologists Clark and Mills (1993) identified
two types of interpersonal relationships that also help explain the desired nature
of the relationship between an organization and a public. One type, a communal
relationship, describes the kind of relationship cultivated by a public relations
program, in comparison with the exchange type of relationship produced by
other fields such as marketing.

In an **exchange relationship,** one party gives benefits to the other only because the other has provided benefits in the past or is expected to do so in the future. In an exchange relationship, a party is willing to give benefits to the other
because it expects to receive benefits of comparable value from the other. In essence, a party that receives benefits incurs an obligation or debt to return the favor. Exchange is the essence of marketing relationships between organizations
and customers and is the central concept of marketing theory. However, an exchange relationship usually is not enough for a public. Publics expect an organization to do things for the community and its stakeholders for which organizations sometimes get little or nothing in return—at least in the short run.

In a **communal relationship,** both parties provide benefits to the other because they are concerned for the welfare of the other—even when they get
nothing in return. The role of public relations is to convince management that it
also needs communal relationships with publics such as employees, the com-

---

[3]We acknowledge the contribution of Chun-ju Hung, a doctoral student at the University of
Maryland, who identified these types of relationships in the literature.

munity, and the media. Public relations professionals add value to an organization when they develop communal relationships with all publics affected by organizational behaviors—not just those who give the organization something in return. Communal relationships are important if organizations are to be socially responsible and to add value to society as well as to client organizations.

This is not to say, however, that exchange relationships are bad for an organization or that public relations professionals do not attempt to develop them. Relationships often begin as exchanges and then develop into communal relationships as they mature. At other times, public relations professionals may need to build a communal relationship with a public before an exchange can occur. Nevertheless, a measure of the degree to which a public perceives that it has a communal relationship with an organization is perhaps the purest indicator of the success of the public relations management function.

Relationship Outcomes.   Researchers have identified many characteristics that define the quality of a relationship. However, Huang (1997, 2001), J. Grunig and Huang (2000), and Hon and J. Grunig (1999) isolated four of these characteristics that we believe are especially important for measuring the quality of organization–public relationships. Of the four, our research suggests that indicators at the top of the following list are most important and that the importance of the characteristics declines as we move down the list:

- **Control mutuality**—the degree to which parties agree on who has rightful power to influence one another. Although some degree of power imbalance is natural in organization–public relationships, the most stable, positive relationships exist when organizations and publics have some degree of control over the other.
- **Trust**—one party's level of confidence in and willingness to open oneself to the other party. Trust is a complicated concept, which has several underlying dimensions. One of these is integrity, the belief that an organization is fair and just. A second is dependability, the belief that an organization will do what it says it will do. A third is competence, the belief that an organization has the ability to do what it says it will do.
- **Commitment**—the extent to which one party believes that the relationship is worth spending energy on to maintain and promote.
- **Satisfaction**—the extent to which one party feels favorably toward the other because positive expectations about the relationship are reinforced. A satisfying relationship is one in which the benefits outweigh the costs. Satisfaction also can occur when one party believes the other party is engaging in positive steps to maintain the relationship.

Research on public relations as relationship management represents one of the most important new areas of research in the discipline. In addition to the initial research that we and our colleagues have conducted, other scholars such as Ledingham and Bruning (1998, 2000) and Bruning and Ledingham (2000) have developed concepts of relationship outcomes similar to ours. We recommend again additional research on relationships as a way of developing a powerful, integrated theory of public relations management.

PUBLIC RELATIONS AND ETHICS

At the end of the earlier section in this chapter on globalization of public relations, we added the notion of public relations and ethics to our generic principles of public relations. Public relations professionals in Slovenia, as we noted there, suggested ethics as an additional generic concept when we asked them if the list of principles from the Excellence study was complete. If we are to add ethics as a generic principle to our global theory of public relations, however, we must acknowledge the need for additional research to develop a theory of ethical decision making in public relations.

Public relations scholars and practitioners have written a great deal about ethics, and most public relations societies have codes of ethics. However, most of what has been written has concerned the personal ethics of practitioners and the relationships among practitioners and their clients. Such ethical problems have included the giving and taking of gifts, dealing with the media, competing for new business, service to clients, fee structures, lying, accuracy, concealment, accountability for results, confidentiality, whistle blowing, gender and diversity, and multicultural issues. In addition, much has been written about the ethics of public relations as a profession, including the role of advocacy and the balancing of loyalty to a client or employer vis-à-vis the public interest.

We have far too little research on these problems, and few, if any, formal ethical theories to deal with them. Even more important than these personal questions, however, is the role of public relations in the ethical decision making of organizations. Our research on excellent public relations suggests that public relations can be the ethical conscience of an organization—the management function primarily responsible for introducing moral values and social responsibility into organizational decisions.

Management theorists have suggested the need for such an ethics role, although few have realized that public relations can fill it. For example, Freeman and Gilbert (1988) pointed out that management theorists have made two "discoveries": (a) organizations consist of human beings who have values, values that help to explain how managers make strategic decisions; and (b) in making strategic choices organizations have found that outside groups—stakeholders—such as customers, suppliers, communities, governments, owners, and employees affect and are affected by the choices organizations make. Thus Freeman and Gilbert stated two axioms of corporate strategy:

- Corporate strategy must reflect an understanding of the values of organizational members and stakeholders.
- Corporate strategy must reflect an understanding of the ethical nature of strategic choice. (pp. 6–7)

Many organizations have developed the position of an ethics officer to monitor the ethics of behavior in those organizations (Petry & Tietz, 1992). Ethics officers can incorporate ethics and responsibility into the formal rules and structure and the cultural values of those organizations; but most ethics officers are not public relations practitioners or even part of a public relations department. Nevertheless, as Budd (1992) said, public relations can be the formal mechanism that incorporates questions of ethics and responsibility into organizational decision making. Public relations is the function that introduces the values and problems of stakeholders into strategic decisions and that introduces a moral element to those decisions.

For public relations practitioners to serve as ethics officers for organizations, however, we believe it is necessary to address the ethics of public relations as a profession and to incorporate ethics and social responsibility into our normative theories of how public relations should contribute to the strategic decision processes of organizations. Most important, we must build our theories of ethical public relations from established philosophical theories of ethics—something rarely done in the literature on public relations ethics.

Ethicists throughout history have developed two major kinds of theories: (a) teleological theories, which emphasize the consequences of one's behavior on others, and (b) deontological or rules-based theories. *Consequentialist* theories seem to be a relevant starting point for public relations ethics because of the central role of consequences in public relations. We believe that a public relations problem exists when an organization has consequences on a public or a public on an organization. In addition, organizations have a social responsibility when they have consequences on publics or on society as a whole.

By contrast, Pearson (1989) developed a *deontological* theory of public relations ethics based on the idea of an ideal communication situation proposed by the German communication scholar Jurgen Habermas. Pearson proposed two rules of ethical public relations:

1. It is a moral imperative to establish and maintain communication relationships with all publics affected by organizational action.
2. It is a moral imperative to improve the quality of these communication relationships, that is, to make them increasingly dialogical [symmetrical]. (p. 377)

The first of these rules essentially specifies that it is necessary for an organization to take consequences on publics into account when it makes strategic decisions. The second states that organizations have the moral obligation to communicate with those publics even though the organization cannot always accommodate the public.

J. Grunig and L. Grunig (1996) proposed that Pearson's two moral imperatives can be translated into an ethical theory of public relations that incorporates both a teleological and a deontological perspective:

- Teleology: Ethical public relations professionals ask what consequences potential organizational decisions have on publics.
- Deontology: Ethical public relations professionals then have the moral obligation to disclose these consequences to publics that are affected and to engage in dialogue with the publics about the potential decisions.

Bowen (2000) developed a deontological theory of ethical decision making in public relations based on Immanuel Kant's concept of a categorical imperative and extensive interviews with public relations professionals in case studies of two highly ethical organizations. Her model proceeds in stages that essentially elaborate on the two principles of Pearson (1989) and J. Grunig and L. Grunig (1996):

- Stage 1 asks whether one is acting on the basis of reason alone and not because of political influence, monetary influence, or pure self-interest.
- Stage 2 applies the Categorical Imperative and asks questions such as, "Would this organization accept this decision if it were on the receiving end?"
- Stage 3 asks the organization to consider its duty, its intention, and dignity and respect for the organization, publics, and society.
- Stage 4 calls for symmetrical communication about the results of the decision-making process.

We believe that the most important question for public relations ethics is the problem of divided loyalties that is inherent in public relations: How can one balance the interests of the organization with the interests of its publics, as well as the interests of society, of the public relations profession, and of the individual professional? We do not believe that pure advocacy or total loyalty to the client organization is the answer to this problem. Rather, we believe ethical principles that help one balance divided loyalties and engage in symmetrical communication provide a better answer. Bowen (2000) has made great progress toward such an ethical theory. As is the case with other research problems discussed in this chapter, however, we believe additional research is necessary.

PUBLIC RELATIONS AND CHANGE

In the very first book on public relations, Edward L. Bernays described this new profession as an applied social science with a capacity to bring order out of the *chaos* of accelerating social changes people have a problem dealing with. Unfortunately, anthropologists have shown us that the source of resistance to bad, frivolous, and dangerous change is the same as the resistance to good, necessary, and positive change. Sociological and psychological theorists have found that groups particularly hate change that is forced on them. Thus, the challenge lies in using communication to develop an understanding of, and by, all parties involved in the impending change.

In the Excellence project, we found that five main types of change significantly affect both organizational culture and the practice of public relations. They are:

- *Personnel.* There is a remarkable amount of turnover in the typical organization. Our backgrounds in sociology may have predisposed us on the Excellence research team to devalue the importance of any individual in today's complex corporation or government agency. However, we came to acknowledge that individuals—through their worldviews and their skills—actually do transform organizational processes.
- *Crises* represent the most dramatic of the changes we observed. Participants in most organizations talked about increased appreciation for their function on the part of others in the organization, greater access to the dominant coalition as a result, more openness in communication, a new willingness to cooperate with pressure groups, and greater support for or at least understanding of the organization from its community, its clients or customers, the media, and even government regulators.
- *Diversity* is a third major type of change—in the form of both multiculturalism and feminization of the field of public relations. Perhaps as a result, we heard a lot about the glass ceiling—and we learned what the most effective organizations in our sample of more than 300 were trying to do to overcome any lingering discrimination.
- *Quality programs* such as TQM represent a fourth type of change. We heard much skepticism about the real effects of such programs; but because of their emphasis on teamwork, many quality initiatives did seem to empower employees. Another aspect of most quality initiatives is benchmarking, or doing research continuously to measure products or services against best practice. To engage in this kind of communication research requires measurement instruments that help determine the value communication adds to achieving the organization's goals. Sadly, we found that this

know-how both in management and in research is sorely lacking almost across the board.

- The fifth and final type of change we found to be reshaping the way communication is done in contemporary organizations comes about through *interventions by professional associations* such as the IABC or PRSA. The seminars and workshops they sponsor make a real difference in increasing the knowledge base of public relations practitioners.

Nevertheless, change, and especially improvement, in the communication function comes only gradually or incrementally. Change in culture is at least equally slow. We learned that effective, two-way communication actually could transform organizations. At the same time, public relations research has only begun to expand our theories of strategic management, symmetrical communication, and relationship management in a way that will help organizations deal with change. Change is a constant theme in professional publications and at professional conferences, and we repeatedly are asked after presentations on the Excellence project what public relations people can do to manage organizational and public responses to change.

Stroh (1999) is among the forerunners of what we are convinced will represent a major line of inquiry for our field. She reasoned that change, occurring in organizations because of change in their environment, causes conflict. Small clashes may escalate into disordered crises and, ultimately, chaos. Building on the chaos theory, she also hypothesized that strategic communication management could lead to what she considered "positive chaos" and a culture of constant change. Thus public relations serves as a "strange attractor," helping bring order out of disorder. She concluded that strategic communication emerges as more important than ever but will be reconfigured from a premise of control and prediction to scenario planning. The emphasis will be on relationship building.

With change as our backdrop, then, what areas of research related to the strategic management of public relations will be most critical for scholars in our field to pursue in this new millennium? In our view, there are four: globalization; feminization; new technology; and downsizing, mergers, and acquisitions.

New Technology

Let us begin with new technology. The Internet, for just one example, offers two-way, interactive approaches to environmental scanning, symmetrical relationships with publics such as the media and shareholders, and more comprehensive databases than ever before. We need to understand how e-mail, newsgroups, listservs, and online chat rooms are conducive to creating good relationships. The Internet also allows for more potent and far-reaching social inquiry than many other methodologies. However, use of the Internet varies by culture, class, economic status, ethnicity, age, geographical location, and gender.

Feminization

Thus, the discussion of new technology intersects with a second major trend that we have discussed extensively in this book: feminization of the field. The new female majority has been overrepresented in the technical, versus managerial, role in public relations. However, feminist scholars have found no essential differences in the way women and men practice or prefer to practice public relations.

One study explicitly linked new communication technologies with helping women in public relations crash the glass ceiling and ascend to the managerial ranks. Kornegay and L. Grunig (1998) proposed that cyberbridging might help all boundary spanners go beyond their tactical, craft-based function to contribute to the dominant coalition. The cyberbridge is an Internet or electronic means for public relations practitioners to gather information valuable to top-level decision makers in their organizations. By using online databases to monitor issues or conducting e-mail surveys of members of strategic publics, communication managers have the potential to connect with and influence the dominant coalition. This cyberscanning, of course, furthers one's own power base—critically important to women who have been relegated inordinately to the technician's role.

Globalization, Downsizing, Mergers, and Acquisitions

Because of its reach, the Internet leads to a consideration of global issues in public relations practice and scholarship that we discussed earlier in this chapter. In sum, the dynamics of today's chaotic environment require a public relations professional, whether male or female, to assume the responsibility for identifying the organization's most strategic publics as part of the management process. Those publics, typically increasing in their diversity, may be scattered throughout the globe.

Globalization has had several effects. One, which we already discussed in this chapter, has been the spread of activism throughout the world. In addition, globalization itself has been the object of activist pressure, as evidenced by demonstrations against the World Bank and the International Monetary Fund.

The other effect of globalization has been the rush to mergers, acquisitions, and downsizing. We believe the theories of symmetrical internal communication developed in chapter 10 offer promise for organizations dealing with these major changes. However, Guiniven (2001) found that employees in seven organizations he studied that have experienced downsizing developed relationships and loyalty more with each other than with the organization that still employed them. As a result, we believe that much research is needed to develop ways of developing symmetrical communication systems in organizations experiencing major change.

Using research to develop communication programs helps develop effective, long-term relationships with strategic constituencies. Such relationships help the organization achieve its long-term mission because it chooses appropriate goals in the first place—goals consistent with the legitimate yet frequently changing expectations of its stakeholders. Public relations professionals who must deal with change thus are likely to find themselves in the role predicted by Holtzhausen (2000). She envisioned public relations people as in-house activists, actually pushing the organization toward needed change.

REFERENCES

Ali, D. J. (1995). *Societal culture and public relations: A comparative analysis of Trinidad and Antigua, West Indies.* Unpublished master's thesis, University of Maryland, College Park.

Aula, P. S. (1996). Chaos and the double function of communication. In W. Sulis & A. Combs (Eds.), *Non-linear dynamics in human behavior* (Vol. 5, pp. 191–206). Singapore: World Scientific.

Baxter, L. A., & Montgomery, B. M. (1996). *Relating: Dialogues & dialectics.* New York: Guilford.

Black, S. (1990–1991). Public relations in China today. *Public Relations Quarterly, 35*(4), 29–30.

Bowen, S. A. (2000). *A theory of ethical issues management: Contributions of Kantian deontology to public relations' ethics and decision making.* Unpublished doctoral dissertation, University of Maryland, College Park.

Broom, G. M., Casey, S., & Ritchey, J. (1997). Toward a concept and theory of organization–public relationships. *Journal of Public Relations Research, 9*, 83–98.

Bruning, S. D., & Ledingham, J. A. (2000). Organizations and key public relationships: Testing the influence of the relationship dimensions in a business to business context. In J. A. Ledingham & S. D. Bruning (Eds.), *Public relations as relationship management: A relational approach to the study and practice of public relations* (pp. 159–173). Mahwah, NJ: Lawrence Erlbaum Associates.

Budd, J. F., Jr. (1992). *Street smart public relations.* Lakeville, CT: Turtle.

Buechler, S. M. (2000). *Social movements in advanced capitalism.* New York: Oxford University Press.

Chang, Y. C. (2000). *A normative exploration into environmental scanning in public relations.* Unpublished master's thesis, University of Maryland, College Park.

Clark, M. S., & Mills, J. (1993). The difference between communal and exchange relationships: What it is and is not. *Personality and Social Psychology Bulletin, 19*, 684–691.

Culbertson, H. M., & Chen, N. (Eds.). (1996). *International public relations: A comparative analysis.* Mahwah, NJ: Lawrence Erlbaum Associates.

Dozier, D. M., & Lauzen, M. M. (2000). Liberating the intellectual domain from the practice: Public relations, activism, and the role of the scholar. *Journal of Public Relations Research, 12*, 3–22.

Eshkol, D. (1992). PR in Israel: An up-to-date overview. *International Public Relations Review, 15*(2), 5–8.

Ferguson, M. A. (1984, August). *Building theory in public relations: Interorganizational relationships as a public relations paradigm.* Paper presented at the meeting of the Association for Education in Journalism, Gainesville, FL.

Freeman, R. E., & Gilbert, D. R., Jr. (1988). *Corporate strategy and the search for ethics.* Englewood Cliffs, NJ: Prentice-Hall.

Giagrande, V. (1991). Public relations in Brazil. *International Public Relations Review, 14*(3), 21–23.

Grunig, J. E. (1989). Sierra Club study shows who become activists. *Public Relations Review, 15*(3), 3–24.

Grunig, J. E. (1997). A situational theory of publics: Conceptual history, recent challenges and new research. In D. Moss, T. MacManus, & D. Verčič (Eds.), *Public relations research: An international perspective* (pp. 3–46). London: International Thomson Business Press.

Grunig, J. E. (2000). Collectivism, collaboration, and societal corporatism as core professional values in public relations. *Journal of Public Relations Research, 12,* 23–48.

Grunig, J. E., & Grunig, L. A. (1996, May). *Implications of symmetry for a theory of ethics and social responsibility in public relations.* Paper presented at the meeting of the International Communication Association, Chicago.

Grunig, J. E., & Grunig, L. A. (1997, July). *Review of a program of research on activism: Incidence in four countries, activist publics, strategies of activist groups, and organizational responses to activism.* Paper presented at the Fourth Public Relations Research Symposium, Managing Environmental Issues, Bled, Slovenia.

Grunig, J. E., Grunig, L. A., Sriramesh, K., Huang, Y. H., & Lyra, A. (1995). Models of public relations in an international setting. *Journal of Public Relations Research, 7,* 163–186.

Grunig, J. E., & Huang, Y. H. (2000). From organizational effectiveness to relationship indicators: Antecedents of relationships, public relations strategies, and relationship outcomes. In J. A. Ledingham & S. D. Bruning (Eds.), *Public relations as relationship management: A relational approach to the study and practice of public relations* (pp. 23–53). Mahwah, NJ: Lawrence Erlbaum Associates.

Grunig, L. A., Grunig, J. E., & Verčič, D. (1998). Are the IABC's excellence principles generic? Comparing Slovenia and the United States, the United Kingdom and Canada. *Journal of Communication Management, 2,* 335–356.

Guiniven, J. E. (2001). *Communicating with the changing workforce: The role of internal public relations in the transactional cost era of human resources management.* Unpublished doctoral dissertation, University of Maryland, College Park.

Heath, R. L. (1997). *Strategic issues management.* Thousand Oaks, CA: Sage.

Holtzhausen, D. R. (2000). Postmodern values in public relations. *Journal of Public Relations Research, 12,* 93–114.

Hon, L. C., & Grunig, J. E. (1999). *Guidelines for measuring relationships in public relations.* Gainesville, FL: The Institute for Public Relations, Commission on PR Measurement and Evaluation.

Huang, Y. H. (1997). *Public relations strategies, relational outcomes, and conflict management strategies.* Unpublished doctoral dissertation, University of Maryland, College Park.

Huang, Y. H. (2001). OPRA: A cross-cultural, multiple-item scale for measuring organization–public relationships. *Journal of Public Relations Research, 13,* 61–90.

Japan PR Directory. (1991). *Japan's PR industry: Current status and outlook.* Tokyo: Public Relations Society of Japan.

Karlberg, M. (1996). Remembering the public in public relations research: From theoretical to operational symmetry. *Journal of Public Relations Research, 8,* 263–278.

Kaur, K. (1997). *The impact of privatization on public relations and the role of public relations and management in the privatization process: A qualitative analysis of the Malaysian case.* Unpublished doctoral dissertation, University of Maryland, College Park.

Kornegay, J., & Grunig, L. A. (1998). Cyberbridging: How the communication manager role can link with the dominant coalition. *Journal of Communication Management, 3*(2), 140–156.

Kovacs, R. S. (1998). *Pressure group strategies and accountability in British public service broadcasting.* Unpublished doctoral dissertation, University of Maryland, College Park.

Ledingham, J. A., & Bruning, S. D. (1998). Relationship management and public relations: Dimensions of an organization–public relationship. *Public Relations Review, 24,* 55–65.

Ledingham, J. A., & Bruning, S. D. (2000). A longitudinal study of organization-public relationships: Defining the role of communication in the practice of relationship management. In J. A. Ledingham & S. D. Bruning (Eds.), *Public relations as relationship management: A relational approach to the study and practice of public relations* (pp. 55–69). Mahwah, NJ: Lawrence Erlbaum Associates.

McAdam, D., McCarthy, J. D., & Zald, M. N. (1988). Social movements. In N. J. Smelser (Ed.), *Handbook of sociology* (pp. 695–737). Newbury Park, CA: Sage.

Nieva, R. (1993). Public relations in the Philippines. *International Public Relations Review, 16*(2), 5–7.

Norguero i Grau, A. (1992, October). *The structure of Spanish public relations: 1980–1990.* Paper presented at the CERP Education Research Committee Meeting, Brussels, Belgium.

Noriega de Aragon, M. (1990). The communicator's environment in Mexico. *Communication World, 7*(12), 47.

Pearson, R. A. (1989). *A theory of public relations ethics.* Unpublished doctoral dissertation, Ohio University, Athens.

Petry, E. S., Jr., & Tietz, F. (1992). Can ethics officers improve office ethics? *Business and Society Review, 82*(3), 21–25.

Pintak, L. (1992). Counselors eye business in Asia. *Public Relations Journal, 48*(7), 8–9.

Plowman, K. D. (1996). *Congruence between public relations and conflict resolution: Negotiating in the organization.* Unpublished doctoral dissertation, University of Maryland, College Park.

Rhee, Y. (1999). *Confucian culture and excellent public relations: A study of generic principles and specific applications in South Korean public relations practice.* Unpublished master's thesis, University of Maryland, College Park.

Scholz, J. (1998). *A normative approach to the practice of public relations in the Eastern part of Germany.* Unpublished master's thesis, University of Maryland, College Park.

Sriramesh, K. (1992). Societal culture and public relations: Ethnographic evidence from India. *Public Relations Review, 18,* 201–212.

Stoffels, J. D. (1994). *Strategic issues management: A comprehensive guide to environmental scanning.* Tarrytown, NY: Elsevier.

Stohl, C. (1993). European managers' interpretations of participation: A semantic network analysis. *Human Communication Research, 20,* 97–117.

Stroh, U. (1999, May). *Communication management in a millennium of chaos and change.* Paper presented at the meeting of the International Communication Association, San Francisco.

Tixier, M. (1993). Approaches to the communication function in France and abroad. *International Public Relations Review, 16*(2), 22–30.

VanLeuven, J. K. (1994, July). *Developing criteria for explaining public relations practices in international contexts: Advances in Singapore and Malaysia.* Paper presented at the meeting of the International Communication Association, Sydney, Australia.

Verčič, D., & Grunig, J. E. (2000). The origins of public relations theory in economics and strategic management. In D. Moss, D. Verčič, & G. Warnaby (Eds.), *Perspectives on public relations research* (pp. 7–58). London: Routledge.

Verčič, D., Grunig, L. A., & Grunig, J. E. (1996). Global and specific principles of public relations: Evidence from Slovenia. In H. M. Culbertson & N. Chen (Eds.), *International public relations: A comparative analysis* (pp. 31–65). Mahwah NJ: Lawrence Erlbaum Associates.

Wakefield, R. I. (1996). Interdisciplinary theoretical foundations for international public relations. In H. M. Culbertson & N. Chen (Eds.), *International public relations: A comparative analysis* (pp. 17–30). Mahwah NJ: Lawrence Erlbaum Associates.

Wakefield, R. I. (1997). *International public relations: A theoretical approach to excellence based on a worldwide Delphi study.* Unpublished doctoral dissertation, University of Maryland, College Park.

Wakefield, R. I. (2000). World-class public relations: A model for effective public relations in the multinational. *Journal of Communication Management, 5*(1), 59–71.

Wakefield, R. I. (2001). Effective public relations in the multinational organization. In R. E. Heath (Ed.), *Handbook of public relations* (pp. 639–647). Thousand Oaks, CA: Sage.

Questionnaires for Heads
of Public Relations Departments

(Full Questionnaire)
Excellence in Public Relations
and Communication Management:
An International Study

Questionnaire for Head
of a Public Relations Department

By completing this questionnaire, you will help to determine the contribution that public relations and communication make to the success of an organization. You also will help to determine how communication programs should be organized and managed to make the greatest contribution to the bottom line. This questionnaire is one of three that will be completed by representatives of your organization. Another will be completed by the CEO or other senior manager. A third questionnaire will be completed by about 20 other employees throughout the organization.

Your organization has been chosen as one of 300 to be studied in the United States, Canada, and the United Kingdom—including corporations, associations, government agencies, and other nonprofit organizations. The survey is part of a 6-year study funded by the IABC Research Foundation of the International Association of Business Communicators and several corporations. The questionnaires have been developed by researchers at the University of Maryland, Syracuse University, San Diego State University, and the Cranfield Institute of Technology in the UK.

Thank you, in advance, for completing this questionnaire. Your cooperation will help to ensure the success of one of the most important research projects in the history of public relations and business communication.

How to complete this questionnaire. This questionnaire uses a numbering system that allows you to give a wider range of answers to questions than do other systems. Your best estimate or even your best guess is sufficient. Do not be overly concerned about the precision of your answers. You may choose any number that you believe represents the extent to which an item in the questionnaire describes what your organization does. A score of 100 is the *average* score that a typical head of a public relations department would give to *an average item* in the questionnaire. A score of 0 means that your organization *never* does the activity described by an item. You may choose a number as high as you want, such as 450 or 500. The following scale should help you. It will appear throughout the questionnaire.

0.........25.........50.........75.........100.........150.........200.........300.........?

Does not	Half the	Average for a	Twice the	As high as
describe	average	typical item	average	you want to go

It is important that you answer every item in the questionnaire, but if you feel you do not know the answer to a question, please leave it blank rather than answering with a zero. For this questionnaire, "department" refers to the unit of which you are a part, such as public relations or communication. "Organization" refers to the overall organization. If you work for a local organization that is part of a national one, your answers should refer to the local unit.

PART I
Characteristics of Public Relations
or Communication Programs

1. Listed below are several publics for which organizations often have public relations programs. Please indicate whether a program for each public is handled by your department, is handled by another department in the organization, or is not part of the public relations function in this organization. If the program is handled by another department, please name that department. Next, please estimate how much of the total time and money that your organization devoted to public relations and communication last year was devoted to each of these programs, including those managed in departments other than the one you manage. Make these estimates with a percentage for each program. These percentages should add to 100.

Program	Managed by: Your Dept. (Circle)	Other Dept. (Name)	No Program (Circle)	Percentage of PR/ Communication Effort
Employees	YD	_____	NP (4)	_____ Percent (5–7)
Media	YD	_____	NP (8)	_____ Percent (9–11)
Stockholders/investors	YD	_____	NP (12)	_____ Percent (13–15)
Community	YD	_____	NP (16)	_____ Percent (17–19)
Local government	YD	_____	NP (20)	_____ Percent (21–23)
State government	YD	_____	NP (24)	_____ Percent (25–27)
National government	YD	_____	NP (28)	_____ Percent (29–31)
Foreign governments	YD	_____	NP (32)	_____ Percent (33–35)
New customers/clients	YD	_____	NP (36)	_____ Percent (37–39)
Existing customers/clients	YD	_____	NP (40)	_____ Percent (41–43)
Activist groups	YD	_____	NP (44)	_____ Percent (45–47)
Labor organizations	YD	_____	NP (48)	_____ Percent (49–51)
Members/volunteers	YD	_____	NP (52)	_____ Percent (53–55)
Suppliers	YD	_____	NP (56)	_____ Percent (57–59)
Competitors	YD	_____	NP (60)	_____ Percent (61–63)
Donors	YD	_____	NP (64)	_____ Percent (65–67)
Educators	YD	_____	NP (68)	_____ Percent (69–71)
Other	YD	_____	NP (72)	_____ Percent (73–75)
Other	YD	_____	NP (76)	_____ Percent (77–79)
Other	YD	_____	NP (80)	_____ Percent (1–3)

Total = 100 Percent

Now, please select the three programs from the list above that have the highest percentage of the public relations/communication budget and that are managed by your department. Write the names of the programs in the space indicated in Question 2 on the next page and subsequent questions as you come to them. Answer the questions for each of the three programs. If your department handles fewer than three programs, enter one or two names only. You may find that you can answer the questions that follow more easily if you think of a more specific program or campaign within this broad category that is representative of the larger category. An example would be an employee magazine within the category of employees—as long as the magazine is typical of your overall employee communication program. Please enter the name of the broad category, however, if you choose this option.

2. The following items describe ways in which your organization could have made the decision to initiate a public relations program for each of these three publics. For each of these programs, use the open-end scale explained on the first page to select any number that describes the extent to which each of the items in the first column describes how the decision was made to initiate that program.

0.........25.........50.........75.........100.........150.........200.........300.........?

Does not describe	Half the average	Average for a typical item	Twice the average	As high as you want to go

	Program 1	*Program 2*	*Program 3*

ROLE OF PR IN STRATEGIC MANAGEMENT OF PR. INDIVIDUAL ITEMS

_____   _____   _____

(Enter Names)

We continue the program because we have had it for many years.

_____ (4–7)   _____ (8–11)   _____ (12–15)

We started the program after strategic planning showed the public could hurt or help the organization.

_____ (16–19)   _____ (20–23)   _____ (24–27)

Senior management made the decision with little input from the public relations head and instructed the public relations department to implement the program.

_____ (28–31)   _____ (32–35)   _____ (36–39)

The public relations head was a part of senior management and participated fully in the decision to conduct the program.

_____ (40–43)   _____ (44–47)   _____ (48–51)

Although the public relations head was not a part of senior management, senior management asked for input from public relations before making the decision to begin the program.

_____ (52–55)   _____ (56–59)   _____ (60–63)

For this program, public relations produces publications, news releases, video tapes and the like but did not participate in the decision to begin the program.

_____ (64–67)   _____ (68–71)   _____ (72–75)

3. The next series of items describe different ways in which public relations programs could be conducted. Some of them may describe your programs. Others may not. Again, please enter the names of the three most important programs from the list on Page 1 and use the open-end scale to estimate how well each of the following items describes each of the three programs.

0.........25.........50.........75.........100.........150.........200.........300.........?

Does not describe	Half the average	Average for a typical item	Twice the average	As high as you want to go

	Program 1	*Program 2*	*Program 3*

MODELS OF PUBLIC RELATIONS:

_____   _____   _____

(Enter Names)

**PA = PRESS AGENTRY PI = PUBLIC INFORMATION
2A = TWO-WAY ASYMMETRICAL   2S =
TWO-WAY SYMMETRICAL**

The purpose of this program was, quite simply, to get publicity for this organization. **PA**

_____ (76–79)   _____ (1–4)   _____ (5–8)

0.........25.........50.........75.........100.........150.........200.........300.........?

Does not describe	Half the average	Average for a typical item	Twice the average	As high as you want to go

	Program 1	Program 2	Program 3
	___	___	___
		(Enter Names)	

After completing this program, we did research to determine how effective it had been in changing people's attitudes. **2A**

	Program 1	Program 2	Program 3
	(9–12)	(13–16)	(17–20)

For this program, nearly everyone was so busy writing news stories or producing publications that there was no time to do research. **PI**

	(21–24)	(25–28)	(29–32)

In this program, our broad goal was to persuade publics to behave as the organization wants them to behave. **2A**

	(33–36)	(37–40)	(41–44)

The purpose of this program was to develop mutual understanding between the management of the organization and publics the organization affects. **2S**

	(45–48)	(49–52)	(53–56)

Before starting this program, we looked at attitude surveys to make sure we described the organization and its policies in ways our publics would be most likely to accept. **2A**

	(57–60)	(61–64)	(65–68)

In this program, we disseminated accurate information but did not volunteer unfavorable information. **PI**

	(69–72)	(73–76)	(77–80)

Before starting this program, we did surveys or informal research to find out how much management and our publics understood each other. **2S**

	(1–4)	(5–8)	(9–12)

In this program, we mostly attempted to get favorable publicity into the media and to keep unfavorable publicity out. **PA**

	(13–16)	(17–20)	(21–24)

Before beginning this program, we did research to determine public attitudes toward the organization and how they might be changed. **2A**

	(25–28)	(29–32)	(33–36)

We determined how successful this program was from the number of people who attended an event or who used our products or services. **PA**

	(37–40)	(41–44)	(45–48)

For this program, public relations and publicity meant essentially the same thing. **PA**

	(49–52)	(53–56)	(57–60)

The purpose of this program was to change the attitudes and behavior of management as much as it was to change the attitudes and behaviors of publics. **2S**

	(61–64)	(65–68)	(69–72)

0.........25.........50.........75.........100.........150.........200.........300.........?

| Does not describe | Half the average | Average for a typical item | Twice the average | As high as you want to go |

			Program 1	Program 2	Program 3
			___	___	___
				(Enter Names)	

Keeping a clipping file was about the only way we had to determine the success of this program. **PI**

       (73–76)   (77–80)   (1–4)

For this program, the organization believed public relations should provide mediation for the organization—to help management and publics negotiate conflict. **2S**

       (5–8)   (9–12)   (13–16)

For this program, public relations was more of a neutral disseminator of information than an advocate for the organization or a mediator between management and publics. **PI**

       (17–20)   (21–24)   (25–28)

4. Each of the following describes a possible objective for a public relations program. Please use the same scale you have been using to estimate the extent to which your organization chose each of the objectives listed below for each of the three programs you selected from the list on Page 1.

	Program 1	Program 2	Program 3
	___	___	___
		(Enter Names)	

COMMUNICATION OBJECTIVES: EACH ANALYZED SEPARATELY

Placing articles in the news media.

       (29–32)   (33–36)   (37–40)

Making certain that people are exposed to a message in the media or a controlled publication.

       (41–44)   (45–48)   (49–52)

Getting the target public to remember the message.

       (53–56)   (57–60)   (61–64)

Getting the target public to believe the message.

       (65–68)   (69–72)   (73–76)

Creating or maintaining a favorable attitude by the target public.

       (77–80)   (1–4)   (5–8)

Changing or maintaining the behavior of the target public.

       (9–12)   (13–16)   (17–20)

5. Here is a list of activities that can be used in planning and implementing public relations programs. Choose a number on the open-end scale you have been using to describe the extent to which each item characterizes how each of the three programs you chose from the list on Page 1 has been planned and carried out in the last 3 years.

0.........25.........50.........75.........100.........150.........200.........300.........?

Does not describe	Half the average	Average for a typical item	Twice the average	As high as you want to go

	Program 1	*Program 2*	*Program 3*
	___	___	___
		(Enter Names)	

STEPS IN STRATEGIC MANAGEMENT

Reviewed management decisions to identify public relations problems. **PROBLEMS**

	___	___	___
	(21–24)	(25–28)	(29–32)

Identified a public relations problem by reviewing the extent to which the organization has been socially responsible. **PROBLEMS**

	___	___	___
	(33–36)	(37–40)	(41–44)

Formal research studies are used to track public reactions to the organization. **SCIENTIFIC SCANNING**

	___	___	___
	(45–48)	(49–52)	(53–56)

Phone calls are made to members of target publics to keep in touch. **INFORMAL SCANNING**

	___	___	___
	(57–60)	(61–64)	(65–68)

Surveys are conducted of key publics. **SCIENTIFIC SCANNING**

	___	___	___
	(69–72)	(73–76)	(77–80)

In-depth interviews are conducted with members of the organization's publics. **INFORMAL SCANNING**

	___	___	___
	(1–4)	(5–8)	(9–12)

Communication or public relations audits are conducted to find out about publics. **SCIENTIFIC SCANNING**

	___	___	___
	(13–16)	(17–20)	(21–24)

After the organization conducts special events, people are called back to get their reaction. **INFORMAL SCANNING**

	___	___	___
	(25–28)	(29–32)	(33–36)

The program subscribes to or uses the services of public opinion research agencies. **SCIENTIFIC SCANNING**

	___	___	___
	(37–40)	(41–44)	(45–48)

Demographic data are used to help make decisions concerning publics. **SCIENTIFIC SCANNING**

	___	___	___
	(49–52)	(53–56)	(57–60)

Program managers talk with field personnel to find out about key publics. **INFORMAL SCANNING**

	___	___	___
	(61–64)	(65–68)	(69–72)

Complaints are reviewed to find out how publics feel about the organization. **INFORMAL SCANNING**

	___	___	___
	(73–76)	(77–80)	(1–4)

Techniques such as VALS or PRIZM are used to segment publics. **PUBLICS**

	___	___	___
	(5–8)	(9–12)	(13–16)

Focus groups are used to research the target public. **PUBLICS**

	___	___	___
	(17–20)	(21–24)	(25–28)

A committee or other formal mechanism is used to track issues. **ISSUES**

	___	___	___
	(29–32)	(33–36)	(37–40)

0.........25.........50.........75.........100.........150.........200.........300.........?

Does not describe	Half the average	Average for a typical item	Twice the average	As high as you want to go

			Program 1	Program 2	Program 3
			___	___	___
				(Enter Names)	

The program was developed because of a specific issue or set of related issues. **ISSUES**

	(41–44)	(45–48)	(49–52)

A crisis communication plan exists in this program. **PLANNING**

	(53–56)	(57–60)	(61–64)

The actual communication program is based on research on the issue and public. **FORMATIVE RESEARCH**

	(65–68)	(69–72)	(73–76)

This program changes every year or two as issues and publics change. **PLANNING**

	(77–80)	(1–4)	(5–8)

This program was developed and is reviewed through a formal planning process. **PLANNING**

	(9–12)	(13–16)	(17–20)

This program has written objectives. **OBJECTIVES**

	(21–24)	(25–28)	(29–32)

Management by Objectives (MBO) is used in this program. **OBJECTIVES**

	(33–36)	(37–40)	(41–44)

At budget time, funding depends on the demonstrated effectiveness of this program. **EVALUATION**

	(45–48)	(49–52)	(53–56)

This program utilizes press releases, press conferences, or other contacts with the media. **EXECUTION**

	(57–60)	(61–64)	(65–68)

Magazines, newsletters, brochures, or other publications are produced in this program. **EXECUTION**

	(69–72)	(73–76)	(77–80)

This program uses special events, tours, or open houses. **EXECUTION**

	(1–4)	(5–8)	(9–12)

This program uses tapes, films, or other AV materials. **EXECUTION**

	(13–16)	(17–20)	(21–24)

This program uses advertising or other forms of paid space in the media. **EXECUTION**

	(25–28)	(29–32)	(33–36)

Contacts are made with government officials in this program. **EXECUTION**

	(37–40)	(41–44)	(45–48)

Personnel in this program write speeches or position papers. **EXECUTION**

	(49–52)	(53–56)	(57–60)

This program publicizes products or services. **EXECUTION**

	(61–64)	(65–68)	(69–72)

0.........25.........50.........75.........100.........150.........200.........300.........?

Does not describe	Half the average	Average for a typical item	Twice the average	As high as you want to go

	Program 1	Program 2	Program 3
		(Enter Names)	

Public relations personnel or senior managers meet personally with leaders of activist groups. **EXECUTION**

	(73–76)	(77–80)	(1–4)

Public relations personnel provide management with information gained through this program. **EXECUTION**

	(5–8)	(9–12)	(13–16)

This program uses interpersonal negotiating techniques to resolve conflicts. **EXECUTION**

	(17–20)	(21–24)	(25–28)

This program makes contact with financial analysts, specialized reporters, or other experts. **EXECUTION**

	(29–32)	(33–36)	(37–40)

The effectiveness of the program is checked through interviews with a scientifically selected cross-section of significant publics. **SCIENTIFIC EVALUATION**

	(41–44)	(45–48)	(49–52)

This program monitors the dissemination of messages (news stories, editorials, letters to editors) through a formal, ongoing content analysis of items in a clip file. **CLIP-FILE EVALUATION**

	(53–56)	(57–60)	(61–64)

Personnel in this program check its impact by keeping their eyes and ears open to the reactions of their personal and public contacts. **SEAT-OF-PANTS EVALUATION**

	(65–68)	(69–72)	(73–76)

Communications are prepared in this program after first reviewing published surveys (Gallup, Harris) on attitudes of publics involved. **SCIENTIFIC EVALUATION**

	(77–80)	(1–4)	(5–8)

This program tracks news releases and other placements through a comprehensive clip file. **CLIP-FILE EVALUATION**

	(9–12)	(13–16)	(17–20)

Personnel working on this program prepare communications by drawing on their own professional experience. **SEAT-OF-PANTS EVALUATION**

	(21–24)	(25–28)	(29–32)

The communication effectiveness of this program is measured by comparing before-program and after-program measures of publics. **SCIENTIFIC EVALUATION**

	(33–36)	(37–40)	(41–44)

In this program the number of inches placed, reach, and other vital statistics are logged for clip files. **CLIP-FILE EVALUATION**

	(45–48)	(49–52)	(53–56)

0.........25.........50.........75.........100.........150.........200.........300.........?

Does not describe	Half the average	Average for a typical item	Twice the average	As high as you want to go

	Program 1	Program 2	Program 3
	____	____	____
		(Enter Names)	

The impact of this communication program is checked by having personnel attend meetings and hearings of groups representative of key publics. **SEAT-OF-PANTS EVALUATION**

	____	____	____
	(57–60)	(61–64)	(65–68)

This communication program is designed as though it were a field experiment of communication effects. **SCIENTIFIC EVALUATION**

	____	____	____
	(69–72)	(73–76)	(77–80)

Personnel in this program monitor dissemination of messages through close personal contacts among mass media professionals. **CLIP-FILE EVALUATION**

	____	____	____
	(1–4)	(5–8)	(9–12)

Personnel working on this program can tell how effective it is by their own gut-level reactions and those of other communicators. **SEAT-OF-PANTS EVALUATION**

	____	____	____
	(13–16)	(17–20)	(21–24)

6. Now, for each of the three programs you have been describing, please estimate the extent to which you believe observable evidence shows that the program has had one of the effects listed below. Continue to use the open-end scale you have been using. In this case, a score of 100 would indicate that the program has had an average effect for a typical public relations program.

0.........25.........50.........75.........100.........150.........200.........300.........?

No effect	Half the average	Average for a typical program	Twice the average	As high as you want to go

	Program 1	Program 2	Program 3
	____	____	____
		(Enter Names)	

OUTCOMES

Positive media coverage resulted.

	____	____	____
	(25–28)	(29–32)	(33–36)

Our message was received accurately.

	____	____	____
	(37–40)	(41–44)	(45–48)

Attitudes of publics changed in support of our position.

	____	____	____
	(49–52)	(53–56)	(57–60)

Litigation was avoided.

	____	____	____
	(61–64)	(65–68)	(69–72)

A strike or boycott was averted.

	____	____	____
	(73–76)	(77–80)	(1–4)

Complaints from publics were reduced.

	____	____	____
	(5–8)	(9–12)	(13–16)

There were fewer disagreements and disputes with the relevant public.

	____	____	____
	(17–20)	(21–24)	(25–28)

0.........25.........50.........75.........100.........150.........200.........300.........?

No effect	Half the average	Average for a typical program	Twice the average	As high as you want to go

	Program 1	Program 2	Program 3
		(Enter Names)	
The quality of communication with the relevant public improved.	(29–32)	(33–36)	(37–40)
Desirable legislation was passed or undesirable legislation was defeated.	(33–36)	(37–40)	(41–44)
A stable long-term relationship was developed with the relevant public.	(45–48)	(49–52)	(53–56)
There was greater cooperation between my organization and the relevant public.	(41–44)	(45–48)	(49–52)
The relevant public changed its behavior in the way my organization wanted.	(53–56)	(57–60)	(61–64)
Understanding improved between the organization and the relevant public.	(65–68)	(69–72)	(73–76)
Product sales or use of the organization's services increased.	(77–80)	(1–4)	(5–8)
There was less interference by government in the management of the organization.	(9–12)	(13–16)	(17–20)
Activist groups were willing to negotiate with the organization.	(21–24)	(25–28)	(29–32)
The program helped the organization make money.	(57–60)	(61–64)	(65–68)
The program saved money for the organization.	(69–72)	(73–76)	(77–80)
The program helped the organization meet its goals.	(1–4)	(5–8)	(9–12)

This concludes the questions on these three major public relations programs. The rest of the questionnaire consists of questions about the overall public relations department that you manage in this organization.

PART II
Characteristics of the Public Relations or Communication Department

The first series of questions in Part II asks about your relationship, as head of a public relations or communication department, to senior management.

LEVEL OF MANAGEMENT: QUESTIONS 7–11 ANALYZED SEPARATELY

7. Does your public relations department report directly
   to the most senior manager in your company?   ____ Yes   ____ No (13)
                                                     (Go to Q10)   **(Go to Q8)**

8. **(If your answer to Q7 was no)** Does an indirect reporting relationship exist, then, from the public relations department to the most senior manager (for example, in which the department reports directly on
   some matters but not all)?   ____ Yes   ____ No (14)
                                                     (Go to Q10)   **(Go to Q9)**

9. **(If there is no direct or indirect reporting relationship to the senior manager)** Does the department report, then, to:

   A senior manager who in turn reports to the most
   senior manager?   ____ Yes   ____ No (15)
   A more junior level of management?   ____ Yes   ____ No (16)

10. Please use the open-end scale you used in Part I of this questionnaire to describe the extent to
    which your public relations department makes a contribution to each of the following func-
    tions of your organization. In this case 0 would be no contribution, 100 would be the contribu-
    tion of an average public relations department, and a high score would be a highly significant
    contribution.

0.........25.........50.........75.........100.........150.........200.........300.........?
No **Half the** **Average for a** **Twice the** **As high as**
contribution **average** **typical department** **average** **you want to go**

Strategic planning.
                                                                              _____
                                                                              (17–20)
Response to major social issues.
                                                                              _____
                                                                              (21–24)
Major initiatives (e.g., acquisitions, major new programs, movements into new
markets, launches of new products or services).
                                                                              _____
                                                                              (25–28)
Routine operations (e.g., development and maintenance of employee communication, community relations, or media relations programs).
                                                                              _____
                                                                              (29–32)

**If your department makes no contribution to strategic planning and decision making, go to
Question 12.**

11. Please use the same scale to estimate the extent to which your department makes its contribu-
    tion to strategic planning and decision making through each of the following activities.

Regularly conducted and routine research activities.
                                                                              _____
                                                                              (33–36)
Specific research conducted to answer specific questions.
                                                                              _____
                                                                              (37–40)
Formal approaches to gathering information for use in decision making other than
research.
                                                                              _____
                                                                              (41–44)

Informal approaches to gathering information.
$\overline{\quad\quad\quad\quad}$
(45–48)

Contacts with knowledgeable people outside the organization.
$\overline{\quad\quad\quad\quad}$
(49–52)

Judgment based on experience.
$\overline{\quad\quad\quad\quad}$
(53–56)

Other _____
$\overline{\quad\quad\quad\quad}$
(57–60)

Other _____
$\overline{\quad\quad\quad\quad}$
(61–64)

Other _____
$\overline{\quad\quad\quad\quad}$
(65–68)

12. Today's organizations are so complex that many of them require more than a single leader to operate effectively. Instead of a single powerful person, then, many organizations are controlled by a *group* of powerful people—often called the "dominant coalition." In your organization, who is represented in this power elite? **Please check all that apply.**

DOMINANT COALITION. KEY QUESTION IS WHETHER PR HEAD IS A MEMBER

_____ The chief executive officer. (69)
_____ The chief financial officer. (70)
_____ The chief operating officer. (71)
_____ The head of public relations, public affairs, or communication. (72)

Other top managers specified below.

_____ _____ (73)
_____ _____ (74)
_____ _____ (75)
_____ _____ (76)
_____ _____ (77)

Representatives of external groups specified below.

_____ Owners/stockholders. (78)
_____ Employee associations. (79)
_____ Clients. (80)
_____ Suppliers. (1)
_____ Competitors. (2)
_____ Activist groups. (3)
_____ Other external group specified _____ (4)
_____ Other external group specified _____ (5)
_____ Other external group specified _____ (6)

Any others specified below.

_____ _____ (7)
_____ _____ (8)
_____ _____ (9)

13. Using the same open-end scale, please indicate the extent to which you believe the "dominant coalition" or power elite that you just identified supports the public relations or communication function in this organization. In this case, 0 would indicate no support at all, 100 would indicate the average extent to which organizations support public relations, and a higher score would indicate strong support.

0.........25.........50.........75.........100.........150.........200.........300.........?

| No support | Half the average | Average for all organizations | Twice the average | As high as you want to go |

SUPPORT FOR PR BY DOMINANT COALITION

In my organization, the level of support is _____. (10–13)

14. On the same scale, please choose a number to describe how extensive the clearance process is for public relations practitioners in your organization, where a 0 is no clearance, 100 is an average amount of clearance for most organizations, and a higher score is extensive clearance. _____ (14–17)

POWER AS EXEMPLIFIED THROUGH CLEARANCE PROCESS: QUESTIONS 14–16

15. Please check any of the following reasons that help to explain why you answered the previous question as you did.

_____ I believe I can make final decisions fairly autonomously. (18)

_____ I usually seek informal approval for a project because I believe that is prudent operating procedure in this organization. (19)

_____ I voluntarily submit my writing to a clearance process to avoid mistakes. (20)

_____ I voluntarily submit my activities to a clearance process as a courtesy. (21)

_____ I voluntarily submit my activities to a clearance process as a way of keeping top management informed. (22)

_____ Some decisions are autonomous but most decisions are taken to the boss for his or her okay. (23)

_____ Although my press releases and projects do not require formal clearance, anyone up the ladder can change them or say "no way." (24)

_____ Most of what I write has to be cleared. (25)

_____ The clearance process here depends on who is in power at the time; some top administrators require more clearance than others. (26)

16. Which of the following communication activities conducted by your unit, if any, must be cleared by senior managers outside your unit?

_____ New projects. (27)

_____ Major projects (in terms of expenditure). (28)

_____ Statements, oral or written, that involve *numbers*. (29)

_____ Financial information. (30)

_____ Crisis communications. (31)

_____ Statements that include direct quotes. (32)

_____ Specialized content. (33)

_____ Statements with political ramifications. (34)

_____ "Sensitive" information. (35)

_____ Statements about top administrators. (36)

17. Does your organization have two separate units, one for marketing-related public relations and another for public affairs (public policy)?

EMPHASIS ON MARKETING COMMUNICATION VS. PUBLIC AFFAIRS: QUESTIONS 17–19

____ Yes (37)
____ No (**Go to Question 19**)

18. Which unit has the larger budget?

____ Marketing-related public relations. (1)
____ Public affairs. (2)
____ Budgets are approximately the same. (3)   (38)

19. Regardless of whether you have separate units, which function—public affairs or market-ing-related public relations—receives more support from senior administrators—the dominant coalition?

____ Marketing-related public relations or do not have public affairs. (1)
____ Public affairs or do not have marketing-related public relations. (2)
____ Approximately equal support. (3)   (39)

20. The senior administrators who run an organization—the dominant coalition you were asked to identify—generally have a prevailing idea about how public relations, public affairs, or commu-nication management should be practiced. Sometimes that idea differs from that of the public relations department. The following set of items are similar to those you answered for specific public relations programs. This time, however, please use the open-end scale to indicate the ex-tent to which the dominant coalition in this organization *believes public relations should be prac-ticed*.

0.........25.........50.........75.........100.........150.........200.........300.........?				
Does not	**Half the**	**Average for a**	**Twice the**	**As high as**
describe	**average**	**typical item**	**average**	**you want to go**

MODELS OF PUBLIC RELATIONS IN THE SCHEMA OF THE DOMINANT COALITION

The purpose of public relations is, quite simply, to get publicity for this organiza-tion. **PA**

____
(40–43)

After completing a public relations program, research should be done to deter-mine how effective this program has been in changing people's attitudes. **2A**

____
(44–47)

In public relations, nearly everyone is so busy writing news stories or producing publications that there is no time to do research. **PI**

____
(48–51)

In public relations, the broad goal is to persuade publics to behave as the organi-zation wants them to behave. **2A**

____
(52–55)

The purpose of public relations is to develop mutual understanding between the management of the organization and publics the organization affects. **2S**

____
(56–59)

Before starting a public relations program one should look at attitude surveys to make sure the organization and its policies are described in ways its publics would be most likely to accept. **2A**

____
(60–63)

In public relations accurate information should be disseminated but unfavorable information should not be volunteered. **PI**

____
(64–67)

0.........25.........50.........75.........100.........150.........200.........300.........?

Does not	Half the	Average for a	Twice the	As high as
describe	average	typical item	average	you want to go

Before starting a public relations program, surveys or informal research should be done
to find out how much management and our publics understand each other. **2S**

(68–71)

In public relations, one mostly attempts to get favorable publicity into the media
and to keep unfavorable publicity out. **PA**

(72–75)

Before beginning a public relations program, one should do research to determine
public attitudes toward the organization and how they might be changed. **2A**

(76–79)

The success of a public relations program can be determined from the number of
people who attend an event or who use products or services. **PA**

(1–4)

For this organization, public relations and publicity mean essentially the same
thing. **PA**

(5–8)

The purpose of public relations is to change the attitudes and behavior of management
as much as it is to change the attitudes and behaviors of publics. **2S**

(9–12)

Keeping a clipping file is about the only way there is to determine the success of
public relations. **PI**

(13–16)

Public relations should provide mediation for the organization—to help management and publics negotiate conflict. **2S**

(17–20)

Public relations is more of a neutral disseminator of information than an advocate
for the organization or a mediator between management and publics. **PI**

(21–24)

21. Think next about the value that you think your public relations or communication department
    has to this organization and about the value that members of the dominant coalition think it
    has. Using the open-end scale, estimate the value that *you* think the department has in compari-
    son with a typical other department in this organization and the value that you think members
    of the dominant coalition would choose on the same scale.

VALUE OF PUBLIC RELATIONS TO THE ORGANIZATION: QUESTIONS 21–22

0.........25.........50.........75.........100.........150.........200.........300.........?

No value	Half the	Average value for a	Twice the	As high as
at all	average	typical department	average	you want to go

Your rating of the value of this public relations/communication department.

(25–28)

The dominant coalition's rating of the value of the department.

(29–32)

22. Now think about the value that your public relations or communication department has to this
    organization in terms of a cost–benefit ratio. Think of the money that your organization bud-
    gets for your department each year—both for the department itself and for outside public rela-
    tions consulting firms. Then estimate the value of the department to the organization as a per-
    centage of the department's budget. A percentage less than 100% would indicate that you think
    the department provides benefits worth less than the amount budgeted. 100% would indicate
    that the benefits equal the costs. A percentage greater than 100% would indicate that the bene-

fits are worth more than the amount budgeted. Estimate what you think the percentage is and what you think members of the dominant coalition would estimate the percentage to be.

Your estimate _____ %
_(33–36)

What you think the estimate of the dominant coalition would be _____ %
_(37–40)

In the next series of questions, you will turn from your relationship with senior management to items that ask about your role in the public relations or communication department and the kind of expertise that your department has.

23. On the same open-end scale, please choose a number that indicates how well each of the following items describes the work that *you* do as a public relations practitioner. Please do not score items highly if others in the department do them, but you do not. Again, 100 is the score that an average practitioner would give to a typical one of these items.

0.........25.........50.........75.........100.........150.........200.........300.........?				
Does not describe	**Half the average**	**Average for a typical item**	**Twice the average**	**As high as you want to go**

ROLES: M = MANAGER   T = TECHNICIAN   MR = MEDIA RELATIONS   CL = COMMUNICATION LIAISON

I produce brochures, pamphlets, and other publications. **T**

_____
(41–44)

I create opportunities for management to hear the views of various internal and external publics. **CL**

_____
(45–48)

I take responsibility for the success or failure of my organization's communication or public relations programs. **M**

_____
(49–52)

I am the person who writes communication materials. **T**

_____
(53–56)

I represent the organization at events and meetings. **CL**

_____
(57–60)

I maintain media contacts for my organization. **MR**

_____
(61–64)

I make communication policy decisions. **M**

_____
(65–68)

I observe that others in the organization hold me accountable for the success or failure of communication or public relations programs. **M**

_____
(69–72)

I keep others in the organization informed of what the media report about our organization and important issues. **MR**

_____
(73–76)

Although I don't make communication policy decisions, I provide decision makers with suggestions, recommendations, and plans. **CL**

_____
(77–80)

I do photography and graphics for communication or public relations materials. **T**

_____
(1–4)

I am responsible for placing news releases. **MR**

_____
(5–8)

I edit or rewrite for grammar and spelling the materials written by others in the organization. **T**

_____
(9–12)

0.........25.........50.........75.........100.........150.........200.........300.........?

| Does not describe | Half the average | Average for a typical item | Twice the average | As high as you want to go |

Because of my experience and training, others consider me the organization's expert in solving communication or public relations problems. **M**

_____
(13–16)

I am senior counsel to top decision makers when communication or public relations issues are involved. **CL**

_____
(17–20)

I use my journalistic skills to figure out what the media will consider newsworthy about our organization. **MR**

_____
(21–24)

24. The next series of items list tasks requiring special expertise or knowledge that is available in some public relations or communication departments but not in others. Using the same open-end scale, please choose any number you wish that describes the extent to which your department or someone in the department has the expertise or knowledge to perform each task listed. Again, 100 is the score that an average department would have on a typical one of these items.

KNOWLEDGE AVAILABLE FOR MODELS AND ROLES: SAME CODES AS BEFORE

Determine how publics react to the organization. **2S MODEL**

_____
(25–28)

Coordinate a press conference or arrange media coverage of an event. **T ROLE**

_____
(29–32)

Get publics to behave as your organization wants. **2A MODEL**

_____
(33–36)

Negotiate with an activist group. **2S MODEL**

_____
(37–40)

Manage people. **M ROLE**

_____
(41–44)

Conduct evaluation research. **M ROLE**

_____
(45–48)

Provide objective information about your organization. **PI MODEL**

_____
(59–52)

Produce publications. **T ROLE**

_____
(53–56)

Convince a reporter to publicize your organization. **PA MODEL**

_____
(57–60)

Use theories of conflict resolution in dealing with publics. **2S MODEL**

_____
(61–64)

Write an advertisement. **T ROLE**

_____
(65–68)

Take photographs. **T ROLE**

_____
(69–72)

Understand the news values of journalists. **PI MODEL**

_____
(73–76)

Get your organization's name into the media. **PA MODEL**

_____
(77–80)

Write speeches. **T ROLE**

_____
(1–4)

Keep bad publicity out of the media. **PA MODEL**

_____
(5–8)

0.........25.........50.........75.........100.........150.........200.........300.........?

Does not	Half the	Average for a	Twice the	As high as
describe	average	typical item	average	you want to go

Develop goals and objectives for your department. **M ROLE**

<u>(9–12)</u>

Produce audio/visuals (graphics, slide shows, videos, radio spots). **T ROLE**

<u>(13–16)</u>

Prepare a departmental budget. **M ROLE**

<u>(17–20)</u>

Use attitude theory in a campaign. **2A MODEL**

<u>(21–24)</u>

Manipulate publics scientifically. **2A MODEL**

<u>(25–28)</u>

Get maximum publicity from a staged event. **PA MODEL**

<u>(29–32)</u>

Perform environmental scanning. **M ROLE**

<u>(33–36)</u>

Write news releases and feature articles. **T ROLE**

<u>(37–40)</u>

Develop strategies for solving public relations and communication problems. **M ROLE**

<u>(41–44)</u>

Prepare news stories that reporters will use. **PI MODEL**

<u>(45–48)</u>

Create and manage a speakers' bureau. **T ROLE**

<u>(49–52)</u>

Help management to understand the opinion of particular publics. **2S MODEL**

<u>(53–56)</u>

Use research to segment publics. **M ROLE**

<u>(57–60)</u>

Manage the organization's response to issues. **M ROLE**

<u>(61–64)</u>

Perform as journalists inside your organization. **PI MODEL**

<u>(65–68)</u>

Persuade a public that your organization is right on an issue. **2A MODEL**

<u>(69–72)</u>

The next series of questions asks about the environment of your organization and about some of its internal policies.

PRESSURE FROM ACTIVIST GROUPS: QUESTIONS 25–36. ITEMS ANALYZED SEPARATELY

25. Using the open-end scale, please estimate the extent to which your organization has experienced pressure from activist groups.

0.........25.........50.........75.........100.........150.........200.........300.........?

No pressure	Half the	Average for a	Twice the	As high as
at all	average	typical organization	average	you want to go

My estimate for this organization is ____. (73–76)
(If your answer is 0, go to Question 37)

26. Think of the most recent case or a typical case when your organization was pressured by an activist group. Using the open-end scale, please describe how successful that activist group was in achieving its goals in its dealings with your organization. Then estimate how successful you think your organization's response to the group to have been.

0.........25.........50.........75.........100.........150.........200.........300.........?

| Not successful at all | Half the average | Average success for a typical encounter | Twice the average | As high as you want to go |

The activist group's level of success was _____. (77–80)
My organization's level of success was _____. (1–4)

27. Where do you tend to find out about activist pressure on your organization? (**Check any that apply**)

_____ The pressure group itself. (5)
_____ Media coverage. (6)
_____ Others in your organization. (7)
_____ Other source _____ (8)
_____ Other source _____ (9)
_____ Other source _____ (10)
_____ Other source _____ (11)

28. Does your organization have a standing committee to deal with issues created by activist groups?

_____ Yes
_____ No (12)

29. Who within the organization is responsible for dealing with activist groups? (**Check any that apply**)

_____ The CEO. (13)
_____ The head of public relations or public affairs. (14)
_____ Attorneys. (15)
_____ A special department or committee dedicated to activist affairs. (16)
_____ Other _____ (17)
_____ Other _____ (18)
_____ Other _____ (19)

30. Using the open-end scale, please estimate the extent to which the entire organization, both senior management and other employees, were involved with the response to the activist group:
_____ (20–23)

0.........25.........50.........75.........100.........150.........200.........300.........?

| No involvement | Half the average | Average for a typical organization | Twice the average | As high as you want to go |

31. On the same scale, estimate the extent to which your organization researched the activist group: _____ (24–27)

0.........25.........50.........75.........100.........150.........200.........300.........?

| No research at all | Half the average | Average for a typical organization | Twice the average | As high as you want to go |

32. Was a special program developed to respond to the group?

_____ No (**Go to Question 34**)
_____ Yes (28)

33. What was that response? _____

_____

_____ (29–30)

34. Use the open-end scale to estimate the extent to which activist groups have a direct involvement in planning your organization's response to them: _____ (31–34) (**If your answer is 0, go
to Question 36**)

0.........25.........50.........75.........100.........150.........200.........300.........?				
No involvement	Half the	Average for a	Twice the	As high as
at all	average	typical organization	average	you want to go

35. How does the organization typically involve the activist group? (**Check any that apply**)

____ Informal conversation. (35)
____ Part of a special committee. (36)
____ Inclusion on the board of directors. (37)
____ Other _____ (38)
____ Other _____ (39)
____ Other _____ (40)

36. Use the open-end scale to estimate the extent to which the organization evaluates its response
to activist groups: _____ (41–44)

0.........25.........50.........75.........100.........150.........200.........300.........?				
No evaluation	Half the	Average for a	Twice the	As high as
at all	average	typical organization	average	you want to go

PROGRAMS FOR WOMEN: QUESTIONS 37–38

37. The next set of items moves from the external to the internal environment of your organization—specifically with the way your organization deals with its women employees. For each
item, use the open-end scale to estimate how your overall organization, not just the communication department, compares with an average organization on a typical one of these items.

0.........25.........50.........75.........100.........150.........200.........300.........?				
Does not	Half the	Average for a	Twice the	As high as
describe	average	typical item	average	you want to go
		in most organizations		

This organization has:

Enacted specific policies, procedures, or programs designed to promote an understanding of the concerns of female employees.
_____
(45–48)

Provided a supportive climate for women at work.
_____
(49–52)

Monitored the use of sexist language in all realms of the organization's communication.
_____
(53–56)

Reviewed organizational policies for their effect on women.
_____
(57–60)

Provided opportunities for women who must relocate or who have relocated.
_____
(61–64)

0.........25.........50.........75.........100.........150.........200.........300.........?

Does not describe	Half the average	Average for a typical item in most organizations	Twice the average	As high as you want to go

This organization has:

Allowed flex time for employees.

(65–68)

Avoided "perks" that divide employees on the basis of their gender and tenure, such as all-male clubs or executive dining rooms.

(69–72)

Established effective policies to deal with sexual discrimination.

(73–76)

Developed specific guidelines for handling problems of sexual harassment.

(77–80)

Set up a system of maternity and paternity leave.

(1–4)

Provided child-care services.

(5–8)

Built a system of multiple employment centers that allows mobility for employees.

(9–12)

Furthered the talents of women through mentoring programs.

(13–16)

Fostered women's leadership abilities.

(17–20)

Funded or reimbursed employees for work-related travel.

(21–24)

Included membership in professional associations as an employee benefit.

(25–28)

Provided opportunities for women to take risks.

(29–32)

Encouraged women who may seem less "serious-minded" about their careers than men.

(33–36)

Groomed women for management by selecting them as "informal assistants" to those in the next-higher position.

(37–40)

Included women in the informal informational network.

(41–44)

Made available comparable data to help women in salary negotiations.

(45–48)

Paid men and women equally for equal or comparable work.

(49–52)

The next two questions apply specifically to the public relations or communication department

Included women in all communication roles—managerial as well as technical.

(53–56)

Promoted women from within the department rather than hired men from outside communication or public relations to manage the function.

(57–60)

38. Please estimate the following:

The percentage of female professional employees in the department. _____%

(61–63)

The percentage of the employees who produce brochures, pamphlets and other publications, write public relations material presenting information on issues important to the public, and edit or rewrite for grammar and spelling the materials written by others in the organization who are women? _____%
(64–66)

The percentage of the employees who take responsibility for the success or failure of public relations programs, make communication policy decisions, and keep management informed of public reactions to organizational policies, procedures, or activities who are women. _____%
(67–69)

Finally, there are a few demographic questions about you and your organization.

39. Approximately how many people are employed by your overall organization? _____ (70–80)

40. Approximately how many public relations or communication professionals are employed by your department? _____ (1–6)

41. Does your department or organization use the services of outside public relations firms?

_____ Yes (7)
_____ No **(Go to Question 43)**

42. Please indicate the percentage of the following types of public relations activities that your department or organization purchases from outside public relations firms.

Preparation and placement of publicity and advertising materials. _____%
(8–10)

Preparation of publications directed to employees, stockholders, investors, and similar publics. _____%
(11–13)

Consulting about relations with the news media during periods of actual or potential controversy or disputes. _____%
(14–16)

Consulting about top-level strategic problems related to the relationship this organization has with outside organizations or groups. _____%
(17–19)

Research in support of the public relations function. _____%
(20–22)

Assistance in developing a public relations or communication department or doing a public relations audit of an existing department. _____%
(23–25)

43. You are:
_____ Male. (1)

_____ Female. (2)   (26)

44. Your age is _____. (27–28)

LEVEL OF PROFESSIONALISM: QUESTIONS 45–51 ADDED AFTER STANDARDIZATION

45. Your highest level of education in any field is:

_____ No college. (1)
_____ Some college. (2)
_____ A bachelor's degree. (3)

_____ Some graduate courses. (4)
_____ A master's degree. (5)
_____ A doctoral degree. (6)   (29)

46. The highest level of training you have completed in *public relations* is:

_____ No training in public relations. (1)
_____ Some continuing education courses. (2)
_____ Some college level courses. (3)
_____ A bachelor's degree. (4)
_____ A master's degree. (5)
_____ A doctoral degree. (6)   (30)

47. Check any of the following professional public relations associations to which you belong.

_____ International Association of Business Communicators. (31)
_____ Public Relations Society of America. (32)
_____ Other _____ (33)
_____ Other _____ (34)
_____ Other _____ (35)

If none of the above has been checked, go to Question 51

48. You attend meetings of professional public relations associations about _____ times a year.
(36–38)

49. You have served as an officer of a professional public relations association about _____ times in the last 10 years. (39–41)

50. You have presented a program for a professional public relations association about _____ times in the last 10 years. (42–44)

51. You subscribe to the following public relations periodicals:

_____ *Communication World.* (45)
_____ *Public Relations Journal.* (46)
_____ *Public Relations Review.* (47)
_____ *Public Relations Quarterly.* (48)
_____ *International Public Relations Review.* (49)
_____ *PR Reporter.* (50)
_____ *PR News.* (51)
_____ *O'Dwyer's Newsletter.* (52)
_____ *Communications Briefings.* (53)
_____ *PR Week.* (54)
_____ *Ragan Report.* (55)
_____ Other _____ (56)
_____ Other _____ (57)
_____ Other _____ (58)

52. The title of your position is _____. (59–60)

53. The name of the organization of which your communication department is a part is
_____.

Thank you. That completes the questionnaire.

(Condensed Questionnaire)
Excellence in Public Relations
and Communication Management:
An Audit

Questionnaire for Head
of a Public Relations Department

By completing this questionnaire, you will help to determine the contribution that public relations and communication make to the success of an organization. You also will help to determine how communication programs should be organized and managed to make the greatest contribution to the bottom line. This questionnaire is one of two that will be completed by representatives of your organization. Another will be completed by the CEO or other senior manager.

This instrument has been used in an "Excellence" study of 300 organizations in the United States, Canada, and the United Kingdom—including corporations, associations, government agencies, and other nonprofit organizations. The survey was part of a study funded by the IABC Research Foundation of the International Association of Business Communicators and several corporations. The questionnaires have been developed by researchers at the University of Maryland, Syracuse University, San Diego State University, and the Cranfield Institute of Technology in the UK.

Thank you, in advance, for completing this questionnaire. Your cooperation will help to ensure the success of one of the most important research projects in the history of public relations and business communication.

How to complete this questionnaire. **This questionnaire uses a numbering system that allows you to give a wider range of answers to questions than do other systems. Your best estimate or even your best guess is sufficient. Do not be overly concerned about the precision of your answers. You may choose any number that you believe represents the extent to which an item in the questionnaire describes what your organization does. A score of 100 is the *average* score that a typical head of a public relations department would give *to an average item* in the questionnaire. A score of 0 means that your organization *never* does the activity described by an item. You may choose a number as high as you want, such as 450 or 500. The following scale should help you. It will appear throughout the questionnaire.**

0.........25.........50.........75.........100.........150.........200.........300.........?				
Does not describe	Half the average	Average for a typical item	Twice the average	As high as you want to go

It is important that you answer every item in the questionnaire, but if you feel you do not know the answer to a question, please leave it blank rather than answering with a zero. For this questionnaire, "department" refers to the unit of which you are a part, such as public relations or communication. "Organization" refers to the overall organization. If you work for a local organization that is part of a national one, your answers should refer to the local unit.

PART I
Characteristics of Public Relations
or Communication Department

The first series of questions in Part I asks about your relationship, as head of a public relations or communication department, to senior management.

1. Does your public relations department report directly to the
   most senior manager in your company?   ____ Yes   ____ No
                                                            (Go to Q4)   (Go to Q2)

2. **(If your answer to Q1 was no)** Does an indirect reporting
   relationship exist, then, from the public relations department
   to the most senior manager (for example, in which the department reports directly on some matters but not all)? ____Yes   ____ No
                                                            (Go to Q4)   (Go to Q3)

3. **(If there is no direct or indirect reporting relationship to
   the senior manager)** Does the department report, then, to:

   A senior manager who in turn reports to the most senior
   manager?   ____ Yes   ____ No

   A more junior level of management?   ____ Yes   ____ No

4. Please use the open-end scale you used in Part I of this questionnaire to describe the extent to which your public relations department makes a contribution to each of the following functions of your organization. In this case 0 would be no contribution, 100 would be the contribution of an average public relations department, and a high score would be a highly significant contribution.

0.........25.........50.........75.........100.........150.........200.........300.........?				
No	Half the	Average for a	Twice the	As high as
contribution	average	typical department	average	you want to go

Strategic planning.   ____

Response to major social issues.   ____

Major initiatives (e.g., acquisitions, major new programs, movements into new
markets, launches of new products or services).   ____

Routine operations (e.g., development and maintenance of employee communication, community relations, or media relations programs).   ____

If your department makes no contribution to strategic planning and decision making, go to Question 6.

5. Please use the same scale to estimate the extent to which your department makes its contribution to strategic planning and decision making through each of the following activities.

0.........25.........50.........75.........100.........150.........200.........300.........?

No contribution	Half the average	Average for a typical department	Twice the average	As high as you want to go

Regularly conducted and routine research activities. _____

Specific research conducted to answer specific questions. _____

Formal approaches to gathering information for use in decision making other than research. _____

Informal approaches to gathering information. _____

Contacts with knowledgeable people outside the organization. _____

Judgment based on experience. _____

Other _____ _____

6. Today's organizations are so complex that many of them require more than a single leader to operate effectively. Instead of a single powerful person, then, many organizations are controlled by a *group* of powerful people—often called the "dominant coalition." In your organization, who is represented in this power elite? **Please check all that apply.**

____ The chief executive officer.
____ The chief financial officer.
____ The chief operating officer.
____ The head of public relations, public affairs, or communication.

Other top managers specified below.

____ _____
____ _____
____ _____
____ _____
____ _____

Representatives of external groups specified below.

____ Owners/stockholders.
____ Employee associations.
____ Clients.
____ Suppliers.
____ Competitors
____ Activist groups.
____ Other external group specified _____

Any others specified below.

____ _____
____ _____
____ _____

7. Using the same open-end scale, please indicate the extent to which you believe the "dominant coalition" or power elite that you just identified supports the public relations or communication function in this organization. In this case, 0 would indicate no support at all, 100 would indicate the average extent to which organizations support public relations, and a higher score would indicate strong support.

0.........25.........50.........75.........100.........150.........200.........300.........?				
No	**Half the**	**Average for**	**Twice the**	**As high as**
support	**average**	**all organizations**	**average**	**you want to go**

In my organization, the level of support is _____.

8. Does your organization have two separate units, one for marketing-related public relations and another for public affairs (public policy)?

_____ Yes
_____ No (**Go to Question 10**)

9. Which unit has the larger budget?

_____ Marketing-related public relations.
_____ Public affairs.
_____ Budgets are approximately the same.

10. Regardless of whether you have separate units, which function—public affairs or marketing-related public relations—receives more support from senior administrators—the dominant coalition?

_____ Marketing-related public relations or do not have public affairs.
_____ Public affairs or do not have marketing-related public relations.
_____ Approximately equal support.

11. The senior administrators who run an organization—the dominant coalition you were asked to identify—generally have a prevailing idea about how public relations, public affairs, or communication management should be practiced. Sometimes that idea differs from that of the public relations department. The following items describe the way your department practices public relations and the extent to which you think the dominant coalition in this organization *believes public relations should be practiced.*

0.........25.........50.........75.........100.........150.........200.........300.........?				
Does not	**Half the**	**Average for a**	**Twice the**	**As high as**
describe	**average**	**typical item**	**average**	**you want to go**

	Practiced Behavior	Dominant Coalition
The purpose of public relations is, quite simply, to get publicity for this organization.	_____	_____
After completing a public relations program, research should be done to determine how effective this program has been in changing people's attitudes.	_____	_____

0.........25.........50.........75.........100.........150.........200.........300.........?

Does not describe	Half the average	Average for a typical item	Twice the average	As high as you want to go

		Practiced Behavior	Dominant Coalition

In public relations, nearly everyone is so busy writing news stories or producing publications that there is no time to do research. _____   _____

In public relations, the broad goal is to persuade publics to behave as the organization wants them to behave. _____   _____

The purpose of public relations is to develop mutual understanding between the management of the organization and publics the organization affects. _____   _____

Before starting a public relations program one should look at attitude surveys to make sure the organization and its policies are described in ways its publics would be most likely to accept. _____   _____

In public relations accurate information should be disseminated but unfavorable information should not be volunteered. _____   _____

Before starting a public relations program, surveys or informal research should be done to find out how much management and our publics understand each other. _____   _____

In public relations, one mostly attempts to get favorable publicity into the media and to keep unfavorable publicity out. _____   _____

Before beginning a public relations program, one should do research to determine public attitudes toward the organization and how they might be changed. _____   _____

The success of a public relations program can be determined from the number of people who attend an event or who use products or services. _____   _____

For this organization, public relations and publicity mean essentially same thing. _____   _____

The purpose of public relations is to change the attitudes and behavior of management as much as it is to change the attitudes and behaviors of publics. _____   _____

Keeping a clipping file is about the only way there is to determine the success of public relations. _____   _____

Public relations should provide mediation for the organization—to help management and publics negotiate conflict. _____   _____

Public relations is more of a neutral disseminator of information than an advocate for the organization or a mediator between management and publics. _____   _____

12. Using the same open-end scale, please indicate the extent to which you believe the "dominant coalition" or power elite that you just identified supports the public relations or communication function in this organization. In this case, 0 would indicate no support at all, 100 would indicate the average extent to which organizations support public relations, and a higher score would indicate strong support.

0.........25.........50.........75.........100.........150.........200.........300.........?				
No support	Half the average	Average for all organizations	Twice the average	As high as you want to go

In my organization, the level of support is _____.

13. Think next about the value that you think your public relations or communication department has to this organization and about the value that members of the dominant coalition think it has. Using the open-end scale, estimate the value that *you* think the department has in comparison with a typical other department in this organization and the value that you think members of the dominant coalition would choose on the same scale.

0.........25.........50.........75.........100.........150.........200.........300.........?				
No value at all	Half the average	Average value for a typical department	Twice the average	As high as you want to go

Your rating of the value of this public relations / communication department. _____

The dominant coalition's rating of the value of the department. _____

14. Now think about the value that your public relations or communication department has to this organization in terms of a cost–benefit ratio. Think of the money that your organization budgets for your department each year—both for the department itself and for outside public relations consulting firms. Then estimate the value of the department to the organization as a percentage of the department's budget. A percentage less than 100% would indicate that you think the department provides benefits worth less than the amount budgeted. 100% would indicate that the benefits equal the costs. A percentage greater than 100% would indicate that the benefits are worth more than the amount budgeted. Estimate what you think the percentage is and what you think members of the dominant coalition would estimate the percentage to be.

Your estimate _____ %
What you think the estimate of the dominant coalition would be _____ %

In the next series of questions, you will turn from your relationship with senior management to items that ask about your role in the public relations or communication department and the kind of expertise that your department has.

15. On the same open-end scale, please choose a number that indicates how well each of the following items describes the work that *you* do as a public relations practitioner. Please do not score items highly if others in the department do them, but you do not. Again, 100 is the score that an average practitioner would give to a typical one of these items.

0.........25.........50.........75.........100.........150.........200.........300.........?
| Does not | Half the | Average for a | Twice the | As high as |
| describe | average | typical item | average | you want to go |

I produce brochures, pamphlets, and other publications.   _____

I create opportunities for management to hear the views of various internal and external publics.   _____

I take responsibility for the success or failure of my organization'scommunication or public relations programs.   _____

I am the person who writes communication materials.   _____

I represent the organization at events and meetings.   _____

I maintain media contacts for my organization.   _____

I make communication policy decisions.   _____

I observe that others in the organization hold me accountable for the success or failure of communication or public relations programs.   _____

I keep others in the organization informed of what the media report about our organization and important issues.   _____

Although I don't make communication policy decisions, I provide decision makers with suggestions, recommendations, and plans.   _____

I do photography and graphics for communication or public relations materials.   _____

I am responsible for placing news releases.   _____

I edit or rewrite for grammar and spelling the materials written by others in the organization.   _____

Because of my experience and training, others consider me the organization's expert in solving communication or public relations problems.   _____

I am senior counsel to top decision makers when communication or public relations issues are involved.   _____

I use my journalistic skills to figure out what the media will consider newsworthy about our organization.   _____

16. The next series of items list tasks requiring special expertise or knowledge that is available in some public relations or communication departments but not in others. Using the same open-end scale, please choose any number you wish that describes the extent to which your department or someone in the department has the expertise or knowledge to perform each task listed. Again, 100 is the score an average department would choose.

Determine how publics react to the organization.   _____

Coordinate a press conference or arrange media coverage of an event.   _____

Get publics to behave as your organization wants.   _____

Negotiate with an activist group.   _____

0.........25.........50.........75.........100.........150.........200.........300.........?

Does not describe	Half the average	Average for a typical item	Twice the average	As high as you want to go

Manage people.

Conduct evaluation research. _____

Provide objective information about your organization. _____

Produce publications. _____

Convince a reporter to publicize your organization. _____

Use theories of conflict resolution in dealing with publics. _____

Write an advertisement. _____

Take photographs. _____

Understand the news values of journalists. _____

Get your organization's name into the media. _____

Write speeches. _____

Keep bad publicity out of the media. _____

Develop goals and objectives for your department. _____

Produce audio/visuals (graphics, slide shows, videos, radio spots). _____

Prepare a departmental budget. _____

Use attitude theory in a campaign. _____

Manipulate publics scientifically. _____

Get maximum publicity from a staged event. _____

Perform environmental scanning. _____

Write news releases and feature articles. _____

Develop strategies for solving public relations and communication problems. _____

Prepare news stories that reporters will use. _____

Create and manage a speakers' bureau. _____

Help management to understand the opinion of particular publics. _____

Use research to segment publics. _____

Manage the organization's response to issues. _____

Perform as journalists inside your organization. _____

Persuade a public that your organization is right on an issue. _____

The next series of questions asks about the environment of your organization and about some of its internal policies.

17. Using the open-end scale, please estimate the extent to which your organization has experienced pressure from activist groups.

    0.........25.........50.........75.........100.........150.........200.........300.........?

Does not describe	Half the average	Average for a typical item	Twice the average	As high as you want to go

    My estimate for this organization is _____.
    (**If your answer is 0, go to Question 28**)

18. Think of the most recent case or a typical case when your organization was pressured by an activist group. Using the same open-end scale, please describe how successful that activist group was in achieving its goals in its dealings with your organization. Then estimate how successful you think your organization's response to the group to have been.

    The activist group's level of success was _____.

    My organization's level of success was _____.

19. Where do you tend to find out about activist pressure on your organization? (**Check any that apply**)

    ____ The pressure group itself.
    ____ Media coverage.
    ____ Others in your organization.
    ____ Other source _____
    ____ Other source _____
    ____ Other source _____
    ____ Other source _____

20. Does your organization have a standing committee to deal with issues created by activist groups?

    ____ Yes
    ____ No

21. Who within the organization is responsible for dealing with activist groups? (**Check any that apply**)

    ____ The CEO.
    ____ The head of public relations or public affairs.
    ____ Attorneys.
    ____ A special department or committee dedicated to activist affairs.
    ____ Other _____
    ____ Other _____
    ____ Other _____

22. Using the same open-end scale, please estimate the extent to which the entire organization, both senior management and other employees, were involved with the response to the activist group: _____

23. On the same scale, estimate the extent to which your organization researched the activist group: _____

24. Was a special program developed to respond to the group?

_____ No
_____ Yes

25. Use the open-end scale to estimate the extent to which activist groups have a direct involvement in planning your organization's response to them: _____ (**If your answer is 0, go to Question 27**)

0.........25.........50.........75.........100.........150.........200.........300.........?				
No involvement at all	Half the average	Average for a typical organization	Twice the average	As high as you want to go

26. How does the organization typically involve the activist group? (**Check any that apply**)

_____ Informal conversation.
_____ Part of a special committee.
_____ Inclusion on the board of directors.
_____ Other _____
_____ Other _____
_____ Other _____

27. Use the same open-end scale to estimate the extent to which the organization evaluates its response to activist groups: _____

28. The next set of items moves from the external to the internal environment of your organization—specifically with the way your organization deals with its women employees. For each item, use the open-end scale to estimate how your overall organization, not just the communication department, compares with an average organization on a typical one of these items.

0.........25.........50.........75.........100.........150.........200.........300.........?				
Does not describe	Half the average	Average for a typical item in most organizations	Twice the average	As high as you want to go

This organization has:

Enacted specific policies, procedures, or programs designed to promote an understanding of the concerns of female employees.　_____

Provided a supportive climate for women at work.　_____

Monitored the use of sexist language in all realms of the organization's communication.　_____

Provided opportunities for women who must relocate or who have relocated.　_____

Allowed flex time for employees.　_____

Avoided "perks" that divide employees on the basis of their gender and tenure, such as all-male clubs or executive dining rooms.　_____

0.........25.........50.........75.........100.........150.........200.........300.........?
Does not	Half the	Average for a	Twice the	As high as
describe	average	typical item	average	you want to go
		in most organizations		

Established effective policies to deal with sexual discrimination. _____

Developed specific guidelines for handling problems of sexual harassment. _____

Set up a system of maternity and paternity leave. _____

Provided child-care services. _____

Built a system of multiple employment centers that allows mobility for employees. _____

Furthered the talents of women through mentoring programs. _____

Reviewed organizational policies for their effect on women. _____

Fostered women's leadership abilities. _____

Funded or reimbursed employees for work-related travel. _____

Included membership in professional associations as an employee benefit. _____

Provided opportunities for women to take risks. _____

Encouraged women who may seem less "serious-minded" about their careers than men. _____

Groomed women for management by selecting them as "informal assistants" to those in the next-higher position. _____

Included women in the informal informational network. _____

Made available comparable data to help women in salary negotiations. _____

Paid men and women equally for equal or comparable work. _____

The next two questions apply specifically to the public relations or communication department

Included women in all communication roles—managerial as well as technical. _____

Promoted women from within the department rather than hired men from outside communication or public relations to manage the function. _____

29. Please estimate the following:

The percentage of female professional employees in the department. _____%

The percentage of the employees who produce brochures, pamphlets and other publications, write public relations material presenting information on issues important to the public, and edit or rewrite for grammar and spelling the materials written by others in the organization who are women? _____%

The percentage of the employees who take responsibility for the success or failure of public relations programs, make communication policy decisions, and keep management informed of public reactions to organizational policies, procedures, or activities who are women. _____%

Finally, there are a few demographic questions about you and your organization.

30. Approximately how many people are employed by your overall organization? _____

31. Approximately how many public relations or communication professionals are employed by your department? _____

32. You are:

_____ Male.
_____ Female.

33. Your age is _____.

34. Your highest level of education in any field is:

_____ No college.
_____ Some college.
_____ A bachelor's degree.
_____ Some graduate courses.
_____ A master's degree.
_____ A doctoral degree.

35. The highest level of training you have completed in *public relations* is:

_____ No training in public relations.
_____ Some continuing education courses.
_____ Some college level courses.
_____ A bachelor's degree.
_____ A master's degree.
_____ A doctoral degree.

36. Check any of the following professional public relations associations to which you belong.

_____ International Association of Business Communicators.
_____ Public Relations Society of America.
_____ Other _____

If none of the above has been checked, go to Question 41.

38. You attend meetings of professional public relations associations about _____ times a year.

39. You have served as an officer of a professional public relations association about _____ times in the last 10 years.

40. You have presented a program for a professional public relations association about _____ times in the last 10 years.

41. You subscribe to the following public relations periodicals:

____ *Communication World.*
____ *Public Relations Journal.*
____ *Public Relations Review.*
____ *Public Relations Quarterly.*
____ *Int'l. Public Relations Review.*
____ *PR Reporter.*
____ *PR News.*
____ *O'Dwyer's Newsletter.*
____ *Communications Briefings.*
____ *PR Week.*
____ *Ragan Report.*
____ Other _____

43. The title of your position is _____.

Thank you. That completes the questionnaire.

Questionnaire for CEO
or Other Member
of the Dominant Coalition

Excellence in Public Relations
and Communication Management:
An International Study

Questionnaire for CEO
or Other Senior Manager

By completing this questionnaire, you will help to determine the contribution that public relations and communication make to the success of an organization. You also will help to determine how communication programs should be organized and managed to make the greatest contribution to the bottom line. This questionnaire is one of three that will be completed by representatives of your organization. Another will be completed by the heads of public relations or other communication departments. A third questionnaire will be completed by about 20 other employees throughout the organization. As the CEO or someone close to the CEO, your perspective is extremely important to this study; and your cooperation is crucial.

Your organization has been chosen as one of 300 to be studied in the United States, Canada, and the United Kingdom—including corporations, associations, government agencies, and other nonprofit organizations. The survey is part of a 6-year study funded by the IABC Research Foundation of the International Association of Business Communicators and several corporations. The questionnaires have been developed by researchers at the University of Maryland, Syracuse University, San Diego State University, and the Cranfield Institute of Technology in the UK.

Thank you, in advance, for completing this questionnaire. Your cooperation will help to ensure the success of one of the most important research projects in the history of public relations.

How to complete this questionnaire. This questionnaire uses a numbering system that allows you to give a wider range of answers to questions than do other systems. Your best estimate or even your best guess is sufficient. Do not be overly concerned about the precision of your answers. You may choose any number that you believe represents the extent to which an item in the questionnaire describes what your organization does. A score of 100 is the *average* score that a typical CEO of an organization like yours would give to *an average item* in the questionnaire. A score of 0 means that your organization *never* does the activity described by an item. You may choose a number as high as you want, such as 450 or 500. The following scale should help you. It will appear throughout the questionnaire.

0.........25.........50.........75.........100.........150.........200.........300.........?				
Does not describe	Half the average	Average for a typical item	Twice the average	As high as you want to go

It is important that you answer every item in the questionnaire, but if you feel you do not know the answer to a question, please leave it blank rather than answering with a zero. For this questionnaire, "department" refers to a unit such as public relations or communication. "Organization" refers to the overall organization. If you work for a local organization that is part of a national one, your answers should refer to the local unit.

The first series of questions asks about the relationship of your public relations or communication department to senior management.

LEVEL OF MANAGEMENT: QUESTIONS 1–6 ANALYZED SEPARATELY

1. Does your public relations department report directly to the most senior manager in your company? ____ Yes ____ No (1)
   (Go to Q4) (Go to Q2)

2. **(If your answer to Q1 was no)** Does an indirect reporting relationship exist, then, from the public relations department to the most senior manager (for example, in which the department reports directly on some matters but not all)? ____ Yes ____ No (2)
   (Go to Q4) (Go to Q3)

3. **(If there is no direct or indirect reporting relationship to the senior manager)** Does the department report, then, to:

   A senior manager who in turn reports to the most senior manager? ____ Yes ____ No (3)

   A more junior level of management? ____ Yes ____ No (4)

4. Please use the open-end scale explained on the first page to describe the extent to which your public relations department makes a contribution to each of the following functions of your organization. In this case 0 would be no contribution, 100 would be the contribution of an average public relations department, and a high score would be a highly significant contribution.

0.........25.........50.........75.........100.........150.........200.........300.........?

| No | Half the | Average for a | Twice the | As high as |
| contribution | average | typical department | average | you want to go |

Strategic planning.

(5–8)

Response to major social issues.

(9–12)

Major initiatives (e.g., acquisitions, major new programs, movements into new markets, launches of new products or services).

(13–16)

Routine operations (e.g., development and maintenance of employee communication, community relations, or media relations programs).

(17–20)

If your public relations or communication department makes no contribution to strategic planning and decision making, go to Question 6.

5. Please use the same scale to estimate the extent to which your public relations department makes its contribution to strategic planning and decision making through each of the following activities.

Regularly conducted and routine research activities.

(21–24)

Specific research conducted to answer specific questions.

(25–28)

Formal approaches to gathering information for use in decision making other than research.

(29–32)

Informal approaches to gathering information.

(33–36)

Contacts with knowledgeable people outside the organization.

(37–40)

Judgment based on experience.

(41–44)

Other _____

(45–48)

Other _____

(49–52)

Other _____

(53–56)

DOMINANT COALITION. KEY QUESTION IS WHETHER PR HEAD IS A MEMBER

6. Today's organizations are so complex that many of them require more than a single leader to operate effectively. Instead of a single powerful person, then, many organizations are controlled by a *group* of powerful people—often called the "dominant coalition." In your organization, who is represented in this power elite? **Please check all that apply.**

_____ The chief executive officer. (57)
_____ The chief financial officer. (58)
_____ The chief operating officer. (59)
_____ The head of public relations, public affairs, or communication. (60)

Other top managers specified below.

____ _____ (61)
____ _____ (62)
____ _____ (63)
____ _____ (64)
____ _____ (65)

Representatives of external groups specified below.

____ Owners/stockholders. (66)
____ Employee associations. (67)
____ Clients. (68)
____ Suppliers. (69)
____ Competitors. (70)
____ Activist groups. (71)
____ Other external group specified _____ (72)
____ Other external group specified _____ (73)
____ Other external group specified _____ (74)

Any others specified below.

____ _____ (75)
____ _____ (76)

SUPPORT FOR PR BY DOMINANT COALITION

7. Using the same open-end scale, please indicate the extent to which you believe the "dominant coalition" or power elite that you just identified supports the public relations or communication function in this organization. In this case, 0 would indicate no support at all, 100 would indicate the average extent to which organizations support public relations, and a higher score would indicate strong support.

0.........25.........50.........75.........100.........150.........200.........300.........?				
No	Half the	Average for	Twice the	As high as
support	average	all organizations	average	you want to go

In my organization, the level of support is _____. (77–80)

8. The senior administrators who run an organization—the dominant coalition you were asked to identify—generally have a prevailing idea about how public relations, public affairs, or communication management should be practiced. Please use the open-end scale to indicate how you think the dominant coalition in this organization *believes public relations should be practiced.*

0.........25.........50.........75.........100.........150.........200.........300.........?

| Does not | Half the | Average for a | Twice the | As high as |
| describe | average | typical item | average | you want to go |

MODELS OF PUBLIC RELATIONS IN THE SCHEMA OF THE DOMINANT COALITION

PA = Press Agentry, PI = Public Information, 2A = Two-Way Asymmetrical, 2S = Two-Way Symmetrical

The purpose of public relations is, quite simply, to get publicity for this organization. **PA**

_____ (1–4)

After completing a public relations program, research should be done to determine how effective this program has been in changing people's attitudes. **2A**

_____ (5–8)

In public relations, nearly everyone is so busy writing news stories or producing publications that there is no time to do research. **2A**

_____ (9–12)

In public relations, the broad goal is to persuade publics to behave as the organization wants them to behave. **2A**

_____ (13–16)

The purpose of public relations is to develop mutual understanding between the management of the organization and publics the organization affects. **2S**

_____ (17–20)

Before starting a public relations program one should look at attitude surveys to make sure the organization and its policies are described in ways its publics would be most likely to accept. **2A**

_____ (21–24)

In public relations accurate information should be disseminated but unfavorable information should not be volunteered. **PI**

_____ (25–28)

Before starting a public relations program, surveys or informal research should be done to find out how much management and our publics understand each other. **2S**

_____ (29–32)

In public relations, one mostly attempts to get favorable publicity into the media and to keep unfavorable publicity out. **PA**

_____ (33–36)

Before beginning a public relations program, one should do research to determine public attitudes toward the organization and how they might be changed. **2A**

_____ (37–40)

The success of a public relations program can be determined from the number of people who attend an event or who use products or services. **PA**

_____ (41–44)

For this organization, public relations and publicity mean essentially the same thing. **PA**

_____ (45–48)

The purpose of public relations is to change the attitudes and behavior of management as much as it is to change the attitudes and behaviors of publics. **2S**

_____ (49–52)

Keeping a clipping file is about the only way there is to determine the success of public relations. **PI**

_____ (53–56)

Public relations should provide mediation for the organization—to help management and publics negotiate conflict. **2S**

_____ (57–60)

Public relations is more of a neutral disseminator of information than an advocate for the organization or a mediator between management and publics. **PI**

_____ (61–64)

9. Think next about the value that you think your public relations or communication department has to this organization. Using the open-end scale, estimate the value that *you* think the department has in comparison with a typical other department in this organization.

0.........25.........50.........75.........100.........150.........200.........300.........?				
No value at all	Half the average	Average value for a typical department	Twice the average	As high as you want to go

VALUE OF PUBLIC RELATIONS TO THE ORGANIZATION: QUESTIONS 9–10

Your rating of the value of this public relations / communication department. _____ (65–68)

10. Now think about the value that your public relations or communication department has to this organization in terms of a cost–benefit ratio. Think of the money that your organization budgets for public relations and communication each year—both for the department itself and for outside public relations consulting firms. Then estimate the value of the department to the organization as a percentage of the department's budget. A percentage less than 100% would indicate that you think the department provides benefits worth less than the amount budgeted. 100% would indicate that the benefits equal the costs. A percentage greater than 100% would indicate that the benefits are worth more than the amount budgeted.

Your estimate _____ % (69–72)

11. On the same open-end scale, please choose a number that indicates how well each of the following items describes the work that *you* think the **head of your public relations or communication department** should do. Please do not score items highly if you believe employees in the public relations department other than the head of the department should do the tasks described. Here, 100 is a score that describes the work of an average head of public relations on a typical one of these items.

0.........25.........50.........75.........100.........150.........200.........300.........?				
Does not describe	Half the average	Average for a typical item	Twice the average	As high as you want to go

ROLES: M = MANAGER   T = TECHNICIAN   MR = MEDIA RELATIONS   CL = COMMUNICATION LIAISON

He or she should produce brochures, pamphlets, and other publications. **T** _____ (73–76)

He or she should create opportunities for management to hear the views of various internal and external publics. **CL** _____ (77–80)

He or she should take responsibility for the success or failure of the organization's communication or public relations programs. **M** _____ (1–4)

He or she should be the person who writes communication materials. **T** _____ (5–8)

He or she should represent the organization at events and meetings. **CL** _____ (9–12)

He or she should maintain media contacts for the organization. **MR** _____ (13–16)

He or she should make communication policy decisions. **M** _____ (17–20)

He or she should be held accountable for the success or failure of communication or public relations programs. **M** _____ (21–24)

```
0........25.........50.........75.........100.........150.........200.........300.........?
```

| Does not describe | Half the average | Average for a typical item | Twice the average | As high as you want to go |

He or she should keep others in the organization informed of what the media report about our organization and important issues. **MR**

(25–28)

Although he or she doesn't make communication policy decisions, he or she should provide decision makers with suggestions, recommendations, and plans. **CL**

(29–32)

He or she should do photography and graphics for communication or public relations materials. **T**

(33–36)

He or she should be responsible for placing news releases. **MR**

(37–40)

He or she should edit or rewrite for grammar and spelling the materials written by others in the organization. **T**

(41–44)

Because of his or her experience and training, others should consider him or her the organization's expert in solving communication or public relations problems. **M**

(45–48)

He or she should be senior counsel to top decision makers when communication or public relations issues are involved. **M**

(49–52)

He or she should use journalistic skills to figure out what the media will consider newsworthy about the organization. **MR**

(53–56)

The next series of questions asks about the environment of your organization and your estimate of its importance.

PRESSURE FROM ACTIVIST GROUPS: QUESTIONS 12–14. ITEMS ANALYZED SEPARATELY

12. Using the open-end scale, please estimate the extent to which your organization has experienced pressure from activist groups.

```
0........25.........50.........75.........100.........150.........200.........300.........?
```

| No pressure at all | Half the average | Average for a typical organization | Twice the average | As high as you want to go |

My estimate for this organization is _____. (57–60)
(If your answer is 0, go to Question 15)

13. Think of the most recent case or a typical case when your organization was pressured by an activist group. Using the open-end scale, please describe how successful that activist group was in achieving its goals in its dealings with your organization. Then estimate how successful you think your organization's response to the group to have been.

```
0........25.........50.........75.........100.........150.........200.........300.........?
```

| Not successful at all | Half the average | Average success for a typical encounter | Twice the average | As high as you want to go |

The activist group's level of success was _____. (61–64)
My organization's level of success was _____. (65–68)

14. Where do you tend to find out about activist pressure on your organization? (**Check any that apply**)

   ____ The pressure group itself. (69)
   ____ Media coverage. (70)
   ____ The public relations or communication department. (71)
   ____ Others in your organization. (72)
   ____ Other source _____. (73)
   ____ Other source _____. (74)
   ____ Other source _____. (75)
   ____ Other source _____. (76)

TIME SPENT IN AND IMPORTANCE OF COMMUNICATION TO CEO: QUESTIONS 15–16

15. Please estimate the percentage of your time as a senior administrator that you spend on communication activities inside the organization and outside the organization.

Inside the organization _____ % (77–79)　　Outside the organization _____ % (1–3)

16. Please use the open-end scale to indicate how important it is for you and other senior managers in this organization to be aware of what people outside the organization are doing that may affect the organization. _____ (4–7)

0.........25.........50.........75.........100.........150.........200.........300.........?				
Not important at all	Half the average	Average importance in comparison with my other activities	Twice the average	As high as you want to go

PROGRAMS FOR WOMEN: ITEMS TO BE ADDED OR FACTOR ANALYZED.

17. The next set of items moves from the external to the internal environment of your organization—specifically with the way your organization deals with its women employees. For each item, use the open-end scale to estimate how your overall organization, not just the communication department, compares with an average organization on a typical one of these items.

0.........25.........50.........75.........100.........150.........200.........300.........?				
Does not describe	Half the average	Average for a typical item in most organizations	Twice the average	As high as you want to go

This organization has:

Enacted specific policies, procedures, or programs designed to promote an understanding of the concerns of female employees.
    _____ (8–11)

Provided a supportive climate for women at work.
    _____ (12–15)

Monitored the use of sexist language in all realms of the organization's communication.
    _____ (16–19)

Reviewed organizational policies for their effect on women.
    _____ (20–23)

0.........25.........50.........75.........100.........150.........200.........300.........?

Does not describe	Half the average	Average for a typical item in most organizations	Twice the average	As high as you want to go

Provided opportunities for women who must relocate or who have relocated.

_____ (24–27)

Allowed flex time for employees.

_____ (28–31)

Avoided "perks" that divide employees on the basis of their gender and tenure, such as all-male clubs or executive dining rooms.

_____ (32–35)

Established effective policies to deal with sexual discrimination.

_____ (36–39)

Developed specific guidelines for handling problems of sexual harassment.

_____ (40–43)

Set up a system of maternity and paternity leave.

_____ (44–47)

Provided child-care services.

_____ (48–51)

Built a system of multiple employment centers that allow mobility for employees.

_____ (52–55)

Furthered the talents of women through mentoring programs.

_____ (56–59)

Fostered women's leadership abilities.

_____ (60–63)

Funded or reimbursed employees for work-related travel.

_____ (64–67)

Included membership in professional associations as an employee benefit.

_____ (68–71)

Provided opportunities for women to take risks.

_____ (72–75)

Encouraged women who may seem less "serious-minded" about their careers than men.

_____ (76–79)

Groomed women for management by selecting them as "informal assistants" to those in the next-higher position.

_____ (1–4)

Included women in the informal informational network.

_____ (5–8)

Made available comparable data to help women in salary negotiations.

_____ (9–12)

Paid men and women equally for equal or comparable work.

_____ (13–16)

18. The name of your organization is: _____

19. Your title is: _____ (17–18)

Thank you. That completes the questionnaire.

Employee Questionnaire

Excellence in Public Relations
and Communication Management:
An International Study

Questionnaire for an Employee
of the Organization

By completing this questionnaire, you will help to determine how public relations and communication programs should be managed to make the greatest contribution to the success of an organization. This questionnaire is one of three that will be completed by people in your organization. The head of public relations and the CEO will complete questionnaires. Many characteristics of an organization and its communication system, however, can be recognized only by rank-and-file employees. You have been chosen as one of 20 such employees in this organization to complete this third questionnaire. Thus, your responses are extremely important.

Your organization has been chosen as one of 300 to be studied in the United States, Canada, and the United Kingdom—including corporations, associations, government agencies, and other nonprofit organizations. The survey is part of a 6-year study funded by the IABC Research Foundation of the International Association of Business Communicators and several corporations. The questionnaires have been developed by researchers at the University of Maryland, Syracuse University, San Diego State University, and the Cranfield Institute of Technology in the UK.

Thank you, in advance, for completing this questionnaire. Your cooperation will help to ensure the success of one of the most important research projects in the history of public relations and business communication.

How to complete this questionnaire. **This questionnaire uses a numbering system that allows you to give a wider range of answers to questions than do other systems. Your** best estimate or even your best guess is sufficient. Do not be overly concerned about the precision of your answers. You may choose any number that you believe describes what your organization is like. A score of 100 is the *average* score of employees in an organization like this who agree that *a typical item* in the questionnaire describes their organization. A score of 0 means that you believe that an item does not describe your organization at all. You may choose a number as high as you want, such as 450 or 500, to show how much you agree with an item. The following scale should help you. It will appear throughout the questionnaire.

0.........25.........50.........75.........100.........150.........200.........300.........?

Does not describe	Half the average	Average agreement with a typical item in most organizations	Twice the average	As high as you want to go

It is important that you answer every item in the questionnaire, but if you feel you do not know the answer to a question, please leave it blank rather than answering with a zero. The questions refer to the overall organization and not just your department or unit. If you work for a local organization that is part of a national one, your answers should refer to the local unit.

1. The first set of items describes ways in which communication takes place in many organizations. Some items may describe communication in this organization accurately. Others may not. For each item, please use the open-end scale explained on the first page to select any number that indicates the extent to which you agree that each item describes the system of communication in this organization accurately.

0.........25.........50.........75.........100.........150.........200.........300.........?

Does not describe	Half the average	Average agreement with a typical item in most organizations	Twice the average	As high as you want to go

(AC = Asymmetrical Communication   SC = Symmetrical Communication)

The purpose of communication in this organization is to get employees to behave in the way administrators want them to behave. **AC**

_____
(5–8)

I am comfortable in talking with administrators about my performance. **AC**

_____
(9–12)

Most communication between administrators and other employees in this organization can be said to be two-way communication. **SC**

_____
(13–16)

This organization encourages differences of opinion. **SC**

_____
(17–20)

The purpose of communication in this organization is to help administrators to be responsive to the problems of other employees. **SC**

_____
(21–24)

My supervisor encourages differences of opinion. **SC**

_____
(25–28)

I am usually informed about major changes in policy that affect my job before they take place. **SC**

_____
(29–32)

Most communication in this organization is one-way: from administrators to other employees. **AC**

_____
(33–36)

0.........25.........50.........75.........100.........150.........200.........300.........?

Does not	Half the	Average agreement	Twice the	As high as
describe	average	with a typical item	average	you want to go
		in most organizations		

I am comfortable in talking with my immediate supervisor when things are going wrong. **SC**

(37–40)

I seldom get feedback when I communicate to administrators. **AC**

(41–44)

2. Next, please choose a number on the same scale to indicate the extent to which you agree that each of the following items describes this organization accurately in comparison with other organizations.

In this organization, important decisions generally are made by a few administrators alone rather than by people throughout the organization. **CENTRALIZATION**

(45–48)

I have a personal influence on decisions and policies of this organization. **PARTICIPATION IN DM**

(49–52)

It is difficult for a person who begins in the lower ranks of this organization to move up to an important administrative or supervisory position within about 10 years. **STRATIFICATION**

(53–56)

I have a great deal of freedom in making decisions about my work without clearing those decisions with people at higher levels of the organization. **CENTRALIZATION**

(57–60)

I must keep reading, learning, and studying almost every day to do my job adequately. **COMPLEXITY**

(61–64)

My unit has a printed organization chart, which nearly everyone follows closely. **FORMALIZATION**

(65–68)

In this organization, there are clear and recognized differences between superiors and subordinates. These differences can be seen in larger offices, quality of office furniture, close-in parking spaces, or frequency of superiors and subordinates having lunch together. **STRATIFICATION**

(69–72)

I have a say in decisions that affect my job. **PARTICIPATION IN DM**

(73–76)

My actual work seldom deviates from a written job description for my position. **FORMALIZATION**

(77–80)

(ALL QUESTIONS FOLLOWING ON CULTURE)

This organization has clearly defined goals. **SHARED MISSION**

(1–4)

Each project in this organization, even if it is a complicated one requiring a team effort, usually is divided into tasks and subtasks. Each employee is assigned subtasks and is solely responsible for the results of his or her work. **COLLECTIVE RESPONSIBILITY**

(5–8)

0.........25.........50.........75.........100.........150.........200.........300.........?

Does not describe	Half the average	Average agreement with a typical item in most organizations	Twice the average	As high as you want to go

If I were one of the four or five most powerful executives of this organization, I would manage the organization in the same way as the executives now in power are managing it. **SHARED MISSION**

<u>   </u>
(9–12)

Advancement in this organization is based more on who you know than on how well you perform. **REWARDS**

<u>   </u>
(13–16)

Most decisions in this organization are made by individuals largely working alone. **COLLECTIVE DECISION MAKING**

<u>   </u>
(17–20)

Most employees in this organization share a common sense of mission that most think is worth striving to achieve. **COLLECTIVE VALUES**

<u>   </u>
(21–24)

This organization is a place where people tend to separate their work life from their home and social life. Most superiors feel that it is not their responsibility nor their right to know very much about the personal problems of their subordinates. **HOLISTIC CONCERN FOR PEOPLE**

<u>   </u>
(25–28)

People in this organization move frequently to other employers, including those who are successful as well as those who are not. **LONG-TERM EMPLOYMENT**

<u>   </u>
(29–32)

People who work here meet frequently off the job. **SOCIAL ATMOSPHERE**

<u>   </u>
(33–36)

Most projects are done here through teamwork. Each individual is expected to contribute to the team effort, but the team as a whole is ultimately held accountable and rewarded or punished for its efforts. **COLLECTIVE RESPONSIBILITY**

<u>   </u>
(37–40)

Most departments in this organization do not share a common mission; each has different priorities that conflict with the priorities of other departments. **COLLECTIVE VALUES**

<u>   </u>
(41–44)

Performance is important in this organization, but promotions are made only after careful evaluation of an individual over a long period of time. **SLOW EVALUATION AND PROMOTION**

<u>   </u>
(45–48)

Most people in this organization are specialists who are known outside the organization as experts in engineering, marketing, accounting, or a similar field. **NONSPECIALIZED CAREER PATHS**

<u>   </u>
(49–52)

Senior managers of this organization frequently socialize with other employees off the job. **SOCIAL ATMOSPHERE**

<u>   </u>
(53–56)

The goals of this organization are different from my personal goals. **SHARED MISSION**

<u>   </u>
(57–60)

People are evaluated often in this organization through hard measures such as sales, profitability, or production. For those who receive favorable evaluations, promotion can be rapid. **SLOW EVALUATION AND PROMOTION**

<u>   </u>
(61–64)

0.........25.........50.........75.........100.........150.........200.........300.........?

Does not describe	Half the average	Average agreement with a typical item in most organizations	Twice the average	As high as you want to go

Most decisions in this organization are made after thorough discussion between all people who will be affected in a major way. **COLLECTIVE DECISION MAKING**

_____(65–68)

This organization is open to new ideas from outside. **INNOVATION**

_____(69–72)

The typical career in this organization is long term; the organization rarely has layoffs and terminations. **LONG-TERM EMPLOYMENT**

_____(73–76)

People take interest in each other in this organization. It is common to find supervisors who feel that it is part of their job to know about personal problems that may be bothering their subordinates. **HOLISTIC CONCERN FOR PEOPLE**

_____(77–80)

Senior management in this organization believes that it must have nearly total control over the behavior of subordinates. **AUTHORITARIAN**

_____(1–4)

Most people do not specialize in this organization. They rotate among areas such as marketing, operations, sales, engineering, personnel, or similar functions. **NONSPECIALIZED CAREER PATHS**

_____(5–8)

The departments in this organization seem to work together like a well-oiled machine. **INTEGRATION**

_____(9–12)

Rigid control by management often makes it difficult for me to be innovative in this organization. **AUTHORITARIAN**

_____(13–16)

Managers in this organization seem to believe that employees lack initiative and must constantly be given instructions. **AUTHORITARIAN**

_____(17–20)

This organization seems to look to the future rather than to the past. **TRADITION**

_____(21–24)

This organization can be classified as conservative. **CONSERVATIVE**

_____(25–28)

Nearly everyone feels like he or she is part of a team in this organization. **INTEGRATION**

_____(29–32)

Being on time is extremely important in this organization. **OBJECTIVE CULTURE**

_____(33–36)

Senior managers in this organization care deeply about other employees. **INTEGRATION**

_____(37–40)

Decisions usually are based on tradition here—the way things always have been done. **DECISION MAKING BY TRADITION**

_____(41–44)

Senior administrators in this organization believe that they know best because they have more knowledge than lower level employees. **AUTHORITARIAN**

_____(45–48)

Before decisions can be made here, committees usually are set up to study the issue. **DECISION MAKING BY RATIONAL PROCESS**

_____(49–52)

0.........25.........50.........75.........100.........150.........200.........300.........?

Does not describe	Half the average	Average agreement with a typical item in most organizations	Twice the average	As high as you want to go

This organization usually is willing to negotiate with groups outside that disagree with it. **COOPERATION**

(53–56)

This organization usually is closed to new ideas from outside. **CLOSED SYSTEM**

(57–60)

Major decisions usually are based on open debate in this organization. **DECISION MAKING BY OPEN DEBATE**

(61–64)

Senior managers here believe in the sharing of power and responsibility with lower level employees. **PARTICIPATIVE**

(65–68)

Usually, we make decisions by trial-and-error. We try things and see if they work. **DECISION MAKING BY TRIAL-AND-ERROR**

(69–72)

Everyone is treated as an equal in this organization. **CONSENSUAL**

(73–76)

Decisions here usually are based on scientific research. **DECISION MAKING BY SCIENTIFIC RESEARCH**

(77–80)

Innovation probably is the most important goal of this organization. **INNOVATION**

(1–4)

Most people who work here seem to be afraid of senior managers. **AUTHORITARIAN**

(5–8)

Everyone works together here to make the organization effective. **CONSENSUAL**

(9–12)

Decisions usually are based on authority here—the way the CEO and the people close to him or her want things done. **DECISION MAKING BY AUTHORITY**

(13–16)

This organization can be classified as liberal. **LIBERAL**

(17–20)

This organization tries to dominate people outside who disagree with it. **DOMINATION**

(21–24)

This organization is open to ideas from outside. **OPEN SYSTEM**

(25–28)

Efficiency probably is the most important goal in this organization. **EFFICIENCY**

(29–32)

3. The third set of questions asks how satisfied you are with your job and the quality of life in this organization. Use the same open-end scale to describe the extent to which you agree that each item describes accurately how you feel about this organization in comparison with the answer that an average employee in most organizations would give to a typical one of these items.

JOB SATISFACTION: O = ORGANIZATIONAL   I = INDIVIDUAL

On the whole, my job is interesting and challenging. **I**

(33–36)

In general, this organization has treated me well. **O** _____ (37–40)

I look forward to coming to work almost every day. **I** _____ (41–44)

I feel as though I have a real chance to get ahead in this organization. **O** _____ (45–48)

The best-qualified people usually are chosen for promotion in this organization. **O** _____ (49–52)

My work gives me a sense of accomplishment. **I** _____ (53–56)

I am satisfied with my pay and benefits. **O** _____ (57–60)

This organization has a genuine concern for the welfare of its employees. **O** _____ (61–64)

My work is a dead-end job. **I** _____ (65–68)

I am satisfied with my day-to-day working conditions. **O** _____ (69–72)

I am satisfied with the recognition I receive for good performance in my job. **O** _____ (73–76)

I have found this organization to be a good place to work. **O** _____ (77–80)

Both men and women are treated well in this organization. **O** _____ (1–4)

My immediate supervisor is hard to please. **O** _____ (5–8)

It is easy to work with my coworkers. **O** _____ (9–12)

There is a good opportunity for advancement in my job. **O** _____ (13–16)

Minorities are treated well in this organization. **O** _____ (17–20)

My work is boring. **I** _____ (21–24)

4. The next set of items asks specifically about the way your organization deals with its women employees. For each item, use the open-end scale to estimate the extent to which you agree each item describes accurately how your organization compares with an average organization on a typical one of these items.

0.........25.........50.........75.........100.........150.........200.........300.........?
| Does not describe | Half the average | Average agreement with a typical item in most organizations | Twice the average | As high as you want to go |

NO SCALES. ITEMS TO BE ADDED OR FACTOR ANALYZED

This organization has:

Enacted specific policies, procedures, or programs designed to promote an understanding of the concerns of female employees. _____ (25–28)

Provided a supportive climate for women at work. _____ (29–32)

0.........25.........50.........75.........100.........150.........200.........300.........?

| Does not describe | Half the average | Average agreement with a typical item in most organizations | Twice the average | As high as you want to go |

Monitored the use of sexist language in all realms of the organization's communication.

(33–36)

Reviewed organizational policies for their effect on women.

(37–40)

Provided opportunities for women who must relocate or who have relocated.

(41–44)

Allowed flex time for employees.

(45–48)

Avoided "perks" that divide employees on the basis of their gender and tenure, such as all-male clubs or executive dining rooms.

(49–52)

Established effective policies to deal with sexual discrimination.

(53–56)

Developed specific guidelines for handling problems of sexual harassment.

(57–60)

Set up a system of maternity and paternity leave.

(61–64)

Provided child-care services.

(65–68)

Built a system of multiple employment centers that allow mobility for employees.

(69–72)

Furthered the talents of women through mentoring programs.

(73–76)

Fostered women's leadership abilities.

(77–80)

Funded or reimbursed employees for work-related travel.

(1–4)

Included membership in professional associations as an employee benefit.

(5–8)

Provided opportunities for women to take risks.

(9–12)

Encouraged women who may seem less "serious-minded" about their careers than men.

(13–16)

Groomed women for management by selecting them as "informal assistants" to those in the next-higher position.

(17–20)

Included women in the informal informational network.

(21–24)

Made available comparable data to help women in salary negotiations.

(25–28)

Paid men and women equally for equal or comparable work.

(29–32)

Finally, we have a few questions about you.

5. How much education do you have?

____ High school degree or less. (1)
____ Some college or technical training. (2)
____ Bachelor's degree. (3)
____ Master's degree. (4)
____ Doctoral degree. (5) (33)

6. What is the *minimum* amount of education required for your *job*?

COMPLEXITY

____ High school degree or less. (1)
____ Some college or technical training. (2)
____ Bachelor's degree. (3)
____ Master's degree. (4)
____ Doctoral degree. (5)   (34)

7. How old are you? _____ (35–36)

8. How many years have you worked for this organization? _____ (37–38)

9. Check the item that best describes your supervisory responsibilities.

____ I am mostly supervised by others. (1)
____ I don't supervise others but work with little supervision from others. (2)
____ I am a first-line manager. (3)
____ I am a middle manager. (4)
____ I am a senior manager. (5)   (39)

10. Your job title is _____ (40–41)

11. Are you a:

____ Male. (1)
____ Female. (2)   (42)

12. The name of your organization is _____

Thank you. That completes the questionnaire.

Qualitative Interview Protocol

Excellence in Public Relations and Communication Management

Initial Contact:

[**Note:** The exact wording you use is not important. This is a semistructured rather than highly structured process. The same is true for the actual questions that follow.]

Hi, I'm _____. *A few years ago your organization participated in the Excellence project, which is the largest study ever conducted of public relations and communication in the world. Now we're conducting a series of personal interviews to discuss those research findings and to ask a few follow-up questions with people like yourself in about 18 of the original 300 organizations. When would be the best time for us to talk?*

Interview with the head of public relations (and others in the public relations department):

[**Notes:** (1) Mention—on tape—the tape recording of the interview. (2) Begin with conversational ice-breakers. (3) Continue with the following questions **in any order,** using any phrasing you determine is most likely to elicit the information we need. **Look for opportunities to suggest a conversation with others in the public relations department or in the dominant coalition.** The best strategy may be to take advantage of a "don't know"-type response. At that point, suggest talking with others in the department or the CEO (or both).]

Questions About Public Relations:

* *Tell me a little bit about the history of this public relations department. How did it come to be the way it is?* [**Possible probe, if necessary:** *For example, did a CEO years back determine that public relations was so important that he or she set about to hire the most outstanding professional possible in this arena? Or did some outstanding practitioner, working from within the communication department, lead senior management both to understand and to support the function so that it could operate ideally?*]

* *How, if at all, are public relations practitioners involved in strategic planning here?*

* *How have you gained the knowledge you have of communication management? of strategic planning?*

* *Results of our survey research suggest that strategic management represents a promising career track in public relations. How do you suggest a practitioner make the transition from technician to strategist?*

* *How, in particular, could a public relations practitioner become a member of the dominant coalition, the group of powerful people making policy for the organization?*

* *Given the state of the economy worldwide, it may be impractical for many to leave their current positions for new jobs in companies whose cultures foster excellence in public relations. What advice do you have for practitioners who seem to be "stuck" in their current posts?*

* *How do public relations practitioners here work together (or at cross-purposes) with their counterpart managers throughout the organization—such as in marketing or human resources?*

* *What relationship do you see, if any, between the practice of excellent public relations and "total quality"?*

Questions About CEOs:

* *If CEOs truly value public relations to the extent they indicated in our survey, then why the modest budgets for the function and even the downsizing of public relations in the typical organization? In other words, do you think CEOs are merely paying lip service to a notion they have been counseled to say they consider important?*

* *Why do you think some CEOs place more emphasis than others on internal communication?*

* *Why do you think your CEO values public relations as highly as he (or she) indicated he (or she) does?*

* *Do you know if your CEO has read the Excellence study results? Have you talked about the initial data report together?*

If having a supportive CEO leads to excellent communication, then do you think it would it be possible to achieve organizational excellence simply by hiring such a CEO—regardless of what is going on in the rest of the organization?

Questions About Diversity:

* *How do excellent organizations empower women?*
* *How do you think highly ranked women in public relations manage to crash the glass ceiling?*
* *How—if at all—do our findings from the survey research for women hold up for racial and ethnic groups or any other diverse publics? In other words, where are the parallels and the divergences?*

Questions About Monetary Value:

[**Note:** Here we would probe for concrete examples, good or bad (such as activist pressure). We also want to touch on social responsibility at this point. We hope participants would be very precise. If we are interviewing someone other than the person who responded to our initial questionnaire, then we first would ask that person to estimate the value of public relations.]

* *What, exactly, is public relations worth to your organization? What instances were you thinking about when you attached a monetary value to the contribution public relations makes to organizational effectiveness?* [Recall that we have the survey data to refer back to from each organization.]

* *What examples can you cite for public relations saving money for the organization? for making money? Why?*

[At this point, assuming participants have not been concrete in terms of dollars and cents, we will engage in a process akin to compensating variation or cost–benefit analysis. Review Bill Ehling's chapter 23 in the Excellence book on estimating the value of public relations to an organization.]

* *Let me talk you through a short series of steps that might help us get at the value of public relations in this organization. Think back to that example of _____ that you just gave, where public relations really helped your organization. You had a choice of how to respond in that situation. You chose one option. Approximately how much did that public relations effort cost?*

*That's the easy part. Now I need to know what was it **worth** to your organization to solve the problem.* [If no answer is forthcoming, proceed as follows:] *Was it worth xxxxx dollars?* [give a very high estimate]. *No? Too much? Well, then, would you say* *it was worth xxx dollars?* [give a very low estimate. Then keep see-sawing back and forth until you've struck an amount that the participant agrees is at least close to the value.]

Closing:

At this point, I'll need to talk with [whoever you have alluded to during the interview]. Thanks so much for your time. I need to ask you only one last question: What should I have asked you that I didn't think to ask? And may I call you later on if I find I need to clarify anything you said?

Interview With the CEO or Other Member of the Dominant Coalition

[**Note:** Really push to conduct this interview but know, at the same time, that you won't have much time to pick the brains of the CEO. Thus we have to be parsimonious about the number of questions we plan to ask. If time permits, of course, all of the questions addressed to communication managers would be appropriate for the CEO as well.]

Questions About CEOs:

* *If CEOs truly value public relations to the extent they indicated in our survey, then why the modest budgets for the function and even the downsizing of public relations in the typical organization? In other words, do you think CEOs are merely paying lip service to a notion they have been counseled to say they consider important?*

* *Why do you think some CEOs place more emphasis than others on internal communication?*

* *Why do you value public relations as highly as you (or your predecessor in this organization) indicated you do?*

* *Have you read the Excellence study results? Have you talked about the initial data report with your public relations director?*

* *If having a supportive CEO leads to excellent communication, then do you think it would it be possible to achieve organizational excellence simply by being such a CEO—regardless of what is going on in the rest of the organization?*

Questions About Public Relations:

* *Tell me a little bit about the history of public relations in your organization. How did the department come to be the way it is?*

* *How are public relations practitioners involved in strategic planning here?*

* *Do you consider public relations part of your top-management team? If so, how did your head of public relations become a member of that dominant coalition?*

How do public relations practitioners here work together (or at cross-purposes) with their counterparts throughout the organization?

What relationship do you see, if any, between the practice of excellent public relations and "total quality"?

Questions About Monetary Value:

[**Note:** Here we would probe for concrete examples, good or bad (such as activist pressure). We also want to touch on social responsibility at this point. We hope participants would be very precise. If we are interviewing someone other than the person who responded to our initial questionnaire, then we first would ask that person to estimate the value of public relations.]

What instances were you thinking about when you attached a monetary value to the contribution public relations makes to organizational effectiveness? In other words, what exactly is public relations worth to these organization? [Recall that we have the survey data to refer back to from each organization.]

Do you see public relations more as a way of making money or saving money? What examples can you cite for public relations saving money for the organization? for making money? Why?

[At this point, assuming participants have not been concrete in terms of dollars and cents, we will engage in a process akin to compensating variation or cost–benefit analysis. Review Bill Ehling's chapter 23 in the Excellence book on estimating the value of public relations to an organization.]

Let me talk you through a short series of steps that might help us get at the value of public relations in this organization. Think back to that example of _____ that you just gave, where public relations really helped your organization. You had a choice of how to respond in that situation. You chose one option. Approximately how much did that public relations effort cost?

That's the easy part. Now I need to know what was it **worth** *to your organization to solve the problem.* [If no answer is forthcoming, proceed as follows:] *Was it worth xxxxx dollars?* [give a very high estimate]. No? Too much? *Well, then, would you say it was worth xxx dollars?* [give a very low estimate. Then keep see-sawing back and forth until you're struck an amount that the participant agrees is at least close to the value.]

Questions About Diversity: [**Note:** Ask if time permits.]

American society is being characterized more as a mosaic or a tossed salad than as the melting pot of yesterday. How has your organization managed to empower diverse employees—in the communication department or anywhere else—who may not fit the profile of the professional of yesterday?

* How do you think highly ranked women in public relations, in particular, manage to crash the glass ceiling?

* How—if at all—do our findings from the survey research for women hold up for racial and ethnic groups or any other diverse publics? In other words, where are the parallels and the divergences?

Closing: *Thank you so much for your time.*

Author Index

Subject Index

Q